AMERICAN SOCIOLOGY SERIES

Kimball Young, General Editor

AMERICAN SOCIOLOGY SERIES

Problems of a Changing Social Order
John M. Gillette and James M. Reinhardt

Sociology, A Study of Society and Culture
Kimball Young

Social and Cultural Dynamics, Vols. I–IV
Pitirim A. Sorokin

Isolated Communities
Oscar W. Junek

Administration of Public Welfare
R. Clyde White

Fundamental Concepts of Sociology
(*Gemeinschaft und Gesellschaft*)
Ferdinand Tonnies
Translated and Supplemented by Charles P. Loomis

Crime and Its Treatment
Arthur E. Wood and John B. Waite

Population Problems, A Cultural Interpretation
Paul H. Landis

The Family
Ernest W. Burgess and Harvey J. Locke

Rural Sociology
Lowry Nelson

Social Work, An Introduction to the Field
Herbert H. Stroup

SOCIAL
WORK
AN INTRODUCTION TO THE FIELD

Herbert Hewitt Stroup

Department of Sociology
and Anthropology
Brooklyn College

New York   Cincinnati   Chicago   Boston   Atlanta

Dallas   San Francisco   *American Book Company*

To My Family

Preface

The field of social work is increasingly attractive to a widening number of college students and lay people generally. In terms of personal appeal, it deals with many of the paradoxical elements found in the more hopeful as well as the bitter aspects of human reality. Social work boldly views the seamy side of human experience. It seeks to apply remedies based upon the materials which the all-too-weak human sciences have developed. In carrying out its functions, social work also has had to struggle with its own inadequate past and with a public which has not always been constructively responsive. Many intellectuals have failed to appreciate the modern aspects of social work and continue to talk about social work in the terms of the last century. But, despite these deterrents, social work has progressed—at some points with notable speed—and has provided a community structure and an interpersonal process which, because of their soundness and consequences, are winning broad support from more and more people.

This book has been written to provide a readable but responsible picture of the nature of social work and its various functions at the present time. It should have value not only for the college student for whom it is primarily intended but also for the citizen who wishes to know about social work. Social work will probably always depend upon an enlightened lay leadership. To those who are active already in community affairs of a social welfare character and to those who some day hope to be, this book should provide a basic understanding of this field of interest.

As a result of the author's experience in teaching and in practical social work, certain materials are stressed over others. The reader will find, for one thing, that there is considerable emphasis upon what might be called the "structure" of social work and comparatively less upon its "process." This should not be taken by the reader to imply that the latter is not important; it is very important. But the author believes that the processual aspects fall more properly within the province of graduate study than within that of an introductory text. On the other hand the student needs a minimum of educational background to understand and appreciate the meaning of the various agencies, institutions, organizations, fields of practice, laws and rules, material equipment, interrelationships with other professions and the community itself, traditions, value norms, and other similar organizational features which support the social work processes within the community.

The writer recognizes the fact that social work had a long and significant history (especially in England) preceding its development in this country. But he feels that an understanding of social work in the United States is probably as much as the beginning student needs. To further this understanding, historical perspective is given considerable attention in each of the various chapters.

Public services have received extended treatment in this book for the reason that they are today very prominent factors in the total operation of social work. Particularly since the passage of the Social Security Act (1935), these services have become more numerous and notable.

Group work and community organization have been generously discussed because of the basic conviction of the writer that social work includes three fundamental divisions: casework, group work, and community organization. Many persons mistakenly tend to identify social work with social casework exclusively; this book should help correct that idea.

In order to aid the nontechnical person in his understanding of the nature of social work and its functions, the jargon of the professional workers has been translated into fairly common language. Likewise, the number of footnote references has been kept to a minimum.

The case summaries which have been used throughout most of the book are employed to place before the reader some of the problems of social work and the ways in which these problems have been met or at least are concretely found. They are not necessarily meant to reveal the social work processes in full. If they illustrate points, they will have served their purpose. Similarly, the case summaries have not always been selected because they are ideal representations of problems or solutions. Indeed, not many such summaries exist today, especially for the laity.

The present work includes many of the forms of social work, but it does not include all. The beginning student does not need to be introduced to every aspect of the field. Certainly, the major fields have been discussed herein. But for the student who wishes an even fuller account of certain specialties and subjects within social work, there exists an excellent source, the *Social Work Yearbook,* which has been published biennially since 1929 by the Russell Sage Foundation, New York City.

Acknowledgments. Aside from the author's own work, the book represents the contributions of many others. It is, of course, impossible to give specific credit for each and every idea which is expressed, but most of them are fairly common property by now. In the case of all quotations, however, the writer is grateful to the publishers and authors for their permission to use the materials.

The writer is indebted to the administration, the teaching staff, and the students of Brooklyn College for a number of years of beneficial association. To President Harry D. Gideonse, Dean William R. Gaede, and others, the writer is indebted, especially for their wise administrative ability and cooperation in the establishment and maintenance of the Office of Pre-Social Work Counseling within the College. This Office, probably unique in American colleges, has provided the author with extended experience in counseling students who are interested in discovering what social work is all about. Likewise, within the College, the cooperation of Dr. Willoughby C. Waterman, Chairman of the Department of Sociology and Anthropology, and the various members of the Departmental staff, is most deeply appreciated. The students who have afforded me the privilege of teaching them during the past years have taught me more about social work and other aspects of life than they have realized.

The library workers of Brooklyn College have ever been helpful in this project. The librarians of the Russell Sage Foundation in New York City also cooperated in providing bibliographic and other assistance.

Each of the chapters has been read by at least one authority in the special field represented. To list them here is to indicate only a part of the debt which is owed them for their technical assistance: Chapter 1, Miss Florence R. Day of the Smith College School for Social Work, Mr. Wilber I. Newstetter of the School of Social Work of the University of Pittsburgh, and Miss Charlotte Towle of the School of Social Service Administration of the University of Chicago; Chapter 2, Mr. Donald W. Moreland of the Boston Provident Association; Chapter 3, Miss Elizabeth Dexter of the Brooklyn Bureau of Social Service, and Miss Ann W. Shyne of the Family Service Association of America; Chapter 4, Mr. Howard W. Hopkirk of the Child Welfare League of

America; Chapter 5, Miss Dorothy Hutchinson of the New York School of Social Work; Chapter 6, Miss Shirley Leonard of the Bureau of Child Guidance of the Board of Education of the City of New York; Chapter 7, Mr. Herschel Alt of the Jewish Board of Guardians, New York City; Chapter 8, Mrs. Marjorie Bell of the National Probation and Parole Association; Chapter 9, Miss Grace White of the New York School of Social Work, and Miss Harriett Bartlett of the Simmons College School of Social Work; Chapter 10, Mrs. Helen Harris Perlman of the School of Social Service Administration of the University of Chicago; Chapters 11 and 12, Mr. Alton A. Linford of the School of Social Service Administration of the University of Chicago; Chapter 13, Mr. Clyde Murray of the Union Settlement, New York City; and Chapter 14, Mr. Clarence King of the New York School of Social Work.

In addition to those already mentioned, there have been many others who have helped in the preparation of the volume—too many to be noted here by name, although their assistance is also gratefully acknowledged.

In the reading of the whole manuscript in an early form the writer is obliged to his former students, Miss Jannette Schulman and Mrs. Frances Marcus Roth.

Mr. Hilary Leyendecker of the New York State Department of Social Welfare read an earlier form of the manuscript also and made many suggestive comments.

To Professor Kimball Young, the General Editor of this Series, a principal debt is acknowledged. Not only has he read the entire manuscript with care, but he has made numerous suggestions which have improved its style greatly.

Finally, the greatest debt of all is incurred by the ever diligent and skillful work of my wife, Grace Guldin Stroup. Without her assistance at every turn this work might never have been completed. Also, to Timothy and Trudi, my children, I owe inspiration.

Contents

xi

xii   CONTENTS

FIGURES

TABLES

1

The Nature and Scope of Social Work

Social work is the art of bringing various resources to bear on individual, group, and community needs by the application of a scientific method of helping people to help themselves. Social work, in this sense, is historically of rather recent origin, for there were long periods in history when men did not apply objective methods to interpersonal problems. In fact, according to a number of social workers, prescientific social work ended only recently. Even at present, social work is not wholly scientific in its methods. It depends to a marked degree on the development of exact knowledge among the various social sciences, but, as yet, the latter have not become fully scientific either as to method or fact. Nevertheless, social work seeks to be scientific. Wherever possible, social workers try to apply the results of objective investigation, particularly in the social sciences, to human problems. They also attempt to maintain an unemotional and critical attitude in their own work.

While social work is scientifically oriented in terms of the knowledge and methods it uses, it also involves certain elements of skill which make it akin to an applied or practical art. As a "subject," social work is scientific; as a "practice," it is an art.[1]

[1] In this book the author assumes that only a minimal accounting of the artistic aspects of social work is needed, since this consideration is appropriately the work of the graduate schools of social work. The graduate schools have the means through their programs of field work training of implementing the skill aspects of social work in ways which are generally not suitable to undergraduate instruction. Therefore, this book will be chiefly concerned with social work as a system of social meaning—a definite arrangement within our society—and will not go deeply into the more professional aspects.

I

Social work, in its application of scientific and practical procedures, is not the only organized present-day method for helping individuals, groups, and communities. Closely related to this field is the work of physicians, ministers, nurses, occupational and physical therapists, psychiatrists, teachers and principals, psychologists, and others.

One of the best ways to understand the meaning of social work is to analyze its nature according to a threefold division of: individuals, groups, and communities.

SOCIAL WORK HELPS INDIVIDUALS

Social Casework

Social work as a particular aid to individuals is commonly called *social casework*. Social casework is practiced by a variety of agencies and organizations in the community. As a process it is primarily interested in helping individuals, on a person-by-person basis, to attain the fullest degree of personality development. To the extent to which this aim is achieved a social value is created; therefore, social casework can also be said to be connected with the increase and maintenance of social welfare generally.

Social casework as it deals with individuals has traditionally been concerned with those persons who for one reason or another have been unable to achieve a fairly normal adjustment to life and who need certain "outside" support. Today, however, it is becoming increasingly evident that social casework can be of benefit to all people. Many persons have a generally normal adjustment to life, and, then, a time may come when they face a problem with which they need help. The analogy to the work of the physician will clarify this point. The physician is not only concerned with the chronically ill but also with persons who may enjoy generally favorable health with occasional medical needs. So, social casework currently aims to assist not only those persons who cannot maintain a normal adjustment to their human environment but also all people who may be in circumstances of particular need. Every person can profit by casework services at one time or another.

Concern With Individual and General Welfare

Social casework is concerned, then, both with the individual and his adjustment to life and with general social welfare. It is not responsible for either in an exclusive way. It does not concentrate on the individual to the exclusion of the social factors which have contributed to his situation. In this respect it differs from psychiatry, for example, which

FIG. 1. "The Lord knows there's enough misery and unhappiness in the movies without having it in real life, too."

(John Ruge, *Collier's.*)

traditionally gives its attention almost exclusively to the individual as an isolated entity. On the other hand it is not responsible for the individual only in so far as he contributes to general social improvement. Social welfare is a basic objective of social casework, but its more fundamental focus is upon the individual. Because it relates primarily to individuals, it cannot participate in general movements to improve society without considering the individual as the fundamental basis of all collective action. In fact, social casework most often must face the interaction of the two. This is one of the reasons why its title includes the words *social* and *casework*. Social casework is a personal-social treatment process. It involves the release of individual ability and the alleviation of environmental pressures.

Present-Day Crises Create Needs

The fact that social casework depends upon the interaction between the individual and his environing world points out that there is genuine and extended need for this type of help in our society. Each human being has a wide array of needs requiring satisfaction. In our time these needs are confronted with a complex and oftentimes confused culture, both in its material and in its nonmaterial aspects. The impact of numerous public crises, such as war and depression (to choose only two), upon the well-being of individuals is often highly frustrating. Because of their own inherent strength or the milder nature of their cultural crises, many individuals are able to withstand disorganizing pressures and to establish fairly satisfactory lives. But others, who are not so fortunate because of their own inabilities or the seriousness of social pressures, fall by the way. It seems that the speed of social change in our society is so great and so fraught with personal disaster that most persons at one time or another need the kind of alleviating support which social caseworkers are able to provide. There is no sign on the horizon, moreover, which suggests that social casework will be needed to a lesser degree in the future. (See Figure 2.)

Implicit in this viewpoint is the reliance of social casework upon the moral conviction that individuals are important, that they are entitled, simply because of their humanness, to respect and to aid when it is needed. This valuative element in social casework finds ample support. But whether the basis be the Christian ethic, Kantian moral idealism, humanitarianism, or some other motivating ideology, the generally accepted moral judgment remains relatively the same. Certainly, there is a significant relationship between the acceptance of this value in social casework and the attainment of democracy.

Development of Social Casework Theory

A distinction can easily be made between the development of the theory of social casework and the history of social work, even though they overlap at many points. The development of social casework theory will be presented here; the history of social work from the point of its American origin will be related in the next chapter.

Early Beginnings. It is impossible to date the actual beginnings of social casework theory, and no effort will be made here to do so. But, with

WHO COMES . . .

Trouble Plays No Favorites. In 1945, 6,310 Families Comprising Almost 20,000 Persons — a Cross-section of Society — Used the Family Counseling Service of the Jewish Family Service, New York City

14%
Engaged in Engineering, Law, Teaching, Drafting, Accounting, Research and Other Professions

33%
Included Painters, Electricians, Pattern-makers, Barbers, Tailors, Watchmakers and Other Skilled Workers

10%
Operated Their Own Businesses Such as Retail Shops or Contracting, Printing and Jobbing Enterprises

20%
Were Sales People, Civil Service Employees, and Office Workers

23%
Comprised Students, Housewives, Semiskilled and Unskilled Workers

OF THESE

9 Out of Ten Were American Citizens

7 Out of Ten Were Married People

5 Out of Ten Were Between 30 to 49 Years of Age

1 Out of Ten Was a Veteran or in Service

FOUR OUT OF EVERY FIVE
Who Needed Counseling Were Self-supporting. 895 Families and Individuals — 14 Percent — Paid a Fee for the Service They Wanted

Fig. 2. Types of People Who Come for Help

(Jewish Family Service, New York City.)

5

the founding of the first professional school of social work (the New York School of Social Work) in 1898, a suitable starting point can be set for the purposes of the present study. This date is used because in the establishment of this institution there is the indication that the theory of social work, in general, had become so definite and large a body of knowledge that it properly was the subject of a special professional school. In fact, in the years immediately following the turn of the century other professional schools were also founded with much the same motivation. Of course, these schools also expressed the growing need for better-trained personnel as more and more complicated problems arose which were not adequately handled in traditional ways.

Impact of First World War. Prior to the First World War the major emphasis in social casework was upon the social factors which influenced individuals who had problems. For many it was a time of social and economic determinism. The causes of human misery were found in the environment, with the elements of environmental influence being given broad interpretation. There was a recognition of the importance of the larger social and economic pressures under which people lived; economics, especially, was looked upon as supplying a basic content for social workers. But the smaller, not less significant, factors were also taken into account. The family, the play group, the school, and the various stimuli of the neighborhood were not neglected. Social caseworkers during this period found in all of these the primary basis of human behavior.

The First World War made a definite and widespread impact upon social casework theory. Psychiatry in this period came to the foreground. The contributions of Freud and his followers were making their impress, and sociological explanations gave way to some extent to psychological and even psychiatric ones. The acceptance of this psychological orientation had its effect upon the methods employed by caseworkers in their dealings with persons in need. The child guidance clinic movement with its stress upon early treatment and prevention of mental problems and delinquency encouraged the trend.

Gains in 1920's and 1930's. In the later 1920's, it was seen in social casework theory that acceptance by the worker of the client and his values was essential to successful casework practice. The previous planning done by social caseworkers for the benefit of their clients was found oftentimes to lead nowhere, because the clients themselves had not really been taken into account in terms of allowing them to help themselves. At this time social caseworkers realized that in order to respect the rights of clients as well as to be efficient they were obliged to allow clients much more freedom and responsibility in making life decisions.

In all of the later periods in the development of social casework theory there was a continuance in one form or another of the prior gains. By the early 1930's the conception of "relationship" (between worker and client) which previously had engaged the attention of social caseworkers again became important but with a refinement derived from experience. Certain psychoanalytic contributions also came more to the foreground, such as the value of catharsis and free association interviewing.

The depression of the 1930's burst upon social casework with terrific force. With it came the modification of many features previously extant. Most of the private agencies were forced to reconsider their function in the community, to devise new techniques of helping people in shorter time, to cooperate with fresh-born governmental agencies, and to face a different type of problem presented by their clients.

Gradually, a more conscious appropriation of psychological theory also characterized the times. But social caseworkers were unable to come to any single agreement as to which theory of psychology should guide them in their activities. As a result at least two schools of thought grew up, the "organismic" and the "functional," with many points in common and a few held distinctively. These schools were based upon the teachings of Sigmund Freud and Otto Rank.[2]

Advances During Second World War. Social casework, like some other branches of human knowledge and action, came under profound influences during the period of the Second World War. Many of the advances which characterize modern practice were initiated or strengthened by wartime experience.

For one thing, during the war, social agencies witnessed an increase in personal problems on the part of clients, in contradistinction to material problems. It is true that the disruptions of war caused many persons to suffer financially, but mainly it was the number and variety of emotional, nonmaterial problems that increased. To meet this need the counseling responsibilities of family agencies were enlarged. This development also gave social caseworkers reason to examine the nature of their services to individuals with personal problems and to "grow in wisdom and stature" because of them.

[2]Their significance for the beginning student of social casework will only be noted here as they are dealt with more extensively in the training received in graduate schools of social work as advanced topics of interest. One statement on the subject for the mature student is: Kenneth L. M. Pray, "A Restatement of the Generic Principles of Social Casework Practice," *Journal of Social Casework*, volume 28, number 8, October, 1947, pp. 283–290.

The war also provided opportunities for social work to become known to large numbers of people who previously had not been acquainted with it at all or else with particular aspects of it only. The fact that social caseworkers were widely represented on selective service boards brought them into contact with the lay people on the boards and with the young men who were examined by them. The recognition by the armed services of a definite social work category in personnel also directed attention to social work. In the armed services many men and women came to know the meaning of social work for the first time. Medical and psychiatric social workers were especially in demand during the war.

More persons on the home front became acquainted with social work through the extension of its activities into certain new fields. Day nurseries sprang up throughout the country. While some operated on a basis not completely desirable in all respects, many were expertly run and included within their services the contributions of social caseworkers. The latter were important in considering problems connected with admission to day nurseries and with the relations between children, nurseries, and parents.

In addition to the introduction of casework services in day nurseries, there were other extensions of social work on the home front. Many industries found it convenient (and even necessary) to employ caseworkers to deal with their employees' problems. In war-swollen cities caseworkers helped many families who had not known social work previously. Likewise, social workers were employed in war-relocation centers as well as in army rehabilitation camps.

Where agencies were already in existence, new and manifold obligations were added to older ones. Organizations like the American Red Cross became exceedingly large, with many new types of problems confronting its workers. After the war, social work became an increasingly important part of the Veterans Administration and other veteran-serving organizations, aiding men and women who were disabled, physically and mentally, by the war. So in many ways casework was given new responsibilities and fresh opportunities for service in the Second World War. It may be added that social work by and large met the challenge of the war with greater ability and more efficient responsiveness than it met the challenge of the economic depression of the 1930's.

Current Trends. Following the experience of the Second World War came a period of resettlement and revaluation for social caseworkers, a logical aftermath of the wartime activities.

One of the current trends is the continuing movement of workers from the older and more established agencies and organizations which formerly dominated the field to the newer and more experimental areas of social work.

Social casework at the present time also is more aware of its own distinctive contributions to human welfare than perhaps at any time in the past. Dependent as it always has been upon other fields of knowledge and not always possessing a sound public prestige, social casework has still been able to work out some of its major problems as a profession. It is now receiving increased popular recognition. Gone are the days for social casework when its right to existence was debated, when many social caseworkers were trying to prove that they were something other than social caseworkers. Also the increased awareness on the part of lay people to the benefits of social casework has tended to boost morale in the field.

Social casework has become surer of its place in the community partly because it has developed, through the experience of the past, more definite concepts and methods than it ever had. While much of social casework still depends upon case-by-case understanding of human behavior, there has been built up through the decades of its modern activity enough data to permit a more secure outlook on the part of its personnel. There is much which remains to be done, and, while social caseworkers are not cocksure today about their advances, neither are they hesitant and fearful.

Social casework is increasingly aware of the need for further strength. In part, this will come about through those measures which will encourage and permit more qualified personnel. It will be helped by improving the standards both of practice and of salaries. It will also be aided by maintaining a watchful eye for newer, useful knowledge being developed in allied fields.

The Practice of Social Casework

Social casework is essentially a generic process. It features certain common elements which can be applied in a number of situations. The auspices under which it is practiced comprise the structure of community relations built up in the past and currently giving the process its organizational form.

Initially, social casework was practiced in a relatively few types of agencies and institutions. But, increasingly, through the years it has been utilized in newer settings so that today there are many agencies, institutions, and organizations which find the contributions of social caseworkers valuable. It would be impossible to list all of these, but a

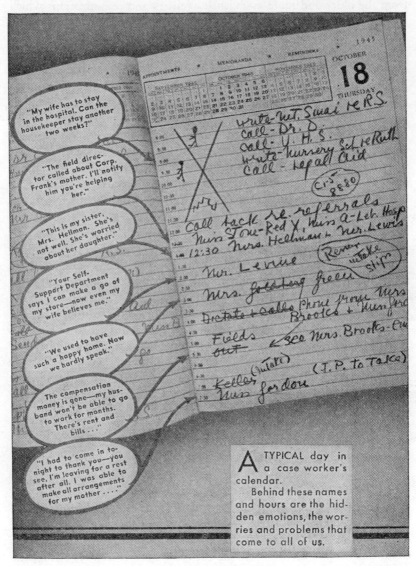

Fig. 3. A Typical Day in a Caseworker's Calendar
(Jewish Family Service, New York City.)

large number can be mentioned to give an idea of the wide scope of the field: hospitals, clinics, courts, industry, military organizations, family welfare agencies both governmental (federal, state, and local) and voluntary, the American Red Cross, travelers' aid societies, immigrant agencies, agencies for the practice of child welfare, institutions for the aged, for criminals and delinquents, for dependent and handicapped children, foster home agencies, day nurseries and schools, adoption agencies, child guidance clinics, mental-hygiene organizations, health organizations, and others.

The importance of the situations in which social casework is practiced varies, even as does the volume of services supplied. (See Figure 3.) In a book such as this, which intends to introduce the beginning student to social casework and to general social work, there is no possibility of giving detailed attention to each and every one of the agencies, institutions, and organizations using casework methods. But, in general, in Chapters 3 to 12 inclusive, social casework will be examined in relation to its organizational settings. It should be borne in mind, however, that social casework is a generic process which is modified by the manner in which it is practiced by specific agencies.

SOCIAL WORK HELPS GROUPS

Social Group Work

That branch of social work which helps individuals in their relations to certain groups is called *social group work*. It is a process of helping individuals through their participation in leisure-time, educational activities conducted under a group leader. While social group work is directed primarily at benefiting individuals, its effects relate to group behavior and even to the broader community and its values. Group work is often spoken of as "character building" in its effect, and in this sense it is rather closely related to the aims of social casework. But, to a considerable measure, the "character building" results of social group work refer to the over-all contribution of the process to the strengthening of wholesome living for individuals within the community, and to the nature of the activities in which such groups engage.

Group work is based upon the conception that all human beings have basic, common needs. These include certain ones which can be satisfied through group association. Not all forms of group association, however, will satisfy these needs. Some, in fact, tend to thwart them. In the recent decades, especially, through increased industrialism, urbanism, and secularism, some of the former means by which individuals were able to satisfy their group needs (such as the church, the family) have lost some of their prestige or influence. In the face of such developments, social group work fulfills a significant function. It promises an even greater contribution to human affairs in the future.

Methods Vary. The method of social group work is somewhat different from that of social casework, although both are concerned with the development of better human relations. Social casework, however, as it is currently practiced is primarily responsible for treatment. It assumes conditions in many instances both within and without the individual which need remedying.[3] Social group work, however, is perhaps more positively oriented. It is responsible for the constructive use made by individuals of group experience, but it is also employed extensively to help people develop more socially acceptable and socially desirable values and abandon socially unacceptable behavior. Social group work, therefore, is not primarily therapeutic, except as that term is used very broadly.

In the application of his knowledge to the social group work situation, the professional worker uses a wide variety of methods. The chief starting point for these methods is the nature of the group in the specific instance. Each group, according to the principles of social group work, has the right to determine its own activities as long as certain broad but fundamental conditions are not violated. This recognition of the particular group's activity means that there can be almost as many means of attaining the goals of group work as there are groups. Actually, however, the activities which have instrumental purposes for the group worker are less numerous. They include the following media, among others: arts and crafts, dramatics, music, dancing, games, sports, pottery, photography, nature study, woodwork, sewing, public affairs, home management, nursing, first aid, prenatal and postnatal care, sex information, and discussion of problems of politics, religion, and labor. (See Table 1 on pages 14 and 15.)

The actual application of knowledge in terms of such activities varies from group to group, according to the inherent interests and abilities of the group, the capacity of the group leader, and the materials available to carry out specific aims. It is conceivable that the concrete methods which might be successful in one situation might be questionable in another. What one group leader will be able to accomplish, with his particular personality and training, may be positive in one group

---

[3]Some people believe social casework will be increasingly sought by individuals wishing to maximize their social functioning, not merely to help them solve some urgent problem.

work situation and negative in another. And yet, there are common elements in group work which can to some degree be charted even at the present time. Leadership, also, definitely is not capricious. But, given the variables in the composition of the group work situation on the part of the group members, the leader, the materials available, and other factors, it is easy to see how great variation exists in practice.

Agencies Dealing With Group Work. Basic to the formulation of methods is the nature of the agency engaged in group work. The agency generally determines the type of program which will characterize it and the methods to be used for the achievement of its aims. In the earlier period of social group work most of the programs were supported by voluntary or private agencies interested in leisure-time and recreational services. The activities in that period also pertained chiefly to children and youth. But, in recent years, group work has been extended to other types of agencies. Often today they deal with others than children and youth. The settlement houses, Y's, Boy Scouts and Girl Scouts, and other similar agencies and organizations which dominated the field of social group work previously are still prominent today, but there are also, at the present time, many new explorations of the values of group work in religious education, housing, adult education, hospitals, child-caring institutions, and elsewhere. In the second chapter, on the history of social work, there is a further analysis of the rise of social group work. Likewise, in Chapter 13, more detailed consideration is given to the structure of this form of social work.

Interaction of Members. Social group work, in part, involves an agency structure in the community. But it is chiefly a process. That is, its chief benefits derive not so much from the agencies which support it as from the actual processes of interaction among the members of groups. In regard to this interaction, there are two focal points—the interaction of the various members with each other, and the interaction between the members as a group and the group leader. The excellence of group leadership can never be a satisfying substitute for the benefits derived from the interaction of the group members themselves. The reliance of the group work process for fulfillment upon the interaction between the members of groups is intrinsic to the practice of social group work. It is among the members that the goals of social group work mainly rest. Without a leader, however, there can be no social group work process. The group worker gives direction to group activities and aspirations. He understands the requirements of the group work process in detail. He can be helpful to groups in providing short-cuts, taken from his knowledge and experience, for

Table 1

PERCENTAGE DISTRIBUTION OF MALES AND FEMALES
BY RECREATIONAL ACTIVITY OF FIRST CHOICE

Recreational Activity of First Choice	Male	Recreational Activity of First Choice	Female
Total*	100.0	Total†	100.0
Travel	16.3	Travel	17.4
Athletics (participation) ..	13.0	Swimming	7.5
Swimming	7.4	Dancing (social)	5.2
Automobile riding	2.3	Tennis	4.8
Boating, fishing	2.1	Movies	2.9
Singing, playing (solo) ...	2.0	Reading	2.9
Tennis	1.9	Singing, playing (solo) ...	2.9
Reading	1.8	Horseback riding	2.2
Movies	1.7	Athletics (participation) ..	1.9
Camping	1.4	Automobile riding	1.8
Dancing (social)	1.3	Concerts (attendance) ...	1.8
Trips	1.3	Parties, socials	1.6
Gymnasium, dancing	1.0	Trips	1.6
Concerts (attendance) ...	0.9	Theater	1.4
Drawing, modeling	0.9	Drawing, modeling	1.0
Theater	0.8	Sewing	0.8
Boxing	0.7	Visiting, entertaining	0.7
Care or repair auto, radio	0.7	Golf	0.6
Horseback riding	0.7	Gymnasium, dancing	0.6
Golf	0.6	Handicraft	0.6
Photography	0.6	Pets (care of)	0.6
Pets (care of)	0.5	Radio (listening)	0.5
Radio (listening)	0.4	Acting (amateur)	0.4
Acting (amateur)	0.3	Camping	0.4
Clubs (not political or civic)	0.3	Clubs (not political or civic)	0.4
Collections (stamp, etc.) .	0.3	Hiking and walking	0.4

(continued on page 15)

the attainment of their purposes. He is a fund of information and wisdom for the successful operation of the group process. It may be possible for a group to achieve its purposes without the assistance of a group leader, but the presence of a group leader should enable the members to attain their goals more efficiently and more rewardingly. Thus the quality of the relationship between the group worker and his group may be compared in importance to the quality of the relationship between the social caseworker and his client.

Individual Approach. Implicit in the methodology of social group work is individualization. By individualization is meant the differential

Table 1 (*continued*)

PERCENTAGE DISTRIBUTION OF MALES AND FEMALES
BY RECREATIONAL ACTIVITY OF FIRST CHOICE

Recreational Activity of First Choice	Male	Recreational Activity of First Choice	Female
Total*	100.0	Total†	100.0
Parties, socials	0.3	Lectures (attendance) ...	0.4
Visiting, entertaining	0.3	Boating, fishing	0.3
Writing (stories, etc.) ...	0.3	Card games	0.3
Card games	0.2	Skating (ice)	0.3
Carpentry, painting, repairing	0.2	Skating (roller)	0.3
		Museums	0.2
Debating, group discussion	0.2	Picnics, outings	0.2
Lectures (attendance) ...	0.2	Writing (stories, etc.) ...	0.2
Pool	0.2	Civic, political	0.1
Skating (ice)	0.2	Collections (stamp, etc.) .	0.1
Church social activities ...	0.1	Photography	0.1
Civic, political	0.1	Singing, playing (group) ..	0.1
Hiking and walking	0.1	Nature study	(††)
Museums	0.1	Pool	(††)
Nature study	0.1	Puzzles, table games	(††)
Picnics, outings	0.1	Other	2.3
Puzzles, table games	0.1	No first choice	32.2
Singing, playing (group) ..	0.1		
Skating (roller)	0.1		
Other	2.5		
No first choice	33.3		

*Based on reports for 3,614 males.   †Based on reports for 3,943 females.
††Less than one tenth of 1 percent.

Source: Nettie P. McGill and Ellen N. Matthews, *The Youth of New York City,* copyright, 1940, by the Macmillan Company, New York, and used with their permission.

approach to the member's stage of growth and his abilities. Obviously, this process is basic to the fulfillment of the aims of social group work. For the individual exists in the social group work situation not merely for the satisfaction of commendable group goals and the meeting of certain community needs under the direction of an efficient group leader, but the group process is also organized to supply him with satisfactions for his basic needs. Group work, in this sense, must be individually oriented. But the group leader cannot assume that the sheer participation of a member in a group will satisfy the member's basic needs. A merely fortuitous arrangement of group activities would probably not go very far toward the meeting of such needs. A general, over-all direction of group activities, moreover, also would not completely meet the requirements of social group work. Instead, the facilities of the group and the leader must be harnessed consciously to meet basic individual satisfactions. This is the meaning of individualization.

As a responsibility, individualization obviously rests more on the shoulders of the leader than upon the membership, for often the membership is not too aware of individual needs. But, by whatever means the individual is taken into account, and this is usually by the group leader, the individual member is one of the chief interests of social group work.

Developments and Trends

Social group work is a relatively recent development. While social casework may still be quite youthful, social group work is even more undeveloped. Of course, in one form or another, group methods have always been used with varying degrees of effectiveness. A large backlog of experience, therefore, was available when group work took on a professional character. However, it is difficult to date the beginnings of modern social group work. Some would put the inception of its modern phase at various times within the latter part of the nineteenth century. Perhaps its rise can be dated back to the use of group methods by city missions or by the social settlements in that period.

In the beginning, social group work agencies frequently stressed their differences. In some cases they championed individual approaches to problems of a general nature without actively joining in cooperative exploration of those problems. With this outlook many forms of social group work came into existence with varying degrees of meaning and effectiveness.

New Outlook. It was not for some years that group work began a more coordinated quest for essential and generic conceptions and methods. The development of these ideas and methods was facilitated by the understanding of human behavior and its application. The increased knowledge of group life available after many years of trial and error, the more pressing needs within the profession for consolidation and improved standards, the development of perspective gained from other fields, and the general tenor of the times—all gave impetus to a distinctive and concrete meaning for social group work. The growth of this process was expressed in the various study groups formed during the 1930's and the courses and sections at state conferences of social work. By 1936 these were well enough developed to permit the organization at the National Conference of Social Work of a national, year-round coordinating agency in the field. As a result the National Association for the Study of Group Work was born. Later, it became the present-day American Association of Group Workers.

Growth of Professional Awareness. The growth of social group work has been steady and notable during the recent years. Certainly, the most significant progress made in the field has been the development of professional awareness. This is evidenced by the attitude of social group workers on every hand. There is a willingness to undertake patient study of the group process which is showing some positive results. Professional standards are higher now than ever before. Persons without a full educational background feel increasingly the need for supplementary knowledge. Social work schools are recognizing the importance of social group work by organizing curricula which will greatly strengthen the professional leadership in the field. Social workers generally are more alert to the possibilities of social group work and in many instances are cooperating with social group work agencies for activities of mutual benefit.

The spread of the method of group work to fresh proving grounds is another significant trend. As was mentioned earlier, the older types of agencies which found group work to be of value no longer dominate the field. The entrance of social group work into various fields (such as religious education, hospitals, and housing) holds the promise of a contribution which is essentially unlimited. In each new application of social group work, additional understanding regarding the nature of the work is created.

Rise of Group Therapy. The rise in recent years of various forms of group therapy indicates another trend.[4] The importance of group therapy is today recognized in many types of agencies. For some years it has been utilized, although in a nascent condition, in child guidance clinics and now has reached its most mature development in such agencies. But experience gained through the war years indicated that the methods of group therapy can have a much wider application. Already there are signs of the development of group therapy into a major type of social group work activity. As such therapy develops, however, it may become a separate specialty within social work, somewhat divorced from group work. Social group work, as mentioned

'Group therapy is the group treatment of individual behavior problems under the direction of a trained leader who combines the principles and methods of individual psychotherapy, social group work, and certain other specialized techniques.

previously, is concerned with the development of normal individuals who wish to take part in definitely constructive experience. Group therapy or "psychiatric group work" is aimed more toward those persons who cannot utilize the benefits of normal group experience. However, the boundaries between normal and abnormal, as is generally known, are uncertain.

SOCIAL WORK HELPS COMMUNITIES

Community Organization

Social work in the form in which it helps communities is called *community organization*. Community organization, as a basic process of social work, concentrates not so much on the individual and his needs or on the group and its growth as upon the larger and more inclusive welfare problems of the whole community. True, it seeks to strengthen the effective accomplishment of casework and group work, but it has other responsibilities as well.

The focus of community organization is upon the activities of groups of people. It is distinguished from casework on the grounds that social casework cooperates with individuals in need. It differs from group work in that group work mostly deals with the activities of specified groups. Community organization begins when a relationship is established between two or more groups to affect community welfare. For this reason, community organization has often been called intergroup work.

Community organization is not exclusively a social work process in its most general terms. It can relate to the processes engaged in by citizens' groups who attempt any particular social gain. The activities of churches, for example, which federate in a community to achieve a social goal might also be termed community organization. Likewise, although on a completer plane, there are those cooperative attempts on the part of entire communities to meet disaster, war, or other tragedy. These too may be called community organization. In fact, the modern community organizer recognizes the fact that the term has no single meaning and that its connotations are broader than social work itself. That this is so does not nullify community organization as a significant factor in the over-all attainment of social work purposes. It simply means that the process is more general than social work, although it is entirely germane to social work.

Existence Required. The need for a process such as community organization is demonstrable not alone on the grounds that there are problems of a community character, relating to social welfare goals, which require the process. Community organization also rests upon the fact that its existence is required by the social work processes of casework and group work. At many points community organization is a logical outgrowth of social casework and social group work problems and perspectives. Thus a caseworker may deal with clients who are delinquent, in part, because of the lack of playground facilities. Group work agencies in the neighborhood may be overtaxed and not able to meet the problem adequately. The creation of new facilities, based on the interests of various agencies and groups within a neighborhood, would be an example of the way in which community organization carries out operations which casework and group work cannot undertake independently.

Community organization has grown, particularly in recent years. Even previously, when social work itself was not a major enterprise as it now is, there was definite need for community organization. But, within the last few decades, social work itself has grown tremendously and the need for community organization has increased at least proportionately.

The rise of the public services in unprecedented volume and range has made new responsibilities for social workers, in general, and especially for community organizers. Today, in many localities there is a need to coordinate the activities not only of the many privately financed social work agencies, but to organize them and the diverse public agencies into a coherent working arrangement. Much has been done to fashion an intelligibly efficient welfare pattern in many places, but much more remains to be accomplished.

Community Organization Activities

There is no easy way of defining and prescribing the activities of community organization. Some of them are especially connected with social work administration. Others are performed by caseworkers and group workers and are felt to be more related to their responsibilities than to those of the professional community organizer. But, in general, some of the activities which can be identified as community organization are the following: coordination, joint financing, public relations work, research, planning, and the initiation of services. These functions may be assumed by an individual agency in regard to its own program. They may involve neighborhood councils, councils of social work agencies, state and regional councils of agencies, national agencies, and international agencies. The details of the community organization process and of the agency structure which gives the process support will be discussed in the last chapter of this book.

Community organization reflects its past development. The bulk of community organization in the past, as in the present, was carried on by casework agencies and group work agencies. In the recent decades, however, since the community needs relating to casework and group work have become extremely complex, agencies have come into existence which are primarily responsible for certain community activities. The trend at present seems to be toward the creation of a more professional operation of these community activities.

Uneven Distribution. Community organization, like the other elements of social work, is presently unevenly distributed. In some cities there are strong community organization agencies which assist the casework and group work agencies in the fulfillment of their obligations. But, in others (and there are a large number), the possibilities of community action have not been realized and developed. In some instances such lack of development is due to the inadequacy of community leadership. Thus a community may see some irritating problems and may vaguely wish to cooperate toward their solution, but may not have anyone available to point the way. In other instances there is a lack of coordination of the various activities aimed at community betterment so that the resulting confusion encourages frustration.

Position of Organizer. The growth and the quality of community organization facilities are always dependent upon the willingness of citizens to cooperate toward a common objective. Without cooperation the community organizer can achieve neither his goals nor the community's. In this respect the community organizer takes a position in regard to his particular problems that the caseworker and the group worker take toward theirs. All three specialists within social work are dependent ultimately upon the desire of persons in need to make a self-initiated response to their needs. They may seek to stimulate this response by their cooperative spirit and their willingness to view problems objectively. But, basically, they seek to help people in terms of the values the people themselves hold and not in terms of the aims they set up *de novo.* This attitude, important in the whole of social work, is fundamental to the community organization process.

The community organizer not only contributes his knowledge to his activities, but he also acts as a positive catalyst in stimulating and encouraging community action. While it is true to say that he does not force his opinions upon the community (or groups within the community), nevertheless he cannot remain absolutely neutral. He does have attitudes formed on the basis of some degree of reliable evidence, and, being involved in concrete situations, it is inevitable that he will be sharing those sentiments with others. His enthusiasm sets the pace and helps to energize those he is leading. His willingness to serve the objective interests of the community leads others to imitate him. So the community organizer is not a passive instrument of groups concerned with community action, but he is a practitioner of the art of democratic leadership. In other words he allows the followership to maintain the basic initiative in achieving their aims, but he still acts as participant leader.

SOCIAL ACTION

Social work has always been concerned with social action. The latter is inherently related to the ultimate objectives of casework, group work, and community organization. An agency which does not have an active interest in community improvement, no matter what its primary tasks may be, is simply not meeting its full responsibility.

Social action is opposed in its meaning to individual action. It is engaged in by groups. It also relates to goals which groups deem to be desirable for the community. While it is not easy to define exactly what actions are socially beneficial, there is a vague but rather effective common consensus as to what is legitimate, at least for a small area such as a local community. Social action also connotes a marked degree of organization on the part of the groups involved in it. This indicates that usually there is a very conscious selection of objectives and a quite definite organization related to the achievement of the aims.

Social action, on one hand, may seek to modify the environment in ways which will not disturb its fundamental structure. Such actions are generally more feasible than others simply because they meet with weaker resistance from certain elements of the community. On the other hand social action may strive to effect a basic revision of the social and economic organization of the community for the benefit of all. Such actions are obviously difficult as they usually meet with the combined resistance of many elements within the community. It is impossible to say which type of social action is more effective, and the validity of whole philosophies of general action are involved in each. But the fact is that not all situations require radical modification, while some do.

Social action, in the sense used here, is not particularly the monopoly of social work. Opinion within the field of social work generally varies on this point and there is no possibility at present of declaring social action either as a basic purpose of social work in an exclusive sense or as a supplementary aim. But, whatever its status, social action is accepted by all social workers as a part of their responsibility.

SOCIAL WORK INTERRELATIONSHIPS

Social work, as can be seen in the preceding discussion, is a method of helping individuals, groups, and communities. It is composed of social casework, social group work, and community organization. Basic to these processes are the assisting elements of social action, social research, and administration. Social research and administration, however, may be conceived not as special and fundamental processes of social work, but as factors which aid in the fulfillment of the three major divisions of social casework, social group work, and community organization.

All three of the processes of social work are united in a philosophy of procedure as well as a philosophy of objectives. In regard to procedures, all are based upon specialized knowledge, most of which is overlapping in actual application. All three, likewise, are founded upon the individualization of problems or situations, whether of an individual, group, or community character. All are limited to specific functions rather than being general means, either alone or together, for the change of social conditions.

In regard to objectives, social casework, social group work, and community organization share in common the aim of increasing and maintaining the well-being of human beings. They are united, moreover, in giving notable attention to those individuals, groups, and communities requiring support and improvement.

No one of the social work processes can be said to be independent of the others. Each requires the others. No one is dominant because of the type of assistance it is able to render. Together, working in harmony to the degree to which it is possible, they can accomplish much. Separately, they tend to frustrate even the activities for which they individually stand.

BASIC CONCEPTS OF SOCIAL WORK

Social work possesses its own body of knowledge. In part it is similar to that held by other professional fields. In its scope and inherent meaning, however, it is distinctive and unique. The body of knowledge which characterizes social work has not been evolved in a brief time, but represents a considerable period of development.

The general concepts which are currently operative in social work are numerous and cannot be treated here in detail. Some, however, need to be mentioned and commented upon briefly.

An Understanding of Individual and Collective Behavior

Social work rests upon the solid knowledge of human behavior. For this understanding, social work must rely for the most part upon the contributing social sciences, but other branches of learning also are of marked value. It looks to sociology to learn the effect of human culture on individual behavior and the meaning of the participation of the individual in his various groups. It turns to psychology to see the nature of mental and behavioral mechanisms and of personality make-up in its ramified detail. Social work is interested in economics because material considerations of income, employment, and other economic factors influence the lives of persons. It finds that political science illuminates many of the problems which individuals possess. History has given social work perspective and detailed understanding of the background factors in the current problems of people. Philosophy challenges social work with its presentation of the relevance of ideas and ideals. Likewise, literature also enriches the understanding of the social worker. In the physical sciences, biology and related subjects appropriately set the stage for many activities of the social worker, as in matters of physical health. In all, there are few contributions in the arts, social sciences, and physical sciences which are not pertinent to social work. Anything which casts light on the nature of human nature—the requirements of social living, the inspiration of the past, the ideas which influence behavior, and other related concerns—comprises part of the knowledge essential for the modern social worker.

General Background Is Essential. To say that the social worker is required to understand individual behavior in terms of the various fields of knowledge which have been suggested, however, is to ask the impossible. No person will ever be completely competent in even a subdivision of one of those fields. But the social worker should seek a first-class understanding of human behavior and should learn to call on the experts in those specialties as required. Some subjects will be more important than others, but all have some place in the preparation of the social worker. Because a general background is so necessary for the social worker, it is appropriate that students not seek to specialize too early in their preparation, but try to gain the widest possible knowledge of human behavior.

Yet specialization is necessary. Diverse fields of knowledge have made their contribution to social work practice, but there also has been knowledge gained about human behavior from social work itself. The graduate schools of social work in large part embody the knowledge gained from this experience, as well as from the other fields of learning. They are able to relate the breadth of this understanding to the specific tasks which are set before the social worker in practice. Beyond the graduate schools of social work lies the field of practice, where success depends upon a sound understanding of individual and collective behavior.

Development of Understanding

Social work rests upon sound knowledge, but it does not end there. It is no "ivory tower" contemplation of human behavior, but the effort to educate individuals, groups, and communities through their exigencies as to the ways in which they may garner strength for future as well as current problems. Information of the most reliable kind must be used, but the effort at education will include other factors as well. The knowledge which the social worker possesses regarding the nature of human behavior must be shared with persons in need so that they will be better able to understand themselves and the problems they face. In that sense, the development of understanding is a basic concept of social work.

But the social worker uses his understanding of human behavior selectively in dealing with people. On the one hand the effort to secure understanding centers around the particular problem presented. Insights[5] are given only when they are relevant. On the other hand the knowledge which the worker employs to aid in the development of understanding is also delimited by the maturity of the persons involved. There may be many insights occurring to the social worker which theoretically may be helpful to specific problems. But the worker must consider not only the problems, but the persons as well. If a caseworker, for example, feels that a client to some degree has a problem because of his attachment to his mother, he may not be able to speak frankly about this because the client may not be prepared to receive any such suggestion. But, whatever modifications are necessary, the basic truth is evident. Social work is, in part, educational. It enables people to grow in the understanding of themselves and in their effectiveness in dealing with the problems they face.

Reliance Upon the Initiative of the Individual

The dynamics of the social work process are also based upon the concept that the persons concerned should take the initiative in meeting their needs. This view has developed out of social workers' actual ex-

[5]Insights are penetrating discernments or intuitions used in interpreting the relationships of events.

perience. Earlier, social caseworkers thought that it was possible to direct others as to how they might meet their problems. But it was discovered in time that there are a number of factors which make such a supposition false. For one thing it is now granted that no social caseworker can even pretend to know the "right" solution to every problem. Others may think that they have such infallibility, but certainly the modern social worker does not claim it. Secondly, the worker realizes, as a result of his experience, that people do not usually like to take advice, and, when they do, it is successful only to the degree to which it is in agreement with their preconceived ideas. It is most difficult for an individual to act upon advice which runs contrary to his preconceptions as to what is proper. Also, there is the matter of responsibility for decisions. Social workers have realized that to make a decision for another places one under certain responsibility. For if the social worker makes a decision for another person, he assumes the blame or praise which the consequences of that decision entail. No social worker wishes to jeopardize his status with his clients or with the public by accepting such responsibility. In actual fact, however, responsibility for outcome rests to some degree with the worker.

These interpretations, however, are essentially negative and they miss the main point. The chief concern of social workers today is that individuals assume responsibility for initiative themselves, since it is only by this means that people can grow in understanding and effectiveness. If the person is simply told what to do, the chances are that the next time he faces a problem, he will have to be told again. If, on the other hand, he will tackle the particular problem himself, he will gain insight and practical experience that will stand him in good stead when future problems arise. Not until the person has made a genuine decision as to what he wishes to do and how he wishes to do it has he understood the real meaning of growth. Again, from the valuative point of view, the worker, being impressed with the inherent dignity and respect of persons, does not feel it within his jurisdiction to encroach upon their prerogatives.

Limitations. Of course, there are limitations which the social worker must set upon the right of the person to determine his own actions. The worker, being part of an organization (usually called a "social work agency"), must represent the conditions for service which are required by his organization. The help he can provide must always be predicated on that condition, and the person in need must abide by such limitations.

Social workers also must limit the individual's use of initiative when such use would seem to work harm upon the person himself or upon others. As has been intimated previously, not all persons or groups are prepared in terms of knowledge or emotional development to make their own decisions. Nautically, we speak about the Plimsoll's mark on a ship. This load-line mark on the sides of vessels indicates the limit of submergence allowed by law. Psychologically, all individuals and groups have their Plimsoll's mark, indicating the amount of responsibility and decision which they can really manage without running into danger.

Judicious Deployment of Resources

Knowledge is a resource for helping people. In its manifold forms it is perhaps the basic resource. It is for this reason that it is so important to the social work process. But knowledge which is usable in social work is of at least two sorts: (1) the knowledge which the social worker has of human behavior and of other resources; (2) the knowledge which the persons they help have of themselves and of other resources. In regard to the first, some attention has been given to the knowledge regarding individual and collective behavior possessed by the social worker. The worker, however, must have other knowledge as well. To the extent to which the social worker knows the resources of the community he will be able to aid people. Thus in casework, for example, a person with tuberculosis may come to an agency which is not equipped to treat such problems. Referring him to an agency which could be of help would be a definite service. Such a referral requires a knowledge of the community's resources.

The social worker also relates to particular circumstances certain resources which his agency makes available, according to its regulations. Thus a club in need of a meeting place may be provided with space by a settlement house.

In regard to the second—the knowledge persons have of themselves and of other resources—some attention has been given to the fact that people have within themselves certain strengths (knowledge, courage, awareness, etc.) which enable them to aid themselves. Also, they may have heard of community resources not known to the worker. They may understand ways of meeting problems missed by the worker. They may recall resources not previously considered in connection with their problem.

Social work, then, is based upon the judicious deployment of resources. Aside from the basic form of knowledge, the facilities of a community are in many localities almost unlimited. The combination of the possibilities of the religious, educational, industrial, medical, and political institutions within large cities presents a picture of resources which is staggering to contemplate.

7 OUT OF TEN FAMILIES IN SYRACUSE USED SOME ONE OR MORE OF THE TOWN'S 114 HEALTH AND WELFARE SERVICES

FIG. 4. Extent of Use of Health and Welfare Services in Syracuse

(Pictograph Corporation for *Social Work and the Joneses,* by Ruth Lerrigo and Bradley Buell, Public Affairs Pamphlet No. 97, published by Public Affairs Committee, Inc., New York, 1944.)

Quality of the Personal Relationship

Practically all that has been suggested in this section of the chapter comes into focus when it is again realized that social work rests ultimately upon the quality of the personal relationship between the worker and the client. This relationship, present in all forms of social work, constitutes the medium through which persons are able to develop themselves by using their knowledge and that presented by the worker. This relationship increases the possibility that people will act on their own initiative. Resources are discovered and explored within the relationship. In fact, a very large part of the social work process ultimately depends upon the quality of the contacts between the worker and the person with whom he is working.

Importance. The importance of the quality of the relationship is shown particularly in casework. In many cases the client will have contradictory feelings about his problem. If the worker should be suspicious, making judgments about the moral implications of the problem or the solutions entered into by the person in need, little of a helpful nature will emerge. But if the worker is able to accept the client, his values, his mistakes, his emotional contradictions, and his uncertain solutions, with a calm assurance that deeply respects his dignity, there may come about a release of tensions, anxieties, guilt feelings, and fears which hitherto may have immobilized the person. Quite often in social casework practice, the actual problems persons face are hardly more important to them than the feelings accompanying the problems. They may need the services of the social caseworker because of all those who have sought to aid them none has approached them and their problems with the idea of accepting them as they actually are. Thus the quality of the relationship should be such that the client is accepted by the social caseworker. Of course, this acceptance on the part of the worker does not mean that he makes the person's problem and values his very own. That would be impossible and undesirable. In fact, it is always necessary and important for the worker to maintain professional standards.

While the above discussion makes evident the importance of the relationship between the social caseworker and the client, the quality of the personal relationships in group work and in community organization is equally important.

The five basic ingredients in social work just discussed are not separate activities which regulate social work practice. They are here analyzed, but in actual practice they are synthesized. This integration, of course, is not easy of achievement. Probably no one can secure it simply by understanding the components. Knowledge is required, but skill is also implied.

SOCIAL WORK AS A PROFESSION

One of the most serious problems in present-day social work is the shortage of adequately trained personnel. This shortage has been persistent and there are few signs to indicate that it will shortly be relieved. It threatens the maintenance, nationally, of high social work standards and cripples at many points the advances social work might make. (See Figures 5 and 6.)

Historically, social work has been very largely staffed by persons who volunteered their services in one way or another for philanthropic activities. In many instances these were persons of independent means with considerable leisure time and social conscience. Even the operations of public welfare for the most part in the past were dependent upon volunteers.

New Understanding of Welfare Rights

Modern social work had its roots in feelings of charitableness. From the financial point of view such feelings often were termed philanthropy. But social work grew in time to a new and different understanding of what is involved in helping others. It recognized that feelings of superiority or even genuine "charity" were not sufficient to meet the requirements of people in need. In many instances such attitudes wrought more harm than good. Gradually, social workers based their work more on philosophies contrary to that of philanthropy. They

SOCIAL WORK — A SMALL PROFESSION

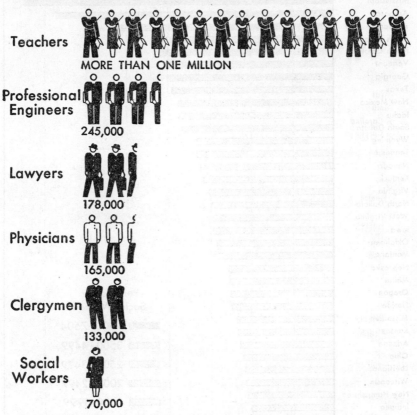

FIG. 5. Number of Social Workers Compared to Other Professions

(Pictograph Corporation for *Social Work and the Joneses,* by Ruth Lerrigo and Bradley Buell, Public Affairs Pamphlet No. 97, published by Public Affairs Committee, Inc., New York, 1944.)

viewed society as a social organism in which the welfare of the individuals affected the well-being of the whole. They saw that a realistic application of democratic theory implied that everyone had certain welfare rights. The "pursuit of happiness" may be somewhat intangible, but it is a powerful sentiment when taken seriously. Calculations indicated furthermore that while social work is expensive to a society it is probably not so expensive as the lack of it. In addition, modern knowledge pointed the way to a more adequate understanding of personal and social failures and the means for overcoming them.

Under the impact of these and other factors in the history of social work, there was a shift from the older outlook of social work as an

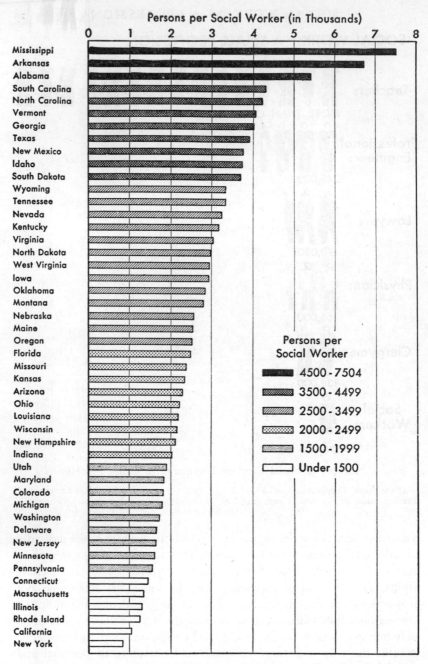

FIG. 6. Rank of States According to Number of Persons per Social Worker, 1940

(Bureau of the Census.)

30

elective activity of a relative few to that of a basic social requirement for the successful and efficient conducting of common social relations. In place of the philanthropist came the social worker.

While it is possible to claim that social work today is not theoretically based on the spirit of philanthropy, it is not possible to claim that philanthropy has been entirely excluded. There are many persons, even today, who engage in social work for motives similar to if not identical with those of the older philanthropist. But, more and more, as adequately trained social workers are made available by the graduate schools of social work, the spirit of philanthropy is diminishing and a newer professional spirit is taking its place.

Rise of Schools of Social Work

The change from philanthropy to social work is mirrored in the rise of the schools of social work. It was not until there was at least some basic redirection of philanthropy that social work as a subject to be taught in organized schools could come into existence. This occurred chiefly at the turn of the present century with the organization of the New York School of Social Work and other schools devoted to the education of social work personnel. By 1919 this development reached such proportions that the American Association of Schools of Social Work could be formed with seventeen charter members. Today, the membership has increased to several times the original figure.

Table 2

SOCIAL AND WELFARE WORKERS IN THE UNITED STATES LABOR FORCE, 1940

	TOTAL		MALE		FEMALE	
	Employed*	Seeking Work	Employed*	Seeking Work	Employed*	Seeking Work†
Total	69,677	2,851	24,868	1,101	44,809	1,750
Urban	58,418	2,532	20,527	972	37,981	1,560
Nonfarm	8,769	240	3,445	104	5,324	136
Farm	2,400	79	896	25	1,504	54
All Rural	11,169	319	4,341	129	6,828	190

*Except those on public emergency work.
†Experienced workers.
Source: United States Census, *Population,* Series P–11, June 9, 1942.

The schools of social work are graduate in nature. Each is connected with a college or university. They offer two general types of experience: (1) course work; and (2) field work. Through these the schools are able to orient their students to the type of understanding required for successful practice and at the same time to provide supervised practical experience in suitable social work agencies. The training, normally leading to a professional Master's degree, regularly requires two years of schooling beyond college. In many of the schools there are organized curricula which prepare specifically for social casework, social group work, community organization, social research, and social work administration.

Undergraduate preparation for social work is increasingly becoming more evident and responsible. The degree of preprofessional specialization varies from college to college, but many today have one or more courses on the subject. These courses, however, should be considered merely as an introduction to later and more extended study of social work in the graduate schools.

Specialized Associations

Professionally, social workers are united in the National Conference of Social Work and the American Association of Social Workers. The first, founded in 1873, holds an annual meeting at which social work themes are discussed. The other, founded in 1921, is similar in organization and program to the professional associations in law and medicine.

In addition to these, social workers often belong to other and more specialized associations. Some of these are the following: American Association of Psychiatric Social Workers, American Association of Group Workers, American Association of Medical Social Workers, American Public Welfare Association, American Association for the Study of Community Organization, National Federation of Settlements, National Association of School Social Workers, and others. Social workers, moreover, may belong to various sectarian organizations.

Several labor unions are open to social workers. Two A. F. of L. unions, the American Federation of Government Employees and the American Federation of State, County, and Municipal Employees, have among their membership social workers employed in government agencies. An even stronger affiliation exists with the C.I.O., in the United Public Workers of America (which includes public welfare workers) and the United Office and Professional Workers of America (which includes workers from voluntary agencies).

Social workers keep up with the advances made in their field through a number of publications as well as through the meetings of the groups previously mentioned. A list of the journals most closely related to social work is included at the close of this book.

The United States Employment Service has developed facilities for the placement and counseling of social workers. Its maintenance of special offices in San Francisco and Cleveland illustrates the importance it places on this type of service.

Requirements for Positions

At present a degree from an accredited school of social work is the chief requirement for positions in the field. In public welfare an important requirement for many positions is qualification according to a merit system. There is also increasing discussion of the values of having registration and certification of social workers generally, similar to those for lawyers and physicians, on a state basis. Puerto Rico has had such a system since 1934 and California passed legislation in 1945 along the same line. In California, social workers who meet the requirements are entitled to use the term "Registered Social Worker" (R.S.W.) in connection with their names.

SOCIAL WORK AND THE SOCIAL SCIENCES

Interrelationships

The student who has been introduced to social work through the reading of this chapter can already piece together something of the relationships between social work and the larger fields of knowledge which make up the social sciences. Social work, as is obvious from this chapter, is not a branch of any of the sciences. In times past a somewhat special relationship existed between social work and departments of sociology in colleges and universities. In some institutions of higher learning, social work is regarded as a kind of applied sociology. Courses in social work are often taught within departments of sociology. Despite the historic ties between social work and sociology, however, it is apparent today that there is no exclusive relationship between the two. As suggested previously, social work draws its insight and skills from many fields of knowledge within the social sciences (and without) and sociology is simply one of them. This does not mean that social work is not indebted to sociology and that it does not depend upon sociological knowledge for its practice; it merely means that the dependence is not absolute or complete. Likewise, social work is not exclusively related to any of the other social sciences: economics, history, philosophy, political science, or psychology. With each of these it maintains and needs cordial relations, but its function is something other than that of any of them. Likewise, social work draws deeply upon knowledge beyond the social sciences.

The student of social work, therefore, should look to all of the social sciences, as well as to the other sciences and the arts, as contributing to his equipment as a professional person. While social work may seem to be a narrow specialization from certain angles, it is in reality very broad. The interrelationships within the field of social work itself are significant and complex. But the relationships of social work with all departments of life are at least as many and certainly as complex. Any happening which affects the well-being of individuals, groups, and communities is of interest to social workers.

Social Work Is a Profession

Social work differs from the various social sciences, moreover, in that it is a profession. Whatever else "profession" may mean, it includes the connotation of skill or artistry. Social work is not a science, comparable to the social sciences, seeking accurate knowledge about man and his social interaction. True, it is fundamentally based upon such knowledge and in no way is antithetical to the spirit of science, broadly conceived. But it has a definite ameliorative and creative function in society. It uses knowledge to meet concrete human needs; in this sense it is an "applied science." The augmenting of skill through the attainment of knowledge is important for social work, but it is not the complete story of the development of professional competence. Knowledge, understanding, and skill—all are parts of the social worker's preparation.

SELECTED READINGS ON THE NATURE AND SCOPE OF SOCIAL WORK

Abbott, Edith, *Social Welfare and Professional Education,* University of Chicago Press, Chicago, 2d edition, revised and enlarged, 1942.

American Association of Schools of Social Work, *Social Work as a Profession,* New York, 1943.

American Association of Social Workers, *Social Case Work: An Outline —A Report of the Milford Conference,* Studies in the Practice of Social Work, number 2, New York, 1929.

Aptekar, Herbert H., *Basic Concepts in Social Case Work,* University of North Carolina Press, Chapel Hill, 1941.

Baxter, Bernice, and Cassidy, Rosalind, *Group Experience: The Democratic Way,* Harper, New York, 1943.

Bingham, Walter V., and Moore, Bruce V., *How to Interview,* Harper, New York, 3d edition, 1941.

Brown, Esther L., *Social Work as a Profession,* Russell Sage Foundation, New York, 4th edition, 1942.

Brown, Josephine C., *The Rural Community and Social Case Work,* Family Welfare Association of America (now Family Service Association of America), New York, 1933.

Bruno, Frank J., *The Theory of Social Work*, Heath, Boston, 1936.

Chapin, F. Stuart, *Contemporary American Institutions: A Sociological Analysis*, Harper, New York, 1935.

Clarke, Helen I., *Principles and Practice of Social Work*, Appleton-Century, New York, 1947.

Coyle, Grace L., editor, *Studies in Group Behavior*, Harper, New York, 1937.

Cuber, John F., and Harper, Robert A., *Problems of American Society: Values in Conflict*, Holt, New York, 1948.

Fink, Arthur E., *The Field of Social Work*, Holt, New York, 1942.

Garrett, Annette, *Interviewing: Its Principles and Methods*, Family Welfare Association of America (now Family Service Association of America), New York, 1944.

Hamilton, Gordon, *Principles of Social Case Recording*, New York School of Social Work Publications, Columbia University Press, New York, 1946.

———, *Theory and Practice of Social Case Work*, New York School of Social Work Publications, Columbia University Press, New York, 1940.

Harrison, S. M., and Andrews, F. E., *American Foundations for Social Welfare*, Russell Sage Foundation, New York, 1946.

Hewes, Amy, *The Contribution of Economics to Social Work*, Forbes Lectures, New York School of Social Work Publications, Columbia University Press, New York, 1930.

King, Edith Shatto, *The Social Service Exchange: A Device for Facilitating the Exchange of Confidential Information Among Welfare and Health Agencies*, Federal Security Agency, Social Security Administration, Bureau of Public Assistance, Bureau Circular number 16, Washington, D.C., 1943.

LaBarre, Maurine Boie; de la Fontaine, Elise; and Blackey, Eileen, *Cultural Problems in Social Case Work*, Family Welfare Association of America (now Family Service Association of America), New York, 1940.

Landis, Benson Y., *Rural Social Work*, Columbia University Press, New York, 1948.

Lee, Porter R., *Social Work as Cause and Function, and Other Papers*, New York School of Social Work Publications, Columbia University Press, New York, 1937.

Lowry, Fern, editor, *Readings in Social Case Work: 1920–1938; Selected Reprints for the Case Work Practitioner*, New York School of Social Work Publications, Columbia University Press, New York, 1939.

MacIver, Robert, *The Contribution of Sociology to Social Work*, Forbes Lectures, New York School of Social Work Publications, Columbia University Press, New York, 1931.

McCormick, Mary J., *Thomistic Philosophy in Social Casework*, Columbia University Press, New York, 1948.

McMillen, A. Wayne, *Community Organization for Social Welfare,* University of Chicago Press, Chicago, 1945.

Niebuhr, Reinhold, *The Contribution of Religion to Social Work,* Forbes Lectures, New York School of Social Work Publications, Columbia University Press, New York, 1932.

Ogden, Jean, and Ogden, Jess, *Small Communities in Action: Stories of Citizen Programs at Work,* Harper, New York, 1946.

Proceedings of the National Conference of Social Work, annually.

Reynolds, Bertha C., *Learning and Teaching in the Practice of Social Work,* Farrar and Rinehart, New York, 1942.

Reynolds, Rosemary, *Evaluating the Field Work of Students,* Family Service Association of America, New York, 1946.

Richmond, Mary, *What Is Social Case Work: An Introductory Description,* Russell Sage Foundation, New York, 1922.

Robinson, Virginia P., *Changing Psychology in Social Case Work,* University of North Carolina Press, Chapel Hill, 1930.

Slavson, Samuel R., *Creative Group Education,* Association Press, New York, 1937.

Steele, Evelyn M., and Blatt, Heiman K., *Careers in Social Service,* In Collaboration with Vocational Guidance Research, Dutton, New York, 1946.

Steiner, Lee R., *Where Do People Take Their Troubles?* Houghton Mifflin, Boston, 1945.

Strode, Josephine, and Strode, P. R., *Introduction to Social Case Work,* Harper, New York, 1940.

Sullivan, Dorothea, editor, *The Practice of Group Work,* American Association for the Study of Group Work (now American Association of Group Workers), Association Press, New York, 1941.

Voiland, Alice L.; Gundelach, Martha Lou; and Corner, Mildred, *Developing Insight in Initial Interviews,* Family Service Association of America, New York, 1947.

Warner, Amos G.; Queen, Stuart A.; and Harper, Ernest B., *American Charities and Social Work,* Crowell, New York, 4th edition, 1930.

Wilson, Gertrude, *Group Work and Case Work: Their Relationship and Practice,* Family Welfare Association of America (now Family Service Association of America), New York, 1941.

Witmer, Helen, *Social Work: An Analysis of a Social Institution,* Farrar and Rinehart, New York, 1942.

Young, Pauline V., *Interviewing in Social Work: A Sociological Analysis,* McGraw-Hill, New York, 1935.

The Social Work Yearbook, *edited by Russell H. Kurtz, published biennially since 1929 by the Russell Sage Foundation, New York, is not mentioned in this bibliography nor in those to follow, because it comprises one of the best current sourcebooks on the many aspects of social work. It can be used with benefit in conjunction with the present study. Likewise, the journals pertaining to social work are not mentioned here but are listed at the end of the book.*

2

The History of American Social Work

Social work in America is related to almost every aspect of our culture. It did not come into being full-blown as an expression of man's humanity to man. Its growth is as long and as devious as that of many other aspects of the American scene.

THE CULTURAL FOUNDATIONS OF SOCIAL WORK

Social work, like other facets of our American tradition, depends for its existence and development upon certain definite social requirements. These social requirements, embracing part of the social structure as well as part of the social process which we usually term "history," will be noted briefly.

Social Mobility

In order for social work to operate as it does today, there must be a significant degree of social mobility, that is, people must have the opportunity of mixing on a rather free basis. If class and caste divisions of a society are pronounced and widely in force, then little social work can exist. For social work depends upon the possibility of a high degree of social interaction—the intermingling of peoples. Thus it is doubtful that social work as it has developed in this country can ever become widely accepted in a country like India, for example, where the caste "lines" are such that a member of one caste could not administer social work services to a member of another. It could exist perhaps in India on a caste basis, each caste and subcaste ministering to its own, but such restriction would undoubtedly handicap its development.

Impersonality

A society with a high degree of impersonality pervading it is rich soil for the growth of social work. Contrariwise, a society with a sensitive appreciation of the highly personal and intimate conditions of life will probably not be so much in need of social work. The contrast can easily be seen in our own country. In the urban communities we find both the highest degree of impersonality and anonymity along with the highest development of the social work services. There are probably other forces at work which account for this correlation, but surely the relationship which we have pointed out bears consideration. So, as might be expected, the lowest development of the social services is found in the rural communities.

A rural society can more or less be characterized as a "primary group" society. By this is meant that there is a high degree of intimate, face-to-face, interpersonal contact among rural people. If someone is disabled, there is more chance of his getting aid from a neighbor or a relative than from a social agency. This is not only because there are fewer social work agencies in the country, but because the distressed person there depends almost completely upon the highly personal relationships he has built up in his rural living. In the city, on the other hand, a distressed person may depend more upon a social work agency for help than upon friends and relatives, possibly because of the predominance of the "secondary group" attitudes he possesses. Undoubtedly, there are many exceptions to these comments.

The Loss of Welfare Function

A part of the general social condition of impersonality is the fact that various institutions in our society have lost their former welfare functions. Since this is so, there has been a more pronounced need for the institution of social work than there otherwise might have been.

Former Role of Family. The family's recreational function is a case in point. There was a time when the family played a much more significant role in the recreational activities of children. Children were prone to organize their recreational life around the family. Johnny played chiefly with his brothers and sisters. In this kind of situation parents were obligated to supply more direction to the recreational pursuits of their children than many do today.

Present-Day Activities. In our time parents are not expected to be the leaders of their children's play experience. This sphere of the lives of their children has been given over to the expert—the person who makes his livelihood through such activity. Thus the modern mother may awaken her young child in the morning and feed him; then she may turn him over to the day nursery for the morning or the whole day. Older children are sent to the public school (which removes a responsibility the family previously shared to a larger extent). When the children come home from school, they may be expected to play with the children on the street, with brothers and sisters perhaps, but certainly without a high degree of parental supervision. For some children the settlement house may be the modern substitute for what formerly was parental obligation. In addition to this, there have grown up in our society various outlets, such as the radio and the movies, which relieve parents of a large part of their recreational responsibilities toward their children and which also define the very meaning of recreation for many children. And what is true of the family's recreational function is true of other family functions also.

Changes in Church Status. Another illustration of the loss of welfare function on the part of a community agency is evident in changes in church function. While the number and importance of the current church-supported philanthropies are not to be overlooked, the church today, instead of being the "hub" of life, has become one of the spokes of the wheel. In earlier times the church was the center of many kinds of activities and concerns which are no longer a part of its program. In the medieval period the church was a prominent motivator for many social functions, art, education, work, and the family. In regard to social service the medieval church was certainly dominant. So much was this true that there was in this prior period very little that could properly be called "public welfare assistance" as the term is now used. The developing complexity of the problems and scope of social service in recent centuries and the development of a more secularistic tradition are two of the more important reasons for the shift in social service from the church.

Social work, then, emerges when various community institutions give up their welfare functions. Social work, from one point of view, is a social substitute for functions that previously were carried on by the home, the church, and other community organizations.

Social Responsibility

Although the growth of social impersonality and the loss of welfare function on the part of some institutions have definitely contributed to the establishment of secular social work as we know it today, nevertheless, its advance probably could not have been possible without a developed sense of social responsibility. An attitude of social responsibility has evolved, it might be said, despite the impersonality of our society and the loss of welfare function on the part of various associations. Because the conception of responsibility may differ from that which religion enjoins (thus being different from the kind of responsibility which has characterized the past), we may be inclined to deny or minimize the significance of that sense in our time. But if one considers the sensitivity of people today to the needs of others, the vast expenditures which go into the effort to prevent and to alleviate social distress, and the numbers of persons who find careers in doing social work and related tasks, the significance of our present-day acceptance of social responsibility is evident. Moreover, the sources of this responsibility in religion and in other ideologies more prevalent in the past are not to be ignored as being presently nonoperative, although in a modified form.

Community Resources

Another of the social requirements for the existence of social work is that of community resources. To engage in social work a society must have the ability to provide above and beyond its primary satisfactions sufficient "surplus value" to make it possible for individuals in need to be given aid. (The term *surplus value* as used here is not to be confused with a similar term in formal economics.) There are certain minimal social requirements, such as food, clothing, and shelter which are fundamentally essential for the maintenance of a social body. A society which is not able to provide for the primal satisfactions of the majority of its citizens will scarcely have the means of extending itself in goods and services to embrace the needs of those who may suffer from the social maladjustments of the society. Thus the type of social service and the amount (and even its very existence) imply a favorable development in the general economy.

THE OLD WORLD HERITAGE

The culture of early colonial America was to a large extent a reflection of the thought and tradition of the "Old World" from which the settlers came. Political forms, economic operations, social distinctions, family habits, religious outlooks—all these in colonial America were highly influenced and shaped by their counterparts in the Old World. A similar relationship holds for social work. The colonists were the inheritors of the ideas and practices of social welfare of their forefathers. A large part of the inheritance was shaped by ideas which had been worked out chiefly in England. Therefore, social work in America has many of its roots in the history of ideas and practices generated and developed there. This holds true for both the private and public welfare services.

PRIVATE SOCIAL WORK IN THE NEW WORLD

One of the chief contributions of the English tradition to social welfare is that of private charity. Part and parcel of English thought for centuries has been the supremacy of private forms of enterprise, even in the field of social welfare. The state, according to this viewpoint, should maintain protective functions but should not maintain welfare functions. This distinction means that the state is responsible for the protection of its citizens against crime, for the prevention of anarchy, for the enforcement of property rights and of contracts, for the protection of the citizens from threat or force from another state. The task of the state in these terms is largely negativistic. It exists mainly to stop certain things from happening. "That government governs best which governs least"—that has been one of the slogans which has expressed the philosophy of the protective state. Of course, recent British governments have greatly modified this view.

While the principle that government should regulate social welfare practices can be traced back at least to thirteenth century England, the idea that government has genuinely positive powers and responsibilities is a concept which has only gradually come into acceptance. Even today the "welfare state" is not accepted in all quarters. But its acceptance is wide enough to enable government currently to maintain many social welfare functions which in colonial America would have been thought to be a direct denial of sound thinking and practice. The historical meaning of governmental participation in social welfare will be discussed presently. At this point we shall review some of the features of the private charity which prevailed in the earlier periods in America.

Church Charities

The church, as a private organization, assumed a major share of the charity of this earlier period.[1] In carrying out this function it assumed that it had support from the teachings of the early Christian leaders and from the then current social and political philosophy. As the center of community life in those former times, it could readily take the role of administering charity. The settlements, moreover, in colonial America were more homogeneous from the religious viewpoint than our mod-

---

[1] An important point in regard to the dominance of the church in charity affairs can be noted for colonial New England where there was a close tie and constant overlapping of offices between church and state.

ern urban communities, thus aiding in the administration of church charity.

Needs Known at First-Hand

The manner of charity distribution in colonial America was significantly different from that which social work agencies employ today. In the early colonial period the church leaders did not need to make rigorous investigations of the needy. This was largely because they generally knew from first-hand and continued experience what the needs were of the members of their communities. But, even later, the church leaders did not devise any investigatory methods which could be classified as modern. In the main their efforts were superficial, if made at all. Much of what was done was done on the basis of sympathy, that is, the religious leader gave assistance because he personally felt touched by the plight of another. It is in this sense that the term "charity" perhaps best characterizes the kind of social work then performed.

Religious Standards of Giving

The religious worker also felt the necessity for making moral judgments. There were certain practices of clients which he felt he could not sanction. Thus assistance was not given to all people. For example, in the early days of church charity in New York City religious workers did not aid persons of a different religious affiliation or those who repeatedly neglected the moral admonitions of the worker. Also, church charity was distinctly limited because its funds came only from its own limited resources.

Usually, assistance for the needy person was given in his own home by a church representative. The clergy of the various denominations took responsibility for the administration of this form of charity. In a number of cases, notably in those communions where there existed the religious philosophy which supported a deaconry, the practical administration of church charity was left to the nonclergy. In New York City, for example, after the colony had taken root, several "sieckentroosters," or comforters of the sick, were sent to care for the needs of the parishioners. While they had some church status, they were not ministers. They visited the sick and gave them spiritual aid.

Early Institutional Care

While the largest amount of service was provided through personal or family contact—this being true for the whole of the colonial settlement—some stress was placed upon the institutional care of dependents. Especially did certain groups of dependents seem to need institutional care. The most common form of institution was the alms-house.[2]

Almshouses. Almshouses varied considerably from place to place. In some localities there apparently was little or no stigma attached to living in them. In 1657 the first Lutheran pastor at Rensselaerswyck, New York, lived in the almshouse in that town. On the other hand, and perhaps in most instances, there commonly was considerable stigma attached to these institutions.

Sometimes the almshouses were organized to house specific types of distressed persons—the sick, the aged, the poor, the young children. At other times the almshouse was a general "catch-all" of the sort which existed in New York State in certain localities where the insane, orphaned children, the aged, prostitutes, and other types of persons were housed without discrimination. In many of the almshouses emphasis was placed on work (for those who were able), and upon protection (largely mere feeding, clothing, and housing) of the dependent persons. Usually, no educational and cultural activities were offered to the inmates. Even children often went without any formal education.

The crippled and the insane fared rather poorly under the private charity work of the colonial days. Mild cases were kept in their own homes or sent to a general institution. In the case of the more violently insane, placement in a public prison or almshouse was a common practice. There was, however, a Quaker contribution to the care of the mentally ill, as they used more humane methods of treatment. There is also evidence of a kindly consideration for mental misfits in the very early colonial period, which was not true somewhat later nor in the first part of the nineteenth century.

Aid to Children. In the care of children, several types of service were offered in the earlier days in America. The indiscriminate almshouse was a popular means of caring for children. However, there were also more specialized institutions as, for example, orphan asylums. Especially after the Civil War did orphan asylums multiply, as a result of the high toll of war casualties.

A form of child care taken from the English also was widely accepted —the *indenture*. The indenture was a system of placing dependent children with families where, under a sort of contractual arrangement, the foster parents were to supply food, lodging, and education in in-

[2]It is well to note here, before the discussion of public services, that it was possible, especially in New England, for needy citizens to be aided by the local government without entering an almshouse. At many points private and official services overlapped.

dustrial skills in return for the labor of the child. A variation in the procedure of indenture was that of the free foster home in which the contractual element of the indenture system was at a minimum.

Later, other forms of aid to children developed on a private basis. In the main they were specialized child-caring agencies, many times with an institution attached, for helping children who were dependent or neglected. Indenturing, however, continued into the later period.

THE PROBLEM OF DESTITUTION

Perhaps the chief problem private agencies faced through the centuries has been the alleviation of destitution. While in the earlier periods of America's history the victims of destitution were not so numerous and so needful of organized relief services as in more recent years, there have always been persons who could not adjust to the economic demands of earning a livelihood or for whom the economy had no place. In the earlier periods a financially disqualified person could migrate to a place where he could adjust. Also, an expanding economy made it possible for many to secure work if they were able and willing. Later, these features were present to a much smaller extent in the economic life of the nation. The exhaustion of the frontier prevented persons from taking advantage of perennially fresh opportunities. The rising industrialization made the individual even more dependent upon tremendously complex economic factors outside of his control. The rise of cities took men away from the more "natural" means of support, such as farming.

In earlier American history it was generally assumed that a person in need of financial help was personally unworthy or had only himself to blame for his plight. This attitude derived largely from the rapidly expanding economy in which it was theoretically possible for all to have gainful employment. Probably it was also due in part to the religious attitude engendered, especially by Calvinism, which laid great stress upon the testing of a man's religiosity by his ability to be successful in employment or business. At any rate the person in need of financial assistance carried a stigma which sometimes prevented him, though his situation was not the result of any clear personal fault, even from seeking help.

In America there have been various means of caring for the destitute. Among them have been private and public almshouses, usually known as "poorhouses." For some years, especially in English history, it was thought a test of a destitute man's sincerity and need to ask him to live in a poorhouse.

New York Society for the Prevention of Pauperism

Another means of caring for the destitute was through private welfare organizations which attempted to render noninstitutional aid. One of the first of these organizations was the New York Society for the Prevention of Pauperism, formed in 1817 by a group of men that included some Quakers. They aimed to attack the problems of destitution, then increasing rapidly in the city. The Society made a study of the causes of destitution and found the following:

1. Ignorance
2. Idleness
3. Intemperance
4. Want of economy
5. Imprudent and hasty marriages
6. Lotteries
7. Pawnbrokers
8. Houses of ill-fame
9. Gambling houses
10. The numerous charitable institutions of the city

In the face of these "causes" the Society instituted a program of action which included dividing the city into small districts manned by two or three visitors of the indigent. Measures werc taken to prevent begging on the streets and to restrict saloons. Positive action involved the establishment of savings banks and employment bureaus, the promotion of life insurance and benefit societies, and the encouragement of Sunday schools. Materials were even supplied for home workers. Finally, means were sought to create one channel for all charitable giving in the city.

While the program of the New York Society for the Prevention of Pauperism is a prominent landmark historically in the field of social work, its chief value lies in its study of causes and its program of alleviation. In the main it was very largely unable to carry out its program. In its purposes, however, it was similar to movements going on about that time in a number of other American cities.

Association for Improving the Condition of the Poor

Another significant development among the private organizations seeking to solve the problem of destitution in a noninstitutional way was the founding of the Association for Improving the Condition of the Poor. It was created in New York City in 1843 to counteract the grave social conditions then existing and to integrate the increasingly large number of small, mushroom-like private agencies which had sprung into existence to meet the crisis of the period. In form and spirit the Association became the dominant charity agency of its kind for the thirty years following its inception.

Robert M. Hartley, one of the founders, being scientifically minded, made a study of the prevalent methods of meeting poverty by visiting a number of cities which had programs of note. However, the plan he finally drew up for New York City differed greatly from what he found elsewhere, although he seems to have been partially influenced by his visits.

Difference Between the Poor and Paupers. The Association sought to distinguish between the poor and paupers. The *poor* were defined as persons not habitually destitute, but with ability and willingness sufficient to enable them, with help, to assume their own responsibility for a livelihood. *Paupers* were those persons, for one reason or another confirmed in their poverty, who were difficult to rehabilitate, usually because of personality factors. The Association endeavored to help the poor. In this purpose the Association did not confine its efforts simply toward the aiding of the unemployed; rather, the stress was placed upon the *condition* of the poor, as the title of the organization suggests.

The Association did not intend to supercede the existing organizations in the same field, although in a relatively short time many organizations did close their doors, thereby placing on the Association an increased responsibility and burden.

"Visitor" System. Following the ideas of the New York Society for the Prevention of Pauperism and of similar organizations in this country and elsewhere, the Association divided the City of New York into twenty-two districts which in turn were divided into two hundred and twenty-five subdistricts. By this means a *visitor* could easily call from each subdistrict to the home of each applicant for assistance.

The visitor usually was a wealthy male who voluntarily gave his time to the needs of the poor. For his work he "pledged himself to withhold all relief from unknown persons, to visit in their homes those who appeared to require benevolent services, and, by discriminating and judicious relief combined with admonitions to prudence, thrift, diligence, and temperance, to help them to discover those hidden springs of virtue within themselves from which alone their prosperity might flow." The Association itself gave no money and only such items of food and clothing which would be least liable to abuse. Any financial aid was given by other agencies, by relatives of the needy person, or by the visitor personally. The Association, further, placed several moral requirements upon the needy as a condition of their receiving aid. These were that all of the recipients of its benefits abstain from drink, send their young children to school, and place their older children in foster homes.

Purposes of Operation. Certain of the bases on which the Association operated have become a lasting part of social work practice even to this day. Some have been summarized in the following statement:

> Relief ought to be based upon an inquiry into the needs of the recipient. A district system equipped with local workers, including volunteers, offers the best method of relief distribution. Certain conditions, such as temperance, school attendance, and vocational training, should be insisted upon. Beggars and the wilfully dependent should be deterred by making their lot less comfortable than that of able-bodied workers.

Various programs, developed out of the Association's efforts, may be noted. The Association took steps to see that tenements met the full provisions of the law. It fought the adulteration of milk. Lotteries, gambling, and intemperance were also on its blacklist. In 1851 the New York Juvenile Asylum was established, and in 1852 a public bathing and washing establishment was founded. The year 1854 marked the creation of The Children's Aid Society. This Society, the Workmen's Home, and the Society for the Relief of the Ruptured and Crippled were largely products of the influence of the Association.

As year followed year, the far-reaching purposes of the Association extended themselves into many American communities, so that by 1875 twenty-nine cities had programs patterned after that founded by Hartley in New York City. But as the Association developed it lost a great part of its reforming and altruistic zeal and became more characteristically a relief-granting agency. The depression of the early 1870's brought to the public's attention the fact that the condition of the poor was still distressing and that the existing machinery for their care was noticeably lacking. The attempts to remedy this situation crystallized in the charity organization movement which is still prominent today, although in modified form.

THE CHARITY ORGANIZATION MOVEMENT

Development in Buffalo

While various efforts at founding a charity organization society were made in Germantown, Pennsylvania, in Boston, Massachusetts, and in New York City, the first city to develop a new form of private agency for the care of the distressed was Buffalo, New York. Prior to this time a great model had developed in the London Charity Organization Society, after which the Buffalo Society was shaped. At Buffalo, a clergyman who had been connected with the London Society proved to be the link between the Old World and the New. As an extension of the social services of his church, Mr. S. Humphreys Gurteen, the clergyman, gathered about himself an enthusiastic band of believers in the principles of social service as developed by the London organization. Together, in 1877, they founded the Buffalo Charity Organization Society.

Aims and Services

The charity organization movement drew heavily upon the experience of the Association for Improving the Condition of the Poor. Thus the Charity Organization Society in Buffalo followed the district plan of operating its services. In that city there were eight districts corresponding to the police districts. Male district committeemen carried on the work of each district office. Regarding its service the Buffalo Society declared that it exclusively needed men, "for this is especially a man's work." (In view of the current overrepresentation of women in the field of social work, the stress upon the need for male workers on the part of the Buffalo Society is interesting to note.) Assisting the district workers in Buffalo, however, were "friendly visitors." These were women enlisted from the wealthier groups in the city.

The idea behind the arrangement of mingling the rich and poor was that of bringing the "rich into such close relations with the poor as cannot fail to have a civilizing and healing influence." While the Buffalo Society sought at first to have one visitor for each disabled family, this goal was not realized. The number of families under the responsibility of a visitor, however, was definitely limited.

The Society was able to establish warm cooperative relationships with the already existing private social work organizations. Such cooperation was possible because the Society strongly stressed its function as one which would not endanger the existence of other agencies. It aimed to build on what already existed. Moreover, the Society declared itself to be impartial in the treatment of its cases. It made no distinctions as to religion, nationality, or politics. Another of its convictions which aided its acceptance by other agencies was that it should not administer financial assistance directly to any client, but should make referrals to such agencies as could aid the client directly. To do otherwise, "would bring the Society's career to a speedy and ignominious ending."

Outdoor and Indoor Relief

One of the prominent efforts of the Buffalo Society was to decrease the amount of money the city appropriated and administered to the poor in the form of *outdoor relief*. Outdoor relief is assistance granted to families or individuals on a noninstitutional basis, that is, not requiring clients to enter an institution in order to benefit. It was felt by the Society that the city government should confine its charity to *indoor relief*, or assistance that does require the client to enter an institution in order to get help. The Society argued that greater possibilities of fraud were inherent in a public program of outdoor relief and that a public relief fund had deleterious psychological effects on the poor. It felt that such a program increased the dependency of the poor on public relief. In a period of three years (1876–1879) of active social-political pressure and examination of all outdoor cases carried by the city, the Society saw the appropriations for this purpose decrease from about $100,000 to about $28,000. Apparently, this decrease was possible without a marked increase in suffering on the part of the poor.

On this point, however, there may be some variance of opinion. It may be that the charity organization movement, in general, was faulty in its attitude toward the problem of relief. In a sense the movement sought to solve the problem on the basis of private philanthropy without involving governmental responsibility to a serious measure. Possibly—though it is easy to judge the past—the movement would have been more helpful if its leaders had thrown the weight of their support toward expanding and bettering the public welfare system of their time rather than seeking to limit and destroy it. If the leaders had given such support, public welfare might not have had to wait until the depression of the 1930's for the period of its greatest development.

The charity organization movement, following the example of the Society in Buffalo, spread to other cities: New Haven, Philadelphia, Brooklyn, Boston, Indianapolis, Detroit, Cincinnati, Baltimore, Washington, New York, Newark, and many other places.

New Features

As the charity organization movement grew and spread to various American cities, new features were attached:

1. The relationship between poverty and the poor man's banker, the pawnbroker, was recognized. It was felt that a legitimate loan society would better enable the poor to help themselves financially. So, in a number of cities, loan departments were established.

2. The societies saw a need for creating living quarters for homeless men and women so that they would not be forced into sleeping out-of-doors, in jails, or elsewhere.

3. The societies learned, through the experience of the flood in the Ohio River valley in 1884, the great fire in 1889 in Lynn, Massachusetts, the severe tornado of 1890 in Louisville, Kentucky, and the Park Place

disaster of 1891 in New York City, that some sort of disaster relief should become a part of their programs.

4. The need was seen early for publications which would bring intelligent information to the public and also to social workers themselves. The present-day *Survey Graphic* and *Survey Midmonthly* date back to this period.

5. The growth of various private welfare organizations indicated to the leaders of the charity organization movement the need for the interrelation of the various agencies in the field. The Council of Charity Officers was one of the first supra-agency organizations founded to meet that need. It was followed on a national basis by the American Association for Organizing Family Social Work, and later, the Family Welfare Association of America (now the Family Service Association of America). In addition to these specific organizations, the charity organization movement, because of the nature of its community interests, laid the framework of the current council of social agency pattern which is evident in many American cities. Through a council of social work agencies the activities of private and public agencies are coordinated and certain common services provided.

6. Bad housing was looked upon as a source of difficulty for poor persons. The societies in many localities took strong measures to enforce existing legislation on this matter and to encourage new legislation to improve housing.

7. Tuberculosis was seen as a special handicap of the poorer classes. Efforts were made to provide health education, medical examination, and medical care for those who suffered.

8. The distinction between the criminal and the delinquent was one which was early made by the societies. Steps were taken to provide separate courts, workers, and institutions for juveniles.

9. The fact that in a number of instances the needs of clients could be better served through detailed legal services impressed the societies with their responsibility for cooperating with the legal aid societies which existed in numerous cities.

10. Gradually, it was seen that training for social work practice was an important part of the administration of social work. Several present-day graduate professional schools grew out of training programs initiated by charity organization societies.

11. The method by which the social worker (or friendly visitor) approached the client was also modified. Chiefly through the insights of Mary Richmond in her book, *Social Diagnosis*, the client came to be viewed in terms of the various social influences which converged upon him and of the need for individual, social treatment.

The American Red Cross

In the period of the founding and growth of the charity organization movement, a new organization with somewhat similar purposes—the American Red Cross—came into being. The Red Cross may be traced in its origin to the writings of Jean Henry Dunant, a Frenchman who depicted in 1862 the sufferings of men on the battlefield and pleaded for an international organization to give relief to such victims. In 1864 an international convention was held in Geneva which established the Red Cross officially. While at first the attention of the International Red Cross was given to the relief of the war-wounded, it later turned to peacetime problems. According to the organization of the International Red Cross, each national constituency is self-governing. The headquarters in Geneva acts as a clearinghouse for national problems and plans.

The American branch of the Red Cross was established by Clara Barton in 1881 and has been under governmental supervision since 1905. Special emphasis in peacetime has been laid on public health services and disaster relief. Since 1929, however, unemployment assistance has been included in the program in some of the smaller communities. In a war period the Red Cross maintains an immense staff to care

RED CROSS EXPENDITURES

The Dollar may be Used as a Measure of Total National and Chapter Expenditures, but it is an Inadequate Measure of Red Cross Services...

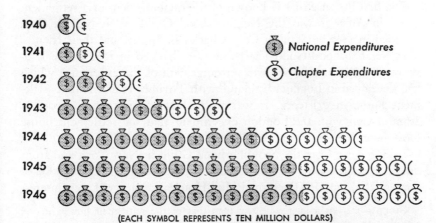

(EACH SYMBOL REPRESENTS TEN MILLION DOLLARS)

Fig. 7. Increase in Red Cross Expenditures

(*Red Cross Service Record: Accomplishments of Seven Years,* The American National Red Cross, Washington, D.C., 1946.)

for the personal and family problems which occur both at home and among military personnel. (See Figure 7.)

Although the Red Cross may be classified as a voluntary or private charity primarily, it also is related in this country to government in so far as there is Congressional supervision of the organization.

Recent Developments

While agencies of the charity organization society type are still active in helping people with a wide variety of personal and family problems, recently many specialized agencies have come upon the scene. Those interested in child care became prominent and were often even further specialized to include agencies for placing children in foster homes, agencies for handling the educational problems of children, agencies for aiding the handicapped, child guidance clinics, and so on. Also, social work, in its efforts to help individuals, began to move into such fields as children's courts, hospital social service, and psychiatric clinics. The history of these various developments is included in the succeeding chapters.

GROUP WORK

While the history of social work for individuals is long and complex, group work activities have been notably recent and relatively undeveloped.

Establishment of Settlement Houses

The first instance that is known of the establishment of a settlement house in America was the Neighborhood Guild of New York City, founded in 1887 by Stanton Coit, Charles B. Stover, and their friends. The Neighborhood Guild (its name was changed in 1891 to the University Settlement House) was an outgrowth of the experience which had developed in London, England, with Toynbee Hall, the first settlement house in existence. It was from direct contact on the part of Stanton Coit with the London experiment that the settlement house movement got under way in this country.[3]

Taking a cue from the Neighborhood Guild in New York and from direct experience with the London effort, Jane Addams and Ellen Gates Starr in 1889 founded the famed Hull House in Chicago. Later, interest

[3]Group work has a longer history than that of the settlement houses if one considers the early missions as a form of social group work. The Five Points Mission in New York City is an outstanding representative of these religiously inspired centers. In the latter half of the nineteenth century there were quite a few missions in the larger cities.

in the settlement house as a means of aiding the poorer groups in the growing American cities spread to other communities.

Purposes. The establishment of settlement houses was motivated by a variety of reasons. The founders (usually wealthy university men who wished to "do good" for the poor) were often impressed by the harsh conditions brought by the developing industrialization of cities. They looked upon the houses as appropriate means of providing educational and recreational facilities for those who otherwise would not have them and who might as a result turn to unwholesome activities. Attempts to integrate the poorer and mainly immigrant groups into the American culture were made by offering courses for those who wished to learn to speak and write English. Classes in civics were organized to do away with the problem of "hyphenization" and to create good citizens. Another objective was to interpret the foreign-born to the people of the United States and to interpret Americans to the foreign-born. There also was some effort on the part of the settlement houses to initiate social reform movements against poor housing, unsanitary conditions, and low wages. Another purpose, undoubtedly, was to give a higher degree of community feeling to areas within cities which had suffered serious social disorganization. Religious conversion was another.

Although the settlement house movement began rather late in the history of American social work, it has steadily increased both in size and in the quality of service rendered.

Other Agencies

In addition to the settlement houses, founded to serve groups rather than individuals, a number of other agencies came into existence to accomplish somewhat similar ends. The Young Men's Christian Association was founded in this country in 1851 for the improvement of conditions and opportunities for young men. Although there were important precursors, the Young Women's Christian Association was formally introduced into American life in Boston in 1866. Likewise, the Boy Scout movement, founded in England, was incorporated in this country in 1910 with a nonmilitary, nonsectarian, educational and recreational program for boys over twelve years of age. With similar purposes the organization of Girl Scouts was established in 1912 in Savannah, Georgia, by Juliette Gordon Low. The community center movement, getting its start about the time of the First World War, sought to provide on a community plane a program which differed little from the settlement house program, except that it was commonly intended not alone for the poorer people of the community.

Although group work has been dominantly a nongovernmental type of social work in its heritage, it no longer is completely so. At the present time there are many developments in the publicly sponsored agencies which involve group work.

COMMUNITY ORGANIZATION

Like group work, social work as it seeks to help communities has only a brief history. The main lines of growth have been in the collaboration of private social work agencies for ends which are essentially self-contributing. Thus, as has been seen, the charity organization societies grouped themselves together for the purpose of creating greater consistency in their programs and to achieve certain generally held goals. The social service exchange movement followed from the development of the charity organization movement. The community chest movement, by which social agencies in a particular community engage in a federated financial drive, was instituted in Denver in 1888, and adopted by Cleveland in 1913 and later by other cities. It provides an example of social work organizing for the benefit of the whole community. The unifying of social services in the community under a council of social agencies suggests still another of the recent developments in this field.

SECTARIAN SERVICES

Private agencies are organized either on a nonsectarian or sectarian basis. There are many nonsectarian agencies offering a multiplicity of social services at the present time. In the main the nonsectarian agencies are more numerous and more influential than the sectarian agencies. And yet, the fact that there are private, sectarian agencies calls for special attention. Naturally, they fall chiefly under the following headings: Roman Catholic, Jewish, and Protestant. These will be discussed briefly here.

Roman Catholic Social Work

Roman Catholic social work is considered by Catholics as deriving from the nature of the Christian religion. Concern for Catholic social work is primarily a matter for each parish, of which there are over 14,000 in the United States. To the Catholic social worker the element of the supernatural is the distinguishing factor between themselves and other social workers. They believe that social work is not only a scientific procedure but also an expression of divine grace which aids both the worker and the client.

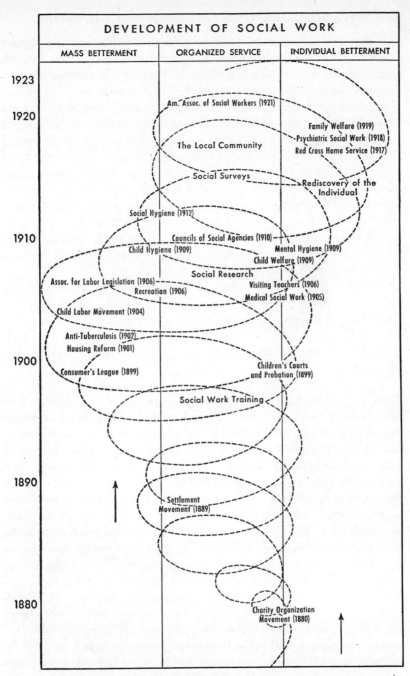

DEVELOPMENT OF SOCIAL WORK

| MASS BETTERMENT | ORGANIZED SERVICE | INDIVIDUAL BETTERMENT |

1923

1920

Am. Assoc. of Social Workers (1921)

Family Welfare (1919)
Psychiatric Social Work (1918)
Red Cross Home Service (1917)

The Local Community

Social Surveys

Rediscovery of the
Individual

Social Hygiene (1912)

1910

Councils of Social Agencies (1910)

Child Hygiene (1909)

Mental Hygiene (1909)
Child Welfare (1909)

Social Research

Assoc. for Labor Legislation (1906)

Visiting Teachers (1906)

Recreation (1906)

Medical Social Work (1905)

Child Labor Movement (1904)

Anti-Tuberculosis (1902)
Housing Reform (1901)

1900

Children's Courts
and Probation (1899)

Consumer's League (1899)

Social Work Training

1890

Settlement
Movement (1889)

1880

Charity Organization
Movement (1880)

FIG. 8. The Rhythm of Social Work

(*The Long View: Papers and Addresses by Mary E. Richmond,* Russell Sage Foundation, New York, 1930.)

55

National Conference of Catholic Charities. Although the Roman Catholic Church is represented in the field of social welfare by such organizations as the National Catholic Welfare Conference and the National Catholic Community Service, Catholic social work, more particularly defined, is represented nationally by the National Conference of Catholic Charities (N.C.C.C.). This organization has been active since 1910 in bringing together on a national basis all groups interested in Catholic social work. Under a bishop appointed by the Hierarchy of the United States, the Conference seeks to bring about an interchange of views on the theory and practice of Catholic social work, to encourage and publish literature pertaining to Catholic social work, to aid in the discussion of standards in relief and prevention work, and to assist in the organizing of additional Catholic social work facilities where there is need. Since 1920 an annual meeting of the Conference has been held to help in the attainment of these goals.

Within each diocese, of which there are 115, the presiding bishop plans and directs the social work activities. Usually, the bishop's responsibility is delegated to a trained priest who is called a "Director of Charities" or by a similar title. The social work carried on in each diocese under the Director of Charities generally includes all branches of social work.

Society of St. Vincent de Paul. In addition to the organizations already mentioned, there are other Roman Catholic agencies interested in meeting clients' needs. Perhaps the chief of these is the Society of St. Vincent de Paul. Founded in France originally, in 1833, the Society was inaugurated in the United States in 1845. While the Society operates on the parish plan, it is not entirely identified with the diocesan programs of social work. The Society in this country maintains its own organizational structure, extending from the local parish to the Superior Council of the United States. The chief work of the Society is the visitation of the poor and unfortunate in their own homes. The visitors by and large are unpaid workers who are supervised by trained, paid workers. A list of the activities of the Society includes: religious counseling, supplementing family income, help in religious training of children, assistance in obtaining dental or medical care, the maintenance of rest rooms, lodging homes, homes for transient and homeless men, visitations to hospitals and penal institutions, work on behalf of Catholic seamen, support of boarding homes for working boys, and the placement of dependent children in free foster homes.

The following organizations also are active on a national basis in Catholic social work: the Diocesan Council of Catholic Women, Ladies of Charity, Christ Child Society, Catholic Daughters of America, Catholic Big Sisters, Sword of the Spirit.

Jewish Social Work

Jewish social work in its present form can be traced back to Biblical times and writings. Wherever Jewish communities have been founded, there have been arrangements set up to care for the less fortunate members within the group.

Influential Factors. The nature of Jewish social work is a result of the ecological and social conditions in which Jews live. Of the 5,000,000 Jews in the United States, almost half of this number live within one city, New York, with an additional quarter scattered in about a dozen other cities. In addition to the factor of distribution, the Jews of America present widely differing cultural backgrounds, giving representation to many Old World cultures. Likewise, in religion, the Jews differ significantly among themselves. All of these conditions affect the nature of Jewish social work. In the main, as a result of the situation just described, Jewish social work lacks a highly integrated form of central coordination and management. Often the services parallel those already existing in the larger community.

Jewish social work appropriately reaches its more extensive and organized form in the Jewish agencies in New York City. It oftentimes lacks a significant degree of professional competence in the smaller localities.

As in the case of the other sectarian types, Jewish social work consists of many kinds of service. Family social work, however, is one of the strong elements of the Jewish social work program.

National Jewish Welfare Board. The National Jewish Welfare Board, consisting in 1948 of a membership of 314 local organizations and 450,-000 individuals, is one of the most effective of the national, coordinating Jewish social work organizations. Founded in 1917, it promotes the creation of Jewish community centers and Y's, gives counsel to such agencies and correlates their activities, cooperates with other organizations for the promotion of Judaism and good citizenship, and contributes to the social welfare of members of the armed forces.

Other Agencies. The National Conference of Jewish Social Welfare is an organization which provides forums for the discussion of problems and aims of Jewish social work. In addition, on a national scale, there is the Council of Jewish Federations and Welfare Funds which has as its purpose the study of the best means of financing local social work activities, the organizing of local financial drives, and similarly related concerns. In the overseas field there have been several organizations operating. The United Jewish Appeal, with a national budget of $250,000,000 for 1948, is one of the largest of the fund-raising agencies.

Protestant Social Work

Protestant social work also is religiously grounded and inspired. It is based on the conviction that one of the vital expressions of religious faith is the serving of those in need. In the history of Protestant social work the widest kinds of social services have been offered. These services are not always clearly attached to a particular denomination, but have sprung up, as have other types of agencies, through the interest and motivation of persons in the community who later have sought (after the agency was an established fact) to secure the "blessing" of some denomination. Sometimes this "blessing" has meant merely that a church official should be an honorary member of the board of directors. On other occasions agencies have requested that the religious ministry of the agency be supplied by a particular denomination. Because of these conditions it is not easy to trace the full scope of Protestant social work or its exact social meaning.

Various Organizations. Such organizations as the Young Men's Christian Association, the Young Women's Christian Association, and the Salvation Army further confuse the definition of Protestant social work. These organizations owe allegiance to no particular denomination and not even to the various Protestant denominations, but rather are largely supported by Protestants, although a nonsectarian program generally is offered. Furthermore, a large number of agencies which formerly were rather distinctively Protestant in establishment and direction have in more recent years become nonsectarian in personnel composition and in client constituency. In addition to these variations there are other interdenominational efforts in a number of cities.

Institutional Services. While the Protestant denominations themselves have never developed casework services to the extent organized elsewhere, they have created and maintained notable institutional services. Settlement houses, for example, in many localities are the direct outgrowth of the community concern of Protestant churches. Institutions for dependent and neglected children, day nurseries, foster home programs, counseling, summer camps, schools, and colleges are also part of the institutional program for youth of the various denominations. Homes for the aged are profusely represented in Protestant welfare activities, six of the largest denominations reporting a total of over 200 such institutions. Hospitals also abound.

City Missions. Some of the Protestant denominations have established city missions. Through these city missions several kinds of services are supplied: summer camps for children, nursing care, religious services, group work activities with foreign-born, temporary shelters, convalescent homes. Special groups of persons, such as seamen and the handicapped, have also received aid from denominational programs of social service. Especially have the Lutheran and Episcopal denominations engaged in work with seamen, in running hostels, homes, and counseling services. The Goodwill Industries, closely attached to the Methodist Church, is an example of the services offered by some of the Protestant denominations for the rehabilitation of the handicapped. Of course, in wartime the services of the various denominations were greatly expanded in many ways to provide for the problems and needs of members of the armed forces and those returning to civilian life. Growing out of the wartime experience of the churches also are numerous and financially far-reaching programs for European reconstruction.

American Friends Service Committee. In this connection the social service activities of the American Friends Service Committee bear mention. Organized in 1917, the Committee has been active in war and peace in bringing about improved conditions for a wide range of people, both at home and abroad. Its present services include relief and rehabilitation in connection with the Second World War, concern for the mentally ill and prisoners, work camps for achieving various community benefits, and education for peace, race harmony, and international understanding. In addition to the American Friends Service Committee, there are similar organizations attached to several other religious bodies.

Efforts at Coordination. The problem of creating coordination among the Protestant social work agencies has been difficult because of denominational loyalties and the separatistic founding and functioning of the agencies. In recent years, however, significant efforts in cooperation have been made. The Church Conference of Social Work, founded in 1930 as a part of the activities of the Federal Council of the Churches of Christ in America, has brought church social workers together for acquaintance and discussion of common problems. In 1934 the Association of Church Social Workers was formed to assist Protestant agencies with the recruitment, training, and placement of social workers. Denominationally, several coordinating boards are rather effective in integrating the services of their churches: the Department of Welfare of the National Lutheran Council; the National Council Division of Christian Social Relations of the Episcopal Church; and the Board of

Missions and Church Extension of the Methodist Church. Local and state federations of churches also offer some aid.

PUBLIC SOCIAL WORK IN AMERICA

There is an impression that the chief, if not the only, history of social work in America is that of the private agencies. According to this view the development of public welfare services is something of late vintage and does not properly represent the basic spirit of this country. Nothing, of course, can be further from the truth, as a history of the whole of American social work should carefully point out.

It is true that public social work has made especially significant advances and expansions in the recent decades. The economic depression of the 1930's made such enlargement not only possible, but inevitable. For, in that period, the private agencies, modeled after the original charity organization societies, found it impossible to care for the widespread and overwhelming economic needs of the unemployed. Limited financial resources prevented them from meeting such extended unemployment, even though they seriously and faithfully tried for a time.

Since the 1930's the attitude of citizens toward such issues as governmental assistance has undergone some change. What formerly to a great many was a strictly private matter has become, in these recent years of changing viewpoints, a concern of the federal, state, and local governments. As has been suggested previously, the idea of a protective state gave way to the idea of the social service state. Economic problems having been so complex and far-reaching and the attitudes of people so modified, it was more or less inevitable that government should share more largely in welfare matters than it ever had in the past. But to say that government has only recently become interested in social work is false. For, government, as we shall see, has been interested in social work for a long, long time.

Furthermore, while the distinction between private and public social work is of the greatest significance for an understanding of the history and present character of social work, it should not be inferred that these two areas are separated by a wide gap. The fact in many places and times is quite the opposite. For example, when in New York State from 1825 to 1866 the number of private orphan asylums increased due to the increased needs for such services, the State of New York contributed tens of thousands of dollars to aid the programs of these private organizations. In a large number of situations there have been mutual, cooperative arrangements between private and public agencies which have greatly benefited both kinds of programs.

Welfare Services in Colonial Times

In colonial America the existence of public welfare services was an obvious fact. For many of the colonies the adoption of the English Poor Laws made public concern for the poor an integral part of public responsibility. Early legislation in the State of Rhode Island made the following provision for welfare services:[4]

And as necessary concomitants hereof, to prevent Murder, Theft, and Perjury. We do joyntlie agree in the present Assemblie to make or produce such Lawes as concerne provision for the poore, soe that the impotent shall be mainteyned and the able employed. And to prevent Poverties, it is agreed that such Lawes be made and produced as concern y ordering of Alehouses, and Taverns, Drunkenness and unlawfuly gamin therein.

Following the passage of this intention, the legislative record of the state contained the following:

It is agreed and ordered, by this present Assembly, that each Towne shall provide carefully for the reliefe of the poore, to maintayne the impotent, and to employ the able, and shall appoint an overseer for the same purpose.

This legislation was passed in 1647.

Overseers of the Poor

In those early days the overseer of the poor was an important part of the governmental machinery. In fact, so important was his responsibility that few men could be found who would assume it voluntarily. Finally, towns had to impose fines upon those who would not accept the office. While at first the position of overseer was a sideline for some official such as the town treasurer, it later became an office in itself.

The overseer had many duties to perform. He assessed a rate of payment on the citizens and was responsible for its collection. The money in the earlier days was spent for such services as medical care of the sick, board, clothing, and washing for the destitute, the expense of "warning" persons out of town, and for moving strangers. Overseers also were called upon to enforce residence requirements not intended to benefit strangers. The investigation of the resources of relatives was a further responsibility. In working out assistance with a townsman, the overseer sought to have the relatives of the distressed person assume

[4]The discussion of the development of early public welfare in Rhode Island is mainly taken from Margaret Creech, *Three Centuries of Poor Law Administration: A Study of Legislation in Rhode Island,* University of Chicago Press, Social Service Monographs, number 24, Chicago, 1936.

the obligation for aid before he would allow the town to obligate itself. An indigent person who possessed property was required to transfer the property to the town, which thereafter administered it for his welfare, assisting him according to his particular circumstances.

Special cases of need were brought before the town meetings for more direct public action. The whole colony assumed responsibility for conditions not locally caused, such as the destitution which resulted from the Revolutionary War. In most cases, however, the overseer carried a high degree of personal authority for decisions relating to the needs of people.

Public Almshouses

A further step in the development of public welfare in the State of Rhode Island (which we are using simply as an example) was the inauguration of public almshouses. The first almshouse was established in Newport in 1723. The inmates of this institution were allowed to beg in the streets of Newport in order to secure part of the expenses of keeping them. In 1753 a project for a Providence County workhouse was carried out. The towns in the county shared in the costs of construction. The administration was lodged in a board of representatives chosen from each town. An executive administrator was chosen by the board of representatives to carry out their will. This administrator was called a "workhouse overseer." The workhouse overseer had the power to take up such "persons as could not give a good account of themselves, or of their way of living." He also had the power to bind out for a period, not to exceed four years, anyone who was unlikely to maintain himself through work in the institution. This provision also held for children.

Other Methods of Treatment

Dependent children were cared for by the widely used system of indenture. The sick were sometimes given into the charge of the destitute so that a "bargain" could be contracted between the town and the destitute, both for the care of the sick and for the financial assistance thereby of the poor. The insane were cared for in two ways: by having the town take over and manage their financial assets and supplying care; and by their being placed in the homes of townspeople, often the poor, so that they would be given the essential care that they needed. Later, special institutions for various types of the needy were established.

Responsibility of Local Community

The situation in Rhode Island was essentially that found throughout New England and in many other sections of the country. The placing of responsibility for the maintenance of public social work services upon the local community is as characteristic of the social services as it is of almost every other aspect of government. In some instances the authority was given to the township or the county instead of the town or parish, but ordinarily such delegation of power was for its locality the counterpart of the town responsibility of New England. Thus, for example, the township and county organization of poor relief was accepted and maintained in the Northwest Territory and the Missouri Territory. As the pioneers moved west they took with them the relief practices they had known further east. Local responsibility for public social work was in keeping with the ecological and transportation conditions which existed in the colonial period. It was, moreover, in keeping with the religious-political-social philosophy of the times.

STATE RESPONSIBILITY IN SOCIAL WELFARE

The assumption by the states of public welfare responsibility came relatively late in the development of the nation, and only when conditions forced it. Some states (notably Massachusetts and Connecticut) did, however, from colonial times assume obligation for their "unsettled poor." By the very definition and operation of the local public welfare laws, individuals who had not maintained residence for a period (the period ranged from a few months to several years) were excluded from assistance by the locality. The majority of states did not themselves undertake jurisdiction for their unsettled poor until about 1930. Thus a person who did not qualify by legal residence for local assistance usually could not secure state assistance, and, consequently, no public assistance at all.

Disaster Relief

Most states did assume early responsibility, however, in the case of disaster relief. Some states offered seed loans when crops failed, some made appropriations when scourges affected crops, some provided coal during depressions, some granted aid to flood victims. In all of these instances, however, it must be noted that the obligation was assumed only for times of disaster.

Veterans' Care

Veterans' relief was another matter which won state support. By 1910 all but six states had provisions for Civil War veterans. Since 1918 a majority of the states have had programs to assist veterans of the First World War. Also, the veterans of the Mexican, Spanish-American,

THE WHY

CAUSES OF ECONOMIC AND SOCIAL NEEDS

> *These conditions stop wages, exhaust savings, and produce dependency in good times and in bad*

SICKNESS AND ACCIDENTS

700,000 Persons Incapacitated on any Given Day

DEATH OF THE BREADWINNER

40,000 Breadwinners Die Each Year

THE AGED

1,050,000 Persons are 65 Years of Age or Over

CHIDREN IN SOCIAL NEED

12,500 Children from Broken Homes Require Foster Care Annually

12,000 Delinquency Cases in Court Each Year

7,000 Neglect Cases Referred to Authorities Annually

6,000 Other Children in Social Need Every Year

BLINDNESS

15,400 Persons are Registered as Blind

UNEMPLOYMENT

500,000 Jobless in March 1946

FIG. 9. Causes of Economic and Social Needs

(*Public Social Services in 1945*, 79th Annual Report, New York State Department of Social Welfare, New York.)

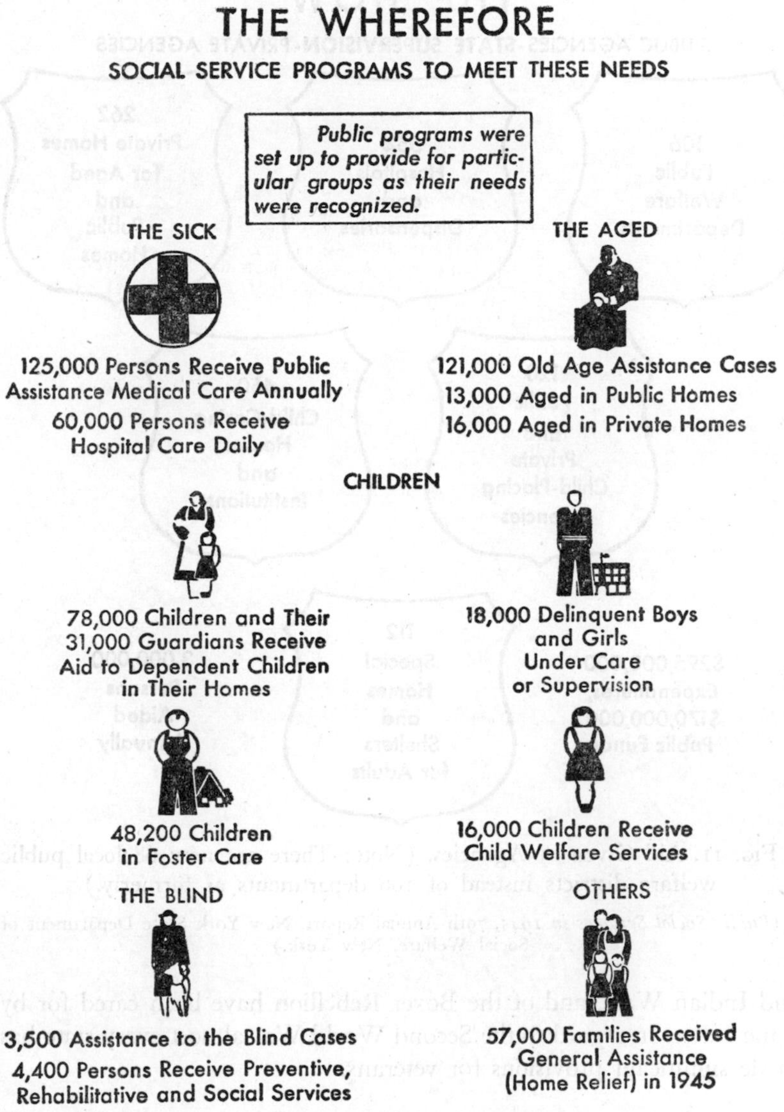

THE WHEREFORE

SOCIAL SERVICE PROGRAMS TO MEET THESE NEEDS

> *Public programs were set up to provide for particular groups as their needs were recognized.*

THE SICK

125,000 Persons Receive Public Assistance Medical Care Annually

60,000 Persons Receive Hospital Care Daily

THE AGED

121,000 Old Age Assistance Cases

13,000 Aged in Public Homes

16,000 Aged in Private Homes

CHILDREN

78,000 Children and Their 31,000 Guardians Receive Aid to Dependent Children in Their Homes

18,000 Delinquent Boys and Girls Under Care or Supervision

48,200 Children in Foster Care

16,000 Children Receive Child Welfare Services

THE BLIND

3,500 Assistance to the Blind Cases

4,400 Persons Receive Preventive, Rehabilitative and Social Services

OTHERS

57,000 Families Received General Assistance (Home Relief) in 1945

Fig. 10. Social Service Programs Set up to Meet Economic and Social Needs

(*Public Social Services in 1945*, 79th Annual Report, New York State Department of Social Welfare, New York.)

THE HOW

PUBLIC AGENCIES-STATE SUPERVISION-PRIVATE AGENCIES

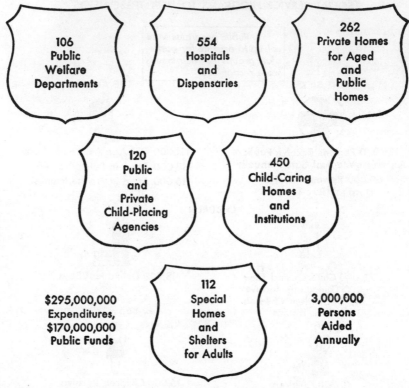

FIG. 11. Aid Given by Agencies. (Note: There are now 68 local public welfare districts instead of 106 departments as formerly.)

(*Public Social Services in 1945*, 79th Annual Report, New York State Department of Social Welfare, New York.)

and Indian Wars, and of the Boxer Rebellion have been cared for by some states. In regard to the Second World War almost every state has made significant provisions for veterans.

Institutional Care

In addition to public welfare work for the unsettled poor, for the victims of natural disasters, and for veterans, the states have developed several programs of institutional care. Those persons who were early recognized as state charges were the insane, the deaf, and the dumb. Later, institutions were created for juvenile delinquents, the feeble-minded, the crippled, and the blind. It was not until the middle of the nineteenth century, however, that the states assumed an active responsibility for dependent children not classifiable under one of the previous heads.

Departments of Welfare

An outgrowth of the assumption by the states of more and more responsibility in public welfare in recent years has been the state departments of welfare. These have acted in various capacities: as a means of coordinating the varied public welfare services of a state, as state supervisory agencies over local and county services, and in the main as informational and educational sources. While the first of such departments was set up in Massachusetts in 1863, by 1904 only fifteen states had followed suit. In 1931, however, the White House Conference on Child Health and Protection reported that only five states had not founded public welfare departments: Arkansas, Idaho, Mississippi, Nevada, and Utah. Today, all of these states have some sort of welfare department.

FEDERAL RESPONSIBILITY IN SOCIAL WELFARE

Federal empowerment to act in the area of public welfare derives from that part of the Constitution which specifically permits Congress "to lay and collect taxes, duties, imports, and excises, to pay debts, and to provide for the common defense and general welfare of the United States." Before the economic depression of the 1930's this passage of the Constitution was not generally thought to be indicative of the kind of social services which are now rather taken for granted as part of the functions of the federal government.

Former Attitude Toward Public Aid

In 1854, philanthropic Dorothea Dix happily saw Congress pass a bill which she had encouraged on the federal care of the insane. But, in his veto of the bill, President Pierce argued that if the federal government assumed responsibility for the insane of the country, it would also have to care for the poor—another class of needy persons; thus the government would be taking on a burden it could not well discharge. In the light of his veto message, President Pierce no doubt would be amazed to see how the Constitution has been interpreted in these latter days. The fact is, however, that President Pierce's veto decision limited federal participation in social service work until the passage of the Federal Emergency Relief Act in 1933.

While the federal government could hardly be termed a "social service state" before the 1930's, some of its earlier acts may be considered broadly as social work. Since 1785 the federal government has made grants in the form of lands to the various states. Sometimes these grants have been for public buildings, sometimes for state universities, sometimes for agricultural experiment stations. The federal government has also appropriated money for various projects carried on by the states: reforestation, highways, forest-fire prevention, the National Guard. It has also assigned money for activities which are perhaps even more closely allied with social work: vocational guidance, maternity and infant care ($900,000 having been appropriated under the Sheppard-Towner Act of 1921), and disaster relief. There was actually a Congressional provision for public works (S. 2749) during the presidency of Warren G. Harding.

Depression of the 1930's

The economic depression of the 1930's was largely responsible for the changed role of the federal government in social welfare in recent years. The magnitude of the problem of unemployment was such as the country had never before faced. The number of unemployed increased from about 2,500,000 in the spring of 1929 to about 15,000,000 in the spring of 1933—the peak year.

Efforts at Alleviation. In the beginning stages of the depression, following the stock market crash of 1929, the social work agencies already in existence sought to meet the needs of the dependent. Each stretched its facilities more and more in order to handle the ever-increasing wants. The Family Welfare Association of America (now the Family Service Association of America) and the Community Chests and Councils, Inc. accomplished a great deal on the organizational and promotional level among the private agencies. The American Association of Public Welfare Officials (the name was changed in 1932 to the American Public Welfare Association) was responsible for significant achievements in the public field. New York State, under the administration of Franklin D. Roosevelt, was among the states notable for programs of alleviation. Its program was instituted on a financial basis of $20,000,000 on September 23, 1931, under the leadership of three unpaid administrators (Temporary Emergency Relief Administration), and Harry L. Hopkins was appointed as executive director. This state experiment was the forerunner of the program instituted by the federal government in March of 1933.

Early Federal Action. Even by 1930, however, the federal government recognized the fact that the existing resources were all too small in relation to the requirements. Consequently, it stepped into the relief scene in that year with the appointment by President Herbert Hoover of an Emergency Committee for Employment, with Colonel Arthur Woods as chairman. The purpose of the Committee, as the name implies, was to deal with the emergency aspects of the unemployment situation from an optimistic or constructive point of view. The Committee stated and restated that among its aims it did not intend to disturb seriously local responsibility for relief. Indeed, the specific purposes of the Committee were later defended publicly:

> With funds only for its own expenses and with a limited staff, the Committee acted as a clearing house for measures found effective in the emergency, gave assistance on specific problems, and reinforced state and local efforts.

Actually, the work of financing and administering relief was carried on by the social work agencies interested in this work before the Committee came into existence.

Passage of Federal Emergency Relief Act

Although Congress considered numerous bills to give the federal government declared responsibility for relief (some were passed but were vetoed by President Hoover), no really significant federal legislation was secured until May 12, 1933, when the Federal Emergency Relief Act was signed by President Roosevelt and the Federal Emergency Relief Administration created. Under the terms of the Act, $500,000,000 was appropriated by Congress to meet the needs of the unemployed. Part of the money was to be matched by state governments, but where state resources were too depleted or the needs were too great this was not required.

Three Aspects of the Program. Three aspects of the program bear special note. First, the federal government for the first time in such a situation and on such a scale had assumed responsibility for the needs of the destitute. This undertaking, in itself, as has been inferred previously, was one of the major changes in the whole of the social and political life of America. Second, the federal government maintained its long-standing respect for local obligation. That is, the Act left the local communities responsible for meeting some part of the total financial needs and for the detailed administration of the program. Third, the federal government envisaged its program of financial help to individuals through state and local governments not as resting on the basis of loans, but as outright appropriations on which there was to be no repayment by the states or local communities or individual recipients.

While the funds appropriated by Congress for the Federal Emergency Relief Administration were larger than any former single contribution by any agency, private or public, the money was not sufficient. So, from time to time, and for various purposes, additional funds were raised. Up to June, 1936, these were:

1. National Industrial Recovery Act of 1933........	$148,035,000
2. Act of February 15, 1934.......................	605,000,000
3. Emergency Appropriation Act, 1935	
Title II, par. 1	257,000,000
Title II, par. 2	223,590,000
Title II, par. 3	500,000,000
4. Emergency Relief Appropriation Act, 1935......	944,005,625
	$2,677,630,625

The state and local governments, moreover, increased their contributions during this period to about double what they had been in 1933.

Kinds of Aid

The kinds of aid, in addition to direct financial assistance, which the federal government administered through the states and localities were manifold. For one thing, the Federal Surplus Relief Corporation (1933) was created to "serve as the instrument through which price-depressing surplus commodities might be removed from the open market, processed, and distributed to relief clients in such forms as foodstuffs and clothing." The relief given to families and individuals through this means was in addition to other grants rather than as a substitute for part of their relief allowance.

Medical assistance was also given to recipients of relief. Accredited lists of physicians and dentists were provided to clients who then were able to receive free medical attention. The payment of the physicians and dentists was from federal funds. No hospital bills, however, could be paid by the national government.

Another kind of service offered through the federal program of social work was that for transients. During the depression adventurous persons oftentimes left the place where they had settled and tried to secure work elsewhere. Others left, simply to roam. For such transients the State Transient Bureaus were established by federal action. They aided persons "who have no legal settlement in any one State or community."

Through the Bureaus transients could receive medical care and hospitalization, clothing, food, education, and recreation.

The federal government also invested about $3,000,000 in various self-help arrangements which had sprung up in large part as a result of the depression. The self-help, cooperative associations performed the following types of activities: dairying, butchering, poultry-raising, carpentry, growing foodstuffs, canning, fuel-wood cutting, making clothing; running bakery shops, beauty shops, laundries, cafeterias; making soap, jams, pickles; and the repair of automobiles. Through this means the unemployed were aided in providing mutually the services and materials which they needed.

The Civil Works Administration which was begun on November 9, 1933, five months after the Federal Emergency Relief Administration came into being, represented another kind of federal service to the unemployed. For a time the "pump-priming" conception of the Civil Works Administration apparently defeated its social usefulness. During its brief history, however, it did supply work to many of the unemployed and gave them a sense of dignity in their relations with government. In 1935 and beyond, the general federal works program which followed the C.W.A. provided job opportunities for many.

Features of the Emergency Program

Requirements for Eligibility. In order to secure any kind of assistance from the governmentally financed and administered program of relief, it was necessary for each applicant to appear before a Social Service Division station to have his eligibility reviewed. The applicant would

GENERAL RELIEF ASSISTANCE PER FAMILY, JULY 1942

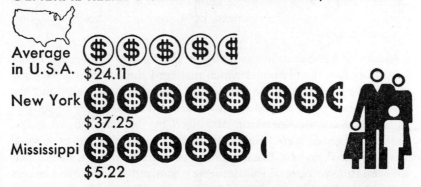

Average in U.S.A. $24.11

New York $37.25

Mississippi $5.22

Fig. 12. Variation in General Relief Assistance per Family, 1942

(Pictograph Corporation for *Social Work and the Joneses,* by Ruth Lerrigo and Bradley Buell, Public Affairs Pamphlet No. 97, New York, 1944.)

then be informed concerning the possibilities of his situation. Technically the Federal Emergency Relief Administration maintained eligibility requirements in the broadest of terms, permitting the states and localities to interpret the exact meaning of the phraseology. The Administration said that all persons unemployed and/or their dependents were eligible for relief. Beyond this requirement two further stipulations were made: (1) that the person have genuine need; (2) that there be no discrimination because of race, political affiliation, religion, color, noncitizenship, or because of membership in any special group. Under these broad injunctions, states and local communities offered relief programs of widely varying natures. The programs displayed such regional discrepancies as an allotment of $6.78 a month for a family of four in Kentucky, in contrast to the $42.12 available in New York. This variation has continued, as is illustrated by Figure 12.

Direct Relief and Work Relief. If the prospective client was able to meet the eligibility requirements in his particular locality, he thereupon could receive either "direct relief" or "work relief." Direct relief was given in the form of food, shelter, clothing, light, fuel, and necessary household supplies, medicine, medical supplies, medical attendance, or the cash equivalent of these to the person in his own home. Work relief was paid to the employable at a fair rate of return on the work which they performed. During the depression the employee, however, was to work only those hours (at a "fair rate") which would enable him to earn his relief allotment. At times the work-relief wages were paid in direct relief. The standard conception of "fair rate" at one point was a thirty cent per hour minimum, but in the fall of 1934 this standard was abandoned. The "fair rate" then became in each locality that one determined by a committee composed of a representative of the relief administration, of organized labor, and of the business or professional groups.

Quality of Personnel. In the period of the Federal Emergency Relief Administration the personnel which managed the Administration was not always of the highest quality. The pressure of the times and the lack of a reservoir of trained social workers led to the hiring of persons with inadequate qualifications, as judged by the standards of today. Various programs were originated for the training of workers while they were at their jobs. Local agencies conducted their own staff conferences. In some places, institutes were organized at which the workers could get a fair idea of the more professional aspects of their work. During 1934-1935 the federal government, as a means of improving the qualifications of its welfare personnel, appropriated about $420,000 for the education of 1,000 persons in accredited schools of social work. The personnel of the public agencies has been advancing steadily in quality in recent years.

Trend of Private Agency Help

While the inclusion of private social work agencies in the administration of federal assistance was considered in many quarters, it was judged advisable that governmental funds not be given to private agencies. The private agencies during this period, therefore, were obliged to concentrate their efforts on a sphere of social services somewhat different from that of the public agencies. The private agencies, not having to maintain clients financially for long periods or in great numbers, were able to devote more attention to personality and community needs. In other words, private social workers turned more and more to those cases which had no strong or permanent financial basis, but involved problems of a social or emotional character. While there has been no trend among the private agencies to assume the responsibilities for economic assistance which the federal government took over in the early 1930's, there has been an increasing trend among the public agencies to expand their conception of service to include many of the personality needs of clients. In the light of this development the problem of the place of private agencies in a social work system so largely and effectively cared for by public means may become acute. At present, however, workers both in private and public agencies are of the opinion that there is so great a need for both types of agencies that the more theoretical problem of the future organization of the social services should be left to the future.

The Social Security Act

As the emergency aspect of the federal program of 1933–1935 began to decline, the need for a more permanent social welfare organization under national auspices was sensed. In line with this, President Roosevelt announced in 1935 that the federal government had to relinquish its practice of relief in favor of a more farsighted program of social welfare. The resulting social legislation was the Social Security Act (August 14, 1935)—an epoch-making action on the part of the American government.

The following types of federal assistance were provided for by the original Act:

1. Old-Age Assistance
2. Aid to Dependent Children
3. Unemployment Compensation

4. Maternal and Child Welfare, including maternal and child health services, services for crippled children, child welfare services, vocational rehabilitation.
5. Public Health Work
6. Aid to the Blind

Significant in this change of emphasis from relief to social security by the federal government was the integration of the general assistance program through the states with a categoric program of assistance.[5] During the years immediately following the Act, though, the federal government not only stressed categorical relief, but also introduced strongly the principle of social insurance. Thus the government implemented a widely held point of view among social workers, namely, that the kind of service in which the federal government had been engaged for several years should be organized on an insurance rather than on a "dole" basis. The huge governmental enterprise in social welfare was put under the management of the specially created Social Security Agency (now the Federal Security Agency).

Thus the public welfare field has progressed from the local charity responsibility of the early period of the country's history to the categorical assistance and social insurance role of the federal government today.

White House Conferences on Children

The federal government has taken part in welfare activities along other lines. The organization of the White House Conferences for Children is an example of the planning and study activities of the national government.

Theodore Roosevelt called the first Conference (named the Conference on the Care of Dependent Children) in 1909. This Conference collected the leaders in the child welfare field from all over the country. The main subject of the Conference was the use of institutions for the care of children. It also considered the rapidly rising method of child care called foster home placement (which today is one of the most important child welfare procedures). It was this Conference, also, which stressed the importance of the home as "the highest and finest product of civilization." It stated that "children should not be deprived of it [the home] except for urgent and compelling reasons." This stand aided the development of "mothers' aid" programs in that period and led to the present "aid to dependent children" activities of the federal government under the Social Security Act and its amendments. This

[5]Categoric assistance is assistance given to persons who have no margin of self-creatable independence, such as the blind, the insane, and the crippled.

Conference, moreover, aided in the creation of the United States Children's Bureau (1912) which has as its purpose: "to investigate and report upon all matters pertaining to the welfare of children and child life among all classes of our people." The Conference also assisted in the establishment of the Child Welfare League of America, a private agency concerned with child welfare problems on a national basis.

The second of the Conferences was not properly a "White House Conference," although it was sponsored by President Wilson. Its title was "Children's Bureau Conference on Child Welfare Standards." Held in 1919, it continued the general work of the first Conference.

The third Conference on Child Health and Protection, held in 1930, was called by President Hoover. It continued and expanded the fundamental work of the first two Conferences. Its results have been published in more than 30 volumes.

The fourth Conference was called by President Franklin D. Roosevelt on the brink of the Second World War. Its title appropriately was "Conference on Children in a Democracy." Almost 700 persons attended, representing every field directly or indirectly related to the welfare of children. Probably, this Conference had the broadest scope of all, for it included not only social services for children, but health and education planning as well. The proceedings were published by the Childen's Bureau. The Conference significantly stated that it too believed that the home was the primary living unit for the child and that governmental services should constantly seek to strengthen the home life of America.

SELECTED READINGS ON THE HISTORY OF AMERICAN SOCIAL WORK

Abbott, Edith, *Some American Pioneers in Social Welfare: Select Documents With Editorial Notes,* University of Chicago Press, Chicago, 1937.

Abbott, Grace, *The Child and the State: Select Documents With Introductory Notes,* Social Service Series, 2 volumes, University of Chicago Press, Chicago, 1938.

Addams, Jane, *Twenty Years at Hull House: With Autobiographical Notes,* Macmillan, New York, 1910.

Addams, Jane, and others, *Philanthropy and Social Progress,* Crowell, New York, 1893.

Bosanquet, Helen, *Social Work in London: A History of the Charity Organization Society: 1869–1912,* Dutton, New York, 1914.

Boylan, Marguerite, *Social Welfare in the Catholic Church: Organization and Planning Through Diocesan Bureaus,* Columbia University Press, New York, 1941.

Breckinridge, Sophonisba P., *Public Welfare Administration in the United States: Select Documents*, University of Chicago Press, Chicago, revised edition, 1938.

Bruno, Frank J., *Trends in Social Work: As Reflected in the Proceedings of the National Conference on Social Work, 1874–1946*, Columbia University Press, New York, 1948.

de Schweinitz, Karl, *England's Road to Social Security: From the Statutes of Laborers in 1349 to the Beveridge Report of 1942*, University of Pennsylvania Press, Philadelphia, 1943.

———, *The Art of Helping People Out of Trouble*, Houghton Mifflin, Boston, 1924.

Deutsch, Albert, *The Mentally Ill in America: A History of Their Care and Treatment From Colonial Times*, Columbia University Press, New York, new printing, 1946.

Devine, Edward T., *When Social Work Was Young: Personal Recollections of the Time, Some Forty Years Ago, When Organized Charities, Public Relief Agencies, Social Settlements, and Others Were Developing What Has Come to be Called Social Work*, Macmillan, New York, 1939.

Devine, Edward T., and Brandt, Lillian, *American Social Work in the Twentieth Century*, Frontier Press, New York, 1921.

Dicks, Russell L., *Pastoral Work and Personal Counseling*, Macmillan, New York, 1945.

Federal Council of the Churches of Christ in America, *The Pattern of Protestant Social Work*, papers presented at the Church Conference of Social Work, New York, 1946.

Fosdick, Harry Emerson, *On Being a Real Person*, Harper, New York, 1943.

Glenn, John M; Brandt, Lillian; and Andrews, F. Emerson, *Russell Sage Foundation, 1907–1946: A History*, Russell Sage Foundation, New York, 1947.

Gurteen, Stephen Humphreys, *Handbook of Charity Organization*, The Author, Buffalo, 1882.

Hendry, Charles E., editor, *Decade of Group Work*, Association Press, New York, 1947.

Hiltner, Seward, *Religion and Health*, Macmillan, New York, 1943.

Karpf, Maurice J., *Jewish Community Organization in the United States*, Bloch Publishing Company, New York, 1938.

Lauerman, Lucian L., *Catholic Education for Social Work*, The Catholic University of America Studies in Sociology, volume 9, Washington, D.C., 1943.

Leonard, E. M., *The Early History of English Poor Relief*, Cambridge University, Cambridge, England, 1900.

Lundberg, Emma O., *Unto the Least of These: Social Services for Children*, Appleton-Century, New York, 1947.

Mangold, George, *Problems of Child Welfare,* Macmillan, New York, 3d edition, 1936.

O'Grady, John, *Catholic Charities in the United States,* National Conference of Catholic Charities, Washington, D.C., 1930.

Owen, Arthur D., *British Social Services,* Longmans, New York, 2d edition, revised and enlarged, 1943.

Pimlott, John A., *Toynbee Hall: Fifty Years of Social Progress: 1884–1934,* Dent, London, 1935.

Queen, Stuart, *Social Work in the Light of History,* Lippincott, Philadelphia, 1922.

Richmond, Mary E., *Social Diagnosis,* Russell Sage Foundation, New York, 1917.

——, *The Long View: Papers and Addresses Selected and Edited by J. C. Colcord and R. Z. S. Mann,* Russell Sage Foundation, New York, 1930.

Riis, Jacob A., *How the Other Half Lives: Studies Among the Tenements of New York,* Scribners, New York, 1890.

Robinson, Virginia P., *Changing Psychology in Social Case Work,* University of North Carolina Press, Chapel Hill, 1930.

Sims, Mary S., *The Natural History of a Social Institution: The Young Women's Christian Association,* Woman's Press, New York, 1936.

Stidley, Leonard A., *Sectarian Welfare Federation Among Protestants: A Comparative Study of the Protestant, Jewish, and Roman Catholic Welfare Federations, With an Especial Emphasis Upon the Federation of Protestant Welfare Agencies, New York City,* Association Press, New York, 1944.

Thurston, Henry W., *The Dependent Child: A Story of Changing Aims and Methods in the Care of Dependent Children,* New York School of Social Work Publications, Columbia University Press, New York, 1930.

Warner, Amos G., *American Charities: A Study in Philanthropy and Economics,* Crowell, New York, 1894.

Watson, Frank D., *The Charity Organization Society Movement in the United States: A Study in American Philanthropy,* Macmillan, New York, 1922.

Wright, Helen R., editor, *Social Service in Wartime,* Charles R. Walgreen Foundation Lectures, University of Chicago Press, Chicago, 1944.

No notation has been made here of the numerous studies of state histories of social work, because of the more generalized interest of the chapter.

Family Casework

3

Social caseworkers almost always are employed by social work agencies. Very few engage in private practice today. The following account provides some understanding of the function of a family caseworker in an agency setting. Written by a community leader who was asked to serve on the Board of Directors of the Brooklyn Bureau of Social Service, it describes his attempt to learn of the structure and function of that organization:

Helping Individuals and Families Who Are in Trouble. . . . I could understand and appreciate this broad purpose of the Bureau's Family Service from my talks with General Secretary Daniels and Elizabeth Dexter, Director of the Family Service Department. But I could not get any picture of how our Family Service differed from that of the public agencies—Home Relief, for instance.

Neither could I understand casework, the method by which this help for families is given. Frankly, I had always rather questioned the cases I read about or heard discussed because they almost invariably seemed to work out successfully and it did not seem natural to me that there should always be a happy ending for problems of people in serious trouble.

I realized how difficult it must be to explain something as intangible as casework, but it seemed to me that I had to get this knowledge if I were to function conscientiously as a member of the Board. To get a picture of the whole setup I made arrangements to visit one of the six district offices of the Bureau. Who comes to the Family Service for help? What do they want? What happens after they get there? These were some of the things I wanted to know.

Mrs. Schmidt met me on my arrival at the Northern district office. I found that, as district secretary, she is directly responsible for all the Bureau's work in that part of Brooklyn. And many and diverse are her

78

other duties; administration of the office and of relief funds; supervision and teaching of staff; the responsibility for knowing her community and for making the Brooklyn Bureau known in the community. In this particular office there are also an associate district secretary, four caseworkers, and three clerical workers. For economy, one of the latter doubles as receptionist and switchboard operator.

On our way to Mrs. Schmidt's office we passed through the waiting-room, a large, cheerful place, simply but comfortably furnished. Two people were waiting—a burly older man who looked so strong physically that I wondered what he was doing there; and a thin, worried-looking young fellow who appeared to have only one arm. I found out later that his arm was withered.

Many People Came Through Friends. I asked her about these people. The older man, she said, had been referred by his minister who frequently used the agency as a source of help for his parishioners. The other younger man had come at the suggestion of a neighbor who had been helped by the Bureau at one time. I discovered that out of a total of 4,994 applications during the year, 47 percent had applied personally, probably as a result of publicity or on the advice of a friend or relative. Ministers referred 8 percent; schools 4 percent; hospitals, clinics, etc., 9 percent. The remainder came from varied sources, said Mrs. Schmidt, mentioning specifically the courts, other private or public agencies, employers, and the like. I had never before realized the number of individuals in different jobs and professions who found it helpful to consult a family agency either about their own difficulties or the difficulties of others whom they knew.

These two clients, Mrs. Schmidt said, were waiting for their appointments with the caseworkers who were to see them. Why appointments? I asked. I had assumed that this was the first time they had come in. If not, was this some of the red tape and delay I had heard about in connection with social agencies?

Mrs. Schmidt explained that both of them had previously made their applications and at that time appointments for interviews had been given. Mr. Burton,[1] the older man, had written two days ago, saying that he was having trouble and asking if we could help. A caseworker had immediately replied, making an appointment for today. Mr. Nelson came in yesterday and was seen by the receptionist to whom he had said only that he wanted to talk with someone about employment. He, too, had been given an appointment for today.

Why hadn't he been seen yesterday when he came in? I questioned. Mrs. Schmidt said that if he had asked to be seen immediately because his situation was urgent, he would have been seen at once. However, when possible, it seems preferable to give appointments so that the applicant may be sure of having sufficient time set aside for him to discuss his difficulties unhurriedly and without interruption. This also affords the

---

[1]All names of clients used in this book are fictitious.

caseworker an opportunity to clear the name of the applicant through the social service exchange, so as to prevent duplication of services by other agencies.

Another frequently heard criticism occurred to me. Do people always have to come to the Bureau office? Aren't caseworkers ever sent to people's homes when problems are reported?

A worker would go at once, said Mrs. Schmidt, if a client requested it and it was difficult for him, or her, to come to the office because of illness or heavy family responsibilities. However, in most instances, it is better for the client to take the initiative in coming to the agency because it seems that when he does so, he makes better use of the help offered. In other words, said Mrs. Schmidt, caseworkers have found from experience that usually the people who take and really use help, are those who come voluntarily to the agency, since that in itself is an indication of their genuine concern about their situation and desire to change it. Moreover, leaving it to the applicant to take the initiative reassures him that the Bureau's help will not be thrust upon him.

Individual and Private Interviews. The next time I glanced in the waiting-room, others were waiting, and I asked about the two I had seen originally. Each was now talking with a caseworker in one of the individual offices, said Mrs. Schmidt. She showed me one of these offices— small but light and well ventilated and so arranged as to insure privacy. I could understand the necessity of privacy for I had a feeling that Mr. Nelson, the handicapped man, would not have felt free to talk except under these conditions. Mrs. Schmidt agreed that it was essential to assure people their interviews were absolutely confidential.

A large map showing the boundaries and locations of the six district offices caught my attention as we went through the hall. It brought to mind another question about which I had wondered since becoming a board member. Why was it necessary to district the work of Family Service? Would it not be more economical, both financially and administratively, for the services to be centralized in one office? I recognized that centralization would mean a good deal of traveling for clients coming from various parts of the borough, but that it did not seem too difficult in view of ample transportation facilities, particularly since some of the district offices themselves are inconveniently located for outlying parts of their own communities.

Districts for Better Community Contact. True, agreed Mrs. Schmidt, but a more important reason exists for districting the work. Brooklyn is a borough of small communities, each possessing distinctive characteristics, social, racial, economic. Also each community has its own problems: one because of low-grade housing; another because of lack of recreational facilities; and so on.

It was important, said Mrs. Schmidt, for the district secretary and her staff to know the character of their particular district so that they might be better able to meet the local needs. This would be better possible, as I could readily see, if the district office were a real part of the community life. Having the office located in the neighborhood was one way of bringing this about.

I began to see that there were complexities in the Family Service. Already this brief visit had raised questions and had brought up many new phases of the work about which I wanted to know more. I suggested to Mrs. Schmidt a series of talks in which she could tell me more of the Bureau's services to families, and in which I might have an opportunity to ask questions as they occurred to me. For instance, I would like to know what those two people I had seen in the waiting-room had wanted, and how the Bureau was able to help them.

A week later, in my office, Mrs. Schmidt told me what had happened in those first interviews. Mr. Burton, the older man, had been greatly worried over money matters. He is a cab driver, whose earnings vary between $15 and $18 a week, sometimes less. This income barely covers current living expenses for himself, his wife and three children. They had had a lot of illness during the past year which has resulted in an accumulation of debts. Some time ago he took and passed a civil service examination for maintenance men in the City subway and he expects this appointment to come through in another three months. While this will mean more adequate wages eventually, it does not pay the bills now. If the debts continue to pile up, even the higher wages will not meet living expenses because they will be constantly paying off arrears. The Burtons had thought about their problem until "their heads were going in circles." He had finally decided to ask the Bureau for temporary financial aid until he could find himself able to manage. He verified for us the information about his prospects for a better job and the need for assistance.

The problem here as in every case, said Mrs. Schmidt, was to help the Burtons find not only a way out of their present crisis but a way which would be most likely to obviate the recurrence of another similar crisis. I agreed but did not see how this could be accomplished unless the Bureau took responsibility for supplementing their income.

We Help the Client to Help Himself. That was one possibility, said Mrs. Schmidt, but the purpose of the Bureau's help is to make it possible for people to mobilize whatever resources they have either within themselves or within their environment, in order that they themselves can take responsibility for bringing about a real change in their situation. For the Bureau simply to step in and pay all the Burtons' back bills would be a way of meeting their present needs, but it might not be a particularly good experience for the Burtons themselves, since it would mean that someone else was taking over a part of their problem, which they had the right and the duty to handle themselves.

In her discussions with the family about possible resources, the worker had learned that they had several insurance policies which could be so adjusted as to free enough cash to meet most of their outstanding debts and reduce payments on the premiums without losing protection. This would relieve their immediate worry. And because the Burtons had been willing to use these resources of their own, the Family Service was willing to help with financial assistance. The caseworker had arranged with Mr. and Mrs. Burton a regular weekly supplementation of their income until the new job came through. Thus they would be enabled to get along without incurring new debts and would gradually be able to pay off the remaining bills. When Mrs. Burton expressed an interest in better household planning, the caseworker arranged for her to have some help from our home economist in budgeting and preparing low-cost meals.

I thought this was a good solution. But why hadn't the Burtons ever seen for themselves the possibilities in adjusting their insurance? That puzzled me. Why did they have to come to the Bureau to find this out?

Caseworkers know from experience, Mrs. Schmidt explained, that when people's troubles mount to a certain point, they become confused and a kind of panic develops which keeps them from doing, or thinking, as clearly as they might otherwise be able to do. At such times, it helps to talk with somebody outside the whole difficulty who may aid you to get a clearer perspective and so find a way out. I could go along with that, because it seemed to me that we have all probably been in spots where it's been hard to "see the woods for the trees." One of the most essential parts of the job of the private agency, said Mrs. Schmidt, was this offering to people who are frightened and unsure of themselves, an opportunity to talk with someone who understands how they feel and who can help them regain confidence in themselves and find ways to handle their own affairs.

But something else puzzled me about this. What if the Burtons had not had insurance? That seemed too easy, somehow. Mrs. Schmidt agreed that this had been less complex than many problems brought to the Family Service, but had there not been this way out, she said, the caseworker would have tried to help the family think out some other plan which would eventually make it possible for them to manage for themselves. If some plan had been worked out, and it had been practical, the agency would again have been able to help the family carry it out.

Sometimes "Talking It Out" Releases Energy. For example, sometimes a solution might involve re-training for the wage-earner so that he could get a better job. Sometimes it might mean vocational counseling for an adolescent child who could then contribute to the family income. Again it might mean arrangements for medical care which otherwise would be a continuous drain on a tight budget. On the other hand sometimes none of these helps is necessary, as the client finds, after a few interviews, that because he *feels* differently—less confused and anxious and upset—he doesn't need any outside assistance but is able to move along again under his own steam. It is easy to see how a person may become so "tied up in knots" that he cannot use whatever potentialities he may have and that, being freed from part of this worry will in itself release enough energy so that he can go on by himself.

Mr. Nelson, the young man whom I had seen in the waiting-room, was a case in point, Mrs. Schmidt said. In his first interviews with the worker, he had been very antagonistic, demanding emergency appointments and claiming that he was being given the "run-around." He was not so much resentful toward the worker, said Mrs. Schmidt, as resentful toward the world because he was unable to find the work he considered his right, and because he was handicapped, which made everything more difficult for him. Besides, it is not easy to ask for help, she said, and most of us get a little angry at the person whom we must ask, because we are afraid of what he will demand from us in return.

That was a new idea to me; I had accepted the conventional attitude toward a donor as one of gratitude. But I could see that it is not always easy to feel under obligation to others for what you consider your right.

In these complex emotional situations of fear and anger and frustration, Mrs. Schmidt said, the caseworker's understanding and skill have real meaning for people, enabling her to recognize their feelings and to know the basis for them. By accepting these conflicts of feeling or helping the client to express them, the worker sometimes makes it easier for him to go ahead, since the inability to get one's feelings off one's chest can be fairly paralyzing.

Mr. Nelson, for instance, really was an employable person and yet it did not look as if he had been making particularly good use of his abilities recently. In succeeding interviews with the caseworker, he was able to talk about some of these feelings about his handicap which had been hampering him in trying to get work, and at the same time to recognize some of his assets. He has not found a job yet, Mrs. Schmidt said, but he has been able to follow out the worker's suggestions for seeking employment more effectively because he is no longer standing in his own way by being mad at the world.

Service of Private Agency Is More Flexible. This all seemed convincing to me, and I felt that I was beginning to see through the popular misconception that the services of a private agency are a duplication of the public welfare services. The distinction, as I now grasped it, was that the public agency is set up with a legal responsibility to meet the need for subsistence alone. This frees the private agency to offer help to families who have the capacity to use such help as a springboard to independence. I could see the need for both kinds of services because, while it seems necessary and important that the public agency administer relief according to strictly defined requirements, it seems equally essential that the private agency be geared to greater flexibility so as to meet the other kinds of problems— personal, psychological, vocational—that trouble individuals and families.

I noticed that Mr. Nelson had received no financial aid from the Family Service, and that brought up another question, the extent to which families in Bureau care receive relief. I was interested to learn that 57.2 percent of those helped over a period of months last year did not receive any financial assistance at all. Mrs. Schmidt said that it was true that much of the Bureau's help had always gone, and would probably continue to go, to low-income families who are caught in some emergency requiring money. However, we find more and more that those with marginal incomes are seeking us out for one or the other of our special services.

For instance, said Mrs. Schmidt, Mrs. Murray came to Northern office several weeks ago, asking for train fare for herself and her two children to return to her mother's home in New Jersey. She and her husband had been married for twelve years. In talking with her, the caseworker found that they had apparently always gotten along reasonably well together until about three years ago when they began to have increasing difficulty. Mrs. Murray did not know where it started or exactly what was wrong. All she knew now was that she was fed up with it, and she wanted to leave. What she sought of the Family Service was $11.50 for train fare.

A Service of Consultation. The caseworker had told Mrs. Murray that she knew how troubled and unhappy she was, but that we could not really help until we understood more about what had led up to this, and what was to come in the future. For instance, how did she plan to manage after she got to her mother's? And how did her husband feel about this separation? What was it going to mean to the children? What did it mean to her? The caseworker knew that after twelve years of marriage it is not easy to break off a relationship and that even though one may be angry and hurt, there are apt to be remembrances of happier times and strong attachments.

Why hadn't the caseworker given the $11.50 anyway? I asked. This would have made Mrs. Murray decide whether she really wanted to leave her husband or not. Maybe if she did and had a chance to get away and think it over, she'd be glad to come back.

That was possibly true, said Mrs. Schmidt. But any separation leaves its scars. And running away with the children might make the future even more complicated for Mr. and Mrs. Murray. When people are in trouble like this, their first impulse is either to run away from it or to ask somebody to show them a way out. I agreed that the solution could never really be that simple, because the trouble had been a long time coming; it could not be solved in a single day or a single interview.

The job of the caseworker, she said, is to help the individual to face his problem and decide what alternatives are open to him. In this way he himself can decide what seems best for him in the light of all the things that are involved. This is not easy, either for the client or the caseworker, because invariably so much feeling complicates the situation.

Client Must Make Own Decision. In this particular case it was sensible to question the wisdom of an impulsive decision to break off a relationship of 12-years duration. The worker could help most by giving Mrs. Murray an opportunity to think through her feelings about her husband—what her marriage meant to her—and what she wanted to do about it. At some point, when she was willing, it might be necessary to talk with Mr. Murray. The Murrays might in the end decide that separation was the best solution for them; or they might decide that there was enough left of their marriage to make it worthwhile to try to work it out together. But, whatever their decision might be, it would be more considered than just to run away, as Mrs. Murray had suggested.

I wondered about the children. What was happening to them while their parents were in this turmoil? They would undoubtedly be affected by it, said Mrs. Schmidt. While they could not be entirely protected, the caseworker was making plans for them to go to Shelter Island Camp for a month so that for a while, at least, they would not be too involved in their parents' difficulties. I knew that Shelter Island was a camp maintained by the Bureau for children, but I had always thought of it as offering merely a recreational opportunity, not realizing how closely it ties in with the other work of the Family Service.

I began to get a sense of the kind of help which casework offers. I could see how helpful it would be to a person in trouble to talk with someone who has no stake in it, and who has had a lot of experience. Friends or relatives inevitably side with one or the other partner, and give advice based more on sympathy or prejudice than on real understanding.

Self-discipline—understanding of people's feelings—knowledge of how to handle them. . . It was much more than "good common sense," as I had previously thought, which enables the caseworker to give help based on the individual needs of the people with whom she works. What is that extra something? I asked.

Mrs. Schmidt said that it is a combination of training and experience given to one who is, at the outset, adapted to work with people. Every caseworker has had at least two years of graduate training in an approved school of social work. The curriculum is designed to give her an increasing understanding of people, and how and why they react as they do to things which happen to them.

Schooling Plus Casework Interneship. Along with this academic training, time is set aside for practical experience which the student gets in agencies such as ours. In this particular district office, there are two students from a school of social work who, as part of their academic training, are learning to practice casework under the close supervision of an experienced worker. Mrs. Schmidt said that a large part of her job is the continual supervision and further training of her caseworking staff in order that the best possible kind of service can be given to those coming to the Bureau of Social Service.

It seemed to me that even in these two brief talks with Mrs. Schmidt I had acquired an appreciation of the complexity of this kind of work. And I had a growing conviction as to its value. In the cases we had discussed, the thing which impressed me was the worthwhileness of these people who came to the agency for help. I realized how much courage it takes to ask for help, and that the very asking for aid implies accepting responsibility for one's problem and for finding a solution. In all three cases, as Mrs. Schmidt pointed out, the worker had in no sense relieved the client of his responsibility. All her effort had been to help him mobilize and use his own strength to meet his difficulties himself.

Obviously this kind of help is a service not only to the individual in trouble but to the community in which he lives. I was glad that the people of Brooklyn feel that agencies such as the Bureau of Social Service should be supported.[2]

From this account it is clear how a family agency functions in a large community. Not only does one see the organization of the agency to some extent, but the process of social casework as well.

FAMILY CASEWORK AND SOCIAL WORK

Social work has been described in the first chapter as a process by which various kinds of resources are placed in a judicious and helpful position for the use of individuals, groups, and communities in meeting their needs. Family casework is one of the types of services social workers engage in with individuals, and it will be the topic for discussion in this chapter. Other specialties which deal with individuals and with the ways in which social work helps groups and communities will be examined in following chapters.

While our interest at the moment is in family casework, we must bear in mind that the various divisions within the casework field are not viewed by most social workers as being as separate in their operations as the chapter divisions in this book would seemingly indicate. It is only by reason of professional specialization and volume of business that agencies customarily devote their energies to a particular type of service. Actually, there is considerable reason to believe that there is a common process of social casework underlying the whole collection of casework specialties we shall survey.

In this chapter, as we discuss family casework, it must further be borne in mind that we are surveying only a part of the services existing in the modern community for families in need. We will consider here those agencies which rely upon private or voluntary means of financing themselves, and reserve the discussion of publicly-financed agencies to two later chapters on public welfare. In terms of ultimate logic there is perhaps little to justify a division, within this book or elsewhere, of the public and private family services. But, taken together, the materials are so plentiful in these fields that efficiency in organization is served by dividing the public services from the private. Also, there have been historically accepted distinctions between them.

[2] "As I Saw It," 63rd Annual Report, Brooklyn Bureau of Charities (now the Brooklyn Bureau of Social Service), Brooklyn, 1940–1941, pp. 13–22.

THE FAMILY AND ITS PROBLEMS

The family is a small social grouping, but, in it, individuals secure most of their basic satisfactions. It is the primary molder of human personality.

The child is not born as a fully developed social being. What gradually becomes his distinctive personality is created by his interaction with many and diffuse elements within the culture which surrounds him. Heredity sets limits to the development of the individual, but it is through the intimate association he has within the family that he assimilates the culture of his society and formulates his own personality, including his attitudes toward other people.

Democratic Changes

The family in itself is not stationary, however. It is constantly, if slowly, changing. For example, it is shifting generally from an institutional basis of existence to a companionship formation. The older pressures of law, authority, tradition, elaborate ritual, and other external factors are fast disappearing or being seriously modified in our American family form. There is increasingly a more democratic spirit pervading our family organization. The signs of greater democracy in the American family have been described by Burgess and Locke as the following:[3]

1. Freedom of choice of a mate on the basis of romance, companionship, compatibility, and common interests.
2. Independence from the parents of the young people after marriage.
3. The assumption of equality of husband and wife.
4. Decisions reached by discussion between husband and wife in which children participate increasingly with advancing age.
5. The maximum freedom for its members consistent with the achieving of family objectives.

The democratizing of the family has many positive aspects and has removed certain factors which interfered in the past with personality development and healthy adjustment. But this trend toward a more democratically conceived family is not an unmixed blessing. It brings in its train many of the sad dislocations which characterize the condition of the modern family and which give rise to the deep need for family caseworkers, as well as other workers. While the modern family is trending toward greater democracy, it also is involved with the

[3]Ernest W. Burgess and Harvey J. Locke, *The Family: From Institution to Companionship*, American Book Company, New York, 1945, pp. 21–22.

consequences of being a changed institution. Also, it is not easy for people to live between the rigid requirements of the old and the more easy-going offerings of the new. The conflict between the older and the newer family traditions is, in itself, the genesis of many present-day family problems.

Other Influential Factors

Aside from the element of democracy, several other forces are affecting the family today. There is the notable shift from rural to urban

FIG. 13. Shift of Population from Rural Areas to Cities, 1790 to 1940

(Evelyn M. Duvall, *Keeping Up With Teen-Agers,* Public Affairs Pamphlet No. 127, published by Public Affairs Committee, Inc., New York, 1944.)

living with all of its complications. (See Figure 13.) Housing has undergone modifications; there are now many more multifamily dwellings than at any time previously. Apartment living also means periodic shifting from place to place within the urban setting. Birth control has become another important factor in the changed situation of the modern family. Our easing attitudes toward illegitimacy play their part in influencing social behavior. The "women's rights movement" has brought new problems to the family. Women are more active than previously, economically; they are assuming more responsibility, politically and socially. The increased number of technological conveniences within the home makes many of these changes possible or easier. The modern family, moreover, has given over many of its responsibilities to experts within the community: teachers, recreational leaders, camp counselors, policemen, clergymen, and others. Finally, attitudes toward sex have changed so that a so-called puritanical view has given way to a more spontaneous and practical conception of the function of sexuality in human affairs. All of these changes and conditions have greatly influenced the stability of the modern family.

Increased Recognition of Problems

When it is realized that the family, especially today, is burdened with pressures and problems such as those derived from the factors just mentioned, it is easy to see how there is marked need for family caseworkers. For, the family caseworker, along with other experts, seeks to aid individuals who have problems and needs primarily related to their being members of families.

It should be pointed out, however, that the increased need for family caseworkers today may not be due so much to a growing number of problems as to an increased recognition that problems exist. Because of the experience of the various social and biological sciences and the professional applications of their knowledge, many of the family problems which formerly went unanswered or even unnoticed are currently being diagnosed and treated.

A change, too, in the attitude of people in need has increased the responsibility of family caseworkers. In times past it was not always deemed proper for a person in need to ask for assistance. Many felt that each individual should steer his own course without too much interference or support from others (especially from organized social work agencies). But this view is passing to a large degree, and today individuals and families realize that the services which are available should be used.

Family casework, then, finds a basis of existence in many of the aspects of our modern living.

THE NATURE OF FAMILY CASEWORK

Family casework is principally concerned with aiding families to secure and maintain a normal, healthy existence. It is based, as are other aspects of social work, upon an underlying philosophy that the family is a desirable social institution, that individuals should be helped to realize the full benefits from family living, and that family problems should be treated so as to relieve exacting pressures from family members. There would be disagreements as to the specific ways in which such an outlook should be applied in given situations by various workers, but some such motivation is the foundation of all family casework.

There are many organizational instruments in the community for the strengthening of family relations, aside from family casework agencies. It is not always possible to distinguish between these organizations and family agencies. At many points they overlap. No one of them has to claim exclusiveness for family services, for there are enough cases for all of the existing facilities. Of course, many family problems are not brought to family caseworkers for the simple reason that most persons manage most of the time to handle their own needs without extended and detailed help from others. Then too, when some needs go unmet, there is no certainty that they could be met by a family casework agency.[4]

Three Types of Needs

The needs people have which can be met by family caseworkers are of three sorts: (1) those primarily located within the external situation; (2) those fundamentally within the persons themselves; and (3) those combining external and internal factors. Probably, for the most part the problems of clients of family casework agencies fall into the third category, but there are some problems more distinctly or exclusively personal or environmental.

Emotional Elements

The people who come to family casework agencies not only have problems of the types just described, but they usually have some tradition of adjustment to their problems. They do not have problems in the same way a student would in facing a mathematical question on the blackboard. They have feelings of a deeply personal character about their problems. If, for example, a client approaches a caseworker in a private family casework agency about a mentally retarded child who is disrupting the happiness of the home, he cannot do so with complete objectivity. He will wonder what the immediate response of the worker will be to him. Will the worker condemn him? Will the worker feel superior to him? Will the worker seek to force a solution on him and his situation which he already has decided he cannot bear? What kind

[4]*Families in Trouble* by Earl Lomon Koos, with a Preface by Robert S. Lynd, King's Crown Press, New York, 1946, makes these points with disturbing effectiveness.

of information should he reveal and what kind should he strictly hide? What would be the reaction of others involved in the case? These and 'other questions may occur to the client who is seeking help.

In other words the objective problem a client presents to a family caseworker almost always presents a concomitant emotional response. This emotional reaction is created in part by the ways in which the client has responded to situations in the past. It also includes the fears and anxieties resulting from having to face the casework situation itself, where the traditional way of adjustment may be threatened and brought into a sharp focus. Thus the help a family caseworker provides must be built not only upon the nature of the client's need, but also upon the attitude of the client toward his problem and toward the person aiding in its solution. Sometimes it is possible to deal directly with the objective factors in a given case and thus relieve the emotional tensions which have developed around them. In other instances it may be more desirable to work first with the emotional elements so that the objective ones may be viewed more readily and more realistically. Obviously, the objective factors in a given problem may include both personal and environmental conditions. These dynamics of the social casework process (as well as certain others) are realized by the client and the social worker in the interview.

Part in Community Programs

Aside from their interest in individuals and families in need, family agencies also aim to preserve and to extend normal family life on a community basis. The family social worker recognizes the fact that individuals and families do not live in a social vacuum. The pressures upon family living from various factors in the community are important to the full functioning of family casework. Family agencies, therefore, take part in all those movements within the community which aim at strengthening the family in general. It is becoming more evident that family agencies are thinking in terms of preventing family dislocations rather than dealing with them after they happen. This viewpoint, represented by varying efforts, is important because it signifies the broader and more social aspects of social work's responsibility. Advising young mothers on the problems of child-rearing may be more important ultimately in strengthening family life in the community than counseling parents whose children have gotten into trouble of one kind or another. Cooperating with those services in the community which are sympathetic with the goals of family casework is oftentimes as significant as the maintenance of the curative functions of the family agency.

While the family casework agency is seriously concerned with the development of community programs to abet the family in general, it is chiefly involved, in terms of expertness of staff, quantity of cases, and bulk of time, with individuals and their families directly.

Changing Emphases

The nature of cases over a period of several decades has changed considerably. The stress upon personal problems without any great financial need, which is characteristic of the family agency in many localities, has been a long time developing. The ways of looking at these personal problems has changed from a lay to a sociological to a psychological to a psychiatric approach. The First World War, especially, gave impetus to the psychiatric interests of social workers and increased the application of psychiatric concepts to casework thinking. But whatever development there was along the lines of personality treatment was for the most part sadly threatened by the great depression of the 1930's which led family agencies back again to more material considerations. There was no other practical possibility at the time. Family agencies, being always responsive to the general need, reorganized their programs to permit the granting of financial assistance mainly. The rise of the social security program of the federal government in the later 1930's subsequently relieved the private family agencies of their heavy relief load.

War-Increased Family Counseling

The Second World War, with the resultant stresses and strains created for family living, reintroduced the importance of family counseling. From military psychiatry it was seen that personal breakdowns were possible for all people if the circumstances were unfortunately arranged to develop them. The need for counseling on the part of many persons who were anticipating sudden marriage, who were separated by the fortunes of war, who faced anxieties and fears which might have been dormant in another period, and who had other problems, was everywhere apparent. The fact, too, that the boom years of a wartime economy made it unnecessary for family agencies to receive so many cases involving material need also increased the possibilities for a service primarily oriented toward helping people psychologically.

Range of Counseling Services

Thus it is that family casework agencies currently devote much time and interest to counseling services. These services have a wide range and actually include all disturbances to normal family living. Health

problems affect many families and need the attention of a family casework agency. Problems centering in economic adjustment also are dealt
with by family agencies. Sometimes, moreover, a family may not be in
need of financial assistance, but of such counseling as will enable it
to solve problems created by a lack of proper budgeting. In these and
in many other ways the family casework agency aids people through
counseling. (See Figure 14.)

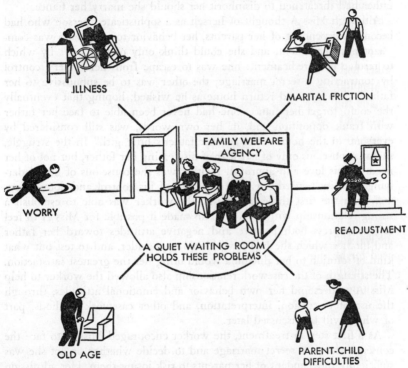

TYPES OF PROBLEMS MET IN A FAMILY CASEWORK AGENCY

ILLNESS

MARITAL FRICTION

FAMILY WELFARE AGENCY

WORRY

READJUSTMENT

A QUIET WAITING ROOM
HOLDS THESE PROBLEMS

OLD AGE

PARENT-CHILD
DIFFICULTIES

Fig. 14. Types of Problems Met in a Family Casework Agency

(Jewish Family Service, New York City.)

Three types of counseling services, however, may be singled out for
special attention here to illustrate the family agency at work. These are:
(1) counseling with premarital problems; (2) husband-wife conflicts;
and (3) parent-child relationships.

Type 1: Premarital Problems. These are shown by the case of Miss
"A," a young lady who utilized the services of a family casework agency
to resolve certain problems that she had regarding her proposed marriage.

Miss A[5], aged 24, had been in conflict about her marriage plans for nearly a year when she applied to the agency. She was involved in a struggle with her parents, who objected to her fiance, whom they considered socially inferior. He was a young New York man who was completing his professional training and had promise of a successful career. The couple had a sound love relationship, full of trust and respect. Since they were convinced that they were in love and were well matched, they had set a date for their wedding. The date was only a few weeks away, but Miss A had not been able to tell her parents of her plans because her father had threatened to disinherit her should she marry her fiance.

Although Miss A thought of herself as a sophisticated person who had become independent of her parents, her behavior toward them was compliant and dependent, and she could think only of two ways by which to resolve her predicament: one was to escape from her father's control by contracting a secret marriage; the other was to be submissive to her father's demands and return home as he wished, hoping that eventually she could forget her fiance. She had never been able to face her father with frank opposition and, in her own words, was still considered by everyone in the home town as "her father's little girl." In the struggle, she was conscious only of her fear of displeasing her father, but not of her need for his love and approval. Neither was she conscious of her underlying hostility toward her father because of his control and domination.

Within the first three interviews, the worker was able to establish a strong relationship with Miss A. This made it possible for Miss A to feel safe to express both positive and negative attitudes toward her father and mother which she had never dared to consider, and to test out what kind of solution to her dilemma would bring her the greatest satisfaction. The strength of the casework relationship also allowed the worker to help Miss A understand her own behavior and emotional attitudes, through the use of discussion, interpretation, and other casework methods, part of which will be discussed later.

As a first step in treatment, the worker encouraged Miss A to face the consequences of a secret marriage and to decide whether or not she was sufficiently independent of her parents to risk losing them. Her admission of her need for them made it necessary for her to arrange a postponement of the marriage date so that she would have time to understand why she was in such a state of confusion about her parents and her marriage.

Later, as the family pressed her to break off with her fiance and return home, she became panic-stricken, and had the impulse to regress into her "good little girl" role and return home. The worker urged strongly that Miss A not make a decision about her fiance or her parents while she was in this state of confusion. Since this move actually denied to Miss A the satisfactions she yearned to secure from her parents, the worker allowed her to satisfy further dependency needs in the treatment relationship. Because of the emotional support that Miss A felt in the relationship, it

[5]The real name of a client is never publicly divulged.

was possible to discuss with her how she had almost capitulated to her parents, how she actually relied on them far more than she had ever suspected, and that she was not so independent as she thought she was.

About this time Miss A was offered a better position than the one she held. Although it offered her professional opportunities and adequate salary, which she desired, she expressed ambivalence about taking it. She had many contradictory reasons for her hesitancy. However, it was evident to the caseworker that Miss A was immobilized because she felt guilty about deserting her employer, and it was clear that her position in relation to her employer was similar to that of her child-parent relationship. The employer was a person who inhibited and controlled the employees. The worker utilized this experience to help Miss A see how she was displacing her feelings about her father onto her employer, and that her feelings of anxiety were immobilizing her assertiveness. She was able to accept this and became aware that her compliant acceptance of the employer's control was self-defeating. She accepted the new position.

The next important step in the treatment began when Miss A's mother visited her. Up to this time, she had always spoken of her parents as of one parental figure. Her mother seemed to be a shadow of the dominating father. Actually, the mother was an affectionate parent who had accommodated herself to her rigid husband by agreeing with his decisions. By now, the worker felt that, while Miss A had a strong need for the worker's emotional support, actually she had relinquished part of her dependence in the casework relationship when she had changed her employment and moved out of the parental situation that the first position re-created.

The worker indicated that some of the remarks Miss A repeatedly made about her mother suggested that her mother had more importance than she was willing to admit to herself, and encouraged her to understand the differences in her feelings toward her two parents. Miss A became aware that she was freer to express opinions and affection when she was alone with her mother. She discovered that this was similar to her relationship with the worker, with whom she felt secure, but with whom she could think and take responsibility in making her own plans. She found that her mother was not prejudiced against her fiance but admired and respected him.

For the first time, Miss A began to separate the attitudes of her parents, and to realize that she had been attempting to hold the affection of her father by complying with his demands; that he was a person who would always seek to control a person weaker in will than himself. She expressed rebellion against the inevitable outcome of having to give up all of her important wishes in the interest of remaining "her father's little girl." The worker now helped her see that part of her failure to appreciate her mother was due to resentment of her mother's submissiveness to the father, and to recognize that her mother's behavior toward her was essentially different from that of her father. As the worker helped her separate her two parents, Miss A's feelings of affection for her mother grew, and she began to see that the relationship between her mother and herself was that of two women who felt secure with each other.

Her failure to feel affectionate toward her mother had been a serious lack of her development and had blocked her from moving on to a more mature relationship with her father. As Miss A was helped to develop more identification with her mother, she began to relinquish her child-like relationship with her father and to accept a more adult role with both parents. The worker reinforced this move by helping her see that her fears of losing her father were unfounded since he expressed in many ways his need to keep her affection. The worker also assured her that as she changed her behavior toward her father from that of a submissive child to that of a young adult he would be pressed to relinquish his behavior of domination toward her.

Miss A sustained her conviction that the marriage was good and right for her. She and her fiance set the date for their wedding. She invited her parents to attend. Neither one attended but her mother immediately sent good wishes to both; and a month after the marriage her father telephoned on Christmas day and extended his good wishes. For several months she did not see her father but continued to feel about him more as one adult feels about another. She continued to grow in her understanding of the kind of person he was. The worker helped her to anticipate his probable behavior when they finally met, so that she could be prepared in advance.

Subsequently, Miss A tested her progress by visiting home. She was pleased to find that she could maintain her own position with her father and did not relapse into a "little girl" role. She was grateful to perceive that, although he was rigid and prejudiced and would probably never change, actually he was a loving father. She felt little anxiety in opposing him, and found herself to be more spontaneous in the presence of both parents—alone or together. She was able to deal with her father's strong ideas in an objective way, and to establish a separate and different kind of relationship with each parent. As she realized that her father could no longer hold her in a dependent-submissive role, she was able to give more affection to her parents and found an increasing ability to give herself more completely in the marriage relationship.

Prior to marriage Miss A was a virgin. While she and her fiance were always able to discuss sexual questions freely before and after marriage, Miss A had never been able to discuss sex with her mother. She turned to the worker to discuss some of her apprehensions about her sexual adjustment. In the interviews, her feelings of anxiety were allayed and she made a gradual satisfactory sexual adjustment.

The marriage has been satisfactory for both partners. Miss A's husband has now started his professional career in another city and the couple are planning for their first child. Their last report testified that after more than two years both feel their happiness and compatibility are increasing.

In a sense it was fortunate for Miss A that she fell in love with someone who was bound to bring strong parental disapproval, because this brought her conflict out into the open and caused her to seek help with her dilemma. The caseworker was able to help her see that her relationship with her father was holding her in a childish role, and that she had failed to develop a mature identification with her mother. The casework treatment kept her from trying to resolve her conflict with her parents by running away from them or by regressing into further dependence upon them. Either solution would have been hazardous for her continued emotional growth. Instead, she was assisted to enter marriage in a thoughtful way, after she understood her emotional difficulties and needs and tested out several possible solutions. Finally, she contracted marriage after she was free to relinquish her childish relationship with her father and to move forward to the more mature relationship with her husband.[6]

Type 2: Husband-Wife Conflicts. The family caseworker treats family problems of persons who are already married. There is a wide range to these problems and there are no two quite alike. They must be handled with varying techniques and insights. Some are relatively simple (or so it would seem) while some are very complex. With some of the problems the social worker may feel entirely competent. On others he may feel that he should consult a psychiatrist for help with the client's problem or refer the client directly to a psychiatrist. The following three examples of marital problems point up just a few of the possibilities:[7]

Mrs. A brought her confusion to a worker when her husband wrote from overseas that he was being discharged, but would not return to her mother's home where the couple had lived since marriage. Mrs. A was an only child whose father had died during her infancy. Her mother, a capable business woman, had centered her emotional life around her daughter. Before marriage, all Mrs. A's social life was with her mother. The mother was jealous of Mr. A, first tried to prevent the marriage, and later made it almost impossible for the couple to have any privacy.

There was no question in Mrs. A's mind about her husband. She loved him and wanted him to return to her. She sympathized with his feeling about her mother, and agreed that Jeanette, the 3-year-old daughter, was becoming a problem because her mother interfered with her care of Jeanette. The child was learning to play her mother against her grandmother.

However, Mrs. A thought her husband was unreasonable to make such

[6]Katherine McElroy, "Marriage Counseling," *Journal of Social Casework*, volume 28, number 6, June, 1947, pp. 213–215.
[7]Elsie M. Waelder, "Casework With Marital Problems," *Journal of Social Casework*, volume 28, number 5, May, 1947, pp. 169–171.

an ultimatum when he knew she could not leave her mother. What would relatives and neighbors say? Her mother had devoted her life to her—was it fair to desert her now? With the housing situation almost impossible, where would they go? He shouldn't have forced this on her so suddenly.

*   *   *

Confusion over loyalty to husband and parents had Mrs. B so upset that she thought she would give up and return with her children to be a child again in her parents' home. "If Ed isn't man enough to stand up against my parents for me, he's a dope, and why should I stay with him?"

Married at 20, and now the mother of two children, Mrs. B was still, for all her eight years of marriage, looking to her parents for her standards. She lived next door to them; they interfered with her discipline of the children, and controlled her by their disapproval. "I can't even wear silk stockings in the house because my mother thinks it is extravagant." Throughout her complaints, it was her parents who seemed to cause the difficulty, but she blamed her husband because he took it quietly, didn't fight her battles. She wanted him to move her away from her family but wasn't agreeable to his suggestion that they buy an old house. "No one takes my opinions seriously."

Mrs. B stuttered and stammered when excited, said she had always done this. Now her young daughter had a similar speech defect. She wondered if Ellen was imitating her, or whether Ellen's stammering was caused by her "personality." Eddie did not stammer. Mrs. B described him as an outgoing, lively youngster.

But not only were the children affected. Mrs. B said "deeper things" were wrong—the sexual adjustment was quite poor. Perhaps this was because she and her husband both had inadequate sex information and the early marriage was difficult because they were "so ignorant."

*   *   *

"My husband has stopped loving me," was Mrs. G's statement of her marriage problem. She was unhappy, cried frequently in the interview, and seemed completely bewildered by Mr. G's attitude because the first few years of their marriage had been so happy. In response to the worker's questions about the change, this story developed.

Mr. G had no particular industrial skill and so had been employed on low-paid jobs. The family managed well while she worked, and by careful planning had gotten by after the birth of the first child. Then a second pregnancy had produced twins. The income, barely adequate for three, suddenly had to be stretched to cover five.

Mrs. G was in very poor health. She needed an operation following her confinement but had not returned for this because she had no money for hospital and doctor bills, and no one to care for the three children while she was hospitalized. She was continually tired and had frequent pain.

She no longer could keep up with the laundry, housecleaning, and cooking as she had been accustomed to. And on top of this her husband had stopped loving her!

Type 3: Parent-Child Relationships. In addition to problems which affect two adults, married or unmarried, family agencies treat many problems involving parents and children. In fact, since so much of the work of family casework agencies is of this nature, there has been considerable discussion in many localities of combining family and children's agencies. The integration of the two types of agencies has occurred rather frequently in recent years. But, where mergers have not taken place, there is still responsibility on the part of the family agencies for the treatment of parent-child problems. While there is difference of opinion regarding the function of both types of agencies in the treatment of these problems, there is some reason to suppose that the problems of a child living with his own family are more likely to come to the family agency, while concern with children placed outside of their own homes or to be placed outside of their own homes falls to the children's agency. Child welfare will be discussed in succeeding chapters.

Many times, parent-child conflicts involve the relationship between a parent or parents and an adult child, and these cases usually come within the province of the family casework agency.

Treatment of Unmarried Mothers

Aside from the services just suggested, family casework agencies have long been interested in the problems of unmarried mothers. The treatment of unmarried mothers comprises for some family agencies a considerable part of their activities; other agencies are entirely devoted to such care.

Emotional Problems. Caseworkers are greatly interested in the emotional problems of unmarried mothers. It is difficult to describe the psychology of the girl who becomes pregnant out of wedlock. Certain sociological explanations may be helpful, but they may fail to go deep enough into the personal motives of such girls. One worker who analyzed the personality patterns of unmarried mothers found that throughout all the cases studied it seemed evident that the girls were using the experience of pregnancy out of marriage as a means of solving some emotional dilemma.[8] According to the report, the unconscious motiva-

[8]Leontine R. Young, "Personality Patterns in Unmarried Mothers," *Understanding the Psychology of the Unmarried Mother,* Family Service Association of America, New York, 1945–1947, pp. 7–13.

tions of the girls hinge on their relations with their families. Usually, unquestioned domination by one member of the family, particularly the mother, characterized the family situation. This was true even in the cases of broken families where dominance by one parent, by a relative, or even by the girl over her parents or relatives, gave rise to emotional stresses of one sort or another. At any rate it would seem that girls who have babies out of wedlock tend to come from families where there is not a healthy, happy relationship between the parents and the children.

It is clear, then, that the social worker must deal not only with surface factors in the cases of unmarried mothers, but with those oftentimes hidden and unconscious aspects of behavior. Unless some relief can be secured for such problems, the unmarried mother may continue expressing her dilemma in the same or in other ways. It is not always easy to assist an unmarried mother to attain such insight regarding herself and her behavior so that she is able to understand and control the basis of her emotional response. Social casework, however, has never been claimed as a perfect adjustor of human problems. There is generally a significant margin of failure. But, for those cases which succeed, there is the hope that the unmarried mother will be able to manage her own life on the basis of the strengths she has acquired through her contact with a social work agency.

Decisions Regarding Children. Unmarried mothers also have problems in connection with their decisions regarding their children. Most unmarried mothers place their children in adoptive homes, although some take their children home with them; others place their children in foster homes. But, whatever the decision, it is a difficult one for the mother to make. Both the emotional and the social implications must be taken into consideration. It is the responsibility of the family caseworker to help unmarried mothers make satisfying decisions in this regard. The following case of "Ruth" shows how such a decision is made and what its consequences are, in part:

When Ruth came to an agency for help, she was pregnant with her second child. She had placed her first for adoption on the insistence of her mother and the local authorities—not social workers—who had felt simply that she had disgraced herself and that in any case her first responsibility was the care and support of her widowed and aging mother. Ruth had never had any fun, any period of normal carefree youth. Born late in her mother's life, she had grown up in a home deserted by the father and shadowed by her mother's bitterness and unhappiness. She had never had any right to a life of her own, to seek answers for her own needs and desires.

Fundamentally, Ruth was not a seriously sick girl and she wanted help and could use it. With the caseworker's help she could begin to express her resentment toward her mother, her feeling of her being trapped, her desire for some fun, for a more normal way of life. She could begin to see that this was her baby, that she had a right not only to make a decision but to use the help and support of the caseworker in making that decision. The caseworker helped her to see that her first obligation was to her baby and to herself, not to her mother. What did she really want for herself? Ruth wanted very simple, normal things—a job she could enjoy, freedom from repressive home restrictions, money for new clothes, and recreation, some fun with young people her own age. She could see for herself that these wishes did not include responsibility for a child and, with the support and reassurance of the caseworker, could see that there was nothing wrong about this. She surrendered the baby for adoption.[9]

Material Assistance

From the foregoing it is evident that family casework agencies currently treat many problems which are nonfinancial. The family counseling services which have been explained and illustrated show one of the most important aspects of the activities of family agencies. But one should not conclude that family agencies do not still grant financial assistance to some clients. The chief problem of the privately financed and managed family casework agency is not whether or not to give money to clients in need, but under what circumstances money should be offered. At the present time many clients who formerly were helped materially by private agencies no longer look to such agencies for assistance. The development of the manifold public services has made many of the financial services of the private agencies unneeded, especially in certain categories of assistance. Indeed, it is certainly impossible for family casework agencies to finance the material burdens of all people who are in genuine need. No system of private financing could today accomplish that gigantic task. It is, therefore, to government that most people must look for material assistance. Only in particular circumstances do the private agencies still grant financial assistance to clients. In 1946, for example, it was found that less than one third of the families and individuals coming to private agencies were given material aid. (See Figure 15.)

It is difficult to know exactly what circumstances should determine whether a private agency should aid clients materially. The Committee

[9] Leontine R. Young, "The Unmarried Mother's Decision About Her Baby," *Understanding the Psychology of the Unmarried Mother,* Family Service Association of America, New York, 1945–1947, p. 16.

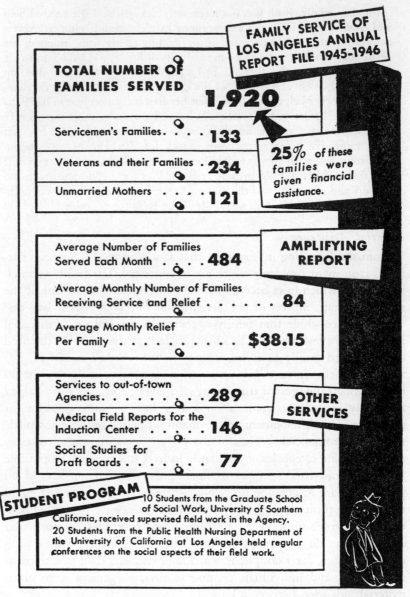

FAMILY SERVICE OF LOS ANGELES ANNUAL REPORT FILE 1945-1946

TOTAL NUMBER OF FAMILIES SERVED **1,920**

Servicemen's Families. . . . **133**

Veterans and their Families . **234**

Unmarried Mothers . . . **121**

25% of these families were given financial assistance.

Average Number of Families Served Each Month **484**

Average Monthly Number of Families Receiving Service and Relief **84**

Average Monthly Relief Per Family **$38.15**

AMPLIFYING REPORT

Services to out-of-town Agencies. **289**

Medical Field Reports for the Induction Center **146**

Social Studies for Draft Boards **77**

OTHER SERVICES

STUDENT PROGRAM

10 Students from the Graduate School of Social Work, University of Southern California, received supervised field work in the Agency.
20 Students from the Public Health Nursing Department of the University of California at Los Angeles held regular conferences on the social aspects of their field work.

FIG. 15. Report of a Family Service Agency on Its Annual Activities

(*The Case of the Empty Mirror*, Family Service of Los Angeles, California, 1946.)

on Current and Future Planning of the Family Service Association, however, has reported on this problem in the following way:[10]

The Place of Financial Assistance in Family Service Program. The Committee on Current and Future Planning recognizes that for the present the use of financial assistance in the voluntary family agency will differ from community to community according to variations in available community resources.

In the immediate years ahead, the voluntary family agency will need a budget for financial assistance to families to implement its program. The giving of financial assistance should not be regarded as something apart but, when required, it should be considered as an integral part of the family casework process. The use of financial assistance to implement a family service program may grow relatively less important as community resources outside the voluntary family agency are expanded and made more flexible, and as the clientele of the agency changes to include a larger number of economically independent families.

Such a program implies the possibility of great variation in the special uses to be made of financial assistance. The following are examples:

1. Granting financial assistance for special educational, recreational, or vocational purposes.
2. Giving financial assistance for maintenance purposes during a period of exploration, where the maintenance during this period will facilitate the casework process or where the agency is undecided about the wisdom of making an immediate referral to another agency.
3. Providing financial assistance for maintenance purposes, during a brief emergency, to families already receiving other services from the agency.

It is the further opinion of the Committee that the financial assistance funds of the family service agency should not be used to supplement inadequate grants of the public department. The supplementation of defined and legally permissible public relief responsibilities is basically unsound in principle.

THE EXTENSION OF FAMILY WELFARE WORK

As has been suggested, family casework has been somewhat troubled in recent years over the nature of its function in the local community. Often, agencies have seen their services to clients in need of financial assistance alone decline markedly. For example, one agency reported that it gave financial aid to 3,354 persons in 1932, to 1,847 in 1939, and to 871 in 1943. The creation of services which in former times might have been considered as part of the function of the private family

[10]*Report of the Committee on Current and Future Planning,* Family Service Association of America, New York, 1946, p. 9.

agency, but which are now attached to some other community organization or group, has also affected family casework. Other influences, too, have been at work.

Establishment of Outposts

In the face of this unsettlement, family agencies have originated several new devices which have allowed them not only to maintain their services to the community as previously, but also have given a rejuvenating promise to the field. One of these newer developments is that of *outposts*. Outposts involve the placement of workers from an agency into extra-agency situations, so that clients and potential clients need not contact the agency directly. Outposts have been established in a variety of ways, and in many instances have been found to be quite helpful in adapting family casework facilities to changing conditions.

Some of the outpost arrangements came about as a result of experience in the Second World War, when war workers did not have time for the more usual type of agency contact. To require the regular procedure might have meant slower production and financial loss for the employee. Thus it was logical for family casework agencies to send their workers into warplants so that workers could receive on-the-spot consideration.

Outposts have also been used by agencies not able to hire their own caseworkers. This also was especially true during the past war. For example, new day nurseries were founded in large numbers. Many of these, as well as other child care centers, were unable to hire social caseworkers to aid them with their programs. Family casework agencies stepped in and lent their workers to such agencies. In some cases a newly founded agency, upon expansion, has been able to cancel the outpost relation and establish its own casework services.

Extension of Contacts. Family agencies have been interested in outpost arrangements from the point of view of strengthening their own relations with the community. During the economic depression of the 1930's some clients knew the family agencies primarily as sources of financial assistance. Unfortunately, many of these persons assumed that this was the only function of the family agency. The establishment of outposts in various community locations enabled the family agencies to come into contact with people who may have failed to appreciate the wide scope of services a family agency can offer.

Value. One of the chief values of the outpost system is the experimentalism involved. The new efforts of family agencies have brought them in direct contact with many fresh and developing aspects of family welfare in the community, and this contact has heightened their sensitivity to their community responsibility. Aside from this the fact that the services of family agencies have been introduced or reintroduced to a large number of people who otherwise might not have had relationships with them has proved to be of value.

Use of Fee-Charging

Another of the recent devices of family casework agencies (and of other agencies) has been that of fee-charging. Fee-charging has arisen as a means of providing social work service for those who wish and can afford to pay for it.

In nonfee-charging agencies the client is asked to make no payment of any kind to the agency giving him assistance. He may, as a result of his appreciation of the service rendered, contribute something either to the agency which has helped him or to some other privately supported community service. But whether or not the client contributes is his own affair.

A fee-charging agency is operated on the assumption that clients wish to pay a fee for the services granted them just as they would pay for services rendered by any other professional person—the physician, the dentist, or the lawyer. In most cases where fee-charging is in practice, a graduated scale for payment has been devised so that a client pays according to his income. While there is something to be said for charging a client a "flat fee" (determined by his income), notwithstanding the complexity of his case, most fee-charging agencies determine the charges on a visit-basis.

Fee-charging agencies have found that they have met a real need in the community. They have made contact with many persons who otherwise might not come to a social work agency. The kinds of people who now generally avail themselves of the resources of the fee-charging agencies are businessmen, factory workers, doctors, students, housewives, and others. The assumption underlying their use of the agency is their ability to pay, as well as the character of their need.

At present about thirty family welfare agencies charge a fee to at least some of their clients. They exist in about fifteen cities. The future will probably see a further development of this practice.

The following examples show that some clients do not wish to receive charity.[11]

[11] Lotte Seelig, "Applicability of a Fee System to a Family Agency," *Smith College Studies in Social Work*, volume 16, number 3, March, 1946, pp. 212–213. See the entire article for a detailed analysis of many factors regarding fee-charging.

Example 1: In requesting camp placement for his little boy Mr. Brown first remarked, "We do not want charity; we are quite able to pay all Sonny's expenses." To dispel Mr. Brown's reluctance in accepting the agency's help with summer plans for his child, the caseworker briefly explained that financial assistance to the needy was a very small part of our work.

*   *   *

Example 2: Placement of the wife's aged father was the plan eventually decided upon by the worker and a young couple. The man and wife were fearful of having the worker make the arrangements with the Home for the Aged because they did not want their contact with the agency to be known. "People will think we came to you for charity," they said.

*   *   *

Example 3: Rather than face the humiliation of a personal application, one man, member of a once prominent family, applied by letter and requested recommendation of an inexpensive eating place. He demanded strictest confidence and justified his application by saying, "I contribute to the Community Chest, and I mentioned the Jewish Charities as beneficiaries."

Wider Community Relationships

The use of outposts and fee-charging by family casework agencies involves certain reorientations for the agencies themselves. These newer extensions of family welfare service are indicative of the way family agencies are seeking to enrich their contribution to the total community. But they raise questions regarding the very bases on which family welfare work exists and should exist in the future. Of interest here is the fact that family welfare work, by its extended program, is proceeding to set up social service relationships with an even wider economic segment of the community. The full meaning of this development is not yet known or appreciated, often even among social workers themselves.

In the past, family casework was largely identified with the lower economic groups of the community—those who could not afford to pay. This fact has placed in the minds of many a stigma on those who avail themselves of the services of agencies. Some persons who as unemployed had to appeal to family agencies during the depression of the 1930's now find it hard in different circumstances to return to them, because they feel that the agencies exist only to aid those who are dependently poor. Those within the community who have never needed financial aid do not realize that the agencies are interested in other problems and needs. Some may think that social work agencies are not equipped to deal with persons who suffer from no marked financial need, but have troublesome personal, social, and emotional problems. To all these persons, then, the recent practices of the family casework agencies should appeal.

The efforts of family casework agencies to extend themselves further into the community are based upon a philosophy of social work which gained credence in the years preceding the newer developments. For some time now social work agencies, in general, have felt that they are more than class instruments bringing aid to the lower and more dependent groups in the population. They have believed that they are an expression of community responsibility which includes all members of the community on the basis of personal rights. Thus a private, non-sectarian, social work agency might reason that since it is dependent for its existence upon the financial support of the general community, an obligation to less than the whole community is not in keeping with the purpose of its establishment. Social work agencies for some time have preferred to think that clients are entitled to the services they can render if the clients meet the particular requirements of the agencies.

For social work itself, these new devices of the family welfare agencies suggest a large, unfolding field of potential activity. While the existing facilities of social work have never been adequate to meet the needs of the poor in the community, it is not known and can scarcely be imagined what quantitative developments will be necessary to extend social work to the whole community. Probably, out of this effort on the part of social workers and clients will come a greatly changed orientation to the social work process itself.

AGENCY INTERRELATIONS

While family casework agencies are instituting new services to strengthen their democratic foundations, they are also extending themselves more in the direction of greater interagency cooperation. That such interagency cooperation was vital and necessary even before the present is attested to by the various attempts made in the past to coordinate family welfare agencies, both locally and nationally.

Locally, many family casework agencies have joined councils of social work agencies.[12] Family agencies have also cooperated for years with other casework agencies. The mutual arrangement between the Family Welfare Association of Minneapolis and the Veterans Administration

[12]Councils of social agencies, as well as the various other cooperative relationships between agencies, will be discussed in Chapter 14.

Facility of St. Cloud, Minnesota, although atypical, shows what can be done in interagency cooperation:

At the time when the mental casualties of World War II began returning to their homes, the staff of the Veterans Administration Facility at St. Cloud, Minnesota, recognized the need for adequate follow-up care of veterans after hospitalization had been completed. There seemed to be little possibility of securing this under the provisions of the Administration. Suitable follow-up care was deemed important by the Facility because of the significant implications of the discharge process and the fact that veterans returning home could be harmed if not received properly. Social work services to the veterans and their families seemed to be a practical solution to the problem.

With these things in mind the social worker and the manager of the Facility sought a conference with the general secretary of the Family Welfare Association of Minneapolis. As a result of a meeting, both groups thought that cooperative arrangements could be set up. Members of the Association visited the Facility to become better informed about the possibilities of coordination.

After these preliminaries, the Family Welfare Association drew up a statement of what services it felt prepared to offer and of the limitations apparently involved for both agencies. It was suggested that the plan of cooperation be modified from time to time as necessity suggested. The Veterans Administration, in turn, outlined a referral procedure which was accepted by the Association. The relationship was changed at some points during the course of time.

The terms of the agreement included: veterans had to have residence in Hennepin County (Minneapolis); they could have served in any war, but they were especially sought for if they served in World War II.

A wide variety of mental cases were represented among the first fifty-one considered. In selecting referral cases the social worker at the Facility took into account not only the nature of the problem which the veteran had, but the relatives to whom he would eventually go. Sometimes, too, the serviceman needed some specific service which the arrangement might well meet.

Usually, sometime before the release of the veteran, the family would be given opportunity to contact the family casework agency cooperating with the plan. Most families were eager to help but knew little about the helping process. The family agency assisted them by clarifying the ways in which they could aid in receiving the veterans into their homes. Patients also were generally willing to have contact with the family agency to assist them individually in thinking through their own adjustments to their families. These contacts were worked out easily between the families, the veterans, and the family agency.

The family agency and the Facility cooperated in many ways in order to perfect this plan. An example of this is the sending by the Facility to the agency the complete history (upon the willingness of the patient and his family) so that the agency would be able to work concretely and with a saving of time. Conferences were also repeatedly required.

The worker at the Facility, in summarizing her experiences in this co-operative enterprise, said: "Teamwork, understanding, tolerance, and respect for the other's job all played a part in the success of the plan."[13]

Casework and Group Work Cooperation

Again, locally, various family social work agencies, especially in more recent years, have developed cooperative programs with social group work organizations. In some instances the arrangements entail the release of time for caseworkers so that they can engage in activities of different sorts in group work situations. Definite relationships are obviously needed because of the common factors involved in casework and group work from a theoretical viewpoint and in light of the cross-referrals constantly made between these two types of social work agencies. The caseworker can often be of help by referring clients as a part of treatment to group work agencies. Likewise, group workers often find that they can advantageously refer their group members to case-work agencies for more intensified and personal treatment. In some instances family caseworkers are available to group members in group work agencies for personal counseling. In others, the caseworker is a group leader, group member, or group aide, assisting the professional group leader in some way. Whatever the relationships (to be deter-mined by the nature of the casework-group work situation, and the adequacy of the personnel involved), they are on the increase.

National Organizations

While family social work agencies have set up effective and beneficial interagency relationships on a local basis, they also have been interested in certain noteworthy national affiliations and developments. The charity organization societies of the past were actively interested in fed-erated services. That is an essential part of the meaning of the move-ment. But it was not until 1909 that they were brought together in significant, national cooperation. The instrument of the accomplish-ment was the Charity Organization Department of the Russell Sage Foundation. Miss Mary Richmond, the Director of that Department, was a pioneer in the development of those skills now known as social

---

[13]This account is taken from "Co-operation Between a Veterans Hospital and a Family Agency," especially Part I, by Helen M. Donaldson, in *The Family* (now *Journal of Social Casework*), volume 26, number 10, October, 1945, pp. 208–211. Part II of the same article, written by Grace C. Mayberg, presents the point of view of the worker within the family agency.

casework. To her office as Director she brought, therefore, an enlightened experience and a professional attitude which counted heavily in the formulation of the fundamental procedures of social casework.

Family Service Association of America. In the year following the establishment of the Charity Organization Department, another national organization appeared on the scene, the National Association of Societies for Organizing Charity, with Francis H. McLean as Director.[14] This organization was established for the interchange of experience and for joint counsel on the part of the member family social work agencies. From 1930 to 1946 it was known as the Family Welfare Association of America; in 1946 the title of Family Service Association of America was adopted. It is by far the most important coordinating organization in the field of family social work. It is a voluntary organization made up of various family casework agencies throughout the nation which control its policies and program. In 1948 the number of agencies participating in the Association was 233, including many of the most prominent family social work agencies of this country and a few from Canada. Of the total the great majority are private social work agencies, although some public welfare agencies are members. Membership in the Association is carefully controlled so that only those agencies which maintain high standards of social casework may belong. Some of the requirements for membership include:

1. A responsible and active lay governing board.
2. Joint participation by the board, the executive of the agency, and the staff, in conducting the activities of the agency.
3. A paid staff which has qualified training for the practice of family social work.
4. A well-defined financial policy with the larger amount of support (for the private agencies) from private funds.
5. A lay constituency which understands and supports the work of the agency.

The Association provides a number of services to the member agencies. For one, it furnishes sound literature on their field. This literature includes two periodicals, namely, *Journal of Social Casework* (formerly known as *The Family*), and *Highlights*. Pamphlets on specialized aspects of family casework, occasional books, and bulletins are also published as the need arises. The Association is equipped to bring professional aid to local family agencies which have special problems. It

[14] See the general contributions of this leader of social work in the special issue of *The Family* (now *Journal of Social Casework*), volume 27, number 1, March, 1946.

offers a personnel service to member agencies. It also is responsible for the interpretation of family social work to the general public.

Important among special studies instituted by the Association was one in 1943 which explored the possibilities of greater cooperation between family welfare agencies and children's agencies.[15] An important social action program of the Association was its efforts in the founding and operation of the American War-Community Services, Inc. (A.W.C.S.), during the war years. Joining with five other national health and welfare organizations, the Association cooperatively developed health and welfare agencies in about fifty American communities which had been particularly affected by wartime conditions and which conspicuously lacked facilities adequate to meet their needs.

SPECIAL SERVICES RELATED TO FAMILY CASEWORK

There are many social casework services which cannot at present be drawn within a strictly logical scheme of things. Some seem to be rather close to family casework, and yet, they are not always considered by family caseworkers to be an intrinsic part of their field. Thus they may be termed special services related to family casework. Any complete accounting of the manifold services of social work agencies should, however, take these special services into account. Some are clearly more important than others in terms of the volume of their operations. Others may be extremely significant in showing the ways social caseworkers can be of help to people regardless of the definitive lines which may be drawn.

The Aged

The aged are one of the special interests of family casework agencies. The increase in the attention which family casework agencies are giving to the aged is in line with the growing proportion of the aged in the general population. It is a fairly familiar fact that the number of the aged is increasing markedly. In 1940, according to the census, 6.8 percent of the population was sixty-five years of age or older. According to the population trend, by 1980 possibly 14.4 percent of the total population will be in the same category. (See Figure 16.)

The aged have many occasions on which to call upon family casework agencies for assistance. They may contact a family agency to discuss institutional placement. They may require the services of a family agency to find a housekeeper. Also, and especially in recent years, the aged are coming to family agencies to be counseled regarding home

[15]Mentioned at the beginning of the next chapter.

problems not requiring too much environmental manipulation. The personal counseling aspects of family casework with the aged have become so noticeable in the last few years that they give promise of a whole new development in casework itself. Already, the science of old age, *gerontology,* is spoken of with increased interest and knowledge.

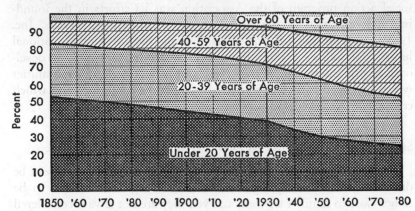

Fig. 16. Proportion of the U.S. Population in Various Age Groups, 1850–1930, and Thompson and Whelpton's "Low" Estimate for 1940–1980

(Paul H. Landis, *Population Problems,* American Book Company, New York, 1943.)

Assistance for Social Needs. Oftentimes the need of an older person is primarily social. As an individual grows older he is apt to lose his relatives and friends. The loneliness attached to old age is traditionally known. Social workers can be of assistance to the aged in encouraging them to find interesting and constructive activity. The following case illustrates this point:

Seventy-five-year-old Mr. Simon thought he had nothing to look forward to when the supply department of a family agency closed and he no longer had his job as tailor. Outside his interest in his family and in the synagogue, there was nothing in Mr. Simon's life. Illiterate in his native language and busy earning a living for his growing family, he had never found time to learn to read and write English. He found his way of living completely satisfactory. Feeling secure for life, the loss of his work was a tremendous shock, and, as he said, "I felt as though something was taken from my life and I was cast off." Financial worry was allayed by a pension, but that was not enough, and even with his interest in the synagogue, time hung heavy on his hands. He missed the daily travel back and forth, forgetting the discomfort of the crowded subway and the stair climbing that had begun to bother him. He missed the pleasantness of the department, his work, and co-workers.

Essentially a well man, he began to develop all sorts of physical symptoms for which the doctor found no organic basis. He begged for a job, but the caseworker could be of no help in that direction. She tried to interest him in developing an interest or hobby, describing the various W.P.A. handicraft classes and the occupational work, particularly rug making done in homes for the aged. She offered extra assistance as required. She also suggested learning English in one of the special classes set up for adult foreigners. He was scornful of the class, feeling that "he was too old to go to school," and politely turned aside every other suggestion.

All that winter he was a miserably unhappy, complaining little man, a general nuisance both to himself and to his family. The idea of a hobby had apparently seeded itself, however, for in the spring he became interested in the landlord's backyard vegetable garden, and eventually took over full responsibility for it. And it was his idea to plant flowers. Although he had never before had any experience with gardening, he had marvelous results. His success and the praise of the neighbors did much to stimulate and foster the interest. It has continued ever since, almost three years, manifesting itself during the winter months in the care of beautiful house plants.

Because this did not occupy enough time, of his own accord he enrolled in the English class and was as proud as a child when he learned to write his name. The family is delighted, for once more he is his old, smiling self.[16]

Federal Financial Aid. Not all of the problems of the aged are cared for by private family casework agencies. The Social Security program of the federal government has done much since 1935 basically to relieve the aged of financial dependency. The effects of this will be felt in greater measure in the future. The following case, involving Mr. "Morales," describes how the Social Security program may significantly meet the material needs of the aged. It also points out the fact that the social worker can do much beyond the requirements of the federal provisions for the enrichment of the lives of the aged:

Mr. Morales, a well-preserved, cultured, South American gentleman of 74, was a construction engineer of international reputation, who had led a busy and exciting life, as his work took him all over the world. An ample income made possible a comfortable mode of living as well as savings and investments for his old age. Possessed of good health, he was able to continue active in work with a railroad until failing eyesight forced him to give up his job. Provident and far-seeing, he had laid away savings and invested in stocks for his retirement from business. When retirement came, even though it was sooner than he expected, he found

[16]Amy S. Powell and Flora Fox, "Growth in Old Age," *Case Work With the Aged,* Family Welfare Association of America (now Family Service Association of America), New York, 1938–1939, p. 19.

adjustment to leisure comparatively easy, for he had financial security, friends, and an absorbing, satisfying hobby in sculpturing.

Five happy years were spent before the market crash of early depression days swept away his income. Savings were soon used up and, penniless, he found himself a recipient of old-age assistance. When the investigator called, he found a worried, crushed, despondent old man, unable to face dependence. Even interest in sculpturing had waned.

The investigator, recognizing not only Mr. Morales' talent, but also his need to have some earning power, suggested that he model small objects which might be salable. Encouraged by the interest and understanding of his new friend, Mr. Morales experimented with some book ends which sold very well. Other articles he has exchanged for food supplies and tobacco. The sculptured head of a child earned him a radio. Mr. Morales, his depression gone, finds life meaningful again and leads a happy existence in his studio apartment.[17]

Institutional Care. There are many institutions which serve the aged. Originally, under the optimism of the federal program, some people thought that the need for institutions for the aged would rapidly disappear. This has not been the case. The actual need for institutions has remained about the same, if it has not increased. The type of person who can best utilize institutional treatment, however, has changed somewhat. Instead of institutions being general catch-alls of the aged, irrespective of their problems, they now are looked upon as being suitable for certain specific types of the aged. Clearly, much depends upon the problem the aged person presents as to whether he should be placed in an institution or not. The sick person who is unable to manage for himself may use the facilities of an institution to advantage. The aged person who is able to take care of himself, except that he is financially dependent, should not be placed in an institution. He should be maintained in his own home or in a private home. There is at present great need for private boarding homes where aged individuals and couples may be cared for. Facilities of all sorts for the Negro aged are notably lacking.

Many of the aged suffer from health problems. Some of them could be treated in their own homes if there were sufficient health services available. Visiting nurses or homemakers could keep many in their own homes. There is need currently for special housing, neither private nor institutional, for the care of the aged. In such special housing a varied program of services to the aged could be established.

Foster Home Placement. One of the newer ways of assisting the aged is through foster home placement. The foster home is able to provide

[17]*Ibid*, p. 18.

more intimate personal relations than other forms of care for the aged. In the foster home care of the aged, the emphasis is upon only a few people, at the most, living under one roof with the protection and care of a private family. Preferably, only one aged person is placed in a home, but in some instances there may be two or three. Much depends upon the personal requirements of the aged person or persons and the foster family. There are problems, of course, of finding acceptable foster homes.

It is obvious that the foster home placement of the aged is suited especially to certain old people. Not all would wish this kind of service. It is unusually attractive to those aged who feel the need to live in small family groups. Some aged persons who seek foster home placement are emotionally immature and insecure. They feel that a close family environment may help them recover the security they had as children:

Miss Walter was such a person. Crippled from infancy by infantile paralysis, her grotesquely distorted body had dragged with the weight of a stone on her keen mind. Her red hair and violent temper portrayed emotional intensity that had never found a satisfactory outlet. As a child she was unwanted and made to feel in the way. She fought desperately for her rights in a family that had included two stepmothers and three sets of children. She was unable to win any one of the group and finally completely alienated her family. As soon as she was old enough she withdrew to live by herself. Her strong arms swung a limp body on crutches and she had to ask help of people she disliked. Knowing no love, she could give none and suspected the motive behind every friendly act. As she grew older and increasingly helpless, she tried again and again to reach out to her family and even to force them into assuming some responsibility for her, but each time she was met with a stern rebuff.

At last, in her sixty-first year, she admitted defeat and on her own initiative gained admission to a home for incurables. The caseworker, although dubious about such a plan, helped her complete the arrangements. Anticipating possible failure, she arranged for Miss W's household goods to be stored temporarily. Miss W's arrival in the institution was a shock. Her queer, outlandish clothing added to the grotesqueness of her appearance, but her superior mind caused her to be labeled as an eccentric intellectual. When ignored, she began telling romantic stories of the love life of her beautiful mother and her liaison with a national political figure, and offered proof that she was the offspring of this union. This intrigued her audience but the lady board of managers was shocked and asked for her immediate removal.

Once again Miss W and her furnishings were united in a solitary existence. A room was found in a run-down residential hotel where she could cook, but before long the office help, the maids, and her neighbors were harassed and bedeviled by her arrogant demands.

Then came her appeal, "I want to live with a family." With many misgivings the caseworker advertised for a home for Miss W. This presented difficulties, for although Miss W sought security through acceptance and affection, she was the kind of person who engendered hostility. An advertisement in the paper brought two possibilities and both prospective foster families were asked to call on Miss W in order to know her and give her the opportunity to choose with whom she would like to live. Miss W chose the home of Mr. and Mrs. Bernard. Mrs. B is a woman in her forties, an energetic, outgoing, hearty kind of person. Her husband, a plumber, is like her in character. They had two children in the armed forces and two at home. They accepted Miss W and gave her their favorite downstairs room, the sun porch, and Mr. B put a washbowl in the corner. She sat with them at the table and they showed both patience and tolerance with her temper outbursts and sulky spells due to imagined slights. To give her some feeling of importance and usefulness, Mrs. B told her cleaning woman to take orders from Miss W. On her first Christmas there, Mr. B carried her into the living-room, danced around the tree with her, and placed her in the family circle. This was her first experience, in a lifetime, of being included in a family Christmas celebration.

It would be wrong to leave you with the picture that Miss W is sublimely happy. Her attitudes are too deeply rooted in the unhappiness of earlier years. She is still easily hurt, often irritable, and still yearning for her own family. On the whole, however, she has been accepted, has found a place for herself in the family where she has spent the four happiest years of her life.[18]

Aliens and Foreign-Born

Traditionally, family casework agencies have been interested in aliens and the foreign-born. While the number of foreign-born residents in the United States has declined within recent years in agreement with the basic intent of the Naturalization Act of 1906 and the Quota Act of 1924, there are still many persons who are foreign-born. (See Table 3.)

The census of 1940 indicated that over 11,000,000 persons fell into this category. This is a sizable aggregate of social work potential. Wartime migration has increased the total somewhat.

The evacuation of West Coast Japanese under the Presidential proclamations of December 8, 1941, also increased the need for social service to those displaced. While the evacuation was of relatively short duration, it posed many family problems for those involved. The loss in

[18]Margaret W. Wagner, "Foster Home Care for the Aged," *Journal of Social Casework*, volume 27, number 6, October, 1946, pp. 238–239. This article has been reprinted in a pamphlet, *Personalized Care for the Aged Client*, Family Service Association of America, New York, 1945–1946, p. 7.

Table 3

QUOTA IMMIGRANTS ADMITTED, 1936 TO 1946

Year	Immigrants Admitted	Year	Immigrants Admitted
1936	18,675	1942	14,597
1937	27,762	1943	9,045
1938	42,494	1944	9,394
1939	62,402	1945	11,623
1940	51,997	1946	29,095
1941	36,220		

Source: *Social Work Yearbook: 1947,* Russell H. Kurtz, editor, Russell Sage Foundation, New York, 1947, p. 52.

emotional security for them was incalculable. Problems were also created in the West Coast area which was economically disrupted for a time through the forced migration of over 100,000 of its former inhabitants.

The problems which aliens and the foreign-born present to family agencies are chiefly those arising from their status. The fact that they are not American citizens or may not have become thoroughly Americanized often places them at a disadvantage in regard to employment and economic activity. In a period of prosperity the pressures upon these people are lessened, but not abolished. But in times of economic depression, noncitizens are generally the first to suffer.

The trying experience of migration also contributes to the need of aliens and foreign-born for social work attention. Their uprootal from an Old World culture to a new life necessitates a series of personal and group adjustments which every foreign-born person is called upon to make. The incidence of personal problems among these "marginal men" runs high, as several studies have shown.[19] Casework agencies, then, serve the foreign-born in their problems of adjustment to this country. The specific meaning of this kind of adjustment varies from individual to individual.

Group work agencies also have participated in the task of acclimating the foreign-born to the United States. Especially in the past, when the numbers of immigrants ran even higher than they now do, settlement houses, community centers, Y's, and other group work organizations operated "Americanization" programs to aid the assimilation of the foreign-born through language, civics, cooking, discussion, and other forms of class work.

[19]See Everett V. Stonequist, *The Marginal Man,* Charles Scribner's Sons, New York, 1937.

Aside from the private agencies in this field there is the Immigration and Naturalization Service of the Department of Justice, which is the government agency primarily responsible for the induction of the foreign-born into American life. Since its program is minimal and short-term, however, the private agencies must still bear the bulk of the problems of the foreign-born.

The pressure of war-created conditions, when over 2,000 persons were being admitted to the United States each month, led in 1946 to the establishment of the United Service for New Americans, Inc. This organization combined the former National Refugee Service, Inc., and the National Service to Foreign-Born Department of the National Council of Jewish Women.

An agency which is at present providing casework services on an international level is the International Social Service. The following three cases illustrate the type of contribution which the Service makes:[20]

Jim, 8, and Joan, 5, lost both parents suddenly, in this country. The children's agency interested in planning for the children discovered that their mother was a native of France where she still had a mother, sisters, and brothers. Before final plans for these children can be made the children's agency wishes to know what part these relatives can play. What is their social and economic adjustment? What was their attitude toward the mother of the children, her leaving home for a foreign country, and her marriage to an American? How does this affect their attitude toward the children of this marriage? Can they offer a wholesome home for two children born and reared in this country?

* * *

Mrs. Ricardo, a resident of New York, where she lives in childless marriage with her second husband, had heard that her first husband, whom she divorced eight years ago in Puerto Rico, died in battle. At the time of the divorce the then 5-year old son remained with the father in Puerto Rico because the mother was considered incompetent by the court. Now the mother wishes to have the child come to this country and live with her.

The family agency which the mother asked for help requested aid from the International Migration Service in learning how the child feels toward his mother, from whom he has been separated for the greater part of his life. This will have to be seen in the light of the affection the boy has been getting from his paternal relatives with whom he is living. Eventually, we shall need to know whether the soundest plan from a social point of view can be reconciled with the legal situation.

* * *

[20]Frank L. Auerbach, "Inter-Country Case Work," The Family (now Journal of Social Casework), volume 26, number 6, October, 1945, pp. 221–226.

A merchant seaman on a Swedish ship became suddenly ill with active tuberculosis while his boat was in New York harbor. He had to be hospitalized and the expense for his hospitalization will be covered by his employer. However, he left in Sweden his wife and two infant children without resources. He worries greatly about their condition. His doctors and medical social worker consider it an important factor for his recovery that he be reassured about the situation of his family and plans made for them.

The International Migration Service was asked to use its connections in Sweden to have the family visited by a local agency and obtain a report on what steps can be taken locally to help the woman and children with all their problems.

Travelers Aid

While many family casework agencies assist travelers who have problems, their main function is to deal with the more general types of cases. However, there are specialized agencies, the travelers aid societies, whose chief concern is travelers' problems.

The travelers aid societies work on a short-term basis with their clients. This circumstance creates particular limitations and opportunities for the societies. It calls for quick analysis of the client's problem by the worker. It involves decisive actions on the part of worker and client. It requires the widest knowledge of community resources.

Usually, the representatives of travelers aid societies are stationed in train stations, bus terminals, steamship piers, and other places of transit. Offering information is one of their fundamental contributions to the well-being of travelers. The information may concern hotel accommodations, employment facilities, means of travel, or other interests of travelers. In all cases, however, the societies try not to duplicate commercial information services.

Social workers in travelers aid societies also offer more complex services to travelers. The supervision of a runaway child, for example, from the place where he has been caught until his return to his home community may be done by prearrangement through the travelers aid societies. In a community where a society is in operation, a representative can meet the train of the runaway, care for his needs while in the community, and see him off again on leaving.

The intercity service of the societies has many other implications. By its nature a local society must have extended contact with social work agencies existing in distant places. The fact that it does enables it to assist the agencies in its own community with their intercity problems. In turn, the society must know well the local agencies so that it can cooperate with the out-of-town agencies in making arrangements for services.

Travelers aid societies at present are located in about a hundred cities throughout the country. Through cooperative relationships as many as 1,900 communities are served. The National Travelers Aid Association, organized in 1917, is the coordinating agency of the various local societies. During the war years, especially, when so many persons were in transit (members of the armed services, defense workers, families of both), the importance of the travelers aid societies was impressed upon those who previously had had no contact with social work.

The following are examples of the types of problems that are treated by a travelers aid society. They are taken from the 1945 Annual Report of the Travelers Aid Society of Baltimore entitled, "Waitin' for the Train to Come in":

"'Im An' 'Er An' It."

She came into Baltimore at a railroad station, with her crushing memories and her baby—like so many others.

She was filled with secret fears.

Bitter, burning tears told of her hidden misery.

"*He* does not know about the baby. His letters stopped suddenly. I do not know where he is."

This confidence came out several days after her arrival, in the privacy of the central office.

"I want to live and work in Baltimore where no one knows me.

"I love my baby and will never give him up.

"My parents *know*, but I couldn't stay in my home town because of my younger sisters."

Like so many others . . .

Financial assistance was necessary for only a short period because a position was soon found in a pleasant family.

After many weeks, Travelers Aid working through Red Cross channels located *him*. He was still in Europe, ill and hospitalized when he received the first news that Travelers Aid in Baltimore was anxious to correspond with him about a certain young lady.

"Go ahead," he told Red Cross.

"I'm just as anxious as they are."

He was told about *her* in the correspondence. The information about the baby was withheld at her insistence, when she learned of his hospitalization. She would allow nothing to go into the letters that would be disturbing to him.

Many weeks later, completely recovered, he arrived in Baltimore.

"Her letters stopped," he said.

"I thought she was through with me. After that I didn't care much whether or not I came back all in one piece.

"Where is she?"

Carefully, he was told that it was no longer a case of just her; but that now the situation comprised a third party, a pretty, healthy baby boy.

Just as carefully it was explained to him that *she* was making no demands on *him*.

"We were both very deeply in love," *she* had said to Travelers Aid when told he had been located, "but he may not care for me now.

"I will not force myself and the baby on him."

All this Travelers Aid told *him* as *she* had insisted.

"*Where* are *they?*"

His words were tensely uttered but Travelers Aid understands inflections.

The meeting was arranged.

Only time enough elapsed to secure a modest trousseau and a minister, before a previously agonized young woman, a sincere and very ardent young man, and a baby entirely unaware of the threat of life's most intolerable burden hanging over his tiny head, were translated into Kipling's:

"'Im an' 'Er an' It,
        Our blessed one in three,"

than which we know of no finer descriptive phrase for the institution we call the family.

*   *   *

When *you* speak of families, dear Contributing Public, you naturally think at once of the normal family, husband, wife, child. But in Travelers Aid, families do not always come ready made.

This story illustrates what Travelers Aid means by *service* as distinguished from *financial assistance*.

It is easy to look at the annual statistics and then at Travelers Aid financial expenditures for relief and to decide that so small a cash outlay for relief against such a large number of services is indicative of problems that are unimportant.

Like some others of the 2,097 Major Problems handled by Travelers Aid during the year, this situation required only incidental expenditures for *financial assistance,* but weeks of careful, painstaking *service* preceded the happy ending.

Always remember that there are many of life's travelers who can pay as they go, but who, once they have fallen upon the "thorns of life," are helpless for many reasons which are not too hard to understand.

Shelley implored the West Wind "thou breath of Autumn's being" to lift him "as a wave, a leaf, a flower."

"So, and no otherwise" does Travelers Aid attempt to do with wisdom and gentleness.

A word apart, no other ear to harken, is often the main boon provided by Travelers Aid for troubled people en route.

It is social work's answer to the moving person, who has the same yearning as other human hearts for the sympathy of its kind.

Though nearly all of the so-called social problems coming to Travelers Aid border on the tragic, there is often a touch of humor somewhere in the situation.

An elderly couple with genuine need for financial help and many other services appeared for the first time with a pair of eyeglasses pinned to the rim of the wife's felt hat. They both used the same glasses but it was understood that the husband had first choice. The location was evidently in the interest of saving words.

A young couple, recently arrived in the city, had secured their own room and a good job for the man before coming to Travelers Aid, yet they still had what was to them an insuperable difficulty. They could not buy an alarm clock, and they knew they would sleep through the morning and lose the man's job unless there was an alarm to waken them.

Travelers Aid obliged with the loan of the alarm clock from the Central Office until another one was located.

Sitting in Travelers Aid booth when the worker returned from placing a young child on a train was a boy, 16, she had never seen before.

"Just saw an empty chair and sat down," he said.

His only baggage was another hat which he had on top of the one he wore. There was a serious problem under those two hats, which took several weeks of financial assistance and service, while Travelers Aid worked with an agency in another city on a plan to give this boy an opportunity to start living a normal life in a supervised boarding home.

And there was the colored woman who was completely lost and whose first name turned out to be "Bewilder."

Sometimes pathos was present even when the immediate problem was slight.

A young ex-serviceman ran into an unexpected lack of funds which made it necessary for him to secure a small loan of $1.70 from Travelers Aid for food and lodging for one night. A salary check from another city had not caught up with him.

Within 24 hours he returned and insisted on giving $5.00 to Travelers Aid. His appearance did not indicate affluence and noting the caseworker's surprise his only remark was:

"I've learned about kindness from Travelers Aid."

It made us remember Bernard Shaw's comment: "Love and affection never came to me by way of my own family." This ex-serviceman, hardly more than a boy, looked very sad and lonely, but a reserve that could not be encroached upon enveloped him. He had learned about kindness from Travelers Aid, down there in the depot by the railroad tracks, and for the time being, at least, that was all the Travelers Aid could do for him.

Travelers Aid is a special aspect of family casework service, employing casework methods to some degree in many of the cases treated.

Industrial Social Work

Industrial counseling (a term commonly used for some forms of social work in industry) is not new to the American scene. Actually, during the First World War such counseling came into existence in many industrial plants as a means of coping with those personnel problems which are a concomitant of modern war. During the 1920's several organizations, such as the Metropolitan Life Insurance Company and R. H. Macy & Co. in New York City, sought to apply the values of psychiatry to their personnel difficulties. Perhaps the most significant of these efforts was made at the Hawthorne Works of the Western Electric Company, Chicago, beginning in 1927. These programs are fairly well known. In recent years industrial counseling has been greatly expanded under the impetus of the Second World War. Probably, an increase in the number of trained social workers seeking employment in industry, capitalizing on a current trend, will influence the further development of this type of social work.

The social worker in industry has a number of functions. The Counseling Committee of the Office of Community War Services presented in 1944 the following description of the work of the industrial counselor:[21]

1. In Relation to Workers.
  a. Inform workers about services and facilities available to them in the plant or community (such as day-care centers, savings and loan funds, rationing boards, housing centers, recreation departments, and social service agencies).
  b. Help workers with personal problems which originate outside the plant and which affect their well-being and productivity on the job (arrangements for day care of children, transportation and shopping, housing, medical care, and other domestic and financial problems).
  c. Help workers with personal difficulties which cause "job problems" (such as need to work on a different shift because of home responsibilities; lack of acceptance by his supervisor or fellow workers because of factors such as race, nationality, or personal habits).
2. In Relation to Stewards, Foremen, and Other Management Representatives.
  a. Encourage and participate in programs which train stewards and foremen in "human relations."
  b. Interpret the effect of production and employment policies on the worker's personal and family life, and the relationship between personal problems and job performance.

[21] *A Guide for Establishment and Operation of In-Plant and Community Information and Counseling Services for Workers,* Office of Community War Services, Federal Security Agency, Washington, D.C., 1944, pp. 3-4.

    c. Inform management of physical conditions within the plant that can be corrected to improve the efficiency and well-being of workers.

    d. Upon request, discuss with stewards and foremen the handling of employee "job problems" affected by personal factors.

    e. Upon request, advise with stewards and foremen on leaves of absence, transfers, and granting of certificates of availability requested for personal reasons only.

    f. Offer the services of the counselors to other in-plant departments (such as medical and safety) in giving workers supplementary interpretation of health and safety measures.

3. General.

    a. Keep in touch with community agencies to obtain information about existing community resources and to interpret the needs of workers.

    b. Promote joint action of community, labor, and management groups to secure needed community facilities and services.

Industrial counselors are not always social workers. In fact, at present there are no rigid requirements as to what educational and experiential background a person should ideally have to engage in this work. But many social workers are accepted in industrial situations as having the prerequisite training for counseling.

Many of the problems treated by social workers in industry are similar to those encountered in a family casework agency. It is for this reason that we are relating this type of social work to family casework. Specifically, the industrial counselor meets a variety of problems. He takes part in effecting better job adjustments for workers. The means of producing better job adjustments may be directed toward problems which exist within the industrial organization itself or toward home conditions which cause a worker to be maladjusted at work. Physical and mental illnesses also play their part in creating industrial problems. The social worker who is an industrial counselor will try to make arrangements for those who fall ill, either physically or mentally, so that they may be treated at the first possible moment and aided in whatever accommodations their illnesses may require. Sometimes the employee is overburdened with worry, feelings of discouragement, and other symptoms of physical or mental disorder. In addition, the social worker in industry is generally active in marriage counseling. Also, the problems of children may affect the efficiency of workers and, therefore, need the attention of a trained social worker. In these and other ways the social worker can bring aid to workers.

The increasing rapprochement between labor and social work has inspired several projects of joint responsibility of this sort. The program in effect in Chicago illustrates the cooperative way in which labor and social work are aiding workers:

The Social Service Employees Union in this city selected the United Packinghouse Workers of America as a co-sponsor for a counseling project to be used by the members of the latter union. This union was chosen because it is a progressive C.I.O. union with a membership of 25,000, of whom 25 per cent are women and 50 per cent are Negroes. The Social Service Employees Union provided the volunteer services of twelve professional social workers on a rotating basis, each volunteer contributing ten hours a month. Services were made available in the union halls once a week during evening hours. The Packinghouse Workers Union supplied the space, the telephone, clerical services, and, in addition, printed and distributed leaflets announcing the service. In bold face type, the leaflets said, "Do You Need Help? Have You a Problem? You don't have to go to Dr. Anthony. Your Union has set up a special social service office at the disposal of all union members . . ."

During the first year of operation, the workers handled 135 applications, most of which had been referred by shop stewards. Lack of housing, especially for Negroes, was a serious problem. There were many problems connected with workmen's compensation, wage garnishments, and other problems of indebtedness. By previous arrangement with the family agencies, the majority of these cases were referred to them for further care. When the union realized how many legal problems were being discussed with the social workers, it engaged a lawyer to supplement the services of the Legal Aid Bureau. As another by-product of the social workers' experience with housing problems, the union launched a campaign of action in cooperation with the Chicago Housing Administration to obtain additional housing units. The regional director of the union, who had been quite skeptical about the value of social work in any form was won over to the point of becoming a member of the advisory committee of the Stock Yards District of the United Charities.

Two additional projects were subsequently made available in locals of the United Electrical, Radio, and Machine Workers, and there are demands for similar projects in other unions in Chicago.[22]

From the present prospects of social work in industry it would seem that only a beginning has been made and that a great future lies awaiting development.

Legal Aid

The problems of the clients of family casework agencies often involve legal considerations. Family caseworkers through their training and experience have some knowledge of legal matters, but certainly not

[22]"Social Work in Trade Unions," unpublished master's thesis by Ruth Altman, School of Social Administration, University of Chicago. Quoted by Mary Palevsky in *Counseling Services for Industrial Workers,* Family Welfare Association of America (now Family Service Association of America), New York, 1945, pp. 36–37.

enough to give advice on complicated problems. It is important, then, that social workers have recourse to legal counsel.

Because of the legal needs of the poor (often those who were known to social work agencies) legal aid agencies came into being as a kind of social service. The first agency in this country to provide clients with the free services of attorneys was the New York Legal Aid Society (1876). Since 1923, societies offering such assistance have been organized nationally through the National Association of Legal Aid Organizations. This national body holds an annual meeting for the participants, collects information from the member agencies, and attempts cooperative programs of legal aid improvement.

According to the *1946 Committee Reports and Proceedings of the National Association of Legal Aid Organizations,* facilities in the United States in 1946 consisted of 64 legal aid offices, 49 volunteer committees, and 24 public and voluntary defenders. The legal aid offices may be divided into the following types of services: (1) Autonomous legal aid societies under the supervision of independent boards of directors and usually supported in part by community chests—31 of these were reported; (2) Departments of government or private social agencies—there were 15 of this type; (3) Bar association offices—in addition to the 9 bar associations which offered direct services to clients, numerous bar association committees engaged in studying or promoting legal aid work; (4) Law school clinics, attached to the law schools themselves or located in cities near such schools—the law students intern in the clinics—6 of these rendered direct legal aid service and an additional 11 assisted existing legal aid offices; (5) Public bureaus, supported by government—there were 3 of these in 1946.

The problems treated in legal aid agencies vary with the times. In periods of depression the cases are mainly concerned with material problems: eviction, mortgages, sick pay, budget-collection, indebtedness. In more prosperous times the problems tend to be less material: domestic relations, adoptions, and other general interests. Of course, in all periods there are a sizable number of both material and nonmaterial problems.

Legal aid cannot, however, be considered a casework service. It is strictly a legal service, similar to that regularly offered by private lawyers. But it does implement family casework by helping to solve family difficulties.

Homemaker Service

Homemaker service has been a rather new but expedient development in social work.[23] The development of such service under the

[23] The older term for *homemaker* is *visiting housekeeper.*

W.P.A. brought to the attention of many agencies a permanent need. Child-caring agencies, family casework agencies, and some independent agencies created programs of this kind in recent years. The practice, growing out of the variety of agencies offering the service, has been diversified.

There are cases in which the problems of a family could be solved if there were someone to come into the home and act as a substitute homemaker. If, for example, a mother must be hospitalized for a period, there may be no one who can manage the home in her absence. The need in such an instance would be increased if there were several children and a working father. In such a predicament a homemaker would be able to provide the necessary continuity in the family life until the mother was well again. The emphasis in this kind of service obviously is upon its short-term character; only a very few agencies have set up long-term homemaker service. In most cases the family is asked to share in the cost to the extent it is able.

The agency considers several problems in placing a homemaker into a needy home. First, it is necessary to examine the basis of eligibility of the family. Usually, the requirements which agencies have established are flexible, allowing the clients many means of meeting agency standards. Once the family's need has been surveyed, it is then suitable for the agency to consider the exact relationship the worker should have with the specific family. If a wife or mother must leave the home temporarily, it is well for the homemaker to have an interview with her to discover what her wishes are for the family's care. This will mitigate any feeling the woman might have of the worker's usurping her place in the home. In general, it is best for the worker to continue the procedures of home care which are familiar to and wanted by the family.

The agency must supply supervision of the homemaker. A further responsibility of the agency is the recruitment of suitable workers and their training, both from the viewpoint of home management and social work interests. To establish means of paying the homemaker is also the agency's problem.

The value of homemaker service is shown in the following two cases:[24]

A housekeeper was placed with an Italian family when the mother became too ill to continue with the household tasks. As the mother grew less able to carry on, the housekeeper took over each responsibility as it was given up by the mother. The children, after the death of their mother,

[24] Thelma Harris, *Safeguarding Motherless Children: Problems Involved in Placement of Housekeepers in Motherless Homes,* Child Welfare League of America, New York, 1939, pp. 17–18.

turned to the housekeeper, as she had been accepted and approved of by their mother. This is a family bound by strong family ties, quite Americanized, and one that has been economically independent. To this father, housekeeper service has been a means of continuing to keep his children and the home which has meant so much to him. His whole life has centered around his home, and with this plan his place in the family is retained, is not even temporarily encroached upon by a foster father. There is not the deprivation of his children and home that placement would have necessitated. To this father the housekeeper is a person who helps make these things possible, while her role in relation to the children is more of a mother substitute.

*   *   *

Since August, 1934, the same housekeeper has been in a colored motherless family consisting of the father and six children. She was placed in the home a few months prior to the mother's death and thus had an opportunity to become familiar with the family setup before they were faced with the loss of the mother. This mother had unusual managerial ability and had assumed almost the total responsibility except that of being wage earner. The housekeeper's role in this family is that of mother substitute. There seems to have been a very real acceptance of her both by the children and the father, who may well be considered a seventh child as he is quite dependent and assumes little responsibility other than that of wage earner. With the older girls in this family, great emphasis is being placed on training them in the performing of household tasks, as it is felt that they will soon be able to take over the responsibility of the home, and care for the younger brothers and sisters. With such a plan the worker would continue to supervise after the housekeeper has been removed.

Of course, homemakers are not family caseworkers, although they are under the supervision of caseworkers. Rather, homemakers comprise an auxiliary service to family casework by aiding the furtherance of social work objectives for family living.

SELECTED READINGS ON FAMILY CASEWORK

Adamic, Louis, *A Nation of Nations,* Harper, New York, 1945.

Beattie, Anna B., and Hollis, Florence, *Family Case Work: A Good Profession to Choose,* Family Welfare Association of America (now Family Service Association of America), New York, 1945.

Beck, Joseph E., and others, *Family Case Work Services for Refugees,* Family Welfare Association of America (now Family Service Association of America), New York, 1941.

Book, Dorothy L., editor, *Family Budget Counseling,* Family Welfare Association of America (now Family Service Association of America), New York, 1944.

Brunot, Helen H., *Old Age in New York City*, Welfare Council of New York City, New York, 1943.

Burgess, Ernest W., and Locke, Harvey J., *The Family: From Institution to Companionship*, American Book, New York, 1945.

Cantor, Nathaniel F., *Employees Counseling: A New Viewpoint in Industrial Psychology*, McGraw-Hill, New York, 1945.

Carter, Jean, *Parents in Perplexity*, American Association for Adult Education, New York, 1938.

Children's Bureau, *Supervised Homemaker Service: A Method of Child Care*, United States Department of Labor, Publication number 296, Washington, D.C., 1943.

Clarke, Helen I., *Social Legislation: American Laws Dealing With Family, Child, and Dependent*, Appleton-Century, New York, 1940.

Cuber, John F., *Marriage Counseling Practice*, Appleton-Century-Crofts, New York, 1948.

Dixon, Elizabeth, and Browning, Grace, editors, *Social Case Records: Family Welfare*, Social Service Series, University of Chicago Press, Chicago, 1938.

Garrett, Annette, *Counseling Methods for Personnel Workers*, Family Welfare Association of America (now Family Service Association of America), New York, 1945.

Goldstein, Sidney E., *Marriage and Family Counseling: A Manual for Ministers, Doctors, Lawyers, Teachers, Social Workers, and Others Engaged in Counseling Service*, McGraw-Hill, New York, 1945.

Groves, Ernest R., *Conserving Marriage and the Family*, Macmillan, New York, 1944.

Hollis, Florence, *Social Case Work in Practice: Six Case Studies*, Family Welfare Association of America (now Family Service Association of America), New York, 1939.

Karpf, Maurice J., *The Scientific Basis of Social Work: A Study in Family Case Work*, Columbia University Press, New York, 1931.

Kasius, Cora, editor, *Relief Practice in a Family Agency*, Family Welfare Association of America (now Family Service Association of America), New York, 1942.

Kimble, Grace E., *Social Work With Travelers and Transients: A Study of Travelers Aid Work in the United States*, Social Service Monographs, number 32, University of Chicago Press, Chicago, 1935.

Koos, Earl, *Families in Trouble*, King's Crown Press, New York, 1946.

Lawton, George, *Aging Successfully*, Columbia University Press, New York, 1946.

Levy, John, and Monroe, Ruth, *The Happy Family*, Knopf, New York, 1938.

Manginelli, Madeleine V. H., *Homemaker Service: Meeting Crises in Family Life With a New Horizon in Child Care*, Child Welfare League of America, New York, 1941.

McLean, Francis H., *The Family Society: Joint Responsibilities of Board, Staff, and Members,* Family Welfare Association of America (now Family Service Association of America), New York, 1927.

Mowrer, Harriet R., *Personality Adjustment and Domestic Discord,* American Book, New York, 1935.

Palevsky, Mary, *Counseling Services for Industrial Workers,* Family Welfare Association of America (now Family Service Association of America), New York, 1945.

Reynolds, Bertha C., *An Experiment in Short Contact Interviewing,* Smith College Studies in Social Work, volume 3, number 1, Northampton, September, 1932.

Rogers, Carl R., *Counseling and Psychotherapy: Newer Concepts in Practice,* Houghton Mifflin, Boston, 1942.

Schmiedler, Edgar, *An Introductory Study of the Family,* Century, New York, 1930.

Smith, Marjorie J., *Rural Case Work Services,* Family Welfare Association of America (now Family Service Association of America), New York, 1943.

Stein, Herman D., *Careers for Men in Family Social Work,* Family Service Association of America, New York, 1946.

Stieglitz, Edward J., *The Second Forty Years,* Lippincott, Philadelphia, 1946.

Swift, Linton B., *The Board Member of a Family Agency,* Family Welfare Association of America (now Family Service Association of America), New York, 1944.

Taft, Jessie, editor, *Counseling and Protective Service as Family Case Work: A Functional Approach,* Pennsylvania School of Social Work, Philadelphia, 1946.

——, *Functional Approach to Family Case Work,* Social Process Series, Pennsylvania School of Social Work, University of Pennsylvania Press, Philadelphia, 1944.

Taggart, Alice D., and others, *Fee Charging in a Family Agency,* Family Welfare Association of America (now Family Service Association of America), New York, 1944.

Wilson, R. S., *The Short Contact in Social Work: A Study of Treatment in Time-Limited Relationships in Social Work,* National Association for Travelers Aid and Transient Service, 2 volumes, New York, 1937.

4

Children in Institutions

Another of the broad types of social work deals with children. One of the ways in which children are cared for is in institutions. Life for a child in an institution is somewhat different from that he would enjoy in his own home. The following account of a typical day's experience in a children's institution gives a vivid picture of this contrast:

December, 1937. "It's time to get up," is the 6:30 greeting from Henry's housemother. Always, or almost always, Henry gets up promptly, airs his bed, washes, combs his hair, and reaches the dining room just as the cow bell used for cottage signals is rung for a 7 o'clock breakfast.

Cottage tasks, which may consist of cleaning the bathroom, the front porch, or the dining room, or washing the dishes, occupy the time following breakfast until Henry leaves for school. Were the early morning schedule interpreted through sound effects it would include, "Aw, do I have to get up?" "I'm coming!" "Tom crooked my comb." "I can't find a broom." "Eddie took my dust pan."

More zealous about playing en route to school than in cleaning the house, Henry may leave with his job unfinished. At the front door his housemother calls, "Henry! Come back!" When confronted with a corner unswept, Henry is astounded. "But I thought I did it *all,* this morning!"

His older cottage fellows leave for high school at 7:50 and begin their school day at 8:30. They take with them school lunches and return between three and four in the afternoon.

Henry, in the sixth grade, can leave as late as 8:30 and still be in time for his classes at nine. He has time to kick a football for a few minutes on the school grounds or throw snowballs at his friends. His going to school and his return are his own obligation. He may go entirely alone, with other boys from the Home, with neighborhood boys, or with his girl friend. The only requirements are that he should avoid tardiness, come home with reasonable promptness, and obey traffic regulations, crossing streets only where there is an officer.

Home for lunch at 11:45, he barely has time to eat in the cottage dining room, help with the dishes, and return to school by one o'clock.

After school he has a task which may be sweeping the hall in the Administration Building, cleaning the gymnasium, or shoveling snow. His promptness and diligence determine whether this task keeps him for thirty minutes or an hour. There is no janitor on the Home's payroll and only one maid, whose entire time is required in Lathrop Cottage where the youngest children live. The older boys and girls, therefore, supervised by the workers, do most of the cleaning in the ten buildings at the Home and keep the premises out-of-doors fairly presentable. This work is done as part of the plan under which each child of suitable age performs some simple task and receives as a return some spending money. The harder tasks merit more pay. Children under twelve years of age have no regular after-school tasks, having this time free for recreation.

Supper is usually served at 5:15 so that a long evening can be available for study and play. All excepting those who work in kitchens and dining rooms have thirty or forty minutes to themselves after supper.

Study hour lasts from 6:30 to 7:30. Children too young to have homework are on their way to bed; or they may have quiet play in their cottages, or a period of supervised play in the Van Alstyne Memorial Recreation Building, or on the campus. The high-school students may remain at their studies from 6:30 until 9:30 or occasionally even later. This varies greatly according to the difficulty of each student's course of study, his ability to study, and his ambition. The library is open before supper and afterward until 8 to 8:30. There, books of reference, encyclopedias, and periodicals are used and children come to read for pleasure only, as well as for study.

Promptly at 7:30 are periods for athletics in the gymnasium, dramatics in the auditorium, cooking classes (which both boys and girls regard as recreation), or meetings of the troops of girl scouts or boy scouts—all scheduled and supervised by the Director of Activities. Bedtime follows these activities. Children are classified by their housemothers and the nurse according to their ages and their health needs as those who go to bed at 7:30, 8:30, or 9:30.[1]

CHILD WELFARE

If family social work is complicated because of the wide variety of cases treated, child welfare work also is equally involved. In some ways

[1]An excerpt from the "Albany Diary," by Howard W. Hopkirk, as recorded in his *Institutions Serving Children*, Russell Sage Foundation, New York, 1944, pp. 224–225.

child welfare is a part, definitionally speaking, of family social work, for the child obviously is part of the family. Historically, the two fields have not been too distinct, and there is increasing evidence that greater cooperation will mark the future. This trend toward synthesis in family and child welfare work is a part of the general trend in casework, as well as in the whole of social work, to find a more generic basis for operation.

That family casework and child welfare work have been moving closer together in recent years is shown in a report published in 1944 by a subcommittee of the Family Welfare Association of America's (now the Family Service Association of America) Committee on Relations Within the Social Casework Field. The subcommittee reported that there were certain "theoretical and practical distinctions between family agencies and children's agencies" made by social caseworkers today, but that these are becoming less sharp and important. The subcommittee also found "as casework skills and diagnosis become more fully developed in an agency, that the difficulties of undertaking child placement or any other specialized service will diminish." A "Joint Intake Plan" in operation in St. Paul, Minnesota, was mentioned by the subcommittee as providing an example of cooperative work by family and children's agencies. Interagency conferences were also mentioned as being helpful to efficient relations between the two fields. Mergers, too, were viewed as contributing to a solution of interagency problems.[2]

When the child welfare field is analyzed into the types of services which social workers render to children, three spheres, not mutually exclusive, become apparent. These are: care of children in institutions, care of children in foster homes, and treatment of children living in their own homes by various community services. These types of activity will be examined here and in succeeding chapters. But again it may be said that there are many interpenetrations among the three.

BRIEF HISTORY OF INSTITUTIONAL CARE OF CHILDREN

Elizabethan Poor Laws

The division of social work for children into three somewhat distinctive services is by no means a new development. As far back as 1601, in

[2]For further details see *Report of the Committee on Family and Children's Work*, by Jean L. Gregory and Ralph Ormsby, Family Welfare Association of America (now Family Service Association of America), New York, 1944. Also see *The Generic and Specific Aspect of Case Work in a Merged Agency*, a summary of a concrete instance by Edith L. Lauer, with a foreword by Virginia Robinson, Child Welfare League of America, New York, 1942.

England, the Elizabethan Poor Laws made provision for all three types of aid. If a child was not supported by his parents, he could be given over to a townsman who would employ him as an apprentice, providing him with protection and work. Or the child could be left in his own home and given work materials by a townsman in order to augment the family income. Or if these means were not available or suitable, the child might then be placed in an almshouse. While such care was provided by the government, the private church charities of the time supplemented these arrangements with their own.

Spread of Child Care Movement

In this country, before the eighteenth century, the most popular means of caring for children was the indenture system. In this system, children were farmed out to adults who needed labor in their homes and farms and were willing to keep a child in return for his work. From the start of the eighteenth century, however, the institutional care of children gained rapidly. It was thought to be one tangible way of expressing religious impulses. The religious motives so expressed were held by both Protestant and Catholic groups. But, in addition to the churches, various fraternal orders also took part in the establishment of child-caring institutions. Usually, their institutional programs were not different from those created by the churches. As the institutional movement spread, government took a hand in it, developing services commonly on a local basis.

Inadequate Treatment

The notoriously inadequate treatment in the early stages of the movement's development are well known to students of history. Often the institutions, whatever their sponsorship, were entirely divorced from local community life. This fact, in itself, tended to make child-caring institutions socially unique, to be viewed as curiosities by visitors and others. Again, such seclusion robbed the children of the many normal community contacts which are important for full development. There was in many institutions, moreover, little provision made for the education of the children beyond the three "R's." In such an environment the children were not given the opportunity to understand themselves or their society, and often they were given no chance to learn a useful trade. While work was a part of the program of such institutions, it was not especially geared to the needs of the children in terms of their ultimate prospect of leaving the institution at a proper age (or for other reasons) to take their places in the life of the community. Within many of the institutions, also, there was substandard provision for health and recreation. In some ways, moreover, the very physical arrangement of the buildings worked against the finer principles held by those who were motivated to serve children in this way. The fact that several hundred children were often housed in one building gave little opportunity for individualized living.

Period of Greatest Expansion

The post-Civil War period saw a notable increase in the number and variety of children's institutions. In fact, the years from the Civil War to the First World War can be taken as the period of the greatest expansion in the institutional care of children. The Civil War, for one thing, increased the numbers of children who were in need of permanent care, for the homeless and orphaned were one of the aftermaths of that war, as of most wars. The philosophy of child care held by the majority of social workers of that time was geared to meet the war-created need, as it stressed the value of institutional care. Unfortunately, however, the intense and dramatic needs of children in this period coupled with the inadequate facilities for their care produced negative effects which have come down to us today.

Since private charity was not sufficient to meet the needs adequately, city and state governments oftentimes aided financially in supporting the institutions. This was especially true, for example, of New York State. Usually, the state governments gave aid to the institutions on a per-capita child basis, but the amounts given were not intended to be sufficient for the whole maintenance of the children. This dual financing generally resulted in conflicts over such matters as administration, selection of children, distribution of funds, and placement of blame for inadequacies.

TYPES OF NEEDS SERVED BY INSTITUTIONS

Children placed in institutions have a variety of needs. Possibly, no child has only one special status which qualifies him for admission into an institution. Usually, there are a number of factors absent or present in his situation which warrant his admission.

Disturbed Parental Relationship

Perhaps the most notable reason for child placement in institutions is that of disturbed parental relationship. The nature of disturbed parental relationships, however, is broad. Take, for example, the case of a family consisting of a mother and four children who have been deserted by the father. It may be possible for the mother to find employment and to care for one or more of her children in her own home, especially with the addition of other community services, such as housekeeping or day nursery service. But, probably, it would be difficult for the mother to support and care for all of the children and herself. In such a situation, the mother might place one or more of her children in an institution. (This would be one solution to the problem; obviously, there are others.) Perhaps the placement would be intended as temporary, until the father is discovered and made to support the whole family, or until he wishes to return to the family as head, or is divorced. If there is a divorce and a remarriage for the mother, she may desire to take into the home again the child or children placed in the institution. In other cases both parents may have deserted.

Death of Parents

Another reason for child placement in institutions is the death of one or both parents. In the case of the death of one parent, some of the problems suggested above might hold. In case both parents die, a more permanent plan for the care of the children of the family would have to be provided. Today, this more extended program might include institutional care at first with foster home placement coming later. At any rate, status as an orphan is one reason for child placement in institutions.

Familial Inadequacy

In situations where both parents are active in the family, children may still be committed to institutions because of other family shortcomings. The family income may be sorely inadequate, one or both parents may be incompetent as parents, or conditions for proper upbringing, such as strong familial control, may be absent. Thus a child who has been judged of being neglected by his parents may qualify for institutional care. In such cases the term of placement may be for a long or for a short period, depending upon the nature of the family difficulty. In cases of incompetence there may be a court decision to enforce the placement of the child, but there also are parents who voluntarily seek placement for their children because they consider themselves deficient.

Mental Disabilities

There are various other reasons for placing children in institutions. Sometimes one parent or both may suffer from a mental disorder. In such an event it might be suitable to place the child or children in an institution until one of the parents can assume normal responsibility. At other times the mental disability of the parent or parents is of such a nature that some permanent rearrangement of the life of the child or children is suggested. Again, the parents may be suffering from a mental condition that might endanger the mental health of the child, thus necessitating outside placement. If a child's stability has already been disturbed, however, institutional treatment is a doubtful method of care before the child has been treated on a more individual basis.

The example of "Mary" illustrates how a child's mental conflict may prevent adjustment to the institution:

Strong, dominant, aggressive, Mary fought any frustration of her wishes with blind primitive violence. Alternately forgotten and over-indulged by a rejecting and neurotic mother she was trapped by her own hate and anger, her fear and guilt about that hate, and her desperate need for love. Mary had real qualities of leadership, executive ability, great energy, dramatic talent, a quick sense of humor, and a vital, driving personality. Entangled in conflicts which she could not face she struggled frantically to escape them. Her resultant behavior was, not strangely, a maze of contradictions. For a time she would take responsibility well only to react to some small, inevitable disappointment with complete irresponsibility and disinterest. She would become bitterly angry with us if we thwarted a wish of hers, but a few hours later she could turn to us with a lovable appeal and an impulsive warmth. She could display the brash egotism and self-confidence of a supersalesman, and the shy, almost panic-stricken unsureness of a novice on Broadway.

She was a leader in the group but she did not know how to use that leadership wisely, nor could she discipline herself sufficiently to give direction to it. Sometimes she sought to bully the others, to force them into compliance with her wishes. At other times she could be surprisingly gentle and sensitive to the feelings of someone who had been hurt. Her conflicts shackled the expression of her talents, while the strength of her feelings drove her on to increasingly destructive expressions of her strivings. We fought to break the vicious circle, to give her some understanding of her own feelings. Through the activities of the group, through giving her opportunities for constructive self-expression, such as chances to organize parties and programs, through casework and personal relationships to understanding adults, we sought to build up a strong enough relationship with her so that gradually she could afford to release the fantasy that she was a loved, wanted, and protected child, a fantasy which fundamentally she knew was not and never could be true. We failed. Mary's suspicion of adults was too great, too deeply rooted, and her need of love and security was too desperate to risk looking at the truth. Mary returned home, still hoping by some miracle to translate her fantasy into reality. Today, she is in a correctional institution.[3]

[3]Leontine R. Young, *The Treatment of Adolescent Girls in an Institution,* Child Welfare League of America, New York, 1945, pp. 26–27.

In the same vein, there are situations in which children are placed in institutions because of emotional disturbances which are not wholly related to the conditions of their homes. In such cases, individual treatment is usually indicated until the child is in a position to utilize the opportunities of an institution. In spite of what has just been said, however, significant numbers of children with mental problems have been placed in institutions without first receiving more direct and individualized attention.

FACTORS AFFECTING INSTITUTIONAL PLACEMENT

Age Conditions

That social workers today believe that children with serious emotional problems should not be sent to institutions has been elaborated upon briefly above. But there are other conditions in current practice which regulate the placement of a child in an institution. Age is such a factor. At present it is admitted by most workers that foster home placement is better for young children. In fact, the rule might be stated thus: The younger the child the more desirable it is to have him placed in a foster home; the older the child the more desirable it is to have him placed in an institution. Of course, there are exceptions to this rule. But for the very young child there are health dangers in prolonged group association. Also, the very young child needs affectional relationships closely resembling those in a home more than do socially gregarious adolescents.

Element of Time

Another criterion which guides workers today in making institutional placements of children is that of time. As has been suggested previously, social workers think of institutional placement as being suitable for those children whose problems possibly can be cleared up within a period of months or even a few years. There are presently very few advocates of institutional care as a permanent placement device except for unusual cases. For short periods an institution can oftentimes offer more and better protection for a child than his own home or a foster home. In an institution there is opportunity of using a social situation of great potency for the control and production of certain desired habits in children. The institution frequently is better able to regulate diet requirements than a private home; it can more readily provide special services, such as tutoring and health care; it enables the social worker and others to maintain a close scrutiny over the behavior of children. In sum, the institution gives an opportunity for the highest degree of control over the conditions under which the social workers and others desire the children to live.

Sibling Relationships

In planning to meet the needs of children through institutional placement, social workers are careful to bear in mind the importance of not disturbing sibling relationships. Only a few child-caring institutions, however, have made adequate provision on this point. As happens frequently when a child is separated from his parents, he may first turn for affection and security to his brothers and sisters (if there are any). If the physical setup of the institution does not make it possible for him to have the love and companionship of his brothers and sisters, then a serious, negative complication may enter the picture. Moreover, through the placement of brothers and sisters together in institutions, the organization of the family is to that extent maintained rather than dissolved. Again, as with so many general rules, there may well be exceptions, i. e., the case where there are siblings who contribute harmfully to each other's emotional problems.

Community Resources

Another important consideration which determines the type of placement a child may receive is the resources of the community. Obviously, not all localities have available sufficient or proper foster homes. Parents may not wish their children to be separated from them by too great a distance. Moreover, the auspices of the institutions available may influence placement. It may not be deemed proper, for example, by the social worker or by the parent to place a Protestant child into a Roman Catholic institution, and vice versa. Or the institution most suitable in terms of geographic availability may itself limit admittance to members of a particular denomination or fraternal order. In such cases, placement naturally must take these conditions into account.

Efficiency

Efficiency may also be a criterion for placement. It is better to place a child in a foster home rather than in an institution if in the judgment of all concerned the foster home is a more favorable environment for the child. There has been considerable generalized thinking in recent years which has more or less blindly preferred one type of placement over another, regardless of the specific conditions bearing upon a given child in a particular community.

No one type of child welfare service can be said to be perfect and always desirable. All have their part to play. Evaluations for placement should include at least: age of child, emotional disturbance, possible length of placement, quality of the services possible in the situation, the wishes of parents, and the wishes of the child.

THE PHYSICAL SETUP OF THE INSTITUTION

Large Buildings Formerly Used

Many of the present-day, child-caring institutions owe their physical setup to the philosophy of institutional practice prevalent many years ago. Formerly, institutions were built on the *congregate* style, that is, with large buildings which housed all of the children and supporting facilities. In these buildings, dormitory space was provided for sleeping; mass dining rooms fed large numbers of children; classrooms and recreation halls were also included. These structures were thought by some to be advantageous because they permitted the easy and concentrated handling of large numbers of children, because the buildings perhaps cost less than any other kind, and because the control factor was relatively simple. In most of the early institutions, boys were separated from girls.

Cottage Plan Now Favored

Recently, social workers (and others) have realized the benefits which come from a more informal physical atmosphere. So, for some years now, the *cottage* plan has been highly favored. (See Figure 17.) In this plan various smaller houses are used, usually on a wide expanse of land. Each house or cottage provides living quarters for a smaller number of children. The living requirements of each group are broken down so that for many purposes each cottage maintains its own independence. Since the conception of more individualized treatment has been in vogue, many of the congregate type of institutions have sought to modify their housing arrangements wherever possible. In some cases considerable change has been possible, but in others very little has been feasible. Too often, social workers and others interested in institutional care for children have been more imbued theoretically with the values of the cottage system than they have been able to show or accomplish practically. For example, cottages have been built which are smaller than the dormitories of old but certainly not small enough to approximate actual family living. But, despite these handicaps, the cottage plan of treatment has very definitely been an improvement over the older and more congregate type of physical arrangement.

In surveying the physical needs of an institution there are many factors which come to mind. Certainly, there is no one conclusion to any one or to all of them, and in each particular situation the best answers

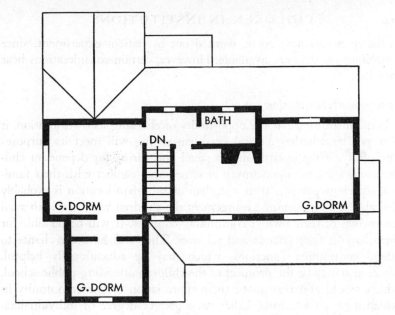

Second Floor

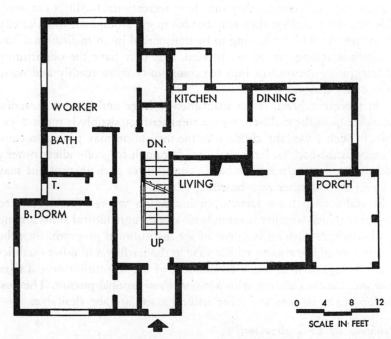

SCALE IN FEET

FIG. 17. Two-Story Cottage for 11 Boys and Girls, Children's Village, the Methodist Children's Home Society, Detroit (one unit of a duplex building)

(Hopkirk, op. cit.)

141

to the questions have to be worked out by patient experiment, since little objective data are available. However, certain considerations bear mention.

Location of Institution

If the institution has the opportunity of choosing its own location, it may ponder whether a rural or urban setting will meet its purposes more fully. If the institution is a small one, caring for dependent children who have the opportunity of some social contact with their families, especially parents, then an urban or suburban location is probably desirable. Under such an arrangement the children will be able to avail themselves of their former community contacts. It will be possible for them to visit their friends and relatives. They will have the chance to attend community functions, which may be educationally helpful. There also may be the prospect of the children attending public school, which would add realism to their appreciation of the community in which they are to adjust. Likewise, a greater degree of individualization is possible under such a community-related program. The children may attend local movies; they may have recreational facilities not available in a rural setting; they may be able to get around the town or city by themselves without having to be transported in an institutional bus, a stigma-attaching procedure. In sum, they may have the opportunity of integrating themselves into the community more readily and naturally than otherwise.

On the other hand, if the institution is large and bears a custodial relationship to the children, then a rural setting possibly is more advisable. In such a case the children of the institution may provide a community in themselves, large and varied enough to give endless novelty and opportunity. Under the best circumstances such institutions may take on the character of a boarding school.

In addition to these factors, an institution where suitably located should consider whether it intends to develop agricultural skills among its children. If farming is a part of the institutional program, then the location should be chosen with a view to the fertility and other qualities of the land. Furthermore, establishment of the institution near a river may provide the children with a singular recreational pursuit. The possession of shade trees and other natural assets are also desirable.

Problem of Centralization

The problem of whether to have a centralized or decentralized physical layout also bears consideration. Of course, in terms of current philosophy, the cottage plan of housing is rather taken for granted as the more advantageous. But, on this point, it is not clear whether there is greater or lesser expenditure in construction and maintenance costs for one type of institution over another. Thus a large institution with a central heating plant presents certain advantages, such as central control and the presence of skilled workmen. In view of home oil burners, however, such advantages seem to be minimized.

Centralized versus decentralized food preparation and dining rooms also proves a knotty problem. Both procedures have advantages and disadvantages, as does the problem of centralized or decentralized sewing and mending of clothes. Some institutions find one plan more suited to their requirements; others find the opposite. In all of these matters, however, where centralization and decentralization seem to be the fundamental problems, the criterion perhaps most useful in settling the issues is that of the welfare of the children. Admittedly, in many instances either plan is for the welfare of the children. But in some cases this criterion may provide a ready answer to the problem. For example, it might hold for the decentralization of sewing where the children in question are adolescent girls who might very well learn this skill by making or mending their own clothes. Thus one aspect at least of the issue of centralization versus decentralization could be solved by subjection to such a test.

Requirements for Cottages

In regard to the cottages themselves, certain considerations may be noted. If at all possible, the cottage should be planned so as to accommodate both boys and girls. The children should live in as small groups as is possible, so as to simulate most closely the conditions in the private home. In no event should the cottage be planned for more than twenty children. Even such a number clearly works against the very principles of institutional care which originated the cottage system. The dormitory style of sleeping quarters should give way to single rooms, or to rooms for two, three, or four children. Living rooms and dining rooms should be of adequate size, with equipment which provides a home-like atmosphere.

The organization of the cottage should be such as to allow for easy supervision by the cottage parents. Their sleeping quarters should be close to those of the children. The cottage should be arranged physically so that there is the least possible exertion for the workers. It should be built so that there is a minimum of fire and accident hazards. While the cottage may be a two-story structure, it is well to note that a one-story building enables better supervision, reduces fire hazards, eliminates stair climbing, and reduces waste space. (See Figure 18.)

In terms of durability the cottage should be built to last perhaps twenty to thirty years. Such a length of time is suitable, for it is short enough to allow for new improvements in design yet long enough to permit hard usage of the building by the children.

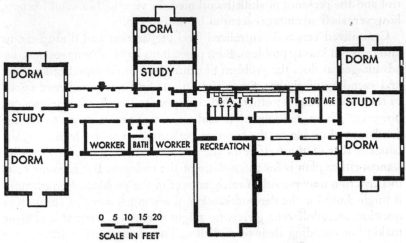

FIG. 18. One-Story Cottage for 30 Boys, Mission of the Immaculate Virgin, Mount Loretto, Staten Island, New York

(Howard W. Hopkirk, *Institutions Serving Children*, Russell Sage Foundation, New York, 1944.)

Throughout all of the planning for the institutional cottage, the requirement of home-likeness is important. The obvious purpose of all institutional management is not the establishment of an inexpensive and efficiency-excelling cottage system. While these features are desirable, the primary aim is to provide facilities which will enable children to feel that the institution is a suitable home. No other value surpasses this one.

WORK AND PLAY IN AN INSTITUTION

Most institutions believe that it is beneficial to operate a work schedule in which the special limits and abilities of the children can be utilized. The nature of the tasks given to institutional children is described in the following account from the "Albany Diary":

> *October, 1938.* Even the little ones in Lathrop Cottage are taught to make their beds. Those who have reached the advanced ages of six or seven years may be seen helping to set tables. It is a valuable part of their training for life to learn how to take care of their own possessions and to do their part in the household's daily activities.

Lathrop Cottage is the only house in which there is a maid to do the routine housework, nearly all of which is too heavy for these little children. In all other buildings, girls or boys may be found doing all kinds of cleaning such as might be expected of members of a large family. The Van Alstyne gymnasium and the Administration building are swept, mopped, and dusted by boys or girls under supervision of the Director of Activities. Other duties include waxing floors and washing walls. The only janitorial service for which men are required is the stoking of heating plants and hot-water heaters. Even in the furnace rooms it is older boys who remove the ash cans and haul them to the dump.

Snow shovelling, lawn mowing, and the raking of leaves are boys' jobs. Some of the oldest boys have sawed up the trees felled by the September storm and have stored the wood so that it may be used in the cottage fireplaces. Outdoor tasks also include work in the gardens. Such tasks are occasionally performed for pay in the neighborhood. Older girls also earn some spending money in nearby homes taking care of children or assisting occasionally with housework. (Such earnings are not to be confused with allowances of spending money, which early in 1939 were introduced as an important element in the program of the Home.)

Boys, as well as girls, assist the cooks in preparing meals, serving, and in washing the dishes. There are no dishwashing machines, so this work, like the preparation of vegetables, requires many hours of boy or girl labor weekly in each cottage. Those who assist the cooks learn elements of cookery, and, in emergencies, some of the oldest girls and boys have prepared a meal for as many as thirty children and adults eating in a cottage. Several fourteen- and fifteen-year-olds can bake good cakes. The cottage groups are too large, however, to permit cooking in appropriate quantities for ordinary families.

Girls have instruction in sewing and those of senior-high-school ages make skirts, dresses, and other articles of clothing.

Two of the oldest girls having single rooms of their own in Lathrop Cottage give daily assistance in dressing, washing, and putting to bed the thirty-four children under eight years of age who live in the same cottage. A third assists in the kitchen. Two of these girls have substituted for workers who were ill or on vacation.

Some of the oldest boys can help capably with repairs or with gardening. One has twice been in charge of the gardens for an entire week when an emergency cut down the number of men necessary to operate the plant. He expects to be a farmer and shows definite promise of success in terms of good work habits, general reliability, and his efforts to understand agriculture. He has a small flock of chickens which finally has paid for its cost. From these chickens he now earns a small but regular amount of egg money.[4]

[4]Howard W. Hopkirk, *Institutions Serving Children*, Russell Sage Foundation, New York, 1944, pp. 167–168.

It can readily be seen that the kinds of work activities listed above are of much benefit to the children in their preparation for normal adult living.

Life in an institution, however, is not all work. There is considerable play also. Calling again upon the "Albany Diary," a rich source of institutional data, the play activities of one institution may show what, in general, obtains in the field:

August, 1939. Many have remarked on the happiness of the children and their freedom from irritation during this summer as compared with previous summers. Much was due to the splendid recreational program supervised by Miss Martha Sheehy, our director of activities. It is from her own report that the following is quoted.

The Lawn Festival was a Circus. A member of the Junior League coached the children and made the occasion a grand success; the children found it more fun than work. It was their production to such an extent that no one, not even their leader, knew on June first what was to be shown to our guests on June fifteenth. She was skillful in handling the children as they chose, rejected, and changed their acts. They treated her as a jolly companion but gave her all the cooperation that a more austere leader might have demanded. A week after the Lawn Festival, we attended the Barnum & Bailey, Ringling Bros. Circus. From the youngest to the oldest present, all enjoyed it. Our Junior League friend was our guest, and the children made many comparisons of this circus with their own.

Early this summer, our oldest children showed an interest in volley ball, newcomb,[5] and games similar to these which they themselves worked out. This interest has been continued, but by those a little younger. Dodge ball and soccer have taken up some of their time, too. Then there have been a number of games, variations of those already mentioned, which the children themselves originated. This planning is beneficial, for it encourages initiative and oftentimes proves fascinating when the regular game has turned boring. This has been encouraged by the recreational staff, for we feel that it is an important accomplishment on the part of the children.

An activity new on our campus this year which provoked a great deal of enthusiasm was archery. Even our most sophisticated adolescents were able to show enthusiasm for this sport. Some of the girls' efforts compared favorably with the boys'. But the sport which has universal appeal is, of course, swimming. Our own wading pool has attracted large groups, both in the afternoons and in the evenings. We have taken swimming parties to Lincoln Park in the afternoon, on the average of six times a week, and some in the evening, attracting many of our older boys and girls. Every week, we have taken a bus load of youngsters, either to Herrington's pond, Schifferdecker's pond, or Camp Cogswell. In these places as well as

[5]*Newcomb* is an excellent "lead-up" game for basketball, and similar sports, involving two teams throwing and catching a ball over a high net.

at Lincoln pond the staff have given instructions to the children in swimming.

Every week there has been at least one visit to some Albany industry: the Coca Cola works, the potato-chip factory, the ice-cream plant, and a bakery. Visits like these are beneficial from several viewpoints: the children enjoy them a great deal; they prove to be of vocational value, because they bring the children in contact with occupations that otherwise they would never know; these visits are of civic value—not only do the individuals see some of the industries of their community, but they also begin to have a little understanding of just what is behind many of the products that they take for granted. Unconsciously, they get a broader background of the world they live in and consequently a better understanding, too. Besides these visits to industries, they have again this summer visited the Schuyler Mansion, the State Educational Building, and the State Office Building.

They have made trips to the hills, those on our grounds and those just off our premises. On these visits, they have had some nature study. In fact, these younger children are now able to recognize trees, flowers, and the well-known poison ivy.

Four mornings a week there has been a class in art in which the children have had lessons in crafts, drawing, etc. They have been tremendously proud of their work, showing their results to the staff. Art work, however, has not been confined to these classes. We have had a large stock of cardboards that have come from the laundry. The children have asked for these on which to draw cartoons and pictures.

Much use has been made of the Builz-em set. Although in many instances the results have been quite crude, they have, none-the-less, been creative efforts. Along this line, too, has been the making of airplanes. Paper, clips, paste—the materials; the result—a lot of excitement and fun.

Time, industry, and ingenuity have been spent on making carts of all kinds. Some have been awkward affairs, merely two bicycle wheels and a handle (perhaps this accounts for the recent disappearance of broom and mop handles). Others have taken several hours, many boards, a large number of nails, skill, and thought. In all, these have been products of the children's own initiative and endeavor.

Another activity which may seem unimportant, but which in my mind has outstanding possibilities, is the playing of the victrola. Many children have asked if they might come into the gym to play it. Just listening to the music meets a certain craving in the child. But other than that, the child is acquiring a taste for good music. That this is true is evident by the frequency with which they select light classics. And often I have heard them playing selections from well-known operas and symphonies.

Social recreation has not been neglected, either. Personally, I feel that this phase of recreation is more beneficial to promoting a happy adult life than any other. Through this type of activity, the child learns how to carry on a conversation, how to conduct himself in the social world, and also develops poise and confidence. Feelings of insecurity frequently disappear as the child learns how to get along with others well. Games, too, are learned which they may make use of in later life, and many organized games, such as head-on, various tags and hide-and-go-seeks, kick-the-can, and capture-the-flag.

There have been some movies. Throughout the whole summer, only three movies have been planned for the group as a whole. Movies are enough patronized by our children so that further encouragement is not necessary. If they want to see a picture, they can use either their allowance or earn the money in some way. Too often movies prove to be an easy means of providing recreation—result, the "movie habit."

On several occasions when some of the boys or girls have asked for permission to pop corn or to make fudge in the gym, they have been allowed to do so. In the Ping Pong room, children have often played this game provided there was a staff member working in the gym.

The most important part of our social program has been the parties. Every group except a few of the very oldest has had a party this summer. Practically every child has had a chance to serve on some committee planning these parties (with some guidance by a staff member—guidance, in its true sense). Because of this, there were all kinds of parties—swimming with outdoor suppers, a scavenger hunt, a fudge-making party, parties with games and refreshments.

An important part of our work is Scouting which we continued this year throughout the summer. The Boy Scouts have made a Totem Pole, woven rings from beads, and made whistle cords and bracelets from shiny leather. The Girl Scouts have had nature study, hikes, a picnic at Schifferdecker's pond, a visit to a model home, fire building, folk dancing, a marshmallow roast, and games in the gym.

Camping has been the most popular form of vacational activity for our children. We've had nine Boy Scouts and five Girl Scouts at camp. The following camps also had some of our children: Y.M.C.A., Trinity Camp, Fresh Air Camp, and Y.M.C.A. Day Camp. Our older boys went camping for two weeks at Pine Lake under the leadership of a member of our regular staff. Several of our oldest girls spent one grand week at the cottage of our secretary. The girls were her guests and she proved a very popular and capable leader. Others have spent part of their vacations at the homes of relatives and friends. A number of boys became farmers for the summer. There were picnics and swimming parties organized by friends.

This gives some idea of the extent of the recreational program. It was made possible only through the cooperation and suggestions of a great many individuals—staff, board members, friends, and the children themselves. The several assistants on the recreation staff were very capable and really were responsible for this program. The volunteer staff were quite unusual and made possible the wide variety and extent of this program.[6]

[6]Howard W. Hopkirk, *Institutions Serving Children,* Russell Sage Foundation, New York, 1944, pp. 177–180.

COTTAGE PARENTS

While our primary interest in discussing the institutional care of children is the relationship of the social worker and the child in need, nevertheless we must examine the place of the personnel within child-caring institutions, and especially the function of cottage parents. First, let us consider the personnel other than cottage parents.

Administrative Officers

An institution must have a director or superintendent. This person is in general charge of all of its activities and is responsible to the board of directors of the institution. In some cases the director is the general "catch-all" of responsibility. If so, he may become more of a "glorified office worker" than an administrative officer concerned with the welfare of the children. One means of avoiding this condition is by distributing some of the responsibility to various subadministrative officers. In some cases we find as administrative assistants a publicity secretary, a purchasing agent, supervisors of cottage parents, and others. Such an organization permits the chief executive to give more time to the planning of those activities and services which bear directly on the welfare of the children.

Other Personnel

Within an institution various other kinds of personnel are needed. Although there is no reason why an institution should have all of the following types of workers, some undoubtedly are needed by all institutions: recreational leader, secretary-stenographer, librarian, accountant, dietitian, cook, physician, psychiatrist, psychologist, assistant houseparent, relief worker, dentist, nurse, storekeeper, purchaser, night watchman, volunteer worker, mechanic. The specific needs of an institution for such workers could only be determined in individual cases.

Caliber of Staff

In general there has been a disregard for the development of staff in charge of nonphysical services to children. That is, child-caring institutions have commonly stressed material advantages and facilities for their children rather than their nonmaterial facilities. A small part of this may be due to the notable shortage of trained workers available for all of the social work specialties. But it may be questioned whether in many instances the leadership of the institutions has been alert, farsighted, and interested enough to develop their social work and psychiatric services for the children. There are still many institutions which do not have qualified social workers on their staffs, and only a conspicuous few have psychiatrists. Of course, only the largest or most specialized institutions need a full-time psychiatrist, as the children served may not require such attention. Even so, a large number of institutions which might well benefit from the development of their social services have thus far not done so.

It is obvious that cottage parents (or houseparents), who have the most personal relationships with the children in institutions, should be of the highest caliber. No matter how underdeveloped the rest of the staff may be, the cottage parents, because of their responsibility, should be able to provide the most positive kind of experience for the children. All too often cottage parents are chosen because they are willing to work for the low salaries offered in the institutional field, rather than because of their previous training and present desirability. (See Table 4.)

Table 4

DISTRIBUTION OF 447 HOUSEMOTHERS ALSO RECEIVING FULL
MAINTENANCE, BY AMOUNT OF CASH SALARY

Annual Cash Salary	Equivalent Monthly Salary	Number of Housemothers	Percent
$ 240 to $ 359	$ 20 to $29.99	10	2
360 to 479	30 to 39.99	22	5
480 to 599	40 to 49.99	131	29
600 to 719	50 to 59.99	133	30
720 to 839	60 to 69.99	69	16
840 to 959	70 to 79.99	37	8
960 to 1,079	80 to 89.99	24	5
1,180 to 1,199	90 to 99.99	4	4
1,200 or more	100 or more	17	1
Total		447	100

Source: Howard W. Hopkirk, *Institutions Serving Children,* Russell Sage Foundation, New York, 1944, p. 92.

Aged Cottage Parents

In many cases cottage parents are elderly persons who for one reason or another are willing to serve in this capacity. Some aged cottage parents genuinely love children. They may possess along with their love of children a reasonably intelligent understanding of the needs of their charges. On the other hand the very fact of their agedness may incapacitate them from a sympathetic understanding. They may be cranky in their personal relationships and easily provoked or irritated by the vigor of young people. Or they may be overindulgent, playing the role of the "spoiled grandparent." But while these things may be true for some aged people, there are also compensations in their cottage leadership. At present, however, the general age of cottage parents in institutions is decidedly too high, and an infusion of younger blood is sorely needed. The war years in this country, with the attractiveness and availability of wartime jobs, added an additional handicap to the recruitment of younger personnel for cottages. In the future a more definite and publicized plan of enlisting the interest of suitable cottage parents will be needed. (See Table 5.)

Table 5

AGE DISTRIBUTION OF HOUSEPARENTS IN 89 INSTITUTIONS FOR
DEPENDENT CHILDREN IN 1940 OR 1941

Age	Number of Houseparents	Percent
Under 20 years	3	1
20 to 29	63	12
30 to 39	105	20
40 to 49	144	28
50 to 59	133	26
60 to 69	49	10
70 years or over	1	—
Age not reported	17	3
Total	515	100

Source: Same, p. 72, as Table 4.

Health Considerations

The health of cottage parents is another consideration to be noted. Older cottage parents are more likely to have physical handicaps which may interfere with the proper discharge of cottage duties or the establishing of sound relationships with the children. Thus they may be ailing and unable to climb stairs; they may be unable to play active games with the children or go on hikes. But, aside from age, the physical fitness of the cottage parent is important. Likewise, cottage parents should be able to withstand considerable mental and nervous strain. The fact that the parents may deal on a day-to-day basis with twenty or more children, usually all of whom are characteristically active and noisy, makes the need for steady nerves a prime requisite.

One means of strengthening institutional practices along this line is through a required health examination upon acceptance as cottage parents. While relatively few institutions require a general health examination, the advantages of one are obvious. It acts not only as a protection to the children, but also to the institution and even to the prospective worker.

Personality Requirements

The personality of cottage parents is also important. For most children in institutions there has been some disturbance in the family situation. This unsettlement, as has been explained, may be for a variety of reasons. Whatever the causes of a child's being placed in an institution, it may be assumed that, in general, he is in need of a strong, healthy, positive personality on the part of his cottage parents. If the child has come from a home where he has not been accepted by his parents, he needs love and security supplied by a cottage parent. If he has witnessed quarrels between his parents, he needs to see the loving and peaceful relationships which can exist between married people. If his parents have distrusted him and spied on him, as though he were constantly doing unethical or illegal acts, he needs cottage parents who will trust him and encourage him to build up his own independence and individuality. In most instances cottage parents have to present more than the usual personality requirements. They must possess additional qualities sufficient to meet the hard and challenging relationship they are bound to have with the children. The character traits most desired in the children for the most part must exist first in the cottage parents. The cottage parents become for the child under their care the image of correctness and idealism. Naturally, it is difficult to set up perfect requirements for the personality of cottage parents. This is at present a theoretical subject of interest, but its importance should encourage institutional leaders to examine closely the suitability of prospective cottage parents for the kind of work their position involves.

The influence which cottage parents may exert on a child under their care is depicted in the following case:

> To have arrived at the age of fourteen meant little in terms of accomplishment or of self-direction to a boy who was without knowledge of his own parents, who had suffered a severe burn caused by neglect in a foster home, who was being bullied by other boys living in the same institutional cottage, and who had been removed from school because of his failure to keep up with others. He personified the underdog, and because of his unkempt appearance the boys had nicknamed him "the pig." He had a cheerfulness and willingness which could be quickly

recognized by anyone trying to understand him. But had he been left to his own resources without encouragement he might have failed dismally.

A new cottage mother and father found him very much in need of a friend. Even though he was awkward and inclined to be dirty, disheveled, and unattractive, the cottage mother undertook to give him the attention and encouragement he craved. In righteous indignation she forbade the other boys to call him "pig." The superintendent and the cottage mother agreed on the plan of returning the boy to school, in the belief that with the patient encouragement she was providing, he might give a very different account of himself. It was also decided to enroll him in the troop of Boy Scouts, in spite of jeers from a few who thought he never would qualify even as a tenderfoot.

He was like a plant responding to sunlight. Personal appearance picked up, school reports improved, and he qualified as a scout. It took effort, and he perspired over lessons that were easy for other boys. He soon became distinguished for tenacity in his work habits, and was in demand by neighbors who wanted their lawns mowed. He became the thriftiest boy in his cottage. When the scouts got ready for a brief period at a summer camp, he was the only member of the troop who had saved enough money to pay his own expenses for one week at camp. This was properly recognized, and he found that in certain other activities as well as in scouting, he could compete effectively with other boys. He showed, more than most boys, consideration for adults. An old woman whose years of service entitled her to board and room at the institution was growing frail. He was attentive to her in many ways, making sure, for instance, that on cold nights she had a hot water bottle to warm her bed.

After leaving the institution he found situations for himself which were greatly to his credit. His good work habits, friendliness, and extreme honesty helped him to keep any position. Throughout the depression decade following 1929 he was unemployed for less than one week. He had worked on various construction projects. When asked why he had never lost a job, he smilingly observed, "I always help pick up the tools of those who leave when the whistle blows." He went to night school and studied accounting. He became a timekeeper and often served as custodian of payrolls. His recreational life, his choice of friends, and his present personal habits mark him as a good citizen. He has avoided indebtedness but has proved a generous friend. In the heart of the depression he made an unsuccessful effort to locate his mother, of whom he had no memory. However she might have neglected him, he wanted to help her because after all she was his mother.

For twenty years he kept in touch with his cottage parents. They had not attempted to become lasting substitute parents, but a fine friendship grew out of their experience in sharing with him for less than two years the daily life in an institutional cottage.

He could hardly have done better had he grown up in a foster home in which affection and the sense of security might have been more easily bestowed. The experience of this young man suggests that some basic planning together with confidence and faith, seasoned with even a little affection, can carry a young person far toward a happy adult life, and that for some children such emotional satisfactions can be provided effectively by those who work in institutions.[7]

PERSONNEL TRAINING

Not only should an institution be careful about the kind of cottage parents who are hired, but it should also be concerned with the training of these persons after they are hired. As yet cottage parents have to meet no prescribed educational or experiential requirements. (See Table 6.)

Table 6

EXTENT OF EDUCATION OF HOUSEPARENTS IN 89 INSTITUTIONS FOR
DEPENDENT CHILDREN IN 1940 OR 1941

Extent of Education	Number of Houseparents	Percent
College and some graduate work	26	5
College, 4 years	65	13
College, less than 4 years	99	19
Normal school	39	8
School of nursing	26	5
Other education beyond high school	5	1
High school only	185	36
No high school	28	5
Education not reported	42	8
Total	515	100

Source: Same, p. 78, as Table 4

Possibly it is not now desirable to demand a rigid background for the work of cottage parents. In one sense they are parents and not experts, and perhaps their greatest contribution to institutional life is in their status of substitute parents. Although fortunately there is current emphasis on preparation for parenthood, we do not require that parents in private homes pass examinations or finish a certain grade in order to qualify as parents. Since the requirements for parenthood are so slight in our society, it does not seem entirely justifiable to ask that cot-

[7]*Ibid*, pp. 132–133.

tage parents have formal, specialized training for their role. Such training may not be possible before they are employed. But, once on the job, the cottage parent can greatly benefit from some kind of training or educational experience. Some experts, however, would ask for definite requirements before hiring. (See Table 7.)

Table 7

CLASSIFICATION OF HOUSEPARENTS BY LAST PREVIOUS PAID POSITION
BEFORE PRESENT EMPLOYMENT, 1941

Last Previous Paid Position	Number of Houseparents
Houseparents in another children's institution	63
No previous paid position	44
Teaching in public or private school	38
Social work	30
Clerical or business position	28
Nursing	20
School or college matron or food service worker	12
Hospital employee	5
Housekeeper or nursemaid in private family	3
Other positions	7*
Not reported	73
Total	323

*Includes 2 librarians, 2 psychologists, 1 church worker, 1 sewing teacher in girl's club, 1 W.P.A. housekeeper.

Source: Same, p. 74, as Table 4.

Two Methods of Training

There are two means of educating cottage parents, as well as other personnel, to fuller understanding of their positions in child-caring institutions. One is the "institute" method which has been applied in various parts of the country. The other is the training which workers may receive within their own institution.

In a number of localities, training institutes are held, with workers from various institutions in the vicinity attending. These meetings usually feature lecture and discussion groups for cottage parents, as well as for other personnel of institutions. Commonly, they are divided into sections for different types of workers: nurses, purchasers, executives, cottage parents, social workers. Such institutes generally are successful in the larger cities or more populated places where a fairly large attendance is possible. Several of the graduate schools of social work have provided such facilities plus educational work on other bases for institutional workers.

The programs of education for cottage parents within institutions are most varied. The extremes indicate that in some little or no work is being done along this line, while in others a very careful program of education is practiced. In some of the better institutions newly appointed workers are accepted on an apprenticeship basis, so that they will be able slowly to grasp the significance of the work they are to do. Through such a program, cottage parents are not plunged immediately into responsibilities which might overcome their zeal for the work. It also saves them from certain embarrassing learning-situations in which they may have to be told about cottage practices by the cottage children. Usually, along with the apprenticeship, some sort of more formal training course is arranged for the cottage parents. In this way they not only will be introduced to the practical procedures of their positions but also may be given an opportunity to learn some of the more theoretical considerations pertaining to their jobs.

Use of Literature and Case Records

In addition to the apprenticeship type or training, other devices have been used to increase the effectiveness of cottage parents. While there is a noticeable scarcity in the literature bearing directly on the work of cottage parents, nevertheless, there are a number of booklets available for their use. The reading of case records is another training practice used in some institutions. While there are advantages in this procedure, there is the feeling among social workers and institutional directors that cottage parents should not be given access to case records. There are two chief reasons for this opinion: (1) Cottage parents are not trained to understand the full implications of the records, and they might thereby gain a perverted picture of the children's problems and needs; and (2) cottage parents, through such knowledge, might be deterred from engaging in a more general and spontaneous parental relationship with the children while worrying about the peculiarities of behavior noted in the case record. Possibly, for in-service training of this type, the maturity of the cottage parents, the nature of the children's problems, and the availability of proper staff supervision in the reading of the records, comprise some of the important considerations for securing an intelligent solution to the problem.

Staff Conferences

In many institutions, regular staff conferences help to educate the cottage parents. Sometimes these conferences are divided in time so that the first part is devoted to consideration of practical administration and the latter part is devoted to a study and discussion of the ways in which the personnel might improve its services to the children. These periods may be formally or informally organized. At other times provision is made for the holding of separate conferences for administrative problems and for staff education. There seem to be some advantages to this latter procedure because a divided conference hour often leaves little time for education. While both of these types of educational service to workers are centered chiefly in the cottage parents, the other workers should not be forgotten. Usually, however, it is thought wisest to focus the educational discussion upon cottage parents and their problems because, as has been stated previously, the cottage parents commonly have the most intimate relationships with the children.

THE SOCIAL WORKER AND THE INSTITUTIONAL CHILD

Thus far we have been examining the general organization of the institutional program for children without too much stress upon the role of the social worker in it. From one angle the whole of the institutional program is essential social work service, even though it is not always and completely controlled by professional workers. Certainly, the professional knowledge and skill of the social worker should be brought to bear on as many segments of the institutional care of children as possible. And yet, the social worker makes up a distinctive but related category of assistance for the child in a child-caring institution.

The professionally trained and qualified social worker in the institutional field is able to examine the social and emotional problems of children at the time their admission is being considered. Such a professionally trained person is also able to aid the child with his social and emotional problems while he is in the institution. Finally, the professionally trained social worker is able to assist the child in leaving the institution and in making an adequate and satisfying adjustment to the community. These functions of the social worker will be examined in some detail.

INTAKE

The social worker is usually the first and chief person to have actual contact with a child (and his family if such are present) being considered for admission. Referrals for admission may come from any one or more of the following: ministers, physicians, neighbors, other social work agencies, teachers, friends of the institution, courts, clinics, summer camps, or hospital departments of social service. An example of the intake process as it involves a referring agency is provided in the case of "Alice Davidson." The social worker in the institution has done the recording:

1-13-41. Miss Mills of the F.A. [Family Agency] here for conference about our requirements and the possibility of Alice Davidson entering Bethesda [a children's institution in Philadelphia]. Alice is fifteen years old and is in the 8B grade at Kearney School. The school reports that she has average intelligence and ability and is probably back in her work because she has no encouragement at home. They think she could go on into high school. Miss Mills describes Alice as an attractive, friendly girl who feels her need of social life.

The problem revolves around the fact that Alice is not a child of the Davidsons. The F.A. has been working with the family for two months. They entered to supplement Mr. D's allowance from the D.P.A. [Department of Public Assistance] because after Mrs. D's death three months ago his relief status changed to that of a single man because Alice is not a legal member of the family even though she has been living with them for a number of years and uses their name. The F.A. entered with the idea of working toward a separation. Alice seems to have no relatives and they have been unable to learn anything definite of her history, but Mr. D is old and in poor health and conditions there are bad for her. Mr. D is extremely strict and overprotective of Alice. This may have resulted from an incident three years ago when he took Alice with him begging, and allowed her to get in a car with a chauffeur who later assaulted her. The S.P.C.C. [Society for the Prevention of Cruelty to Children] and other agencies became active and an effort was made to take Alice out of the Davidson home. Mr. D has been opposed to letting her go and seems very fond of her. He resents the financial situation which is forcing him toward letting her leave, but Alice seems to want a change.

Miss Mills has not talked with either Mr. D or Alice about any specific plan but thinks this might be what Alice needs. We talked about our requirements, the necessity of application coming from Mr. D and Alice, the preliminary examination, and possibilities of support. I suggested that we might ask for support through the dependency court, but as Alice will be sixteen within two months this does not seem practical. Miss Mills questioned Mr. D's willingness to go to court anyway but was anxious that this should not keep us from taking Alice and thought F.A. might pay board if we could not take her free. Since Alice is eligible to come to Bethesda, Miss Mills will approach the Davidsons with this plan.

1-17-41. Miss Mills telephoned. She has talked with Alice and Mr. D and they both seem interested in Alice coming to Bethesda. I said that I had talked with my supervisor about our conference and she had suggested support from the D.P.W. [Department of Public Welfare] for Alice until she is seventeen since she is probably legally an orphan. Miss Mills felt that it would be inadvisable to ask Mr. D to go to court as he is suspicious of anything which suggests anyone taking Alice away from him. The F.A. would be willing to support Alice here for the school term and think they could make arrangements to continue. I questioned the soundness of this plan and of further action with Mr. D taking so little real part in the separation. He will be bound to feel that we are taking Alice from him after she comes if he does not face it beforehand. I asked whether Alice has been able to tell him she wants to leave. Apparently she has taken a definite stand that she wants to come to Bethesda. It was decided that if Mr. D were willing to come out to talk with me, we would see whether we could work something out rather than make an issue of D.P.W. support.[8]

Information Needed

Often the referring person or agency further provide the social worker in the institution with important information. The gathering of data concerning the child and his family is one of the first steps which the worker takes. Determining whether a child meets the requirements for admission into an institution is never easy. Each casework situation is unique and should be treated as such.

In building up information regarding the prospective client, the social worker avails himself of the primary resources of the child's family. The parents are seen and talked with in order that their viewpoints may be known. What are their motives in seeking placement? What do they think will happen to the child within the institution? What do they think will be the future of the child in terms of his post-institutional life? Is the institution the type of placement which they desire or are they confused regarding the alternatives: institutional care, foster home care, care for the child in his own home? What kind of life have the parents afforded the child? What are their special habits and attitudes? What behavioral problems does the child represent to them and how well grounded is their opinion? What is the condition of the home? What is the situation in regard to the relatives of the family and the child?

These are a few of the questions which the social worker must ask of the family before the child is admitted. In some instances the parents have been mistaken in their impressions regarding their own ability to handle the problem. Sometimes they have misunderstood the nature of the child-caring institution and need to be referred elsewhere. Other times they discover aspects of their situation which need the attention both of a child-caring institution and some other community resource.

[8]Grace I. Bishopp, *The Role of Case Work in Institutional Service for Adolescents,* Child Welfare League of America, New York, 1943, pp. 12–13.

In some cases talking over the meaning which placement will have for them and their child may make the parents reconsider the whole idea of placement as a solution to their problem.

The difficulties sometimes met in dealing with parents who wish to place children in an institution are shown by the following incident:

The intake worker realized that a young woman who came to the agency with the idea of placing her three children without having given any thought as to how their care would be paid for, and who expected to retain all of her pension for herself, was not likely to participate in a very responsible way in planning for herself or for her three children. When pressed by the intake worker to consider ways in which the board bill might be met, she commented, "But I thought you would arrange all this for me," thus expressing her dependent attitude toward life.

The information she had previously given showed that she had married very young, that she was only 25 at the time of application and that her husband, who had recently died, was 15 years her senior. She was rather a hard-looking young person, but the children who had accompanied her were attractive and were carefully dressed. They seemed at ease in our office, were friendly with the worker, and quite free with their mother. Their behavior and appearance made the worker think that the mother had more feeling for them than she had indicated up to that point. She wondered whether there was basis for referral to a family agency and described the services of a family agency, but the mother was not interested. She wanted placement and reiterated her inability to pay for it.

The worker explained again that private arrangements could not be made on those terms and that the Department of Welfare would not be able to assume complete responsibility for board because her income, though small, was sufficient to make it possible for her to meet part of the expense. The mother repeated that she could not do that. The worker said she could see that she really felt she could not but that she had not told her why it would be impossible. Perhaps together they might run over her expenses, so that each might have a better understanding of what they were. The mother again referred to her expectation that the agency would relieve her of the board bill.

The worker was professionally trained and had considerable sensitivity to people. She felt that the mother was in need of help of some kind, and it troubled her not to be able to get beyond her rigid attitude. However, she realized that unless the mother was willing to meet the conditions which would make it possible for the agency to help, it was unlikely that she would be able to use help. It is a basic principle in casework that a caseworker's ability to help is conditioned by her own acceptance of the realities involved for the client.[9]

[9]Edith May Holmes, "Intake Service for Children's Institutions," *The Family* (now *Journal of Social Casework*), volume 22, number 6, October, 1941, pp. 186–187.

Other Factors

The social worker must also take the child into consideration. Even the smallest child can express certain needs, and it is important that the social worker determine whether those needs will best be met by institutional care. Older children can more fully provide the worker with extensive information and insight on the advisability of their placement. The modern social worker in a child-caring institution does not make plans for a family and child without consulting with and being led by the wishes of the members involved. The social worker, too, has no Rosetta stone to enable him to size up a complicated situation and bring out an easy answer. He is the assister of persons who present their problems. So the worker does not wish to "railroad" the child into an institutional placement, or any kind of service, if the child is not fully aware of what is going on or disapproves of it. The worker, wherever possible, is under obligation to probe the mind of the child under consideration for institutional care and to discover his side of the problem.

The social service exchange is a valuable informational resource for the child care worker, if a family has previously used the health and welfare facilities of the community.[10]

Placement Sometimes Not Desirable

In many cases it is determined that the placement of a child in an institution would not be the most desirable course of action. The case of Mrs. "G" illustrates this:

Mrs. G, a young Swedish woman, was referred by the minister of the church she attended. She was neatly dressed and looked like a simple, substantial sort of person. She was very much upset. At times her accent made her difficult to understand although in calmer moments she spoke clearly and grammatically. She wanted to arrange for her three-year-old child to be cared for, saying that things could not go on as they had been going. Six years ago she and her husband came from Sweden. They had been led to understand that there would be no difficulty in making a living here and that they might even become rich, but they had had nothing but trouble since they came. Her husband's brother had urged them to come and had promised her husband a job, which had not materialized. He lost interest as soon as the financial situation of the G family became critical.

The G's moved from place to place, each time looking for cheaper quarters. At first their savings had carried them but now they were gone and the rent was due and there was hardly enough food in the house for

[10]The social service exchange is discussed in Chapter 14.

the next two days. Recently Mr. G had started to drink, and Mrs. G simply would not put up with that. She had not been used to it in her father's home, and she would not tolerate it in her own. Last night her husband had not come in at all. Olaf, the child, needed shoes. He used to be a good child, but now he was unmanageable. Yesterday morning Mrs. G went to the "Relief." She did not know whether she would get help or not. She was told to come back with papers. She understood that people waited a long time for help and if you did get on relief you did not get much money. She had noticed an ad in the newspaper which she answered in the afternoon. A lady was looking for a maid and would pay $40 a month, without living. Mrs. G thought she might get the position; the lady had seemed to like her. She hoped she would get it because then she wouldn't need the relief, and she would be able to support herself if she decided to leave her husband. She would pay for Olaf's care in an institution.

The worker listened attentively, occasionally asking questions. She wondered whether it was the possibility of being on relief or the opportunity to leave her husband that made the job seem important. Mrs. G answered hesitatingly that it was both. She would not like being on relief but she wouldn't like leaving her husband either. The worker learned that Mrs. G had worked intermittently at cleaning jobs since her arrival in this country, but that she had always planned her work around Olaf's care, working while he took his nap or when her husband could be at home. It had not occurred to her to consider placement until her minister had suggested it. He thought she could work, pay a small amount for the child's board, and leave her husband. She could start a new life alone. He thought that a woman should not feel she had to live with a man who drank. Mrs. G asked how the worker felt. The worker thought it important for her to be sure. Had she ever thought of leaving him before? Mrs. G looked somewhat shocked and said no, there had been no reason for her to think of it before. In Sweden they had been very happy together. They had planned to buy the place they rented and had expected to live there when they were old.

The worker was sympathetic. She thought Mrs. G must often have wished she had not come to this country. Mrs. G described how reluctant she had been to come and how she dreaded leaving her mother and sisters and brothers. She had not let them know how hard things had been here, and she hadn't written to her husband's people either. It did no good to worry old people. She would like to go back to Sweden if she could, but the war made that impossible, and besides, Mr. G had taken out his first papers. They had made very few friends here because they had so little money, and then, too, caring for the child had taken up much of their time. The worker commented that she must have been very lonely. She asked whether she would not miss Olaf if she separated herself from him. Mrs. G said she would but that she would visit him often. She asked anxiously what the place would be like. The worker said that was something they needed to talk about because she thought that Mrs. G probably did not realize that in this country children as young as Olaf were taken care of in private homes rather than in institutions. The worker went into detail explaining why we felt that institutional care was not good for little children. She told something of the process by which boarding homes were selected and said that if Mrs. G wanted to consider boarding home care she would send her to another agency since we did not have that service to offer. Mrs. G did not like the idea of a boarding home. She thought Olaf would miss her. He might wonder why he had to live in someone else's home. The worker said that children sometimes did wonder about that, but that the agency and the foster mother tried to help them understand.

The worker mentioned the cost of such a plan. She thought it would be at least $25 a month, and she wondered whether Mrs. G would be very far ahead financially, since she would have to pay for her own living out of the $15 that remained. Mrs. G thought that she might not be able to manage on $15. It was not very much considering how expensive things were. She thought life in a rooming house might be lonely too.

The worker then directed the discussion to Mr. G. She gathered the impression that while he was drinking heavily at the moment, he had started to drink only recently. Mrs. G thought it was due to the men who hung around the place where they lived. The worker said that sometimes people drank because they were unhappy. Did she think that Mr. G was unhappy because he had not been able to find work or because he, too, missed Sweden? Mrs. G said solemnly that she thought it was very possible. He was ashamed of his drinking, she knew he was, because he never spoke of it unless she did, and sometimes he went out of the house without looking at her. She worried about what was going to become of all of them. The worker said that she did have a good many things to worry her. Would she like the worker to send her to a place where she could talk over her worries? Mrs. G wanted to know what good talking would do. The worker said that wasn't all there was to it. When you talked with a person who was expert in helping people with troubles like yours you came to understand your own troubles better. You could see how they had come about and often that made you able to do something about them. Mrs. G looked perplexed but interested. What would the "place" be like? The worker said it was called a family agency because it helped people with family troubles. It was a social agency like our agency only it helped people in this other way.

Mrs. G had not liked the idea of a boarding home for Olaf so perhaps the family agency could help her find a solution without sending him away. Mrs. G said slowly that she would prefer not to send Olaf away, but how were they going to live? The worker said that the family agency would be able to help Mr. G with suggestions about work and that they would also be able to advise Mrs. G about part-time work. There was the possibility of a day nursery for Olaf. Would they find work for Mr. G?

The worker said that she knew they would be able to advise him about where to look for the kind of work he was fitted to do but that they would not find it for him. Mrs. G wondered whether his drinking might not be a handicap. The worker thought that Mrs. G would find it helpful to talk with the worker in the family agency about that. She was sure the agency would help Mr. G if he wanted them to. But what about the rent and the fact that they had no money? The worker pointed out that Mrs. G had already been to the public agency about that and had been given a return appointment. She thought perhaps she would want to let her application stand until things straightened out because the family agency would not be able to help them that way. Mrs. G was afraid that the public agency would not help them in time, so the worker offered to explain the situation and if possible secure an earlier appointment for Mrs. G. Mrs. G was pleased with this suggestion and the worker had no difficulty in changing the appointment.

Mrs. G was with the worker a little over an hour. When she left, her manner was confident and she looked happier. She went away from the office holding tightly to a referral card to the family agency, where an appointment had been made for her.[11]

In some institutions the responsibility for admittance of children rests fully with the social worker or with a committee of social workers. This is especially true if the institution is large. However, a number of institutions lodge the authority for admission of children in a committee of the board of directors. Fortunately, this practice is on the decline.

INSTITUTIONAL CARE

If and when the child is acceptable for institutional care, the social worker has the responsibility for introducing him into the new experience. The change from a private home to an institution is a hard adjustment for many children to make. Indeed, not only may children with problems be affected negatively by placement, but new problems may arise.

After the child has been admitted to the institution the duties of the social worker should not be relaxed, although they often are. It is at present an unfortunate commentary on the practices of many institutions that their social work services are expressly directed toward intake and discharge of children, but not equally directed toward the care of children while they are in the institution.

The family and relatives of the children are also a proper concern of the social worker during this period. From one viewpoint the institutional social worker is a family caseworker in that he is interested,

[11]Edith May Holmes, *op. cit.,* pp. 188-189.

where possible, in reconstituting the family at the earliest moment. To this end, he should keep close watch on the living conditions of the parents, which may change from time to time. The father may secure a better job; the illness of the mother may pass; or other circumstances may arise to assist the child's return to the home. In all these considerations the social worker is interested in helping the parents to assume responsibility for the child when they are able.

Parent-Child Relationship After Placement

The social worker also is concerned with the relationship the child will have with his parents after he has been placed. For example, if the institution does not charge the parents for the child's upkeep, the parents may assume that they no longer have any economic responsibility for the child. This unfortunate attitude might seriously hamper the relationships between the child and his parents as well as that between the institution and the parents. If the child's parents are asked to contribute where possible to the maintenance of their child, they tend to keep an attitude of at least partial responsibility. This response, while important to the solution financially, is also significant for the continuance of normal parent-child bonds. Again, the possibilities of the child returning to his parents for short stays, for weekends, holidays, or for considerable parts of the year, may also constitute a problem for all involved.

Sometimes the social worker must give considerable time to the parents regarding the parents' or the institution's relationship with the child. The discussion with the father of "Alice Davidson," mentioned previously, shows this aspect of the social worker's job:

3–7–41. Mr. D here early. He started out by saying how bad he feels and how hard it is to be alone. I agreed that he must be feeling Alice's absence very keenly. Yes, he is, and especially when she has turned against him so. He is all alone and doesn't have anyone to talk with about it. He wandered from this into a long rapid discussion of how much his wife had meant to him and the kind of work they had done and how much they had tried to do for Alice. I listened for some time, then said I thought Alice appreciated what he had done for her. I assured him she had not been having other company Sunday afternoon and told him how Mrs. Lougee had found her crying after he left. This seemed to satisfy him a little but he went into a long tirade against a friend called Doris. He would like us to keep Doris from seeing her. She came between him and Alice before and encouraged Alice to defy him and run to movies and neglect her work.

I told him we would not be able to stop Doris from visiting here, or Alice from visiting her during free time. Mr. D contradicted me sharply saying, "Where there's a will, there's a way." I admitted that he was right and put it on the basis that we would not stop her and went from this into the subject of Alice having to be free to do the things the other girls do. We had rather sharp conflict for a few minutes, but I continued to insist that he would not want us to make Alice obey the rules the other girls had to obey and yet seem unjust to her by not giving her the same privileges.

He picked this up quickly. No, nobody could do that to him and he wouldn't want anyone to do it to "his Alice." He had been insisting that he wanted us to make her behave herself, and I emphasized the point that we had to have freedom to do this in our own way, explaining that Alice wouldn't be allowed to go out if she neglected her work or disobeyed the rules, and that he should come and fight with me when he had a quarrel with what she was doing. Surprisingly, he grinned and said it was a little too snowy for us to go out and fight.

We both laughed and he seemed to feel much better. We talked a little about how Alice would be affected if we all pulled her different ways and he told of the trouble he and Mrs. D had always had that way. He branched off into his treatment of an incident when Alice became interested in a married man, but when I asked plainly if she is too fond of boys, said no, she's always been good except for Doris. He talked again about what a bad influence she is.

I explained how such attachments die when girls are separated if no one interferes. At first he threatened that if we wouldn't do anything about it, he would go to court for an injunction against her but finally seemed to drop the idea and said it had done him good to come out here and talk. He felt better. He seemed quite able to accept my suggestion that he and Alice fought because they were both feeling hurt and agreed that he did want her to enjoy herself and be happy. He could not accept the idea of not coming at least once a week to see her. He would like to come every Sunday afternoon. I did not oppose this but told him it might be an aggravation to him because Alice would grow more and more engrossed with girls and seem less interested in him. I said we had that experience with girls and their own parents and it seemed quite natural. It didn't mean that they cared less for their parents but just that they were young and interested in what they were doing and what was going on.

Mr. D said something about "there isn't as much feeling between Alice and me as though she was my own daughter." I assured him that I thought she had a very warm feeling for him but probably he was right in thinking their tie was not as close.

We talked a little about the value of him having some interests of his own, but he doesn't seem to know how to accomplish this and is critical and distrustful of people and very pitiful in his hope of a job. He would like to cook for us and offered some flour he has. He said again as he left that he felt much better about everything now. Miss Mills and I are the only people he has to talk to. I said the secretary would make an appointment for him to see me whenever anything came up about Alice or her progress here.[12]

Interpreting the Child's Needs

Within the institution the social worker has responsibilities for the interpretation of the child's needs and problems to the rest of the staff. This is especially so with regard to the cottage parents. In this instance, whether case records are used or not, the social worker tries to give the cottage parents a background for understanding the child. This, in turn, should enable them to meet the needs of their charge intelligently. If the child's background has indicated a need for strong love attachments, the cottage parents can make note of it in their personal relationships with him. If he has been left to himself in his own home and has developed little sense of corporate or social responsibility, then they may, by having this information from the social worker, be able to structure his experience in such a manner as to benefit him. If there are certain secret aspects of his past life, such as a father in prison or a mother who is a prostitute, they will want to avoid situations or conversations which may prove embarrassing to him. Thus the cottage parents are a rich source of influence for the social worker in his indirect relationships with the child.

The social worker may also have more direct relationships. He may give the child an opportunity to discuss any grievances toward fellow cottage friends. Sometimes the child may become involved in such activities as homosexuality or stealing of institutional supplies, about which he does not wish to speak to his cottage parents. Or he may have grievances toward the cottage parents themselves. In all such circumstances the social worker may be able to provide a sympathetic and understanding ear.

Continuing Assistance

Sometimes a child will not have specific grievances, but will need the assistance of a caseworker in order to work through some continuing personal or family problem. The case of "Alice Davidson" again makes this point:

> *11-18-41.* I asked to see Alice after school. She came to the office willingly, but seemed to have some question about why I might want to talk with her. I said we had not seen each other recently, and the last time we talked she had been having some trouble. I wondered how things are going now. Alice said, "Things are much better. What you said last time was true and I've been able to work things out." I thought that was good news, and went on to say how interested I am in knowing something

[12]Grace I. Bishopp, *op. cit.,* pp. 24–26.

of her general feeling about living here now that she has been here some time. I have been wondering what values she is finding for herself in this experience, and how constructively she is using her free time and what it all means to her. I mentioned the question both of us knew, that is, whether she should continue to live at the institution, how Mr. D felt about it, and our feeling that it was good but depended mostly on the girl's use of it. Alice didn't respond, and as this had been rather complicated, I wondered if she understood what I meant.

She said, Yes, she does. She was just thinking about it. She thinks it has been very good for her to live here. She had been talking to her father the other day and he was after her again to know if she wouldn't like to come home if he could get her out. She hated to hurt his feelings, but finally had to tell him she wouldn't want to go back to the way they had lived before. She went on to say that at home they always lived in an uproar. One time she could do something and the next time she did the same thing it was wrong, and there was a constant battle between her and her father. She knows what is right and wrong here. There are rules and regulations, and if there is a change you are notified in advance so that you know what you are doing.

It is true that she finds routine work and doing things immediately when people ask you hard, and sometimes she gets checks, but as soon as she gets over being mad she knows that it is better for her. At home she was sloppy and got out of a lot of things she should have done, although on other days she would work her head off. Her father still feels the same about her being out so late on Saturday nights and often says, "Alice, why don't you get in early? You don't have to stay out until eleven." She doesn't think that is too late, though, and she doesn't do anything she shouldn't when she is out. She and Bill usually go to a movie and then stop for some ice cream, and it takes that much time when you count in the going back and forth. She talked quite a bit about Bill, telling me about his parents and his job, and how since they are both Italian and have hot tempers they are trying to learn self-control, and how he has been helping her to understand Mrs. Brooks, the housemother, too.

I asked occasional questions, and Alice went on to say that she doesn't understand why it is so hard for her to control herself unless it is because she learned to get her own way at home by fighting. Whoever got the maddest got what they wanted. It does seem different here, where unless you could have something anyway, nobody ever gives in to you. She told of an incident in which she recently became angry in school and talked so badly to the teacher that she had given her a day to apologize or be suspended. She was terribly worried and apologized and resolved that wouldn't happen again. I was surprised and wondered if she didn't feel she could let us know when she was in trouble. She knows she could, but felt it was up to her not to let it get that far, and I thought that true.[13]

[13]Grace I. Bishopp, *op. cit.*, pp. 27–28.

Other Duties

Not only may the child seek out the social worker for direct contact, but the social worker, as indicated above, may initiate contacts with the child. Such consultations may be arranged on the basis of a weekly or monthly period which is "written into the schedule." Or the social worker may on his own initiative see only those children of the institution who have special personal problems. While many institutions guard against accepting children for institutional placement if they obviously are in need of intense individual treatment, the rule cannot always knowingly be kept. Sometimes a child who has been judged as capable of appropriating the values of group experience in an institution is actually unable to perform in a cottage group and needs to be referred elsewhere. Or, if the case is not too serious, he may be given special attention by the social worker within the institution.

The social worker also has other duties in caring for the child. If the child attends a school off the premises, the social worker will want to cooperate in various ways with the school authorities so as to help the child adjust to his school obligations. If the child goes to school within the institution, the problem and responsibility may be much the same. It may, indeed, call for even closer cooperation. Some institutions, however, may have a staff member other than the social worker to care for the school adjustments of the children.

An extreme type of educational need on the part of a child under institutional care is expressed in the following account:

February, 1937. A member of the special class conducted at the Home is a ten-year-old boy. When he came to us last month he had not even completed his first grade. An incompetent relative with whom he lived had moved about from one farm to another. The result was a lack of any continuous school attendance and inexcusable absences for periods lasting for weeks and months. Emotional problems created by the same incompetent relative made it doubly important that he receive individual attention. He has faulty reading habits which must be patiently corrected before he can make any real progress. It is too early to tell how intelligent he really is, but we are hopeful that he is not subnormal. During ten years of neglect much retardation can accumulate. Our picture of this boy, neglected as he is, is not entirely a matter of shadows. His acquaintance with animals is unusual for a child of his age. He has musical ability which permits him to entertain other children with a harmonica and he has a certain way with him of singing cowboy songs.[14]

[14]An excerpt from the "Albany Diary," by Howard W. Hopkirk, as recorded in his *Institutions Serving Children,* Russell Sage Foundation, New York, 1944, pp. 161–162.

Psychiatric Aspects

If the child is attending an outside psychiatric clinic, the social worker will prepare a report on the child for the use of the psychiatrist. If there is a psychologist within the institution or if the institution uses the services of an outside psychologist, there may also be duties in this connection.

In some instances the social worker finds it necessary to work with the parents of placed children or to refer them to other aid in order to create the best possible social and psychological environment for the children. Mr. "B" provides an illustration of this:

Some time ago, Mr. B, a man in his early forties, came to us for placement of his two little girls. He was a widower and described himself as having been "father and mother" to the children since his wife's death four years before. He could not continue caring for them because of poor health and lack of regular employment and there were no relatives to assume responsibility. A housekeeping arrangement would not do because of a previous unsuccessful experience with a housekeeper, and he was unwilling to consider boarding home care, feeling threatened by a foster father. Throughout his contact with us he was seen as a rather unstable, immature person, dependent upon superficial things—the kind of house in which he lived, the cultural status of the people with whom he boarded—but we felt that in spite of this he was truly fond of his children and concerned about their welfare.

Arrangements were eventually made for the children to go to an institution near the city. Mr. B was asked not to visit too frequently at first and not to come at times that would interfere with the routine of the children's lives. There was no further discussion of the visiting regulations since he made no objection. Several weeks later we learned with some surprise that he was visiting frequently and that he often came at inconvenient hours. The children were not settling down to the life of the institution and seemed unable to accept the placement as anything more than a temporary arrangement. Further acquaintance with Mr. B on the part of the institution revealed that his feeling for his children was something quite different from fatherly affection and amounted to a dependence which was jeopardizing the children's emotional development. It was felt that he needed the help of a psychiatrist.

In reviewing our contact with Mr. B we realized that the indications of his instability, which were apparent throughout, were not considered in evaluating his feeling for his children and that there was little realization of the fact that he was using the children to work out his own difficulties. It is questionable whether he would have been able to recognize this if it had been pointed out, but whether he could or not, a decision as to the degree of responsibility he could assume for his behavior should have been made before the children went to the institution. Placement will have little value for the children unless they are free to take advantage of the constructive things about it.[15]

DISCHARGE AND AFTERCARE

The problem of assisting the child to leave the institution and adjust to the community is as important as that of intake and institutional care. The social worker, therefore, spends considerable time in planning for the discharge and aftercare of children who have met the qualifications for return to the community. In too many instances the requirements for the discharge of institutional children are rigid, unintelligent, and harmful. Too often they center chiefly about age. There is much to be done in building up discharge standards which will reflect the individualized interest of the social worker in the child.

Social Worker's Responsibility

In aiding the older child to leave the institution and seek an adjustment in the community, the social worker very often becomes in effect a vocational guidance worker in that he is called upon to assist the child practically, in becoming economically independent. This responsibility calls for keen insight, good community contacts, and helpful counseling of the child about to be discharged.

For the younger child the discharge from the institution may mean his assumption of new conditions which may be a threat to his security. The child returning to his own home may face the problem of making or remaking an accommodation which in many instances is trying and worrying. In such a situation the social worker maintains a responsibility both to the child and to the parents for his reception. If there are other children who have remained in the family or who have been placed either in an institution (the same or a different one) or in a foster home, the problem becomes more complex.

Guiding the Adjustive Process

The case of "Joan Ross" shows the adjustive process as guided by a social worker. Joan, a fourteen-year-old, was an intelligent, well-adjusted, almost overresponsible girl. She had been placed in an institution during a time of great family conflict due to the father's desertion.

11-3-41. On our way home from clinic Joan began to talk about when she came to Bethesda two years ago last Wednesday. She remembers how different it felt when she was new. She really likes it here and enjoys the

[15]Edith May Holmes, *op. cit.,* p. 191.

other girls now. She feels sorry for new girls like Marilyn, though, who have no father or mother. Her mother's visits always helped her so much when she was homesick. I agreed that she probably never felt completely alone at Bethesda when her mother had been so close to her all the time. She talked for a few minutes about how frequently she visits on week ends, and then rather abruptly asked how she would be able to arrange to go home to live. Things are different for her mother now and she has a good job and a nice apartment.

I said I would be glad to talk to Mrs. R about it if she felt she could care for Joan now. Joan answered that her mother and she could decide whether she wants to stay at Bethesda or go home. I said we felt this to be the parent's responsibility. She said she knows, and then asked something about whether there would be much red tape in such a way that I felt she was trying to protect her mother. I said that we would help her mother make the arrangements if it was going back to court which was bothering her, and Joan talked freely about her mother's shyness and the way things are at home with her aunt in the same house, too.

She chatted quite easily about her experience here and at school. She said once that she thinks it is a good thing she came here for these two years anyway. She has grown up from being an innocent child and has learned how to do things. As we passed the station, she remembered that last year I used to take the train and expressed pleasure that I was coming home to dinner with her tonight.

11–5–41. Letter sent to Mrs. R asking for appointment.

11–11–41. Mrs. R here for appointment. After talking a moment about her job and the difficulty she had getting here on time, I said Joan had told me she was thinking she might be able to take her home. She is. Things are better for her now than when she brought Joan here. She is working pretty steadily. She does not want to criticize us. She thinks it has been very good for Joan to be here, but of course the best place for a girl is in her own home. If she is with her mother, she can have special things to eat, which might help her skin. She hopes that doesn't sound too critical of us. I said we understand why she would want Joan and that it would be better. We have enjoyed working with Joan and her too but we are glad if she can have Joan home with her now. We have always thought it better for a girl to be with her own mother if she could be. Mrs. R talked about how hard it had been to get Joan here because Miss Johnson had said she was a good mother and should keep her home. She wondered if it would be as hard to get her out. We talked about her going back to court and she seemed to feel that she could and decided when to go.

Mrs. R reported her progress in a number of telephone calls, finally saying she had decided not to have Joan change until she would change schools anyway. This was not convenient for us, so I asked if she would come out to talk about it again.

12–22–41. Mrs. R here very early. I picked up the subject where we had dropped it and Mrs. R talked freely about herself and Joan deciding to wait until the end of the term and the court worker saying she could do either thing she wished.

I wondered whether there is any other reason Mrs. R does not want to take Joan now. "No, that is all. Joan does not want to change schools for a month." I explained that a month will make quite a difference to us because of the girls who are waiting to come. It did not seem to me that Joan would find a change so hard when she gets along so well, especially when she seems to have finished here and is thinking about being home so much that she hardly seems interested in what is going on here at all.

Mrs. R was a little angry and maintained that while she did not want to change Joan she would take her now if I thought she could go to the same school from home. I thought this could be arranged. Mrs. R decided to do that, then, but hoped we would not want her to take Joan out before Christmas. I said we wouldn't; she talked a little about our not knowing what it means to Joan to be in the holiday play and being left out of things here, even though she does want to go home, too. I understood this and talked of the values she was going to miss in companionships of her own age. Mrs. R talked about thinking she is too old in some ways, but went on to tell of the young friends she would have. She could not express herself very well, but seemed to be saying they were of a better class and could say with much more conviction and less apology that she thought it was time Joan was with her again.

She had a little difficulty making up her mind when she would want to take her, though. I said something about this being a big chance for her as well as for Joan, and her antagonism seemed to disappear. She talked freely about what having Joan would mean and how she is looking forward to it. She also expressed her fear of still having to appear in court. It is so hard, like a disgrace. I agreed that it was hard and that this might have made her want to put it off, too. Yes, she always is afraid of things. The only other thing she worries about is the war. She wonders if Joan would be safer here than at home. I said I could understand this because I knew she had worried about Joan being safe when she wanted to come here. Mrs. R said Joan is older now, though, and maybe it will be all right.

She and Joan both seemed very pleased over her decision to come for Joan Christmas morning so that she will not have to come back after the holidays.

12-24-41. I talked with Joan this afternoon. She told me again of the dream she had about being home on a Sunday afternoon and going to sleep and waking up frightened that she had slept so long that she would be late getting back to Bethesda. Then she had remembered that she was home to stay and didn't need to worry. She is thrilled to think it may come true during these holidays. We talked about how ready to leave she is. Yes, she wants to go, but it is hard, too. She was a little tearful over leaving the girls and the staff and showed me some of the things the girls have given her to remember them by. She was glad Miss Johnson asked to say good-bye to her. Joan also talked a bit about how she has learned to do things and said she is going to make things easier for her mother.

Later: I saw Joan and Mrs. R briefly after the play. Mrs. R seemed quite free and happy. She said good-bye with much feeling and added that she will bring Joan back to visit.[16]

Aftercare Service

Beyond the period of initial reintroduction into the family the child and the family need an aftercare service for meeting problems which may then arise.

On the other hand, if the younger child is to be discharged from the institution and placed in a foster home, the social worker also has certain functions to carry out. He makes contact with the foster home agency, if the institution does not maintain its own foster home department. He passes on his understanding of the child to those who will deal with him from then on. Readjustments of the parents may be a part of the discharge process of the child from the institution.

Some institutions maintain alumni clubs which meet at regular intervals so that discharged children may not have to face a complete separation from the institution. There are undoubtedly some values in such a procedure. It can be doubted whether those most in need of such a group, however, will appropriate its services. Conversely, those who do use it may be those who need it least. In some cases children who have been in an institution for a long period may cling too tenaciously to an alumni organization and fail to make a clean break between their experience in the institution and the future they face in the community.

It may be mentioned finally that the social worker does not maintain an independent and exclusive service to the children he serves. There are many other persons who may be involved in the case of a particular child: teacher, psychologist, parent, psychiatrist, nurse. Moreover, the institution itself, despite whatever its own resources may be, is not unconnected to other agencies and resources of the community. Part of that relationship will be pointed out in other ways throughout this book.

Child Welfare League of America

Of special importance in the field of child welfare is the work of the Child Welfare League of America. Founded in 1920, it is composed of 200 accredited agencies engaged in child care and protection. Provisional membership includes about 40 others. Its purpose and activities have been described as follows: "To develop standards of service for child

---

[16]Grace I. Bishopp, *op. cit.,* pp. 31–34.

protection and care in children's agencies, institutions, and day nurseries, and in community programs through the following means: cooperation with governmental departments of child care, publications, information exchange service, loan library and record forms, case record exhibit, general information and education in the field, field service consultation, and regional conferences."[17] Its monthly *Bulletin* (October through July) contains information of interest to all child welfare workers. Its operations are of importance even to those who are not active practitioners in the child welfare field.

SELECTED READINGS ON CHILDREN'S INSTITUTIONS

Abbott, Grace, *The Child and the State: Select Documents With Introductory Notes,* Social Service Series, 2 volumes, University of Chicago Press, Chicago, 1938.

Agnew, David H., and others, *History and Reminiscences of the Philadelphia Almshouse and Philadelphia Hospital,* Detre and Blackburn, Philadelphia, 1890.

Austin, Harriet, *Your Loving Daughter,* Doubleday, New York, 1939.

Bishopp, Grace I., *Role of Case Work in Institutional Service for Adolescents,* Child Welfare League of America, New York, 1943.

Bowler, Alida C., and Bloodgood, Ruth, *Institutional Treatment of Delinquent Boys: Part I—Treatment Programs of Five State Institutions,* United States Children's Bureau Publication, number 228, Washington, D.C., 1935.

Brownell, Abigail F., *Child Care Facilities for Dependent and Neglected Negro Children in Three Cities: New York City; Philadelphia; Cleveland,* Child Welfare League of America, New York, 1945.

Child Welfare League of America, *Understanding Children: A Study Outline for Children's Institutions,* prepared by the New York State Committee on Mental Hygiene and the Child Welfare League of America, New York, 1945.

Cooper, John M., *Children's Institutions: A Study of Programs and Policies in Catholic Children's Institutions in the United States Made Under the Auspices of the National Conference of Catholic Charities and the Commonwealth Fund of New York City,* Dolphin Press, Philadelphia, 1931.

Crissey, Orlo L., *Child in the Institution,* Child Welfare League of America, New York, revised, 1940.

Dillon, Edmonia B., *Case Work in a Children's Institution When Provided by a Separate Child Placing Agency,* Child Welfare League of America, New York, 1943.

[17] *Social Work Yearbook: 1947,* Russell H. Kurtz, editor, Russell Sage Foundation, New York, 1947, p. 609.

Fredericksen, Hazel, *The Child and His Welfare,* Freeman, San Francisco, 1948.

Gesell, Arnold L., and Ilg, Francis F. L., *The Child From 5 to 10,* Harper, New York, 1943.

Gesell, Arnold L., and others, *Infant and Child in the Culture of Today: The Guidance and Development in Home and Nursery School,* Harper, New York, 1943.

Hart, Hastings H., *Cottage and Congregate Institutions for Children,* Charities Publication Committee, Russell Sage Foundation, New York, 1910.

Hopkirk, Howard W., *Institutions Serving Children,* Russell Sage Foundation, New York, 1944.

Jamison, A. T., *The Institution for Children,* Baptist Book Depository, Columbia, South Carolina, undated.

Lundberg, Emma O., *Unto the Least of These: Social Services for Children,* Appleton-Century, New York, 1947.

Putsch, Lorene, *Self-Government in a Children's Institution,* Child Welfare League of America, New York, 1945.

Stern, Edith M., in collaboration with Hopkirk, Howard W., *The Housemother's Guide,* Commonwealth Fund, New York, 1946.

Thurston, Henry W., *The Dependent Child: A Story of Changing Aims and Methods in the Care of Dependent Children,* New York School of Social Work Publications, Columbia University Press, New York, 1930.

Trotsky, Elias, *Institutional Care and Placing-Out: The Place of Each in the Care of Dependent Children,* Marks Nathan Jewish Orphan Home, Chicago, 1930.

White House Conference on Child Health and Protection, *Report of the Committee on Socially Handicapped, Dependency, and Neglect,* Appleton-Century, New York, 1933.

White House Conference on Children in a Democracy, *Final Report,* Superintendent of Documents, Washington, D.C., 1940.

Williamson, Margaretta, *The Social Worker in Child Care and Protection,* American Association of Social Workers, Job Analysis Series, volume 3, Harper, New York, 1931.

Young, Leontine R., *Treatment of Adolescent Girls in an Institution,* Child Welfare League of America, New York, 1945.

For additional related readings, consult the bibliographies at the end of the other child welfare chapters.

5

Children in Foster Homes

A currently popular method of caring for children is foster home placement. The following excerpts, provided by The Children's Aid Society of New York City, illustrate the types of needs that may be served in this manner:

Nobody questioned the Scherers when they moved into a shabby furnished room with their four-year-old Eric and his six-year-old sister, Freda. It was their own affair. But when one night a few months later the landlady heard the children sobbing, all the neighbors gathered. It seemed that Mr. and Mrs. Scherer owed rent and had left the previous night when Eric and Freda were asleep. When they wakened, there were no parents and no breakfast.

The children were used to going hungry and waited patiently all day playing quietly with an old teddy bear. But when it grew dark again, they were frightened and lay down on the bed and cried quietly. Kind neighbors fed, but could not keep these modern babies in the wood in their crowded flats. After waiting forlornly in a shelter for several weeks while police searched for their parents, The Children's Aid Society placed Eric and Freda in a family who know and love children.

Here they've been happier than ever before in their short lives. Mr. and Mrs. Barlow's devotion to them helps to fill the ache left by the desertion of their own parents. They live in a little suburban house, have nourishing, well-cooked food, and medical care, and what is more important to the children, nice warm clothes and two white bunnies which are the envy of the neighborhood.

Last week the children's "Aunt Chris" of whose existence we never knew, came to our office in search of her sister, their mother. She hadn't seen her sister in years and knew nothing about the children's plight. Best of all—she wants to take them home to live with her and her husband.

* * *

177

The Gordons had always been a spunky little clan, especially Jeannie, with her fair hair and sparkling gray eyes. It was Jeannie who took charge of the four little sisters when her mother died of cancer. Ellen and Cathie cried and went to pieces, so Jeannie kept a stiff upper lip and tried to do the things her mother said were important, like seeing all the children ate a good breakfast. Of course, Mary, the baby, was too young to understand anyhow.

That was two years ago and Mr. Gordon, handicapped by a serious heart condition complicated by asthma, struggled to keep the little family together. He could only work intermittently and after months of illness he felt obliged to accept the offer of relatives to take Ellen. The hardest blow was when he consented to little Mary's going to friends.

" 'Twill be best for baby, and we can't give her the care she needs," he comforted the two remaining little girls.

Perhaps Mr. Gordon had seen the handwriting on the wall. His condition grew continually worse. Unable to care even for Jeannie and Cathie, he was obliged to ask us to find a foster home for them, still hoping he could have them with him again later on.

Now he is in the hospital on the danger list but Jeannie and Cathie are together and determined to remain together in a foster home.

*   *   *

Three days before Christmas last year the janitor of a rooming house in the New York theatrical district heard a faint cry in the front hall. He hurried upstairs and found near the radiator a warmly wrapped baby boy.

No one knew how the baby had got there, though sometimes the roomers left the latch off the door when they slipped out to buy cigarettes. The police took the baby to a hospital where according to city regulations foundlings are given in rotation the Protestant, Jewish, or Catholic religion and a name. Our baby was declared a Protestant and given the name Philip Warren.

There were few clues to follow and no trace of either parent. Perhaps Philip's mother had just received news of a soldier husband's death, or perhaps Philip's father was frantic following his wife's death in childbirth.

By not permitting the adoption of children until a year and a day following their abandonment, New York's law leaves the door open for parents and children to be reunited. Philip's parents have not been found, however, and he has never left the hospital where the police brought him. Though he received some attention, the overworked nursing staff have not been able to give him the cuddling and fondling babies need. His development has been slower than that of children who have loving attention, and consequently he is described as having "institutional retardation."

Now Philip has been referred to The Children's Aid Society for boarding care until he can be legally adopted.

The Society has a foster home in mind for Philip where he will get all the love and attention he has missed so far in his short life. Like other foundlings we have placed, Philip will probably quickly develop into a normal, responsive baby who crows and holds his arms out to be picked up.

*   *   *

Sigrid is a real Norse baby, with flaxen hair and serious gray-blue eyes which look out with confidence on a strange new world. To her, life in a temporary shelter is the natural life for new babies. She doesn't know that her mother has been in a mental hospital since her birth and may not be able to care for her for many months.

Sigrid's father is devoted to her and would love to keep her with him at home, but he has no women relatives who can help and it is impossible to find a housekeeper for what he can pay.

He wants Sigrid to have the right start—the love and attention every baby needs to develop normally, so he has asked us to find a foster boarding home for Sigrid.

*   *   *

Pam and Polly had been as happy in their shabby flat their porter father's salary afforded, as though surrounded with all the luxuries, because they were secure in their parents' love and devotion.

Then their mother had a nervous breakdown and had to "go away." She told eight-year-old Pam that she must mother five-year-old Polly and "try to do the way you seen me do." Pam tried, but the food didn't taste right and the iron burned a big hole in Polly's one good dress. Their father realized the little girls were getting thin and peaked and yet with his irregular hours he could not care for them. Their mother, too, was worrying about them and so they asked us to find a temporary foster home.

When our worker talked to the children, Pam kept her arm around Polly as she explained, "Mummy said I should take care of baby chile— and she must go where I go." Assured that the foster mother wanted both children, Pam said, "And will the lady we live with comb our hair and iron our dresses and even buy us a pair of shoes?"

*   *   *

Betty was only seventeen when, while visiting relatives in New Orleans, she met a nineteen-year-old soldier. After a wartime courtship these youngsters were married with high hopes. A month later Johnny went overseas, and eight months later a little girl was born. Betty was a devoted mother and learned to take good care of the baby, managing nicely on Johnny's allotment by living with her aunt.

Two years later Johnny returned like many other men, not wounded, but a changed man. Restless, moody and unreliable, he "flew off the handle" if the baby cried. Four months before his son was born, Johnny deserted his family.

Her aunt couldn't care for both children, so Betty paid a neighbor to care for the baby. It wasn't very good care and it cost more than Betty could earn.

Then Betty heard about The Children's Aid Society and brought Johnny Jr. to us to place with a foster mother who loved and understood babies. Betty showed the dignity and maturity few twenty-one-year olds have today as she discussed her plans for having her baby with her just as soon as he is old enough to go to a day nursery from nine to five. She explained that after finishing her job at the office she helps the caretaker of the apartment house with the cleaning so that her room costs only $5.00 a week.

It costs $68.74 a month to give a young baby like Johnny a fine foster home with medical care, clothing and supervision, but Johnny's mother is paying all but $23.74 of this. $5.46 a week seems a ridiculously small sum to insure a baby loving foster care until his own mother can care for him.

*   *   *

It was about a year ago when John and Susan were brought before a children's court because they were neglected and left without proper supervision, and were subsequently referred to The Children's Aid Society for care because it cares for more Negro children than any other New York agency. Their father was a sailor, a dimly remembered person whom they had not seen in many years; their mother a domestic, doing day work. Their home was a succession of basements and garrets in deserted Harlem buildings. They had never known or heard of a relative—they had no friends except playmates.

The mother was patently a mentally disturbed person, uncommunicative, unpredictable, barely able to care for herself. With the months she has grown more ill and more furtive about avoiding medical attention. Yet there has never been any question about her love for the children or their love for her. Each time she disappears, John and Susan, with adult concern, wait anxiously and wistfully for some word that she is all right.

Susan is doing well in her foster home. She is one of those remarkable children who can come through the most damaging experiences and still grow in poise and self-sufficiency. Expertly, she is directing her school training so that in three more years she will be equipped to be self-supporting.

Slim, frail, asthmatic, little John finds life more difficult. He misses his mother intensely, he reaches out hesitantly to others in his anxiety to please and to receive affection; yet it took a little while for him to get ready to take into his heart any substitute for that mother he loves so much. John has been at our Brace Farm and now is ready to go into a foster home.

But John, the quiet, the seclusive, the lonely one, has a dream. He wants a home where he can have music lessons, and he wants it with all the loneliness and pent-up frustration of a child who has never had anything satisfactory in his whole life. Probably he will never be a Maurice Rocco or a Duke Ellington, but we think that if this is the way to feed his starved little soul, we must try and provide it along with his more basic needs.

As has been suggested previously, the field of child welfare can be divided into three areas of activity: care for children in institutions, care for children in foster homes, and care for children in their own homes through various community services. The first of these subdivisions of the field—care for children in institutions—has been surveyed in the preceding chapter. This chapter will describe the way social work aids children through placement in foster homes.

BRIEF HISTORY OF THE FOSTER HOME MOVEMENT

The Indenture System

The foster home movement of today is quite different from what it was in former times. The movement as such can be traced historically at least to the Middle Ages. In this period, dependent children were placed in the hands of persons who: (1) supplied their physical and social wants, and (2) were compensated for such service by the children's work. This system of indenture, as it was called, met a large part of the burden of caring for dependent children during the latter period of feudalism. Indeed, with certain modifications the indenturing system continued long past the feudal period. Even during colonial times in the United States the indenture proved a popular method of child care, along with the institutional method of providing for dependent children.

The system of indenturing, while it had certain positive features, also possessed definite drawbacks. Although it did offer a plan whereby children could be given apprenticeship experience in learning a trade for later self-support, it rested upon a contractual agreement which many times placed the child in the position of being a "child laborer" rather than an apprentice. The persons who took children were sometimes unscrupulously intent on finding cheap labor. Looking upon the indenture as a business enterprise, they exploited the children by giving inferior service, food, and clothing in return for the children's work. It is difficult to see how the substitute parental role could be fully appreciated and developed by "parents" who were chiefly interested in the economic advantages of the relationship. Thus, for many, the more altruistic parental role was submerged in favor of the less altruistic one of employer. In this sense it is understandable that many enlightened persons preferred the child-caring institution to the indentured foster home.

The New York Children's Aid Society

The quality of foster homes was greatly improved through the work of The New York Children's Aid Society and other agencies modeled after it, from 1853 on. The New York Children's Aid Society was founded under the influence of Mr. Charles Loring Brace, a student of theology, who believed that he could realize his religious ideals by working with children. In the 1850's in New York City there was a high prevalence of homeless and needy children and an inadequate supply of facilities for their care. Many of the needy were the children of immigrants, who were pouring into the city in almost overwhelming numbers. The schools, for one, were unable to meet the challenge of the large numbers of children. At one time, for example, it was estimated that approximately half of the children in the city were without schooling of any kind. Even the additional city facilities maintained by the various private and public institutions and nurseries were unable to meet the demands imposed by the severe conditions.

The Children's Aid Society, then, came into existence primarily as a means of meeting the widespread needs of children during this decade. Assisting Mr. Brace in the establishment of the Society was, among others, Robert M. Hartley, the executive of the Association for Improving the Condition of the Poor.

After surveying its possible contribution to the needs of the city's children, the Society created several methods of service: industrial schools, religious meetings for boys, workshops, assisting children to find work outside of the city, placing children in families which were economically strong, and providing lodging for boys. Some of these activities were not permanently maintained, such as workshops and religious meetings for boys, but others were continued, some even to the present time. Of interest to us at this point is the Society's program regarding foster homes.

Foster Home Program. The foster home program of the Society retained the essential form of the indenture. At its own expense, the Society placed needy children in homes where some work was required. Stress was put on getting the children placed outside of New York City. At times, groups of children were taken by train to other parts of the country, a practice which encouraged applications from would-be foster parents in rural areas.

The Society improved the placement practices which had previously existed. It insisted upon "good Christian homes." Practically, this meant some sort of selection of the foster homes into which children might be placed. There was also a fairly strong emphasis on the more altruistic reasons for the acceptance of children into foster homes. Children were not to be economic assets alone; they were also to be protected and guided by thoughtful and religious foster parents. The Society, too, inquired into the relationship which a foster home established with a child in order to judge the effectiveness of the home-child-agency relationship. It must be admitted, though, that these investigations were sometimes made from a defensive point of view because of the criticisms against the program and sometimes without the best of scientific procedures. On the whole, however, the quality of the program distinguished it from prior efforts.

While the Society managed to improve the practices of foster home placement, it continued certain features of child care which, under modern standards, are considered to be inadequate. The placement of children in foster homes was not done with sufficient discrimination, but in a more or less wholesale manner. Also, there was too great freedom in the agency-child-foster home arrangement to permit uniformly good results. The economic element was still prominent in the motives of those who took children. The Society's program did not include financial reimbursement to the foster parents, an apparently necessary arrangement if the bad effects of indenturing are to be avoided. The Society's plan, furthermore, placed undue hardship on the parents of those children who had to be released on a permanent basis for care, usually in a distant place. For the children, too, the same criticism held true. In addition, while the usual foster home was fairly positive in its influence on the children, some were not.

The pattern of foster home placement developed in New York City in The Children's Aid Society was adopted in other cities within a relatively short time. All of these agencies were privately organized and financed.

National Children's Home and Welfare Society

A society which apparently developed somewhat independently of the pattern given in The Children's Aid Society of New York City was the American Educational Society founded in 1883 by Martin Van Buren Van Arsdale in Illinois. In terms of personal motivation the American Educational Society grew out of a pledge Van Arsdale made to himself, during his theological training, that he would seek by every means to deliver children from the bane of the almshouse. The Society was formed to aid young girls educationally and to place children with families. The Society first had state-wide coverage of cases; later it became the National Children's Home Society and, as such, granted charters to similar agencies in other states.

In addition to the various privately founded and financed organizations for placing children in foster homes, there were certain developments within the public field which may be mentioned. Public placement of children in foster homes came about in part as an outgrowth of the state basis of operation of the American Educational Society and its counterparts. Public participation in the foster home movement was increased through the organization of state departments of welfare. These departments tended to consolidate the values of the American Educational Society and The Children's Aid Society, but on a public basis. With the growth of these public departments the National Children's Home Society had greatly lessened responsibility, especially as an instigating and controlling force in placement. In its later days it sought to federate on a voluntary basis the foster home services of the various public programs. In 1916 its name was changed to the National Children's Home and Welfare Society.

Development of State Programs

The first state department of welfare to develop foster home placement was in Massachusetts in 1863. Under this department newer and better programs of child care were sought than were provided by the almshouse and the indenture system. Through several years of experimentation it was found that the placing of dependent children in foster homes was a more satisfactory procedure in many of the cases than allowing them either to wander about the streets, to leave state institutions without aftercare, to live in almshouses, or to be placed under the older indenturing system. The state-administered program sought to incorporate the best of the values of The Children's Aid Society and the American Educational Society.

Other states followed the lead of Massachusetts in the establishment of state departments of public welfare. In 1899 New Jersey adopted a state policy which encouraged placement of dependent children in foster homes. In this case the state assumed responsibility for dependent children even to the extent of supplying funds to encourage boarding homes. Heretofore, the usual practice of both private and public agencies had been to place children in foster homes without involving an expenditure for the support of the child. New Jersey, in agreeing to supplement the resources of the family and the child's work by additional financial assistance, made a noteworthy innovation.

Pennsylvania did not assume quite the degree of responsibility that was characteristic of some other states. In that state there was a cooperative arrangement between the state and the Pennsylvania Children's Aid Society. The state contributed in certain ways and under certain circumstances, but the Society carried the responsibility of inquiry and contact with prospective foster homes, and arranged for supplementary financial support. The counties of the state also had a responsibility in the administration of this program.

Although private agencies still carry a large part of the responsibility in foster home placement, the state departments of public welfare currently maintain the states' responsibility for neglected and dependent children. The program of foster home placement has become so popular for state-administered child care that in some instances, such as in Michigan, the state uses only the foster home method of care. In some states the responsibility of the state departments is largely financial and administrative; the actual responsibility for carrying out foster home placement and supervision rests upon the counties. Ohio and Indiana are examples of this practice today. In a few states the responsibility is mutually shared by the private and the supporting public agencies. And, in a few states, there is no state responsibility. Here the placement of children is entirely dependent upon private agencies, if and where they exist. State programs in foster home placement usually tend to rely heavily upon local resources, while offering supplemental assistance only.

INSTITUTIONAL *VERSUS* FOSTER HOME CARE

In theory the foster home is a suitable environment for almost all neglected and dependent children. In actual practice, however, the foster home is utilized as a placement possibility for fairly definite types of children. The present feeling among workers in the child welfare field is a decided preference for foster home rather than for institutional care, unless special circumstances in individual cases determine otherwise. Of course, a child's own home is still more desirable as the first and best choice of locale for giving him aid when he has need for it. Social workers are currently of the opinion that there is not any genuinely satisfactory substitute for the original family life of the child. No foster home or institution can compare in benefit, all other things being equal, with the child's own home. In line with this belief, social workers first strive, whenever possible, to aid children in their own homes; or, if that is not feasible, to seek the construction or reconstruction of the child's natural home as quickly as possible. Yet in many cases it is not physically possible for the child to be with his parents; sometimes it is not advisable in terms of the child's welfare. The parents may be deceased or have deserted. They may be in prison or may be exerting an unhealthy influence upon the child. Or they may not be able to keep their children because of illness. So instead of being able or eager to keep all children with their families, social workers increasingly recognize that there are some children who cannot be cared for in this manner. For these there are essentially two choices: the foster home, or the institution. The foster home has taken precedence in the minds of many workers because of its more homelike qualities. (See Figure 19.)

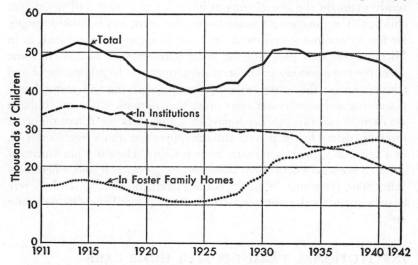

FIG. 19. Dependent and Neglected Children Under Foster Care in New York State, 1911 to 1942

(Howard W. Hopkirk, *Institutions Serving Children,* Russell Sage Foundation, New York, 1944.)

Personal Relationships

In the foster home the child can usually have closer familial relationships than in an institution. The belief now is that in order to grow into an integrated person a child must have close personal and affectional relationships. These are of more importance than any amount of hygiene, education, psychiatric care, etc.[1] This view has been responsible for the attitude of social caseworkers in this special field who believe that preschool children and babies should not be placed in institutions where it is almost impossible to give them this personal attention be-

[1]See Anna Freud and Dorothy T. Burlingham, *Infants Without Families,* International Universities Press, New York, 1944.

cause of the nature and size of the group. In the institution the child is perhaps but one of twenty who call their cottage parents "mother" and "father." He seldom has any kinship ties with the other children in the cottage or with the cottage parents. As much as the institution seeks to inculcate family habits in its cottage system, there are always the apparent differences between the institutional and the natural home setting.

The foster home, on the other hand, is by design suitable for more personal relationships between foster children and foster parents. There are seldom more than a few children in one foster home. The parents, while not "real" parents, can be more attentive to the children than cottage parents. In some situations, where the need for affection on the part of a child is especially great and where the therapy seems suitable, he may be placed in a foster home where he is the only child. Obviously, such an arrangement is not possible in an institution. Thus the parents in the foster home can offer more direct affection to a child than can be offered in an institution.

Institutional Adjustments

The community relationships of the foster child and the institutional child differ widely. For most institutional children there is a "mass" problem of adjusting to the community. The child in the institution makes really two "community" adjustments. The first is to the institutional community. In the case of some institutions the number of the members makes assimilation a fundamental problem. The institutional child, for example, not only has to adapt himself possibly to nineteen other children in his group, but also to the children in other cottages—in some instances a group of two or three hundred people. That is the first adjustment which the institutional child has to make.

The second is to the larger community—to the neighborhood, town, or city. Full participation in the life of the community may be hampered by the possibility that the child will be looked upon by community members as being "an institutional child." This means that a certain amount of stigma may rest upon him as an institutional ward. He may be pitied or distrusted by the larger community. He may, moreover, find it more difficult to fit in to school, church, and other institutions in the larger community. He may come in special garb to a public school, thus being pointed out especially as an institutional child. Instead of being able to play with the children of the larger community, he may be restricted in his athletic activities to institutional teams. There are other factors, too, which may make it difficult for the institutional child to find his place in the larger community.

There are some institutions, however, which permit rather wide community contacts on the part of their children. An example of this is provided in the "Albany Diary":

January, 1937. Many of our neighbors are helpful in educating our children in ordinary social amenities. There are invitations to birthday parties in the homes of school friends, Sunday dinners in such homes, and occasional visits after school. School friends are welcomed in our cottage, although more visiting of this sort would be desirable. Some of the older children have opportunities to earn money in the neighborhood. All these experiences help our children to find their way as individuals and to have that self-respect which comes with happy neighborhood life.

There are few runaways from the Home. The oldest children consider it silly for anyone to run away from a place where there is so much freedom. Last fall during the week of the World Series baseball games four boys ran away, taking with them a radio. In Tom Sawyer style they found their way to the river and were en route to an island hideout. The man from whom they took a boat without permission caught one of the boys and helped us find the others. One of the venturesome spirits later led two successive runaway parties which involved truancies from school. Finally, he was committed to an institution for delinquents where his school attendance will be more assured. He is the only child who in the years 1935 to 1937 has gone directly from the Home to such an institution.

On holidays, including Sundays, there is much visiting with relatives and friends. Dinner invitations from the relatives, Sunday school teachers, neighbors, and other friends usually are accepted. Most of the children have several opportunities each year to enjoy such hospitality in the homes and in the company of friends they like.

Membership in a radio club at Trinity Institute is a privilege enjoyed by several boys. School clubs have a generous representation from our girls and boys. In the elementary as well as the high schools our boys have opportunities to try for places on athletic teams. The oldest boy under our care was on the 1936 varsity football squad at Albany High School. He played in enough games to give him his letter. Another was on the Schuyler Junior High School football squad.

The Girl Scout and Boy Scout troops at the Home are encouraged to compete with other troops and to participate in community activities with other troops. Both of our troops have been well represented for several years at Camp Cogswell and Camp Hawley. From these experiences, girls and boys of scout age have learned to mingle happily with their peers and to acquire the resourcefulness and skills which both scout organizations encourage.

We are happy to emphasize this policy in our work—that children must learn from living.[2]

---

[2]An excerpt from the "Albany Diary," by Howard W. Hopkirk, as recorded in his *Institutions Serving Children,* Russell Sage Foundation, New York, 1944, pp. 225–226.

Foster Home Adjustments

The foster home child, on the other hand, is required to make adjustments of a somewhat different sort. He usually is not cut off as sharply from the community as some institutional children. Living himself in a private house, he has open to him the many possibilities presented to children everywhere who live in their own homes. If he wishes to join in recreational activities, he plays with the other children on his street or in the neighborhood. He may be able to attend sessions at the local "Y," but no one of necessity would be able to distinguish him in his pursuits from the child who lives with his own family. In attending school he is simply another child. He is not marked off formally or actually from the other children. On the whole he does not receive the social stigma which falls on the institutional child. Occasionally, there may be speculation about him, whence he came, what happened to his original family, or how he gets along with his foster parents, but the attitudes which go into such expressions are usually much less organized and direct than those pertaining to the institutional child. So in the foster child's relationships with the larger community he is not usually set apart in any way from the children who live with their own families.

Of importance to the value of foster home care also is the fact that the child within his foster home must adjust to fewer people. In one sense there is no "community," for there usually are only foster father and mother and possibly one or more children within the home. The adjustments for the foster child, therefore, are direct, primary, and informal. Thus it probably is easier for the foster child to adapt himself both to his home situation and to the community than it is for the institutional child to fit in to the institution and the larger community.

This description of the experience of the child in a foster home implies a much more homelike atmosphere. Thus, if it is not possible or desirable for a child to be or remain in his own home, a foster home placement is considered to be the next best location. Omitting exceptions, the institution is today generally looked upon as a means of treating only certain special types of child needs.

Actually, in the placement of children there is no easy rule for the social worker to use. All systems of classification, whether of children or agency services, fail because they are general. The specific child and his situation are everlastingly unique—different in many ways from all other cases. There is no easy way, therefore, of applying a simplified rule to the placement of children. Each child must be considered for what he is, and for what his situation reveals.

Evaluating Community Resources

The nature of the community resources also must be evaluated. The fact that the child's situation suggests a foster home as being most suitable for placement does not necessarily mean that the child can or should be placed in a foster home. Perhaps there are no suitable foster homes available in the community, and it would not be ultimately desirable to locate the child in a distant community because of possible interference with the later reconstruction of the child's own home. Perhaps there are foster homes available in the community, but none for the moment which would suitably meet the needs of the particular child. Again, the institutional facilities of the community may be of such marked quality that placement in an institution would be better than in an average foster home.

Parental Attitudes

Moreover, much depends upon the attitudes of the child's parents, if they are active in the placement. Perhaps they do not wish the child to live in a foster home for fear of parental competition. A case of this sort is clearly seen in the request of Mrs. "C" for the placement of her nine-year-old son:

Mrs. C had been having marital difficulty. Her husband had never maintained her or their son, David, adequately. Soon the family had to apply for relief. Mrs. C separated from her husband. Her dissatisfaction mounted until finally she decided that for her the solution lay in the placement of her child and a job for herself. Her ambivalence was clear at intake. She would find it difficult to see her child in the care of another mother. It was arranged, therefore, that she would not visit in the foster home for the first six months. Soon she was working as a practical nurse and was much happier.

David, however, was finding it difficult to take to the foster home. He seemed happy there but in the semimonthly visits with his mother at the office he was asking her when she would take him home. The placement worker in her interviews with the mother was supporting her decision to leave the child in placement, through reviewing with her the difficulties she had experienced before his placement. At the end of six months, the child was replaced in a permanent home, and the mother permitted to visit. She soon complained about the distance to the foster home, that the foster mother was not motherly enough and her children were unfriendly, and insisted on replacement. In several interviews she cried about the boy's begging her to take him home, and about her guilt in not doing it. When the boy questioned both mother and worker as to how long he would be placed, the worker was at a loss as to what to tell him, and the mother would say, "For a little while."

Mrs. C's criticism of the foster home and the requests for replacement made it clear to the caseworker that the problem lay in the mother's feeling of responsibility for the rearing of her child, but since the "diagnosis" had been that she could function best with her child away and since that seemed to be borne out by her very happy adjustment in her work, the worker decided to try to let the mother have some share in the rearing of her child through discussion as to what kind of a home she thought her child would be happy in. Mrs. C's prompt reply was, "I can't tell you; that's your job." She seemed clear that whereas her difficulty was around her feeling of responsibility for rearing her child, she could not solve that by taking over part of the agency function, in decisions about placement. She must decide whether she would take her child or would temporarily or permanently surrender her claim to rearing him. It became clear to the worker that the job was a solution to part of the mother's problem, but that the problem that led her to placing David was in her relationship to him; that her conflict was being projected on the question of type of home and the length of placement.

Now the worker was able to help Mrs. C face it more clearly. Mrs. C kept insisting that the child be moved to see if he could be happier elsewhere and stated that in the meantime she had applied for relief, adding laughingly, "I'll never get it on the terms I'm insisting upon." When the worker could accept that the mother was wanting and yet not wanting placement, and that it was all right for her to decide either way, she could then be firm that no other plan could be made for the boy until Mrs. C decided for how long she would want this service. Mrs. C soon agreed that that would have to be done, that her confusion was upsetting David, so that he could not really use the foster home. Finally she came to the decision that, having found work so satisfying, she would have to find a way of living with her boy that could allow her to go on with the job. This she did within a month, and the boy was discharged for a two months' trial period. At the end of that period, Mrs. C reported how happy she and David were and how much more grown up David had become.[3]

Deciding on Type of Placement

Perhaps the social worker's active espousal of the foster home as the most advantageous environment for children aside from their own homes may prejudice her habitually toward foster home placement for all children. At any rate, there is no easy, general way of determining which kind of placement or aid a child might need. Even in particular cases the decision for one type of service as against another cannot be made with ease.

Before a child is placed in a foster home, the social worker makes a

[3]Henrietta L. Gordon, "Discharge: An Integral Aspect of the Placement Process," *The Family* (now *Journal of Social Casework*), volume 22, number 2, April, 1941, p. 39.

detailed inquiry concerning the exact nature of the case. Placement is made on the basis of this investigation. In many ways the placement of a child in a foster home is more complex and difficult than the placement of a child in an institution, for the foster child must be placed in a home which will very closely and directly fit his needs. Although it is desirable that an institutional placement be made according to the needs of the child, the problem is usually of a more general character. In foster home placement *this* child must be placed in *this* family and *that* child in *that* family. While there may possibly be more than one family which could meet the needs of a particular child, the problem usually is that of making the closest possible approximations to ideal circumstances. Thus both the child and the foster home have to be examined in a most careful manner by the child welfare worker doing foster home placement.

But, more than the child and the foster home, the child's own parents need the close attention of the foster home worker. The following case of Mrs. "B" illustrates how a parent's motives may play a part in the desired placement of a child:

Mrs. B is an immature and sickly person who suffers acutely from competition with her 6-year-old son George. She speaks openly of her hatred for him and is actively cruel and punishing with him. George, at 6, is a highly anxious child who vacillates between depressions and destructive activity of a terrorizing nature. Day after day becomes a battle of wills and an outwitting of each other on the part of mother and son. Mrs. B asks for placement as the only way of keeping her sanity and as the means by which her suffering can be mitigated.

She is fairly intelligent, is able to acknowledge her hatred of George and her feeling of competition with him. To the caseworker she speaks of wanting to feel happier and to become different and she sees this as essential before the child can ever be returned to her. Mr. B, 20 years older than his wife, is fond of George and is willing to place him in order to have peace at home. Through the efforts of the caseworker Mrs. B voluntarily seeks the services of a psychiatrist for herself and seems eager for the forthcoming help. However, after a few interviews she refuses to continue, preferring her misery. She makes herself more and more sick so she will surely not have to take the child back home. To do so would mean giving up her competition with George and, back of this, her possessive love for her husband. Her desire to change "falls short." It was only possible on her own terms, those of an unconditional love from her husband. He must love no one but herself, not even their child.[4]

'Dorothy Hutchinson, "The Request for Placement Has Meaning." *The Family* (now *Journal of Social Casework*), volume 25, number 4, June, 1944, p. 129.

THE FOSTER HOME

Both the worker and the foster parents have their particular contributions to make to the child, and both are of equal importance. The foster mother has the day-by-day care; the worker helps both the foster mother and the child with their problems and difficulties. But in addition to the worker and the foster parents, there are other influences upon the life of the foster child, such as the quality of the community and the physical adequacy of the home. The social worker considers various factors in evaluating a foster home.

The Community

The social worker who wishes to place a child in a foster home must consider the quality of the community of which the foster home is a part. Obviously, it would not be desirable to place a child in a neighborhood noted for its ill effects upon human personality. The social worker also must consider with whom the foster child will play. Will his playmates be of the sort that would encourage delinquency on his part? What recreational facilities does the community offer? The size of the community also is a matter for consideration by the social worker. From materials readily available the social worker can know what the effects would be of placing a city child in the country and vice versa. The organization of the total mores in the community is significant, and different effects can be secured through placement in different communities.

Also of interest to the social worker are the schools available to the child. Will the child be placed in a community where the teachers will cooperate with the home and with the social worker in solving problems connected with the child's adjustment to the school? Does the community feature special trade schools which might be valuable for the educational training of the child? How far are the schools from the foster home?

Similar questions might arise in regard to churches. Is there a church of the child's faith? How interested and helpful would the minister be? What facilities for recreation and education do the churches offer?

Again, the social worker must be interested in the economic standing of the community. It is not considered suitable for a child to be placed in an environment where the economic advantages would be smaller or markedly greater than those he previously enjoyed. To introduce a very poor child into a very wealthy community would create problems for the child which he did not have before. The reverse is also true. In some cases, however, it may be possible and desirable to introduce a child into a neighborhood with somewhat better living standards than those to which he was accustomed. Through such means the worker may be able to increase the amount of economic advantage and emotional security the child may have and may need.

The Home

While the quality of the community is a primary consideration for the worker in the placement of children in foster homes, the quality of the home itself can be of no less significance. To begin with, the very physical facilities of the home are important. The child should have his own bedroom. He should be in a home which is spacious enough to provide him with indoor play opportunities. The home should have sufficient windows to allow for proper light and ventilation. The ordinary safeguards of sanitation should be required. There should also be no pronounced dangers in the construction of the house which might prove to be fire or accident hazards.

The Foster Parents

Quality. Without a doubt it is the foster parents themselves who are the most important factor in any foster home placement. The community is important, as are the physical and intellectual qualities of the home, but these are superficial by comparison with the first value, namely, the quality of the foster parents. In this regard, placement workers look for two things. First of all, they look for a healthy relationship between husband and wife and their own children. This sets the pattern for family response on the part of the foster child and establishes standards which are quickly imitated by him. Secondly, foster parents are sought who have a real interest in and a feeling for children. The child placed in a foster home requires sensitive understanding and affection. If the foster parents are genuinely concerned about the well-being of the child and give him such attention, he will be able to achieve those patterns of personality development which are basic to an integrated life and are the goal of foster home placement.

Motives. In this connection the motives of the foster parents in accepting a child into their home need to be considered. The question "For what reasons did the foster parents really choose to have a foster child?" must be raised. To this question the foster parents should be able to give an answer which is true and which is satisfactory to themselves as well as to the social worker. Unhealthy motives, even if naively held as being altruistic by the foster parents, should put the worker on his guard about the efficacy of the arrangement. Motives are held suspect by most workers if they seem to relate only to values the prospective foster parents wish to derive for themselves from having foster children. Moreover, when a large element of financial motivation is undoubtedly present, the social worker is sharply reminded that the foster home arrangement is not exactly a business enterprise, at least not at its best. One of the hardest tasks, and yet one of the most necessary, which the child welfare worker has is that of refusing to accept people who would like to be foster parents. Sometimes the refusal can be turned by the worker into a means of referring an applicant to other social work agencies able to aid him with his personal problems.

The following comments by a placement worker indicate the complexity of motivation some placements entail. The couple mentioned applied for a child of five or six years of age to board as a "companion" for their own child:

Mr. J took the initiative in applying for a foster child. He evidently has considerable drive to achieve, has continued his education through college and partly through a law course by attending night school. His desire for a foster child is possibly motivated by his identification with Tommy and his need for him to achieve. He seems to think a foster child would help mold T into the kind of child he thinks he should be in contrast to what he sees T to be now—an only child "spoiled" by indulgent parents. Mr. J also shows a need to be an adequate father. Actually, he gives a lot of evidence of being very insecure and of lacking warmth for children and understanding of them. It is possible that he is resentful of T because the latter's birth terminated his law studies, at least temporarily, due to a reduction in the family income when Mrs. J had to stop work.

Mrs. J appears to be a better integrated person than Mr. J and has some positive qualifications in her relationship with children, but they seem insufficient to balance the negative as shown in her relationship with Tommy. She is overprotective of him, indicates a need to keep him a baby, and an inability to place any limitation on his behavior. She is inflexible in her requirements of the agency, and there is some evidence that basically she does not want a foster child but needs to have the application approved in order to maintain her status, particularly with Mr. J. She shows total inability to identify with a foster child. She is ambitious, too, and there are indications she may be resentful of T because his birth has delayed Mr. J's completion of law school and probably terminated permanently her plan of getting a college education herself after Mr. J finishes.[5]

Age. The age of the foster parents is also a factor to consider. For many children the finest kind of parental relationship may be possible

---

[5]Dorothy Hutchinson, *In Quest of Foster Parents: A Point of View on Homefinding,* Columbia University Press, New York, 1943, p. 15.

if the ages of the foster parents correspond roughly to the ages of their own parents. Ordinarily, elderly foster parents are not too satisfactory. They may not understand the ways of children; they may spoil them; they may be irritated by them; they may not be able to establish and maintain desirable personal relationships. On the other hand elderly foster parents are not always undesirable. Their use depends upon the child, his age, and situation, as well as on the foster parents themselves. Frequently, children need grandparents more than they need parents, and there are elderly people, 55 to 60, who are still vigorous and young in spirit.

Religion. The foster parents should be of the same religious faith as the child. This aids the child in his adjustment to the home and provides the foster parents with a means of abetting the moral growth of the child.

Health. The parents should be possessed of reasonably good health. Communicable diseases or chronic illness would be highly detrimental to the proper care of a child and would possibly have an adverse effect on the child's physical and mental health.

Education. The educational achievements of the parents need to be noted, chiefly to guard against the child's not being able to receive parental support in his intellectual strivings.

Analysis of Foster Home

The following detailed report provides in summary fashion a description of the social worker's analysis of a foster home—in this case a "wage home." While wage homes are being used less and less, the description does serve to point out the aspects of the foster home which are of concern to the worker in child placement:

THE FOSTER HOME

Family. Carl E. Harrington, 29; Grace (Saunders) Harrington, 27; Ruth, 6; George, 3; Mary, 1.

Community. The community is a residential suburb of Boston, developed during the past seven or eight years from an area of extensive farms. Substantial single houses have been built and into them have moved people of moderate means who are for the most part young and enthusiastic, with the result that there is evidence of a splendid community spirit.

All the town schools have a high academic rating and an excellent teaching staff. The junior high school contains many groups interested in nature study, reading, dramatics, etc.

attitude. She doesn't intend to have her do more than she is able to do, but will insist upon her doing what she does efficiently and wishes for a girl who will above everything else be willing. The visitor believes that the atmosphere and relationships in this home are ideal. Mr. and Mrs. Harrington spoke with great affection of each other and seem to have a real understanding. They have a large group of friends and are cordial and hospitable. They are devoted to their children and seem perfectly congenial and happy.

Both Mr. and Mrs. Harrington attend the Methodist Church regularly.

Children. Little George was playing outdoors during most of the visitor's call, but his mother asked him to come in for a few moments. He is rosy cheeked, robust, healthy, and quite large for his age. The older child, Ruth, came home from kindergarten just before the visitor left. When introduced to the visitor she shook hands politely and withdrew from the room as soon as she could. The children appeared to be obedient and well trained. Mrs. Harrington discussed her methods of caring for the baby, who is being brought up under the supervision of a pediatrician. She appears to have a thorough understanding of infant care and to follow directions scrupulously. Her theories about the training and discipline of the older children are excellent, but whether or not she is able to carry them out the visitor does not know.

Health. All the members of the family are in good health. The children seldom have even a cold. Mr. Harrington is the picture of health, and the fact that he does much outdoor work keeps him in good condition. Mrs. Harrington says that she is well and she appears to have an abundance of energy.

Finances. The Harringtons have every appearance of having an adequate income in spite of Mr. Harrington's temporary unemployment. They both come from families of means. They own their own house and evidently live comfortably.

Interests. Both Mr. and Mrs. Harrington have broad interests. At the present time their chief concern is their home and their children. They belong to few clubs, etc., but entertain frequently. They have an active connection with their college groups. Mr. Harrington is doing scout work at present and is interested in recreation for boys. He devotes a great deal of time and thought to his own children. Both Mr. and Mrs. Harrington read widely and are well informed.

Type of Girl Wanted. The Harringtons wish a girl to help in the home primarily because they need assistance, but in return they expect to give a girl a real home and to share generously with her. At the present time they feel that they cannot do a great deal for a girl financially, but believe that the advantages of their home life may compensate for this lack. They can pay $4 a week, and hope that during the summer they will be able to increase this. The summer plans for the family are not definite. They will probably take a cottage at the seashore. In this case they would like very much to take the girl with them. Above everything else, they want a girl who can be depended upon.

ANALYSIS OF HOME

Assets	Liabilities
Very intelligent foster parents with a great deal of background and education who are socially minded and see what the agency is trying to do for its girls.	Question of Mr. Harrington's temporary unemployment. This is not a real problem at the present time, but might become so if prolonged.
A home which is simple in its appointments, but which has an atmosphere of refinement and culture that is real.	Inability to pay girl adequately while Mr. Harrington is unemployed.
Foster parents well adjusted in their personal relationships, not limited in their social contacts, and will share their home life with Children's Aid Association girl and make her a member of the family.	Mrs. Harrington gives the impression of being somewhat timid and perhaps less resourceful than her husband. She may not be able to analyze the girl and her problems.
Foster father who is coopera tive and who takes as much inter est and responsibility as does fos ter mother in working out a plan.	

REFERENCES

Dr. L. H. Brown, Family Physician. Dr. Brown is a busy, serious, efficient, middle-aged physician with a strong personality. He says that physically there is nothing wrong with the family. There is no chronic, contagious, or communicable disease. Mr. and Mrs. Harrington are reliable, refined people. Their home is happy and efficient. Any child or older girl placed here would be taken in as a member of the family group. They would both be patient and understanding with an adolescent girl. The children in the family are happy and normal. Dr. Brown added, "This in itself is enough of a recommendation."

Mrs. Arthur I. Clough, a Neighbor. Talked with Mrs. Clough, a refined person who stated that the Harringtons are excellent people in every respect. Mrs. Clough knows nothing about the intimate family life, but feels sure there is no question about it. Both Mr. and Mrs. Harrington have had many advantages. Mrs. Clough does not hesitate to recommend the home. She speaks of the children as being beautifully brought up.

Mrs. Thomas Gordon, a Neighbor. Mrs. Gordon, an acquaintance of the visitor, is a most interesting matron, who was very happy to give her recommendation of this home. She grew up with Mrs. Harrington. Both families lived in New Hampshire at the time, and she and Mrs. Harrington went through school together. "She is one of the finest girls I have ever known," she said, "very capable and has a splendid mind." Her family is one of the "Four Hundred" in her home town. Mr. and Mrs. Harrington are well suited to each other and their life is congenial. The Association is fortunate in having this kind of home for an older girl.

Mrs. Carleton Dodge, a Neighbor. Visitor talked with Mrs. Dodge. She is a charming woman, refined, intelligent and conservative. Is probably a person who has always lived in an environment of culture. Was cautious in her statements, and yet gave a most enthusiastic recommendation. The Dodges have known Mr. Harrington since he came East. He is almost like a son to them. Mrs. Dodge said that of all the homes which she knows intimately, this is about the finest one. Mr. and Mrs. Harrington are well suited to each other and their home life is happy and congenial. Their interests are similar. They have three lovely children. Mrs. Dodge speaks particularly about how sane they are in solving their problems. Both of them are equal to handling an older girl. Mr. Harrington has had vast experience with young people, principally with boys, but Mrs. Dodge feels sure that he would show the same good judgment in dealing with any young person. Mr. Harrington comes from a very fine family, all the members of which are engaged in worth-while enterprises. If the right girl is placed, she will have the advantage of real home life. Mrs. Dodge has no way of knowing how much Mrs. Harrington would expect of a girl, but feels sure she would not impose upon her.

Mrs. Charles M. Cook, a Neighbor. Mrs. Cook is a young person about Mrs. Harrington's age. She speaks very highly of Mrs. Harrington, who she feels is a rather unusual person. Mrs. Cook says that the children are being brought up very nicely. Mrs. Harrington is not a gadder. Her home responsibilities come first. As far as Mrs. Cook knows, there is a united, happy atmosphere in the home. The family and all their relations have many good times together. Both Mr. and Mrs. Harrington would have a good understanding of young people and would, she feels sure, deal with firmness, but fairness. She has always made the girls who have worked for her members of the family and given them a feeling of freedom in her home. However, she would expect them to do their part. Both she and Mr. Harrington are well balanced. They are responsible, sensible people. They have had many advantages and yet would not look down on a girl who had had less than they. Everyone in the community likes the Harringtons very much and Mrs. Cook feels safe in recommending them unreservedly.

Other equally favorable references were obtained.[6]

[6]Edith M. H. Baylor and Elio D. Monachesi, *The Rehabilitation of Children: The Theory and Practice of Child Placement,* Harper and Brothers, New York, 1939, pp. 202–208

RELATIONSHIPS BETWEEN AGENCY, CHILD, PARENTS, AND FOSTER PARENTS

After applicants are accepted as foster parents, there are at present three general types of relationships which can be set up between the agency, the child, the parents, and the foster parents.

Boarding Basis

The child may be placed on a *boarding basis*. In this relationship the child is expected to do certain small tasks about the house, but this work is not intended as a means of paying for the care granted by the

Table 8

AN ITEMIZED GUIDE FOR BOARD RATES TO FOSTER PARENTS

(Based on Estimated Costs and Present Practice of Placement Agencies)

	Monthly Costs		
		Boys and Girls	
	Infants to 5 years	6 to 12 years	13 years and over
Based on estimates of the New York Budget Council:			
Food	$14.00	$18.50	$22.50
Gas and electricity	1.00	1.00	1.00
Cleaning supplies and household replacements	1.90	1.90	1.90
Medicine chest supplies	.25	.25	.25
Laundry	1.50	1.50	1.50
Based on agency experience:			
Rent including heat	10.00	10.00	10.00
Personal incidentals	1.00	1.00	1.00
Social and educational activities	.50	.75	1.00
Service	11.00	6.00	6.00
Total, regular rate monthly	$41.15*	$40.90	$45.15

*An extra allowance of $5.00 a month is recommended for infants, some preschool children, physically handicapped and seriously emotionally disturbed children, and for those in temporary care.

Source: *Final Report of the Committee on Relationships With Public Departments of the Standing Committee on Welfare and Health Services,* Welfare Council of New York City, New York, February, 1946, p. 9.

foster parents. Under this arrangement the child's parents, relatives, or the agency—singly or together—contribute toward the upkeep of the child. The foster parents are asked actually to supply no financial assistance except that which is indirectly expressed, such as the ownership of a home or the possession of house furnishings. Usually, the foster parents are given money on a budgeted basis which is planned as being adequate for the child's needs. (See Tables 8 and 9.) The foster parents are not paid for the service they render; only the additional expense incurred by having the child in the home is considered. This type of foster home relationship is probably the most popular and the most used.

The new idea, however, is that foster parents really do a big job and should be paid for actual service rendered over and above what it costs them to take a child. This paying for service is still slight, but the trend in the field is in that direction.

Usually, an agency will rely as much as possible upon the financial resources of the child's parents for his support in the foster home. This procedure oftentimes enables the parents and relatives to continue their responsibility and possibly their attention and interest. It gives the placing agency an opportunity of controlling the foster home, because the foster parents are paid through the agency. It places the whole relationship on a business basis which was not possible under the former

Table 9

PER CAPITA COSTS OF FOSTER CARE SERVICE: CASEWORK AND
ADMINISTRATION, 1944

	Agency A		Agency B		Agency C		Agency D	
	Amount	Per cent	Amount	Per cent	Amount	Per cent	Amount	Per cent
Casework salaries	$ 59.86	57.8	$ 91.25	42.9	$101.11	44.1	$144.18	47.0
Other salaries and pensions	28.11	27.1	70.08	33.0	88.33	38.5	86.14	28.1
Total salary cost	87.97	84.9	161.33	75.9	189.44	82.6	230.32	75.1
Operation of office	15.33	14.8	26.28	12.4	25.18	11.0	38.32	12.5
Other expenses	0.36	0.3	24.82	11.7	14.60	6.4	37.96	12.4
Total	$103.66	100.0	$212.43	100.0	$229.22	100.0	$306.60	100.0

Source: Same, p. 28, as Table 8.

indenture system. On this basis the foster parents are supposed to feel that they are being aided by the agency and that they have a responsibility to the agency and to the child. Moreover, while the amount of money paid can never be taken as full payment for the care of the foster child, it does enable the foster parents to provide otherwise unobtainable benefits. There are dangers, however, where foster parents have no other incentive than a financial one.

The Wage Home

Another type of relationship which may be set up between the child, the agency, the parents, and the foster parents is that of the *wage home*. In this type of arrangement the child is placed in a foster home where he is to pay by his work for the services and benefits the foster parents provide. The agency, the parents, and relatives are not expected to contribute toward the support of the child, although exceptions in degree are made. Fortunately, this setup is no longer widely used. Often, these foster parents are simply looking for cheap maid service. The wage home may place too great a strain upon the child by making him essentially dependent upon himself through his work. He may not be able to assume this responsibility without also developing personal problems of an emotional character. He may not actually be able always to earn enough to keep himself on a paying basis with the foster parents. This arrangement, furthermore, removes considerable responsibility from the agency and from the parents and relatives. It means that the parents may not maintain as deep a concern for the child as they otherwise might. The agency, too, will lose a valuable tool for controlling the foster home situation. It is advantageous, however, where the parents cannot pay for the support of the child, where the agency does not have funds to support the child, and where the child is quite capable of caring for himself. In regard to the last, there is still a modest place for the wage home in relation to adolescent girls who wish to take on domestic responsibilities as a job and who need a protective setting, but there are not too many of these.

The Free Home

Finally, the agency, the child, the parents, and the foster parents may create a relationship in which the agency and the parents are not expected to pay for the upkeep of the child and in which the child himself is not expected to work, except at small household tasks. The cost of maintenance is borne by the foster parents. This type is known as the *free home*.[7] This arrangement relies too heavily on the philanthropic

[7]Adoptive homes will be discussed later in the chapter.

impulses of the foster parents, since it permits them to assume the whole financial burden. It may lead to undesirable emotional developments on the part of the parents. It again removes responsibility from the agency and from the parents. It places the child in a position where he is the recipient of charity. It has the obvious merits of relieving the agency, the parents, and the child from financial responsibility.

THE CHILD DURING FOSTER HOME PLACEMENT

While a large part of the activities of the social worker in foster home placement centers in the operations attached to getting the child properly placed, nevertheless the social worker is also interested in and responsible for the actual adjustment of the child to his new home situation. The demands of the adjustment may be such that the child is unable to orient himself smoothly. Placement may create social and emotional problems which previously did not exist for the child. Thus in one case a child began to wet his bed during his first night in a foster home, a practice he had not evidenced previously. While such a development may be viewed as only a "practical" problem by the foster parents, it is not so with the social worker, who realizes that such behavior may have significant emotional roots and consequences for the child.

One of the tasks of the social worker is to interpret the child's conduct to the foster parents. This means that the social worker plans with the foster parents regarding their approach to the child and his problems. In regard to enuresis, for example, possible questions might be: What does it mean to the child? Is such behavior a subject for discipline? If so, what kind of discipline? What is meant by that term? What is hoped to be accomplished by whatever is done? Will any given procedure help or hinder the child in his desire to conquer his enuresis? Does the child wish to conquer it? Does it make him feel guilty? To what experience is the guilt attached? So, conferences of the social worker and foster parents may be needed to meet the problems which the foster parents do not feel entirely qualified to handle. These problems range widely in category and depth.

The foster parents themselves always need the understanding of the placement worker. The ability of foster parents to handle children may vary with the child, as is pointed out in the following case:

Following study, the Parker home was approved for the use of an adolescent boy. The Parkers, whose own children had recently married and left the home, were persons with real warmth and a genuine interest in children, but it was believed that they had not had experience that could be expected to fit them for dealing with particularly difficult children. At the time the study was completed, it became necessary to find a home for Jack, a boy whose difficult behavior had so upset his foster parents that they felt they could no longer continue his care and had at last asked for his immediate removal.

The agency's only choices at the time were of placing him in an already crowded home or of placing him with the Parkers, and the latter plan was decided upon. As had been the case in previous placements, Jack appeared to get along well at first but soon his difficulties were again expressed overtly. He became destructive in the home and stole several valuable articles. The worker was able to work very closely with the family and give much help, but the situation exploded when Jack encouraged a girl neighbor to steal money with him from a store and both children were apprehended by the police.

Before Jack's placement with the Parkers, a preplacement visit had been made by the worker, who attempted to prepare them for Jack's difficulties; but the Parkers had not had any previous experience with foster children and were not able to accept this behavior. Jack had had several replacements up to this time and the worker knew well that his problems had been aggravated each time he was again uprooted; she became so identified with him that she was unable to see the situation of the foster parents and recommended the immediate disapproval of the home of these foster parents who had "no understanding of children whatsoever." In her preplacement visit and in her contacts in the foster home during the first months of the placement, the worker had been enthusiastic about the foster parents' "way with Jack," but when the foster parents revealed their inexperience in the face of his difficult behavior, the worker, in her concern for the boy, appeared to lose sight altogether of the foster parents' needs.

Later, when the situation was discussed in conference and the home was re-evaluated, the worker was able to observe the case more objectively; and then she could recognize the positive qualities in the home as well as its possibilities for the kind of child for whom it had originally been recommended. There were found to be many assets in the home when it was used for such a child, and later placements were much more successful.[8]

The social worker also acts as a liaison between the child and his actual parents, if they are in any measure still in the picture. The child within the foster home may develop a conflict of interest between his foster parents and his real parents. In such a situation the social worker tries to interpret the child, the parents, the foster parents—each to the

[8]Connie Fish, "Maintaining Foster Homes," in *Some Practices in Home-Finding,* Child Welfare League of America, New York, 1942, 2d edition, pp. 31-32.

other—and in all these relationships the function of the agency. The interpretation may involve general attitudes, feelings of dependency, possessive inclinations, guilt responses. It may also involve less theoretical and emotional (yet derivative) concerns; such as, how often will the child see his parents?

AFTERCARE

Permanent placement is not usually sought for foster children. For them there is some possibility of their own homes being reconstructed so that they may again live with their families. The child welfare worker plays a part in the development of this possibility, and from this angle may be regarded as being something of a family caseworker. He also has the responsibility for the transfer of the child from the foster home to the original home. In this work the processes of placement are somewhat reversed, that is, the child is again to be placed, this time in his own home. The discharge of the child from the foster home rests upon the proper investigation of the child's own home in order to establish the suitability of such action. The social worker is also concerned with the social and emotional problems which may accompany the transfer. Many of the problems encountered by the child in adjusting to his foster home may reappear when he is returned to his own home. Indeed, the new placement may revive certain problems which the child had before he was placed in the foster home and may, in addition, create new problems which were not present either in the foster home or in his own home previously. On top of this the social worker is aware of the problems of adjustment to the community the child has to make in returning to his own home. Here the questions of the quality of the schools, churches, recreational facilities, and so forth, may all be revived but in a changed context.

Sometimes a foster child is unable to return to his own home and may achieve such a relationship with his foster parents that they will in effect adopt him. The case of "Harry" suggests this course and some of its difficulties:

When Harry, a bright, attractive youngster, was placed at the age of ten, it was clear that he would need foster care "forever," since he had no parents and was not eligible for adoption. The home chosen was that of a family financially comfortable. The foster parents both expressed a desire for a child who could become a member of their family. They had only two sons and had always wanted a larger family. Soon the foster mother was telling with pride that Harry was taken for one of her children; there was such a close relationship. The foster parents both talked about how gladly they would help him through college should he be interested. The foster mother made demands on the agency for all the boy's special needs, while she was supplying him with many luxuries of her own. Fearing the boy might feel deprived or discriminated against, the agency continued for seven years to carry full responsibility. Distressed about its implications, but because of her feeling for the boy, the worker, whenever possible, met all requests for additional clothing, carfare, and incidentals.

Naturally, Harry knew of all these discussions. How he felt about them can only be conjectured. He knew also of the foster mother's deep concern about him. As he grew older, she would not let him work summers; he needed a vacation, she thought, as did her children. When the boy was approaching his eighteenth birthday, the foster mother was told there would be no more funds for Harry, except for a partial scholarship for a short period. This was the first attempt to clarify what obligations are imposed in taking a child on such a basis. Experience had taught the foster mother that persistence was fruitful but the worker stood firmly on the reality that there was no money. Harry expressed some concern about how the foster mother felt about the matter though he knew he would in any event remain in the home. Soon the foster mother realized her persistence was of no avail. Her whole attitude changed and her husband confirmed her feeling. Of course this boy was a part of her family, no matter what the partial scholarship would amount to. There was no question about it; Harry would continue his schooling. For the first time it was made clear to the boy, too, what he really meant to the family.[9]

Earning a Living

Another concern of the social worker is the discharge of the child from the foster home to make his own way socially and economically in the community. The primary reason for such discharge is that of age. Agencies commonly have an age limit, usually 16 or 18, applied to the children they support. If it is impossible or inadvisable for the child to return at this time to his own family and either the foster home no longer wishes to keep him or he does not want to be kept by the foster parents, the social worker is faced with the problem of aiding the child to adapt himself on a more or less adult basis to the larger community.

Prior to such discharge the subject of vocational training and opportunities should be discussed realistically and thoroughly. The child may need help in finding employment; in his employment, at least initially, he may need counseling. Furthermore, if he has to establish his own living quarters, he may want advice on such matters as location and rent.

[9]Henrietta L. Gordon, "Discharge: An Integral Aspect of the Placement Process," *The Family* (now *Journal of Social Casework*), volume 22, number 2, April, 1941, p. 41.

Social Adjustments

Beyond these considerations there are the problems which are attached to the social adjustment of the person in the community. How will he meet persons who might become his friends? What standards should one have in regard to personal relationships? How should one spend money? How should one secure additional education or training, if these are desired? These and other questions suggest the counseling relationships which may be set up by the social worker and the person who is leaving a foster home to make his own way, economically and socially, in the outside world.

In all regards the primary purpose of the social worker in discharge is to make possible a positive and satisfying adjustment of the foster child to the community, whatever the circumstances and problems may be.

ADOPTION

Procedures of Placement

The procedure of adoptive placement is similar to that of foster home placement. Many of the same problems exist. The investigation involved is usually more intensive, however, because placement for adoption looks toward a permanent arrangement. Since the arrangement is to be permanent, the social worker is happy that many states prohibit would-be parents from adopting children before they have had them in their homes on a foster home basis for a period of six months to a year. It is increasingly apparent that such a span of time is necessary in order to protect both the child and the adopting parents from various misconceptions and problems which might otherwise be disastrous for the adoption relationship. This is true largely because, in adoption, the legal aspects are so prominent. Once the child is legally adopted, the foster parents have all the legal rights of the real parents, and the agency withdraws. Therefore, the initial placement of the child in a home for six months to a year can provide all concerned with a trial period in which compatibility can be tested.

In adoption, the child's surname is changed legally to that of the adopting parents. In foster home placements this is not done, although sometimes the child does change his name for the sake of convenience, but not legally. Some states permit the adopted child's new name to be entered even upon a birth certificate and other papers in order to erase any discrepancies which may appear between the adopted name and the birth name.

Illegal Activities

The adoptive cases chiefly concern very young children, often those of unmarried mothers. Illegitimate children are liable to all sorts of harmful and illegal schemes of adoption. Although many states have taken active measures to curb such activity, certainly not enough has yet been done. Unlawful schemes flourish for several reasons. On one hand the unmarried mother, because of her situation, may wish to have her child adopted as quickly as possible after its birth and surely without any publicity. On the other hand there are many persons who would like to adopt children but cannot qualify under the terms laid down by professionally run agencies. These people oftentimes are willing to go to extremes in their efforts to have an adopted child. The fact that many of them are willing to pay to have a child given them is sufficient grounds for numerous rackets in the handling of illegitimate children. While there are difficulties in the way of detecting many of the cases of "black-market babies," the states probably could and should take vigorous steps to crush out this type of adoptive practice. A couple desirous of having an adopted child also should realize that if they are not eligible, as judged by the standards of a professionally operated agency, they should very seriously reconsider their decision to adopt. Likewise, an unmarried mother who has a genuine interest in the future welfare of her child should plan to contact a professional agency, whose placement procedures are personally and socially desirable. Of course, no agency would seek to create a problem for an unmarried mother, such as unwelcome publicity or exorbitant fee-charging.

Problems of an Unmarried Mother

It is not always easy for an unmarried mother to bring her problem to an adoptive agency. Usually, there is considerable questioning on her part as to the requirements the agency might make of her, her child, and the child's father. Receiving assistance is often not a pleasurable experience, despite the fact that it may be greatly desired. The following account of an application by an unmarried mother makes this point clear:

3–13–40. Miss D is in the office. She is not a particularly well-groomed girl and has a sullen, unhappy expression most of the time. When she came into the room, she started to take off her gloves, and consumed almost five minutes at this. She worked very slowly and deliberately and finally remarked that she guessed her hands were wet when she put them on, as the gloves did not come off easily. When she finally sat down, she looked so uncomfortable that I suggested that she remove her coat, and she replied that it was hot, and proceeded to get up again and take off her coat. There was no urgency in any of her movements and I felt that she was purposely delaying getting into the interview.

I said that Miss K of the Maternity House had phoned that she wanted to talk about a plan of adoption for her baby, but I did not know how much she had explained to Miss D about the way we worked. She answered in a tone of finality that Miss K had told her nothing at all. She did volunteer that she did not know just when she would be leaving the House. The rule was that a girl who was going to keep her baby could leave at the end of two months, but a girl who wanted to place her baby must stay the full three months. I said that I had not known about that rule. She remarked with a good deal of bitterness, "I can't make out myself just how it works, because I have certainly known some girls who have left before that time, even though they were going to give their babies for adoption. I guess it just depends on how Miss K and the Board feel." I agreed that I had known of some girls whose babies had come to us at a very early age because of some special situation which made it important for the mothers to get home. She said yes, she knew about these, too, but there were others who left for no good reason that she could find out.

I then turned the conversation to a discussion of her own plans. I said that we can arrange for placement of a baby, first in a boarding home, and later for adoption, if that is what the mother wants. I described the temporary foster home care as a period of observation which we wanted to have before a permanent plan is made. That gives us a chance to know the baby, and it also gives the mother time to find out whether placement for adoption is the thing she really wants or whether when she gets back into the community she may work out some different solution. She said she had thought a lot about taking the baby home, and if something turned up so that she got a really good job, she would consider it. However, that didn't seem likely and she thought it probably would be adoption. Her people have expressed a willingness to have her bring the baby home if that is what she wants to do, but she does not think that will be the right thing. Really they are too old to take on a baby. Her mother is 52 and her father 49! I asked her how the baby would be received in the neighborhood, and she answered quickly, "That is another thing, she wouldn't be received at all. There are some children like that who have come back home, and I can see how other children treat them on the street."

She has one married sister, though, who has no children and has brought up the possibility of adoption of her baby; but her brother-in-law doesn't have a permanent job. She added immediately, "I don't suppose you would approve of her going to my sister anyway." I said I didn't know what we would think; that really wouldn't be up to us. How did she feel? She said there were some things she liked about it and some things she didn't. She really didn't know at this point just how she did feel. She did know one thing, however, if she decided to keep the baby, it would mean actually taking her herself, not placing her in a boarding home. She has seen so many girls come back to the home whose babies were being boarded and she thought it was an awfully unsatisfactory plan. They didn't seem like real mothers to the babies, and for her own part she didn't think anybody got very much out of that kind of an arrangement.

She has a teacher's certificate, but she definitely has no interest in teaching. A period of practice teaching was enough to convince her of that. What she would really like would be to take a technician's course, but she will not know about that until she sees her family.

I said that we would have to discuss arrangements for the baby's board if she wishes to place her. The temporary placement would cost six dollars a week, and our budget was planned on the expectation that the parent would reimburse us for the major part of this. We tried to make some adjustment according to the mother's ability to pay. She said she knew that payment would be necessary, but until she goes home she cannot make any definite plans.

I realized at this point that she really wanted to include the father of the baby in the plans, and asked her about him. She said at once that she wanted to see him when she goes home. She has already talked to him, but it has been very unsatisfactory. She really thinks he won't do much, as he knows that it would be just as painful publicity for her as for him if she were to bring action against him. He is very much pampered at home, and can do everything just the way he wants to. She showed great bitterness toward him. When I mentioned the fact that we wanted to know about the father's family, she said that she would try to get all that information from him. She hopes to see him when she is home this time, but in all probability won't be seeing him afterwards. She seemed to have no confidence that she would be able to get help from him.

She spoke with real feeling about the baby. At the same time, I got the impression that she was able to take no real pleasure in her, as she is so uncomfortable both in her present situation and in her relation to the father. I asked her whether she had expected to visit the baby during the temporary placement. She wasn't sure—if she stayed in Philadelphia, she thought she would want to. I explained that we had definite arrangements for visiting—once a week, not in the evening, and with the understanding that the mother could not take the baby away from the foster home. That seemed all right to her, and I had the feeling that she actually did not expect to be visiting at all.

(She certainly does not have the pleasant feeling about her stay in the maternity home which most of the girls express, but I did not gather that there were any specific reasons for her dislike of the place.) She did seem quite free in talking about her feeling before the interview was over—it was almost impossible to terminate the interview, and when she finally rose to leave, she spoke with more spontaneity than she had shown at any other time, thanking me with real cordiality for seeing her and talking these things over with her. She agreed to get in touch with us again after her visit home. Then she would know whether she really wanted placement, and how she could meet payment of the board.

Before leaving the office, she took at least five more minutes to put on her gloves, working in the same unhurried, almost trance-like way, that she had done at the beginning.[10]

The social worker, in the case of adoption, gives the same kind of attention to the process as is given to foster home placement. After the child is legally adopted the services of the social worker are reduced or abandoned entirely. This does not necessarily mean an abrupt break in the relationship, but rather that the services of the social worker should no longer be required unless unusual circumstances arise.

FOSTER DAY CARE

The type of foster home placement discussed so far has assumed that children are placed for complete and possibly long-term foster family care. There is another kind of foster home placement based on day-by-day relations between children and foster homes. For this reason alone it is often termed "foster day care." Under this type of arrangement a child is placed in a foster home during the daytime with the expectation that his relationships with his own home will not otherwise be broken. Foster day care is suitable in cases where the mother must for one reason or another be out of the home during the day.

Responsibility of Parents

Naturally, this arrangement places greater responsibility upon the parents of children than upon the foster parents. It means that a parent must be so concerned with his child that he shall not want to be separated more or less permanently from him. This emotional fact in itself is significant. The social worker must take it into account in such ways that the parent will not feel that he is genuinely competing with the foster day parents, but that he has the primary obligation toward the child. It also means that the parent will usually contribute much more to the actual care of the child than under the regular foster home plan. The mother, for example, must get the child up in the morning, dress

[10]Mary Frances Smith, "The Case Work Process With the Parent as a Factor in the Adoption Decision," in *Adoption Practice: Case Work With Parent, Child, and Foster Parents,* Child Welfare League of America, New York, 1941, pp. 39–40.

him, feed him, and provide other attention in the early hours, preparatory to the child's going to the foster day parents. If the mother works, this additional morning burden may be noticeable. Likewise, at the end of the day the common parental care must be shown the child. The psychological need for the child must in some manner outweigh these added obligations.

Advantages and Disadvantages

From this discussion it is evident that the day placement of a child in a foster home has certain handicaps, as well as certain advantages. Additional limitations to foster day care have been listed by Luna E. Kenney in *A Ten-Year Experiment in Foster Day Care*.[11] They are:

1. Lack of formal group contacts for those children who particularly need it.
2. Lack of provisions for nursery school.
3. Difficulty of home-finding in certain neighborhoods.
4. Expense of home-finding for temporary placements.
5. Lack of speed in placement.
6. Potential confusion in child's mind regarding role of own and foster parents.
7. Difficulty in keeping community aware of the service offered.

These difficulties are not without their compensations, as further explained in the study mentioned. According to Miss Kenney the following are the advantages to foster day care:

1. The ability to serve a large and varied territory without regard to the distance of home from the nursery headquarters.
2. Greater opportunity for families who live in desirable neighborhoods.
3. Provision of service which is less likely to mark child and family as atypical in neighborhood.
4. Lessened health hazards.
5. Provision of care for otherwise neglected children of school age.
6. Elimination of group conflicts.
7. Service to varying social and economic groups.
8. Constructive effects of foster family upon child's family life.
9. Extreme flexibility of plan to meet varying needs of family.

The two following cases provided by Miss Kenney illustrate the way in which a children's agency may be of help to parents who can utilize foster day care. In the first the emphasis is upon a specific need on the

[11]Luna E. Kenney, *A Ten-Year Experiment in Foster Day Care*, Child Welfare League of America, New York, Bulletin number 15, February, 1939.

part of an unmarried mother. In the second the advantages of foster day care for middle-class families are made apparent:

Melanie H, a young girl of 15, gave birth to Edwin, who was placed full time in a foster home for two years. At the end of this time, Melanie had secured regular work and was living with her mother and brother, both also working. These two became reconciled to having Edwin in the home though it meant criticism from the neighbors among whom they had lived quietly for many years. Melanie requested day care for Edwin and from the first met the full cost of payments to the foster day mother, Mrs. Cox. Mrs. Cox quietly and voluntarily assumed the responsibility of helping to reestablish Melanie in the eyes of their mutual friends. No chance was lost to assure anyone that Melanie was a "fine girl"—without qualification. Mrs. Cox's daughters, who were near Melanie's age and who were highly esteemed in the neighborhood, invited Melanie to go to shows, etc., with them. Though Melanie was not strong in her training methods with Edwin, her efforts were quietly reinforced by those of Mrs. Cox who instilled into the child a real respect and love for his young mother. Though he is a forceful individual of eight years now, and often disagrees with his mother violently, he will tolerate no breath of criticism of her from anyone else—even if it is implied only by agreement with *his* previous remarks. He is devoted to Mrs. Cox, and refers to her as "Mom" —but from the time of his placement he distinguished between Melanie and Mrs. Cox by saying to the uninformed, "Not *my* Mom, but this Mom —Mom Cox."

*   *   *

The simple need for day care may also be found in "white collar" families. Mrs. G, a former teacher, had come to this city with her two boys, Jim and Joe, to be near Dr. G who was completing his training in a hospital near Philadelphia. She secured work with a local relief agency and established herself and the boys in a small apartment. Here she wrestled with the problem of maid service, finally facing the fact that she could not afford to hire help of the type that she was willing to have in close association with her boys, nor could she stand the strain of working and keeping house. At her request, a foster home was found where she and the children might live. Her understanding of the boys' developmental problems was excellent and she managed the supervision of this very well. The only service really required of the nursery was the selection and supervision of the foster home. Mrs. G paid the full costs of placement and so was able to remain generally as independent as she had always been.

SOCIAL CASEWORK IN DAY NURSERIES

Day nurseries, like the day care of children, provide a kind of foster home arrangement for families. Day nurseries are in large part a developing phase of child care and as such give opportunity for social casework.

Previous Outlook

In the past, day nurseries have implied a custodial purpose. They have often existed so that children would be cared for outside the home as a means of relieving parental responsibility. Just as a woman sent her laundry out for cleaning so as not to have to do the work herself, so many parents used day nurseries as a means of escaping obligation. Since this was so, most parents did not insist upon social services to their children. They simply wanted them out of the way for a time during each day.

Present Threefold Care of Children

Recently, however, this conception of the day nursery has been greatly modified. No longer do day nurseries consider their task to be basically custodial. They feel that they are providing a threefold care of children which is highly complex. One part of the work of the day nursery is that of health. The modern day nursery believes that it has a health responsibility when young children are brought together. This means specifically that the newer nurseries provide for the health needs of children either through a nurse under a physician's consultative direction or directly through a physician. Another part of the work of the day nursery is that of education. It is not enough to bring children together and allow them to do as they please. The services of someone who is trained and experienced in educational work with children are needed. This person, usually a teacher, creates the content of the daytime experience of the children. A third feature of the day nursery is the provision for social work services. Thus the day nursery today places the activities of the children in a setting of nurse or physician, teachers, and social caseworker. In day nurseries there is every reason for mutual respect and cooperation between these three types of workers. Because of the nature of this text, it is the contributions of the social workers that will be elaborated upon here.

Investigating Applications

The social caseworker is responsible for the applications of parents to the nursery. In many nurseries the beginning and the end of the social worker's job is this responsibility. Briefly, the social worker can be of help to the nursery and to parents by applying casework methods to the needs and problems of the parents in relation to the resources of the nursery. The parent seeking acceptance of her child into a nursery is met by the worker who analyzes the basis on which the application is made. What are the purposes of the woman in asking for nursery care? Does she propose nursery care as a more or less permanent solution to her problem? Is she primarily interested in the service as a means to solve her own problem or as a way of genuinely helping the child, or both? Are there other means of child care aside from the nursery which might better be used? What obligations is the woman willing to accept in regard to the nursery? Is she financially able to pay for the service? To what degree? Does she reveal family difficulties which day nursery care will not alleviate, but which require other social work services? What are her expectations of the nursery? Does she think that it will "save" her child?

By questions of this sort the worker seeks to make the best possible use of the nursery's facilities for the best possible help of child and parents. Also, by securing such data from the parents regarding themselves and their child the social worker may be of help to the nurse and teachers. The knowledge of the worker is significant in orienting the other personnel of the nursery to the fundamental personality aspects of their job. As a child takes part in the nursery program, he may reveal problems which call for special attention by the whole staff. The information the social worker has uncovered should be of notable help in meeting these problems.

Nursery Responsibilities

Day nurseries do not necessarily believe that it is their responsibility to guide parents, aside from the problems their children present. For the most part, nurseries are primarily engaged in the daytime care of children with other than social work concerns. Many are financially limited and thus are prevented from carrying out a full program of social service care. But, in some instances, and happily these seem to be increasing, nurseries are accepting a more complete family responsibility. In such cases it would seem that the nursery almost becomes a family casework agency in a share of its activities, although nurseries do not commonly consider themselves as being family agencies. The amount of benefit, however, which nurseries are able to create under adequate social casework leadership is inestimable. The following case illustrates the ways in which a social worker in a day nursery can be of help to the family:

> Mr. and Mrs. Lawrence had had their eleven-year-old boy in our nursery nine years ago. In June of 1942 Mrs. L came in to apply for their only other child, Lucille, who was then fifteen months old.
> Mrs. L was dissatisfied with practically everything in her living situa-

tion. Her husband was not intelligent enough to earn more money; she hated the apartment in one of the new housing projects; she was worried because they had done nothing to straighten Jack's crooked teeth. Although she is a stenographer, she was planning to go that night to a job of scrubbing in a theater if we would take Lucille. She struggled hard to have me make an exception and take Lucille at fifteen instead of eighteen months, which is our age limit. When I could not accede to her request but discussed with her instead the possibilities of foster day care, she began to plan a little less frantically. Four days later she telephoned to thank me for the interview, saying that she felt better about staying at home and managing on her husband's money.

9/24/42. Mrs. L made reapplication but came too late for her appointment.

9/25/42. She came too early and had to wait. It seemed that Mrs. L had just returned home after having deserted Mr. L and Jack, taking Lucille with her. She was feeling so satisfied at being at home that she did not seem to be ready to go to work, although she had a stenographic job to go to. She agreed to the application process, but I doubted ever seeing her again.

11/12/42. Mrs. L came in, her old self. Her appearance and Lucille's indicated her frantic, frustrated, unsuccessful efforts at living. She was working as a stenographer. Hers and her husband's combined wages were $65.00 a week and they had no more. She hated their apartment. She had been taking Lucille to a cousin's because our application seemed useless, but she wasn't satisfied with the care Lucille was getting. Then she proceeded in a long struggle with me to try to change every step of the application procedure. Certainly, if I had not used the application structure long enough to be convinced of its worth I would have given in to such persistent battering, but as Mrs. L organized herself to meet the nursery requirements, she began to consider Lucille and the rest of her family and to be a little less disturbed about herself.

11/22/42. Lucille entered the nursery for beginning half days. Mrs. L began then to try to get the group leader to keep her all day. Up until Christmas Mrs. L struggled to change nursery routine to fit her chaotic unplanned living. But when the whole family came to the Christmas tea, both Mr. and Mrs. L expressed quite frankly that meeting nursery requirements was the best thing that could ever happen to them.

January, 1943. The old struggle began again. Lucille was brought and called for by eleven-year-old Jack. She came late without a bath and her hair uncombed. She was left uncalled for after the nursery had closed. In an interview in the home with both Mr. and Mrs. L concerning these things, Mrs. L, after expressing her hurt feelings and having a good cry, began to plan some organization of her day. She and Mr. L then actually planned to bring Lucille and call for her themselves, which they did fairly regularly. Mrs. L combed Lucille's hair, although sometimes not until she arrived at the nursery. Interestingly enough, Mrs. L's appearance improved also. Through all of this, Lucille was growing happily by leaps and bounds in the nursery school. I saw Mrs. L frequently, supporting her in her efforts and holding her to all nursery requirements. In this I had the complete support and close cooperation of the nursery school teacher and group leader.

3/25/43. Mrs. L came to see me after telling the group leader that she was going to take Lucille to another nursery near home, which would be easier.

3/26/43. Mrs. L came on time but was rushed and out of breath. She began by saying that she wasn't going to take Lucille away from here— she just could not do it, Lucille was too happy. I said that Lucille could be happy in another school also, and perhaps it would be easier for Mrs. L. Then she began to tell me all the things about the other school which would be easier for her, especially the fact that Jack could take and call for Lucille. She understood my reason for wanting a parent to contact the nursery and said that Jack wasn't old enough to take so much responsibility, but just the same it was hard. Then she went into a long story of all the work she has to do, and how little sleep she was getting and how irritable she was with her husband and her children. She thinks that she has high blood pressure, and is on her way to a doctor tonight. But she really supposes it is her nerves. I said that perhaps she wanted to see a psychiatrist. She jumped at this, saying that she had often thought about it, but couldn't admit it to anyone. If anyone else had suggested it to her except me, it would have made her mad. I thought it made her a little mad for me to suggest it. She admitted that it wasn't pleasant, but somehow she knows that I want to help her and not to hurt her. Then she began to plan to have a thorough physical examination, and see what came of that. She wanted to know if she could come back to see me next Thursday, and we made an appointment.

3/27/43. The nursery school teacher (Miss Olsen) of the school near Mrs. L's home telephoned to say that Jack had said that Lucille was coming to her school Monday. I thought perhaps she might come, but I hoped not until she had a good-bye party and ended her experience with us. This teacher will insist upon that before she admits her.

4/1/43. Mrs. L telephoned to break her appointment just ten minutes before I was expecting her. She was having to work late. She wanted to know if I was disappointed. I told her that I had saved time for her and had been expecting her. Eagerly she wanted to know if I was really looking for her. I assured her that I was. She was sorry that she just hadn't left work and come.

4/2/43. Mrs. L asked the group leader to have me telephone her at work. This I did to find that she wanted an appointment for the following Thursday. I told Mrs. L about the waffle party, and asked if she could plan to stay next Thursday to work with a group of mothers. This pleased her and she agreed to come.

4/8/43. Mrs. L came late to her appointment, but dressed so well that

I commented on her appearance. She beamed, saying that she thought I'd like it. I said that she and Lucille had such beautiful red hair and she did so little with it. That's what her sisters say and her employer hints at it. What she likes about me is that I'm frank, and she thinks I like her. I just smiled. She went on to tell me about the physical examination. She did have high blood pressure, but the doctor says it is the irregular hours she lives. She has decided to get hold of herself. She's trying to organize her day and if she sends Lucille to a closer school, she'll have more time. I agreed with her and commented on the fact that I knew there was a good teacher in that school. Mrs. L didn't like the equipment. We talked a bit about how people rather than equipment make a school. Mrs. L then planned that Lucille would end her coming here the last Friday in the month. I told her that we would begin on the Monday of her last week to help her want to leave. We made arrangements that Mrs. L would work with Miss Olsen about Lucille's good-bye party. Mrs. L was sorry that she hadn't had Lucille's birthday party here. (She had wanted us to have it with Jack representing her, which we had refused.) With this planned, Mrs. L went back to her old worries: wanting to own a home (she says that's an obsession); disappointment in her husband; and Jack's teeth, which she has started to have fixed. I had another mother coming in for an appointment and told Mrs. L I was sorry that she had not had all of her time. She knows that it is her fault—not mine. I took her over to the room where mothers and staff were making Easter baskets, book marks, and sun suits for the bazaar. She worked interestedly all evening and really got acquainted with Lucille's group leader. She had always expressed a fear that Lucille's "Cappie"[12] did not like her.

4/16/43. Mrs. L telephoned me today to forget about any farewell for Lucille. She wasn't going to take her out. Lucille is happy and why should she have to change schools because her mother has a hard time arranging her day. I said that we would be glad for Lucille to stay or we would be glad to plan for her leaving. Again she said that she wasn't leaving, and for us not to say anything about it to Lucille.

4/17/43. Mrs. L, Jack, and Lucille came to the waffle party. Mrs. L had to go back to work and left Lucille with Jack. Mrs. L made an appointment to see me the following Thursday.

4/22/43. Mrs. L came in smiling, saying that she had come in to end up this spell of trouble. I thought that she certainly had been mixed up for awhile, but I thought that she planned for Lucille and Jack in spite of her nerves. Then she burst out that $5.00 was a lot of money to pay here. Maybe some people didn't want to save for a home. Maybe some people wouldn't bother to pay $400.00 to have a child's teeth fixed. I thought that she was possibly right, but that I wouldn't have any right to judge how anyone spent money. She agreed of course I wouldn't. She hadn't thought of it that way. Then I got out the fee scale and she went over it carefully.

[12]The name children give to Salvation Army Officers who help with the groups.

It seemed sound and fair to her. It's just that she's a poor manager. Then she told me that the other school charged only $3.20 and that had been a factor in their favor. "Now that's out, everything is out, and I've been perfectly frank about everything." I said that she could still take Lucille out anytime she wanted, and that she could reapply whenever she wanted. She believed that was so and that's one of the reasons she likes it here. She can come in to see me and be frank about everything and know that it doesn't affect what we do for Lucille. And it's so nice to think of Lucille upstairs here when she's at work. And she likes her work and she's really succeeding. I was sure that she was. Then she told me about how they were giving her more and more responsibility.[13]

SELECTED READINGS ON CHILDREN IN FOSTER HOMES

Arlitt, A. H., *Psychology of Infancy and Early Childhood*, McGraw-Hill, New York, 1946.

Baylor, Edith M. H., and Monachesi, Elio D., *The Rehabilitation of Children: The Theory and Practice of Child Placement*, Harper, New York, 1939.

Blatz, William E., *Understanding the Young Child*, Morrow, New York, 1944.

Child Welfare League of America, *A Manual for Foster Parents*, prepared by a committee of the Child Welfare League of America, New York, 1945.

Copelan, Ethel A.; Fish, Connie; and Deemer, Albert E., *Some Practices in Homefinding*, Child Welfare League of America, New York, 1942.

Dashiell, Alice T., *Health Program of a Day Nursery*, Child Welfare League of America, New York, 1944.

Freud, Anna, and Burlingham, Dorothy I., *Infants Without Families*, International Universities Press, New York, 1944.

Harral, Elizabeth; Smith, Mary F.; and Bishop, Julia A., *Adoption Practice With Parent, Child, and Foster Parents*, Child Welfare League of America, New York, 1941.

Hosley, Eleanor M., *A Manual for the Beginning Worker in a Day Nursery*, Child Welfare League of America, New York, 1946.

Hutchinson, Dorothy, *In Quest of Foster Parents: A Point of View on Homefinding*, New York School of Social Work Publications, Columbia University Press, New York, 1943.

Kenney, Luna E., *A Ten-Year Experiment in Foster Day Care*, Child Welfare League of America, New York, Bulletin number 15, February, 1939.

[13]Dorothy Curtis Melby, "The Place of Social Casework in the Day Nursery: Its Relation to Administration and to the Nursery School," *Day Nursery Care as a Social Service: A Discussion of Current Viewpoints With Case Material*, Pennsylvania School of Social Work, Philadelphia, 1943, pp. 21–25.

Meyer, Gladys, editor, *Studies of Children*, with an introduction by Dorothy Hutchinson, King's Crown Press, New York, 1948.

Ribble, Margaret A., *The Rights of Infants: Early Psychological Needs and Their Satisfaction*, Columbia University Press, New York, 1943.

Sayles, Mary B., *Substitute Parents: A Study of Foster Families*, Commonwealth Fund, New York, 1936.

Stone, Sybil A.; Castendyck, Elsa; and Hanson, Harold B., *Children in the Community: The St. Paul Experiment in Child Welfare*, Federal Security Agency, Social Security Administration, Children's Bureau, Publication number 317, Washington, D.C., 1946.

Taft, Jessie, editor, *Social Case Work With Children: Studies in Structure and Process*, Journal of Social Work Process, Pennsylvania School of Social Work, volume 3, number 1, Philadelphia, 1939.

Walker, Wilma, editor, *Child Welfare Case Records*, Social Service Series, University of Chicago Press, Chicago, 1937.

For additional related readings, consult the bibliographies at the end of the other child welfare chapters.

6

School Social Work

Another of the ways in which social casework helps children is through school social work. The following excerpts illustrate some of the activities of the social caseworker in a school setting:[1]

LOST AND FOUND

Headache, sore throat, toothache, dizziness, not feeling well—so read the excuses on Edna's attendance card. Then one day Edna was truant and wrote herself an excuse.

Conferences—with the school nurse, and physician; with the counselor and psychologist; with parents and classroom teachers; and finally with the psychiatrist. A thorough examination by the family physician showed that there was no condition warranting school absence.

According to the expert findings, a serious reading disability existed, as well as an inability to memorize. "Everything goes black for a minute when I try to say my poetry," Edna insisted. Instruction in a remedial reading class and an explanation to the regular English teacher of certain deep-lying timidities brought the first improvement.

"Edna likes to manage—really can take responsibility for practical things," mother said. When the visiting teacher[2] described different school activities—in the lunchroom, in the halls, in the library, in the lost and found department, Edna exclaimed, "I'd love to manage the lost and found department!"

And never was the lost and found department in better hands. Stray mittens, vagrant mufflers, weary old caps, wandering notebooks, and the hundreds of other objects belonging to such departments—all were

[1] These excerpts are taken from *Meet the Visiting Teacher*, published by the Child Study Department of the Minneapolis Public Schools, undated, pp. 5–10.
[2] *School social worker* is the newer, more acceptable term.

carefully classified and neatly arranged. Every evening there was Edna presiding over her wares, smiling, attractive, and happy; and many a Romeo leaned gallantly on Edna's balcony reclaiming raincoats and sweaters left accidentally on purpose in her department.

English remained Edna's most difficult subject. Nevertheless, twice, original poems signed "The Lost and Found Lady," appeared in the school paper advertising lost articles or commending the pupils for their cooperation.

At the close of the term, the most valuable things found in that department were Edna's good attendance and school citizenship.

The visiting teacher discovered that this child was frustrated by her inability to learn to read satisfactorily, and so provided specific remedial reading measures. In addition the child was given a chance to earn school success in spite of her academic handicap. Children of this sort were formerly taken to Juvenile Court for punishment, with no understanding of what "ailed them."

*   *   *

SUCCESS COMES TO TOMMY

There sat Tommy as though glued to his kindergarten chair. For six months he had refused to take part in any class activities. His vocabulary seemed to consist of just one word, and he was sparing in his use of that.

"Do you think he might be subnormal?" asked his teacher anxiously.

The visiting teacher found that, although bashful, withdrawn, and retiring at home, Tommy talked and played a little. She found from intelligence tests the psychologist gave that he was of average intelligence.

Then she discovered Leonard, a brother fourteen months younger.

Leonard greeted relatives and guests. Leonard entertained with stunts and nursery rhymes. Leonard this and Leonard that. Praise for Leonard; criticism for stolid Tommy. Tommy became daily more shy and withdrawn, finally refusing to attempt anything new. His behavior, apparently stubborn and mean, brought punishment. A rejected, insecure little chap was Tommy.

When the real causes were interpreted by the visiting teacher, sympathetic understanding came from both home and school. Soon Tommy's short legs were flying on errands to the store, to relatives, to neighbors. At school these same legs were very handy in bringing articles for work projects, helping teacher, or going on errands (very important) to the principal's office. Tommy took on a playmate or two; then the group.

Leonard was sent to visit relatives and mother invited playmates for Tommy. Father took him on trips and mother took him on shopping tours, allowing initiative and giving responsibilities wherever possible. Many new experiences came during a summer vacation at Aunt Mary's.

For every success he was praised, encouraged, reassured. His need for affection was met both at school and at home. By September, Tommy could bear Leonard's successes because he now had successes of his own.

The visiting teacher's experience in understanding children led her to a correct appraisal of his handicaps. Her interpretation of the situation to the parents and teachers resulted in a wholly different life for him. Formerly, such children were often thought to be feeble-minded.

* * *

SOMETHING GALLANT

"Oh, by the way, Miss Lawrence, what about the McGlone boys? They seem to be calming down. No mother—no father— What have you done to them?" Mr. James, the principal, looked puzzled and amused as he made the inquiry.

"I'm afraid I can't take much credit, Mr. James, except that I did refer the family to the Children's Protective Society."

Miss Lawrence, the visiting teacher, summarized a few of the main events—the father's hospitalization, the installing of Mrs. Murphy as housekeeper for the three motherless McGlones, and later on, the arrangements for the father's funeral—all managed so kindly and carefully by the social worker.

"Then the calming down began when Mrs. Murphy took over the family? That Mrs. Murphy must be a gallant soul!" Mr. James remarked.

"I think it's because they saw so much improvement that the C.P.S. consented to Mrs. Murphy's staying on with the boys until they're either through school or employed."

"Then, after all, what those kids needed was a mother!" mused Mr. James. "And there seemed no way of ever getting under their skins! Have that Mrs. Murphy here for Mother's Day, will you? We should give her a medal or at least pin a posy on her!"

A few days later, Miss Lawrence visited the McGlone home. Mrs. Murphy, tall and rangy, met her with a flashing smile and a merry twinkle in her eye.

"And it's glad I am to be with the lads," she said; "they're rough but goodhearted. I don't mind a little hell-raisin' once in a while. Brought up three of me own, by hand, y' might say. And well I know what the McGlones'd be if the Society had separated them and placed them out! Just bums! Plain bums, that's what!"

"Well, you've done one grand job, anyway! Mr. James wants to know if you received the invitation to Mother's Day?"

"Yes, the lads wants me to go, too. They chipped in and bought me a new waist. Will everyone be dressed up swell?"

She brought out a black silk blouse for Miss Lawrence to appraise.

"Just the thing, Mrs. Murphy, just the thing! You'll be as grand as anyone. And we'll be looking for you."

As she was leaving, Miss Lawrence said, "Our school thinks you should have a medal. Look well hanging on that new blouse!"

"For just doin' what I like to do—bossin' boys around?" Mrs. Murphy threw back her head and laughed merrily.

Yes, there was something gallant about that woman!

A visiting teacher often learns of children who have needs which cannot be met by the resources of the school system itself. In this case, the visiting teacher's part was to know the community resources so well that the social agency which was organized to provide the needed service could be called in to help. Formerly, children of this type drifted from one relative's home to another, or were sent to an orphanage.

* * *

"HE'S AWFUL"

"Harry is impossible in my room," the teacher told the principal. "He is defiant, won't work, fights with other children. Eleven years old, in 7B, but he's failing."

"And you've tried everything?"

"Yes, praise, punishment, nothing helps."

The visiting teacher went to his home and found he was living in a comfortable house with the grandmother, his parents having died when he was a young child.

"Don't tell me," his grandmother said. "He's stubborn, sullen. Only reads and writes poetry. Runs around for birds and insects. Won't help me. And children won't play with him. Fights them. How can I help it? If it were not for him, I could spend my old age traveling around."

His grandmother spoke of her own talent in art and of how she had always wanted Harry to be an artist. "But he's awful! Doesn't mind me in anything. I scold and scold. I'm fed up with him."

His past teachers were consulted. Since he entered kindergarten he was a problem. "An attractive child," one teacher said, "but always demanding attention. Talked loud, shuffled his feet, slammed doors, laughed at children, at teachers." For several years he had been a problem!

The visiting teacher called on the assistance of the psychologist and psychiatrist.

Harry was found to be very bright, tests giving him a rating in the upper 2% of the population. In reading he was four years beyond his grade.

He told the psychiatrist that teachers did not like him, children would not play with him. "Books are my friends. I like to walk alone."

Harry was a sick boy emotionally. He was sure his grandmother did not love him. To cover his loneliness he fought with children, and with teachers.

In conference it was agreed that Harry be double-promoted, that teachers build up his confidence by praise, by encouragement. His grandmother was given an insight into her own and Harry's difficulties, which made a change in her attitude. His social activities were programmed through the Boy Scouts, Big Brothers, and Y.M.C.A.

Here was a boy whose whole life was being blighted and his character distorted because he could not find love at home, at school, or with other children. Everyone disliked him. The visiting teacher was able to discover what was causing his problem, and through skillful work was able to change the attitude of his grandmother and teachers, so that he could give up his retaliating behavior and become a reasonably good boy.

Of course, the duties of a school social worker vary from place to place. In general, however, they include the type of functions indicated above.

THE CHILD AT HOME

In recent decades, social services for children at home have been on the increase. In many ways they comprise the broadest and most intensive types of services rendered children by social workers, although at the present stage of development the importance of the other forms should not be minimized. But more and more it is recognized that the first choice of the social worker (as well as of the enlightened citizen) lies in keeping children within their own homes, if such procedure is at all possible. The most ideal and natural location of the child is in his own home; therefore those services which predicate that the child must leave his home suggest conditions in need of very careful attention from the point of view of the child, the family, and the well-being of society. The normal home possesses just those experiences which the child, any child, needs. No other sort of group can take its place.

The home life of countless children, however, is not normal, oftentimes for reasons over which they themselves have no control. Repeatedly, special aids are required to be supplied by various agencies in the community in order to provide or maintain a minimal standard of normality within the home. Social work aid to children in their own homes is only one of the many services available. And even where the child receives help from a social worker, there are generally other specialists who also contribute their skills and knowledge to the strengthening of home relationships.

Chapters 6, 7, and 8 will describe the kinds of child welfare work which aim at improving the conditions of children who, in the main, live at home.[3] It must be borne in mind, however, that the divisions of labor discussed within these chapters (and within the book as a whole) are rather artificial because there is much overlapping in the services given children. A child may, for example, be treated by a child welfare agency for his inability to get along in school. Or he may be treated by a family caseworker who has happened to establish the contact through an interest in the problems of the parents. Or he can be helped by a social worker attached directly to the school. The problem might also be handled by others.

The remainder of this chapter will be devoted to a description of school social work. The following chapter will be concerned with child guidance clinics. Still another chapter will discuss the courts, probation, and parole.

Again, it must be remembered that within the limits of these chapters only those services to children in their own homes, which are conducted along casework lines and chiefly by social workers, will be surveyed. Group work activities for children will be mentioned at a later point. Governmental services will also be considered later.

SCHOOL SOCIAL WORK

The broadening responsibilities of schools for the maintenance and development of children's welfare accounts in part for the rise of school social work. In a prior period, when the purpose of the schools was merely the teaching of the three "R's," there was very little call for the practice of casework in the schools. It was enough for the school to perform its rather narrow function and to leave to other community agencies, especially the home and the church, the private problems of students. But today the relationship of the school to the community has greatly changed, so that now the school has programs which in another day would have seemed entirely inappropriate. One of these activities is school social work.

Adjustments Between School and Child

Perhaps the most significant change that has occurred in the history of American education is the relatively recent effort to fit the school to the needs of the child rather than insist on the child's adjustment to the school, without aid from the school. While this statement may seem somewhat extreme, it does point out an important innovation in educational philosophy. (All too often, unfortunately, there is only theoretical acceptance of this philosophy.) Today it is recognized that

[3]Children in foster homes and institutions may also benefit from these services.

children often fail to fit in to the school situation unless aided by facilities within the school itself. No longer do educators believe that the child's adaptation to the school is a relatively simple thing; they see it as a complex and compelling demand being made upon personalities not always willing or able to adjust. The child's failure to adjust may not be due necessarily to causes within the school, but whatever the source, a child's emotional instability often expresses itself in his school behavior. The child, thus, may be delinquent. He may fail to attend school regularly. He may feel that the work the school maintains is childish and unmanly. He may be primarily engaged in asserting his own supposed maturity or his own independence. In the classroom he may refuse to be attentive to the required work. He may seldom come prepared for the day's work. He may be a disciplinary problem for the teacher and the principal.

If these responses exist, it may be assumed that something is possibly wrong with the organization and function of the school. It may also be granted that something is wrong with the personal make-up or background of the child. But, whatever the rock on which the school or child is foundering, a new course must be charted. In this task both the school and the child must do their share. One cannot always obliterate the school and begin afresh with all of the best rational insights that advanced educators possess. Nor is it possible to scrap the child or to insist that come-what-may he must adapt himself to the school. Rather, as the term "adjustment" suggests, there must be a settling of the conflicts on the basis of what both the school and the individual are able to do, in order that both may get along together for their mutual well-being. Here the school social worker can play an important role.

Types of Problems

The types of children with whom school social workers mostly deal are the following: (1) children who are failing in their work; (2) children who are aggressive and give evidence of antisocial conduct; (3) children who are withdrawn in their normal social contacts; (4) children who present unusual behavior, especially that which is deemed socially regressive; (5) truants; (6) neglected and sick children; (7) delinquents; (8) children who have needs as a result of their poverty status; and (9) children who without warning drop out of school.

THE HISTORY OF SCHOOL SOCIAL WORK

School social work began in 1906 and 1907 in New York City, Boston, and Hartford. Each of these origins will be examined briefly.

Development in New York City

In New York City, school social work started when the workers in two settlement houses, Hartley House and Greenwich House, felt that they needed to know the teachers of the children who came to their settlement houses. Because of their broad interest in the individual child in the settlements, these workers wished to extend their concern into the school relationships of their charges. Through a school contact the settlement house workers believed they would be better able to create a "tailor-made" recreational program to meet the needs of these children. Oftentimes, too, they were in a position to hear complaints concerning the school and to deal with students who were unadjusted in ways of which the school authorities were ignorant. The settlement house workers also were quite aware of the interconnections between the school, the settlement houses, and the children's homes. For these reasons, then, the settlement workers tried to articulate these relationships in a manner beneficial to all three.

The schools, however, were not wholly unaware of the problems of student adjustment. The thinking and activity of a teacher, Mary Marot, for example, did much to crystallize the misgivings which many teachers had with the then inadequate methods of aiding the students in meeting their problems. In this period new ideas regarding education were beginning to come to the fore among teachers. Under the impact of the developing science of psychology, teachers became alert to individual differences in intellectual capacity and emotional make-up. Changing theories of motivation, especially, played a part in increasing the teachers' use of scientific approaches to student learning. Sociology, as a science of human relations, was at this time suggesting the complex and influencing ramifications of modern culture and of the relation of the individual to it in terms of learning. Teachers, moreover, came to realize the added responsibilities the schools had to assume in the face of the declining functions of the home and the church. All of these changes gave momentum to the school social work movement.

Within a short time after the possibilities of school social work in New York City began to be explored, the Public Education Association appointed a committee to develop this type of service to children. Six years later the Board of Education took over the responsibility for school social work. Administratively, however, the New York City setup has suffered through its lack of genuine integration within the public school system. As it stands at present, the school social work department is more a related function of the school system than an integral one. Even so, the New York City development is one of the most adequate in the country.

Boston Beginnings

In Boston, school social work was maintained through private auspices. The settlement house background of the movement was lacking. Actually, school social work began here in 1906 through the efforts of the Women's Education Association. This parent-teacher organization saw the need for a "bridge" between the home and the school because "lack of understanding between home and school often results in loss, sometimes in serious injustice to the child." The bridge which the Association set up was a social worker, appointed first to the Winthrop School District. Later, as this plan seemed to fill a real need, it was expanded and other organizations developed similar services. By 1923 there were seven such workers in the elementary schools of Boston and two in the high schools.

Growth in Hartford

While the work in New York City received its initial impetus from two settlement houses and the work in Boston from a parent-teacher association, the work in Hartford, Connecticut, grew out of the experience of the Henry Barnard School and its Psychological Clinic. The director of the Clinic felt that some sort of home-school arrangement was called for in order to make the treatment of problem children more effective. Part of the job of the school social worker in the Henry Barnard School was to investigate the home background of children and to prepare case histories for the psychologist in the Clinic. The worker also took part in aiding in the social adjustments called for in the treatment process.

Programs in Other Cities

The programs of school social work in New York City, Boston, and Hartford were used in modified form elsewhere. Philadelphia began such a program in 1909; Worcester, Massachusetts, in 1910; Rochester, in 1913; Kansas City, in 1915; Minneapolis, in 1916; and Chicago, in 1919. The work in Rochester was important because it represented the first instance where school social work was incorporated from the beginning in the school system. Here school social work became a separate department of the city's educational program. The workers were required to have not only a license to teach but also social work training through having been employed in a social work agency of quality.

National Expansion

National impetus was given to the school social work movement in 1921 when the National Committee on Visiting Teachers, affiliated with the Public Education Association, was granted a sum of money by the Commonwealth Fund of New York for the development of a country-wide demonstration program. The committee placed thirty school social workers in as many different communities. Cities, towns, and rural counties presenting a wide array of different social conditions were chosen in order that the program might be studied from as broad a perspective as possible. While the initial goal of the demonstration was to create a mass of concrete data by which school social work could be judged and appreciated by local communities, its final purpose was to enable such communities not only to see the values of the program but to accept it and adapt it to their local requirements. Although the National Committee paid most of the salaries of the workers chosen for the demonstration, local boards of education were called upon to pay part. Later, as the program proved itself, the boards completely took over the program, both financially and administratively.

All these early efforts put the movement well under way. It continued to develop notably and at present is a significant part of the general social work contribution to American life. In recent years many localities have realized the importance of school social work and have added trained staffs to their school systems. In addition to the outstanding program of the Bureau of Child Guidance in New York City which will be discussed later in the chapter, several recent developments bear comment here.

Philadelphia Plan

In Philadelphia, a Division of Pupil Personnel and Counseling was created by the Board of Education in 1942. Its purposes were to "coordinate the work of the attendance officers, home and school visitors, employment certificating officials, and counselors, and give a common direction and continuity to these closely related services." To fulfill these purposes there are at present a central administrative staff, a counseling section, and a staff of counselors and counseling teachers assigned to various public schools in Philadelphia. In the counseling section there are several consultants who both teach and counsel. They also are responsible for the in-training program of the Division.

In the first year forty-two elementary teachers were selected from the regular teaching staff to counsel. These were freed during the five mornings of each week of the school year in order that they might take special courses in counseling education. In the second year certain courses were continued, although for only a half day a week. During both years there was supervision of the actual counseling they did when not teaching courses. Beyond the second year no formal training program was conducted, but some of the counseling teachers did extend their education. In time, additional groups were added to the program and given similar training and experience.

The approach of the Division to the problem of secondary-school children was somewhat different. In Pennsylvania, secondary-school counselors possess certificates from the state to act as "guidance counselors." They qualify for this certificate by taking written and oral examinations administered by the school system of the city.

In the Philadelphia program, a special room is provided for the worker, as is generally true in other situations. The workers have been agreeably pleased to find many children coming of their own volition to the counseling offices for aid.

Provisions in Louisiana

In Louisiana there has been open recognition through law that the provision for school social work is definitely a state responsibility. Under the terms of the current legislation, each parish must provide at least the part-time services of a school social worker. While the law lays particular stress upon the attendance duties of the school social workers, there is no doubt that more than attendance duties legitimately fall to their lot. The additional responsibilities are indicated in the twofold program enunciated by the State Superintendent of Public Instruction: (1) preventive measures to keep children well adjusted to their school work; (2) corrective measures that remedy conditions deterrent to the child's normal development and regular attendance. The clearly positive function of the school social work is apparent, particularly in the first of these provisions. Also, there is recognition in the requirements of the position for genuine social work skills. While a teaching certificate is obligatory, the school social worker in Louisiana must also have additional training of a type related to the responsibilities of school social work.

Operations in Michigan

The Michigan plan does not operate on a compulsory state-wide basis, as do school social work services in Louisiana. But it may in time be extended throughout the state. The aim of the legislation in Michigan is to encourage local initiative by providing state funds for communities wishing to develop a school social work program. Moreover, in Michigan the primary motivation seems not to have been that of attendance problems but rather that of juvenile delinquency.

Local boards in Michigan draw on state money to meet the greater part of their financial burden. In 1944, the first year of operation of this program, $200,000 was appropriated by the state. The state also created two classifications of school social work personnel. One looks forward to the time when fully professional workers will be available. The other, and more practical at the moment, recognizes qualified teachers who have partial social work training. There is, moreover, a definite provision for the establishment of a training program to increase the number of workers available to the schools.

The programs in Philadelphia, Louisiana, and Michigan are instructive in that they represent some of the present-day organizational developments within school social work.

National Association of School Social Workers

The professional workers engaged in school social work joined together in 1919 to form the National Association of Visiting Teachers, later known as the American Association of Visiting Teachers, and now called the National Association of School Social Workers. This group, supported by the dues of its members, exists to exchange information, to interpret the work to the community, and to establish proper standards of practice.

CURRENT TRENDS

At present there are several notable trends in school social work. Three of the more important, general ones will be mentioned here.

Awareness of Functions

First, there is a trend toward a fuller understanding of the nature of the work itself. As experience has been built up, school social workers are realizing that they should not attempt to treat all the cases referred to them. In other words they now believe that they cannot and should not take over the whole burden of child welfare work in the community. They are as a result formulating their approach to those children who can best use their services. As another product of increased experience, school social workers are today more and more aware that they have two primary functions in regard to the school child: (1) *social diagnostic,* that is, they may well fulfill their responsibility if they are simply able to detect problems and to make referrals to the proper community resources equipped to handle them, rather than to attempt themselves to apply lengthy and elaborate treatment processes; (2) *coordinative,* that is, to marshal the existing community facilities for children, especially as they may be brought to focus upon school children with problems.

Integration of Work Within Schools

Second, there is a trend toward a greater integration of school social work within schools, especially with attendance and personality work. This development is logical for the future of school social work, for it relates readily to the elaboration of school services suggested by modern educational theory and practice. The example of the Board of Education of San Diego makes clear the possibilities. In that city, school social work is a part of the program of the Bureau of Child Guidance, the head of which is a former school social worker. Within this Bureau there are school social workers, attendance supervisors (trained in social work), psychologists, home tutors, and speech-correction teachers.

Increasing Group and Community Participation

Third, there is a trend toward increasing the amount of group and community participation in educational problems. There is growing need for school social workers to interpret their efforts through group meetings of parents and others. To parents the worker can give insight into the problems confronting both children and schools as they seek to do their work. The parents can also be taught the value of home well-being for school adjustment. In addition, school social workers should interpret their functions to the social work agencies and other interested groups in the community so that there may be the highest degree of sensitivity on the part of lay and professional persons to the problems of children at school.

THE FUNCTIONS OF SCHOOL SOCIAL WORKERS

A study made by the United States Office of Education of the Federal Security Agency on the place of school social work services in the schools notes that 266 cities had such services as of 1945. (See Table 10.) In 159 of these cities, only one full-time or part-time worker was employed. In 65 cities, one and three-quarters to three workers were available; in 15 cities, three and a half to six workers; in 10 cities, seven to ten; and in 17 cities, above ten workers were used. This means, among other things, that the representation of school social work in American cities is relatively slight, although the trend indicates the field is growing. It signifies further that the functions of school social

Table 10

VISITING TEACHER SERVICES PROVIDED IN CITIES REPLYING
TO QUESTIONNAIRE, BY STATE IN WHICH LOCATED

	Number of Cities Reporting			
State in Which Located	Full or part-time visiting teacher service	No visiting teacher service	Some service provided by other than trained visiting teachers	Interest in or plans to provide visiting teacher service*
Alabama	3	2	2	—
Arizona	—	2	—	1
Arkansas	3	2	—	—
California	17	18	3	—
Colorado	5	3	—	—
Connecticut	3	8	1	—
Delaware	1	—	—	—
District of Columbia	—	1	—	1
Georgia	6	2	1	1
Idaho	2	1	—	—
Illinois	14	23	8	2
Indiana	13	7	5	—
Iowa	5	4	5	1
Kansas	2	7	5	—
Kentucky	6	2	3	—
Louisiana	1	1	—	—
Maine	—	5	—	—
Maryland	1	—	—	—
Massachusetts	12	47	3	3
Michigan	15	18	3	8
Minnesota	3	6	5	—
Mississippi	2	5	3	1
Missouri	5	9	4	1
Montana	2	2	1	—
Nebraska	2	1	2	—

(continued on page 237)

workers vary with the locality. In one city the school social worker may perform as a general practitioner, that is, he may undertake all of the variety of problems found among students. In other instances, and quite in the extreme, he may enjoy a rather high degree of specialization, largely engaging in one particular type of activity.

In general, the activities of school social workers fall into five categories.

Attendance

In many localities the school social worker is undistinguished from the attendance officer in charge of truancy cases. In other places special

Table 10 (*continued*)

VISITING TEACHER SERVICES PROVIDED IN CITIES REPLYING
TO QUESTIONNAIRE, BY STATE IN WHICH LOCATED

State in Which Located	Number of Cities Reporting			
	Full or part-time visiting teacher service	No visiting teacher service	Some service provided by other than trained visiting teachers	Interest in or plans to provide visiting teacher service*
New Hampshire	—	8	1	—
New Jersey	14	36	3	5
New Mexico	2	1	—	—
New York	16	31	10	1
North Carolina	4	9	2	2
North Dakota	2	—	—	—
Ohio	28	16	7	3
Oklahoma	5	9	1	2
Oregon	3	1	1	—
Pennsylvania	33	30	12	2
Rhode Island	2	6	—	—
South Carolina	3	3	1	—
South Dakota	—	3	1	—
Tennessee	6	3	—	1
Texas	8	17	1	2
Utah	2	1	—	—
Vermont	—	2	1	—
Virginia	1	7	3	1
Washington	3	9	—	1
Wisconsin	10	13	3	—
Wyoming	1	—	1	—
Total	266	381	102	39

*Included in 2d column.

Source: Katherine M. Cook, *The Place of Visiting Teacher Services in the School Program,* U.S. Office of Education, Bulletin 1945, number 6, Washington, D.C., p. 42.

workers are employed as attendance officers. But where the two positions are synonymous, we see one of the functions that the school social worker may perform.

It would be erroneous to assume that the task of an attendance officer at best is merely mechanical or legal. Too often indeed this assumption is made, but there is little to support it in terms of reason or results. Above all, the results suggest that only a program aimed at understanding truants in the manner in which social workers try to understand their clients will prove basically successful. This is not to say that when school social workers operate in truancy cases, positive effects ensue automatically, but the general possibilities seem to be stronger in that direction than when programs fail to include social work training for attendance workers.

The following case of "Harry" shows how a school social worker as an attendance officer was called upon to solve a truancy problem:

The school referral said Harry was a chronic truant and they wished some help. He was not interested in school and did not care to learn.

The attendance officer assigned to this situation talked with the school to get some further information about Harry. His teachers thought he was a bully, thought he was a slow learner, and were disgusted with his truancy. They knew nothing about his home situation. His brothers were attending school regularly, the attendance officer learned by checking with the school they attended.

A note left at the home for the father or the mother to come to the office brought the father in. He was worried and upset. The mother was quite ill in the hospital, the family had no place to live, and he had not been able to do much in the way of supervision of the children. In fact he gets so mad with Harry he beats him sometimes. They are living temporarily with a relative in very crowded quarters. Father said, "I'd like to have you put Harry in the Detention Home." The worker said she hardly felt that was the place for Harry. She thought maybe he needed a bit of care and a friend. She added, "And I think you need some help, too, don't you? You are worried, and trouble comes from every angle."

The father settled himself in his chair a little and the worker said, "If I can have your help on this, let's see whether we can help Harry. I think you really want Harry to get along and be a young man you can be proud of but you are hurt and angry and worried and hardly know which way to turn." Father nodded and the worker asked, "Do you believe Harry might be looking for a friend? He doesn't have his mother now. Is there anyone in your family that could look after the children until you come home from work?" Father thought a while and presented a plan to have the children stay with an aunt until he called for them in the evenings. He felt the aunt would be willing to do this.

The worker talked with Harry about school and about his truancy. The boy was timid and fearful, not able to say much. Then the worker talked with Harry and the father together about the plan to stay with the aunt and told Harry she would come to see him tomorrow; would he be thinking a little about all this?

Next day Harry smiled hurriedly and a little fearfully when the worker came. He could say that he did not know the things he should in school, that he was "all mixed up" inside, and he was scared in school too. At the same time he was rather belligerent in asserting that he did not care because he did not know anything in school; he did not have to learn anything. The worker replied that she guessed it would not do much good to go to school if he felt that way really but "I believe you would like school if you felt good there, felt that your teachers wanted to help you. Now I would like to help you out of this trouble but I can't if you are not willing to do your share. Think it over, Harry, and I will see you tomorrow for your answer."

The following day Harry's greeting was a little more certain. He thought he ought to try. He and the worker decided she would talk with his teacher about the fact that Harry would like to try to do things a bit differently in school. The teacher was interested in changing her attitude toward Harry and suggested that if he seemed really to try she could perhaps give him some responsibility that would make him feel he had some value.

Two weeks later the worker stopped by to see Harry. He beamed a greeting and walked confidently toward her saying, "I'm a J.P.O. I've been in school every day. I like my teacher. She is very kind to me." Harry may have relapses but he, his teacher, and his family all feel better, and Harry is taking some steps toward being more responsible for himself.[4]

In Harry's case, a solution was effected relatively easily. Many truancy problems are more complex and deep-seated, however, and may require much skill and months of patient effort on the part of the worker.

Behavior-Problems Adjustment

Although the primary function of the teacher in the classroom is the imparting of knowledge, this task is colored both by the personality of the teacher and by the interacting personalities of the students with the teacher. As many teachers can readily affirm, the problem of teaching may involve more time and energy in the direction of creating and maintaining the conditions most conducive to learning than strictly in the direct transmission of information.

To a certain degree a class progresses successfully when it assumes that all of its members are "normal." In other words all of the persons within the classroom situation must be capable of that extent of cooperation and mutual adjustment which will permit a group process. Occasionally, there are in class groups children who are unable to curb their own individualistic needs sufficiently to permit the group process to function. When this occurs, something definite usually happens. Either the group becomes centered about the needs of the unadjusted individual, or it is disrupted to the point where it is incapable of functioning at all, or the unadjusted member is forced out.

[4]Mildred Sikkema, "Sharing Responsibility in the School Guidance Program: A Case Study," *Hawaii Educational Review*, volume 35, number 1, September, 1946, pp. 22–23.

The first alternative occurs frequently and the second can be found in group after group. The third alternative is not usually possible in the school.

The duties of the school social worker in part pertain to the more efficient social functioning of the class members. While the chief responsibility for handling problems of behavior rightfully rests upon the classroom teacher, there are some instances, especially in a large school, where the teacher becomes something other than a teacher if too much is expected of him in this regard. In such cases the imparting of knowledge may suffer so remarkably, through a diversion of interest on the part of the teacher and the class, that the important educational goals of the classroom are lost or severely mitigated.

In situations where the teacher is confronted with a behavioral problem of great intensity and complexity, there are several courses open. On the one hand he may find that talking the matter over with the school social worker may give him sufficient insight to enable him to work out the solution himself. On the other hand teachers commonly find it helpful to refer the student or students to the school social worker directly. In the latter event the school social worker can perform his tasks most efficiently when the referral truly represents an individual problem and not a group problem; but aiding the individual student to make a suitable school adjustment may result in fortifying the group objectives of the school.

The following is a teachers' check list of observable symptoms of potential or incipient delinquency:[5]

Extremely restless
Extremely excitable—lacks self-control
Extremely tense or inhibited
Often left out of play groups
Bullies other children
Is bullied by other children
Self-conscious over physical anomalies
Self-conscious because aware of socio-economic differentness
Resentful of criticism
Teases maliciously or with intent to hurt or annoy other children
Shows cruelty toward animals
Extremely self-important
Not a good sport
Cheats
Lies

[5]Schools Against Delinquency: A Guide for New York Schools, The University of the State of New York, The State Education Department, Albany, 1944, p. 18.

Steals
Is frequently truant
Shows evidence of abnormal interest in sex
Unable to persevere in any mental effort
Mentally preoccupied—day dreams
Easily upset, depressed, or angered by frustration
Wants constant reassurance
Not able to make decisions and stick to them
Afraid in many situations
Dogmatic: insists on having own way

Disciplinary Case. The school social worker usually has responsibility for behavior-problem cases which involve disciplinary action on the part of school officials. While many school officials are equipped to meet problem children who need discipline in an intelligent and therapeutic manner, nevertheless it is the special responsibility of the school social worker to try to cure unruly behavior through social casework methods. The following case of "James" illustrates how a suspension case was handled by a school social worker:

On March 30, 1944, the principal of our high school suspended Jim, age not quite sixteen, from school and referred him to the school social worker. The principal had taken a poll of the teachers' opinions which revealed that Jim had a way of completely riling his teachers, five of whom were men. They thought that he was off on the wrong foot from the time he entered the previous fall. He was quiet to the point that some called him withdrawn, but he was defiant in the way he cut school or cut classes and offered no explanation. He was thought to be dull, uninterested, and lazy. He was failing everything.

Early next morning, Jim's mother, Mrs. Leo, appeared at the social worker's office to say he had not come home all night. She had called the principal and she was very angry. She thought she never understood Jim. Of course, she had little time to think about it with nine children to take care of. Louis was the oldest; then James. Admittedly she had trouble on her hands with Mr. Leo, too, who always had to be the boss and never had had any time for Jim. She could just see what would happen. Jim would come home and then his father would have to give him a "good beating." Jim would have nothing to say (not that it would make any difference if he did say something), and the next thing she knew Jim would be doing something else that he shouldn't do. Maybe Mr. Leo was right, she thought aloud, "Jim ought to have enough sense to look at how Louis acts and learn a lesson for himself."

The social worker talked with Mr. Leo that same evening. In the meantime Jim had come home and in spite of Mrs. Leo's entreaties bolstered by the social worker, Jim got the beating. Mr. Leo with his

Old World ideas and his broken English poured out his complaints. There was just nothing that he would have but for the court to be called in and Jim to be sent away. "It's like a rotten apple. If you've got one bad one, you can't have him around to spoil the others." Mr. Leo substantiated how he had made big sacrifices for his family. He had had no education himself and had come to the United States at fifteen and shifted entirely for himself from that time on.

The one thing the social worker seemed to accomplish in this interview with Mr. Leo was to get him to refer the boy to the worker in a constructive way. Mr. Leo knew that what Jim said was not to be reported back to the father later. He told Jim to talk. Jim talked. It wasn't like him. He had never done such a thing before. He was scared but it did not stop him. He brought out extreme resentment toward Louis who actually seemed to be encouraged by the family in his childish abuse of Jim. Jim also expressed resentment toward his father. In Jim's mind this was a cruel world anyway. There was little or no self-respect or confidence left in the boy. What did it matter what he did? Nobody cared. Least of all, Jim.

With Jim there seemed to be a job for the social worker to do in three areas: with the family's attitudes, the faculty's attitudes, and most of all with Jim's own. There was a period of three months when the worker concentrated on these. The family attitudes did not change more than a very little. The father would seem to go along on a plan but then he would always rescind his consent. Mrs. Leo did not stand her ground against Mr. Leo. Moreover, there had to be an emergency or the social worker did not really have an audience with the parents. With the faculty there was a different situation. They could see that Jim had reasons to be angry and no natural outlets for his resentment. They were pleased with a psychological study which showed not only good average intelligence but unusual performance ability. They made all kinds of exceptions in program to fit the boy's interests and abilities. In two months every teacher was reporting improvement.

Probably this consideration proved to Jim that people in the high school were interested after all. In preparation for his return to school, the social worker talked with him several times. After the pressure of the first emergency was gone, Jim did not talk as much of his inner feelings. When Jim, his family, and the social worker would work out some plan, and then Mr. Leo would queer the whole thing and they would have to start over again, no doubt Jim felt that at least there was someone on his side. Jim had had his troubles in elementary school, too, but in the new environment of some 1,500 people he had felt lost altogether. He needed someone to pull up his self-esteem, until satisfactory adjustment in school had a chance to take hold with him. This was the social worker's job.

By June, Jim had work in a grocery store after school hours, and in the next eighteen months the worker's only contacts with him were during her shopping trips there. The manager liked Jim because, as he said, "He does what I tell him and I always know where he is." For some time Jim had been itching to get into service. He was pretty disgusted when the war was over last summer before his father had consented to his enlistment. However, he had long since made up his mind to put up with the family restrictions until he was eighteen when he would be on his own. Jim spent his eighteenth birthday last month at an Army training center. He enlisted with two and a half years full high-school credit for work in line with his ability. The high-school teachers do not even remember now that, in the spring of 1944, they had given up hope for Jim.[6]

"Jim" illustrates one type of behavior problem that the school social worker may meet; actually there are many. The child may be over-aggressive; he may be overly withdrawn. He may be belligerent toward his teacher; he may be a bully toward his classmates. The manifold forms that behavior abnormalities may assume elude any simple analysis.

Home-School Relationships

The school is increasingly recognized as being dependent for its success upon the homes from which its students come. For example, a child who is emotionally disturbed because of conditions within his family is scarcely able to do his best in school. Or a child whose parents are not concerned with providing study supervision at home will probably miss some of the values for which the school stands. So the modern educator must be interested not alone in what goes on in the classroom, but also in how the school and its program fit into the family backgrounds from which the students come.

Consequently, the school social worker must often deal with pupils whose lack of school adjustment is due to home difficulties. These cases cover many and wide variations. Probably, in some sense or other, every case which the school social worker treats on an individual basis is connected in greater or smaller degree with family conditions.

The following case of "Mary" (age 7) shows how dependent a child may be for the success of her school performance upon harmonious and secure home conditions. It also shows the activities of the school social worker in the furtherance of improved school-home relationships:

Mary told the school nurse that Betty, who was in kindergarten, was not in school because she was sick and home alone. She said her father was in the "South Seas" but her mother worked but didn't come home

[6]Joyce Winberg, "The School Social Worker's Contribution to the Child's Social Development," *The Bulletin of the National Association of School Social Workers*, volume 22, number 2, December, 1946, pp. 11–12.

at night because she was living with an aunt. A 17-year-old girl stayed with Betty and Mary at night.

Because Mary seemed so tense and anxious, the school principal asked the school social worker if she would find out more about the child's home situation.

Information available through other social agencies revealed that this was an illegitimate child. The mother had subsequently married and had two other children. The mother's family was of the middle class as to economic, social, and educational standards.

The mother's sister had recommended that she not return to her own home after birth of Mary because the maternal grandmother was a mentally disturbed person and had been in a mental hospital for 6 years. The mother did go home and Mary remained with the grandparents at the time of the mother's marriage until after the first child was born.

The Child Welfare Division had supervised mother and child until her subsequent marriage and until the mother took Mary out of the State to her new home. The Child Welfare Division felt it would not be logical for them to go back into the case now because they were definitely associated with the illegitimacy and with the child apart from her family picture.

The school social worker called and found that the mother had returned to her parents when the father went into the Army. She was employed during the day but returned home each evening at 5:00 p. m. The grandparents were there all day and seldom left the house.

Mary was at home when the worker called and began to cry as soon as she realized the worker was from school.

The mother could see no reason for Mary's story at school. She indicated that she wanted to see the worker alone in the near future.

The social worker reported the information from her call to the school, and in a few days the school called again saying that Mary had reported to the nurse again that her mother had left home, that the father was coming home on a furlough, and the mother was going to get a new daddy, and that there was no one at home to take care of her. The school social worker called the mother who came into the office the following day. She expressed anxiety over Mary's "stories," saying that she had been telling such stories in the neighborhood and at home for the past year or so. Mary was always tense, worried, fearful, had nightmares and a very poor appetite. The mother felt Mary was turning away from her. The younger children were relaxed, happy, and affectionate.

The possibility of study and treatment at the Child Guidance Clinic was presented to the mother. She was definitely interested and the school social worker made an appointment and introduced her to the Child Guidance Clinic worker.

The school social worker again reported to the school the plan for study and treatment.

In this case the school social worker has not carried any further responsibility for the case because the mother is able to accept and follow up on treatment with the Clinic. The child does not present any particular problem at school at present, so the need for a frequent continuous contact with school is not indicated. Responsibility for reporting any new developments as to her behavior at school was left for the school to report directly to the Clinic.[7]

Aid to Parents. The school social worker also deals with the parents of child clients. This means that at times the function of the school social worker comes very close to that of family casework. When a parent, however, requires considerable casework attention, the usual practice is to refer him to another agency in the community, most probably a family agency.

The need for some casework aid to parents can be seen in the following illustration, where a parent responded negatively to the school's requirement of her signed consent for the study of her child:

William R, a 12-year-old boy recently transferred to an opportunity class in a new school, was referred by his teacher as "one of the worst boys in the class—he seems unable to control himself." His mother had responded to reports about his behavior with extreme irritation. Approached first by the principal and then at his suggestion by the Bureau social worker by letter, Mrs. R had expressed willingness for William to be studied at the Bureau but flatly refused to sign the consent blank.

Urged by the principal, who in turn had been urged by the boy's teacher, the social worker again wrote the mother, asking her to call at the school and finally managed to interview her in the Teachers' Room where school staff members were constantly coming and going. (This was the only available spot.) Mrs. R repeated that she would not sign the consent blank. The worker wondered what the mother feared. The answer was, "A widow has to be afraid." She was worried lest her children would be taken away from her. All assurances that the Bureau neither could nor would do this were of no avail, so it was suggested that she might like to take William to a clinic that would not require a signed consent. She thought she would and agreed to tell the principal of her decision.

Ten days later the social worker received a letter from a public agency enclosing Mrs. R's signed consent, and immediately wrote her for a clinic appointment. This was not kept but instead Mrs. R called at another time when it was not possible for the worker to interview her. A home visit was promised as a substitute, even though the mother showed little enthusiasm over the suggestion. There was a certain under-

---

[7]Alma Laabs, "Coordination of School and Social Agency Resources: Role of the School Social Worker," *Education for Victory,* volume 3, number 5, September 4, 1944, p. 23.

tone of hopelessness and anxiety in her conversation which, plus the fact that the school would insist that the Bureau take some action in regard to William, strengthened the worker's persistence. She called at the home a few days later and talked with Mrs. R as she sat by her kitchen table, tapping it nervously with her fingers and answering in brief, clipped sentences. She was obviously antagonized.

The worker said she realized that Mrs. R had signed the blank against her will. She affirmed this and said she still resented it. Again, as in the previous interview, it was made clear that the Bureau wished her to go through with the clinic study only if it would be helpful to her and the boy. She said she remembered that and therefore had not returned and now she was again being annoyed by the school's recurring complaints. She found William for the most part gentle and obedient at home and able to get along well with his brothers and sisters. Of course he was nervous but even when he showed terrific outbursts she never whipped him because it did no good.

She realized what the trouble was at home and went on to mention her husband's death. (The worker had learned from an agency record that Mrs. R had married a man much older than herself, had quarrelled with him and finally taken him to court, that he had then registered a counter-charge against her.) The worker took this opportunity to say that she knew of Mrs. R's difficult time with her husband and of the court action. At first it was denied vehemently. Then slowly, with much feeling, Mrs. R told of her constant fear of having more than the five children who had come in such rapid succession; of her quarrels with her husband and frequent flights to her mother's home; of her swearing out a warrant against him; of her bitterness about his countercharge against her; and finally of his death.

Eventually, Mrs. R herself brought the conversation back to the subject of signing the consent blank. She had decided it would be safe and she proceeded to give considerable information about William's early childhood.[8]

Aside from their direct work with families, school social workers throughout the country cooperate with their communities to further mental hygiene benefits. Much of the history of school social work has stressed the mental hygiene contribution to normal living. School social workers have seen that they are are in a strategic position in many communities to assist in this direction.

Referral to Community Agencies

As has been mentioned, a current trend in school social work is that which emphasizes the various general services which communities

[8]Shirley Leonard, "Intake Policies in a School Setting," *The Family* (now *Journal of Social Casework*), volume 22, number 8, December, 1941, p. 266.

commonly provide for persons in need. Increasingly, it is being seen by school social workers that they should not initiate a program which might duplicate services already existing in the community. Wherever such prior services are adequate, the modern worker is interested in relying upon them rather than in competing with them.

Aside from duplication, there are other reasons why the school social worker does not wish to develop all types of social service to students. For one thing, some services are too expensive. It is not possible, for example, for the school social worker to organize a relief program to assist unemployed parents of school children; schools simply do not have the financial resources to enter the field of unemployment assistance. Again, there is the matter of staff availability. (See Tables 11 and 12.)

Table 11

NUMBER OF PUPILS ENROLLED FOR EACH VISITING TEACHER,
BY NUMBER OF CITIES REPORTING

Number of Pupils	Cities Reporting	Number of Pupils	Cities Reporting
1,000 or under	6	7,001 to 8,000	10
1,001 to 2,000	29	8,001 to 9,000	4
2,001 to 3,000	57	10,001 to 15,000	8
3,001 to 4,000	29	18,000 to 25,000	1
4,001 to 5,000	19	More than 25,000	1
5,001 to 6,000	11	Not reporting	77
6,001 to 7,000	14		
		Total	266

Source: Same, p. 21, as Table 10.

Table 12

ANNUAL COST OF VISITING TEACHER SERVICES PER PUPIL ENROLLED,
BY NUMBER OF CITIES REPORTING

Cost per Pupil	Cities Reporting	Cost per Pupil	Cities Reporting
$0.10 or less	10	$1.01 to $3	28
$0.11 to $0.40	52	More than $3	8
$0.41 to $0.70	52	Not reporting	67
$0.71 to $1	49	Total	266

Source: Same, p. 24, as Table 10.

The school social worker has enough to do to discharge his own functions efficiently without attempting to assume several other roles. Thus if he finds that some children would be benefited by activities of a group work nature, he can refer them to various neighborhood facilities where there already exist trained staffs for just this purpose. Then, too, there is the question of competence. If a child's difficulties seem to stem from some physical disability, referral to the clinic of a hospital may be helpful. Or, in cases of extreme emotional instability, treatment in a psychiatric clinic may be indicated.

Need of Child's Parents. Sometimes it is the child's parents who need to be referred to some community agency. The following is a case summary in which the needs of a child, "Jane," in relation to her performance at school led to family considerations which ultimately necessitated a referral of the mother to a family casework agency:

Jane, fourteen, was referred to the worker in the schools because her frequent absences were seriously retarding her school progress. Although illness had been given as an excuse, it was thought by the school, based on the mother's reports, that Jane was not physically ill, but emotionally upset due to conflicts in the home.

Mrs. B was introduced to the worker when she came to school to discuss Jane's absences. The principal explained that the worker was someone in the school to help children who had special problems. Mrs. B accepted this and said that she hoped the worker could help Jane, who was very unhappy.

During the first three interviews, Mrs. B confined her discussion to a consideration of Jane's problems, their causes, and implications. She explained that the absences followed quarrels between Jane and Mr. B. After these quarrels and punishment, Jane cried all night and was unable to come to school the next morning.

Mrs. B showed some insight into the causes of her husband's behavior and discussed with the worker ways of dealing with it. Although she commented that she herself was unhappy, she said that she was resigned to her lot but wanted something different for Jane. She asked for suggestions about how she might help Jane with her social relationships, discussing particular situations in which there was difficulty.

During these interviews, Mrs. B seemed to make constructive use of the help which the worker was equipped to give. However, she then attempted to use the worker in another area of her problem.

Mrs. B came to the fourth appointment looking worried and nervous. Mr. B had been drinking again. He had been abusing her and the children and threatened to move the family to a cheap four-room apartment. She wondered if the worker could help in forcing Mr. B to remain in their present home. The worker explained that she, herself, could not help with this problem and again interpreted her function in the school. She suggested that Mrs. B contact the Family Society (previously active), explaining their ability to help with a problem of this kind. Mrs. B showed some resistance to this suggestion, complaining of the previous family worker and saying that she had never known why the worker had been "sent in" before. Mrs. B was helped to bring out her feelings about this and it was pointed out that the situation would be different this time as Mrs. B would be going to them asking for help with a problem that was bothering her. Mrs. B agreed that she would like to "try again" and asked the worker's help in making an appointment. It was agreed that Mrs. B would continue to see the worker for help with Jane and her difficulty in school.

A conference was held with the Family Society, in which it was decided that that agency would work with Mrs. B on the domestic problem and the school worker would continue to see both Mrs. B and Jane about problems presenting themselves in relationship to Jane's activity in the school.

Jane accepted interviews with the worker readily, saying that her mother had told her that this was a person with whom she could "talk it out." During the early interviews there were frequent complaints about her father, his abusiveness to her, and his accusations against her. There was discussion about how she and her mother handled these situations and an attempt was made on the part of the worker to understand Jane's feeling about them. During the time that Mrs. B was upset about the domestic problem, Jane's interviews seemed almost to have been prompted by her mother. This material was handled on the basis of Jane's own feeling, and an effort was made to encourage her when she differentiated her feelings from those of her mother and discussed constructive ways of dealing with her relationship to her father. In one interview she told of a party which she was planning to give. Her father had opened one of the invitations and objected strenuously. Jane commented, "My mother would stop here, but I won't." Later she described enthusiastically how well her father behaved at the party, "even helping with the refreshments."

In every interview Jane also discussed problems related to the school—grades, friendships, and activities. The importance of this area was stressed with an explanation to Jane that here she could receive satisfactions regardless of the problems at home. Jane responded to the worker's interest in her academic achievement and extracurricular activities. She brought out her ability in art and her attempts to enter a special art class. As her interest in school increased she became enthusiastic about plans for high school next year. The worker pointed out that her frequent absence would create a more serious problem in high school than it had in elementary school. Jane recognized this and agreed to make an effort to come to school regardless of her feelings and to talk with the worker if she felt too upset to attend classes.

There was a noticeable improvement in Jane's school work, attendance, and social relationships. If, after further work and study, it is felt that the problem with her father is of such a fundamental nature that it impedes further progress, referral for help in this area will be considered.[9]

Cooperation Between Workers. The school social worker does not merely refer cases in many instances; he stands by to contribute his share to the assistance of the child client. This means that he cooperates with other agencies in the community whenever possible and to the extent to which such cooperation lies within his defined function as a school social worker. The school social worker, then, cannot fulfill his entire purpose unless he avails himself of the information and skill of other social workers within the community. The need for cooperation between workers concerned with the welfare of clients is made vivid in the following illustration taken from an address by Miss Shirley Leonard, Chief School Psychiatric Social Worker of the Bureau of Child Guidance in New York City (part of the Board of Education) to the New York State Youth Commission:

> Throughout the recent war period, great progress has been made in closer contact between schools and community agencies—which is all to the good. But what we need to recognize is that most schools cannot even make full use of community agencies unless they have social workers on their school staffs. The following incident is a good illustration: Several years ago, a school social worker gave a course in the summer session of the University of Washington. It was called "The Social Adjustment of School Children" and had in it thirty students, about half of them teachers and half of them social workers employed in several of the states in the northwest. Class discussion focused around specific problems of children with which either a teacher or a social worker needed some special help.
>
> One day one of the members who had been a teacher and recently became a principal brought to class a long written report of a family she had been struggling with for years. It was one of those families social workers know so well—with a somewhat inadequate father who was an unskilled worker, a harassed, intellectually low-grade mother, frequent family illnesses, too little income, and too many children. As each new child entered the school, teachers groaned. Irregular attendance, uncleanliness, tardiness were the problems at first. The principal described her long-suffering attempts to correct conditions by sending for the parents, visiting the home, and encouraging the children. Nothing helped. Finally,

[9]Florence Poole, "The Child and the Social Case Worker in the Schools," *Social Case Work in Public Schools,* published by the American Association of Visiting Teachers (now National Association of School Social Workers), October, 1941, pp. 38–40.

when one of the older children became a full-blown behavior problem, with stealing and defiant outbursts in the classroom, she resorted to corporal punishment. She told this to the class with considerable feeling ending with, "I don't think, after this summer, I'd do that again."

Immediately she was bombarded with questions from members of the group—several of them in county welfare work. What was the family budget, had the children had physical examinations, what was this boy's intellectual ability and was he in the right class, what was known about the parents' attitudes toward each child, etc. The bell rang and the class adjourned for that day. Next morning, the school principal led off at the beginning of the session, "Since yesterday I have learned that Miss ——— (she turned to the person next to her) is a worker in the County Department and has known this family for six years. She will answer some of the questions I couldn't yesterday." By the end of the course, the school principal and the county welfare worker left Seattle for their small city in North Dakota, with a plan to work together not just with this family but with others. Neither one expected any Utopian results but each realized the importance of concerted effort. This school principal, if she had had her own social worker, would have been working in close touch with the county welfare worker long before, and especially with new school entrants from this particular home.[10]

Thus the school social worker fulfills his diagnostic function by making referrals where necessary to other community resources, and fulfills his coordinative function by cooperating with those community resources for the ultimate well-being of the child.

Direct Treatment

From one point of view, every phase of the school social worker's task involves some direct treatment of the adjustment problems of school children. What usually differs from case to case is the extent to which the worker deals with the individual's problem without calling in others from the community. There are times when the worker cannot effectively use community resources outside the school but must rely upon his own facilities. This may be true where appropriate community resources do not exist or where they are already overburdened. In those cases where they are absent, the worker, both for the sake of the community in general and his own special function in particular, would feel called upon to organize such services. Where they already exist but are impractical either because a fee is charged, because the facilities are not geared to the needs of school children, or because they are already overtaxed with clients, the school social worker seeks to correct these deficiencies.

[10]From an unpublished manuscript.

Teacher Assistance. The school itself, however, is an important resource for the school social worker. It is often necessary to include the staff of the school as being in strategic positions for the influencing of their charges. Especially is this true of teachers. Where this is so, the teacher and the social worker may comprise a team for the direct treatment of a child. The following case summary provides an example:

Aged twelve, physically attractive, of better than average mental capacity, living in an economically secure home, Mary Jane suddenly amazed her teacher by becoming quarrelsome with her classmates and generally disagreeable and uncooperative in the classroom. The visiting teacher found her pretty glad to have someone with whom she might discuss her troubles although she confessed she was so fearful the youngsters might find out about her worry that she had refrained from going to her teacher. In fact she thought her teacher was "too nice to know about me." It seemed she had recently learned she was an adopted daughter and that no one knew who her real parents were. Apprehension about her heritage and insecurity about her status with the foster brothers she had considered her own, were reflected in her school relationships. With the worker's assistance Mary Jane was able to gain some understanding of what the situation meant to her as well as ability to discuss it with her teacher and foster parents. The teacher worked faithfully with the caseworker and Mary Jane on plans which helped her feel comfortable with her classmates and others. In school she is once more her old happy self and the teacher is glad he realized the importance of seeking assistance.[11]

Summary of Five Functions

By way of summary, the functions of the school social worker include:

1. Attendance duties
2. Behavior-problems adjustment
3. Home-school relationships
4. Referral to community agencies
5. Direct treatment

In this connection it cannot be supposed that the duties of the worker neatly fall from moment to moment into one or another of these categories. These divisions simply serve to picture the roles which the worker is asked to assume. Usually, as in some of the cases presented in this section, the worker in handling a problem may be involved with several of the functions concurrently.

[11]Gladys E. Hall, "The Function of the Caseworker in a School Setting," *The Bulletin of the Virginia Conference of Social Work,* Visiting Teacher Issue, volume 1, number 2, January, 1946, p. 14.

List of Duties

The five functions of the school social worker, moreover, which have been mentioned, do not comprise all of his duties. A conference called by the U. S. Commissioner of Education, held in Washington in June, 1945, and attended by representatives of the United States Children's Bureau, the United States Office of Education, and others connected with the actual practice of school social work in one way or another, issued a longer list of duties. The Conference's special statement was as follows:[12]

GENERAL DUTIES

1. The responsibilities and duties of visiting teachers are, to a considerable extent, influenced by the number of visiting teachers employed, the resources of the school, and the community which each services.

2. The general function of the visiting teacher is to serve individual pupils who need special understanding and help in problems of social adjustment so that they may derive the utmost benefit from their school experiences, and to assist those responsible to make adjustments in school experiences, where necessary, to meet each pupil's needs and help him find opportunities to continue his educational program to the maximum of his capacity and adjustment.

3. The work of the visiting teacher augments and supplements rather than replaces the help given by the classroom teachers, the school psychologist, and the educational counselor. The success of the visiting teacher service depends, to a large degree, upon adequate preparation of personnel to do the job, as well as the sympathetic understanding of the total school program on the part of the whole school personnel, the child, and the parents, and upon the mutual understanding of how each can utilize the services of the others.

SPECIFIC DUTIES

1. Organize a visiting teacher program.

2. Work with children on both elementary and secondary levels who present difficulties in their adjustment to school situations.

3. Act as consultant to parents, pupils, and school personnel, on problems of children. This assumes:

    a. a thorough knowledge of the problems most common to children and specifically the symptoms indicative of such problems so that

[12]*Visiting Teacher Services,* Report of a Conference Called by the Commissioner of Education and Held in the United States Office of Education, Washington, D. C., June, 1945, Leaflet 75, written by Katherine M. Cook, United States Office of Education, Federal Security Agency, United States Government Printing Office, Washington, D. C., 1946, pp. 8–9.

prevention can be considered as a main objective of the visiting teacher program;

b. skill in helping children to assume responsibility for these problems and work toward ultimate improvement.

4. Interpret the program to the community, to the various lay and professional agencies, to the school staff, to parents and children.

5. Work with parents, community agencies, and individuals to modify whatever conditions are necessary to meet the problems of children.

6. Cooperate in stimulating total faculty planning on the problems of children, to assist in adjusting the program to the individual needs, and/or assist the children to adjust themselves to socially acceptable patterns.

7. Work with school officials to achieve a community-wide understanding of the school and the community agencies and how they are related in their functions.

8. Study children and home and school conditions which promote good educational relationships, and make such study of variations as will make it possible for individuals to receive all that education may offer.

9. Assume responsibility for referral to appropriate community agencies. This involves a knowledge of all the agencies, local and state, which serve children, and of how to secure and use their services.

10. Devise and maintain an adequate system of records.

11. Through cooperative effort of all interested groups, stimulate the development of such necessary services to children as are not available at the present time.

Combination of Functions. The following account shows how a school social worker in a small city combines many of the above functions in her daily activities:

Just what sort of thing does a visiting teacher do in a small city? Let's glance at her date-book notes. Every day from 8:30 to 3:30 she visits two or more schools. As the only person, except the superintendent, to cover all school levels, she has a big "laboratory" from a study of which she can recommend coordinated action for the whole school system. Today, she has finished a study on proper age for admission to kindergarten and grade 1, in cooperation with the school psychologist. Tomorrow, she may begin a study of the underage child.

For this afternoon, she has arranged a meeting of the student teachers practicing in the various schools. Here the superintendent and the woman member of the board of education explain the philosophy of the school and the type of community. The members of the Child Guidance Department discuss their contribution to the children. In this way, students know something about the whole system and are given an introduction into the possibilities of their profession. Both student teachers and colleges have found such meetings helpful.

Friday, she will meet the last of the new pupils entering the high school this year because this is the most difficult adjustment for them to make. Tuesday, a visit with foreign-born parents to help them with various problems of self-adjustment. A new teacher is given a thumbnail sketch of some of the pupils she is taking on. Another teacher has difficulty with the backward children in her group and consults the visiting teacher about techniques.

One mother wants to know why her Sheila can't get to sleep nights— so high-strung! How can she be told that dinner at eight is too late for third-graders? George Washington Lincoln is throwing rocks; "Dosie Doats" bites her nails! Jimmy James cries at home but not at school; Angelica is scared of pets; Jonesy tells some "whoppers" daily; Mary May "acquires" things . . . Conference with principal, teacher, then child, then parent; perhaps with doctor, pastor, social worker, or public health nurse.

George bullies because papa is out of a job. Sheila's mother is out all the time. Henry's father has married again. John's mother has six children and is worn out. Follow them all up. Get help somewhere, or send them to it.

Three street lights near Floral School have been smashed in recent months. The big brothers of the boys tell visiting teacher it is because the youngsters are hanging around outside the recreation center. Get age lowered for admission to recreation center. Suggest a summer library in distant schools. How about a cub scout troup? Lots of sickness in Mercy School. Nurses report families of eight living in rooms without adequate ventilation, heat, or baths. Call board of health nurse. Get civic groups on it.[13]

It is important at this point to stress the fact that the school social worker's interest embraces not only the child, but the teachers and school administrations as well. In this regard the worker cooperates closely with the school officials in the carrying out of their functions. The teacher may not find it feasible to send all disciplinary problems to the school social worker, but may himself get much help from the mutual interchange of experience and ideas in consultation with the worker. Where the child is referred directly, the school social worker aids the teacher's understanding by discussing the case with him. School administrators on occasion may be similarly involved.

Bureau of Child Guidance. In some localities there are psychologists and psychiatrists who also take part in the treatment of children. Here the school social work program closely resembles that of the child guidance clinic. An example is provided by the school social work unit

[13]Condensed from Nora Alice Way, "The Visiting Teacher in the Small Community," *Education for Victory,* volume 2, number 24, June 20, 1944, p. 29.

of the Board of Education in New York City, the Bureau of Child Guidance. The following is a description of the Bureau's organization and service:

The New York Bureau of Child Guidance was established by the New York Board of Education in 1931 for the study and treatment of school children showing academic, behavior, or personality problems. A second and equally important part of its function is the mental hygiene education of school personnel. The Clinic was organized in various boroughs through Child Guidance Units, each Unit consisting of a psychiatrist acting as administrative head, from two to four psychologists, and several psychiatric social workers. The latter are assigned to all the schools in the district for which their Unit is responsible, and serve as intake workers.

Referrals come largely from school principals or other administrative persons in the schools. The social worker, in close touch with principals and teachers, may help them to make use of other agencies and clinics if the problem seems not an appropriate one for the Bureau of Child Guidance. Some of the cases referred may require only a few contacts with the parent, others may indicate clearly that the child needs psychological study. Frequently the parent will accept help from the school but is threatened by even the thought of any agency outside. In such a situation, the social worker may continue contacts with child or parent only long enough to reassure them and enable them to accept the services of the agency whose program meets their need.

For the most seriously upset children the Clinic operates as a team. The social worker talks with the principal and the teachers who know the child, in order to get as complete a picture as possible of his school experience. She then sees the mother or the father, sometimes both, learning from them about their child's early developmental and health history, his family situation, and the attitudes and relationships which are patterning his behavior. The social worker's next step is to see that the psychiatrist and the psychologist study the child. An initial conference is then held which consists of a pooling of the material that has emerged from the social worker's picture of the child in his family and school setting, the psychologist's findings as to his intelligence level, special abilities and disabilities, school achievement, and his educational needs. To this the psychiatrist adds what he has learned about the child's physical and emotional condition, his feelings about himself, his parents, his brothers and sisters. The psychiatrist determines the kind and extent of the personality disturbance. As often as possible the school principal or the teacher is present at this initial conference to present the classroom aspect of the child's behavior.

A tentative diagnosis is then made which gives a dynamic picture of the forces operating in the child's life to produce his behavior, and a treatment plan is evolved. This may mean that the psychiatrist takes the child on for treatment or that the psychologist or a teacher tutors him, or that the social worker sees the parent at regular times to help him in better understanding and handling of the child. All three of these services may be used or any one of them according to the seriousness of the problem and the areas in which the child needs help. Soon after the initial conference the social worker sees the parent to interpret the findings of the study, and does the same with the school personnel. She follows the school visit with a written report which is a simple, untechnical explanation of what has entered into the child's problem and what the school may do to help. Further contacts with the teacher and the principal may be frequent and often result in the better handling of the child in the classroom as well as at home.[14]

A description of the child guidance clinic follows in Chapter 7.

CERTIFICATION

Social workers in general do not have to secure state licenses before they can practice; the profession generally is regulated on a less formal basis. The schools of social work graduate students with diplomas, certificates, or degrees, and these tend to take the place of public certification of competence. The intelligent employer of social workers today will want to know from a job candidate whether he has graduated from a social work school or not. At present about fifty of these schools exist, distributed through almost all sections of the country.

Another means of judging the reliability of the social worker in general is his membership status with the American Association of Social Workers or with some other equally valued professional association such as the American Association of Psychiatric Social Workers or the National Association of School Social Workers. The standards of these Associations are of such a nature that they tend to establish safeguards for agencies seeking fully qualified social workers.

State Requirements Vary

At present there are few examinations which can evaluate the ability of social workers, although the American Association of Schools of Social Work has been considering for some time the advisability of creating one. Such a test could then possibly be used by the different states in setting up licensure practices.

In the field of school social work the problem of certification is especially important since so many of the workers are employed by school systems which commonly rely on some form of licensing. In some states

[14]Description supplied by Miss Shirley Leonard of the Bureau of Child Guidance, New York City.

Table 13

CERTIFICATES REQUIRED OR HELD BY VISITING TEACHERS, BY STATE, NUMBER OF CITIES, AND TYPE OF CERTIFICATE

State	Number of cities reporting	Type of Certificate					None	No information
		Special		Teachers		Both teachers and special		
		State visiting teachers	Other*	State teachers	Other†			
Alabama	3	—	1	2	—	—	—	—
Arkansas	3	—	—	1	—	—	2	—
California	17	—	4	8	—	3	—	2
Colorado	5	1	—	2	—	—	2	—
Connecticut	3	—	1	1	1	—	—	—
Delaware	1	—	—	—	—	—	1	—
Georgia	6	—	—	1	1	—	4	—
Idaho	2	—	—	—	—	—	2	—
Illinois	14	—	1	7	—	2	3	1
Indiana	13	—	5	3	—	2	3	—
Iowa	5	—	—	4	—	1	—	—
Kansas	2	—	—	1	—	—	1	—
Kentucky	6	—	2	3	—	1	—	—
Louisiana	1	—	—	—	—	—	1	—
Maryland	1	—	—	—	—	—	1	—
Massachusetts	12	—	—	—	—	—	12	—
Michigan	18	—	2	9	3	1	3	—
Mississippi	2	—	—	1	—	—	1	—
Missouri	5	—	—	4	—	—	1	—
Montana	2	—	—	2	—	—	—	—
Nebraska	2	—	—	2	—	—	—	—
New Jersey	14	4	—	2	—	2	5	1
New Mexico	2	—	1	—	—	—	1	—
New York	16	—	5	5	—	3	2	1
North Carolina	4	—	—	—	—	—	4	—

(continued on page 259)

the state teaching examination and license may be adequate for local appointment as a school social worker. In other states there may be local requirements more exacting than those made by the state. (See Table 13.)

Other states and localities, however, feel that in the area of school social work no license is at present practicable. It is becoming increasingly evident that school social workers need not be both trained teachers and social workers. It is fortunate indeed when the social worker in the school system has definite knowledge and appreciation of the schools out of which referrals come. This background, however, is no more specialized for school social work practice than that of the hospital

Table 13 (*continued*)

CERTIFICATES REQUIRED OR HELD BY VISITING TEACHERS,
BY STATE, NUMBER OF CITIES, AND TYPE OF CERTIFICATE

State	Number of cities reporting	Type of Certificate				Both teachers and special	None	No information
		Special		Teachers				
		State visiting teachers	Other*	State teachers	Other†			
North Dakota	2	—	—	1	1	—	—	—
Ohio	28	—	3	15	1	3	6	—
Oklahoma	5	—	1	1	2	—	—	1
Oregon	3	—	1	1	—	1	—	—
Pennsylvania	33	—	6	11	4	3	6	3
Rhode Island	2	—	—	1	—	—	1	—
South Carolina	3	—	—	2	—	—	—	1
Tennessee	6	—	—	3	—	—	2	1
Texas	8	—	—	3	—	—	5	—
Utah	2	—	2	—	—	—	—	—
Virginia	1	—	—	1	—	—	—	—
Washington	3	—	—	1	1	—	1	—
Wisconsin	10	—	—	5	1	1	3	—
Wyoming	1	—	—	—	—	1	—	—
Total	266	5	35	103	15	24	73	11

*Includes "special," "special attendance," "child welfare and attendance," "special school-nurse-teacher certificate," "visiting teacher certificate."
†Includes "regular," "teaching certificate," "normal diploma," "college permanent," "standard."

Source: Same, p. 44, as Table 10.

for the medical social worker, and yet it is not a requirement that a medical social worker also be a licensed nurse. The education—in the classroom and in field work—received today by school social workers in accredited schools of social work amply prepares them for practice without additional specialization. The fact that some places require the school social worker to be a licensed teacher also reduces the chances of the schools to get a sufficient number of qualified school social workers, for there are only a relatively few persons who happily combine both teaching and social work backgrounds. It seems clear that no real harm can come and certain genuine advantages may accrue from the removal of this dual requirement.

Licensing Practices

In those states that require licensing of one type or another, the school social worker is given either a special license which indicates his status as a school social worker (although the actual titling may differ from place to place) or a license which certifies that he is merely a teacher. Where the latter procedure holds, local boards of education may set informal requirements for school social workers, making sure that the teacher is "more than a teacher," that he has some knowledge and skill in social work. According to a recent study only about 32% of the cities having school social workers require licensing of some sort. In those cities where no licensing is required, informal arrangements for the hiring of school social workers usually are used. These differ rather widely from place to place.

Terms Used for Workers

The name most commonly used for workers in this field is "visiting teacher," but this is gradually being replaced by "school social worker." Other terms in use are: "home or school visitor," "nurse, school nurse, or visiting nurse," "school visitor," "attendance supervisor," "coordinator," "director of individual guidance," "truant, probation officer, or school patrolman," and "visiting counselor." Other terms used in a relatively few locations are: "adjustment service worker," "dean," "director," "family life coordinator," "guidance counselor," "personnel worker," "principal," "school caseworker," "welfare director," and "child welfare worker." The variety of titles under which school social workers operate indicates the lack of uniformity which pervades the field as a whole. Certainly, one of the needs in the field is a greater degree of consistency.

SELECTED READINGS ON SCHOOL SOCIAL WORK

American Council on Education, Commission on Teacher Education, *Helping Teachers Understand Children,* Washington, D.C., 1945.

Benedict, Agnes E., *Children at the Crossroads,* Commonwealth Fund, New York, 1930.

Cook, Katherine M., *The Place of Visiting Teacher Services in the School Program,* United States Office of Education, Bulletin 1945, Washington, D.C.

――――, *Visiting Teacher Services,* United States Office of Education, Leaflet number 75, Washington, D.C., 1946.

Culbert, Jane F., *The Visiting Teacher at Work,* Commonwealth Fund, New York, 1929.

Ellis, Mabel E., *The Visiting Teacher in Rochester: Report of a Study,* Joint Committee on Methods of Preventing Delinquency, Commonwealth Fund, New York, 1925.

Everett, Edith M., *Visiting Teacher Service Today,* American Association of School Social Workers (now National Association of School Social Workers), New York, 1940.

Kvaraceus, William V., *Juvenile Delinquency and the School*, World Book, Yonkers, New York, 1945.

Louttit, Chauncey M., *Clinical Psychology: A Handbook of Children's Behavior Problems*, Harper, New York, 1936.

Oppenheimer, Julius J., *The Visiting Teacher Movement: With Special Reference to Administrative Relationships*, Commonwealth Fund, New York, 1925.

Sayles, Mary B., *The Problem Child in School: Narratives From Case Records of Visiting Teachers*, Commonwealth Fund, New York, 1929.

For additional related readings, consult the bibliographies at the end of the other child welfare chapters.

The Child Guidance Clinic

The child guidance clinic plays an important part in the modern treatment of children. Its work is shown in the case of "Caroline G." Her case is taken from the records of the Institute for Juvenile Research, a child guidance clinic in Chicago:

> Caroline G was an eighteen-year-old girl, the older of two children. The family lived in a small town some distance from Chicago where they owned their home and were well thought of in the community. In contrast to her brother, aged sixteen, who was serious-minded, ambitious, and who conformed to the family pattern and selected his friends from among the "best people," Caroline was uninterested in school, resisted all attempts at control by her parents and showed little discrimination in her choice of friends. In fact, she seemed to prefer to associate with the "bad girls" of the town and was much talked about for this. She had a marked interest in men, including some of bad repute. For these reasons and because her mother, Mrs. G, wished vocational advice for her daughter, Caroline was brought to the clinic. Caroline had left high school at the end of her third year and had come to Chicago to attend an art school for the summer. At the time of the examination she was insisting that she be allowed to remain in the city without her parents and to continue in art school during the coming winter.
>
> The history disclosed that there was always considerable antagonism between brother and sister, that she had always hated school, had repeated several grades, and had exhibited indifference to her teachers. However, she had been regarded as a "sweet, lovable child" and the mother reported no difficulty with her until about the age of thirteen. At that time the family moved to another town and Caroline made friends with a girl whom the parents felt to be socially inferior, as she was the daughter of a gas-station attendant. Caroline's father was very proud of his ancestry

and in his devotion to his daughter was much disturbed over her association with any one whom he felt to be inferior. The parents tried to break up this new friendship only to have Caroline insist on seeing her friend, resorting to subterfuge if necessary to carry out her wishes. After a time this friendship gave way to another, equally disfavored, which the mother again sought vainly to dissolve. She probably felt the "disgrace of inferior associates" less than did the father, but was the one responsible for the active steps taken to combat it.

Finally Caroline made friends with a charming girl, the daughter of a physician, and over this the mother was quite happy. Nearly two years later she learned through town gossip that Caroline had been initiated into various types of sex play by her latest friend and the latter's young brother. In spite of heroic efforts the family was unable to break up this friendship until they finally left town. In their new community Caroline again selected as companions two girls of whom her parents disapproved because of their reputations, and her interests now were chiefly in dates and petting. Her rebelliousness to her parents increased steadily and she lied to them almost constantly. She had frequent temper tantrums and much of her behavior was described as "willful disobedience." Some of it was quite bizarre and the mother was especially shocked by Caroline's interest in sex terms and vulgar phrases and her absorption in people of unsavory character. She protested that the girl was ruining her reputation and bewailed the fact that in her behavior Caroline never considered "a mother's feelings." The father considered the mother's methods too easy and demanded vigorous action to curb the daughter, but on the other hand he was almost lavish in the amount of money he gave her. This was particularly true even in view of a definitely reduced family income.

The study at the Institute revealed a very slender, rather attractive-looking girl of superior intelligence whose energies were poorly directed. She was quite self-centered, much interested in her attractiveness to men, but showed no warm feeling for any one except some of her girl friends. She was dissatisfied with everything, even with her art work, although it was the one thing she had always wanted to do. Much of her behavior was felt to be rebellion against overprotective parents who were quite moralistic in their attitudes and overly interested in social position. It was decided that an opportunity for her to develop in her particular field, art, was important and that recognition here, together with a less restricted social environment, might make her problems less acute.

The director of the art school reported that Caroline had good ability and the parents were willing for her to continue there through the winter and live at a girls' club maintained under religious auspices. It was probably not so much recognition of the girl's need that prompted this decision, as sheer hopelessness, for the parents were at the end of their resources. The father expressed it well when he said to the psychiatrist that, although she ought to be at home, they would not know what to do with her if she were. She was completely out of hand.

It was felt by the Institute staff that Caroline needed some steering and some support in this new situation, but that it would have to be done skillfully and subtly so as not to arouse her antagonism further. She needed the experience of making her own decisions and accepting the consequences of them. But she could not be cut loose to sink or swim when her training had obviously never been the kind to foster a gradual development from the dependency of childhood to an adult responsibility for herself. She craved independence but lacked the in-between experiences calculated to develop judgment.

With these points in mind a social worker was selected who, it was planned, would make friends with Caroline and give her some support without becoming authoritative. The worker was a young person herself, not too much older than Caroline, but with enough maturity to understand many of Caroline's difficulties. Her own interests were somewhat similar to those of the girl and she was acceptable to Caroline as a friend whom she could comfortably introduce to her other friends. The worker met Caroline for tea after school, they had dinner together occasionally at the girls' club where she lived, downtown, and at the worker's apartment, and Caroline came occasionally to the Institute for interviews.

Throughout this time she was encouraged to discuss with the worker whatever interested her: her school work and plans for the future; her girl friends at the club; the various men she had known and liked, with reason therefor; the parties she attended; and her relationships with her family and the people in her home town, where she returned to spend nearly every week end at the parents' suggestion. While maintaining a noncriticizing attitude, the worker helped Caroline express and examine her confused feelings toward various people, to evaluate her own behavior and gradually to come to understand somewhat not only why she felt and acted as she did but also what lay back of her parents' attitudes. The worker suggested reading to Caroline which might be helpful to her. Together they discussed some of the personal implications of the ideas in this reading.

During this period Caroline's dissatisfaction with the school and with herself continued. She attended irregularly and finally changed to another school where the emphasis was chiefly on costume design. Her own interest in exotic and bizarre effects in clothes continued. She dyed her hair and was delighted with the excitement this caused at the club. Her extravagance, of which the family had previously complained, continued even in the face of a somewhat diminished family income. After a time, however, she began to be concerned over finances and conceived the idea of doing part-time work as a model in a dress shop in order to lessen her financial demands on the family as well as to get more spending money for herself. The worker pointed out the advantages and disadvantages of this, but left the decision to Caroline, who finally dropped the idea. In the spring, quite on her own initiative she obtained for herself a housework job as a mother's helper. She evidently hoped her father would continue to send the full amount of money for her board and she would thus have more to use for clothes, but this he declined to do, agreeing to send her half the usual amount. She made no objection to this plan and by this time she was quite able to see his point of view. The fact that her job would keep her at home every evening, taking care of the baby in the family and give her practically no chance to attend the frequent parties, which she had enjoyed, apparently disturbed her not at all.

Without doing any declaiming about it, she settled down to much more serious work at school, discontinued her frequent absences there, and took on the added responsibilities of her job with credit to herself and satisfaction to her employer. The worker, acting as consultant and confidante, was impressed with Caroline's judgment of situations and her growing insight into her own behavior. It became apparent, too, that while Caroline had a flair for the unconventional, her behavior as seen from the larger perspective was much less bizarre than it had appeared to the family in their smaller community. When faced with the opportunities for somewhat more unconventional activities in Chicago than at home, she evaluated these situations sensibly and patterned her behavior along wholly acceptable lines. These decisions were the result of her own thinking and judgment rather than of restrictive or coercive measures applied from without.

During the spring the mother came to Chicago and the worker had some opportunity to become better acquainted with her. She proved to be quite proud of her daughter's ingenuity and resourcefulness and admired the "spirit" she had shown. The mother disclosed a certain sympathy herself for behavior which deviated from the rigidly conservative mold in which she was forced to live, at the same time recognizing the practical necessity of conformity. The worker, utilizing this attitude, was able to interpret Caroline's behavior to her mother and, in turn, to bring to Caroline a fuller understanding of the mother's position and of her underlying hopes and aspirations for her daughter. In this and in previous contacts with the mother through letters, the worker's role was one of mediator and interpreter.

In June, Caroline returned to live with her family, thus carrying out a plan she had been considering for some time, namely, to live at home and to attend the college there and to take a business course through the summer which would later enable her to get work. She planned, also, to study sculpture with an artist in the town. Interestingly, the suggestion of the business course had originally come from her brother whom formerly she had heartily disliked. He, too, was planning to take the same course that summer.

In making and carrying out these plans, Caroline was able to proceed in a much more matter-of-fact way than had characterized her thinking and planning of a year before when she left home to study in Chicago. With much more clarity she could understand her situation. The insight she had gained increased her tolerance for her family and lessened her need to oppose them. The plan initiated by herself met with the parents' hearty approval in contrast to their grudging consent of the year before.

If the family does not reassume repressive measures or insist upon planning and managing her life as before, but encourages the independent, responsible, growing-into-adulthood behavior which she is now manifesting, the prognosis for Caroline's ultimate adjustment is felt to be highly favorable.[1]

The case of "Caroline" illustrates one type of problem that is met in child guidance clinics and shows how treatment was effected. The child guidance clinic is designed to cope with a wide range of problems and to serve children of all ages.

THE PLACE OF THE CHILD GUIDANCE CLINIC

It is apparent that with all of the many services for children offered by modern communities there should be room for child guidance clinics; for the clinic, as the name bespeaks, provides opportunity for specific study and treatment of childhood problems. Not that the clinic is the only place where child guidance is carried on, for, in the most general sense, child guidance is within the province of parents, nursery school leaders, teachers, clergymen, judges, social workers, psychiatrists, and others in many different situations. The clinic can be described as being highly similar at points with other community facilities that serve children, but differing in that its fundamental objective is to aid socially and emotionally maladjusted children who live at home. While parents, teachers, clergymen, and others may on occasion deal with a problem child, they do not function primarily to serve problem children. The child guidance clinic, on the other hand, is designed especially to handle children's problems on an individual treatment basis.

In this connection, it is well to note that some child welfare agencies, which are not essentially clinics, may provide a variety of services to children, including those of a clinical nature. Thus, for example, an institution may offer child guidance services as part of its larger program for helping children. But, aside from such clinical services, there is a genuine place in the community for "unattached" clinics. What characterizes these clinics usually is that the use of psychotherapy is their first and foremost responsibility. It is true that they also find it necessary oftentimes to maintain such other services as medical treatment, foster home care, and institutional care, but this is as a means of fulfilling their primary obligation. Where child guidance clinics do not

[1]The Staff of the Institute for Juvenile Research, *Child Guidance Procedures: Methods and Techniques Employed at the Institute for Juvenile Research,* The Century Psychology Series, D. Appleton-Century, New York, 1937, pp. 169–175.

maintain such programs of their own, they may find referrals to other community agencies necessary and helpful. Referrals may be made either prior to or as a result of treatment.

HISTORICAL PRECEDENTS

While the term *child guidance clinic* first appeared in 1922, there is evidence that some agencies before that time were, in actual organization, a fair representation of what the movement later became. But before the first child guidance clinic was founded, even in nascent form, there were historic needs which made it possible for the movement to originate. Three of the factors, culturally speaking, contributing to the rise of child guidance clinics will be mentioned here.

Mental Disease

Interest in childhood experiences was one of the results of the scientific study of the mentally ill. This interest was founded on at least two major influences.

Psychoanalytic View. First, there was the psychoanalytic theory of Sigmund Freud, which held that the first five or six years were exceedingly important for the formulation of later character traits. This view modified the conception of the origins of mental disease and stressed the significance of early care of the mentally disordered. It also encouraged investigators to discover the detailed meaning of early life experience as a means of dealing with later disturbances. Psychoanalysis in its origin and development has contributed to the better understanding of the importance of childhood adjustment.

Mental Hygiene Movement. The second influence in developing an interest in children was the mental hygiene movement. The mental hygiene movement has been concerned primarily with the preservation of mental health. It has sought this preservation through a variety of measures. Its origins are ancient, but, nationally, the movement came into being through the crusading activities of Dorothea Dix and William Sweetser. Its modern phase and current effectiveness developed from the initiative supplied by Clifford Beers. Beers published an account in 1908 of his own mental illness and the treatment which he received in a mental hospital. The title of his classic work is: *A Mind That Found Itself.* Upon his recovery he pledged himself to work with vigor for the betterment of the conditions under which mental patients suffered. Dr. Adolf Meyer, to whom he turned in his efforts, advised a very broad approach to the institutional problem. Meyer suggested that a program be established which would for the most part aim at the prevention of mental disease. It was basically with this philosophy of action that Beers helped found the National Committee for Mental Hygiene in 1909. At present the Committee includes some 800 elected members, about 1,200 public memberships, and 30 state mental hygiene societies. It publishes *Mental Hygiene* and *Understanding the Child,* journals which aid its program. The purpose of the Committee is effectively summarized in the following sentence: "The Committee works for the conservation of mental health."

It was natural that the Committee, and other groups formed with the same or similar purposes, should be concerned with children and their mental health. For, in preventing mental illness among children, the logic ran, the incidence of mental illness among older persons in the population would be decreased. The child guidance clinics were one of the devices utilized early in the mental hygiene movement to implement its basic aims.

Delinquency

With the general growth of willingness to understand children and their problems in terms of a more scientific methodology of analysis and treatment, there came about during the period of the early 1900's an interest in the delinquent child as being a special problem, in contrast to the adult criminal. In this period, juvenile courts in which the unique needs of the delinquent could be presented and treated came into being. Moreover, under the impact of the evidence which was being assembled in the social sciences, it was becoming more and more difficult to distinguish, except perhaps for legal purposes, the delinquent, the predelinquent, and the nondelinquent. Seemingly, the behavior of each category even in relation to the law was not as simple as it had been assumed. This discovery threw open the whole problem of children's variant social behavior and gave ground for the rise of the child guidance clinic with its individual and objective methods of study and treatment.

Recidivism also stirred child welfare workers to realize the essentially preventive task which was theirs. So often the adult criminal showed that his growth into criminal behavior habits began at an early age. While curative efforts were made then as now with the adult criminal, it was early seen that the most fruitful period of attention was childhood and that the most beneficial type of work was basically preventive. The task of the child welfare worker in many instances was to save the child from a criminal's career before he was fully on the road to such a future. Again, interest in the delinquent and in child guidance clinics went hand in hand.

Increase in Scientific Understanding

Despite the fact that mental disease and delinquency contributed to the rise of the child guidance clinic movement in genuine ways, their significance would not have been realized unless there had been a concomitant growth in scientific understanding of human behavior generally. Part of this increase has been intimated in regard to the contribution of psychoanalysis to the movement. But there were other contributions as well.

Sociology and psychology especially, among the behavioral sciences, made rapid strides from the time of the First World War to the present. Before that they had had a significant history, but scarcely as developed and as reliable as in the later period. Psychology, for example, aided in the development of guidance procedures through the refinement of mental tests. The First World War itself was an impetus to psychologists to devise more dependable mental tests than had been previously possible. Sociologists also were active in showing that individual behavior is often determined by cultural features which influence the person. Thus, to this way of thinking, delinquency was not always a condition brought about by the inadequacy of the intrapsychic forces within the individual child, but was culturally derived from the groups in which children participated.

In addition to psychology and sociology there were other advances on which the child guidance movement relied. These were as broad as the human sciences themselves. The growth of knowledge within social work itself should not be neglected, for the accumulating experience of social workers in their various specialties gave strength to the guidance movement.

A PANORAMA OF GROWTH

Given the background of need in mental illness and delinquency and the increase in scientific knowledge, the rise of the child guidance clinic movement was assured. The earlier forms which it took were not always in accord with its latest developments, but they tend to throw some light on current procedure. For purposes of brevity, only three fundamental historical contributions to modern clinics for children will be mentioned.

State Hospitals and Institutions for the Feeble-Minded

The earliest clinic founded to meet the needs of children was that established by Dr. John B. Chapin in the Pennsylvania General Hospital in 1885. This clinic had as its purpose the "treatment of mental diseases in their early or incipient stages occurring among the poor and indigent." The emphasis upon "early or incipient stages" reminds one of the "preventive" stress which was to develop so thoroughly in the child guidance clinic field.

Other institutions soon followed the example of the Pennsylvania General Hospital. The Warren State Hospital in Pennsylvania developed a similar program for children. In 1897 the Boston Dispensary was opened under the leadership of Dr. Walter Channing. This clinic was chiefly interested in feeble-minded children and probably contributed to the founding of the Massachusetts School for the Feeble-Minded. In time, clinics also appeared in other states. Massachusetts and New York, early recognizing that hospitals should exert community leadership in the prevention of mental illness, encouraged them to establish outpatient departments and clinics. In the main, however, the clinics founded in the earlier years were undifferentiated as to the age groups they served and actually included mostly adults. In some places one of the chief functions of the clinic was to act in probation or parole cases where some kind of psychological or psychiatric attention seemed desirable.

First Formal Beginnings. Because the first clinics dealt mainly with adults, it is to the Outpatient Department of the Boston Psychopathic Hospital, which regularly accepted children as clients from 1912, that we must look for the first formal beginnings of the child guidance clinic movement in hospitals. This institution, under the direction of Dr. E. Southard, was the first one that actually received fairly large numbers of children for study and treatment. Other clinics for children followed quickly. In 1915 a clinic attached to the Allentown State Hospital was founded in Easton, Pennsylvania. Special provision was made in its charter for public-school children who gave evidence of abnormal social behavior. In 1919 a series of school clinics were set up in Massachusetts to examine children who were retarded in their school work. Other states followed this lead and from the early part of the twentieth century to the present an increasing number of services to children have sprung out of hospital experience.

Juvenile Court Clinics

The originator and leader of the child guidance clinic devoted to the delinquent child was William Healy. His experience was influenced heavily by the five-year study of delinquents which he made while employed in the Juvenile Court of Cook County, Illinois. From this study and from other experiences as well, Healy realized that while the new juvenile courts were a marked improvement over the older indiscriminate adult criminal courts they were not wholly satisfactory in themselves. They were not able to deal with the total personal problem of youthful offenders. While they had assets which deserved further exploration, such as history-taking, classification, semilegalistic approaches, extension of the probation idea, nevertheless they still needed to be supplemented by a clinic which would treat the juvenile offender primarily as a human being, and only secondarily as a lawbreaker. So, under the sponsorship of Mrs. W. F. Dummer and others, William Healy founded the Juvenile Psychopathic Institute in Chicago in 1909. (The name of "Institute for Juvenile Research" was adopted in 1920.) In his book, *The Individual Delinquent*, Healy gave a classic statement of the approach of his clinic to the problems of "youth in the toils."

Another attempt to create a child guidance clinic was made in 1915 by the Department of Public Welfare of the State of Ohio. This clinic was called the Ohio Bureau of Juvenile Research, in keeping with its interest in studying children's behavior. Like the clinic established by Healy, the Ohio Bureau affirmed as its purpose the study, case by case, of young people who were adjudged to be delinquents. In addition to study the Bureau also declared its intention of taking those steps which generally would mitigate the amount and variety of juvenile delinquency. While the approach of the Bureau at first was obviously toward the juvenile delinquent, it later was expanded to include many other types of child guidance need.

A further advance was the establishment in 1917 of the Judge Baker Guidance Center in Boston. This clinic was named in honor of a judge who showed a most intense interest in the creation of an institute in Boston similar to Healy's in Chicago. Upon the founding of the Guidance Center, Healy himself was invited to become its director. Along with his assistant, Augusta Bronner, he began in Boston to develop further those ideas which in Chicago had attracted the attention of the entire country.

The creation of these clinics designed to study and treat delinquents put the movement off to a very good start. Today one of the recognized contributions of the child guidance clinic is that of helping potential delinquents.

The Demonstration Program of the Commonwealth Fund

As the clinics that were established in connection with hospitals and juvenile courts came to be recognized as valuable instruments for the treatment of children, need was seen for further development of the movement. A national demonstration program was envisaged to stimulate the interest of many localities which knew of the significance of the child guidance clinic movement only through the channels of communication. Many times in the history of social work the demonstration method has been an effective device for the extension of a worthy idea which has not found popular acceptance. It is based on the assumption that someone or some organization will support an idea to the point that its value will be proved by observation and real experience to others. The demonstration method seeks to convince communities of values which these communities can then appropriate and utilize for themselves.

The program which the National Committee for Mental Hygiene developed for the extension of child guidance clinics is an example in point. The Committee obtained the cooperation of the Commonwealth Fund for the purpose of financing a series of demonstrations throughout the country. In 1920, as a part of the initial conception of the task, Professor Henry Thurston of the New York School of Social Work, along with members of an assisting committee, was asked by the Fund to work out a suitable plan. Professor Thurston's report to the Fund was finally accepted and reprinted in the Fund's annual report for 1922. The plan, to cover a five-year period, contained the following suggestions:

1. To develop the psychiatric study of difficult, predelinquent, and delinquent children in the schools and the juvenile courts; and to develop sound methods of treatment based on such study.
2. To develop the work of the visiting teacher whereby the invaluable early contacts which school systems make possible with every child might be utilized for the understanding and development of the child.
3. To provide courses of training along sound lines for those qualified and desiring to work in this field.
4. To extend by various educational efforts the knowledge and use of these methods.

While the fourth of these suggestions could be carried out by the Commonwealth Fund itself because of its organizational character, responsibility for the other three provisions was allocated to three agencies equipped to assume the assignment:

1. *The New York School of Social Work* was enabled to offer a more extended program in psychiatric social work and to offer increased instruction for visiting teachers. It also was aided in the establishment of a Bureau of Children's Guidance for the study and treatment of children and as an opportunity of field work experience for those

students who were specially preparing themselves for future work of that type.

2. *The National Committee for Mental Hygiene* was assisted in the creation of a Division on the Prevention of Delinquency, which was to conduct demonstrations of the application of child guidance principles to juvenile offenders.

3. *The Public Education Association of New York* was aided in the formation of a National Committee on Visiting Teachers, which was to develop a demonstration program on the value of visiting teacher work. The work of the Division on the Prevention of Delinquency of the National Committee on Mental Hygiene, which pertains most directly to the subject of this chapter, will be elaborated upon here.

Trial Location at St. Louis. Through a careful method of selecting sites for demonstrating the values of the child guidance clinic, the Division selected St. Louis as the initial trial location. The St. Louis clinic, with the backing of the experience and leadership of that community, began its work in the spring of 1922. A psychiatrist, a psychologist, and a psychiatric social worker made up the staff of the clinic. In addition to these full-time workers, some volunteer professional service was made available, and two students from the Smith College School for Social Work were placed in the clinic for their field work training. Within a few months two more social workers were added to the staff. The clients treated were mainly from the courts, although there was opportunity for referrals by schools, parents, and institutions. During the first eight months, 344 cases were accepted by the clinic, the large part of them having been referred by the juvenile court. In accepting the 344 cases the clinic took only those with definite mental aspects. Experience with the cases seemed to show that the clinic (as well as the court) was getting the problem children too late and that provisions were needed to locate and treat potential delinquents and disturbed children long before they came to the juvenile court or, on the basis of referral, to the clinic. The clinic did seem of value, despite its limitations, as a training place for workers, and this type of experience was further developed.

One of the original aims of the Commonwealth Fund in establishing the demonstration program was to encourage local communities ultimately to take over full responsibility for the clinics. In St. Louis, after early difficulties, the city did assume responsibility, although on an inadequate basis. In fact, one of the results of the demonstration in St. Louis was the discovery that public financing of such clinics creates certain impediments to the unrestricted use of clinic facilities.

Experiences in Other Cities. The experiences of the other demonstration programs varied with the locality. At Norfolk, Virginia, it was learned that a clinic must rely to a considerable extent on community services for the fulfillment of its program. In Dallas, Texas, it was discovered that the child guidance clinic need not be too dependent upon the courts for referrals in order to run a successful and worthwhile program. In Monmouth County, New Jersey, clinics worked best in cities and were assumed to have general educational obligations toward the job which they sought to do. The Minneapolis clinic discovered that workers from other private agencies could be used on a loan basis. In Los Angeles, clinics were found to be more serviceable if they maintained an interpretative service in the community for other professionals such as doctors, clergymen, lawyers, and teachers. So each location provided its special conclusions to the whole study.

But, while the several clinics established throughout the country developed their own particular features, they held the majority of their basic conclusions in common. They uncovered a common body of knowledge regarding the etiology of behavior problems and a shared set of techniques for meeting them.

At the end of the demonstration period the number of clinics throughout the country had increased fourfold. While many problems still were unsolved, nevertheless a firmer footing had been achieved. When, in 1927, the Commonwealth Fund withdrew its support of the program, it did arrange for an advisory service to clinics. The Division on the Prevention of Delinquency became, thereupon, the Division on Community Clinics.

Future Trends

In an interview with Dr. William Healy and Dr. Augusta F. Bronner the following question was asked by students at the Smith College School for Social Work: "What do you see as some of the future needs and trends in child guidance work?" To this inquiry they answered:

> It is usually a rather thankless job to attempt the part of a prophet; this is true in thinking about the future of child guidance work as in any other matter. It is probable that guidance clinics will increase in number, perhaps sponsored sometimes publicly, sometimes privately. Doubtless, there will be introduced new techniques as these become available. It is likely that there will be continued growth in the field of psychometrics, that experimental methods and treatment will continue. All the work in group therapy and play therapy is still relatively new and likely to be modified with further experience. Psychiatry, in general, is still in a state of continual expansion of knowledge. Training in research is a vital part

of the clinic program and, in all these directions, there is likely to be a continuing modification and growth.[2]

THE ORGANIZATION OF THE CLINIC

The child guidance clinic differs somewhat from other social work agencies in its organization and approach.

The Total Approach

In the first place it attempts a "total" approach to its clients. The social worker in most agencies does not deal with the total personality of clients for several reasons, the chief reason being that of functional specialization. There are certain knowledges and skills of other professionals which the social worker does not possess and makes no pretense of possessing. Thus the social worker is content to recognize the need as the case may be and make the proper referrals. However, it is becoming more apparent in modern social work practice that clients should on occasion have available the resources which deal with their whole personality. In family casework agencies, for example, there is increasing development of services which are somewhat different but definitely related to social work. Specialists who can bear upon other aspects of clients' lives than those for which the social worker is trained are regularly being utilized in these agencies. Some of these experts, in the case of large agencies, make up a rather essential part of their functioning: psychiatrists, psychologists, home economists, homemakers.

But, while the growth of additional special services in modern social work agencies is notable, it is nowhere more apparent than in the case of child guidance clinics. Here, even from the first, the obvious need for the supplementation of social work services was appreciated and met. In its attempt to see the child as a whole, the child guidance clinic has found that the services of social workers, psychologists, and psychiatrists may be readily utilized. The ideal ratio between these workers has been suggested as two or three social workers to every psychologist and psychiatrist. In actual practice, however, there are often five or six social workers to each of the other workers.

The important point about the current organization and operation of the child guidance clinic is the fact that the social worker does not exclusively handle the cases but relies on a cooperative arrangement between psychiatrist, psychologist, and social worker. Through the

[2]Dolores Wing, Sylvia Fuhrer, and Gertrude Rotenberg, "The Growth and Development of the Child Guidance Movement," *Focus* (an annual publication of the students of Smith College School for Social Work), Northampton, 1946, p. 9.

media of these three types of personnel the whole personality of the child is approached and treated.

In addition to recognizing the value of a diversified staff, clinics have also been willing to use supplementary instruments—such as foster home care, institutional care—to meet the needs of the "total" child.

Types of Cases

Just as the approach of the workers in other agencies limits their practices, so the effort of the child guidance clinic to deal with the whole personality of the child clearly restricts the types of cases it is prepared to accept. While child guidance clinics can and often do extend services to those children who have a limited need, they more commonly are interested in accepting those cases which are "total life problems." For instance, if "Johnny" wishes, because he and his parents have little money, to find an inexpensive summer camp placement, his case might be handled by a child guidance clinic, especially by those clinics which have elaborate community relations and programs. But he probably would do better to apply to another kind of agency, like a children's aid society.

The simplicity of Johnny's case suggests another significant basis on which acceptances are usually made by child guidance clinics. Just as a placement in a summer camp (all other things being equal) does not involve the entire needs of the child, so also it does not signify very much mental complication. Johnny can go to camp without being seen by a psychiatrist. Around this point the distinctiveness of the child guidance clinic can be seen. Usually, by its very organization, the child guidance clinic accepts only those children who have some definite, complex, and fairly profound emotional difficulty. Since cases taken are usually broad in their mental dimensions there is additional reason for saying that the clinic works with the total personality of clients.

The following cases represent some of the problems that engage the attention of a child guidance clinic. They point out the complexity and the seriousness of the problems treated.[3]

Dave's family has been known to the agency for nine years. Dave is now 18, has an older brother, 19. The parents have been divorced since Dave was five. Following the divorce, the children were shunted about to relatives on both sides and to foster homes, the mother taking the responsibility sometimes, again the father. The boys had no consistent early training. The mother is a hysterical, demanding woman, said by the father often to be cruel and abusive to the children. The father has been

[3]Helen Ross, "The Case Worker and the Adolescent," The Family (now Journal of Social Casework), volume 22, number 7, November, 1941, pp. 234–235.

a peddler most of the time since coming to this country after tne World War. Neither parent had much education. The father was known by the family to go often to prostitutes and the mother is said to have had men friends in the home. Dave is a very bright, attractive boy with an I.Q. of 127. He was the mother's favorite until recently when Henry became a wage earner and thereby gained status with the mother. At 14, Dave was enticed by another boy, a delinquent known to the agency, to cooperate in a theft and was put in jail and sent to the detention home for two weeks. Following this episode, the mother turned on Dave and accused him of being worthless like his father.

Since Dave graduated from high school last year, the caseworker has seen him frequently in order to help him secure work. Dave has secured and lost several jobs. He has recently shown open resentment to his father and wants to try to make him support him and his mother. Henry, who seems to have been a stabilizing factor in Dave's life and the only real authority figure, is now in the Air Corps. This makes the social worker of great importance to Dave at the moment and Dave comes to him to ask help. It is as if he were saying, "I need a father or a big brother to help me get along." The social worker is friendly; a good rapport is established, so that Dave is able to confide in him concerning certain sexual fears; he is anxious lest something is wrong with his genitalia. His mother is at this time in the hospital having a gynecological operation. The worker arranges for him to see the agency doctor who assures him he is normal. Following this verdict, before the boy sees the worker again, he takes a girl to his home and has sexual relations with her. Though he confesses being somewhat disappointed in the whole episode, he says he "now feels like a man." Since this time, he has confessed gambling adventures, trying the worker out with a story of having gambled away his allowance. Recently he has confessed gambling debts up to $70 and his effort to borrow $80 so that he might play the balance in order to win back his losses.

* * *

Herbert is a 15-year-old boy with one older sister, Marion, 17. The parents are almost old enough to be grandparents: the mother, 56; the father, 65, unable to work for many years because of a heart ailment, bedridden for several years, now given only six months to live. This family, once well off, is on relief. The girl, an excellent student, is now working and doing well. She is active and responsible, and is held up as an example to Herbert, who is timid, nonaggressive, poor in sports, has no friends. The mother makes all these complaints of him and threatens him with psychiatry. The father, once active and ambitious, is disappointed in Herbert and berates him constantly. When the father had a serious heart attack recently and had to go to the hospital, the mother held the boy responsible. The sister is impatient and disparaging in her attitude. The boy is utterly discouraged. To avoid going to gymnasium, which he detests, he recently forged a teacher's signature. This the parents accept as proof of his worthlessness. Herbert has superior intelligence, is inclined to be studious, and seeks his consolation in books. He likes most of his teachers.

*   *   *

Paul is 12 years old, the only child of an Italian father and a Jewish mother, divorced when Paul was eight. At that time, the mother requested the Juvenile Court that he be placed in a trade school. She refused foster home placement when the Court referred the case to the agency. Paul had infantile paralysis when small and a consequent lameness was corrected a year ago by a successful operation. He now limps very slightly. The agency found it hard to convince Paul's mother of the necessity for this operation. She has always infantilized him, she keeps him closely with her—he sleeps in the same room with her in their small quarters—does not let him stay out after 7 o'clock, keeps him out of school on the slightest pretext, so that he is one year retarded at school, plans he shall be a radio announcer. Her interests are largely dramatic; she entertains stage groups in her home and she frequently takes part in performances. The worker suspects that she is alcoholic.

It was with great effort that the worker succeeded in getting the boy to camp the summer after his operation. At camp, he was slow at first to assert himself and to make friends, but he became more aggressive as the season advanced and he has continued this attitude, showing marked tendency to identify himself with his father, whom he sees occasionally. The father is often engaged in study pursuits and is frequently in the courts. The mother uses the boy to get money from the father. Paul is a fine looking, well-built boy, of masculine appearance. The worker notes that his rebellion to his mother seemed to break out after the operation, which she had resisted. The mother is not pleased with this change in the boy and complains bitterly. She expresses fears that he will become homosexual, she demands that he be known as a Jew, not as an Italian, she is firm in her resolve to make him take up radio work, for which he has only dislike. The mother is a highly unstable character, apparently always in competition with men. Whether her unconscious motive is revenge on all men or the need to keep the boy as an extension of her own ego is unimportant for our plans. In either case, she is a menace to the boy's proper development and must be encouraged to let the boy be placed outside the home.

These cases may suggest that children always come to the clinics indirectly in connection with other family problems. While it is true that many cases come by way of referral, there are also many direct requests for help. Parents often seek out the services of child guidance clinics in their efforts to secure help with problem children.

It should also be pointed out that the child guidance clinic currently treats other behavior problems than the types suggested above. Many of the children served today are younger than the adolescent delinquents and predelinquents who were formerly the chief concern of the clinics, and their problems are appropriately different. At the present time, clinics are responsible for the whole range of childhood problems. More and more they are also acting in the capacity of consultants to parents on the everyday problems of rearing normal children.

Direct Treatment

Aside from the type of problem that receives its attention, the child guidance clinic also differs somewhat from other agencies in the type of treatment it affords. The clinic is characteristically concerned with *direct* treatment. Elsewhere in social welfare the worker in many instances is called upon to administer not direct but rather *environmental* treatment, that is, treatment concerned with the changing of conditions external to the client and his emotional life. In environmental treatment the client is somewhat divorced from his own feelings about what is going on by the external problem which presses upon him. Just as the "causative" factors in such cases often do not originate within the individual, so the treatment can oftentimes be achieved without too much attention to the intrapsychic life of the client. Thus a man who is unemployed may need little more than to find a job. His unemployment may for a time be emotionally disturbing, but this disturbance may in many cases be dependent simply upon the fact of his unemployment and not upon his psychic disposition. Such a case is properly within the province of a casework agency.

Another unemployed person, however, may be in need of direct treatment. The implication here is that his emotional disturbance may not be caused fundamentally by his inability simply to find work, but may be a reflection in his work relations of his personal, emotional inadequacy. Merely finding such a person a job might utterly fail to solve his personal problem. What may be needed is a therapy which will enable the man to face most or all of his life situations with personal adequacy.

Yet, while the stress in child guidance clinics is upon the treatment of the child, it should not be inferred that the child guidance clinic is not interested in environmental changes as they pertain to clients' needs and problems. In fact, a considerable part of clinic programs, and one which is enlarging, is directed toward improving the social conditions in which clients have to live. Indeed, one reason for the rise in the ratio of social workers compared to psychiatrists and psychologists in clinic work is the fact that the social needs of child clients are known to be very important. This point will be further emphasized later in the chapter.

THE CHILD GUIDANCE CLINIC AT WORK

Range of Problems

What are the kinds of problems handled in child guidance clinics?[4] The range of problems accepted for treatment is broad, but not all clinics specialize in all type of problems. For some clinics there may be a greater development of one specialization, due to peculiarities of staff, to community needs and resources, or to special circumstances of the moment, such as delinquency in wartime. The Institute for Child Guidance (now the Bureau of Child Guidance of the Board of Education) of New York City reported that, over an intake period of six years, the most common reasons for referral, in order of their frequency, were as follows:

1. Disobedience, negativism, stubbornness, rebelliousness
2. "Nervousness"
3. Temper
4. Stealing
5. Truancy, home and school
6. Lying
7. Feeding difficulties
8. "Does not get along with other children"
9. Retardation in school
10. Enuresis
11. School failure
12. Speech difficulties
13. Disturbing behavior in school
14. Fingersucking and nailbiting
15. Placement, adoption
16. Overactivity
17. Shyness, withdrawal
18. Sleep disturbances
19. Fears
20. Excessive phantasy

The types of acceptances made in this instance indicate the range of problems that the child guidance clinic may treat. Obviously, there may also be other factors.

[4] There will be no discussion in this chapter of the role of group therapy and play therapy in the activities of the child guidance clinic, although this is an interesting and important aspect of current clinic practice. Group therapy is treated in Chapter 13 (Group Work), since it can be practiced in other agency settings than clinics for children.

Source of Referrals

How, it may be asked, do children having such problems secure the services of the clinic? This question is answerable only on a local basis, for there are wide variations of practice throughout the country. It is fair to say, however, that in general many of the referrals are made by other social work agencies in cases where they feel that they are not equipped, for one reason or another, to undertake the necessary treatment themselves. A child guidance clinic in Richmond, Virginia, as an illustration, does not accept applications from individuals, such as parents and relatives, but mainly relies upon referrals from other social work or community agencies and the formal offices of the city (the courts, for example).

On the other hand in some locations the chief source of referrals may be the parents of disturbed children. They, of course, constitute a very natural source. If a child suffers from one of the disturbances mentioned above (as being the experience of the Institute for Child Guidance), it is easy to see how the problem would strike hardest upon his parents who, then, might seek relief through contacting a clinic.

The schools also comprise an important source of referrals for the child guidance clinic. This is especially true of communities where there are no school social work developments or where the child guidance clinics are not synonymous with the school social work programs.

Initial Inquiry

When an application for service is received by a clinic, an appointment is made for an interview with the referring person and the child in order to determine the nature of the problem. In those instances where a referral is made by a social work agency, some other means of initial analysis may be used. Usually, a social worker would be the person of the clinic staff to undertake the intake work. The purpose of the initial inquiry is to ascertain whether or not the clinic is prepared to accept the case. If the case is accepted there remains the further obligation on the part of the social worker, although sometimes this is accomplished through staff consultation, to determine the extent to which the clinic can be committed to the case. That is, will the case involve a long-term study of the child? Will it necessitate the setting up of cooperative relations between the clinic and a social work agency? These and other questions would be raised. Obviously, it is important for the child guidance clinic to formulate a specific and clear program of care for each individual so that its resources may be put to the best advantage.

Tests Given

Once the case is accepted and its specific terms made clear, the child is deemed a client of the clinic. If his case seems to warrant a physical examination, this may be the first step in the treatment process. Some clinics have their own pediatricians. In others the psychiatrist, because of his medical background, does the medical analysis. In still others the physical examination may be attended to by a supporting agency, that is, an agency which has made the referral and is continuing contact with the case in a supplementary manner.

After the physical examination, or in some cases concurrently with it, the psychologist may enter the picture to administer tests of a basic and preliminary sort. In certain cases the giving of tests may occur later in the clinic process, according to the developing and specific needs of the child as uncovered by the staff. At any rate if the child's needs, on the basis of the preliminary investigation, seem to advise mental testing, such a procedure would be initiated by the psychologist. The following is a generalized report on a child by a psychologist. It illustrates the type of contribution which the psychologist makes to the casework process:

CONFERENCE ON "D" (15 years)

Psychological Examination. D was observed to be a tall, slim girl, who was dressed in neat, attractive clothes, and used cosmetics. She appeared apprehensive and tense during the verbal aspects of the examination, though she never verbalized her feelings. She was quiet, restrained, and spoke and performed chiefly in answer to specific questions and directions. She needed no urging, however, and was completely compliant. She demonstrated stable attention and performed with good concentration and persistence. In her concrete adjustments, she was careful, controlled, observant, and exact, yet fairly rapid.

A Rorschach Examination was given and was of interest in that it indicated a state of general disturbance and a repressed, inert, impoverished personality with a tendency to withdrawal. Difficulty in meeting new situations was evidenced in a lack of vigor in her adjustments.

She demonstrated normal intelligence, though it was easily apparent that she was distinctly more effective, more even, more confident, and more controlled in her concrete nonlanguage adjustments than in situations requiring verbal-social communication. Further, in a test combining mechanical intelligence with manipulative skills, she showed good ability.

She has completed the work of the elementary grades in slightly more than the usual amount of time and is at present in the 9B grade in a junior high school. She has progressed approximately at an average rate for her age though she did repeat the 2A grade. Her conduct ratings have consistently been A and B+. Her proficiency grades have been B to B+, except when she failed in 2A. However, in 9A she received a C grade. It appears likely that she is now slightly overgraded for her verbal ability which is more in accord with that of the average 8th-year pupil. Her C rating last semester reflected to a large extent a state of disturbance and difficult home adjustment. However, a growing difficulty with school was probably also reflected, on the basis of sheer verbal or academic level.

At present, she demonstrates 8A reading comprehension and 7B ability in the fundamental processes of arithmetic. These achievements, although in fair agreement with her abstract ability, verify the need for individual help in her present grade.[5]

Social History Secured

During this period, when the child is being examined physically and is undergoing psychological tests, the social worker is busy too. He is delving into the social history of the case. He is collecting information as to what the configurations of the problem are as they reveal themselves in the child's thinking and action, in the responses of his parents, his teachers, and others interested. The following example of an interview with a child's mother shows the complications which developed from the mother's impression of her son's problems:

The reason for referring this boy was originally given as disobedience at home and at school, with demotion at school because of misconduct. The mother's real concern, as it emerges in this interview, centers around the resemblance of this child to his father who she feels has not realized his potentialities and toward whom she has strong but unrecognized feelings of hostility.

The mother almost burst into discussion, leaving practically no opening for the worker to explain Center procedure or discuss fees. When the interview was half completed, the mother began looking at her watch saying that she had to be home by four o'clock exactly to take the boys to church choir. "I try to be an example of punctuality and good behavior for the children . . . I never make a promise that I don't keep to the letter . . . I not only do this, but stress this to them." Although the mother said that she expected the worker to have questions for her to answer, she was so much concerned with the problem that she could hardly pause for answers to questions of her own or discussion of the Center.

The mother began by saying that Jimmy is a very attractive child physically, perhaps the most attractive member of the family. She has put a great deal of thought on the problem, and, as she sees it, she thinks that he "got off to a bad start." For the first three months he had colic and cried continually. The neighbors can vouch for this because it was so

[5]William Goldfarb, "A Psychologist's Services in a Child-Placing Agency," *The Family* (now *Journal of Social Casework*), volume 22, number 4, June, 1941, pp. 125–126.

marked. As his mother sees it, Jimmy has never been well behaved and has always "acted up" when someone was around. The siblings are perfect hosts, "and are the kind who will push a chair under a guest, while Jimmy is always the kind who pulls the chair out from under them."

The second factor, as the mother sees it, is that the older brother, Donald, has always had an attractive personality—"he holds the center of the stage no matter how many babies come in the home." Donald makes good grades and is one of the highest paid members of the Boys' Choir (a feat which he accomplished within a year when it takes other children five years), has many dinner invitations, and parents of other children telephone the mother saying how much they enjoy him and that he is welcome to return at any time he wishes. "Jimmy has good competition in an older brother like this . . . I know what it's like myself because I had a brother like that with whom I had to compete." The third factor is that when Jimmy was two, Ellen was born, "Girl babies are always attractive and she took the stage at a time when Jimmy would normally be getting attention." He then began to do such things as throwing a brick through the window, cutting a tent with a knife, and doing other drastic things to get attention. "It wasn't as though he didn't get attention enough. We probably paid more attention to him than to the others but the other children are the kind who always do the right thing at the right time." The mother said that Jimmy cannot be driven but must be led.

Jimmy has begun to smoke, buys cigarettes, and two weeks ago when the parents were at a dinner party, his father telephoned home to see how things were going and found that the neighbors had their fire hoses out as Jimmy was smoking behind the hedge and had caught the hedge on fire. One time adults were having a party and were serving beer and children were told to go in through the back door. Jimmy took a glass and poured himself a glass of beer from the left-overs from the different glasses. He became "really tight."

The mother thinks that Donald has many of the interests she had when she was a child, whereas Jimmy is more like his father. Father was an exceptionally naughty child and mother has heard "terrible tales" of things father did. He was so troublesome that when paternal grandfather had his last illness, he arranged to have father sent to a military school. The mother says that this school was really "four walls" and the boys were not allowed to leave even for the funeral of a parent. Father went to this school and paternal grandfather died while he was there. Father ran away and went overseas. He had many adventurous travels before he settled down and was married. Mother says that in looking back, she sees how much more father could have made of himself if he had not squandered his childhood opportunities. Father talks with her about this and agrees. This is one reason that she is so concerned about Jimmy.[6]

[6]Dorothea McClure, "Intake Practice in a Child Guidance Center," *Intake Policies and Practices,* Family Welfare Association of America (now Family Service Association of America), New York, 1940–1941, pp. 23–24.

Interpretation and Action

The interpretation of materials and the directing of the case, while in actuality shared with the psychologist and social worker, are primarily the responsibility of the psychiatrist. His contribution specifically to the understanding of the child and his behavior includes the interpretation of the whole of the materials given him by the other workers in the clinic, the uncovering of the more fundamental and psychiatric implications of the child's problem, and the application of medical treatment appropriate to his training.

Following an initial survey of the child and his needs from the different directions of interest and skill that the various workers in the clinic represent, the staff may hold a conference on the case. Before this conference the workers may have consulted with one another informally and repeatedly, but at this first staff conference the case is reviewed and discussed, perhaps differences even argued out, from several points of view by all of the staff members. Usually, at this stage some plan of further action is formulated. From this point on various approaches with a common purpose may be used, but the predetermined interpretation guides each worker in his efforts to be of assistance to the child. Other staff conferences may be held to check on progress. Probably, much informal consultation will go on until the case is declared closed.

THE CHILD AND HIS PARENTS

From this description one might think that the sole attention of the child guidance clinic is directed toward the child. This is not so. In current practice the direct and environmental aspects of general treatment are clearly seen as fused in most instances.

In the earliest period of the clinic movement the child himself was the chief source of attention. Following that, parents were "found." That is, workers who sought to alleviate child problems found themselves very often confronted with the need for changing parental attitudes. "For every problem child there is a problem parent" became almost a slogan in the second period. Today, however, it is seen that both extremes of attitude are unrealistic and that both the child and the parents are involved in most cases but in a way that no one can easily describe or even work with, except on an individual basis. On the one hand the child feels certain things. He is implicated whether he is the "cause" of his involvement or not. He must make an adjustment to his problem and the demands of the outer world. He must rationalize his dilemma somehow. No amount of work with his parents will obliterate the personal aspects of his problem for him. On the other hand, in many instances, merely seeking to alleviate the problem of a child by easing his essential situation may be like trying to smother a fire by throwing more logs of wood on it. Children are in large part the creatures of the environment which influences them. Chief among the social influences of children is the family. In the family the basic habit patterns toward self and society are early formed. These patterns also are maintained through the sheer stability and permanence of most families. Thus the social worker in the child guidance clinic plays an obviously important role when he seeks to understand and modify the social environment of the child client.

The child and his parents are not separated in their problem any more than they can be separated in the treatment which the child guidance clinic offers. The child and his parents are involved in the problem even before the clinic. For example, a child and his mother may both face pressure from the school to improve the quality of the child's work. Again, a child and his father may both feel pressure because of the predelinquent behavior of the child. Together, the child and the parent may come to the clinic anxiously seeking for some easement of their problem. The close bond which usually exists between the child and his parents must be recognized by the clinic as a most important factor in the treatment of both. (See Figure 20.)

There are, however, cases where the parents do not wish to cooperate with the clinic. Certainly, there is no possibility (and little desirability) of the worker reaching out, as it were, to pull into the clinic a recalcitrant parent who does not feel emotionally involved in the plight of his child. Unless the parents do have an intensely active interest in the problem, there is usually little chance for effective, total treatment of the child except of a quite direct sort which, then, may or may not be permanent. Of course, the success of direct treatment is dependent among other things upon the age of the child. Obviously, a very young child could be helped very little without the cooperation of his parents, simply because of his own immaturity.

Child guidance workers often need to take into account the fact that parents contact clinics with considerable pain to themselves. The worker usually seeks to accept the discomfort of parents in ways that will lessen their anxiety. The comment of such a worker explains this:

"I recoil from this experience," says one mother when she comes for her first interview at the Child Guidance Center; "We wouldn't have come here if we hadn't tried everything else we knew of," says another mother. "When my little boy is bad, I feel sick and worried, and when he behaves

FIG. 20. What Will Help in Child Guidance

(Evelyn M. Duvall, *Keeping Up With Teen-Agers*, Public Affairs Pamphlet No. 127, New York, 1940.)

a little better I feel foolish to think I decided to come to you for help," says a third mother. Through such comments, the more articulate of our parents tell us how difficult making an application for help is for them, and we know that they are voicing feelings shared to some degree by the majority of parents who come for a first interview. Some parents, who are constantly seeking advice from many sources and who are unable to make use of any help offered them except for temporary relief, may tell their story eagerly in the initial interview, but because the caseworker cannot accede to their demands for sympathy or for criticism, they, too, find the experience difficult. Still other parents may partially protect themselves from anxiety by bringing their own diagnosis of what is wrong and what should be done about it.

In general, we may say that the purpose of our first interview is to provide the parent with an opportunity to present his problem and for the caseworker to describe the services that her agency offers so that parent and caseworker may decide together whether the parent may expect to find the help he needs at the agency to which he has applied. As clearly indicated in the statements quoted, the matter is not so simple. The parent would not have come to us at all had he been able to treat the trouble himself. Often by the time he arrives he is in a state approaching despair, has lost any perspective he may have had, and feels baffled, angry, and guilty. His distress has been sufficient to make him take a step he had probably contemplated for some time but rejected earlier. He believes that he is in some measure inadequate or he would not need help. One mother very aptly expressed her distress by saying, "When you come to a place like this, you are sick enough to need a doctor yourself. You want help; you want to be made to feel good."[7]

It is evident that the child, too, must cooperate if much is to be accomplished. Some parents fail to appreciate this point. They simply want their children to change their ways. They themselves may be partially willing also to do some changing. But they would like the child to be spared the personal and emotional cost of altering strongly established life-patterns. For such cases it is clear that no amount of willingness on the part of parents can automatically solve anything for the child. It is of great help if the child also wishes to solve his dilemma and is intelligently supported by his parents.

The responsibility of the child in the treatment process is suggested by the following case:

Hazel's mother had come to discuss the study of her 16-year-old daughter who she thought was too much interested in boys, stayed out too late at night, and was rebellious and untruthful. In response to the caseworker's question as to how the mother could best present Center study

[7] *Ibid*, p. 21.

to Hazel, the mother replied quickly, with much feeling, "I've already had trouble about that. Hazel saw my letter to you and flew into a rage. I told her that unless she would come here I would take her to the Juvenile Court." The mother added that she would hate to take Hazel to Court because the school would know. "The school doesn't think Hazel is a bad girl. . . . You won't talk to the school, will you?" The mother was assured that the school would not be consulted until she was ready for such a step, and the caseworker suggested that the mother make no issue of Hazel's coming to the Center but report to her that the mother had found that people at the Center were friendly and interested in helping young people work out their problems. The mother later reported that Hazel herself raised the question of coming to the Center by asking her mother, "When are you going to the Center again?" The mother replied that she might not be going since she and Hazel could not work out their misunderstandings unless Hazel was interested. Hazel responded with, "When you go to the Center again, I'm going along."[8]

THE CLINIC AND THE COMMUNITY

The relationship of the clinic to the community must also be considered. While this has been touched upon previously, it may be recalled here that the clinic, if it is to function well, must think not only in terms of children and parents but also about the whole community.

The following example shows how a child welfare worker can utilize the presence of a client for the education of community leaders. The case of "Tommy" aided the appreciation in this instance of a teacher and a school superintendent for the problems of all children:

The school adjustment of a child placed in a home carefully selected to meet his needs is creating difficulties for the school superintendent, who feels that the agency is making unfair demands on the school to leave the child there. Mr. W, the superintendent, had telephoned demanding Tommy's removal from school. Tommy's behavior is so disturbing to the teacher and the other eight children in the one-room school that Mr. W is afraid the community may discharge the teacher, close the school, and send the children to the consolidated school five miles away. Mr. W feels the community does not have to put up with such behavior in a county child; he is ruining the school. He is obstreperous and defiant, and the teacher finds him completely impossible.

Tommy is an 8-year-old illegitimate twin boy whose parents are deceased. The twins were referred for adoption at the age of 2½ months. At 14 months Tommy was admitted to the hospital with a tubercular knee and remained there for over 6 years. His leg was in a plaster cast for 3 years. He was then fitted to a long leg brace with pelvic band. When he

[8]*Ibid*, p. 24.

was removed from the hospital and placed in a foster home at the age of 7½ years, he still wore this brace day and night. Tommy proved to be too much of a care in this foster home and six months later was transferred to his present placement. Tommy has average native intelligence.

Mr. W was aggressive and single-minded in his determination to have Tommy removed. Children's agency supervisor told Mr. W that Tommy presented problems to us, too, and suggested it might be helpful if he and the teacher met with her and the worker who supervises Tommy in his foster home. Supervisor learned from Mr. W in the course of this discussion that the school factors affecting the school situation are complicated. Mr. W believes that the small school is valuable to the community, but there is considerable feeling in the school board that it might be better for the children to go to the consolidated school in the neighboring village. Mr. W hopes that by keeping a good teacher there he can prove his point.

The superintendent of schools pointed out that the community is watching the school situation anyway, and it is unfair to "saddle" such a problem on the school. The children's agency is interested in "charity" and although the superintendent considers himself a charitable man, this is too much. The children's agency supervisor said we didn't consider trying to find out what Tommy needed quite in the light of charity. Tommy had been taken under care by the county because there is no one in his normal family group who can provide for him. He is really our child, and we have the parental responsibility of doing the best we can for him.

The superintendent considered that our problem, not his. His problem was that the community was going to be after him any moment to make him account for the fact that one child, a nonresident, was depriving their children of the teacher's time and attention. The other eight children come from only three other families in the community, but the community is so small that three families are important. Children's agency supervisor said the whole problem is certainly complicated, and that we very well know how delicately it must be handled. We recognize that Tommy could not only try the patience but would tax the ingenuity of any teacher, and we wanted to offer the teacher all the help we possibly could. At this point the superintendent said all the help they wanted was to have Tommy removed from the school.

The children's agency supervisor agreed that of course he saw it that way but that we had even more of a problem. We couldn't pass the child on. We had to find some way, however inadequate, of giving him what he needs. That seemed a bit of a new idea to Mr. W but he rallied quickly, as if for fear he would weaken, and demanded sharply if we knew how much power he had over children's agency. The children's agency supervisor replied that we did recognize that as a public official he could bring pressure against us; that it might even be that by such a procedure he could force us to act against our best judgment of what is our responsibility to Tommy. She didn't think, however, that it really had to be that way. It seemed to her that we both had problems, although they were different. There ought to be some way of balancing the two without harm to the child.

The superintendent pointed out that he wasn't interested in the one child, he had perforce to consider the good of the whole as his working unit. Children's agency supervisor agreed but said that she felt we had a common concern, the education of the child. It was her opinion that children's agency had a right to turn to the superintendent of schools as an educator and to expect him to be thoughtful about the individual educational needs of such a child. He admitted this but pointed out that his chief responsibility is administrative. He cannot bear to jeopardize the teacher's professional reputation for Tommy. The caseworker and children's agency supervisor agreed that this child is enough to distress any teacher, and that we thought our job was definitely to try to be helpful to her, for she carried the brunt of the trouble. The teacher said it was not knowing what to do that was hard. We pointed out that with a child like Tommy, no one really knew the answer. Even if Tommy were in another school, he would still present a serious educational problem. Children's agency supervisor asked Mr. W a direct question as to what he would suggest. He suggested having Tommy taught at home under the Crippled Children Service. Tommy is not eligible for this, however, because he is able to walk. Also, Tommy is not a defective child and is therefore not a subject for Opportunity or Special Class.

Special coaching at home was considered. The foster mother has been trying to do this, and feels Tommy is showing some improvement. The caseworker stressed the fact that Tommy has not learned to have confidence in anyone, and perhaps that is the most important thing for him to learn just now. Children's agency worker injected the thought that it might be that Tommy really does hate other children who compete with him. The teacher thought this might be true, but if he did, wasn't that a criminal trait and wouldn't it lead him into serious trouble? We all felt that unless some way could be found for him to develop a different sort of behavior, he could pile up hate and revenge into ultimate antisocial activity. Children's agency supervisor pointed out that if we thought of the incessant activity of a child who has just recently learned to walk, and realize that during all the time Tommy was developing the strong desire to use his large muscles he had been bound in casts or braces, we could see the strong feeling that might result. The teacher said that Tommy's learning to trust just one person seemed important, and perhaps that was something tangible to use. We all agreed that this might be true. Since he knows what is expected of him, it is important also that he be held up to conform to rules. Punishment is not unfair when he comprehends but disobeys deliberately. It was evident that when the teacher began to think of possible ways of helping Tommy, Mr. W relaxed a bit. It was agreed that the teacher would try further with Tommy, and that the caseworker would discuss with the foster mother some of the things the teacher had told us of Tommy's reaction in school so that she could do what she could to help. We all agreed that perhaps Tommy couldn't change right away but that we had gained something by discussing it from all angles.

Later the superintendent of schools said that in a recent trip to visit crippled children receiving home teaching, he had found himself more curious than he ever had been about the individual circumstances of each child. Some weeks afterward the teacher came in to the children's agency office. Tommy was still difficult, she said, but "I find myself fascinated by trying to find out how he learns." She has tried to show him individual interest, but has maintained that he must conform to the rules he understands. Recently one of the other children said Tommy was learning how to play more easily and the other children liked him more. The teacher said it is evident that he is showing better capacity to follow the rules of the game and regard the rights of other children. She was particularly pleased that the other children had noticed it.[9]

The clinic also has a preventive role to play in the community. One of the excellent features of the child guidance clinic movement in the past has been its insistence that its work is effectively tied up with the mental hygiene approach to personal and community behavior. Intrinsic to the mental hygiene approach, as the child guidance clinics have represented it, is prevention. If the community has essentially destructive and disturbing elements, it is not enough for a clinic to be interested merely in salvaging human beings from them. It must seek to act upon the community in ways that will mitigate or abolish these forces which cause child problems. The number and variety of forces which tend to work deleteriously on the well-being of children call for a multi-approach on the part of the clinics. The type of preventive program will, of course, have to be in accord with community and clinic resources, but, whatever the approach, the responsibility is quite the same.

Aside from their obligation to promote those measures which will remedy or abolish harmful social factors, child guidance clinics have a more positive role to play in regard to child welfare in the community. One responsibility is to evaluate the various agencies and organizations which play a part in the lives of children. These include other social work agencies, the schools, courts, and other organized social influences. Even the family as a social institution calls for constant appraisal by clinics, for within families children find their basic emo-

[9]Maude Von P. Kemp, "The Child Welfare Service Job and the Community," *The Family* (now *Journal of Social Casework*), volume 23, number 9, January, 1943, pp. 340–342. This case has been condensed with variations for purposes of brevity.

tional satisfactions. So, in whatever way community conditions may suggest, clinic workers are interested in raising the quality of child life. The child guidance clinic also is concerned with the objective understanding of childhood behavior. It believes that, through such study as will lead to understanding, the clinic is providing itself and other agencies and organizations for children with an increasingly sound basis for the improvement of child life. Research of childhood behavior as a part of the clinic movement is as old as the movement itself. In fact, the child guidance clinic is one of the foremost community agencies at present which studies children empirically.

As child guidance clinics develop their programs and are able to serve more efficiently, they are coming to find more and more that they have a contribution to make to the normal relationships of children and parents. While the clinics have never been devoid of this conception of their work, they are taking it more seriously today than ever before. Not only do they deal with problem children; they are currently counseling many parents in regard to the more ordinary troubles of family life as they relate to children. Even before a problem can be deemed serious enough to merit specialized attention, it may be met successfully through counseling services. The clinics appreciate their role in this regard and are making their services available to a larger number of parents and children who do not necessarily have abnormal perplexities.

SELECTED READINGS ON THE CHILD GUIDANCE CLINIC

Ackerman, Luton, *Children's Behavior Problems: A Statistical Study Based Upon 2,113 Boys and 1,181 Girls Examined Consecutively at the Illinois Institute for Juvenile Research,* University of Chicago Press, Chicago, 1942.

Blos, Peter, *The Adolescent Personality: A Study of Individual Behavior,* prepared for the Commission on Secondary School Curriculum, Progressive Education Association, Appleton-Century, New York, 1941.

Burbury, W. Mary; Balint, Edna W.; and Yapp, Bridget J., *An Introduction to Child Guidance,* Macmillan, London, 1946.

Carmichael, Leonard, editor, *Manual of Child Psychology,* Wiley, New York, 1946.

Clifton, Eleanor, and Hollis, Florence, editors, *Child Therapy: A Casework Symposium,* Family Service Association of America, New York, 1948.

Hamilton, Gordon, *Psychotherapy in Child Guidance,* Columbia University Press, New York, 1947.

Isaacs, Susan, *Intellectual Growth in Young Children,* volume 1, Harcourt, New York, 1930.

Isaacs, Susan, *Social Development in Young Children: A Study of Beginnings,* volume 2, Harcourt, New York, 1933.

Jewish Board of Guardians, *Conditioned Environment in Case Work Treatment,* New York, 1944.

Kirkpatrick, Milton E., *The Organization and Function of the Child Guidance Clinic,* National Conference for Mental Hygiene, New York, 1941.

Levine, Maurice, *Psychotherapy in Medical Practice,* Macmillan, New York, 1942.

Lewis, Nolan D. C., and Pacella, Bernard L., editors, *Modern Trends in Child Psychiatry,* International Universities Press, New York, 1945.

Rogers, Carl, *The Clinical Treatment of the Problem Child,* Houghton Mifflin, Boston, 1939.

Sayles, Mary B., *Child Guidance Cases,* Commonwealth Fund, New York, 1932.

Staff of the Institute for Juvenile Research, *Child Guidance Procedures: Methods and Techniques Employed at the Institute for Juvenile Research,* Century Psychology Series, Appleton-Century, New York, 1937.

Stevenson, George, and Smith, Geddes, *Child Guidance Clinics: A Quarter Century of Development,* Commonwealth Fund, New York, 1934.

Taft, Jessie, *The Dynamics of Therapy in a Controlled Relationship,* Macmillan, New York, 1933.

Teagarden, Florence M., *Child Psychology for Professional Workers,* Prentice-Hall, New York, revised, 1946.

Thomas, William I., and Thomas, Dorothy S., *The Child in America: Behavior Problems and Programs,* Knopf, New York, 1928.

Truit, Ralph P., and others, *The Child Guidance Clinic and the Community,* Commonwealth Fund, New York, 1928.

Witmer, Helen L., *Psychiatric Clinics for Children: With Special Reference to State Programs,* Commonwealth Fund, New York, 1940.

———, *Psychiatric Interviews With Children,* Commonwealth Fund, New York, 1946.

Zachry, Caroline B., *Emotion and Conduct in Adolescence,* prepared for the Commission on Secondary School Curriculum, Progressive Education Association, Appleton-Century, New York, 1940.

For additional related readings, consult the bibliographies at the end of the other child welfare chapters.

8

Social Work With
Delinquents and Criminals

Social casework is concerned with helping criminals and delinquents. Casework developed more rapidly in connection with delinquents, but its possibilities with adult offenders are very great. The following case of "Tom" illustrates what may happen to a boy who is involved in social misconduct:

FIRST CONTACTS

Thursday, November 29, 1945. Number 12 Police Station received a phone call from a parking lot attendant: "Hurry up! I'm holding a kid that tried to swipe a car!"

The police picked up 15-year-old Thomas K—; brought him to the Detention Home by the rear entrance; filled out a form giving the name of the child, his age, the reasons for his appearance, and the names of the complainants. The two police exchanged their information sheet with the Detention Home supervisor who gave them a receipt for the boy's custody.

Detention Home Supervisor, Mr. Homer, ushered Tom into a glass-enclosed interviewing booth. There the boy was asked identifying information so that Juvenile Court files could be checked and his parents notified. New record sheets were made out because Tom had never been previously detained. A bath sheet, a valuables' record, and a medical record were made out. Mr. Homer briefly asked Tom about the charge initiated by the parking-lot attendant. The boy did not deny the theft. His attitude was, "Well! So what?"

Tom accompanied Mr. Homer to the Senior Boys Department where Mr. Brush took charge. Preparatory to taking a shower, Tom's body was checked for vermin, bruises, and other injuries. Mr. Brush recorded on the bath sheet that Tom's left calf had a scratch, which had been received in playing "touch tackle last Saturday." After finishing his shower, Tom was given a medical examination and blood test by Dr. Foster, the court's physician. Mr. Brush followed up the examination by assigning Tom a locker for his clothes and a bed in the Senior Boys dormitory. Tom was issued clean institutional clothing except for shoes.

"Time for school," said Mr. Brush . . . Tom followed the supervisor to the classroom where fifteen other boys whose ages ranged from 14 to 17 were already seated . . . With no time lost Tom was in school again, doing classwork and receiving credit for it.

Tom and the other Senior Boys left the classroom and returned to their dormitory's day room for a few minutes before the dinner hour—just enough time to play a game of ping pong, to wash up, and to find out the names of a few fellows.

Dinner. The boys queued up, cafeteria style; each picked up his tray laden with food and made a right turn into the dining room . . .

Tom observed the other boys pick up their trays of used dishes and deposit them on the serving counter where he had obtained the food. The boys stood around until all had finished. Then, like a brigade passing water, the boys began pushing the dining room furniture into the hallway . . . A colored boy grabbed a broom and began making long sweeps with it . . . Others appeared with mops and pails. . . . Mr. Brush beamed, "Good job, good job, let's go!" and the group started towards the Senior Boys day room where they would have free time until the next class.

Miss Stevens was looking forward to seeing the Senior Boys. "Do you want to help me fix Christmas tree ornaments today?" . . . One of the boys helped Miss Stevens distribute the crushed ornaments to the various tables. In a few minutes the entire group seemed absorbed in the stuff of Christmas . . . Miss Stevens . . . glanced at the clock. "Almost finished? Let's put them away and finish up tomorrow." . . . The classroom emptied and the Senior Boys walked into the adjoining classroom for their second session with Mrs. Braun . . .

School dismissed. Tom and the others filed singly out of the room and proceeded to the boys' department day room. Tom was challenged to checkers almost as soon as he entered the room . . .

Mr. Bowser, an Assistant Intake Secretary, came to the day room. "I want to see Thomas K—" Tom bounded up from his chair. "Here!" and followed Mr. Bowser into a small office.

From the Assistant Intake Secretary's Report. Tom was interviewed in the Detention Home. When asked about his troubles he explained that he can't get along at home. His parents nag him about his bad school marks; never allow him to go out with other boys to shows. He said that he pays his own way through money he earns working but his father still will not permit him to go. He goes out anyhow because his father works from 3 to 11 and he doesn't listen to his mother.

Tom's Statement. *Tom, age 15, stated that he was on his way downtown to look for a Christmas holiday job. The weather was wet and cold. As he passed the parking lot he thought he could sit in one of the cars and warm himself. He had no sooner closed the door than the attendant rushed up and accused him of the car theft. Tom admitted he was learning to drive against the wishes of his parents; that he was truant; that he had participated in a joyride previously with a boy whose car ownership was doubtful. Tom seemed to be very much disturbed and upset. He said, "I shouldn't have been in that car . . .", and about that point the tears began flowing. The self-confidence with which the interview had begun melted away.*

Tom wanted to go home. Mr. Bowser informed him that the Court Authorities had already reached Tom's family. His parents would be in the next morning to see him.

"See me? Do I have to stay here?" Mr. Bowser then explained that Tom's release depended on many factors: on the report of the police; on his parents' attitude; on the report of the school; but chiefly on Tom himself and on his realization of the seriousness of his behavior.

Mr. Michaels, the evening Supervisor, announced that it was close to supper time . . . The boys made a column of two's and waited for Mr. Michaels to start them toward the kitchen . . .

The Senior Boys went to the gym on the first floor. Within a few minutes basketballs were thumping . . . The game was stopped. Everybody went upstairs to the classroom. Some pretty girls from a club called "The Junior Council" were there with a lot of packages in their arms . . . The announced program: a Bingo game with prizes for the winners. The hour passed too quickly . . . The boys left the room after they had "policed" it.

Tom and his companions took their showers . . . They went to their assigned beds. Lights out . . . The night Superintendent, writing at his desk, could be seen through the glass partition.

* *Friday, November 30, 1945.* Mr. Giltenboth, the Night Supervisor, opened the door of the dormitory. "Time to get up." . . .

Breakfast . . . When the chores were completed, all the boys with the exception of those assigned to the kitchen went to the classroom. . . . When Mr. Homer peered into Mrs. Braun's classroom, Tom stood up. "Is my Dad here?" Tom preceded Mr. Homer into the office. . .

INTAKE SECRETARY'S REPORT

Friday, November 30, 1945. Tom's father called at the office. He is a youngish man, neat, well dressed, alert in manner. The father stated that he had been contemplating Court action for some time. He said he needed the "power of Law" to impress Tom. Mr. K— stated that he is not as severe as Tom might indicate, but denied that he had been unsuccessful in enforcing rules and regulations at home. "The boy has proven himself untrustworthy at times. He is not careful in the selection of his companions . . . he is a poor student—not because Tom isn't smart, but because he doesn't care."

Mr. K— stated that the allegations of the police were unfounded "because Tom can't drive." When informed that his son was learning to drive the father seemed surprised. "Guess he'll be wanting to buy a car next."

Mr. K— then began asking what he could do about the situation. He paused more frequently than he had in the beginning of the interview to phrase his questions. His concern seemed genuine. "Did Tom tell you that he has had trouble in school and with me about his school marks?" When informed that we were aware of the problem, Mr. K— then volunteered, "I'll bet that's at the bottom of this whole mess!"

The father asked if Tom could be released in his custody. He indicated that he did not object to the Court's interest. The Intake Secretary said that he would check with the police before authorizing release. Mr. K— could visit Tom if he wished.

Later—Mr. McKnight, the Police representative, stated there was no further information on Tom and no objection by the police to his release.

Later—Tom released to the custody of his father. He was informed that there would be a court hearing later.

THE INVESTIGATION

Herewith is the report of the investigation as presented to the Judge the evening before the hearing. (Judge Schramm studies these reports so that he can familiarize himself with each case.)

First Appearance. Name. K—, Thomas (age 15 years); 345 Dormet Street; Pittsburgh, Pa.

November 30, 1945. Petition filed by Mr. Charles Bowser, Assistant Intake Secretary, Juvenile Court of Allegheny County.

Charge. Said Child was brought to the Juvenile Detention Home on November 29, 1945, by officers from Police Station Number Twelve; said child was involved in "attempting larceny of a car." Legal settlement of said child is the City of Pittsburgh, Pa. Your petitioner prays that a hearing be held in Juvenile Court.

Statement of Child. Thomas is a sturdy but unrefined type of boy whose mannerisms and speech suggest recklessness. He is well built, but lean; has regular features from which a skin eruption detracts. Tom squints his eyes. His attitude towards his mother would lead probation officers to believe that he was intolerant of her authority. He was sullen and impolite to her. When the probation officer was alone with Tom, the lad was cooperative and responsive.

"It happened on Thursday morning, November 29. I didn't go to school because I wanted to find a job. I'll be 16 pretty soon; so I thought I would get a Christmas holiday job. It's pretty cold these days; so when I passed this parking lot I didn't see anybody around; so I decided to sit in one;

warm up and maybe listen to a radio a little. The guy got me before I had a chance to do anything. It was a crazy thing to do, but everybody pushes me around these days, especially Mr. Koller. I don't like school, I don't like him!"

Tom agreed with the probation officer that everybody had to follow regulations, even Mr. Koller. He admitted he wasn't very considerate of the rules of his parents. He volunteered: "—especially about that gang of mine and about learning to drive a car." When asked about his truancy, Tom said, "That too!"

Previous Knowledge. He has never appeared before Juvenile Court or any other Court.

School Record. Dr. Koller, Principal of the High School, made a general statement. He said Tom was a member of a gang known as the "Hell Raisers" and they were! No day passed that he didn't receive some information on one of them. However he had no direct evidence. He enumerated the following: breaking a window; interfering with the play activities of small children; jumping street cars; cutting classes. Tom's school marks were: English, D; World History, E; American History, E; Mechanical Drawing, C; Metal Shop, B; Physical Education, E; Citizenship, E. Of the total of 67 days, he was absent 23.

Statement of Parents. Mother was emotional during the initial stage of the interview. She spoke of the humiliation which she would suffer as a result of the proceedings and was horrified by the thought of appearing in Juvenile Court. When P.O. explained Juvenile Court procedure and the general objectives of the Court, mother relaxed and assisted in establishing facts for the investigation.

Mother informed Probation Officer that both the police and the Detention Home had notified her of the boy's arrest.

She admitted that Tom had caused her some concern, especially his saucy attitude, his streetcar-hopping, and the gang with which he was involved. He ridiculed her attempts at punishment. The father had acted wisely by restricting Tom's use of leisure time and money.

Father came in from shopping just as the interview with mother was drawing to a close. He said he didn't believe that his boy had the right to enter the car, but was sure Tom had no intention of taking it. Tom and he had discussed the matter thoroughly. "Tom had no business leaving school; that's his business now!" Probation officer then informed parents of the doctor's examination. The doctor's diagnosis had been: nine pounds underweight, refractive error, wax in both ears. Probation Officer suggested that Tom be taken to a clinic for further examination and correction. "It might help his school work." Parents agreed. Father was composed and judicious when discussing problems with Probation Officer.

The father seemed to feel that perhaps he was at fault in that he had not been close to the boy; had taken little part in supervision. He pointed out that he worked long hours, therefore spent little time with his son.

Social History. The family is composed of the parents and two children.

Tom is the older. The other son, Paul, is four years younger and doing well in parochial school.

Both the parents were born in Pittsburgh. They have resided here their entire lives. Father has been employed regularly at a mill. Father was an only child. Mother had been working prior to her marriage but has had no employment since that time.

Mother is in poor health, a heart condition. Father stated that mother is very much upset by Tom's difficulty.

Home Investigation. The family rents a small four-room house, one of a row, in a quiet residential section.

Statement of Police. "His story sounds fishy! There has been a lot of car-lifting lately by kids. No, we never saw this kid before."

Social Agencies. No social agency has known this family.

Evaluation: Facts revealed in the course of this investigation point up Thomas' inability to meet the limits set up by the community, the school, and his parents. There is some question regarding the adequacy and consistency of parental supervision. Both parents appear to recognize to some degree Tom's inability to meet limitations but are somewhat overprotective. This is evident in their attitude towards Mr. Koller and his criticism of Tom's behavior. They have been unable to accept the constructive help made by the school.

It appears that the authority of the Court may be a constructive factor in assisting Tom to meet some limitations and in bringing the parents to some realization of the possible future if the boy is not corrected.

Recommendation. That Thomas be returned to the custody of his parents on probation.

Reasons: 1. This boy's conduct for several months has shown a definite trend toward habitual delinquency.
2. Remedial measures have already been taken at the probation officer's suggestion for the correction of the eyes.
3. Transfer to a trade school has been arranged by the parents.
4. Although parental control has been weak, the parents have been aroused to their responsibilities by Tom's trouble. A better relationship between Tom and his parents seems possible under supervision by a probation officer.

THE FAMILY IN COURT

Friday, December 21, 1945. Court opened for the day at 9:30 a.m. The Court session began without formality. Mr. Downs, the probation officer who had a written report on Tom, walked up to the desk. He named the child, the reason for the Court's attention, and the information which he had gathered concerning the child. He briefly summarized the problem because the Judge had "studied" the case the evening before the hearing. Mr. Downs ushered the parents individually into the courtroom. The Judge talked over the boy's problem with them. Tom's school adjustment was discussed, his companions, his behavior on the streets and playground, the remedial measures initiated.

After each of the parents had been in the courtroom, the Judge left his chair. He entered a very small room next to the courtroom. The plain-walled room was without furniture save for two or three chairs.

Tom was waiting when Judge Schramm entered. He acted surprised when the Judge extended his hand for a handshake. Tom didn't know what to do. He extended his sweating palm slowly. "I've never shook hands with a Judge before." The ice of conversational restraint was broken.

The Judge encouraged Tom to talk about himself—not only about his recent involvement, which he fully admitted, but about the whole story of his difficulties. The more Tom talked, the more he seemed to be gaining in confidence. Tom indicated penitence for his acts; he said that his folks didn't understand him; his father never did talk to him "man to man" like the Judge did. But lately, after he got into trouble, his father was paying more attention. Father and son went to a movie together, the first in a long time. And last week the father "came down the cellar to help fix my brother's sled." Dad saw Mr. Koller so that Tom could go to Trade School.

Judge Schramm spoke solemnly to the boy. He reminded Tom that the circumstances in which he was arrested were extremely suspicious; that "bad company invites trouble." "I've decided that you can go home on probation. An officer of the Court will see you from time to time. Talk over your problems with him." The Judge again shook hands with Tom, then left the room.

Back in the Courtroom. The parents entered the courtroom together. The Judge told them that Thomas would be on probation. Mr. Downs, the probation officer, would be visiting them.[1]

The procedures used in Pittsburgh are considered good (if not ideal), but it should be realized that other cities have somewhat different methods of treating juvenile offenders which are probably just as good. The details of procedure vary from place to place, but the underlying principles remain the same.

ATTITUDES TOWARD DELINQUENTS AND CRIMINALS

There is a noticeable tendency on the part of all persons to classify others according to rather rigid categories. When a person does a "bad" act, he is not thought of as being bad in one particular incident, he is all too often considered totally bad. Likewise, when a person does "good," we are apt to think that he is thoroughly good. We are prone

[1]These materials are quoted from *Priceless: Handle With Care*, the annual report (1945) of the Juvenile Court of Allegheny County, Pennsylvania.

to use this method of evaluation even when judging whole groups of people, as well as individuals. Thus we say that a certain race, class, or nation is "good" or "bad," according to the spotty and partial evidence which we may have on hand and in the light of predisposing factors within ourselves. Probably few tendencies in the ethical realm are as striking as that by which we tend to judge other individuals and groups in terms of total response.

This tendency to make general judgments is evident throughout human experience, but it is especially demonstrated historically and even at present in the classification and treatment of lawbreakers. So often the history of criminal punishment sounds like a Gertrude Stein parody: "A crime is a crime, is a crime, is a crime, is a crime." When a man violates a law we do not commonly ask, "Who is the man?" but rather, "What law has he broken and what consequences does such lawbreaking enjoin?" If we consider the individual at all, we think of him only in terms of his misdeed. All of the many constructive possibilities which he possesses, all of the kindly and legal acts which he may have performed previously, all of his permanent and generally guiding moral aspirations are usually set aside. If he has committed a crime, we unfortunately say that he is pervasively "bad." And for the most part we treat him as though we believed our statement. Often he is placed in an institution where he lives in a cell block designed for mass living —as though all inhabitants were to be regarded (or disregarded) equally. He wears the same clothes as the other prisoners. He is regulated by the "equal" standards of the prison. The person who commits a criminal act finds himself classified as a member of a particular group of society and is treated almost without question as though he genuinely and inevitably belongs to the group.

While the practice in regard to criminals differs widely within the various jurisdictions of the United States, there have been few genuine exceptions to what has just been said. Fortunately, however, some inroads are being made on the philosophy that a criminal is a criminal and the only place for him is in prison. Probation and parole are two systems that tend to recognize the criminal as an individual rather than as a type. But, even in the past, some lawbreakers were excepted from mass classification and treatment. These traditionally fell into two groups: the insane, and children.

For many years it has been realized that a man who is not in full possession of his mental faculties is not fully responsible for his actions, legal or otherwise. Therefore, recognition has been made of the fact that to punish a person who is psychotic or mentally deficient would be of no avail and would not strengthen justice in the community.

Likewise, children have never been deemed to be as responsible for their actions as have adults. There have been times when children under a certain age have been excused from all criminal responsibility. It seems illogical, whatever our theory of justice, to hold a five-year-old, for example, responsible for his conduct. The fact that children have been viewed as comprising possible exceptions to the common methods of handling criminals has given the basis for very important modern developments in the treatment of juvenile offenders. These developments have taken several forms, but probably none is so important as the rise of the juvenile court.

THE RISE OF THE JUVENILE COURTS

Juvenile courts originated in 1899 out of the age-old sentiment which generally distinguished children from adults on the point of responsibility for behavior. But, specifically, juvenile courts arose out of three other important conditions. (1) *The reaction against the harsh treatment of children in the eighteenth and nineteenth centuries.* An early record of the treatment of an eight-year-old child who set fire to a barn states that the child was summarily tried and hanged for his act. Sensitive minds became increasingly aware that such punishment of child offenders was out of all proportion to what was required. Then too, many persons were appalled at the jails in which accused juveniles were placed. These places were surely breeders of criminality. By not making proper segregation according to age and background, they fed the incarcerated with a hunger after unrighteousness. The brutality and lack of rehabilitative treatment were notorious aspects of jail placement. With the rise of juvenile courts, however, the practice of placing juvenile delinquents in jail has been largely eliminated. (2) *The growth of new information about the nature of human conduct.* While it would be inaccurate to say that the nineteenth century possessed a thoroughgoing scientific understanding of human behavior, the discoveries of the psychologists and sociologists of the last decades of the century at least laid the basis for the modern views of man. In the light of the growing knowledge of how and why people respond, it was realized by relatively large numbers that the older methods of interpreting and treating children's criminal behavior were inadequate and ill-founded. (3) *The common law conception of the state as the protector of children.* In the common law there was the view of the courts as being the ultimate "parents" of the children. According to this outlook the courts possess a responsibility toward children which supersedes that of parents, for the court in some cases needs to direct the relations between parents and children for the benefit of the latter. In this sense, children were thought to be the wards of the state.

Thus the revolt against overly harsh punishment for children who had broken the law, the new findings of the human sciences, and the requirements of the common-law tradition called for a new method of treating child offenders.

Some distinctions were made between juvenile delinquents and adult criminals in the period preceding the introduction of the juvenile court. In some jurisdictions a child offender could be sentenced by standards which applied more specifically to his age classification. These standards were different from those which held for adults. For example, shortly after the Civil War, the state of Massachusetts passed a law which provided for a state "visitor" to be present at the trials of children and to arrange (under certain circumstances) for suitable placement in a foster home. In the same period the Midwest provided in some cases an atmosphere of less condemnation and authority by trying children out of court. Other modifications of court procedure were introduced in various localities about this time until the first full-fledged juvenile court was an actuality. This was the juvenile court founded in Chicago in 1899. The juvenile court of Denver, although of limited jurisdiction, was established in the same year.

Following the development of the juvenile courts in Chicago and Denver, the newer and more satisfactory methods of treating child offenders spread to most of the other states.

Adolescent Court. At this point a type of court for child offenders which oftentimes is not called a "juvenile court" or "children's court," but rather an "adolescent court," bears mention. The differences between the two types of court are relatively minor, the most important being that of age. The adolescent court usually makes a specialty of treating persons from the ages of sixteen to twenty-one. In view of the problems which are generally characteristic of that particular age grouping and of the methods of treatment, the adolescent court is a particularly fitting social instrument for its purposes. However, the procedures used in the adolescent courts are not radically different from those employed in juvenile courts. In fact, adolescent courts may be looked upon as a special variant of the juvenile courts. They exist, moreover, in only a very few cities.

THE PHILOSOPHY OF THE JUVENILE COURT

The juvenile court differs markedly from the regular criminal court. For one thing the juvenile court does not conceive of itself as being opposed to the child brought before it. It does not make charges against children. It does not arrange for a formal series of counterexchanges between debating lawyers. There is no jury to decide the guilt or innocence of those accused. In short, the juvenile court does not sit in judgment. Rather, it seeks to find an explanation for the child's conduct and to help the child live according to the standards of the community. (See Figure 21.)

The ultimate responsibility in the juvenile court is vested in an "expert," a judge, who is eager to include in his treatment-decision all of the scientific elements of evidence which may be had. As the presiding officer he usually does not adhere strictly to juridical rules. The investigation is conducted on a more informal basis and certainly a more private one than in a criminal court. The general public is not allowed to sit in on the cases, although any friends, relatives, or others who have a contribution to make may be present at the hearing. The judge's approach to the accused child is one which seeks the broadest possible interpretation of the conditions which precipitated the offense. Economic and social factors are strongly relevant to the decision which he makes. He does not want to match the existing legal punishments to the offense (as Gilbert and Sullivan put it: "to make the punishment fit the crime"). He wants to understand the child, first and foremost, so that in the final analysis the least important aspect of some cases may be the legal. Similarly, in treatment, the primary intent of the judge is to arrange for that series of experiences which will best enable the child to adjust ultimately in a positive manner to his home and the community. The means of treatment are thus of necessity more numerous in a juvenile court than in a criminal court.

The whole process suggests that much attention is given in the juvenile courts to the individual and his needs. Emphasis is not so much on the actual guilt of the child as on the reasons and circumstances behind the guilt. The question is not so much "How can we punish him?" as "How can we help him?" The adult criminal, on the other hand, usually finds the court more interested in the crime than in himself as an individual.

INVESTIGATIONS

If the principles which motivate the juvenile court are to be operative, certain preliminary steps must be taken. One of the most important procedures, and one which concerns the social worker in the court setting, is that of the preliminary investigation. The preliminary investigation is a device which enables the court to proceed intelligently on

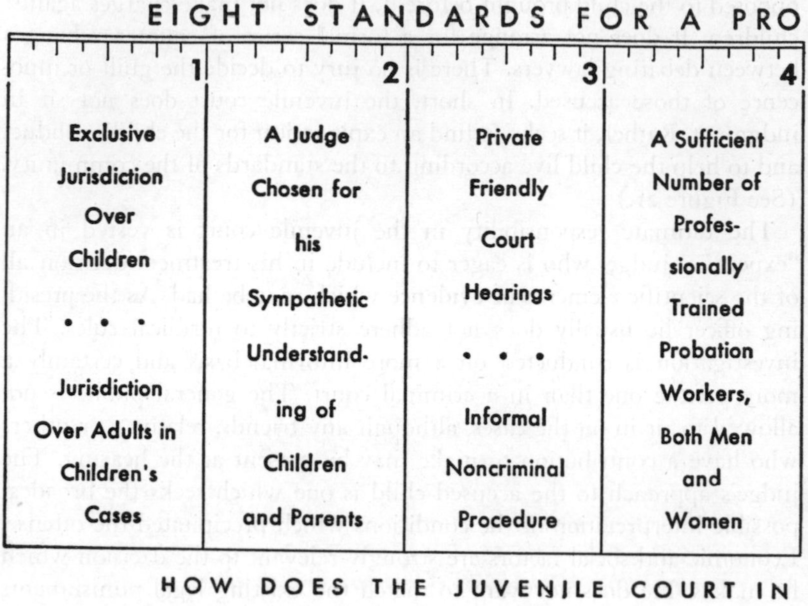

EIGHT STANDARDS FOR A PRO

1	2	3	4
Exclusive Jurisdiction Over Children • • • Jurisdiction Over Adults in Children's Cases	A Judge Chosen for his Sympathetic Understand-ing of Children and Parents	Private Friendly Court Hearings • • • Informal Noncriminal Procedure	A Sufficient Number of Profes-sionally Trained Probation Workers, Both Men and Women

HOW DOES THE JUVENILE COURT IN

FIG. 21. Eight Standards for a Progressive Juvenile Court

the basis of accurate information. It is important that the juvenile court base its conclusions not on the whims of personal prejudice or the half truths of lawyers in opposition, but on the careful, impartial, painstaking uncovering and collating of the facts behind the case. The social worker attached to a juvenile court is given the responsibility of finding the facts and making interpretations which will enable a sound plan of treatment to be devised. Upon this foundation, much of the success of the juvenile court program depends.

The question naturally arises: How does the social worker attached to a juvenile court go about making an investigation of a case? This will be answered briefly, although the actual process differs in its dynamics from case to case. Only the general scope of information desired in most cases will be indicated here.

Preliminary Steps

One of the first steps of the investigating social worker is the clear-ing of the case with the social service exchange.[2] This permits the inves-tigator to discover whether the child and his parents have a history of

[2]The organization and functions of the social service exchange are described in Chapter 14.

GRESSIVE JUVENILE COURT

5	6	7	8
Facilities for Physical Examinations and for Psychiatric Study of Problem Children	A Well-Equipped Detention Home, or Selected Boarding Homes for Temporary Care of Children	An Efficient Record and Statistical System • • • Adequate Clerical Help	Cooperation With Other Agencies • • • Community Support Through Interpretation to the Public

YOUR COMMUNITY MEASURE UP?

(Courtesy of National Probation and Parole Association.)

contact with the social work agencies of the locality. If the child or parents have previously been treated by other social agencies, effort would be made to uncover the nature of the relationships and to incorporate the findings of the assisting agencies into the investigation record of the court social worker.

Another step is the examination of the actual offense to determine its character and its contribution to an understanding of the child's problem. In some cases the type of offense would be an important indication of the child's behavior problem. The mode of committing the specific type of offense might also be enlightening. If the child is accused of stealing valuable equipment out of a closed school, questions such as these might be raised: What factors predisposed him to be interested in stealing? What did he do with the stolen goods? Who assisted him, if anyone, in creating his offense? What special attitudes, if any, did the child reveal in the commission of the act?

Again, the child's health might be an important factor. A health examination arranged by the social worker is a standard prerequisite for all court examinations. While the health evidence may not be of significance where normality is discovered, nevertheless where physical abnormalities are found, there may be a notable connection between the conduct of the child and his state of health. The mental health of the child is also of interest to the social worker. An intelligence test may indicate possibilities both for explanation of conduct and for treatment. A general psychological evaluation may throw considerable light on the etiology and treatment of the case.

The child's performance at school (if he attends school) would be of interest to the court social worker. In connection with school performance the social worker would like to know not only the academic accomplishments of the child but also his social manners—his ways of getting along with people. Likewise, the worker would be concerned with the child's extraschool activities. Does the child participate in the program of a neighborhood settlement house? If so, the leaders at the house may contribute significantly to the understanding of the child. Does the child work? If so, his employers, past and present, may add to the evidence at hand. Who are his friends? If they can be known, they may assist in a fuller understanding. Does the child attend church? If he does, it may be of importance to know whether his church attachment is weak or strong.

Of great significance to the social worker attached to a juvenile court would be an investigation of the family background of the child. Are both parents living? Are they divorced or separated? Are they compatible, emotionally stable, economically independent, sober, healthy? All of this information is vital to the social worker's understanding of the child. Recognizing the fact that the behavior of a child is very largely determined by his experience within the intimate family group in the early years, the social worker would want to know many related details about the organization and operation of the child's family.

The community in which the child and his family live would also be a subject for investigation by the social worker. What is the housing condition of the locality? Does the child live in a slum area in which delinquency is frequent and "normal"? Is the community one where recreational facilities are inadequate or absent? Do neighborhood gangs exist in the area, and, if so, how have they contributed to the development of the child? To know that the community is deficient in some regard might indicate a factor in the past determination of the activity of the child.

These and other sources of information about the child are used by the court social worker in drawing up his case study for the court. While there is no set form to gather information for the court, the following one, prepared by the National Probation and Parole Association and widely used, gives an idea of the nature and organization of the materials sought:

JUVENILE
GUIDE FOR RECORDING INITIAL SOCIAL STUDY
(*Preliminary Investigation*)

Complaint. State date, nature, accompanying circumstances and sources of the complaint, together with complainant's attitude toward offense.

Previous Court or Institutional History. State any previous court experience of the child with date, name of judge, and disposition.

Family History. Use narrative form without topical headings. State sources of information.

State the family background including racial, religious, social, and economic facts, with delinquency records of family members, if any. Give in detail early history, education, and employment data for both parents. Give circumstances preceding marriage, the success or failure of the marriage, and reasons therefor. Describe present living conditions. Note moral and ethical standards of the home.

Give personality data for each member of the family, mental and physical health, education, employment experiences, attitude of parents toward each child and of children toward parents and each other, attitude of family toward the child's situation.

Child's History. Individualize the child.

Include attitude of parents toward birth of child, developmental history, age of weaning, teething, walking, talking, preschool life, status in the family.

Discipline in the home and child's reaction.

Neighborhood and its effect on child's personality, periods of separation from family and reaction of the child.

Physical history, illnesses and their effect, physical and emotional.

Personality traits and behavior trends.

Significance of previous court or institutional experience, of other delinquent experiences.

Practical meaning of religion to the child, application of religious principles to everyday experience.

School experience, grade attained, attendance, reasons for truancy and other misconduct, attitude toward teachers and classmates and vice versa, reasons for leaving school.

Work record, jobs held, how secured, wages, reasons for leaving, vocational interests, results of tests given, attitude toward job or employers.

Recreational outlets, group activities (including organized and supervised), status in group, type of movies, hobbies, type of reading matter, recreation with family or outside, kind of companions.

Child's attitude toward present situation, his explanation of conduct and plans for the future.

Information From Social Agencies and Others. State experience of social agencies with child and family including reasons for agency con-

tact, services rendered, family's response, agency recommendation in reference to present situation.
Analysis, Interpretation, Recommendation.

PROCEDURES AT THE HEARING

As has been described, the hearing of a juvenile case is usually preceded by a rather lengthy investigation of the background factors which have led to the particular behavior under consideration. The purpose of this research is not that of preparing charges against the juvenile or to make more easy a prosecutor's task (there is no prosecutor in the children's court), but to enable the treatment procedures offered by the court to be more intelligently founded and more effective in their application. The true purpose of the court in the final analysis is treatment, not punishment. The spirit of investigation is understanding rather than moral judgment.

The Petition

The hearing procedures in the juvenile court are processually modeled along the lines suggested. Usually, the court's responsibility is formalized in a *petition*. The petition seeks to describe the conditions discovered in the child's situation which have brought him to the attention of the authorities. A sample petition in the case of a delinquent girl is the following:[3]

THE CASE OF AMY STEWART

IN THE JUVENILE COURT OF THE COUNTY OF LOS ANGELES, STATE OF CALIFORNIA

In the Matter of	
Amy Stewart	PETITION
A Person under the age of twenty-one years.	

TO THE HONORABLE JUVENILE COURT OF THE COUNTY OF LOS ANGELES, STATE OF CALIFORNIA:

YOUR PETITIONER   A.L.D.   respectfully represents that the above named person is residing within said county and is a

[3]Pauline V. Young, *Social Treatment in Probation and Delinquency: Treatise and Casebook for Court Workers, Probation Officers and Other Child Welfare Workers,* McGraw-Hill Book Company, New York, 1937, pp. 150-151.

person under the age of twenty-one years, to wit, of the age of sixteen years, on or about the ___3rd___ day of ___September___, 193_5, and is a person defined in subdivisions ___2 and 11___ of Section One, within the meaning of the Act of the Legislature of said State, known as the "Juvenile Court Law," approved June 5th, 1915, and Acts amendatory thereto. In that said person ___Amy Stewart___, who has no parent or guardian; or who has no parent or guardian willing to exercise or capable of exercising proper parental control; or who has no parent or guardian actually exercising such proper parental control and who is in need of such control, in that the parents have been unable to keep this girl from associating with undesirable companions.

In that said person, ___Amy Stewart___ who is leading, or from cause is in danger of leading an idle, dissolute, lewd or immoral life in that for the past year and a half this girl has been associating with one, ___John McFarland___, 19 years of age (Oriental), living at_____. Girl admits being pregnant and admits having sexual relations with ___John McFarland___.

As provided in Section 3, Juvenile Court Law, the Probation Officer of Los Angeles County has made an investigation of the facts herein alleged and has approved the filing of this petition.

That the said person is now in the custody and control of ___Juvenile Hall___. That your petitioner is the ___Policewoman___ of said person, and is entitled to the custody thereof. That the names and residences of the relatives of said person living in the said County are as follows: Parents: _____.

That in order to secure the attendance of said person at the hearing of said matter, it will not be necessary that a warrant be issued for the arrest of said person, ___Amy Stewart___.

WHEREFORE, your petitioner prays that this Honorable Court inquire into such matter and declare said person a ward of the Juvenile Court and deal with said person as provided in the above entitled Act of the Legislature, and make such order in the premises as to this Honorable Court may seem meet and proper, to which order your petitioner now consents.

___A.L.D.___
Petitioner.

Address _____

STATE OF CALIFORNIA,
County of Los Angeles,

_____A.L.D._____, the petitioner above named, being duly sworn, says that ___she___ has read the foregoing petition, and knows the contents thereof, and that the same is true of ___her___ own knowledge, except as to the matters which are therein stated on _____ information or belief, and as to those matters that _____she_____ believes it to be true.

A.L.D.

Subscribed and sworn to before me this
____5th____ day of ____November____ , 193_5_
L. E. LAMPTON, County Clerk.
by _____ , Deputy.

On the basis of the petition, the court comes into session in the presence of the juvenile under examination, the court representatives, and friends and relatives who may be needed. Only those are admitted to the hearing who have something to contribute to the understanding and treatment of the child's problem. Questions are asked by the presiding judge in confirmation of the evidence at hand and toward the securing of additional information. From the information presented to the court by the probation officer and the verbal investigation by the judge, a decision is made as to the best method of treating the juvenile.

Conduct of Hearing

The actual conduct of a hearing is vividly portrayed in the following scene from a former Broadway play. While the hearing is given a fictionalized treatment, it does serve to show the spontaneity which characterizes juvenile court procedure. The case of Elizabeth Collins, a teen-age girl, is being heard:

JUDGE enters D. R. Crosses to chair, sits.

JUDGE. (Immediately resuming, calls.) Oh, yes, Mr. and Mrs. Collins. (Pulls chair closer to desk. Mr. and Mrs. Collins go to platform. Indicating witness chair.) Up here, Mrs. Collins. (She stands near the chair.) Do you swear in the presence of Almighty God to tell the truth?

MRS. COLLINS. I do. (She sits.)

JUDGE. How many children have you, Madam?

MRS. COLLINS. Four.

JUDGE. All of them the children of Mr. Collins?

MRS. COLLINS. (Amazed.) Why—of course! (COLLINS drops hat—picks it up.)

JUDGE. Who's the eldest of your children?

MRS. COLLINS. Lizzie there.

JUDGE. How old are the other three?

MRS. COLLINS. Bobby is six, Mary is seven, Joseph is nine. I had two miscarriages between Joseph and Lizzie. 'Twas in '30 and '32 during the depression, and I was workin' too hard. My husband was idle.

COLLINS. (As if defending himself against a charge of loafing.) I couldn't get no work.

JUDGE. But you are working now.

COLLINS. Yes, sir. In a shipyard. In California.

JUDGE. What is your line of work?

COLLINS. Glass worker, Your Honor.

JUDGE. Are *you* working now, Madam?

MRS. COLLINS. I have to! Him bein' idle most of the time till after Pearl Harbor put us in plenty of debt, and we ain't through payin' up yet.

JUDGE. How many days a week do you work?

MRS. COLLINS. I'm home only on Sundays. And sometimes not then.

JUDGE. At what time do you usually get home from your job?

MRS. COLLINS. About one in the morning, Your Honor. I'm a cook for a theatrical couple, and I have to wait till they get home from their performance at night to serve them a late supper.

JUDGE. (Looking at a document.) Now—this petition alleges truancy. . . Mrs. Busch, read the school attendance record.

MRS. BUSCH. (Reads from a report in her hand.) During April, absent: eight whole days, six half days; during May, absent: seven whole days, three half days. During June, *this* month, not present any school days. (COLLINS shuffles feet.) But, Your Honor, today is the 12th, and it was over two weeks ago that Elizabeth was remanded to the Detention Home.

JUDGE. (Nods.) Mrs. Collins, you heard what the Probation Officer read from the record?

MRS. COLLINS. Well, I don't call it truancy, Your Honor. I mean, Lizzie wasn't playin' hookey. And I told them so at school! Lizzie was home when she wasn't at school. And she told me about it every time.

JUDGE. Why did you permit it?

MRS. COLLINS. Because she had to catch up with the housework! Your Honor, Lizzie's got to help me out a bit. With a family of four and my husband not in town, and workin' such long hours, I've got to have some help. And Lizzie's old enough.

JUDGE. What did she help you with?

MRS. COLLINS. Well—she fixed the meals. Dinner for herself and the three kids. Not for me. You see, I have to get dinner for the people where I work, so I'm not home dinnertime.

JUDGE. Are you home for lunch?

MRS. COLLINS. Well, I leave the house about half-past twelve. But the children eat their lunches at school.

JUDGE. Oh, you put up lunches for them . . . ?

MRS. COLLINS. Well, yes, Lizzie does it. It's easy, Your Honor—a couple of sandwiches for each one.

JUDGE. How about breakfast? Are you home then?

MRS. COLLINS. I am. But the children don't like breakfast. Can't get 'em to swallow a mouthful in the mornin'. It runs in the family, I guess. I was like that when I was a youngster.

JUDGE. You could train them to like breakfast.

MRS. COLLINS. Oh, good Lord—start trainin' four children to eat in the morning! 'Twould take no end of naggin' and they'd never get off to school.

JUDGE. Rise an hour earlier and give yourself time for the job. It's important.

MRS. COLLINS. But if they won't eat breakfast what's the use me gettin' up, Your Honor? It's not that I'm lazy. But I've got to have some rest, too! When I get home at night I'm so tired I can't fall asleep before three in the morning usually. How could I be up at seven and be fit for a day's work?

JUDGE. (Referring again to a document.) Now—the school report states that Elizabeth has decayed teeth. Did you know about it?

MRS. COLLINS. Your Honor, the school nurse told me about it. All my kids have bad teeth. In school they told me, "Get them fixed," and I said I would. But how, Your Honor? (To COLLINS.) With what? Will a dentist do it for nothing?

JUDGE. There are free dental clinics.

MRS. COLLINS. But I haven't the time to take the children there. I have bad teeth, too. On this side no back teeth; on that side four rotten teeth. . . And my husband, too:—*no* back teeth, upper or lower. Charlie, show the Judge I ain't lyin'! (COLLINS starts to, JUDGE stops him.)

JUDGE. No, it's not necessary. . . . Who does the cleaning for your family, Mrs. Collins—housecleaning, I mean? (CLERK enters U. L. Crosses to table 1.)

MRS. COLLINS. I give the apartment a thorough going-over on Sundays, when I'm home—and Lizzie helps me.

JUDGE. Who does the washing and ironing?

MRS. COLLINS. When my husband was idle he used to do it. But now I have an electric washing machine; so it's easy. Lizzie does it.

JUDGE. (Removing his glasses.) Elizabeth has had too much work to do for a girl of fifteen.

MRS. COLLINS. It sounds a lot, Your Honor. But after all, there were the hours from 8:30 till 3:30 when she was in school, and had nothing to do but sit. When I was her age I was workin' ten hours a day in a canning factory.

JUDGE. Mr. Collins, are you considered a good worker in your line?

COLLINS. I know my job all right, Your Honor, but before the war it made no difference how well you knew your work. There was no jobs.

JUDGE. But now that you are working, why hasn't your wife been staying home to look properly after your family?

COLLINS. (Apologetically.) We're terrible in debt, Your Honor. (MRS. COLLINS nods.) We borrowed so much when I was out of work. And now, me livin' away from home, we have a double expense.

MRS. COLLINS. We owe money on the furniture, on the washing machine, and cash we loaned from my relatives and my husband's relatives!

JUDGE. But couldn't you have gotten another job, Madam, one that wouldn't keep you away from home so much?

MRS. COLLINS. Excuse me, Your Honor, that's easy to say—"couldn't you get some other job" . . . I'm a cook. No matter what job I'd have I'd be leavin' at seven in the morning and returnin' eight, nine o'clock at night, or even later!

JUDGE. Mmm . . . Did you know that your daughter was associating with this—Lockwood girl? (COLLINS looks at Elizabeth.)

MRS. COLLINS. Yes, now about Ruby: I knew that Lizzie was goin' around with her, and when I met the girl I didn't like the looks of her. So I told Lizzie not to go with her anymore.

JUDGE. Did you make sure that she had stopped going with her?

MRS. COLLINS. Lizzie usually obeyed me.

JUDGE. Had you heard that Ruby was kind of "wild"?

MRS. COLLINS. (Glances L.) Och, in our neighborhood they're always gossipin' about everybody.

JUDGE. Hadn't your neighbor, Mrs. Marti, told you that Lizzie was staying out late with Ruby?

MRS. COLLINS. (Looks at MRS. MARTI. Flaring up.) Mrs. Marti was always tellin' me things that were none of her business! Half the time I couldn't make out what she was saying, and what I did understand was sure to be a squawk about someone or other. No one was good enough for Peter! (Peter looks at MRS. MARTI—she looks down.) Anyway, Lizzie was always home when I got back from work.

JUDGE. At one in the morning——?

MRS. COLLINS. Well—yes.

JUDGE. Did you allow your daughter any spending money?

MRS. COLLINS. Oh, yes, a little every week, for candy and ice cream and so on for the four of 'em.

JUDGE. Did she at any time seem to be spending more than you allowed her?

MRS. COLLINS. I never noticed it.

JUDGE. Did you buy all of her clothes?

MRS. COLLINS. Certainly! . . . Except for that jacket there. (Looks at ELIZABETH.) She told *me* that she got it from Ruby.

JUDGE. And you believed her?

MRS. COLLINS. My right hand to God! Why shouldn't I've? They say Ruby's mother has money—and people often give away things when they get tired wearin' 'em themselves.

JUDGE. Wasn't the jacket *new* when Elizabeth got it?

MRS. COLLINS. (Fingers her dress.) It was. But even so—I've many times got new things from well-off people. They see something in a store and they like it. When they bring it home they don't like it. Well, sometimes they won't bother to return it, and they give it away when it's still new.

JUDGE. Have you and Elizabeth gotten along well, or have you clashed?

MRS. COLLINS. (Looks at ELIZABETH who stares at her.) Clashed? Why, of all things! I should say not! . . . Though she wasn't always a considerate child.

JUDGE. In what way? Give me an example.

MRS. COLLINS. Well, when I was tryin' to get some sleep, like of a Saturday morning—Lizzie'd be havin' her friends in, laughin' and gigglin' and wakin' me up. Or—what always made me furious—when I'd be wantin' her to help me with something—and she'd be primpin' before a mirror, eternally primpin'—fixin' her hair this way, that way, lookin' at her profile.

COLLINS. (Crosses R. to platform. Interrupting.) Your Honor—if you don't mind my sayin' it—I don't think that should count against Lizzie— I mean this primpin' in front of a mirror. All young girls do it.

MRS. COLLINS. That's the trouble! You were always makin' excuses for her . . . (COLLINS turns. Smiles at ELIZABETH. Crosses up R.) spoilin' her! All young girls *don't* spend hours before a mirror! I never did. (To JUDGE.) And it made me furious when she did it and of course we'd have a row!

JUDGE. (Nods.) All right. You may step down. (MRS. COLLINS rises.) Oh —do you belong to a church, Mrs. Collins?

MRS. COLLINS. (Proudly.) Oh, yes!

JUDGE. Do you take the children to the services?

MRS. COLLINS. (Steps down.) I never have the time, Your Honor! (Stops, turns.)

JUDGE. (Nods.) Go back to your seat. You too, Mr. Collins. (COLLINS goes back to his seat, Bench 1. MRS. COLLINS crosses L. C., turns.)

MRS. COLLINS. (Crosses R. to JUDGE.) Your Honor, may I have Lizzie back at home? What right has the Detention Home to take my daughter away from me, anyway?

JUDGE. The Police Department took Elizabeth away, Madam. She was placed in the Detention Home until we could complete the investigation for this hearing.

MRS. COLLINS. (Worried.) Will she be going back there?

JUDGE. We're trying to decide now, Madam, *where* your child should go —(He makes notes on petition. MRS. COLLINS, looking hopelessly confused, goes back to her seat, bench L. 1.)[4]

This excerpt represents only a portion of the scene, but it is enough to indicate how a hearing is conducted.

THE DETENTION HOME

In some cases while the child is awaiting his hearing he is placed in a detention home. Almost any arrangement which removes the child

[4]*Pick-Up Girl*, a play by Elsa Shelley, copyright, 1946, by Elsa Shelley. Copyright, 1943, by Elsa Shelley, under the title *Elizabeth vs. You and Me*, published by Dramatists Play Service, Inc., New York.

from his own home, whether it be a jail, a boarding home, or a detention home so designated, is here meant as a detention home.

Too many times the care of the child prior to the decision of the juvenile court is inadequate and haphazard. The problem of caring for a child in a detention home is not an ordinary child welfare service inasmuch as the child detained is a special problem with special needs. There should be provided those services which will enable him to adjust as well as possible to the facts of his circumstances and the probable course of his future. More than a mere custodial program is required. The detention home also is not a penal institution, punishing the child before he comes to court. It must respect the rights and dignity of the child in every aspect of its program. Furthermore, it should keep the child for only the minimal amount of time necessary to handle his case effectively. While clinical services should be provided, no long-term treatment should be undertaken.

Type of Children Admitted

According to a study of the problem of detention homes made by the National Probation and Parole Association, the following variety of children at present enter the doors of detention homes:

1) Delinquents who have committed serious offenses or who have severe social problems.
2) Delinquents who have committed minor offenses or whose problems are less serious.
3) Children awaiting transfer to state training or industrial schools.
4) Runaways from institutions and from their own homes, including runaways from other communities.
5) Habitual school truants.
6) Mental defectives, delinquent and nondelinquent.
7) Material witnesses who are not themselves delinquent.
8) Uncared-for children who represent the large, dependent, and neglected group.
9) Lost children needing emergency shelter, perhaps for only a few hours.

It is suggested that some of these children should not be retained in this manner. Rather, the use of detention homes should be kept to a minimum and the great majority of children should be left in their own homes during investigation. The following three types of children, however, should be kept in detention homes:

1) Children so beyond control that parents or guardians may not be able to prevent a repetition of behavior which is menacing to themselves

or the community, such as repeated offenses, armed robbery, serious assault, and certain sex cases.

2) Children who are in physical or moral danger in their own homes or who are temporarily stranded and for whom no other immediate emergency placement (such as with friends, relatives or neighbors) is possible.

3) Children whose presence in court, return to another jurisdiction or community, longer time placement or uninfluenced testimony in another court can only be assured by detention.[5]

It is clear that if these standards are to be maintained, stricter intake procedures will have to be worked out to care for the other types of children in substitute ways.

Types of Service

Since the purpose of the detention home is more inclusive than merely that of custodial care, there are principally three types of service which the detention home can offer the child:

1. Physical Care. The detention home is responsible for the physical care and custody of the child. In regard to care, the child should be examined by a physician to determine his medical needs, and the home itself should be conducive to healthful living in its physical arrangements. As for custody, maximum security should be provided where needed without introducing a jail-like atmosphere.

2. Nonphysical Needs. The detention home is responsible for the nonphysical needs of the child. The assistance of professional persons is required to aid in the adjustment of the child to the home. His presence there should be explained to him so that he has an idea of the procedures not only within the home but for the disposition of his case as well. For children who are emotionally disturbed, casework services are important, along with those of other staff members. Likewise, the daytime activities of the child should be organized so that he will be busy and socially interested. Too often the detention home is lacking in group activities under professional supervision, leaving the children to modes of behavior which are detrimental to the philosophy of child rehabilitation. Assumptions that the child is "not going any place" or is too disorganized to take part in guided social activities have been found to be fallacious. If it is possible for the detention home to render clinical services to the child in conjunction with his detention, a helpful factor will be introduced into his treatment.

[5]Sherwood and Helen Norman, *Detention for the Juvenile Court: A Discussion of Principles and Practices,* National Probation Association (now National Probation and Parole Association), New York, 1946.

3. Pertinent Information. The detention home is responsible to the court for providing information based upon observation of the children in its care. It is actually in the detention home that a part of the investigation needed by the court for intelligent disposition of the cases begins. From the experiences within the home the needs of the children and their abilities are usually strikingly seen. This rich source of knowledge should be utilized in every possible way in determining the future of the children.

In carrying out these three requirements for a suitable detention home, it may be noted that it is probably correct to divide those children who are dependent, neglected, or involved in certain forms of delinquency from those for whom security detention seems to be necessary. In the cases of the former, boarding homes or homes which closely approximate normal home living can be used advantageously. A more informal custodial attention is required, although the quality of the social service care is none the less significant. For the latter cases more highly specialized institutions with adequate staffs are needed. In all circumstances, congregate-styled homes should be avoided, and it is obvious that in no instances should the child be placed with adult offenders.

In short, the successful detention home needs both caseworkers and group workers. Few homes, however, are fully equipped in this regard. The social caseworker can assist the child with his adjustment as an individual to the program of the home and to his probable future. The group worker can supply needed social activities for the child which will help maintain his normalcy or even aid in his treatment. Both caseworkers and group workers will be able to study the children during the detention period and compile useful data for the later disposition of the cases.

DISPOSITION OF CASES

The court may dispose of the cases of delinquents in various ways.[6] Social workers are not necessarily involved in all of them. (See Figure 22.)

[6] If the case is shown to be of insufficient importance to require extended treatment, it may be dismissed. Usually, a trivial case would not find its way to the hearing but, with careful social work preparation, would be evaluated long before the time and attention of the court was given. Oftentimes, too, cases may be dismissed because preceding the hearing certain adjustments have been made independently of the court (or with the court's assistance) which alleviate or abolish the problem. In the practice of dismissals, usually some social work is implied.

NEEDED SERVICES AND FACILITIES FOR THE
TREATMENT OF JUVENILE DELINQUENTS

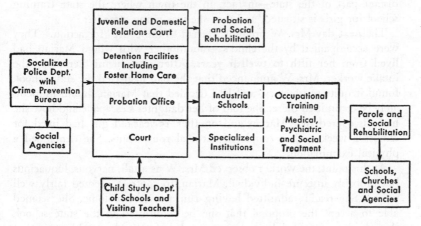

Fig. 22. Needed Services and Facilities for the Treatment of Juvenile Delinquents.

(June P. Guild and Arthur A. Guild, *Social Work Engineering,* Harper, New York, 1940.)

Foster Home Placement

One of the best plans for delinquents, aside from supervision in their own homes, is foster home placement. Foster home placement may be desirable in certain instances for the reasons already given in Chapter 5.

In general, there are several means of accomplishing placement from the juvenile court: (1) the child may be given over to a private agency for placement; (2) the child may be remanded to a public agency for placement—some localities require that children be placed in foster homes by public agencies, although in many places there are few facilities for foster home placement outside of the private agencies; (3) the court itself may have a program of foster home placement.

None of these methods of placement can be considered as ideal aside from the local conditions in which it operates. What might seem to be most desirable in one place would probably not be in another.

The case of "Marian W" illustrates the way in which a youthful delinquent might be placed in a foster home under the probation supervision of a court:

The court first learned of Marian W when her mother telephoned the juvenile court office to report that the girl had disappeared from home and that she strongly suspected Marian had left town with a carnival. We immediately notified the police departments and they routinely broadcast the information on the state police radio. The next information we had was that the mother had located the carnival in a small community in a distant part of the state—in fact, in the town where the state training school for girls is situated, and that she was going after her.

The next day Mrs. W brought Marian to the court "for action." They were accompanied by the child's grandmother with whom Marian had lived from her fifth to twelfth years. After introducing herself to the intake worker, Mrs. W announced that she had inspected the state school, found it quite satisfactory, and had decided that Marian should immediately be committed there. She told of her daughter's escapade and how she had discovered that Marian and another 15-year-old girl had lived for almost a week with a couple of carnival roustabouts. She demanded a physical examination.

At this point, the worker observed Mrs. W as a tall, nervous, loquacious but probably insecure individual. Marian, in contrast, seemed fairly well poised. She readily admitted having run away from home. She seemed able to accept the proposal that she be committed to the state school, though she countered by expressing a belief that she could remain at home without repeating this experience.

The grandmother was a small, rather elderly lady, who appeared concerned not alone with Marian's escapade but with the mother's attitude toward the problem. She impressed the worker as a capable person of high principles who gave affection sincerely, and had quite a little understanding of the girl. She expressed a desire that Marian return to her (the grandmother's) home on a permanent basis.

Though it was apparent that Mrs. W was challenged by this, the worker felt Marian should not return to her own home because of the mother's punishing attitude and recommended that the child be placed in the care of the grandmother, pending a hearing. Such an order was entered.

Before the hearing was called, the case was referred to the Girls' Probation Officer for an appraisal of the circumstances that led up to Marian's antisocial behavior. In the preparation of the social history and recommendations to the court, the worker stood between the court on the one hand and the parent and child on the other, and served to focus attention upon the issues involved. The girl had admittedly been incorrigible. Should the court, acting as an authoritative agency and in conformity with the expressed desire of the parent, punish and control? Was the girl pregnant or diseased? Could she be relied upon in the future to make sound moral decisions? Would acts of the court which Marian would construe as punishment result in ultimate good behavior or would they make her resentful and determined to "get even"? Did she want to be punished? If institutional care was not indicated, what substitute plan could the court consider? These and many other questions were tied up with Marian's background and past experiences, with her mental ability and her emotional conflicts. All these had to be considered, analyzed, and resolved before the case could be presented to the court for an intelligent decision.

During the two weeks following the first office interview, Marian was given a complete physical examination. After several office and home interviews with the girl and her relatives, a social history was prepared and she was referred to the local child guidance clinic, the West Michigan Children's Center. She was prepared for her visit to the Center by a frank discussion of her attitudes, her interests, and her future plans, and helped to understand that psychologists such as she was to meet there can often help all of us more fully to understand ourselves.

When the worker received the physician's report and the results of the Center study, she collected all the information she had about Marian and attempted to evaluate it and to point it up with recommendations for the benefit of the court. Marian was an attractive 15-year-old girl whose difficulties had no basis in physical ailments. She had not contracted a venereal disease, although the doctor was of the opinion that she had indulged in sexual intercourse. She had experienced difficulty in competing in an 8th-grade placement, which was explained by the psychologist's opinion that she was of dull, normal intelligence. Though she gave the outward appearance of poise, she was found to be insecure and lacking in self-confidence in school, home, and other social situations. She talked continually about her mother, complained that her mother spied upon her and that her mother even accused her of attempting to alienate the affections of her stepfather. A brother, aged 12, was reportedly well adjusted; she displayed no definite feelings toward him.

Marian's father had deserted his family when she was 5, and she had visited his home for one week several years ago. She stated that she admired him and would choose to live with him, but his whereabouts were unknown.

Marian had lived with her maternal grandmother, who was a strict Seventh Day Adventist, from her fifth to twelfth years, as stated above. She was unable to accept this religion and showed a feeling of guilt concerning this matter. During the two-week study period she continued to behave excellently at the grandmother's home despite the fact that her mother frequently interfered by criticizing her and upon at least one occasion incited a disturbance with relatives which resulted in police being called.

The mother had continued to insist upon institutional commitment until the possibility of placement in a foster home was mentioned. Mrs. W, at the suggestion of such a possibility, criticized the court and stated that if Marian was not committed she wanted her home. She understood Marian; Marian had been born under a veil; such children have difficulty separating right from wrong; her home was as good as anyone else's.

This reaction substantiated the opinion of the psychiatrist that Mrs. W felt insecure in her relations with her daughter, had pretty strong feelings of guilt about her failure personally to care for Marian during seven of her fifteen years, and had a real need to justify her past actions. He pointed out that Marian was struggling for recognition, was confused by her mother's inconsistent attitudes, and would need pretty intensive casework while isolated from her mother—at least until considerable interpretative work with the mother could be accomplished. He suggested foster home placement.

At the hearing, Marian readily admitted that she was a runaway from home and had been incorrigible. The important question was disposition. The mother reiterated her desire that Marian either be committed to the state school or be returned home. Fortified by the report and recommendations of the casework staff, the court placed Marian in the home of the X's, a middle-aged couple who had acted in similar cases before and understood the needs of adolescent children. This was not so much of a challenge to the mother as placement with relatives would have been. In addition, the court alleviated some of Mrs. W's guilt feelings by ordering that she reimburse the county for the cost of her daughter's care.

During the past year, the Girls' Probation Officer has seen Marian at least once a week. Periodic conferences with the psychiatrist have been held. The worker has attempted to interpret the girl's behavior and needs to her mother.

Marian has maintained a good standard of behavior in the foster home. She has been allowed to discontinue school and has made a fairly good adjustment to her work as an inspector in a soft-drink bottling works. Some progress has been made in bringing Marian and her mother closer together, though it is recognized that both will be in need of help for several years.[7]

Institutional Placement

Not all children can be placed in foster homes. There are some juveniles who need the protection of an institutional environment. Likewise, there are some children who need to be kept from wreaking their special brand of havoc upon communities. But, whatever the purposes (these to be determined in individual cases), some children find their best treatment within an institution. The practices of institutions, in general, as discussed previously in Chapter 4, throw light on procedures for juveniles who are in need of such services as determined by court experience.

An institutional placement of a delinquent child is shown in the case of "Bob J":

Bob J, a rather stubby little 13-year-old boy, was referred by the public school as the truancy gang leader in his community. All his teachers had

[7] Judge Stephen H. Clink and Millard Prichard, "Case Work in a Juvenile Court," *The Family* (now *Journal of Social Casework*), volume 25, number 8, December, 1944, pp. 305-307.

talked to him, the attendance officer had visited the home and threatened the parents; finally in desperation he "put the papers on him." When Bob was first interviewed in the office, he was found to be a genial boy who had unusual poise and ability to express his feelings. Among other statements made were the following: "I don't have trouble getting my lessons, but am tired of going to classes." "I hardly ever see my father since he started his new job." His parents were both intelligent individuals who had given a lot of thought to this problem, had tried everything, and were ready to allow someone else to take over. Bob was referred to the child guidance clinic for diagnostic observation. They found that he had superior intelligence in both abstract and manipulative fields, was probably bored with the low standard of work expected in a normal class room; had ability to converse on the level of a superior adult; and was becoming emotionally unstable and frustrated due to the fact that he had to compete with several siblings for parental attention. It was recommended that Bob be placed in a special boarding school where he could gain recognition through academic accomplishment and develop to full capacity. He has been in this school for one year, has almost a straight "A" average, and whenever home on a visit calls the worker to tell of his accomplishments.[8]

Restitution and Reparation

One of the practices which is widely used in criminal court procedures is that of fining the offender for his crime. This is universally frowned upon for juveniles, as it fails to be in harmony with the chief purposes of the juvenile court—the reconstitution of the individual child as a normal and adjusted member of the community. For the most part it is lacking in educative value, although in some instances it may increase the child's appreciation of the offense which he committed. It may provide him with an opportunity of contributing to the righting of a wrong. It centers his attention upon a tangible rehabilitative program. Actually, restitution and reparation are not in themselves treatment. They are more properly parts of a more comprehensive treatment program and gain whatever effectiveness they may have through connection with other methods. They need to be used sparingly and wisely.

Probation

The chief means of rehabilitation in the court process with juveniles is that of probation. Probation implies that the child is under the protection, guidance, and control of the court. He is not simply dismissed. He is given a supervisor, the probation officer, to help him regain and

[8]*Ibid,* p. 308.

strengthen his social position. It is true that if the child does not respond to the conditions of probation, other means may be employed, such as committal to a training school. But the primary hope in probation is that of the rehabilitation of the youthful offender by a helping process which does not require him to be institutionalized.

The need for probation is suggested in the case of "Jim B":

Jim B, aged 15, presented the court with an adolescent developmental behavior problem somewhat aggravated by the times. The problem as seen by the police department was robbery, unarmed. Jim's first encounter with the police was due to the fact that in company with five other boys of his age he had blackmailed another boy into dividing stolen money. Jim was a physically mature and fairly attractive youth who was rather easygoing. He was able to recognize that he was at fault himself but equally able to place blame on others. He did not spare his parents in his placement of blame for he attributed his school truancy and late hours to the fact that his parents were too strict and would not allow him to use the family car whenever he wanted it. His parents maintained a good home, were conservative, capable individuals. Jim was their youngest child and was expected to conform to the patterns of the older children.

The caseworker recognized the gang activity as a symptom of greater problems that Jim was facing in his attempt to live up to his size, to compensate for feelings of persecution, and to measure up to his intellectual and emotional standards. He was sulky and defensive when taken to his home, and when challenged by the father's statement that they wanted him if he would conform, he replied, "I would rather stay someplace else." Jim was immediately taken to a foster home for detention despite his reported interest in going to an institution. Jim wanted to be punished. After being away for two days he asked to go home. The boy has been placed on probation and is making a good record. The court was able to supplement a good home by providing timely authoritative support for the parents. Jim has been able to accept more limitation, and, in turn, the court has made his home situation more pleasant by interpretation of his needs to the parents.[9]

In view of the complexities which juvenile cases may present, it is important that the workers in charge of probationers be skilled in their task. At present many do not have the best training. Generally speaking, the ideal education requirements for the probation officer would be graduation from college and from a graduate school of social work, with specialization in the period of graduate training in probation courses and field work. In addition to these formal educational qualifications, there is that of experience itself in the field.

[9] *Ibid,* pp. 307–308.

Qualifications for Workers. The National Probation and Parole Association lists the following minimum qualifications for probation workers (or for parole workers) :[10]

1. Education. A bachelor's degree from a college or university of recognized standing, or its educational equivalent, with courses in the social sciences.

The best training for probation and parole work is in a graduate school of social work. However, the educational requirement listed is probably as much as can be required as a minimum in many parts of the country today.

For the purpose of this section, social sciences include the following: sociology, psychology, anthropology, economics, political science, it being preferable that the applicant shall have a balanced program in these subjects. We recommend a minimum of 32 credit hours distributed among these subjects.

2. Experience. One year of paid full-time experience under competent supervision in an approved social agency or related field. One year in an accredited school of social work with field work practice may be substituted. If the probation or parole department is equipped to provide in-service training under adequate supervision the requirement for previous experience may be waived.

By a related field is meant such professional work as teaching; personnel work in industry wherein the applicant did actual adjustment work with individuals, not merely employment service; or casework in an institution or correctional agency. When an in-service training program is provided by the department in lieu of preliminary experience, it should be an organized program of training, sustained over a period of at least one year.

3. Personal Qualifications. A probation or parole officer must be a person of good character and balanced personality.

The following personal traits are essential: good health, physical endurance, intellectual maturity, emotional stability, integrity, tact, dependability, adaptability, resourcefulness, sincerity, humor, ability to work with others, tolerance, patience, objectivity, capacity to win confidence, respect for human personality, and genuine affection for people.

Understanding the Individual Child. The probation officer practically always conducts the preliminary investigations. Because he knows something about the child offender, in such instances, he is prepared to enter into his supervisory work with some understanding of the "causes" of the problem. Obviously, the probation worker cannot approach each child with a stereotyped causative theory. He must individ-

[10]*Standards for Selection of Probation and Parole Officers,* National Probation Association (now National Probation and Parole Association), New York, 1945, pp. 9–10.

ualize his services to each child if he is to make any headway. What he must do and what he must believe in connection with the child in his charge are exceedingly difficult to say since there is no solid body of knowledge or of practice in probation which would provide either an easy or a hard answer. The present state of probationary practice is not such as can be summarized into "handbook" rules for successful probation. This is probably a good thing, as it can be seriously doubted if any set of rules can ever take into account the variations in human personality and circumstance.

Even though the probation worker does not have definitive rules which can help him in each and every situation, he does have some ways of establishing a helpful relationship with juveniles which have proved more successful by experience and insight than some others. For one thing he should present a constructive relationship to the child in which the child sees in the person and the activities of the worker the kind of sympathetic and assisting response that will encourage the child to strive for a positive adjustment in the community. This means that one of the most important assets in probationary work is the personality of the worker. Since the worker will be seeking to set standards of action for the child, he himself must be able through his personality to give evidence of what those criteria really are. Thus nothing is more important in probationary work than the personnel.

Practical Procedure. But there are other elements of successful practice too. The youthful offender, for example, may have fallen into "the wrong company." His friends may have a negative influence upon his adjustment to the community. It is not enough for the worker to tell his client not to associate with his friends. Additional requirements are evident. The worker must be in a position to encourage the child to enter into healthful social relationships by assisting him in making such contacts. This specifically may mean that the worker will encourage the child to join the Y.M.C.A., that the nearby settlement house be informed in a tactful way of the problem so that the child may be given positive opportunities, that the church leader of the child (if such is deemed wise) be given knowledge of the child's predicament so that special care will be given from the standpoint of religion and ethics, or that other means be used to enable the delinquent to form friendships which will issue in an adjusted personality. Naturally, it takes time and skill on the part of the worker to create such contacts. In many cities overburdened workers scarcely have time to do very much detailed work even though it might be important from the long-range point of view.

Various practical considerations on which the behavior of the offender may be dependent also will have to be considered by the probation worker. He will want to know, for example, if the child has spending money. If the child is still in school, it may be necessary to inquire concerning family allowance or to provide opportunities for the child to earn his own spending money. If the offender is no longer in school, he may need a job. Even more important than a job may be the career plan of the client. There is not only the matter of what he can do immediately, but how he will solve the problem of permanent income. In many cases this means counseling the offender along educational and vocational lines.

If the child offender is still in school, the probation officer will wish to examine the school situation of the child. The school adjustment may be the root of the personal problem. If so, the officer, in connection with other services provided by the school and the community, will want to create the possibility of the child's achieving a normal school life.

The probation worker will want also to examine and build upon the child's relations to his parents. He will recognize that within the family many of the fundamental attitudes of the child have been formed, and that within that environment the possibility of permanently changing the behavior of the child may fruitfully lie.

Helping the Child Understand Himself. Thus, in treatment, the probation worker will want to take as many practical steps toward alleviating pressures upon the delinquent child as will enable the child to discover the meaning of normal living. The practical steps which the probation worker takes to rehabilitate the juvenile offender must, however, be combined to increase the degree of insight which the child has regarding himself. It is perhaps not too much to say that the primary objective of all probation work is to enable the child to understand himself. It is impossible for the probation worker to supervise the life of the child until he is an adult. Usually, probation runs for a stated period and then is withdrawn. But, even within the period in which a child is placed on probation, the probation officer cannot be expected to regulate his every action. That indeed is not the purpose of probation. Rather it is to enable the child to guide himself, to act responsibly and constructively for his own welfare.

To help the juvenile gain insight regarding himself is not an easy task. More and more it is recognized that the probation worker must be skilled in psychological or psychiatric methods of helping young people secure insight. Thus, through regular conferences with the probationer, the worker seeks to discuss the factors which have been operative in the juvenile's case. He tries to deal with questions which pertain to guilt and anxiety. He strives to point out those emotional adjustments which will be most rewarding to the child. Above all, however, the child himself must be able to appreciate the contributions of the worker and to wish for self-understanding.

While most of what the worker does will be based on the preliminary investigation which was conducted for the court, the actual developments of each case will go far beyond these findings. New factors may be discovered and greater understanding of the child may be achieved as the probation officer works with him from week to week. The initial record chiefly provides the starting point.

Probation Officer at Work. A concrete example of the probation officer at work is afforded by the following excerpt:

AN OFFICER SUPERVISING BOYS

9:00–10:00 a.m. Office hours (interviews and attending to mail).

Received letter from Child Guidance Department which contains the summary of psychological examination given to J.V., probationer. Letter received from Board of Health stating that T.R., probationer, would be admitted to Farmingdale Preventorium on September 18. Letter sent to father of L.J., requesting him to call in the evening to discuss plan for vocational guidance of his son. 'Phone message received: N.T. absent from school, principal requests that cause of this be ascertained if possible and report given forthwith to her.

Interview. Former probationer requested advice concerning conduct of younger brother. Promised to visit home in the near future. Tentative plan of spare time activities outlined for younger brother.

'Phone message: Cleared A.B. case through social service exchange.

10:15–10:50. Visited Shipping Master to discuss employment possibility for S.D., 16-year-old probationer who is interested in obtaining position in merchant marine.

11:00–11:20. Visited home of V.T. Boy ill, apparently with flu. 'Phoned City Physician to call as soon as possible. Returned to home and told mother that physician would call before 2:00 p.m. Requested her to keep boy in bed and to try and keep an even temperature in the room.

11:25–11:55. Visited ungraded school. Discussed recreational problems with teachers of A.M. and C.M., brothers. Planned to speak to Y.M.C.A. director re membership.

Interviewed A.M. Planned with him to use his time between 3:00 and 6:00 each afternoon, if possible, under the direction of the school playground director. Urged him also to visit Mr. B at the Y.M.C.A. to arrange for membership there. Tried to arrange weekly routine, including lunch and recreation if possible, under supervision of playground director, Y.M.C.A., and Scout leaders.

Interviewed C.M. Discussed with him the possibility of rekindling his interest in boys' books, particularly those which deal with experimental electrical problems. Also planned use of spare time under playground director, as well as Scouting activities. Showed C.M. how in the past the hours between 3:00 and 6:00 had been time during which he became involved in numerous mischievous activities, and how the substitution of this type of recreation would be immeasurably beneficial to him. Boy hoped to be able to follow out plan.

12:00–1:00 p.m. Lunch.

1:00–1:45. Home visit. Parents of R.S. still unemployed, receiving aid through P. & A. department. Father irritable and nagging around household, owing to his unemployment and other problems which are vexing the parents at present. Tried to explain one phase of adolescence to father during this call. Suggested that father attend evening school to study English, particularly during the time he is unemployed. Father agreed to consider this.

1:55–2:15. Home visit, W.L. Good adjustment continued. Mother exhibited latest aeroplane model made by son, who has followed the hobby faithfully during past six months. Suggested further reading on boy's hobby and named facilities available for this, i.e., school library, city library, manual training teacher, and Scout leaders, who were willing and able to give proper information.

2:30–3:00. Home visit, P.H. Mother dissatisfied with boy's conduct because he thinks of nothing but play. Tried to show mother the value of this and soothe her attitude as much as possible. Suggested simple games which could be played at home by children.

3:15–3:45. School visit. Took J.M. from school to dental clinic to fulfill appointment.

4:00. Returned to office.

4:00–4:25. Preparing and dictating re sentence summary, consisting of synopsis of the boy's record while on probation, including his adjustment to the plan made, his school record, the cooperation of the parents, and the boy's attitude toward his own problems.

4:25–4:40. Advice to parents of L.C. concerning naturalization. Filling out naturalization papers and explaining the meaning of certain perplexing questions to the parents; grammatical errors and mistakes in English were corrected also. Parents were instructed to report on the 10th day of January to Room 406, Hall of Records, the Naturalization Clerk, who would give them proper instructions for their final appearance before the Naturalization Judge.

4:40–4:45. Prepared daily report sheet, covering contacts made in office, home, and field, to serve as preliminary abstract for supervisional record.

4:45–5:05. Dictated supervisional work of the day to Ediphone machine. This will be transcribed into permanent records which will show what has been done on each individual case, and which is also for the purpose of complying with the law, which requires that a permanent record be kept of all contacts with probationers.[11]

The relation of the probation worker to the court may differ from locality to locality. There probably is no consistent pattern of personnel organization which obtains everywhere. In some instances the court provides for social workers whose primary responsibility is that of preparing cases for court hearings and who may, in addition, assume probationary responsibility.

Parole

Parole does not properly begin as a disposition of the child offender at the time of the child's court hearing. By definition, it must wait until the child has served a period in an institution. But parole is definitely an important step in rehabilitation. It it often part of the continuity of treatment for young offenders.

The use of the term *parole* in regard to the youthful offender is perhaps misleading. Many may conclude from the word that the programs which operate under that title in most of the states are identical with the parole systems for adult criminals. Because of this conception, some institutions participating in parole programs for juveniles prefer other terms. Institutions like the Sleighton Farm School for Girls in Pennsylvania, the Long Lane Farm in Connecticut, and the New York State Training School for Boys make parole one of the activities of the social service department, foregoing any formal mention of parole itself. The Whittier State School in California prefers "placement." Other terms are also used.

Different From Probation. Parole differs essentially from probation in a number of respects. Certainly, one of the most important of these is the fact that in parole the child has already been institutionalized for a period and thus presents a different need for adjustment to the community following his release. If the probationer requires careful attention so that his return to the community will be facilitated, the parolee's need is even more marked. Quite often the type of living which he has done in an institution has not furthered the ease of his adjustment to the community. In the institution he has been relieved for the most part from the responsibilities which would help develop and maintain his initiative. He has no fundamental problems of food, clothing, shelter,

[11]Margaretta Williamson, *The Social Worker in the Prevention and Treatment of Delinquency,* published for the American Association of Social Workers, Columbia University Press, New York, 1935, pp. 60–62.

and the use of his time. These are decided for him by the institution. In the community he cannot expect such rigid control. The parolee also suffers from the social stigma of having spent time in an institution. The child who passes through the court, whether into probation or not, is marked out by the community in many instances and because of this possesses many adjustive problems. But the child who has been institutionalized faces even greater problems. He bears the additional burden of having been "sentenced" to live in an institution. It is certain that in most cases he will have a harder time being accepted in the community. Similarly, the paroled child will have undergone institutional experiences which will affect the conditions of his adjustment to the community. The child who is placed on probation may be relatively isolated from other delinquents from the beginning of his probation period. But the paroled child comes back to the community with the background of having lived with others who have presented serious behavior problems to society and who may have had tremendous influence over him. Thus the paroled juvenile presents a special problem in treatment.

Two Methods of Operation. Parole is organized in the states chiefly on two bases. One type operates from within the institution which releases child delinquents. In this kind of setup the social service department is usually a segment of the administration of the institution. In the second type of parole organization the social services are offered to children from an agency outside the institution. In this case social service care may be provided for children from more than one institution; in fact, it may be organized on a state basis, as in Massachusetts. There are some obvious advantages to both sorts of parole organization. The first benefits from a greater sense of continuity in treatment, since the children are known both within the institution and at every stage until they are finally released even from parole restrictions. On the other hand the second system enables economies of activity in that the one organization will have a wide geographic coverage without duplication of services.

Of greater importance, however, than the organizational structure of parole is that of personnel standards. No parole system can be efficient in terms of the goals given it unless it has workers who are qualified to accomplish them. As in other fields of activity, the organization is important, but the people running the organization are even more significant.

Parole Worker's Task. The parole worker's task is principally three-fold. (1) He tries to understand the child. He starts his case record.

He wants to know the child's life history. (2) He begins to prepare the child's family and the community for the eventual paroling of the child. He discusses with the child's parents the various aspects of the child's present condition and his possible future. He seeks a foster home suitable to the needs of the child, if placement is deemed necessary. Or he looks up employers who may help in the vocational rehabilitation of the child. (3) He supervises the child after release from the institution. This last duty consumes much of the time and attention of the parole worker, but it is obvious that efficient performance of the first two tasks is essential if the supervision is to be of the most benefit to the child.

While there is considerable need for closer cooperation between the institution and the parole worker, most parole officers do little work with children while they are in an institution. Their real work begins just before the child is ready for release, for it is then that a suitable plan must be evolved for the child's future. Sometimes the child is returned to his own home; sometimes he is placed in a foster home. Wherever the child is to live, the factors which make up the life of the child in the community must be considered: schooling, play, religious activities, work.

The parole worker is responsible for the child's adjustment to his new life. This does not mean that the worker merely helps the parolee in his initial reintroduction to the community, but rather the worker continues his interest for a stated term. He has regular contacts with the child in order to meet problems that may arise, but he should also be available to the child at any time of his need. Too much stress has been placed traditionally on the regular reports which the parolee makes to the worker. The worker is not simply a policeman who checks on the conduct of the child; he should be a friend, a counselor, a social worker —a person who enables the delinquent to realize what he wishes to achieve for himself and others. In other words the social worker as parole officer seeks genuinely positive results from his relationships with children.

THE USE OF AUTHORITY

A discussion of the ways in which the social worker may be of assistance to the juvenile delinquent through the juvenile court and the various modes of treatment seems to be illogical to some reflective individuals. They argue that social casework can scarcely be practiced in a compulsory setting, that it is not a proper restriction upon social casework to have it as an adjunct to the strong arm of the law. On the surface there seems to be considerable logic behind this claim. It is true that the social caseworker does not inflict his values upon the clients whom he serves. He does not cherish the responsibility of having to direct the lives of other people, for in such direction there are many dangers. The social worker would like clients to make up their own minds and to solve their problems within the terms set down by their own consciences. The social worker doing parole work or any type of social work under the law seems to be an anomaly.

The problem of social work and settings which imply or express the use of authority is broader than social work in connection with delinquents. It embraces the social worker in the public welfare agency, in the armed forces, in all basically military organizations, to some extent in medical and psychiatric social work, and elsewhere.[12] In fact, viewing the problem from the standpoint of social work as a social institution there probably is some degree of authority involved in every social work activity.

It is important to understand that in some instances the restraints of law may seemingly be detrimental to the wishes of the offender, as of us all. It is not, however, within his province, when it comes to behavior covered by law, to have his wishes respected. Thus the criminal who wants to break into a store to rob it naturally can be confronted with the fact of law and the restriction contained within it. The social worker does not need to tolerate such conduct, although he can seek to understand what has motivated the person to express it.

Again, no agency with a clear conception of its purpose and its contribution to the community can exist without some standards. These standards tend to regulate the social worker and, indirectly, the clients. They become for some workers in nonlegal agencies what laws are to workers in legal organizations.

THE JUVENILE AID BUREAU

The law-enforcing agencies of a community should be responsible for more than the treatment of those who break the laws. They should be obligated to work toward the prevention of delinquency. A type of organization, usually within police departments, which has been successful in recent years in preventive work is the Juvenile Aid Bureau. Other titles used for it may be: Juvenile Bureau, Youth Guidance Bureau, Delinquency Prevention Bureau.

[12] See especially in this connection, *Short-Term Therapy in an Authoritative Setting,* by Bertram Beck in collaboration with Lewis L. Robbins, Family Service Association of America, New York, 1946.

Functions

The functions of the Juvenile Aid Bureau have been compiled and delineated by the National Advisory Police Committee on Social Protection of the Federal Security Agency as follows:[13]

1. A careful study of the community's juvenile delinquency problem.
2. The treatment of all cases of juveniles taken into custody by the police, and of other cases presenting special problems.
3. Leadership in informing and guiding the entire department in techniques and methods by which police can control and prevent delinquency.
4. Frequent inspection of public places which may attract youth, particularly the young girl. During wartime, these places often also attract servicemen.
5. Patrol duty in parks, preferably by men and women plainclothes officers working together. If young girls are found in compromising situations, the policewoman handles the case of the girl, and the policeman, the man. In the majority of instances the girl's conduct will not be such as to require arrest; however, an intelligent policewoman, recognizing the youth of the girl, realizes that the child may be in a situation which could prove hazardous, and will so advise her and send her or take her home.
6. Interviewing and taking statements from youths involved in sex problems of any type, with particular attention to girls.
7. Interviewing parents of juveniles who may be in difficulty.
8. Investigating complaints received by police concerning adults who may be contributing to or causing delinquency of children.
9. Acting as liaison or referral officers between the department and those welfare agencies, public or private, which can provide redirectional services to the delinquent youth.
10. Cooperating with civic, social, and church groups to improve certain conditions in the community which may be contributing to delinquency.
11. Developing services of various kinds to meet the needs found in the course of the work of the Bureau.

The head of the Juvenile Aid Bureau is commonly given appropriate rank in the police department, because it is important in many cases that he have the authority which successful operation of a Bureau requires. He needs the active cooperation of all police officers and departments. His staff should be competent. If there are no trained social workers on it, those chosen for service should be acquainted with the aims of the Bureau, be sympathetic toward them, and efficient in

[13]*Techniques of Law Enforcement in the Treatment of Juveniles and the Prevention of Juvenile Delinquency,* compiled by the National Advisory Police Committee to the Federal Security Administrator, in consultation with the United States Children's Bureau, Federal Security Agency, Office of Community War Services, Division of Social Protection, Washington, D.C., 1944, pp. 39-40.

achieving them. In some cities qualified social workers are a part of Bureau staffs. As the functions listed above indicate, some of the workers should be women and some men. There is at present some difference of opinion on whether the headquarters of the Bureau should be located in police buildings. Some feel that the realistic tie with the police department can be abetted in this way, while others claim that such a location gives the child a feeling that he is being arrested instead of merely questioned. Whatever the arrangement, it should be such that the youth does not come in contact with adult offenders.

Requirements

The prevention of delinquency will require a number of assets on the part of the Bureau, aside from administrative talent.

1. Trained Workers. It will require that there be trained workers within the Bureau who will be able to treat those children who are referred by policemen. One of the chief aims of the Bureau is to locate and treat cases of incipient delinquency before there can be an actual need for court referral. If the Bureau is really efficient it should prevent many cases from developing and later appearing in the juvenile courts.

2. Relationship With Court. The Bureau should have carefully worked out relationships with the juvenile court. This does not mean that the Bureau will usurp the functions of the court, but that there be mutual understanding and cooperation between them. The Bureau can aid in reducing the number of indiscriminate and unnecessary petitions which are filed in the juvenile court. The Bureau may also aid in reducing the problems of the detention period (while the child is awaiting a hearing) by assuming responsibility for detention arrangements and for supervision. Where cases are to come before the juvenile court the Bureau may assist in the preparation of the case, thus saving the court time.

3. Relationship With Other Agencies. The Bureau should have intelligent relationships with other agencies in the community. It may be that through the treatment of a child the Bureau may uncover problems which exist in the child's family. Where these are serious they can be referred to another agency more suited for the treatment. In practically all localities it is not possible for the Bureau to treat all problems which come before it. By knowing the resources of the community it may be able to provide solutions to problems which indirectly or directly relate to delinquency.

4. Study of Sources of Delinquency. Another way by which the Juvenile Aid Bureau may help diminish or defeat delinquency is by studying the sources of delinquency in the community. By examining its intake of cases the Bureau will be able to conclude where the danger spots are in a community, the types of offenses which are most frequently committed, the age group of offenders, and possibly some of the methods which may be able to combat delinquency. If a study of the community discloses that there are dance halls which are unregulated, bars which admit minors, candy stores which operate rackets, employers who use minors, or other signs and evidences of delinquency creation, the Bureau will be in a position to recommend to the police department that steps be taken to remedy the conditions.

5. *Recreational Services.* The establishment of a recreational unit, usually within the Bureau, to help divert children into legal play channels has been a part of the programs of several Juvenile Aid Bureaus. The pattern of recreational services offered by Bureaus differs somewhat from place to place, as should be expected, but the Police Athletic League of New York City provides an illustration of what can be done:[14]

> The Police Athletic League is concerned with all children. Over a quarter of a million boys and girls took part in P.A.L. physical, social, and cultural activities during 1947. The P.A.L., however, is primarily concerned with the more than half a million youngsters in our town who are not affiliated with any other youth-recreation organization. These boys and girls do not want to be left out . . . but they are . . . simply because no youth serving facilities exist in their neighborhood.
>
> In 1947 P.A.L. provided a year round recreation program for hundreds of thousands of boys and girls. P.A.L. gave these children their only opportunity for recreation. The magnitude of the program is indicated by the following statistics.
>
> 1,310 baseball and softball teams
> 585 basketball teams
> 30,000 in track and field meets, boxing exhibitions, and swimming and soccer
> 78 youth centers
> 475 boys at "Fox Lair," Adirondack summer camp, for three weeks vacation
> 65 supervised play streets and playgrounds
> 21,000 to Bear Mountain for all day boat ride
> 500,000 to professional baseball, football, basketball, hockey games, to rodeo and circus under supervision
> recreational programs in each of 82 Police Precincts
> 72,000 at teen-age dances

[14]Taken from the leaflet "P.A.L., a Bill of Rights for Childhood," issued by the Police Athletic League of New York City, undated.

ADULT OFFENDERS

Thus far in the discussion of the way in which social work relates to the juvenile court and to the various services to children which center in the court, there has been no extended treatment of the role of social work with adult criminals. As in the case of juvenile delinquents, social workers serve adult offenders through probation and parole. The philosophy and practice behind these two types of treatment are essentially the same for adults as for juveniles.

There are a number of services which the social worker can render the adult offender in penal institutions, although at present such services are extremely limited. In many instances the rehabilitative process within penal institutions does not include a place for a trained social worker. Much of the work done toward rehabilitation is performed by clergymen, wardens, and other prison officials—special officers, physicians, psychiatrists, and others—who have social contributions to make. Only as their contributions can roughly be termed social work can social work be said to exist to any degree in many prisons. It is clear, however, that prisons need these other services no matter what they may be called.

Where social workers do exist in institutions for adult offenders, they may have a variety of functions. Six of the ways in which a social worker can serve are here described.

Preparation of the Case History

Obviously, if the prison which has responsibility for a criminal wishes to treat him in an individualized manner it must know something about him. The securing of information in the form of a life history is a contribution of the social worker. He will prepare for the prison officials the data for understanding the inmates. Naturally, not all of the material of the case record can be secured within the prison. Some of it can. The social worker will have opportunity to interview the prisoner and ask pertinent questions about his life. But he will also need to learn about the prisoners from those who knew them in the community, from relatives, friends, and others. Information secured in presentence investigations is also pertinent.

In some prisons the preparation of the life history is left to others than social workers. Sometimes the case record becomes little more than a glorified collection of mere facts. If so, something is lacking. The social worker can make an important contribution here because he is especially trained in professional insights to accomplish history-taking successfully. Usually, a prison officer or administrator is not thus qualified.

Services to Prisoners' Families

A second type of activity in which the social worker participates in a prison is that of relating the prisoner to his family. This is no easy task. The prisoner is taken from the community under compulsion. He does not have time to complete his arrangements for those who may depend upon him. He may leave behind him a worried wife, mother, or child. His interests also may suffer if he has no means of representing himself in the community. Lawyers may be too expensive and not professionally trained to handle the social problems of prisoners. The social worker, however, is equipped for this service.

A large part of the hope of rehabilitating prisoners comes from their response to those whom they love. If a criminal in a prison, sentenced for a period of two or three years, can have the feeling that his family is loyal, sticking by him in his trouble, he may be able to gain that composure and positive reaction to all of the other aspects of his incarceration that will make him a fully adequate citizen in the end. If he knows, for example, that his wife or sweetheart is true to him, that she cares intensely for him and is solicitous for his well-being, he may respond by wanting to be equally worthy of the affection and respect. The social worker, then, has an opportunity to work for the rehabilitation of prisoners, through those whom the prisoners love.

Oftentimes a private social work agency, as for example a family casework agency, can be of help to an inmate indirectly and to his family directly. This service may become direct to the offender once he is released if he is not supervised by a parole agency. The "Cassell" family illustrates this type of work:

The Cassells were referred by the United States Northeastern Penitentiary a few months before our cooperative program was in operation. Mr. Cassell, the prisoner, was greatly upset and worried about his young wife who was expecting their first baby. She was destitute, living with impoverished relatives who did not want her, and quite aside from having very little food and practically no clothing, she had no idea of where she would go for medical care when the baby was due. In addition to all these problems, she had been infected with a venereal disease, and it preyed on her mind all the time.

When the Family Society visitor called, she found Mrs. Cassell living with her mother who was forever threatening to put her out on the street and making her life miserable because she was pregnant and her husband was "no good." Her mother was Catholic and had turned against her daughter because Mr. and Mrs. Cassell had had a civil marriage. There was constant quarreling, for the mother, who was very poor herself, begrudged every mouthful of food Mrs. Cassell ate. Mrs. Cassell could not even go out for a walk to get away from the tension at home because she had no shoes and her clothing was most inadequate.

The Family Society visitor talked with the mother who agreed to give shelter to Mrs. Cassell; the County Relief Board would send a grocery order to cover the food needs of the entire family and a separate milk order for Mrs. Cassell. Arrangements were made to have her registered in the prenatal clinic of one of the hospitals where she would be confined free of charge. Shoes, clothing, and carfare were given Mrs. Cassell, and the doctor in the clinic took a real interest in her and gave her treatments for the venereal infection. With the economic burden thus lightened, the mother, though still resentful, ceased to quarrel with her daughter. Mrs. Cassell was able to come to the Family Society visitor for a chat whenever she was lonely.

In due time Mrs. Cassell gave birth to a boy whom she named Gerald. Mr. Cassell was reassured about the care given to his wife. After twelve days' hospital care, arrangements were made for convalescent care, and for five weeks Mrs. Cassell and Gerald enjoyed rest, fresh air, and good food at a convalescent home in the country.

As the time for Mr. Cassell's release drew near, his wife asked the case-worker if she could help her start a separate household of her own so that her husband could be spared the disagreeableness of being dependent on her mother, who still "had it in for him." After going over the situation with her, she was assisted in renting a neat, comfortable apartment. A milk and grocery order in which her husband was included, was sent to her, and when Mr. Cassell came home from prison, he was able to go directly to his wife and child in their own home. He came to see the Family Society visitor very soon and it was agreed that she would do all she could to help him get work. By chance, the Family Society visitor, in checking his former work references, was able to secure him work at his old job of cabinet finisher, and for a couple of months the family enjoyed a fair income and independence.

It was interesting to notice that as soon as Mr. Cassell was laid off he came directly to the Family Society to ask for help. His wife had feared that he would return to his old cronies and get into trouble again. The visitor talked with him and after resuming the relief orders, he asked for help in other directions. There had been some friction between him and his wife about the care of the baby and also about the venereal infection. By helping Mrs. Cassell continue the treatments at the hospital and having the doctor encourage her on the progress she was making, both Mr. and Mrs. Cassell were reassured about the cure. She was likewise helped in the care of the baby who has won a gold star at the baby clinic for perfect health and normal growth.

By getting various contributors interested in the family, a small trust fund was raised so that their rent could be paid regularly. It was felt that too much economic insecurity might disturb Mr. Cassell to the point of desperation. He is still hunting for work, but is not overwhelmed by discouragement. He is very happy with his wife and Gerald and is only waiting for the time to come when he has a job and can take care of them without outside help.[15]

Prisoner Classification

Social casework services can be utilized to aid in the classification of prisoners. It is important for the rehabilitation of the offender that he be so placed within the prison in terms of varying factors that he may secure the maximum benefit from his prison experience. Work, for example, is an opportunity for treatment. Within most prisons and for most prisoners there are work requirements. But at what work to place which inmate constitutes a puzzle to which the management of the institution needs to give considerable attention. The placement of the prisoner in his living quarters, the forms of activities provided of a recreational character, the educational possibilities needed for rehabilitation, the conditions for the improvement of the individual, the possible use of parole—these and other considerations are based on prisoner classification.

The social caseworker within the prison has an important role to play in the classification process. In most instances the classification of prisoners is done by a board composed of the warden, the physician, the psychologist, the psychiatrist, the social worker, and perhaps some others who are in a position to be of assistance. The social worker can be of special help to such a board because he gathers a great deal of the factual information on which board decisions can rightly rest. In a few cases he has extended first-hand contact not only with the offender himself but with the relatives and friends. His understanding does not dominate the knowledge or skill of the other participants of the board necessarily, but it is of inestimable help to them. The Federal Bureau of Prisons, under the Department of Justice, provides an excellent example of the use of prisoner classification.

Counseling Services

During the time the prisoner is interned it can be assumed that he will have problems. The initial problem is that of adjustment to the prison. The prison regimen may be new and strange to the habits of the criminal. He may object to some parts of the prison routine. He may have real grievances against other prisoners, officials, and things in

[15]John B. Middleton, "Parole and the Family Agency," *Cooperative Case Work,* Family Welfare Association of America (now Family Service Association of America), New York, 1935–1939, pp. 52–53.

general. The social caseworker can do much toward alleviating such pressures in the life of the inmate.

The prisoner also brings an emotional problem (sometimes more than one) into the prison with him. Commonly, he is worried about something. Perhaps he feels guilty for his act. Perhaps he is concerned about the involvement of others in his offense. His prior life may have been left at loose ends and he may be anxious about that. Whatever the problem, it is safe to conclude that each prisoner presents some sort of problem. Naturally, if the man can have an opportunity to express his need, to talk things over with a sympathetic person who may be able to help him, he will feel that the prison is definitely interested in his reconstruction and that there may be some hope left for him. Much can be accomplished by this "talking over" procedure. The prisoner may begin to see himself more objectively. He may have a chance to focus his problem clearly through defining it verbally to another person. He may be given concrete advice as to how he may meet some of the aspects of his problem. He may get to know that there are people who are interested in him sufficiently to sit and listen and respond with genuineness. These and other values may derive from counseling services proffered to prisoners in institutions.

Preparation for Parole

Prison days for criminals, in all but a few cases, fortunately come to an end. The benefit is supposed to be gained, and the prisoner is released. But before he is placed out of the prison on parole there should be a preparation by the social worker for the release. The prisoner should have the chance to think through verbally with someone what he is intending to do once released. What type of work will he do? What attitude should he take toward his old friends? What should be his approach to his wife and children? How should he take critical remarks? The social worker is competent to aid in meeting such questions.

Parole Supervision

Parole is utilized in treatment both for delinquents and criminals. It indicates a probationary period which is served after the adjudged person is released from a correctional institution. The actual conditions of parole operate similarly to those of probation, although some of the factors involved in individual cases would differ. As was suggested in the case of juveniles, the parolee faces a more difficult adjustment to the community, because of his imprisonment, than the probationer.

Both probation and parole have fallen into disfavor with some people because as methods of rehabilitation they seem to be too lenient. Those who are critical often have the least understanding as to what probation and parole mean. Their criticisms, however, in some instances are felt more popularly than the solid opinions of those who have knowledge. To them, probation and parole seem to be methods of evading legal responsibility rather than of assuming it. They sometimes see a rise in delinquency and criminality because of a "laxness" in the courts or the prisons. From the practical point of view, however, there seems little reason to accept criticisms which rest on such flimsy and emotional reasoning. For one thing no one has yet claimed that these methods of treatment are one hundred percent successful. They are recognized by most social workers as being very human tools in a field where human tools are often all too inadequate. But there is certainly no indication that the "tough" forms of treatment are more successful.

Perhaps the most important argument by which such critics of probation and parole can be answered is that these methods seem to relate closely to the obvious and fundamental requirement of a treatment process, namely, that it adjust the offender directly to the community in which he finally will have to live. Obviously, the prison method of treatment for the great bulk of offenders does not contribute sufficiently to this end. The imposing of fines may well fail to accomplish the desired goal. After all is said by the court and done by the punishing agencies of government, the maladjusted person must return to and make his way in a community. Probation and parole are means whereby the offender may return on a trial, guided basis. They are the crucial ways by which the lawbreaker bridges the gap from maladjustment to adjustment (remembering that these are relative terms). No matter what we may think about the efficacy of prisons and of other means of punishing ("treating") criminals, there still must be some apparatus whereby the criminal is released from the pressure and direction of the law to the normal, free associations of the community. If this accommodation can be made without a period in an institution (probation), so much the better; if it must wait until the person has served a term in an institution (parole), even so, it is necessary.

That the procedures of probation and parole need improving cannot be denied, but the basic methods of probation and parole are here to stay. The future will probably only see an extension of them. It is to be hoped that their growth will also mean their improvement.

National Probation and Parole Association

The work of the National Probation and Parole Association is important. Incorporated as the National Probation Association in 1921 and combined with the American Parole Association in 1947, the Association has created a national service for individuals (probation and parole officers, judges, and others) and for agencies which are interested in the betterment of programs and techniques of treating the criminal and the delinquent. The Association's program includes not only probation and parole but also any related subject. It provides for various special studies of problems. Its project in 1946 on the principles and practices of detention homes for juveniles is an example of this service. It has also made its professional staff available to localities wanting expert advice on special problems. It has an interest in legal research, providing information, drafting bills, and making law summaries. It holds state, regional, and national conferences for workers. It seeks to publicize the existing needs and resources. Its publications comprise an important contribution. In these and other ways the Association plays a significant role in the development of improved standards and practices.

Goal Is Prevention

The primary intention of the individualized processes discussed in the present chapter, namely, the juvenile court, probation, and parole, is that of discovering basic reasons for antisocial behavior, not especially for the purpose of punishment but for the goal of stopping it. Since many of the criminal actions listed in the statistics of criminal behavior are caused by recidivism, successful programs in probation and parole may actually help to reduce the amount of crime committed year by year.

SELECTED READINGS ON SOCIAL WORK WITH DELINQUENTS AND CRIMINALS

Aichorn, August, *Wayward Youth,* Viking, revised and adapted from 2d German edition, New York, 1935.

Alexander, Franz, and Healy, William, *Roots of Crime,* Knopf, New York, 1935.

Bates, Sanford, *Prisons and Beyond,* Macmillan, New York, 1936.

Breckinridge, Sophonisba, *Social Work and the Courts: Select Statutes and Judicial Decisions,* University of Chicago Press, Chicago, 1934.

Carr, Lowell, *Delinquency Control,* Harper, New York, 1941.

Committee on Classification and Casework, *Handbook on Classification in Correctional Institutions,* American Prison Association, New York, 1947.

Glueck, Sheldon, and Glueck, E.T., *Criminal Careers in Retrospect,* Commonwealth Fund, New York, 1943.

Glueck, Sheldon, and Glueck, E.T., *Juvenile Delinquents Grown Up*, Commonwealth Fund, New York, 1940.

———, *One Thousand Juvenile Delinquents*, Harvard University Press, Cambridge, 1934.

Healy, William, *The Individual Delinquent: A Textbook of Diagnosis and Prognosis for All Concerned in Understanding Offenders*, Little, Brown, Boston, 1915.

Healy, William, and Bronner, Augusta F., *New Light on Delinquency and Its Treatment*, Yale University Press, New Haven, 1936.

Healy, William, and others, *Reconstructing Behavior in Youth*, Knopf, New York, 1929.

Lindner, Robert M., *Stone Walls and Men*, The Odyssey Press, New York, 1946.

National Probation Association (now National Probation and Parole Association), *A State Administered Adult Probation and Parole System: Draft of a Model Act*, New York, 1940.

———, *John Augustus: First Probation Officer* (a rare old book reprinted), New York, undated.

———, *Standard Juvenile Court Law*, New York, revised, 1943.

Norman, Sherwood, and Norman, Helen, *Detention for the Juvenile Court*, National Probation Association, New York, 1946.

Panken, Jacob, *The Child Speaks: The Prevention of Juvenile Delinquency*, Holt, New York, 1941.

Pigeon, Helen D., *Probation and Parole in Theory and Practice: A Study Manual*, National Probation Association, New York, 1942.

Polier, Justine W., *Everyone's Children: Nobody's Child—A Judge Looks at Underprivileged Children in the United States*, Scribners, New York, 1941.

Porterfield, Austin L., *Youth in Trouble*, The Leo Potishman Foundation, Fort Worth, 1946.

Reckless, Walter C., and Smith, M., *Juvenile Delinquency*, McGraw-Hill, New York, 1932.

Shaw, Clifford R., *The Natural History of a Delinquent Career*, University of Chicago Press, Chicago, 1931.

Shaw, Clifford R., and McKay, H.D., *Juvenile Delinquency and Urban Areas*, University of Chicago Press, Chicago, 1942.

Tappan, Paul W., *Delinquent Girls in Court: A Study of the Wayward Minor Court of New York*, Columbia University Press, New York, 1947.

Thom, Douglas A., *Normal Youth and Its Everyday Problems*, Appleton-Century, New York, 1932.

Waite, John B., *The Prevention of Repeated Crime*, University of Michigan Press, Ann Arbor, 1943.

Wessel, Rosa, editor, *A Casework Approach to Sex Delinquents*, Pennsylvania School of Social Work, Philadelphia, 1947.

Williamson, Margaretta, *The Social Worker in the Prevention and Treatment of Delinquency,* American Association of Social Workers, Job Analysis Series, number 4, Columbia University Press, New York, 1935.

Young, Pauline V., *Social Treatment in Probation and Delinquency,* McGraw-Hill, New York, 1937.

For additional related readings, consult the bibliographies at the end of the other child welfare chapters.

9

Medical Social Work

The following case of Mr. "Sherman" clearly illustrates a situation in medical social work where the patient faces an unexpected and serious diagnosis requiring a complete remaking of his life plans. It indicates how a medical social worker in a hospital can bring the social work process to bear upon patients' problems. While Mr. Sherman's problem was quite serious, even less profound physical difficulties oftentimes result in complex social and emotional troubles.

November 10, 1937. Referral of Case by Nurse. It is the function of the nurse in the Medical Clinic to give instruction in hygiene and nursing care to a patient when indicated by the doctor. It was while explaining necessary precautions to be taken at home by a patient with active pulmonary tuberculosis that she asked him to wait to see the social worker,[1]

[1]Worker is one of three senior staff members of the Medical Service, each one of whom has the equivalent of two days in the clinic in addition to a 25-bed ward and supervision of a second-year student. From 100 to 150 patients are examined in the clinic daily. It is the medical social worker's responsibility on the days when she is "in clinic" to take care of any cases referred to Social Service. These referrals may be made by the doctor, clinic nurse, clinic secretary, dietitian, and others. No attempt at 100 percent contact is made, but a few patients are seen routinely, such as those to be admitted to the hospital from the clinic. The Social Service office adjoins the clinic waiting room and is conveniently near the examining room, so that the doctors may have ready access to it.

The local tuberculosis program is handled through the Metropolitan Tuberculosis Bureau, to which all infectious cases are referred as soon as the diagnosis is made. If immediate hospitalization is advised, every effort is made to get the patient, as soon as possible, into one of the several tuberculosis wards. These are located in the various hospitals of the city and are supervised by the Tuberculosis Bureau. All examinations of contacts are done routinely by neighborhood health stations under the supervision of the Tuberculosis Bureau.

as he had indicated a willingness to do so. Meanwhile the nurse, with the medical record in her hand, outlined to the worker what her contact with the patient had been and her impression of his apparent need for help, saying, "He seems so upset."

From a brief glance at the medical record, worker learned that the patient was making his initial visit to the clinic, but had been under treatment for diabetes by a private physician for 16 years. His present complaints included weight loss, night sweats, and hemoptysis. It was the physician's impression after examination that the patient had active pulmonary tuberculosis. Patient's wife was employed as a stenographer and the couple occupied a five-room apartment, for which they paid $27.50 monthly.

Interview With Patient. The nurse left the social worker's office with a smile and a nod toward the patient, who was seated just outside the door. He smiled back almost imperceptibly. He was out of earshot, but worker could see him plainly through the glass partition. He was a white man in his middle thirties, of average height, who sat with shoulders hunched, giving him an air of dejection. His hat was beside him on the bench. His one hand nervously fingered the brim; the other hand, resting on his knee, hung limp. His face was sallow and his complexion had a yellow cast. His light thin hair seemed to be plastered on his forehead, as though held by perspiration. His grayish eyes, somewhat magnified by thick glasses, seemed to be focused on some distant point. He was clean-shaven and neatly dressed, although his overcoat was slightly ragged at the sleeves.

When the worker rose from her desk to call him, she smiled and said in a low voice, "Won't you come in the office, Mr. Sherman?" The patient looked up blankly, fumbled for his hat, and without a word followed worker into the office. Indicating a chair and quietly closing the door, worker seated herself across the desk from the patient, saying, "Won't you sit down? The nurse tells me you are pretty worried. Perhaps if we talk it over I may be able to help you." He sat down heavily with a deep sigh, stared down at his hat, and then said in a low, scarcely audible voice, "I don't know—I just can't believe it. I can't understand how I could get it."

Realizing the "it" referred to the recent diagnosis of pulmonary tuberculosis, worker felt it best to let the patient express what was uppermost in his mind, so that she might be better able to understand what he considered the problem. She said nothing, but looked directly at the patient. With another sigh he looked up and worker was aware that his chin trembled. Nevertheless, he went on, "How can I do what the doctor tells me I should? How can I go to bed for months?" He shuddered slightly, "Lord knows how many months!"

"Why not, Mr. Sherman?"

"I've got to work. I can't stay in bed at home."

Previously, worker had noticed from the medical record that the patient and his wife were occupying a small apartment. She asked, "Does your wife know of your physical condition, Mr. Sherman?"

Clutching his hat with sudden nervous motions, he said, "That's just it. She'll be so worried. It just means more expense and it's the shock of it all. I've been getting treatment for my diabetes for a long time. In fact, I've doctored most of my life, but I just can't believe that I have tuberculosis. It's almost like being struck by lightning or something. Maybe she has it, too—oh, I just wish I could die."

Worker felt at this point that she needed further knowledge of the patient's understanding of his condition in order to give him any interpretation of the illness and its implication to him as an individual. She said, "Of course it is a shock to you to learn that you have tuberculosis, but what did the doctor tell you about your condition?"

The patient leaned forward slightly and said earnestly, "Well, only that I have tuberculosis. I've been losing weight the last few months. I've been tired all the time and I've sweated a lot at night, but I never supposed that it was anything really wrong with me. It is in my lungs, and that's why I have to be so careful at home, so that my wife doesn't get it, too. The doctor said she'd better be examined right away."

The patient was discussing each thing as it came to him. Worker nodded occasionally. As he paused, worker asked, "What did the doctor advise you to do?"

"Go to bed right away—today, even—and stay there until I can go to Metropolitan Hospital." At the mention of prolonged hospitalization worker saw the patient wince and since she was not sure of the basis for this attitude, asked, "Why don't you want to go to the hospital? That is the best way, you know, or the doctor wouldn't have advised it."

The patient's anxious attitude rather than the reply he gave seemed to indicate more than appeared on the surface.

"Yes, I know, but it's the expense. (Pause) And how long will it be?"

Worker replied, "That is very difficult to tell because no two people will respond alike to treatment. You know that yourself, Mr. Sherman, having diabetes, and seeing how other patients are unable to take the same amount of insulin as you."

The patient nodded, "Yes, I suppose that's right, but staying in the hospital . . ."

Just then the doctor who had examined the patient entered the office, apparently to discuss another case, but stopped as soon as he saw that the worker was busy. However, worker made the most of the opportunity to draw the doctor into the discussion by saying, "Oh, Dr. Williams, if you are not too busy right now, could you talk to Mr. Sherman and me?"

Dr. Williams entered, smiled, and sat on the corner of the desk, between the patient and the worker, half facing each one. "Yes, indeed, I'm not busy now. What's the trouble?"

Worker explained, "Mr. Sherman is pretty worried about his health.

I wonder if you would talk to him so that he will be able to carry out the recommendations that you made."

"The only recommendation that I made was for hygienic precautions at home until he can get into a tuberculosis sanatorium and stay there until he is well."

At this the patient broke in, "Yes, but doctor, I don't see how I can."

"John," in a friendly, emphatic tone, "you must. That's the only way you'll ever get well."

"Then—then, I will get well?"

Dr. Williams, with a laugh, "Of course you will, only it's going to take a good long time. The diagnosis has been made early, and if you do your part by resting and eating now, you probably won't have a bad time at all. It's a pretty tough combination, diabetes and tuberculosis; each disease sort of works against the other. For example, the diet for one has food in it that a patient with the other disease shouldn't eat. The main thing is complete bed rest for a few months."

During Dr. Williams' remarks the patient said nothing, but listened attentively. Then, as the doctor rose to go, he said, "I—I—I don't feel quite so bad about it, I guess. Thanks, Doc."

Dr. Williams turned to worker, "Is that all?" Worker nodded, "Thank you, Dr. Williams." To the patient the doctor said, "No worrying, now, John," and left the office.

When the doctor had gone, the patient remarked, "I guess you know the main reason why I didn't want to go to the hospital."

"No, why?"

"Well, I thought I was going in and would never come out. I always thought that consumption was the end. (Pause) But how about the expense? I can't possibly pay a hospital a big bill. My wife's working, but she don't make much." It seemed best to worker to accept patient's statement of his fear of dying without much comment, as there seemed to be no indication for a need to determine the basis for it.

Worker replied, "Through the Metropolitan Tuberculosis Bureau, arrangements for your hospital care will be made for the county to assume the financial responsibility."

Patient sighed, "Oh, I see."

Worker then asked, "What sort of work had you been doing?"

"I have my own business, selling brake linings, but since I've been sick in the last, say three months, I don't believe I've cleared more than $36."

"You said your wife is employed?"

"Yes, she works at a printing company—she's a stenographer—it's the Eton Envelope Printing Company on Wade Avenue. She's making $85 a month."

"So you have been able to get along?"

"Lord, yes, I would die before I'd accept charity." After a short pause the patient continued, "What if my wife has tuberculosis, too?" At this point the worried expression which had been so apparent on the patient's face at the beginning of the interview, but had gradually disappeared, now returned. Worker ignored his statement that he would not accept charity yet accepted without apparent disapproval that the county pay his hospital bill. "She needs to be examined. Dr. Williams told me to come in tomorrow. She'll come with me then."

"Has your wife any symptoms, do you know, like a cough, weight loss, night sweats, or anything like that?"

"No, she seems perfectly well, but I guess you can't tell anything about it by the way people look. He [the doctor] wants me to come back for a checkup on the X-rays and sputum."

"When you come in tomorrow, and after you have seen the doctor again, we can decide better about an examination for your wife."

"Then when I—I mean, we—come in tomorrow, can I see you right away?"

"Yes, of course, Mr. Sherman. As soon as you have registered downstairs, come directly to the Medical Clinic, and if I'm not here, the clinic secretary will call me."

The patient rose, straightened his shoulders, smiled wanly, and said, "Thank you for taking all this time. I was just about bowled over when he told me I had tuberculosis. I still can't believe it. Maybe there's a mistake. Anyway, I do want you to talk to my wife. You will, won't you?"

"Yes, Mr. Sherman, I will be glad to do anything I can." Worker gave patient her name, and as he went out he repeated it, saying, "Thank you again, Miss Smith. I'll certainly be back tomorrow."

November 12, 1937. Clinic Interview With Patient's Wife. As worker was not in the clinic when the patient and his wife arrived, she went to see them as soon as possible. As she approached, Mrs. Sherman, who was sitting alone on the edge of a bench in the clinic, looked expectantly toward worker. She was a small shy person with a round face and, like patient, wore glasses of a rimless, octagonal type, which tended to make her eyes look large. Worker introduced herself, saying, "I am Miss Smith: you are Mrs. Sherman, aren't you?"

The latter nodded, but before she could speak tears dropped from her eyes and she clutched the worker's hand. Worker sat down beside her and after a moment said, "Has Mr. Sherman seen the doctor yet?"

Wife nodded and replied with her head lowered, "Yes. He's in there now. The doctor told me that he does have tuberculosis." At that point she sobbed and dabbed at her eyes with a handkerchief clasped in her hand. "Oh, it's such a shock. I just can't believe it."

Worker replied, "I can well understand how you feel, Mrs. Sherman. You must have been upset by the knowledge of your husband's condition."

Mrs. Sherman looked up, speaking fast as though she had to tell someone, "It just seems that the bottom has dropped out of everything. Things were going along fine. Of course, we did have to worry some about money, but at least we were happy—and then . . ."

"The doctor advises that your husband go into a hospital as soon as possible. Will such an arrangement be all right with you?" By this time wife seemed more composed.

"The doctor knows best and I suppose that to be in the hospital is the only thing. It'll be awfully hard to be separated from John, but it's for the best. I am rather worried about myself and he wants me to get examined right away." Worker explained the procedure as to examination of contacts at the neighborhood health station. Because of wife's strong desire for an examination, worker made a definite appointment for her by telephone. When this was arranged, wife sighed and said, "It's so good of you to do that, I would not have any idea what to do. Especially now, I can't seem to figure out anything for myself."

At this point worker received a telephone call and had to excuse herself to answer it. Following the call, worker was forced to leave the clinic, so she said, "Mrs. Sherman, I'm sorry, but I must leave without seeing Mr. Sherman today. If you have any difficulty, or if I can be of any assistance I hope you will call me." She then gave wife her telephone number.

Mrs. Sherman remarked, "You have been so kind to us. I do appreciate everything you have done. It has made it easier during this time of difficulty. I surely will call you if I need you."

Feeling that the departure was rather abrupt, worker asked, "Would you mind if I came to see you later at your home, Mrs. Sherman?"

"Oh, would you? I'd like it so much if you would. Thank you again and good-bye."

Later Developments. A few days later the patient was hospitalized, and although both the patient and his wife were still concerned about his physical condition, they were much relieved to learn that wife's examination was entirely negative. Following patient's admission to the hospital, the wife gave up the apartment, placed their furniture in storage, and went to live with her sister, thus reducing the living expenses. This arrangement worked out satisfactorily to all concerned.

Patient has been responding so well to rest and hospital treatment that he was allowed to go home with his wife on New Year's day. Because of his improvement the doctor has told him that he may not have to remain in the hospital as long as was originally thought. As a result, both he and his wife are much more hopeful and are looking forward to the time when they can return to their own home. Finances are not an issue, as the county is paying for patient's care and his wife is working steadily. Worker has been in touch with the wife at her place of employment. It is worker's plan to get in touch with the couple after the patient's discharge, if they indicate a need for further casework.[2]

[2] The case of "John Sherman" was taken from *Some Aspects of Social Casework in a Medical Setting: A Study in the Field of Medical Social Work,* prepared by Harriett M. Bartlett for the Committee on Functions of the American Association of Medical Social Workers, Chicago, 1940, pp. 41–46.

The sufferance of physical pain is an old, old fact of human experience. All of us need little education as to the meaning of illness. And yet, the amount of pain that a person is able to suffer or the length of time that a person is able to undergo suffering seems in the cases of many individuals to be somewhat secondary in importance to the social and emotional concomitants that go along with physical ailments. An amputee, for example, long after physical pain has passed, may have the socially painful experience of trying to get along without a limb, of having people watch him with curiosity, of looking for a job which he can accept, of being received by his family, of renewing friendships with members of the opposite sex. Even a relatively simple illness or hospitalization experience may bring about or aggravate deep-seated problems for the patient.

While the treatment of the social and emotional concomitants of physical illness has not yet caught up with the great strides in the field of medicine, marked advances have been made. Social work is one of the many services in our society which are contributing to this advance. That branch of social work activity which is especially interested in the social and emotional problems of the physically ill and is carried on in a medical setting is called medical social work. The medical setting is usually a hospital or hospital clinic.

THE HISTORY OF MEDICAL SOCIAL WORK

Like the other types of social work practice, modern medical social work is rooted deeply into the past. Although the formal professional organization dates back only a few decades, its foundations rest upon achievements which are much older.

The period preceding the modern professional organization of medical social work was characterized by five types of services, including (1) unorganized services, (2) lady almoners, (3) aftercare of the insane, (4) nursing care, and (5) training of medical students.

Unorganized Services

There probably never has been a time when persons have not been friendly toward the sick. Usually, the friendship shown came for the most part from lay people and friends and relatives of the sick. So, for example, when a widower-father needed to be hospitalized and the children of the family were left without immediate and direct supervision, there have been grandmothers, neighbors, and others willing to lend a helping hand during the period of need.

But not always did the concern for physically ill persons come from a lay person. There have been within the history of the western churches many instances where a religious leader became a sort of non-professional medical social worker and led a person or a family through some crisis connected with physical suffering. Certainly, most of the medical social work attention given by lay and professional people, through the greater number of centuries preceding the formal expression of medical social work as a profession in itself, was undertaken in this relatively unorganized and rather nonprofessional manner.

Lady Almoners

Lady almoners have been a common part of English hospital organization. Before the latter part of the last century they sought to increase the social ease of hospital patients by caring in informal ways for their social problems.

Under the leadership of Charles S. Loch, who was the Secretary of the London Charity Organization Society in the 1890's, the lady almoner came to hold an even more responsible position in English hospitals. Mr. Loch saw in the lady almoner a means of solving a perplexing problem with which charity hospitals at that time (as ever) were confronted. Under the system of medical service then current it was difficult and often impossible for a hospital offering either free or partly free medical service to distinguish between those who were worthy and those who were unworthy of less than fully paid medical service. There were some rather crude and haphazard ways of trying to ascertain whether the patient was worthy of charity, but these were widely known to be sorely inadequate. It was the opinion of Mr. Loch that the lady almoner in those English hospitals offering part-paid or free medical treatment could act as an investigator of the worthiness of patients. This innovation was a far cry from the modern practice of medical social work in all of its varied manifestations, but, at least, it was a step in that direction.

The first lady almoner to undertake the task of investigating patients was appointed in 1895 and practiced at the Royal Free Hospital in London. A paragraph from the report prepared in part under the direction of Mr. Loch for the Select Committee of the House of Lords describes what the functions of the lady almoner were:

> There should be appointed in every medical charitable institution a distributor or referrer of patients, who should see the patients after they have been seen by the medical officer, and who, subject to the requirements of the hospital from the point of view of medical instruction or gravity of illness, should decide as far as possible on the statements of the

petitioners for relief, and also as a rule, by a reference of the case to a charity organization committee or some proper local organization.[3]

The meaning of this statement, then, implies that the lady almoner was to uncover the financial status of the patient in order to judge his acceptability by a charitable hospital and to refer him, if such seemed desirable, to whatever local social work or medical agency could best help him. As the plan worked out, the lady almoner was assigned the responsibility of carrying on liaison relations with the social work and medical resources of the community. This brought the almoner more into the role of the modern medical social worker. Undoubtedly, the lady almoner represents one of the important precursors of professional medical social work.

Aftercare of the Insane

Somewhat before the lady almoner became an important dispenser of medical social service in the English hospitals, there existed in England the Society for After Care of Poor Persons Discharged Recovered From Insane Asylums. The lengthy title of this Society tells its own story. It was intended as a social service to those patients of mental hospitals who were adjudged cured and who, being discharged, were in need of assistance in making community adjustments. While the Society was a voluntary association, still it worked under the general supervision of the medical superintendents of mental hospitals. Its chief practical functions were the placement of homeless mental patients in foster homes and in convalescent institutions, and the guiding of discharged patients in their attempts to orient themselves satisfactorily to their communities.

In the United States this type of social service was not instituted until some years after it was organized in England, and here by the State Charities Aid Association of New York (1906). In this country the work of the State Charities Aid Association came at about the time that hospital social service was beginning on a formal and professional basis.

Nursing Care

Inasmuch as the primary task of a nurse is the medical care of patients, services of a social and emotional character which nurses have rendered in the past might appropriately fall under the heading of unorganized social service. The importance of the nurses' contributions to

[3]Quoted in Ida M. Cannon, *Social Work in Hospitals: A Contribution to Progressive Medicine,* Russell Sage Foundation, New York, new and revised edition, 1930, p. 9.

social service, however, places nursing care in a class by itself as a significant predecessor of medical social work.

Whether a nurse was attached to a hospital and found her duties to patients solely within a hospital or whether the nurse was a home nurse who assumed responsibilities toward patients in their own homes, an important part of her activity was of a social and emotional character. If the nurse was in a hospital, she naturally maintained personal relations with hospital patients. They could ask her about their problems when they did not feel free to speak to their physicians. They could ask social "favors" of nurses because of the service implications of the nursing profession. On the other hand, if the nurse was practicing in a private home, perhaps much more of the social care of the patient was bound to spring up. In many instances the home nurse became the friendly companion and through this office came into very direct contact and knowledge of the personal problems of her patient. Occasionally, the nurse in the home found herself concretely in the midst of family problems without any preliminary discussion or foreknowledge. Obviously, too, there were nurses (as now) who enjoyed both hospital and home contacts with patients.

The personal relationships which many nurses built up with patients quite often took the place of more formal medical social service relationships. Thus the nurse may also be counted as a contributor to the modern medical social work field. Even today nurses contribute to the social work process. They are taught the social components of their profession, and social workers are called in to work with patients only when the problems are complex and can be met more appropriately through casework services. Indeed, one of the functions of the medical social worker is the education of student nurses (and medical students) regarding the social aspects of illness and medical care.

Training of Medical Students

The medical profession was also aware of the need for training medical students in the ways of approaching the social and emotional aspects of patients' problems and of utilizing to the best advantage the social service resources of the hospital and the community in serving their patients. The first example of instruction in medical social work for prospective doctors was provided by the Medical School of Johns Hopkins University in Baltimore, Maryland. There, under the inspiration and direction of Dr. Charles P. Emerson, the training included not only classroom instruction but field work experience as well.

A statement by Dr. Emerson in 1909 indicates in part how this program for medical students was organized and how it functioned:

It was partly to aid their education that seven years ago (1902) some of the medical students of the Johns Hopkins University organized the first student board of the Charity Organization Society of Baltimore. They visit one poor family or at most two poor families, assigned them by this society, for weeks, months, or even for four years. They do what they can to improve conditions in those households. No effort is made to select for these students families in which there is sickness; in fact, the students prefer families where there are boys. But the students learn how the poor man lives, works, and thinks; what his problems are; what burdens he must bear. They learn the intimate relationship between the ills of the physical body and the home environment. They also learn how easy it is to give very good advice which will add burdens that cannot be borne. They find out that the poor man is not always a self-convicted sinner nor a self-confessed ignoramus, and that he has his own ideas as to the necessity, and especially as to the possibility, of his following advice. The poor man loves his vices as truly as does the rich man, and will not abandon them at the offhand suggestion of a strange doctor. The students find that to effect a much needed reform, e.g., to keep the windows open, they must win first the confidence, next the love of the poor patient, and then stick to him closer than a brother to prevent relapses.

In five years there were on the rolls of active volunteer workers of the three students' boards over sixty students, or one quarter of the entire enrollment of the school. They did not meet in the hospital, but in the offices of the Charity Organization Society. The reason for this was that every member of the self-appointed committee which guided this work was connected with the hospital and was also a manager of the Charity Organization Society, hence no conflict between these two interests could arise. All the patients at this hospital who seemed to need special social service were referred directly to this society, but the most interesting and the best cases for the students to study are not these medical cases. This organized student work, with its purpose of training doctors in social service, is, we believe, a very important department of the hospital.[4]

The interest of medical students in the social and emotional concomitants of physical illness continues today.

Expansion of Movement

From such early beginnings, largely nonprofessional in themselves, the modern movement of medical social work has arisen. Specifically, because of the awareness among hospital personnel of the social and emotional needs of patients and because of the accomplishments of the

---

[4]C. P. Emerson, "The Social Service Department of a General Hospital," *National Hospital Record,* March 15, 1909, pp. 5–7, quoted in Ida M. Cannon, *Social Work in Hospitals: A Contribution to Progressive Medicine,* Russell Sage Foundation, New York, new and revised edition, 1930, pp. 12–13.

informal means already at the disposal of hospitals, social workers were introduced into several hospitals about the turn of the last century. Bellevue Hospital in New York City, the Massachusetts General Hospital in Boston, Johns Hopkins Hospital in Baltimore, and the Berkeley Infirmary in Boston were some of the first hospitals in the country to introduce medical social workers as a definite personnel category. Following the acceptance and the demonstration of medical social work in these hospitals the movement spread through the years following until, at present, social service departments are widely accepted parts of hospital organization, at least for the larger hospitals. Unfortunately, many small hospitals throughout the country have no social service department and indeed can hardly afford a full-time social worker.

As the medical social work profession grew it branched out from hospital practice to work in other agencies and organizations. It is now practiced in public health and medical care programs. The introduction of the medical social worker into the public health field was not accomplished until relatively recently because of the nature of the growth of that field. In the beginning, when public health so often was a matter of mass approaches to community health problems, there was little need for caseworkers. It was only as the efforts of public health workers turned to emphasis on the individual that an opening was made for casework. In this sense the medical social worker's responsibility assumes the presence of a patient and a physician related on an individual basis; in other words, his role is predicated on personal relationships.

The most common function of the medical social worker in public health organizations is to act as consultant to other workers who are more basically responsible for the health program, although there are exceptions. Often, medical social workers provide for visiting nurses (and others) a broader and deeper appreciation of the social work aspects of their patients' problems than a nurse receives while in training. The medical social worker in such a program may aid individual health workers to make proper referrals of patients whose social problems are such that simple physical aid cannot produce adequate results.

Medical social consultants, however, also have responsibilities of a community nature. The planning of the total agency program as it relates to the social aspects of health and medical care, and the coordination of the various health and welfare services of the community are increasingly the concern of the medical social worker.

In addition to the medical social worker's role in health programs in places other than hospitals, affiliations exist with agencies where special types of problems are considered. Such, for example, would be an agency which cared for crippled children or for the tubercular. Here the need for medical social workers is apparent. Usually, as in the other health programs just mentioned, there is no formal relationship between such agencies and community hospitals. There probably will be additional applications of medical social work in the future to fields allied in a general way with health. (See Figure 23.)

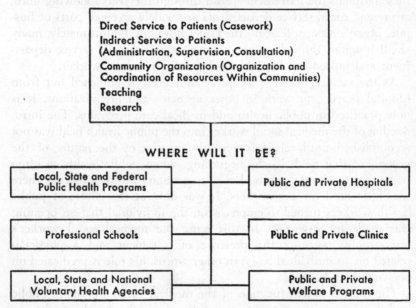

WHAT WILL YOUR WORK BE?

Direct Service to Patients (Casework)

Indirect Service to Patients
(Administration, Supervision, Consultation)

Community Organization (Organization and Coordination of Resources Within Communities)

Teaching

Research

WHERE WILL IT BE?

Local, State and Federal Public Health Programs	Public and Private Hospitals
Professional Schools	Public and Private Clinics
Local, State and National Voluntary Health Agencies	Public and Private Welfare Programs

FIG. 23. Types and Places of Work for Medical Social Workers.

(*Your Future Career,* American Association of Medical Social Workers, Washington, D. C., March, 1947.)

MEDICAL SOCIAL WORK IN A HOSPITAL

The chief setting for medical social work is, however, in hospitals. The fact that this work is practiced within the confines of an institution which serves a larger purpose, creates a prospect for medical social work different from the other specialties of social work.

Organizational Features

The social service department of a hospital is not a thoroughly independent organization but rather is a part of a larger operating unit. Concretely, it is an adjunct to the more basic work of the institution, namely, the treatment of disease by physicians and surgeons. Because this is so, the medical social worker in a hospital setting is called upon to participate in a team—which may include nurses, occupational and physical therapists, and others, as well as physician and social worker—in which the fundamental aims of the social worker are those of the physician. Nothing which the social worker does should fail of this purpose. In the team the doctor is the chief. He decides the ways in which the social worker can be of help to him in his ultimate goal of aiding the patient. The social worker, thus, is an instrument for medical treatment, as are others within the hospital.

The contribution of the medical social worker derives its importance from the well-accepted fact that the physical health of patients is often dependent—even to a surprising degree—upon their social and emotional well-being. The relationships between the "mind"and the "body" are complex, each influencing the other in significant ways under a variety of circumstances. As a rule the approach of the physician is to the "body" of the patient, while that of the social worker is to the "mind," or to the "mind" in social operation. Actually, however, these distinctions of function are at best artificial, since, as has been said, there is no genuine dichotomy of the personality. But it is fair to say that the physician has more skill in the treatment of physical problems, while the social worker is more apt in the skills which social casework implies. Together, their aim is the health of the patient. Each contributes his share in the process of aiding recovery.

The relationships of the social work department and the community are also somewhat different in medical social work from what they are in other forms of social work. Usually, the social worker is responsible for the public relations existing between the agency and the community. In family casework, for example, this task is simplified because the worker represents only the agency itself. The hospital social worker, on the other hand, must familiarize the community not only with the social services of the hospital, but with the services of the hospital as a whole. This obligation has both advantages and handicaps to the worker.

The social service department of a hospital must ever keep before its attention its responsibility to see the patient in his wholeness. The modern hospital, like modern medicine, is noted for a high degree of specialization. The situation sometimes arises in hospitals where the physician knows a great deal about a small need that the patient has almost to the exclusion of the larger, and especially the social, needs of patients. Thus one can unfortunately assume that all too often the more the physician knows about the particular ailment of the patient the less he will know about the patient in his totality. (There are, however, many important exceptions to this rule.) The social service department of a hospital, in view of this tendency, plays an important role in trying to keep the complete picture of the patient before its own workers and the other workers in the hospital. This type of contribution is usually not necessary in less institutionalized forms of social casework.

It is interesting to note, moreover, that the medical social worker in a hospital may have a plethora of administrative problems. Much of this difficulty, however, can be obliterated or at least mitigated if there is a high degree of administrative coordination among the executives of the various departments that comprise a hospital. There are, furthermore, ways of administrative organization for a social service department, as for hospitals, which are more to be preferred in this connection than others. For example, if the social service department is an integral part of the hospital organization, without special financing or outside supervision, there may be a better chance of administrative harmony within the hospital than otherwise.

Type of Patient

The fact that the medical social worker operates within a larger medical setting determines the type of patient that he will be meeting. It will also influence the amount of attention that he can give the patient. The assumption on the part of the medical social worker is that the patient has not come to the hospital to make sole use of him, but to make use of the medical facilities. This means that the relationships which the worker will have with the patient will be somewhat different from those of a caseworker in a child guidance clinic, for example, where the client approaches the agency with a specific request which is primarily in line with the relatively homogeneous function of the agency. Moreover, since the patients of the medical social worker come to hospitals primarily for medical treatment, and since the control over those accepted for such treatment is to a considerable extent determined by other than social workers, the number and the type of clients of social service departments cannot be regulated as easily as they can in some other kinds of agencies. So it is that the medical social worker has patients who never in the first place intended to speak with a social worker but intended merely to secure medical treatment. They must be accepted within the terms of the time and attention possible on the basis of the patient-load prevalent in the hospital.

Positive Features

The factors described above, and others, all comprise organizational features inherent in the practice of medical social work in a hospital.

None is to be taken as negative in itself, although that may be the case in a specific hospital. On the other hand the social worker in a medical setting finds many advantages and opportunities. The atmosphere of the hospital itself is exciting and challenging. Many of the dramatic elements in human experience center in physical and emotional illness and with these the medical social worker has a fair share of contact. The hospital atmosphere, moreover, features a teamwork of scientifically oriented workers. These workers are a constant stimulus to medical social workers, aiding them in their own attainment of a more precise and definite practice. Being in association, in the larger hospitals, with other medical social workers as co-workers and as supervisors, enables the medical social worker to grow in knowledge and skill. The fact, too, that the medical social worker is an accepted part of a hospital staff may enable patients to accept him with considerable ease. In these and other ways the experience of the medical social worker can be enriched and made effective.

Worker's Part

The way in which a social worker can help the physician and hospital is indicated by the following case:

> A boy eleven years of age, a diabetic patient, presented a very difficult medical problem which strained the family budget to provide the necessary diet and medicine. He was a problem also in school and was the center of family friction and resentment because of his behavior difficulty with one of his brothers and sisters. The significance of the illness in his situation is clear, because the family had managed without trouble, either in the emotional or the environmental area, prior to the onset of the diabetes. This family constituted a medical-social problem, whether or not they had been previously known to another type of social agency.[5]

Whenever a patient expresses a problem not directly connected with his principal need of getting well, the social worker refers him to an "outside" agency for treatment. A case which illustrates the times when a social worker within a hospital would not consider it his function to treat a problem of a patient is the following:

> A boy five years of age was in the hospital for an acute upper respiratory infection, of the kind often referred to as "grippe." He had been maltreated by his stepmother and was the bone of contention in a serious family situation. Whether or not this family had been previously known to a social agency, their problem was a social one, because it existed independently of the child's illness, which was self-limiting. The responsibility

[5]Henry B. Richardson, *Patients Have Families*, The Commonwealth Fund, New York, 1945, p. 213.

of the medical social worker was ended when she made it possible for the father to apply to a family agency.[6]

From these two cases it is plain that the medical social worker is hired by the hospital not because the hospital is altruistic and wishes all people to live in peace and in security, but because the worker is a worthy adjunct to a definite purpose—that of obtaining the health of the patient. While this is true, in general, it is difficult in many borderline cases to judge the proper contribution of the hospital and of other community agencies. Here there is no definitive solution; each case must be handled on an individual basis.

PATIENTS AND THEIR PROBLEMS

Although the medical social worker is limited in a hospital setting by the requirements of the institution, there are more personal aspects of his work which comprise, as it were, limitations of a different kind. This means simply that the medical social worker (and here the statement is true for all social workers within their own peculiar agency limits) is restricted by the special needs of the patients who come to social service departments of hospitals. Naturally, the medical social worker will not be confronted with all types of cases, but, as has been suggested, with those cases which have a physical basis or a seeming physical basis.

Patients entering a hospital regularly do so with many misgivings and suspicions. They may regret that they are compelled to undergo medical treatment. They may wonder about the urgency of their need for medical treatment. They may not care to interrupt the otherwise normal course of their living to take up residence in a hospital or to visit in a clinic at stated times. They may wonder about the quality of the treatment which the hospital can offer to them with their specific need. They may be concerned with the whole nature of the medical process. Perhaps, too, they may fear lasting deformity because of treatment. They may believe that something dreadful may happen to them as a result of their hospital experience. Perhaps even death may be faced through their stay in the hospital.

The questions which clients have regarding themselves and others come to focus oftentimes in the very process of admission to hospitals. Sometimes the admission procedures uncover problems on the part of others than clients. The following case of "Helen Abbott" illustrates the complexity of the admission process. From this case it is obvious that

[6]*Ibid*, pp. 213–214.

the use of social work in hospital intake can assist in the primary function of the hospital, namely, good medical care.

July 29, 1938. History. The patient is a 7-year-old girl who was brought to the Orthopedic Clinic, having been sent in by the school nurse from a small town outside the city. The patient dragged one leg. The Orthopedic Clinic advised hospitalization for operation for contracture of the left tendon achilles.

This child was one of four children of a young family. The father worked as an insurance salesman, earning $15 to $20 a week. He stated that he did not secure this amount of money because of work which he actually did week by week, but that his employer had been willing to equalize his wages for the year in order to allow him this amount of money each week. He was an independent young man, who said that he had attempted to keep off relief through the entire depression and up to this point had managed to do so. He refused to consider public assistance for the hospitalization of his child, saying that even if it meant that she was handicapped he would rather have her physically handicapped than have the stigma of having secured public relief. He had come from a self-respecting, independent New England family and was resistant and bitter toward relief of any kind. The mother was a hard-working woman, who appeared somewhat malnourished and who showed the strain of the family situation. There were three other children, all younger than the patient, Helen. The family paid $20 a month rent and there was an insurance policy of $1,000 on the father, which had been borrowed on to the limit. The family had managed by economizing to keep clear of debts, except for current expenses.

The mother took the child home from the clinic and agreed to talk with her husband about the expense of hospital care. The physician estimated that the child would be in the hospital about two weeks. Nothing was heard from the family until the visiting nurse in the town telephoned to say that she was interested in the family and believed this child ought to be operated on, but the family refused assistance. She had tried to secure local private help, but had been unable to do so. She was advised to have the father come to see the admitting officer and discuss the situation with her.

When the father arrived he was quite defensive and resistant. He was not convinced that his child needed the operation and felt that perhaps a brace would remedy the defect. He wondered if the institution was going to experiment on her. He did not want to accept any assistance, but preferred to have the operation postponed indefinitely, until such time as he saw that the child got worse or until he had money to pay for it. As the examining physician had stated that the patient should be operated on as soon as possible in order to prevent further deformity, the admitting officer consulted him in the presence of the father, to ask the various questions which the father wished answered. These were: Is delay a handicap to the child? Can she wear a brace instead of having an operation? When she is operated on, will a brace be necessary? The physician made clear to the admitting officer that the operation was necessary immediately, if the child's handicap was not to be permanent; that the longer there was delay, the greater would be the handicap; that the patient would not need a brace following operation; and that, so far as could be anticipated now, if she were operated on at this time a second operation would not be necessary, but if the operation were postponed now and done later, a second operation would necessarily follow the first.

This was interpreted to the father and he was asked if he had any other questions regarding the advisability of the operation. However, these seemed to satisfy him and he agreed to discuss them with his wife. By this time the admitting officer had overcome his defensive attitude and he appreciated the fact that she was interested in getting for his child what was considered medically advisable. It was explained to him that the hospital as such had no interest in this particular condition, that it was a simple operation, and that our only interest was the benefit of his child.

The admitting officer then discussed the financial situation. The father immediately stated that he could not possibly pay for the child's hospitalization and confirmed the data given above. He said he would be willing to have her come to the hospital if he could pay, but he could not pay. The admitting officer then asked him if he would be willing to have private sources made available for the child's care. This he listened to and said he had never had relief before of any kind, that he would fight rather than take it, that he felt his child might be used for experimental purposes if she were a free case, and gave many other reasons against free hospitalization. Each one of these in turn was interpreted to him; namely, the fact that neither the physician nor the nurse would know whether the child was being paid for by him or by some other source; that to a certain extent we all accept private relief when we accept the services of endowed institutions, such as universities, private schools, or libraries; and that, therefore, the acceptance of a free bed, which would mean the use of money given to the hospital for such a purpose rather than the use of money given to a library, was pretty comparable.

He listened to this interpretation and explanation, and agreed to consider it and discuss it with his wife. Pressure was not brought to bear on any of his attitudes, except to make clear that the child would definitely be handicapped if the operation was postponed. He left the admitting officer in an entirely different frame of mind. He thanked the admitting officer for her consideration and understanding, and said he saw things in a different light. Later that day he telephoned to say that he had discussed it with his wife, they had agreed that they did not want anything to stand in the way of their child's progress, and they would bring her when there was a bed available. He also agreed that if there was any money from private local funds, such as money from the President's Ball, he would be willing to avail himself of that. This was interpreted by the admitting officer to the visiting nurse, with a statement that arrangements were being made so that the child could come in on a free bed, supplemented by private funds which the admitting officer might secure, if possible, and that there would be no delay as soon as a bed was available. The visiting nurse reported that she had seen the family in the interim and they were delighted and grateful, although embarrassed.

The admitting officer then conferred with the individual in charge of the money from the President's Ball in the city. The case was interpreted to him but he did not know whether this patient could be considered eligible for that fund. However, later, fifty dollars were promised from the fund toward the hospital care and the child was admitted, the rest of the hospital bill being paid out of the free bed fund. The patient was discharged to the dispensary and has been reporting to the clinic regularly since that time.

Worker's Comment. The admitting officer, through her casework judgment, recognized the problems which were blocking this father in accepting hospital care for his child. These two problems were lack of conviction of the need for operation and financial difficulty. Both were interpreted satisfactorily to the parents and available resources were brought in to assist in the care that the patient needed. Interpretation was given by the admitting officer to the visiting nurse and to the representative of the President's Ball Fund.[7]

The case of "Helen Abbott" is somewhat unusual in medical social work practice, it must be admitted, for few hospitals presently engage medical social workers in intake work. Intake work is commonly the responsibility of some officer of the hospital, perhaps a clerk. But it does suggest a practice which may become more widespread as more medical social workers are available for such work. It also hints at the possibility that hospitals themselves can be saved considerable time and expense if there is a proper intake procedure where problems of patients, in connection with their medical treatment, are discovered early and by intelligently trained social workers.

Fears for Themselves

Usually, the medical social worker discovers that patients have two kinds of worries, although in any given case they may be co-mingled.

Patients may have certain fears regarding themselves. A very common fear is that concerning ability to pay for medical treatment. A patient who is extremely sensitive regarding his ability to meet the financial standards of the hospital may worry unnecessarily. Without

[7]*Some Aspects of Social Casework in a Medical Setting: A Study in the Field of Medical Social Work*, prepared by Harriett M. Bartlett for the Committee on Functions of the American Association of Medical Social Workers, Chicago, 1940, pp. 181–183.

a clear realization of his financial relation to the hospital, he may retard his recovery or add without foundation to the stress under which he receives medical treatment.

Entering or leaving the hospital may be of serious concern to some patients. A patient may enter a hospital for a period of treatment with pronounced anxiety that he may never be entirely well again. Or a patient whose departure date from the hospital has been set back because of medical reasons may overexaggerate or misinterpret the meaning of this delay. Or a patient who cannot leave when he intended may become troubled because plans that he made will have to be broken.

Some patients have an intense fear of taking anesthetics. To them this process means the surrender of active selfhood and the submission of the person to another individual, usually the surgeon. The experience also has parallels to the death experience which for some patients may be their fundamental and covert anxiety.

Surgery may frighten other patients. It may imply to them that they have a most serious ailment, "maybe cancer, although nobody will say so." They may be concerned about the removal of a part of the body because this may signify to them some loss of individuality or the becoming different from other people. They may feel that any situation which calls for surgery involves the risk of death itself. So, welling up to the central experience of surgery may come all of a lifetime of fears, frustrations, anxieties, doubts, and dependencies.

The following case suggests the implications which surgery may have for some patients. It concerns a woman, thirty-five years old, whose father died of cancer and who herself was going through an operation for tumor of the breast, possibly malignant.

Miss B was taken to the operating room and shortly afterward the surgeon announced that the tumor had proved to be malignant and the radical operation would be performed immediately. During the morning Miss B's fiance, Mr. H, telephoned and was given this information by the social worker, together with the suggestion that he and Miss B's mother come in later in the day. As soon as it seemed expedient, the worker went to Miss B's bedside, after consulting with the nurse who commented upon her restlessness which did not seem to respond to the sedatives she had been given. Miss B was fully awake when the worker entered her room and recognized her at once. She was crying freely and tossing her head from side to side on the pillow. She stopped for a moment to say accusingly: "See what they did to me! And you were so encouraging. All of you said it would come out all right. I should never have let you persuade me. I should have stayed by my Science."

Then followed an outburst of resentment toward her mother and Mr.

H. She sobbed and she said she wanted her mother more than anyone else. Her mother was never around when she needed her. What right did she have to desert her now? She was angry too because of Mr. H's absence and said she guessed it didn't matter anyway because everything would have to be called off. He wouldn't want her now that she was all cut up—just like "chop suey." She would be an imposition on him, anyway. He had an invalid mother who needed all of his attention herself. She wished he wasn't a bartender, anyway. The saloon frightened her because she was afraid of people when they were drunk. "Everything in my life is a mess. I wish I could be born again and start all over." Then very abruptly she said: "I guess my father wants me to go and be with him. That's why he made me have this awful disease."

During the few minutes of the worker's visit she wiped the perspiration from Miss B's face and stroked her forehead. She commented that she knew Miss B was very angry at everyone who had had anything to do with her treatment. She explained that she, herself, was responsible for the absence of Mr. H and her mother, who had called during the morning and had been told to come in during the afternoon since the worker had expected Miss B to be asleep until then. In response to Miss B's comment that "I know I'm acting just like a baby," she replied that all sick people pass through a few days in which they do feel as helpless as a baby and that the nurses expect to give them extra care during that period. She was reassured about her tears and told not to be embarrassed by them. At the termination of the worker's visit Miss B seemed somewhat quieter.

During the days which followed, the worker visited Miss B regularly at the same time every morning. Until the third or fourth day, her dependency was marked and her demands upon the worker great. On one occasion, after her tray had been brought by the nurse and the back of her head elevated so that she could feed herself with her right arm, which was not bandaged, she insisted that the worker feed her. Although there was no physical necessity for this, her request was granted because of her apparent need at that moment for attention from the worker. During the process of being fed she talked freely and referred to the many occasions upon which her father had complained that he had a cold, gone to bed, and made the family wait upon him even though he was well enough to eat a large steak.

One day she expressed anxiety about the discharge from her wound and commented that the odor was just like that which had been present during her father's illness. During these first postoperative days she spoke about the interest she had always felt in the appearance of her body and referred to the fact that now its "lines" would be broken. On one occasion she told the worker about an incident in which she was nearly drowned. At the conclusion of her narrative she said briefly: "That was pretty bad but I came out of it whole." Her mood fluctuated from day to day and she was quite often depressed. However, as she gained in physical strength, her dependency upon the worker lessened and upon the fourth or fifth day she reported eagerly that she was able to go to the bathroom and no longer needed to be waited on. She became curious about the worker.

When the tenth day arrived, some very simple interpretation was attempted in which only the material introduced by Miss B herself was used. She showed considerable acceptance and insight into her situation and commented that she had often wondered why she had ever decided to marry Mr. H, because he was just the same kind of man as her father, domineering and stern. Then she observed that she knew the reason she liked Mr. H was because he reminded her of her father. The worker explained that Miss B might need further help in understanding some of her thoughts which seemed confusing to her and suggested that this could be arranged later, if she thought she would like to try to straighten them out. In the meantime, emphasis was placed upon the various obstacles to recovery which presented themselves from day to day. Miss B's course was steadily upward and she was discharged from the hospital after a minimum period of care. Before she left, she was beginning to arrange the details of her wedding and to reconstruct plans which once seemed so impossible of realization to her. She indicated less and less need of the worker and commented several times upon the fact that she was beginning to "get things straightened out."[8]

Difficult Decisions. Because of the critical nature of illness, patients sometimes find it difficult to make decisions relating to their problems. Usually, the pressure of time makes deciding a difficult matter. For example, the woman who enters a hospital for a general examination may be told that she should undergo an operation. While she may have surmised that entering a hospital for a general checkup might reveal conditions necessitating an operation, still she might be relatively unprepared consciously to face the fact and to make a decision in regard to it. She may, therefore, seek to put the decision off for another time; she may try to get someone else to solve it for her, the physician, the social worker, or a nurse; she may "go to pieces" and not be able to make a decision at all.

The client's need to make decisions and to carry them out reminds us of the responsibilities of the medical social worker in this connection. The medical social worker also is commonly pressed by the time limitations of a particular case. He does not have the possibility of accepting a problem when he chooses and of settling it within time limits which are deemed desirable by him in view of the nature of the case. He, too, must bring himself to act quickly on a crisis which has "hit" the client, and without the possibility for adequate intellectual and emotional preparation. Of course, the medical social worker, like

[8]*Ibid,* pp. 131–132.

social workers in other agencies, does not believe in "taking over" the life of the client. The medical social worker, therefore, would not accept the responsibility of making important decisions for patients, but he would be especially concerned about the special pressures which might be at work on the individual.

Continuous Treatment. In some cases the principal problem of the patient (and the worker) is to meet the detailed implications of recurring or continuous need of hospitalization or treatment. Usually, such cases involve much more for the patient and the worker than those which are of short-term duration. Not only may the patient be faced on occasion with the dread of hospitalization and its specific treatment meanings, but he may be faced, when not in the hospital, with anxieties which are ever-present and which may develop in intensity. It is well for such individuals that there are social service departments in hospitals which give continuous service. The patient receiving such service may not feel as though his contact with the hospital is broken over and over again, and that each time he returns he has to meet in some degree a new situation. He will probably feel that the social service department is a general source of aid and encouragement for him through his long course of illness. If he thinks he needs advice or wishes to "talk out" the growing details of his sickness, he may always approach the medical social worker. This type of service frequently demonstrates the social service department of a hospital as an important "community" agency.

Invalidism. Another of the problems which patients present is that of invalidism. A patient facing difficult adjustment to hospitalization has one problem, but if he must further consider the necessity for permanently lessened activity, a factor is added to his problem which is of no mean weight. Invalidism, thus, is a very hard condition for anyone to accept. It is even harder for one not merely to accept it but to make something of it, that is, to utilize one's remaining strengths in order to carry out as normal a life as possible. The medical social worker will sometimes be concerned with the social implications of invalidism. He must plan with the patient in order that the invalidism may be accepted with as little regret as possible and that the patient may make the most of his existing possibilities.

The value of a social service department is clearly evident in cases of invalidism. The physician may, for example, tell the patient that he no longer can remain in his occupation of milkman with all of the strenuous exercise that such work entails. The patient may on such medical advice wish to change his job. But, usually, the physician is not in a position to inform the patient as to what he can do nor is he commonly available to help the patient to accept the need for a new position. The medical social worker, on the other hand, is engaged in just that sort of work. He may not assume complete responsibility for all such cases himself, but at least he will know the resources of the community that are interested in aiding such persons.

In addition to the problems suggested here as being the direct concern of patients in hospitals, there are, of course, many others. Perhaps most of the activities and services of the medical social worker are less dramatic than some of those which have been here mentioned, and many of those included in the present discussion have their less dramatic moments. But in everything the aim of the medical social worker is the health of the patient and the social and emotional problems which retard health.

Fears for Others

The second general type of problem which patients in hospitals present to medical social workers is that concerning people other than themselves.

For some patients the primary focus of concern is not with themselves. They may be well enough able to accept themselves and to make the most of a difficult situation. But they may be extremely worried about the manner in which they are involving others.

A patient in a hospital may face the hampering of his physical activities due to an organic defect. He may be able to accept his limitation. But he may be fearful of telling his wife. He may feel that she will not understand. She may think that he is seeking to avoid work. He may be judged as less manly because he is restricted by the conditions of his defect.

Another patient may be troubled because he has transmitted disease to someone else. Thus a patient who is being treated in a hospital may worry because he has given his syphilis to his wife. He may be relatively unconcerned for himself. But he may wonder how it will be possible for him to inform his wife. He may consider whether he should tell his wife. The knowledge of her threat in health may cause him no end of difficulty. Guilt feelings may characterize his response to his illness.

Similarly, a man who undergoes hospital treatment may be capable of accepting his need for treatment, but may be greatly worried about the way in which his family will survive during the period of his hospitalization. The man who finds it necessary to start the life of an invalid may not worry about himself, but may be terribly interested in what will happen to his business. The woman in constant need of hospital treatment may be willing to accept this circumstance, but may wonder what the expense connected with treatment will do with the family's plans and dreams of a new home or a new automobile.

In these and other ways patients are concerned with others. These disturbances, while they may seem to be somewhat removed from the primary medical problem of the patient, may actually be at the root of the recovery process. It is well within the function of the medical social worker to be vitally interested in such problems since they often play an important role in the achievement of health for the patient.

Combined Problems

Many times, as it can readily be appreciated, the patient presents fears in regard to both himself and others. Such, perhaps, is the most common experience. Emphasis, clearly, may also differ from case to case. What to one patient may be a problem of importance only to himself will for another be of prime significance to his friends and relatives.

Oftentimes the patient, as in the process of discharge from a hospital, may have no problem to stir intense emotions, but, nevertheless, is beset with genuine social concerns developing out of going home. The following case is illustrative of this:

Worker introduced herself to patient and explained that the doctor had told her that patient was ready to go home soon and might have some problems about care at home. Worker commented that she was interested in helping her with this. Patient is an obese, middle-aged, grey-haired woman with a very pale skin. She has large dark eyes and appeared somewhat depressed. Patient sighed and replied that she was going home, but not to her own home. She was going to her sister-in-law, since she felt that she would need someone to take care of her. At this point, with a good deal of suppressed feeling, patient started sobbing and said she was afraid to go home but she did not want to remain in the hospital. After a short pause, worker replied that it must be difficult for her because of the nature of her operation. Patient continued to tell worker that the operation really involved a radical change. She was terribly ashamed and upset about it. She did not want people to take care of her and she hated taking care of herself. Worker said that she knew about this. Patient with some feeling stated that the odor nauseated her and she was afraid that people around her would not want to stay near. She did not like anyone else to take care of her and she felt she must learn to manage.

Worker wondered whether she had discussed with the doctor the possibility of caring for herself. She replied that he had assured her that the colostomy[9] opening would be closed up in two months. In addition, he

[9] A colostomy—the establishment of an artificial anus by an opening into the colon.

had prescribed a diet so that she would be able to control the colostomy during this interval period. Worker commented that she knew of other patients with similar conditions who had learned to care for themselves. Patient replied that she never knew anyone had this kind of operation. It was something entirely new to her. She really felt disgusted with herself and was fearful about reactions of people coming in contact with her. Worker commented that it was not easy to accustom oneself to something like this, but that perhaps it was her feeling about herself that was the important thing. Worker then suggested that perhaps patient would like to talk about this further. Was it that she might feel others were disgusted because she herself felt that way? With much less feeling, patient nodded and thought that might be the reason. Worker wondered if patient had been told about the nature of the operation. Patient replied that if that had been made known to her, she would rather have died first.

Worker commented that not having known about it must have made it more difficult to accept. Had the doctors explained why it had been necessary? Patient replied that they had. She went on to say that they had promised to close it up, so that it was this present period that concerned her. With a sigh, she added she supposed she would just have to manage for two months. Worker wondered how she felt about the arrangements at her sister-in-law's home. She explained that she felt she was rather weak and did need to be with someone. She would have her own room and did not anticipate any difficulties in staying with the family. It was simply her own feeling about herself. Patient went on to tell worker about her family relationships and her feelings regarding being a free patient. This was the first time she had to accept care without paying for it. She felt that she had received excellent care but was upset about her inability to reimburse the hospital.

After some discussion of the physical arrangements at her sister-in-law's house, patient and worker agreed that at present she would need a public health nurse to help her with her dressings and bed care. Worker arranged to send a nurse. Patient said she could make her own arrangements about leaving the hospital and returning to clinic.[10]

This case also illustrates the fact that the medical social worker's chief concern derives from the hospital's relation to the patient in terms of medical care.

Environmental Conditions. The meaning of environmental conditions must be considered by the medical social worker for each patient on an individual basis. There is no simple solution to any of them. As stated in a previous chapter, there is reason to think that the social

[10]Jeanette Hertzman and Rachel Wyman, "The Beginning Process in Medical Social Case Work," in *The Family* (now *Journal of Social Casework*) volume 26, number 1, March, 1945, p. 26.

worker can operate both in a "direct" way (in regard to the patient's own fears about his illness) and "environmentally" (in regard to the fears which the patient may have concerning others). Usually, as we have seen, both types of treatment are needed. But there are also limitations to both. The social worker cannot always change environmental factors. The ill man in a time of general unemployment may not be able to change his job as quickly and as suitably as in a time of full employment. Such conditions the social worker (and others) must recognize. Wherever environmental conditions cannot be modified to suit the needs of the patient, the medical social worker must seek those alterations in the patient's own personal outlook which will take the objective social conditions into account. If the patient who needs to change his job, for example, cannot because of general economic conditions over which neither the worker nor the patient has control, then a second choice may have to be made by the patient (as, "going on relief") and the basis for such a decision be considered by the patient and the worker. Again, it may be stated that in most cases there is no easy choice between direct and environmental treatment. The patient and the worker are usually involved with degrees of both.

To say, however, that environmental conditions are sometimes such that they cannot be modified readily by the worker and the patient is not to mean that they are never changeable. When an individual can find optimum adjustment to his family and community through effecting environmental changes, the medical social worker and his patient are obliged to act. Indeed, in some instances what appears as an immovable social barrier to the full adjustment of the patient may become upon examination a false obstacle. Much depends upon the ability of the social worker to understand the range of environmental possibilities which exist in a given case and to make these available for the patient's use.

THE MEDICAL SOCIAL WORKER AND TEAMWORK

As suggested previously, the hospital medical social worker does not operate by himself, but in conjunction with other professionals within the hospital and the community.

Within the Hospital

The two principal types of persons with whom the medical social worker has relationships in a hospital are patients and physicians. There are others with whom the social worker has contact, but, chiefly, his association is with these two. Something of the type and quality of

relationship which workers have with patients has already been intimated. Here, consideration will be given to the associations between
workers and physicians.

Physician's Outlook. The relationship which a worker can establish
with a physician will in large part depend upon the conception which
the physician has regarding the value of medical social work and his
own ability to make use of such service. Some physicians may consider
medical care to be merely a matter of treating organic disturbances.
Such a view, obviously, might allow little room for the use of a social
service department in the thinking of the physician. Under such circumstances he may feel that the medical social worker is encroaching
upon his own work or that the social worker is operating in a sphere
of activity which has no genuine basis in reality. On the other hand,
and more happily, the physician may appreciate the close relationship
between bodily and psychic functions and feel the need for a careful
and definite program of interrelationship with the medical social
worker. Thus his conception of the medical process may include social
and emotional factors in addition to organic, and thereby make considerable place for the kind of treatment a medical social worker is capable of performing.

Under the training which is being offered today in the leading schools
of medicine there can be no doubt that the future physician will be
thoroughly trained, as are many today, in the knowledge and treatment-
skill of the social-psychological problems of patients. The concept of the
"total patient" has won acceptance everywhere now in medical circles.
The effect of its acceptance, however, has not been fully felt as yet.
Certainly, the current training of physicians, and of nurses, too, will
have its repercussions in due time, perhaps in ways which will alter
extensively the relationships of hospital professional personnel.

The physician also is an important determinant of the degree to which
the medical social worker can cooperate in the treatment of patients.
If the physician has the outlook that it is strictly his job to treat organic
difficulties and the job of the social worker to treat the social and emotional, he may be inclined to make referrals to the worker without that
degree of cooperation which is necessary oftentimes for the success of
a case. He may be reluctant to divulge medical information, believing
that the social worker will not understand what it signifies or that he
will misuse it. He may be unwilling, even though he may recognize
the importance of social service, to cooperate to the extent of holding
mutual conferences so that patients' problems may have the benefit of
joint effort. But, on the other hand, he may be eager both to recog-

nize the maturity and the value of the social worker and to take part in a mutually cooperative program of aiding patients. Whatever view he may take, however, is conditioning for the social worker and will influence the amount of service which the worker will be able to render to patients in given instances.

Contribution of Social Worker. The social worker also has an important contribution to make to the success of his relationship with the physician. The worker, for example, cannot assume that he knows as much about organic disease as does the physician. He must be willing to admit, voluntarily and generously, that the physician is an expert in his own field. Or, in other words, the worker cannot suppose that his treatment alone is self-sufficient. He must be willing to see what the physician may suggest as having possible value. This does not mean that either the physician or the social worker is dependent upon a kind of blind devotion (they probably will not arrive at it anyway in practice) regarding each other's specialization. But, at least, the worker has to be amenable to relationships with physicians, with a well-grounded philosophy of the place which social service holds in a hospital setting.

More than cooperation or the cooperative spirit, however, is needed from the worker. The worker has an obligation to understand what the physician is attempting to do, and this not in vague, hazy terms, but with the concreteness and technicality which the organic condition of the patient may indicate. The worker, then, must have a fairly certain store of medical information such as will find acceptance by the physician. Through this information the social worker will more promptly and thoroughly be able to understand what is in the mind of the physician and thus be of help to patients.

The worker must also respect the time of the physician. The physician who is an expert, say in brain tumors, will not always have large amounts of time to offer the social worker in discussing the social implications of his operations. What time he is able to give to the social worker should be organized and used to the best possible advantage by the worker. Trivia should be kept to a minimum and consultation take place only when there is a genuine basis for it. Through such means the physician may secure greater respect for the medical social worker and be more cooperative when consulted.

Use of Authority. One of the points on which misunderstanding can arise between the physician and the social worker is over the use of authority. The physician may not appreciate the efforts of the worker to permit the patient to make important decisions for himself. Because the physician is often placed in the position of having to make important and immediate decisions on the basis of his own knowledge and experience, he may assume that such a course should everywhere and at all times be practiced. The social worker obviously will be differently minded. The social worker will recognize that there are indeed times when it is impossible to allow the patient the full use of his decisive powers, but in the main the social worker will want to permit the patient to make up his own mind wherever possible. The social worker believes that if authority is too often used in relation to the important life decisions of the patient, the initiative of the patient may be permanently threatened, if not cancelled. Thus if a patient thinks that upon entering the hospital he can give his life over into the hands of experts to manage for him in that situation until he leaves, he will be sadly misinterpreting the competence of the workers within the hospital and perhaps be forming incorrect impressions regarding his own responsibility inside and outside of the hospital.

The use of authority by the physician does not imply that physicians generally are dictatorial but that the nature of their work permits them to operate with a high degree of expertness in more concrete ways than can social workers. Thus medical treatment is today a more precise field than social treatment. It may be possible to tell a patient what he must do if he is diabetic, but the solution to an unemployment problem may be less clear. Similarly, individuals claim a greater degree of competence to deal with their own social problems than they do with their medical. Oftentimes it is the patients themselves who impute the authority to the physician.

The physician, therefore, has opportunities and responsibility which are not given to the social worker. Usually, however, on the part of well-trained physicians, a method of cure is suggested or recommended, rather than commanded. It is clear that the physician can say to a patient: "If you wish to be cured you must do as I say." The intent of such a statement is not necessarily that the physician is compelling the patient, but that there is no other means of cure in the light of the physician's knowledge than the one which he has prescribed.

To say that the social worker usually exercises less authority than the physician does not mean that the social worker in the hospital condemns the use of authority. If the community requires that venereal patients receive treatment under penalty of the law, there can be no discussion by the worker as to whether such a course of action is desirable or not. The social worker takes a stand on the question by referring the patient to the law. But if there are several ways by which the patient can be medically treated for his disease, there may be reason to allow the patient a choice of methods, if there is no decided advantage in any and if the hospital facilities make one program of treatment as desirable as another. To permit the patient to express his own initiative toward the treatment process, both organic and social, may enable the patient to make better use of the services offered.

Sometimes the social worker is better able than others to accept the desires of patients, to enter more fully into their cases. The following case illustrates this, among other things. It is prefaced by the worker's own introduction:

The following case illustrates how a bedridden patient was blocked in her desire to participate actively in medical care because of factors influencing her relationship with the hospital. The caseworker's help was focused upon enabling her to express feeling that she was afraid to display in the presence of the doctor and the nurse upon whom she was dependent for care.

The patient, a 29-year-old single girl with chronic rheumatoid arthritis, was referred to Social Service by the doctor who had been treating her for over a year as a private case. She had been readmitted to the hospital as a ward patient and her symptoms were more acute than they had been during the former three hospitalizations. Actually, the worker had first learned about this patient through the clinic registrar and thought that there would be many problems because of the complicated medical picture. After talking with the head nurse who was quite interested in the patient, worker asked the doctor whether she might talk with the patient. The doctor suggested waiting a few weeks during which time worker followed the medical developments. The doctor finally agreed that, since patient might be bedridden for a long time, the interest of the Social Service Department would be helpful, particularly with plans for convalescent care. Before interviewing the patient, worker had learned that the patient and her sister were estranged from the father and a stepmother. For seven years they both had maintained an apartment above their financial means. The sisters had always been very close to each other. The patient's present acute exacerbation occurred around the time that her sister became interested in a man of some social status. They were married during the patient's hospitalization.

When the worker first interviewed the patient six weeks following her admission, the patient questioned her directly as to the reasons for her interest. The worker replied that the doctor had thought she might be having some problems in relation to her illness. Patient thought that her problems were no different now than they had been before and asked why doctor had not suggested that worker visit her previously. As the interview progressed, patient brought out a great deal of feeling about not having visitors. At the same time she expressed some relief that no one had seen her in her present condition. Patient had thought herself attractive, but now described herself as "toothless" with hands like "claws." She immediately showed the worker a photograph taken when she was well which the worker thought was quite appealing. In spite of her dejection about her appearance, she indicated that she had hopes of looking better again. Since she repeated that it was better that none of her friends came to see her while she looked so badly, worker wondered how she felt about her visiting. Patient responded that it was good to talk with someone besides the nurses and doctor; and since worker "belongs to the hospital," she knew about patient's illness and was not "shocked at my appearance."

After this statement, patient talked for some time about her younger sister and about the "nice" man she married. Sister had moved patient's clothing and furniture to her new apartment and patient had thought that when she left the hospital she would go to her home. Worker sensed that patient might have some feeling about sister's marriage, particularly since sister was several years younger, appeared more adequate, and was physically more attractive. Worker sensed that patient seemed to be making a controlled effort to cover up her true feelings and had made a great deal of effort to repress her hostility. This was indicated overtly in her rigidity and tenseness, which seemed to be a factor in her illness. Patient seemed to be able to relate positively to the worker and further indicated that she would like to talk with the worker whom she could accept as part of the hospital.

Patient looked even less comfortable physically when the worker saw her again. Her fingers seemed stiff and sore, and her fingernails were coming off. Patient told worker that her sister had visited her the previous week and had brought her some fruit. She emphasized the fact that she realized how busy the sister and her husband were, so that they could not visit often. She then went on to talk about getting well and said that she understood that recovery was slow in certain illnesses. Although she had been in the hospital for two months, she hoped she could leave at the end of another two months. Suddenly, patient burst into tears, after which she seemed embarrassed and began to apologize. She said she had never allowed herself to show her feelings before anyone although she did cry at night. She also mentioned that she hoped her doctor would not be told that she lost control. He has done so much for her and he might think her ungrateful. She really felt she could not tolerate being ill this way all her life. She brought out her fear of dying, which she thought might result from the infectious process reaching her heart just as it had affected her fingernails.

At this point the worker was able to accept patient's fears and the fact that it was not easy for her to be ill. It was her thinking too that patient might be helped through a casework relationship to release some tension and thus lessen her rigidity. In talking with the doctor about this, he expressed discouragement that patient was not showing any progress. The infection seemed to be difficult to check. He felt, too, that patient's emotional state was a large factor in her illness and that, unless she were helped to resolve some of her feelings, the medical treatment would be ineffective.[11]

Patient's Choice of Adviser. Allowance must be made, moreover, in the relationships between the physician and the medical social worker as to the ability of the patient to use one more than the other. There are, as we know from experience, some patients who do not care to be asking "life" questions of physicians but prefer someone who does not represent expressed authority to them. They feel that with social workers there is greater opportunity of making up their own minds. On the other hand there are other patients who reject the independence they must assume when in contact with social workers and prefer the discussion of their problems with physicians. That one patient prefers one relationship and another prefers the other does not necessarily reflect adversely on the efficiency or the reputation of either the physician or the social worker. Both should try to realize what is going on and make adjustments correspondingly. Thus in some cases the social worker may expect to be dominant, and, in others, the physician. In still others the patient, the social worker, and the physician will be able to create and maintain mutually cooperative relationships. All three may sit down together to discuss the meaning of an organic sickness for the social living of the patient.

Sometimes, however, such mutual cooperation is not feasible. The following comment is an example:

> This patient seems to have called on the doctor and the social worker for different types of services. The doctor gave her the support she needed by his authoritative attitude. The social worker gave her an opportunity to think through the emotional implications of the operation. The worker felt drawn into a discussion of factual medical matters which she was not entirely equipped to give and which she could not relate specifically to the patient's physical condition. Because of the interview, which fulfilled the patient's desire to talk, however, worker was perhaps able to coordinate for her the different elements in her problem. The setup of the Gynecological Clinic made it impossible for the doctor, the social worker, and the patient to work together as a unit.[12]

United Front. Certainly, teamwork by the social worker and the physician is important if for no other reason than that it enables both

[11]*Ibid.,* pp. 24–25 (with slight modifications).

[12]*Some Aspects of Social Casework in a Medical Setting: A Study in the Field of Medical Social Work,* prepared by Harriett Bartlett for the Committee on Functions of the American Association of Medical Social Workers, Chicago, 1940, p. 36.

to present a united front before the patient. A "united front" here is not meant as a threat to the patient or a conspiracy which operates necessarily behind his back. It means to express the need for concerted opinion. For example, if a physician tells a patient that he no longer can climb stairs and the patient comes to the social worker with the request that the social worker translate such a direction into practical vocational terms, it would be unsatisfactory and possibly even harmful for the patient not to quote the physician exactly, but to say something like this: "The physician tells me that I should not exercise greatly." It is advantageous, therefore, for the social worker to get his information concerning patients from the attending physicians themselves. By having agreed on the essential elements of the case from the medical and social points of view, both the physician and the social worker will be able to serve the patient in a more intelligent manner. This procedure also means that whatever differences of opinion the physician and the social worker might have, should be "ironed out" cooperatively before either seeks to deal conclusively with the patient.

Oftentimes, the medical worker, instead of being the cooperator with the physician and the patient, feels it necessary to help in the adjustment between the two. If the physician uses authority freely so that the patient is puzzled or irritated, the social worker may consider a valuable function to be that of helping the patient to relieve the friction between him and the physician.

Relationships With Others. Although this discussion of the teamwork responsibilities of the medical social worker in a hospital social service department has considered rather simple relationships between physicians, social workers, and patients, it is well to remember that the personal interconnections can be much more complex. If the social worker operates in a clinic within a hospital, for example, he may have to relate himself to more than one physician. He may be the central connecting link between all of the hospital personnel. The main integrative tie, for example, which the patient may have with the hospital, may be the social worker, if the physicians in the clinic are not assigned generally to a given set of patients. While this type of relationship is hard on patients, it is also difficult for workers, because their problems are multiplied.

The relationships of the social worker also may become more complex when outside individuals are involved in patient relationships. Where there is a friend or relative who has an interest in the patient and who may give him advice or make demands upon him, the client's problem is more complex. Where there is need to refer the patient to a home economist to discuss an aspect of the problem in which the social worker and the physician may not be skilled, another element is added. When the patient is given medical advice which involves muscle training, the occupational or physical therapist may be added to the situation. And so on. It is clear that the more persons who are actively concerned with the case, the more difficult and delicate the social relationships of the worker will become. What has been "spelled out" at some length previously regarding the relationships between the social worker and the physician very often holds true for those of the social worker and the other professional persons who make up a hospital staff. A good rule for the medical social worker to remember in this connection is: The more involved the relationships are, the more conscious definition of relationship there should be.

In the Community

The medical social worker not only has responsibility for relationships and processes within the hospital which are important in caring for patients, but he must also be aware of community relationships and processes.

Points of Contact. The social worker in the hospital has many points of contact with the community. Contact may be made with patients initially, through referrals by other community social work agencies. A family casework agency which is treating a husband-wife quarrel, for example, may come upon the fact that a child in the family is in need of medical attention and may make a referral to the social service department of a local hospital in order that the medical problem of the child be evaluated. Such a contact for the social worker in the hospital would mean, if repeated sufficiently, the growth of definite referral arrangements with the referring agency. On the other hand the medical social worker might come upon the case from the opposite point of contact. That is, the child may come to the clinic for medical treatment and reveal upon investigation some relatively long-term family need requiring the attention of a family caseworker. It would be appropriate (in the hypothetical case referred to) for the medical social worker, because the husband-wife quarrel is not intrinsic to the medical situation, to refer the parents of the child to a family casework agency. Perhaps the family, then, might receive joint treatment: the parents from the family agency, and the child from the hospital. In such a situation the need for cooperation between the hospital and the community agency is clear. Just as the physician and the social worker within the hospital should cooperate for the good of the patient, so a hospital social worker and a community social worker need the same type and degree of cooperation.

The "Connell" case, though rather involved, shows how a social service department of a hospital cooperates with a family agency in providing service to a family:

In the referral letter concerning Mrs. Connell sent to the agency, the hospital social service worker stated frankly, "For some time I have been at a loss to know what treatment is indicated." The family had been known to the social service department of the hospital for four years. At the time of the first contact Mrs. Connell had presented much the same picture as at the time of referral to the family agency four years later. She looked emaciated and ill, complained of innumerable aches and pains, could take no responsibility for herself, was fearful for her children, at the same time able to take no responsibility for them, and had been unable to make any satisfactory marital adjustment.

During the four years of contact, the hospital had given Mrs. Connell several complete physical examinations but could find no organic difficulty. All her teeth had been extracted, artificial dentures provided, and high caloric diet prescribed. At different times convalescent care had been provided, visiting housekeeper assistance engaged, the children placed, an increased food allowance from the public department obtained, and Mr. Connell had been away at C.C.C. camp. None of these things had brought about any change in the situation, however. Mrs. Connell had talked of her happiness before marriage when she had no responsibilities and the hospital believed that possibly, if a very simple environment could be provided for Mrs. Connell in which she had no decisions to make and no responsibilities, she might be able to make a fair adjustment. The hospital believed that the necessity of living on an inadequate allowance from the public agency made life too difficult for Mrs. Connell and asked that the family agency supplement this allowance.

The worker from the family agency discussed this case with the hospital worker and questioned what the family agency could offer, since all possible plans had been tried and had failed. Although the supplementary relief might at first appear to relieve some of Mrs. Connell's anxiety, it would not be likely to contribute toward a permanently more satisfactory adjustment and the family agency could not continue it over an indefinite period of time. The family agency worker stated that if, however, Mrs. Connell had a psychiatric examination and the psychiatrist believed that Mrs. Connell could be helped with psychiatric treatment and through relief from the financial strain, the family agency would be willing to give financial assistance for as long as a year. If the psychiatrist's diagnosis were unfavorable, there would remain the possibility of placement of the children, which would leave Mrs. Connell entirely free since she and her husband were separated at that time. This was agreed upon.

The psychiatrist diagnosed Mrs. Connell's condition as "exhaustion neurosis" and believed that she could be helped if treatment were continued over several months with a prolonged overfeeding diet. On the basis of this report the family agency gave supplementary assistance for four months.

When Mrs. Connell then showed no improvement, plans for a conference at the hospital of all persons interested were initiated by the family agency worker. The family agency supervisor and worker utilized their skill and knowledge to help all persons concerned to express their knowledge gained through experience with the case and to correlate these facts and experiences. Through this interchange and use of each other's experience, it was agreed that there was no possibility of helping Mrs. Connell, that the situation was no better since the family agency had been giving assistance. It was decided that the children should be the chief concern of those interested in the family, and that placement of the children would be the best plan since Mrs. Connell herself had on several occasions indicated a desire for that.[13]

Informing the Public. The medical social worker also has the responsibility of informing the social agencies in the community of the services of the hospital. The medical social worker through his contact with patients has an excellent opportunity of educating patients concerning the value of social service work. Through the contacts which the medical worker has with other community agencies, he can also publicize the work of the hospital so that they may better know what services are available.

The methods of informing the general community of the program of the hospital are manifold, and there is no easy means by which the task can be accomplished. The personal and direct contacts which the worker has with agencies pertaining to referrals and joint cases may be a serviceable means. The medical social worker acting as a medical consultant to a social work agency in the community may be another. The giving of informative talks to lay organizations, such as parent-teacher groups, local ministeriums, chambers of commerce, and fraternal associations, may aid the medical social worker in creating a more exact understanding of the hospital for the community. The publication of descriptive materials for the benefit of lay people provides another way of educating the community concerning medical social service. In addi-

[13]"Our Relationship to the Community as Seen Through Referrals," part of a report of a meeting of twelve family caseworkers called together by the Family Welfare Association of America during the winters of 1937 and 1938, the article being written by Lorna Sylvester and Alice Taggart for the committee, *Cooperative Case Work,* Family Welfare Association of America (now Family Service Association of America), New York, 1935–1939, pp. 4–5.

tion, there are other means by which the social worker may relate himself and his department more closely to the needs of the community.

Development of Facilities. The medical social worker, moreover, has a responsibility for the creation and coordination of local health facilities. If there is no public health organization in the community that can do preventive work or adequate home nursing, a challenge to the medical social worker is presented. It is important to the functioning of the social worker that such facilities exist. Therefore, it is part of the activities of the worker to seek the establishment of such resources where they are lacking. (See Figure 24.)

The development of adequate community health facilities in rural areas is especially important. If the worker is situated in a state hospital where patients are accepted from a wide area, even the whole state, the need for extensive community relations, in terms of the area covered by the hospital in its admissions system, is clear. In most states there is striking unevenness in the medical social service resources of the various communities. Particularly in the rural areas there is a decided lack. The medical social worker cannot consider his job as complete if he deals only with individual patients under such conditions; he must assume responsibility for community resources.

Knowledge of Resources Needed. Among the first prerequisites of the medical social worker in his community relations is a knowledge of community resources, in an exact and detailed fashion. Oftentimes, the success or failure of the medical social worker, as with other workers, hinges on his understanding of what can be done for the patient outside of the resources his own agency presents. If the client must change his job because of health and the medical social worker successfully discusses the problem of accepting such a condition with him, the patient will still need a job which will meet his requirements. Where to send him in the community, what agencies are most suited to his needs, how time can be saved for him and for others (such as agency time), what specifically he can do within the terms of his abilities—these are some of the questions that the worker would have to answer in order to function in a significant manner. If the patient is tubercular and needs to be hospitalized for a period, where are the hospitals the patient can use? What charges do they make, if any? If he has a family, how will geographic location complicate or ease his problem? What is the process of making contact with the hospitals? These and other questions are also part of the medical social worker's responsibility. Thus the social worker cannot always dispense with

NEEDED COMMUNITY FACILITIES FOR PUBLIC HEALTH AND MEDICAL CARE

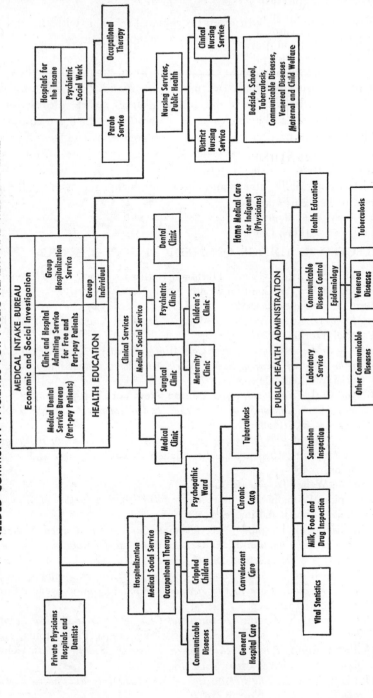

FIG. 24. Needed Facilities for Public Health and Care. (June P. Guild and Arthur A. Guild, *Social Work Engineering*, Harper, New York, 1940.)

patients' problems only through his personal relations with the patient. He must have a keen awareness of community resources.

The medical social worker is also interested in contributing to the prevention of physical sickness and the social maladjustment which derives from such sickness. Because of his strategic position in dealing with developed cases, he is able to bring authoritative information to those individuals and agencies in the community which are concerned with preventive programs. Because of his contact with cases in all degrees of development of personal and social complications, and especially with those which are nascent, the medical social worker is able to detect potentially intense and chronic problems and tries to alleviate them in their early stages.

SELECTED READINGS ON MEDICAL SOCIAL WORK

Backmeyer, Arthur C., and Hartman, Gerhard, editors, *The Hospital in Modern Society,* Commonwealth Fund, New York, 1943.

Bartlett, Harriett M., *Medical Social Work: A Study of Current Aims and Methods in Medical Social Work,* American Association of Medical Social Workers, Chicago, 1934.

———, *Some Aspects of Social Case Work in a Medical Setting: A Study in the Field of Medical Social Work,* American Association of Medical Social Workers, Chicago, 1940.

Binger, Carl, *The Doctor's Job,* Norton, New York, 1945.

Cabot, Richard, *Social Service and the Art of Healing,* Dodd, Mead, New York, revised, 1928.

Cannon, Ida M., *Social Work in Hospitals: A Contribution to Progressive Medicine,* Russell Sage Foundation, New York, new and revised edition, 1930.

Cannon, Walter B., *The Wisdom of the Body,* Norton, New York, 1932.

Champion, William M., editor, *Medical Information for Social Workers,* William Wood, Baltimore, 1938.

Commission on Hospital Care, *Hospital Care in the United States: A Study of the Function of the General Hospital, Its Role in the Care of All Types of Illness, and the Conduct of Activities Related to Patient Service, With Recommendations for Its Extension and Integration for More Adequate Care to the American Public,* Commonwealth Fund, New York, 1947.

Cressman, Edith M., editor, *Functional Case Work in a Medical Setting,* Pennsylvania School of Social Work Publications, Philadelphia, 1944.

Goldman, Franz, *Public Medical Care: Principles and Problems,* Columbia University Press, New York, 1945.

Hinsie, Leland E., *The Person in the Body: An Introduction to Psychosomatic Medicine,* Norton, 1945.

Richardson, Henry B., *Patients Have Families,* Commonwealth Fund, New York, 1945.

Robinson, George C., *The Patient as a Person: A Study of the Social Aspects of Illness,* Commonwealth Fund, New York, 1939.

Shimberg, Myra E., *Health and Employment: A Study of Public Assistance Clients Attending Out-Patient Department Clinics,* National Council on Rehabilitation, New York, 1946.

Sigerist, Henry E., *Medicine and Human Welfare,* The Terry Lectures, Yale University Press, New Haven, 1941.

Thornton, Janet, and Knauth, Marjorie S., *The Social Component in Medical Care: A Study of One Hundred Cases from the Presbyterian Hospital in the City of New York,* Columbia University Press, New York, 1937.

Psychiatric Social Work

Another of the casework specialties is psychiatric social work. Like the others mentioned it does not particularly imply unique methods of treatment; it also involves the utilization of social casework principles. But such social work generally is practiced in psychiatric settings. It is usually defined as that part of social casework which is undertaken in direct responsibility with psychiatry.

TYPES OF CLIENTS AND PROBLEMS

A glimpse into the types of clients and problems that social workers in this specialty may encounter is provided in the following account, *All in the Day's Work of Miss Morton, Psychiatric Social Worker:*[1]

The pages of the letter fluttered and lay still upon the desk, and Miss Morton blessed the slight breeze that saved her office from the oppressive heat. But more essentially she was concerned with glimpses of Agatha's life, brought back to her mind by the letter: Agatha's miserable, deprived childhood, with an early strong desire to make a better life for herself; her long struggle with strenuous, underpaid jobs; her early and unfortunate marriage to a man who drank and was cruel to her; her struggle to support him and the two children who arrived soon after the marriage; and her final realization that another child was on the way. It was then that the crisis had come. For Agatha had grown used to her tragic struggle, but something inside her rebelled at bringing another child to the miserable home. And yet she saw no way out. Her confusion and distress

[1]Mary-Ellen Woodcock, *All in the Day's Work of Miss Morton, Psychiatric Social Worker,* American Association of Psychiatric Social Workers, New York, 1943. The account provided by Mrs. Woodcock has been slightly abbreviated here.

resulted, then, in an illness which showed itself in the form of increasing periods of complete loss of memory when Agatha would wander about the city, dazed and lost. And so she had finally been taken to the hospital where Miss Morton first met her.

While awaiting the arrival of her child she had tried, with the help of the doctors, to sort out the feelings and ideas she had kept to herself for so many years. And after the baby came, and she had seen her three children well cared for in foster homes, Agatha tried to make a new life for herself, alone.

But the old wounds were not yet healed. Without the understanding and security of the hospital to protect her, Agatha soon sensed the approaching return of the old confusion. Worried, and wanting to avoid another breakdown, she had come back to Miss Morton and the doctor for advice, and had taken it. And now came this letter written from a State Hospital:

"Dear Miss Morton:

"Perhaps you wondered what has become of me since I last saw you at the City Hospital. I was glad to leave there. It was so crowded and the doctors were so busy. Now, as you see, I am in the State Hospital. I came because you and Dr. Saunders advised it, but now I know it was the best thing to do. I have a nice doctor here, a woman, and she has time to talk things over. I know it may take a long time, because I am understanding things only slowly. But my doctor does help, and the life here keeps me occupied. We have school and handcraft in the morning, and I have a job in the sewing room afternoons. Now I have 'privileges.' That means I can walk around the grounds when I have free time. There is lots of grass and trees here. And we have movies and dances each once a week.

"I guess that's about all. But I wanted you to know I am all right. And if my husband should ask you, don't tell him anything about me.

> "Your friend,
>> "Agatha Howe."

No, Miss Morton thought, I don't imagine Mr. Howe will turn up. And some day, if she keeps on trying as she is, Agatha will get over her desperate fear of him.

*   *   *

A knock on her door, and Miss Morton glanced at her calendar—Mrs. Vorse, and on the dot, as usual.

The short, stocky woman who entered, plumped herself down, and burst into a torrent of words.

"Here I am again. And did I have a time getting here! I wanted you to see this new dress I made. But when I was trying to press it Paul and his father began arguing. So of course I had to put in my two cents' worth. And Jimmie was yelling, 'Can't we ever have peace in this house?' And my husband told him if he didn't like it he could get out. And I said it was his home, he should stay in it. And my husband hollered that it was no home, with me gadding about, and who was I out with yesterday? I was only trying to save him money by looking for bargains. You know no one can make a dollar go further than I can, but he never appreciates it. And Miss Morton, won't you talk to him and make him see things my way?"

Miss Morton laughed, "You all had a good time, didn't you?"

Mrs. Vorse looked startled, and then burst into jolly laughter.

"I guess you're right. We wouldn't fight if we didn't enjoy a good row. You've told me that, but I forget!" Quickly serious, she added: "But what I want to say is, Paul is going to give up his job and then what? He'll sit around the house and the next thing we know he'll be sick again!"

"Did he say he was going to sit around?"

"No . . . He said he was going to get a better job. But will he? Look at his father, with two trades, and he was out of work, years."

Miss Morton smiled again, for the last year had taught her that kidding was often more effective with Mrs. Vorse than earnest discussion. Even remarks that might seem caustic to another person Mrs. Vorse took in good part. Perhaps, Miss Morton thought, it was because she and Mrs. Vorse sincerely liked one another. So she smiled and remarked:

"You know perfectly well that Paul and his father are two different persons."

"That's right. But you always have to remind me. And next you'll say, 'Quit bossing.' But I have quit!" Mrs. Vorse nodded proudly. "I really am afraid to have Paul leave his job. But you know what I told him? I said, 'Paul, it's your life. Do what you want!' But does he? No! Always he asks my advice about everything."

"And does he take your advice?"

Another chuckle from Mrs. Vorse. "No. If I tell him what I think he argues. And if I say, 'Make up your own mind,' still he argues."

"This arguing, does that look as though he were going to be sick?"

"Of course not. When he was sick he just sat. He never did anything. Oh, I see what you mean. The arguing is a good sign, and so is his trying to get a better job. It means he's growing up to have a mind of his own."

"Yes, you knew it all the time. It's just that it's hard to give up the old habits, isn't it?" This time Miss Morton was gentle, for she appreciated the sincerity of Mrs. Vorse's efforts to change, and she knew the struggle was not over yet.

"You mean being bossy. And what else could I do with three wishy-washy men! But Paul, since he came home, he stands up for himself, and I do try to let him. I guess it was a good day for Paul when he entered this hospital. If you people would just do something about Jimmie and Dad . . ."

"Now, now, one thing at a time. It's Paul we're here to talk about. You do deserve credit for keeping your fears about him to yourself. What do you think now about his quitting?"

An inward struggle was evidenced by Mrs. Vorse's frown and the twisting of her handkerchief. But it resolved itself suddenly, and she beamed again.

"I see! I know! He found this job alone, and the last one, too. And this is better. You mean maybe he'll do better and better each time he gets a new one?"

"Good for you! You're learning. And remember that he is young and healthy, he's had his education, thanks to you, and jobs aren't so scarce now as they used to be. So he's not in the spot his father was. Let's go on hoping, shall we?"

Mrs. Vorse bobbed up. "Yes, and taking things easy—maybe!"

* * *

Miss Morton was sure the address was correct. She had not been there for six months, but often before that. Now the Kellys' name was nowhere to be found, and her letter to them was still lying in the outer hall. Perhaps the superintendent could help.

"Two blocks down, the building on the northeast corner," was his reply.

There she found Mrs. Kelly in the midst of unpacking, but cordial nevertheless.

"I thought you'd be around soon," Mrs. Kelly remarked, clearing off a seat and producing cigarettes. "And I'm glad of an excuse to rest. I've been at this moving for three days. With this terrible heat I wonder I've been able to handle it. But Bob is a great help. And it's such a relief to have a bedroom for the children . . ."

As the casual conversation went on, Miss Morton made a series of mental comments. She and the doctor had been pretty sure that this family would be all right once Mr. Kelly got back to work, and Mrs. Kelly recovered from the shock that his severe mental illness had given her. As she heard Mrs. Kelly telling about their summer at the beach, about Diane's long siege of whooping cough, and about the baby's remarkable development, Miss Morton felt pleased that the hospital had been of service. It looked as though she and the doctor had been on the right track; the Kelly family was back to normal. For Mrs. Kelly was concerned with the minutiae of everyday life and no longer harassed by vague doubts and fears. And she looks so different, Miss Morton thought, remembering the pale lassitude characteristic of Mrs. Kelly the year before. So she risked a question she might otherwise have omitted.

"And your spells of trembling, have they disappeared?"

Mrs. Kelly frowned a moment. "I don't remember . . . Oh, yes; the last one was after Bob was laid up with a bad sore throat and couldn't even eat. You know he was sick like that before he broke down. And so I was afraid this time. I guess those spells may come back again whenever I am really worried."

Miss Morton nodded and said nothing further, but again she was pleased, for this was the first time Mrs. Kelly had spoken of a connection between worry and spells of trembling. Perhaps her recognition of this relationship, at last, accounted for her matter-of-fact attitude now.

Then Miss Morton's full attention was again captured by what Mrs. Kelly was saying.

"Bob wanted me to tell you that he is just fine. But he'd be glad to come to see the doctor whenever you wish. We know you want to check up every so often, because of those special treatments he had. And we want to help in the hospital research if we can."

Miss Morton mentally reviewed her "Outline for Follow-up Visits," then said:

"Yes, of course, the research is part of the reason I'm here now. Dr. Saunders wants to see Mr. Kelly in about three months. In the meantime, I have a few questions to ask . . ."

* * *

As they left the drug store where they had been talking for the last hour, Miss Morton turned to Mrs. Stewart.

"Would you like to have me go to the Family Society with you?"

Mrs. Stewart nodded vigorously, but there was distress in her halting reply, "If you have the time—I am ashamed to do it—and I am afraid I may lose my way."

"But you want to go today, while your mind is made up?"

This time Mrs. Stewart could only nod. But her determined expression made it clear that she would go ahead with her application for financial help, no matter how much it distressed her.

Mrs. Stewart hesitated briefly before entering the remodeled brown stone house, which had a modest sign in the window, "Family Society." But when they were ushered into a sunny reception room she looked around curiously. The simple furniture, bright cretonne curtains, and piles of magazines on the table made it look like any other reception room.

Miss Morton already knew Mrs. Ardsley, the District Supervisor, and talked with her alone, first.

"Ordinarily I would have suggested that Mrs. Stewart come alone. But she has not quite recovered yet. It is hard for her to keep to the point when she is talking, and sometimes she gets really confused. So I thought it might be easier all around if I were to tell you first what the family is facing . . ."

Mrs. Ardsley reached for her pencil and made rapid notes as Miss Morton told of the Stewarts' series of misfortunes. While Mr. Stewart was ill with arthritis, the mortgage on the house was foreclosed. Then Mrs. Stewart's mental illness developed and she was in and out of hospitals for almost two years. In the meantime the family had broken up, different members going to live with various relatives. Now Mr. Stewart was well enough to work, but so far had been unable to find a position. Roy, the eighteen-year-old son, did not earn enough to cover all the family expenses, and relatives had helped as much as they could. If Mrs. Stewart was to continue improving, she needed to be relieved from worry as much as possible. As long as the family was broken up she was constantly anxious about the children. Roy could only manage to visit her occasionally, and Mrs. Stewart was quite upset about the constant complaints of Beatrice, the sixteen-year-old daughter. Beatrice said she was "getting sick and tired of being grateful to relatives who did nothing but boss," and to get away from what she considered "no kind of a life" she was beginning to stay out late nights with an older group of friends whom her mother didn't know. Mrs. Stewart's great desire was to get the family together again.

"And you think some of these problems may straighten out if the family could have their own apartment?" Mrs. Ardsley asked.

"I am sure that Beatrice and Roy would both be happier and behave better. This in itself would be a relief to Mrs. Stewart. Then she would be able to handle other problems better. She has always been the leader of the family and the others are used to depending upon her. Mr. Stewart, for instance, needs her help. He is worried about his difficulty in finding work. Once they have a home again Mrs. Stewart can be a help to him as she was before her illness.

Mrs. Ardsley nodded. "I have known other families like that. We shall have to talk things over pretty thoroughly with both the Stewarts. But I see no reason why, together with them, we can't work out some solution."

Back in the reception room, Mrs. Stewart was sitting on the edge of her chair, clasping her handbag tightly. She looked up expectantly when they came in.

"This is Mrs. Ardsley," Miss Morton said. "I have told her something of what you are up against, but she wants you to tell her more. So I'll say good-bye now. Be sure to let me know how things go with you."

As she left the building, Miss Morton glanced at her watch. Three-thirty already! That meant she would have to hurry if she was to be back at the hospital in time for her next appointment.

* * *

She needn't have rushed so, Miss Morton thought. She might have known Mrs. Thompson would be late! But it gave her time to freshen up after the long hot subway ride, and for that she was thankful.

Back at her desk, she looked over some papers that had arrived during her absence. Well, she thought, it's doubly lucky Mrs. Thompson is late. For among the papers were Dr. Saunders' notes on his recent talk with Mrs. Thompson's daughter, Barbara.

Yes, Dr. Saunders thought that there were some definite signs of progress. This was good news, for it seemed a shame that a youngster like that should be in such trouble. Mrs. Thompson had brought Barbara to the Clinic a few weeks previously, after the school had complained that Barbara was taking money from other girls' pocketbooks. Sturdy and tall,

Barbara might be taken for eighteen instead of fourteen, Miss Morton thought, were it not for the slight awkwardness of the adolescent who has recently grown too fast. In Barbara's regular features and curly blonde hair were indications of the beauty she might show as a woman. And despite her newly acquired bulk, Barbara had managed to keep up and even improve her skill in skating, swimming, and ballet dancing. She was always the star performer in the school water pageant, even designing and making the costumes. Her dancing had resulted in a scholarship with an outstanding teacher who was already talking of a stage debut. In appearance, Barbara seemed much like her contemporaries, more intelligent and talented than some, but mostly just an awkward schoolgirl, clad in sweater and skirt, ankle socks and sport shoes.

But Barbara was growing up in a hard school, as Miss Morton knew only too well. For Barbara had to contend with other things beyond the common confusions of adolescence. In addition to becoming accustomed to her own rapid development towards womanhood, and her discovery that the world was more complicated than she had thought as a child, she had to struggle, too, with poverty, the lack of a father, and the complications of living with her mother in the home of friends. She had not only to find out for herself what was "right" and "wrong," but also had to figure out for herself what her own stand was on the difference between her mother's ideas and the views of the rest of the household.

Miss Morton thought of her own concern after her last talk with Mrs. Thompson. Barbara's mother was an attractive, well-dressed woman, appearing younger than her forty-odd years. But underneath this external appearance of youth, Miss Morton could sense that this was a woman who had accepted and clung to many rigidly conventional ideas and moral yardsticks. She was the kind of person who would think, even if she didn't say it, that the latest generation was "about to go to the dogs." Could Miss Morton help Mrs. Thompson to forget the "sinfulness" of Barbara's "stealing" long enough to think of Barbara as a person, instead of as a "criminal"? I can only try, Miss Morton thought, and there is always the chance that as Barbara improves in her behavior, it will be easier for Mrs. Thompson to look at things in a different light. If I can help her get over her fear that Barbara is going to do something "much worse," that will be a big step, for people who are afraid have difficulty in thinking clearly.

Still, it was good to see that Dr. Saunders' notes again indicated hopes for Barbara. In their last talk the girl was frank and sincere in her attempts to understand the confusion which had led to her "stealing." She had the advantage of the elasticity of youth, and she responded eagerly to Dr. Saunders' efforts to help her develop a "grown-up" attitude of her own. And that meant having ideas which were truly her own and for which she would be responsible, even though some of them might be different from her mother's. For one thing was very clear to the doctor. That was that Barbara's "stealing" was, in part at least, a rebellion against

Mrs. Thompson's strict, puritanical attitude, which allowed for very little fun in life.

The door opened, and Miss Morton came quickly back to the present. "Hello, Mrs. Thompson; I was just thinking about you. I hope you feel as cool as you look! How have things been going with you?"

The day's experience of "Miss Morton," of course, merely illustrates the task of a psychiatric social worker in a particular agency, in this case a clinic attached to a hospital. There are other settings where psychiatric social work is practiced, and, even in a given setting, the responsibilities of the psychiatric social worker may vary. This excerpt does inform us, however, regarding some of the problems to be met.

SOCIAL TREATMENT OF MENTAL AND EMOTIONAL PROBLEMS

As much as we may talk about the freedom of the individual to do as he pleases, we are constantly reminded, nevertheless, of the rigorous restrictions which society places upon everyone's conduct. Often we do not even wish to undertake certain actions because we know that disapproving social pressures will preclude our enjoyment of them. When at times we are deviant in our behavior, it may be at terrific cost. That is, being variantly minded, we may be in opposition to restraints from within us and without. Consider a simple example: A young man no longer believes that it is wise to wear neckties. He abandons the practice altogether. He sees no sense in it. But can his decision be put into practice without the sacrifice of certain values which he cherishes, some perhaps more than his distaste for tie-wearing? Probably not. He must be prepared to withstand the rebuffs and comments of friends who "rib" him about his dress. He must foresee what attitude his girl-friend will take when he shows up for a date without his tie. Also, and not the least important, he must account for his feelings, perhaps even guilt, in questioning and in breaking with the accepted folkways of his society. Thus it is not easy for anyone to deviate too much from the accepted social values without receiving some form of punishment. The punishment will in part be from the "outside" and in part from conscience.

So it is with the much more serious problem of those who diverge in their essential conduct from the standards in our society which are considered necessary and normal. The truth of the adage that "no man lives unto himself" is no more striking than in its application to mental and emotional abnormalities. No one can live a solitary life so far as mentally abnormal conduct is concerned. He must face, if not the very strong restraints of conscience, the very strong pressures of a culture which insists upon a relatively high degree of uniformity in behavior. The person who is not "normal" in our society immediately and persistently feels the impact of social control.

Today, it is increasingly recognized by both professional and lay people that a large proportion of the population suffers from mental and emotional problems of some kind or degree. These range from disturbances created by current crises to severe illnesses which require the person's hospitalization. While at the present time many psychiatric social workers work with hospitalized persons, probably as many or even more find their responsibilities to lie with individuals whose conflicts prevent them from functioning effectively in the community but nevertheless permit them to remain outside of a hospital.

Early Methods of Treating the Mentally Abnormal

Formerly, interest was focused almost exclusively on the extreme expressions of mental disturbances, known as *psychoses*. People who suffered from these maladies were looked upon and treated in various ways. The early means of controlling the deviant behavior of the mentally ill were primarily repressive. They assumed that the mentally sick person was a malicious individual who needed to be coerced into normality by a culture striving for consistency. There are instances in medieval Europe and in early American history where mentally ill persons were actually beaten in order that their demons might be punished and "cast out." As in the cases of the New England witch hunts, some of the mentally abnormal even suffered the death penalty. (See Figure 25.)

The mentally ill in the early American period also were regulated by the isolation method. Under this form of "treatment" the community segregated an abnormal individual so that he would not present a community problem. The case of Jan Vorelissen, as seen in the Upland Court Records of 1676, illustrates this procedure. Jan, according to the Court, was "bereft of his natural senses and is turned quite mad." Because with his madness he was unable to support himself (there is no family mentioned), it was ordered that a "little block house" be built for him "for to put in the said madman."

Another method of supervising the mentally abnormal in the early American period was through a form of the indenture system. In some localities the insane person was given into the charge of someone who: either accepted a single sum of money for the responsibility; operated under an arrangement whereby the unbalanced person paid for his upkeep with work; or received from the government continuous financial support for the individual, giving him care as a kind of foster parent.

A MENTALLY ILL PERSON IS NO CRIMINAL
BUT THIS IS THE WAY HE IS TREATED

FIG. 25. Methods of Treatment of Mentally Ill Persons

(Graphic Associates for *Toward Mental Health*, by George Thorman, Public Affairs Pamphlet No. 120, published by Public Affairs Committee, Inc., New York, 1946.)

At best, however, the indenture means of care was loosely organized and led to many injustices.

Institutional Care

These early means of caring for the abnormal were superseded by institutional treatment. In some places the insane were placed in the general community poorhouse along with dependent children, delinquents, prostitutes, and the aged. Elsewhere, institutions were specialized for separate categories of need. In such places the care of the mentally sick tended to be more responsible, although it was in actuality simply another means of isolating the individual who was not conforming to community standards of normality. These establishments were a far cry from the modern mental institutions.

The results of these methods of managing the mentally ill proved their inadequacy. But, in time, new ideas and fresh approaches were formulated to meet the problem. Attention was given to the possibility of a more scientific understanding of mental abnormality. Leaders in the care of the insane began to be concerned with ways in which the living conditions within mental institutions could be improved. Also interest rose in whether mental sufferers could be cured or at least their plight alleviated. Thus as early as 1824 the first hospital designed exclusively for the use of mental patients was founded in Lexington, Kentucky. It and the hospitals which were to follow are significant because they show the advancing interest and knowledge in the problem of the mentally disordered.

Outstanding Social Reformers

Near the middle of the nineteenth century, Dorothea Dix, a remarkable advocate of social reform, appeared upon the American scene. She, among other things, waved the banner of pitiless publicity so that all could see what horrors existed in the care of the mentally ill. So great at that time were the cruelty and stupidity involved that Miss Dix could write to the Legislature of Massachusetts: "I proceed, Gentlemen, briefly, to call your attention to the state of insane persons confined within the Commonwealth, in cages, closets, cellars, stalls, pens: Chained, naked, beaten with rods, and lashed into obedience." Such indeed were the conditions about a century ago in one of the most "advanced" of our states. But, despite these practices, there were also gains. The formation of the Association of Medical Superintendents of American Institutions (now known as the American Psychiatric Association) in Philadelphia in 1844 was another landmark in the development of a sane treatment of mental patients.

Psychiatry, moreover, then and later was searching for the best possible methods. At the turn of the last century it achieved significant insights into the problems of mental illness. While there was a host of contributors, certainly no one was more important than Sigmund Freud. It was he who not only formulated for the first time the dynamics of personality structure and functioning but also developed a psychotherapeutic method for the treatment of emotional conflicts. The psychobiological theory of Dr. Adolf Meyer also helped to usher in the modern psychiatric period of scientific understanding.

Clifford Beers, another psychiatric pioneer, through his own mental breakdown and later recovery saw the need for a preventive movement and helped organize with enthusiasm and skill the National Committee for Mental Hygiene. This association has played a large role in stimulating an intelligent public interest in mental problems, their causes and prevention.

It was out of this background that psychiatric social work had its origin. From its early interest in the understanding and treatment of the mental and emotional problems of psychotics, psychiatric social work has broadened its concern to include the understanding of normal behavior. Much of its practice and its success in the recent decades is due to the services it has developed for normal persons who suffer from emotional upsets.

HISTORICAL DEVELOPMENT OF PSYCHIATRIC SOCIAL WORK

Social Origin of Mental Disorders

The development of psychiatric social work has been largely dependent upon the rise of social psychiatry in this country, especially that type represented by such leaders as Dr. Adolf Meyer, Dr. E. E. Southard, and Dr. William A. White. The views of these men stressed the social origin of a large number of cases of mental disorder. It was admitted, as it had been stressed too exclusively in the prior period, that some mental problems have their origins in biological conditions which are relatively unaffected by social factors and need medical rather than psychological or social treatment. But it was also emphasized by this early group of psychiatrists that many cases of mental instability were basically social in their causation and accordingly needed social treatment. Even assuming a highly individualized interpretation of mental disorder, they argued, it was not possible to think of treatment as being solely individual. The patient may suffer from a condition which can be treated partially in terms of his individualization, but no problem can ever be wholly so treated. For the patient, no matter what cure may directly affect him, also lives in a social environment which creates its pressures and makes its demands. In other words the patient may be treated successfully on an individual basis, but still may need counsel and direction as to how he may work out an adjustment with his family, with his neighbors, at work, and in other life situations. This kind of social interpretation of the nature of treatment provided the groundwork on which psychiatric social work could build.

It was further suggested that not all cases could be treated by directly influencing the patient. Sometimes a high degree of social manipulation was required. The problem of a patient, for example, may ultimately lodge not so much with his own private concerns as it may with the familial situation in which he finds himself. Or there may be other social factors which are actively involved. At any rate Dr. Meyer and his associates saw mental disease not as something which affects simply a part of the individual patient but his whole personality, and this personality in its social context. Thus the psychiatrist was called upon to understand more than the anatomy of the brain in order to diagnose and treat a mental disorder successfully; he had to know all that went into the organization of the personality of the patient, from within and without. He had to use social information in every step of the psychiatric process.

Need for Detailed Records

Another contribution of this school of psychiatrists which was important was that of record-taking. At the time of Meyer, mental patients were given hasty diagnoses which consisted for the most part of someone's guess as to the central psychological manifestation of the patient. At one time this designation might be correct, and at other times it might be wrong, but certainly by any modern standard it was sadly inadequate. Diagnosis served as little more than a label. It did not relate the individual to his past and to the real relationships which he had with the community of which he was a part. Meyer believed that classification systems were woefully lacking and sought to encourage the securing of case records of a fairly detailed character. Social caseworkers could develop these records.

These developments (and others) within the field of psychiatry were significant for the origin of psychiatric social work because they early defined the function of the psychiatric social worker. In the first place the psychiatrist had to understand the kinds of social information which Meyer's views implied or find someone else who did. Because of the division of labor and the crying need for psychiatrists, among other reasons, it was natural that there should arise a special group of workers who assisted the psychiatrists in appreciating the social evidence of mental cases. If the psychiatrists were most proficient in the psychiatric aspects of mental disease, then the psychiatric social workers were most capable in regard to its social causes and implications.

Just as psychiatric social workers were called upon to make the diagnostic work of psychiatrists more meaningful, so they were needed to participate in the treatment. The same skill used in gathering and understanding the social experience of a patient was also important to the adjustment of the patient beyond the hospital or clinic to his home and community. Thus psychiatric social workers were needed both for analysis and therapy.

Rise of Mental Hygiene Movement

But aside from the need for psychiatric social workers on the part of psychiatrists, social workers generally were interested in the problems of people suffering from mental disorders. As early as 1874 a paper was read at the National Conference of Social Work, with the title "The Duty of the States Toward Their Insane Poor." Soon afterwards, a section of the Conference was formed on insanity and feeble-mindedness to give expression to the rising interest of social workers. This section became in time the present-day Mental Hygiene Section of the National Conference.

The rise of the mental hygiene movement also became an important rallying point for social workers interested in the mental aspects of clients' problems. The mental hygiene movement, in part a monument to the work of Clifford Beers, has had two main purposes. First, it has sought to prevent mental diseases. This has led it into various educational channels involving a wide number of lay and professional people. Secondly, it has attempted to provide people with a general understanding of their behavior for these reasons: such knowledge will tend to increase personal satisfactions; it will enable individuals to accept the world of reality instead of escaping into fantasies; and it will help them realize and live with the various factors which make them distinctive and dynamic personalities. This goal also involves educational procedures of great variety. Both aims reflect the basic desire of the leaders of the movement: "the conservation of mental health."

From this description of the mental hygiene movement's chief aims it can be realized how closely it paralleled the efforts of social workers in certain aspects. Social workers found in the movement an organized effort to achieve many of their own aims. From the movement they learned, according to its stress, the vital significance of mental health.

Aftercare Development

The interest of social workers in the rising importance of psychiatry was further stimulated by their contacts with discharged patients of mental hospitals and institutions. This concrete relationship with the workings of mental disease gave the social workers an appreciation of the special understanding and techniques necessary in work of this sort.

In New York. A specific illustration of the experience of the State Charities Aid Association in New York shows the development of such interest on the part of social workers. In 1906, as a result of a study made on the subject, an "aftercare agent" was appointed by the Association to handle those cases in which some treatment was needed in the home circumstances of patients who no longer needed to be hospitalized or institutionalized. It was the work of this "agent" to ease the adjustment problem of the discharged patient as he sought to reestablish normal personal and community relationships. Half a decade later, on the basis of the experience of the State Charities Aid Association, a worker was provided, out of public funds, to perform a similar function under the State Commission on Lunacy at the Manhattan State Hospital. In 1912 an outpatient department was established at the Long Island State Hospital. Similarly, a clinic, created for mentally ill persons, was established in cooperation with the Manhattan and the Central Islip State Hospitals. In the years immediately following, numerous psychiatric arrangements were made through the cooperation of social workers and psychiatrists, to care chiefly for the social and psychological aspects of psychiatrically disturbed people.

In Massachusetts. Elsewhere than in New York the interest of social workers originated other psychiatric social service facilities. In Massachusetts, beginning in 1913, there was definite concern in formalizing, through the creation of outpatient departments of mental hospitals and institutions, the attention which social workers had been giving informally to discharged mental patients. Also in Massachusetts, as early as 1918, a Division of Social Service was inaugurated which had as its responsibility the planning and coordinating of the various social service activities of the state mental hospitals. This was the first example of coordination in psychiatric social work on a state level.

In General Hospitals. Even general hospitals with psychiatric clinics began to see the need for social work. Bellevue Hospital in New York City, the Cornell Clinic in the same city, and the Massachusetts General Hospital provide excellent illustrations of this movement. In these situations it was readily realized that clinics dealing with mental patients on a less permanent and intense basis than the state hospitals and institutions nevertheless had need for extended social service work. The desire for concrete data regarding the life of the patient was felt no less in the clinic of the general hospital than in the state mental hospital. In fact, general hospital patients needed special instruments of social adjustment even more than state hospital patients, for in the general hospital clinic much of the treatment process had to rely on community forces, while in the state hospitals much more direct therapy could be employed. This means, in other words, that the social worker in the general hospital actually was related more responsibly to treatment than in the state hospital.

Perhaps a large share of the current cooperative treatment practices used by psychiatric social workers and psychiatrists can be traced to their activity in the early general hospitals. Moreover, through the activities of the psychiatric social worker in the general hospital, the social service agencies of the community were reminded rather vividly of the reality and promise of social work as applied to psychiatric cases.

Beginnings of Professional Training

The formulation of psychiatric social work as a definite part of social work was also aided to a noticeable degree by the experiences of the Boston Psychopathic Hospital. From the very beginning of the hospital there was some provision made for such work. A year after the hospital was established under the leadership of Dr. E. E. Southard (1912), Miss Mary C. Jarrett became the head of its social service department. The psychiatric social work of this hospital has been ably described in *The Kingdom of Evils* written by Dr. Southard and Miss Jarrett (1922). This book became one of the first detailed and reliable accounts in the newborn field of psychiatric social work. While the authors made no claim to the use of revolutionary materials in their conception of this work, they did provide a guide for the types of activities which prevailed at the Boston Psychopathic Hospital. In general, the writers saw four kinds of such activity within their hospital: (1) casework service, (2) executive duties, (3) social research, and (4) public education. While they conceived these four divisions, they believed, and it is now accepted generally, that the major energies of the worker should be utilized in the first, that is, in the casework process. The other functions have today mostly fallen to specialists in other areas of social work.

As a means of increasing the number of workers who would be proficient in psychiatric social work, Dr. Southard and Miss Jarrett, at the Boston Psychopathic Hospital, arranged for a number of students to take their social work training in the social service department of the hospital. It was principally through this educational device that the first genuine beginnings of professional training originated. At first the training was related to the professional social work program of the Simmons College School of Social Work. Four years later, in 1918, under the impact of the war-created needs in the psychiatric field, the Smith College School for Social Work was founded to meet the demand for personnel which the new knowledge about mental problems had created. Cooperating in this venture was the National Committee for Mental Hygiene. What began as an eight-month experimental Training School for Psychiatric Social Work under the direction of Miss Jarrett and the joint sponsorship of Smith College, the National Committee, and the Boston Psychopathic Hospital, became in time one of the outstanding schools for the training of social workers.

Treatment of So-Called Normal People

Aside from the growing need for psychiatric social workers in hospitals, social workers, generally, had for a long time been interested in psychiatry because of their constant relationships with so-called normal people in their daily work. These persons often came for many kinds of services other than help with their mental and emotional difficulties, but there were many individuals in whom the social workers detected some kinds of conflict, disorganization, and inability to handle themselves in their life situation. These persons were not so disabled mentally and emotionally that they needed to be placed in a mental hospital. Often they did not require extensive treatment of their psychiatric problems. They were able, by and large, to manage their own affairs in the community, to take part normally in family life, in work, in recreation, and elsewhere. Yet many of them suffered from such emotional disturbances as excessive moroseness, excitability, guiltiness, or some other undesirable personality characteristic. These people, coming as they did in large numbers to social workers either directly or indirectly in connection with such problems, stimulated a wider interest in psychiatry among social workers generally. The mental hospitals taught social workers considerable about the contributions of psychiatry, but the clients that social workers met from day to day certainly taught them as much.

Thus family casework, child welfare work—in fact, all of the specialties of social work—became psychiatrically oriented. Social workers, generally, were seeking to understand why and how the people they dealt with behaved as they did—why it was, for example, that an individual who could see the rationality of a certain way of behavior could not seem to carry through on it. The older, nonpsychiatric theories regarding human motivation and conduct were not able to satisfy the most inquiring minds among the social workers. It was logical, therefore, for them to turn to psychiatry to learn its contributions to a fuller and more profound understanding of human nature and conduct.

Formation of Professional Organization

At any rate, by the second decade of the present century psychiatric social work had been established on a rather firm footing. In 1920 a group of psychiatric social workers met at the Psychopathic Hospital in Boston to discuss the possible formation of a professional body to serve their interests. The fact that the group felt initially that the time might be ripe for establishing a professional organization attests to the intensity of sentiment for psychiatric social work which must have been present in that section of the country and possibly in others. But, after due consideration, the group felt it would be unwise to set up such a body and they relinquished their idea of a formal organization. They did form, however, a Psychiatric Social Workers Club which had as its purpose "to maintain the standard of psychiatric social work throughout the country." Because the American Association of Hospital Social Workers (composed of those social workers employed in hospitals usually not concerned with mental patients) was already in existence, the Psychiatric Social Workers Club decided that it would be suitable to petition that organization for affiliation.

In 1922 the Club became the Section on Psychiatric Social Work of the American Association of Hospital Social Workers. Under the leadership of this Association, psychiatric social work was encouraged and became an active specialty in the field of social work. But because the alliance seemed to imply too exclusive a relationship with one social work service, namely, medical social work, interested psychiatric workers separated from the hospital Association and formed in 1926 the American Association of Psychiatric Social Workers. This organization has been active to the present time in increasing the usefulness of psychiatric social work. In 1947 there were about 850 members.

Definition of Psychiatric Social Worker. In recent years there has been some confusion regarding the exact meaning which *psychiatric social worker* should have. At the present time the psychiatric social worker can be said to be a social worker who deals with mental and emotional problems on the part of clients, either in conjunction with a psychiatrist or with a psychiatrist taking major supervisory responsibility for the cases. This does not deny, however, the values and application of psychiatry in the other divisions of social work.

Developments During Two World Wars

The two World Wars contributed directly to the development of psychiatric social work. In fact there is an impression even among some social workers that the rise of psychiatric social work was the result merely of the needs arising out of the First World War. This is not so. There can be no doubt that the war accented the acuteness of need in the psychiatric field and provided fresh and frequent cases for consideration, but the psychiatric social work movement, like the psychiatric movement itself, was on firm ground even before the inception of the war, as this chapter thus far suggests. The First World War did, however, create a number of benefits for the rising field of psychiatric social work. It stimulated the development of training facilities and defined the scope and function of the psychiatric social worker. It also brought the subject of mental illness to the attention of the general civilian population.

The Second World War, with its increased stress upon the importance of psychiatric treatment, greatly strengthened the possibilities of psychiatric social work by opening for it new and increased responsibilities. The recognition of the personnel category S.S.N. 263 by the armed forces, creating military psychiatric social workers, and the establishment of the classification M.O.S. 3605, giving officer status to those who could qualify for military psychiatric social work, gave positive

IN HEAVY COMBAT 1 OUT OF EVERY 4 SUFFERED FROM NEUROSIS

Fig. 26. Neurosis Caused by Heavy Combat

(Graphic Associates for *Toward Mental Health,* by George Thorman, Public Affairs Pamphlet No. 120, published by Public Affairs Committee, Inc., New York, 1946.)

and new prestige to psychiatric social work. Following the Second World War additional civilian interest has been shown on the part of informed citizens. The employment of psychiatric social workers in the Veterans Administration under Public Law 390 also is doing much to strengthen the field. (See Figure 26.)

National Mental Health Act

The National Mental Health Act, passed by Congress in June, 1946, indicated a growing concern upon the part of many persons and organizations aside from the federal government for the mental well-being of the citizenry. By the Act, $7,500,000 was authorized for the construction and equipment of hospital and laboratory buildings for a National Mental Health Institute. This Institute is under the direction of the United States Public Health Service. It concentrates on mental disease research and the training of psychiatric personnel. An additional $10,000,000 has also been authorized for federal grants-in-aid to governmental and voluntary organizations undertaking the same types of activities as the Institute.

PLACES OF PRACTICE

When the question is asked, "Where is psychiatric social work practiced?" the answer must in part involve what the inquirer means by psychiatric social work. If one accepts the definition previously offered, to the effect that it is social work practiced in conjunction with psychiatric supervision, then the question almost answers itself. But, as was also inferred, the contributions of psychiatry to social work go beyond those found in psychiatric social work. To the extent to which all social workers are oriented to a scientific understanding of the forces in human behavior, there is a connection between all the specialties of social work practice and psychiatry. But, specifically, psychiatric social workers are employed in hospitals and clinics, and also in public health nursing agencies and in educational institutions.

Hospitals

As has been explained above, the psychiatric social work movement has always had close association with hospitals. In the light of what is now known regarding psychosomatic disorders—the sometimes subtle and complex interconnections between illnesses of the body and conditions of the mind—this association certainly has been fortunate. Medicine and social work are now cooperating on the study and treatment of psychosomatic cases.

In the case of mental hospitals, the need for social workers is quite obvious. Historically, the program of the Veterans Administration of the federal government, in the wake of the First World War, contributed to the increasing awareness of the possibilities of psychiatric social work care in veterans' hospitals for the mentally ill. Moreover, in the past, some state hospitals for the mentally ill took the lead in providing psychiatric social work for patients. Actually, though, the development of social work care in mental hospitals has been uneven. On one extreme some states and individual organizations (the Veterans Administration, for example) have created quite admirable programs of social service care. They have involved a more or less complete service to patients, from planned intake, through hospital treatment, and into the community. These programs have also been marked with a high spirit of cooperativeness among the staffs in the mental hospitals. On the other hand there are all too many states and organizations operating in this area of need which have practically ignored the possibilities of adequate social service for the mentally ill. (See Figure 27.)

Intake. The psychiatric social worker in the mental hospital is first of all concerned with intake. When the patient is referred to the hospital, it is generally the responsibility of this specialist to contact the patient's home and community and to make a preliminary contact with the patient himself in order to gather facts which can be used in diagnostic work within the hospital. In some places the nature of this work is low-geared and casual, although generally it is recognized as being

SOME STATE HOSPITALS SPEND ONLY 40¢ A DAY PER PATIENT WHILE PRIVATE HOSPITALS SPEND $8

FIG. 27. Expenditures for Service of Mental Patients

(Graphic Associates for *Toward Mental Health,* by George Thorman, Public Affairs Pamphlet No. 120, published by Public Affairs Committee, Inc., New York, 1946.)

tremendously important. By means of such work the hospital gains an insight into the patient's individual background and the special circumstances of his home and community, and thus is better able to initiate treatment appropriate to the case. Also, a preliminary survey will indicate the possibilities of further home contact, of visits by relatives and friends, and of the later return home of the patient.

Social Treatment. The second responsibility of the psychiatric social worker in a mental hospital is that of social treatment. Treatment in one sense begins on the day of the first contact and is involved in everything that the worker does while in contact with the client. In some hospitals the psychiatric social worker has the social investigation as his main duty and may have little or no therapeutic relation with the patient himself. In other situations quite the opposite is true. The worker may have a shared and cooperative responsibility for treatment in addition to the task of social investigation. The auspices of the hospitals, the availability of psychiatrists, the nature of cases, the skill of psychiatric social workers, the philosophy of treatment held by the staff of hospitals—all have a part in the determination of what role will be given to the psychiatric social worker. Recently, as in the case of the child guidance clinic, psychotherapy has become the responsibility of some psychiatric social workers.

Treatment of the patient may involve the worker not only in direct contact with the patient but also in continuing relationship with the patient's family. An example of the type of work which may be required with the relatives of a mental hospital patient is shown in the problem of gaining consent for treatment. A worker writes about this as follows:

Signing the required consent for shock therapy is in itself a grave responsibility for the relative to take, and when his conflict is heightened by ambivalent feelings, conscious or unconscious guilt, and hostility toward the patient, his indecision and suffering are heightened. Whereas the recommendation for treatment is made by the physician, the responsibility for helping the relative work through his own feelings is more often the responsibility of the social worker. The relative asks innumerable questions which he may have asked the physician previously, or which he has been afraid to ask. About electroconvulsive therapy, for example, he questions whether the memory loss is permanent. Does brain damage occur which affects the higher centers of the brain? What is the voltage? Have there been fatalities? What is the convulsion like? Is it painful? Does the patient remember it? Is his personality going to be changed? Will he be cured? Will he resent the relative for giving consent? Simple, direct replies may prove sufficiently reassuring to the relative. Often it is evident that deeper anxieties prevent his arriving at a decision.

A daughter unable to sign consent for electroconvulsive therapy for her mother discussed several times with the social worker the doctor's recommendation, including the special involvement of the patient's having a mild arteriosclerotic condition. The daughter's anxiety was not alleviated. Alternative possibilities of removing the patient from the hospital and of additional consultation for confirmation of the recommendation were discussed and discarded. Some further exploration revealed that the daughter had experienced similar anxiety regarding every major decision involving the mother's physical welfare in the past.

It was not until this relative brought out her ambivalent feelings toward the patient, her feeling of having been rejected as a child, and her resentment at being in the position of having the mother-daughter role reversed, that she gained insight into the basis of her indecision. Feelings of hostility against the mother and their defense in fear of "hurting" and thus retaliating for previous injustices stood in the way of her signing the necessary consent papers. With this insight into her own attitudes, the daughter was able to face the problem with greater objectivity and arrive at a decision that involved less guilt and suffering for herself.[2]

[2]Rowena Ryerson, "Case Work With Schizophrenic Patients Treated with Shock Therapies," *The Family* (now *Journal of Social Casework*), volume 26, number 8, December, 1945, pp. 293–294.

Release. The release of the mental patient from the hospital or institution sets the time for the third of the psychiatric social worker's responsibilities. In many hospitals the value of the psychiatric social worker is mainly demonstrated in this third period. Usually, the patient admitted to a mental hospital has left a community situation which has contributed in some measure to his problem. It is only a sign of basic intelligence for a mental hospital to want to make sure that the community into which the patient will return will enable him to overcome his previous difficulties and to make the best possible adjustment. While this truth can easily be appreciated, it is not always easy for the psychiatric social worker to secure necessary changes in the families and communities in order to assure their acceptance of the patients on a positive basis. Oftentimes, family members need to rethink their attitudes toward the patient, to settle their own problems, to extend themselves in such ways as will enable the patient to make sure of his complete recovery, if that is possible.

Henry Freeman suggests that the relatives with whom the psychiatric social worker has to deal may fall into three classes.[3] The first of these is the group which seems capable of meeting the patient's needs. These may need little more than some practical interpretation and suggestions from the hospital. The second are those that have problem attitudes but seem capable of modifying them. The third group is composed of those who present rigid and inflexible patterns. Both the second and third categories may require extensive casework attention from the psychiatric social worker if the full adjustment of the patient is to be achieved.

In planning for the patient's successful community adjustment, the psychiatric social worker must also consider the patient's own attitudes. In the time that he has been in the mental hospital, the patient has learned a new mode of life. The removal of economic responsibility for his family during his hospitalization will mean that he must become accustomed again to the assumption of such obligation. Separation from those who have been greatly involved in his problem will mean relearning to adjust to these persons. In these and in other ways the psychiatric social worker helps the patient to establish as normal a life as is possible.

The worker may also form a tie between the patient and himself long after the discharge. The following case is illustrative:

> A young patient who suffered an adolescent schizophrenia has maintained contact with the social worker over a period of four years. He

[3]Henry Freeman, "Casework With Families of Mental Hospital Patients," *Journal of Social Casework*, volume 28, number 3, March, 1947, pp. 107–113.

indicates how often he wishes to come, and what he wishes to discuss, although it is evident that he is not working toward the solution of any definite problems, but rather that the relationship is the important therapeutic factor here. Over a period of years, there has been observed a significant diminution of his anxiety, a certain dulling of his personality, and a restriction of his activities, which include excellent application of himself to a routine clerical job, one movie a week, and living in a home in which the conditions are quite unfavorable. The evidences of slow deterioration point to the possibility of an underlying disease process. He has some concern about being different, and it is in this area that he uses the help of the worker, who accepts him in spite of his being different and puts no pressures upon him to change. It is obvious that the worker could in no way set goals of higher social adjustment with this patient, but that the relationship alone is an important factor in helping him to maintain himself in the community without too much sense of difference.[4]

Summary of Responsibilities. The responsibilities of the psychiatric social worker in a mental hospital—intake, treatment, and release—are portrayed in the following case summary in the fashion in which they most often occur—as a connected series of events:

The ward physician referred John Smith, twenty-three years old, because "he is depressed and needs someone to talk to" and, as a secondary reason, because additional history was needed for diagnosis. During the first interview the patient responded positively to the worker's suggestion that talking over some of his difficulties might be helpful. He mentioned his physical condition and employment as his two chief problems. He had had surgical treatments for a mastoid condition while in service and had been told that about once a year his ear would become infected and would run. This was very disturbing to him. In addition, he had been hospitalized by the army on several occasions because of a varicocele. He felt that the doctors had disagreed about the need for further treatment for it and about the prognosis. Already, he had spent some money on private medical care and was concerned about future expense. He talked at some length about his failure to achieve his lifelong ambition to become a policeman. Although he knew that his limited education would probably have to be supplemented, his greatest frustration came from the fact that he felt that he had been given the "run around" when he inquired at various places about how he could apply for an appointment to a police force. He told the worker that he had attempted suicide at least four times, and emphasized in this connection worry about his health and about work. At the conclusion of the interview the worker said that she thought that she could help him and that she would be able to talk with the ward physician before seeing him again.

[4]Rowena Ryerson, *op. cit.,* pp. 292–293.

During the second interview the patient was in better spirits. He said that he felt that the worker's talk with him had helped him to see that he was not using his energies constructively in solving his problems. Also being on the ward with so many other patients who were worse off than he had made him look at things differently. At times during this interview he was able to make a realistic approach to his difficulties. For instance, he said that in the first place, suicide was contrary to the teachings of his religion, and secondly, that if he really wanted to do something to help his wife and child, killing himself would certainly not be the answer. Also he felt that he had dwelt too much on the importance of his getting a job as a policeman, and that possibly later on when he had additional preparation he might make further application. At present he would concentrate on supporting his family as best he could.

On the next visiting day the worker talked with the wife. She was a very small, pale young girl who seemed to be emotionally unstable and showed very little insight into her husband's condition. On the day the patient was admitted to Lyons she had been discharged from a period of hospitalization resulting from a miscarriage. Although she since had been advised that she needed additional medical care, she refused to consider securing it until the patient left Lyons. She was inclined to be overprotective in her attitude toward her husband and wanted to give the worker the impression that there was nothing wrong with him. The worker interpreted to her that she was not judging the patient but that the staff was interested in his condition and in helping him. Additional history was secured from her which confirmed a particularly poor family background with extreme poverty during the patient's childhood and adolescence and serious delinquency among siblings. Although he later returned it, the patient had picked up a wallet belonging to another soldier during service because he was so distressed over letters received from his wife describing financial difficulties. As a result of this he was reduced in rank to a buck private. His wife continued to write him of difficulties at home and he finally went AWOL, returned home, secured work, and supported his wife and his mother for some time. He was eventually apprehended and court-martialed. While serving the six months guardhouse sentence imposed, he was hospitalized because of somatic symptoms and emotional instability. During this hospitalization a medical discharge from the Army was granted on the basis of a diagnosis of psychoneurosis. The worker felt that Mrs. Smith had considerable guilt about her part in these two incidents, and that probably this was influencing her present protective attitude. Following his discharge Mr. Smith became discouraged about not getting a promotion on his job, which he felt he deserved. Real misfortunes occurred about housing and finances and he began to quarrel frequently with his wife. They finally separated. Shortly afterwards he was admitted to Lyons.

The worker continued to see the patient who maintained his pleasant improved outlook and was able to be very helpful to some of the other patients on the ward. His wife had decided that she wanted him back and they intended to re-establish their home again following his discharge. He said that he was not unhappy in the hospital but that he would like to go out and prove that he could make good. Recognizing that there were serious environmental and emotional problems with which Mr. and Mrs. Smith would have to contend, the worker discussed with them the possibility of a referral to a family agency in order that they might have continued professional assistance in working out their plans, and, after some interpretation, they both decided they wanted to follow this suggestion. When the case was considered by the diagnostic staff, the patient's symptoms were considered to be psychoneurotic in origin. The worker was asked to carry out the plan for referral to a community agency since it was felt that continued hospitalization would not benefit Mr. Smith but that both he and his wife needed additional casework help. The case will be continued as active with social service until the referral has been accomplished.[5]

Use of Foster Home Placement. The possibilities of employing foster home placement for the mentally ill have been demonstrated for some generations, but they have never been so appealing as now to social workers who deal with patients in mental hospitals. The idea that the family in itself is a beneficial and even therapeutic setup which may bring healing to the mentally sick is not new nor the special property of any group. But the use of foster home placement to aid mental patients presents many possibilities to the psychiatric worker. Involved in these foster home programs are all of the problems that have been discussed previously under the foster home placement of children, plus other problems as well. The worker, therefore, who has responsibility for the operation of a foster home program for mental patients must possess a high type of social work competence in order that the objectives of such a program may be achieved. The responsibility breaks down in practice into the following activities: (1) *selection of suitable patients*—obviously, not all mental patients can benefit from foster home placement; (2) *selection of homes*—because of the intricate and profound meaning which foster home placement may have for mental patients, appropriate skill must be shown in the selection of suitable foster homes; (3) *supervision of patients and homes*—after an arrangement has been made to bring a patient and a foster home together, the social worker has continuing obligations to see that the most is made of the resulting relationship.

[5] Emily R. Scanlan, "Case Work With Veterans in a Neuropsychiatric Hospital," *The News-Letter of the American Association of Psychiatric Social Workers* (now *Journal of Psychiatric Social Work*), volume 15, number 2, Autumn, 1945, pp. 18–19.

The following is a case summary which shows the social worker in relation to the foster home placement of a mental patient:

George's case is presented as an example of the adjustment of a continuous-treatment patient for whom many factors had to be considered in finding a home. First of all, the caretaker had to have enough understanding of venereal disease to know that there was no danger whatsoever of infection from the patient, for George was a general paretic. A second thing of importance was to have someone in the home to whom George could talk freely in Italian, for he had been born in Italy and his English was limited and, third, the caretaker had to be a person who could handle George sufficiently firmly to see that he looked after himself adequately and that he did not annoy others. Finally, since George was somewhat infirm physically, he had to be helped up and down steps and watched to see that he did not fall as he walked around the house and yard. A home which answered all these needs and offered many other possibilities for satisfaction was finally found.

Not much was known about George's early life in Italy. During the First World War George served three years in the Italian army. During this time he contracted syphilis, which many years later caused his mental illness. He was a skilled workman who had made a comfortable living for himself for many years. His marital adjustment had been unsatisfactory and terminated in a divorce, but his relationship with his daughter, born before he entered the army, had been pleasant enough until he became mentally ill. He was admitted to a state hospital when he was forty-two years old. As the result of malarial treatment, he improved somewhat and was given parole, although he was far from well both physically and mentally. His daughter tried at this time and on many occasions subsequently to give him care in her home, but she could do nothing with him. She continued to show her interest, however, after he was committed, by providing him with clothing and spending money.

In spite of George's difficulty in adjusting, even for a short visit, at his daughter's, he was placed in a family care home. It was thought that his daughter had always expected too much of him and that perhaps he would respond better to the care of a stranger who would not be upset by the annoying things he did. The home in which George was placed was a most unusual one. Mrs. Van, a widow, her sons and their wives, and her daughters and their husbands, all lived gaily and harmoniously in a large, rambling, old house with a fine garden. All the young people went out to work, which would leave Mrs. Van alone all day if she did not have the patients for company. Mrs. Van knew what had caused George's illness and understood that the infectious stage had long since passed and that he no longer needed any treatment. The social worker had also told her that George had been found very difficult for his daughter to handle. However, with the suggestions which the social worker gave Mrs. Van as to how to help George to do what was expected of him, she said she thought she would like to try caring for him. Mrs. Van had one other patient, a well-educated man who spoke Italian fluently, and she felt that interpreting for George would give this patient something to do that he would enjoy.

When George was first placed in Mrs. Van's home, he behaved exactly as he did at his daughter's—he was untidy, his table manners were terrible, and he was selfish and inconsiderate of everyone. However, Mrs. Van was not daunted. On the advice of the social worker she explained to George that he would have to room alone and eat alone until he had learned to keep himself tidy and to eat sufficiently well to sit at the table with people. She showed him how to handle his knife and fork and made suggestions as to how to eat in a way that was acceptable to others. Mrs. Van gave him this training in much the same way that one would train a child of two. He complained a little and at first there was some question whether he wanted to stay in the home. However, the social worker, in discussing the matter with him, urged him to wait for a few weeks to decide this question, and he consented.

In four months the patient, under the highly individualized care which he received in this home, became neat and tidy and many of his former objectionable habits disappeared. His table manners improved so there was no objection to his eating at the table with the family. He began to keep himself and his clothing clean. Today, while he still rooms alone, he keeps his room clean and attractive and no one would hesitate to share it with him if it were necessary. With the patient's improvement, it became easier to understand his English. He talks with the social worker now in English, confining his remarks chiefly to the statement that it is a nice home and he likes it there, or he may have some little episode to tell about the family, and, while he is not the kind of person who takes part in family activities, it is plain that he observes and takes an interest in what the family is doing. He now is content to listen to the radio and sit quietly looking at the pictures in magazines.

It has been interesting to notice the effect that George has had on the highly educated patient who is also in this home. Apparently, it has given him great satisfaction to feel that he has been an important factor in George's improvement. He himself is an elderly man, and he shows George off and brags about him as if he were his grandchild. The relationship of these two patients, which had been considered so carefully when placement was made, has been mutually beneficial and has resulted in satisfactions to both.

While it is not expected that George will show much further improvement, he is comfortable and happy in family care. His daughter's interest in him is much greater than it was formerly. She is much pleased with his improved manners and his attitude of contentment. She says that now it is a pleasure to come to see him when before it was a duty. George has found a life which offers interests in keeping with his mental and physical limitations. There will, of course, be lapses in George's good behavior, but they will probably not be frequent or prolonged.

With this patient there was little that the social worker could do directly but she was able to help Mrs. Van in training him to be a more socially acceptable human being. Mrs. Van's usually successful method of jollying the other patients under her care into doing things did not work with George. He had to be handled firmly but kindly. He had to be told over and over again what to do and how to do it. At times Mrs. Van called the social worker to come over and support her handling of George. Both Mrs. Van and the social worker had to learn a few Italian words to make George understand them and even then the other patient often had to be called in to explain things (he too had to be cautioned as to how he should speak to the patient). The first weeks were difficult, but as Mrs. Van says, George's improvement is ample reward. George now understands what is expected of him and he is living up to these expectations and derives satisfaction from doing so.[6]

Clinics

The Child Guidance Clinic. A field that presents wide opportunity for psychiatric social workers is the child guidance movement. The nature and functions of child guidance clinics and the role of the psychiatric social worker in them have been discussed in Chapter 7 and need not be gone into again here.

In this connection it is important to recall the close tie that exists in many localities between the child guidance clinic and the school social work movement. Thus school social work suggests another opportunity for psychiatric social workers.

Outpatient Departments of General Hospitals. At the present time many adults with mental and emotional problems are treated in the clinics of general hospitals. The patients in these clinics may be those who come directly for help with their emotional problems, or they may be those who, entering the hospital with a claim to some physical disability, upon analysis are discovered to be suffering from an emotional upset.

The role of the psychiatric social worker in psychiatric clinics is not too well defined. Admittedly, his responsibilities in history-taking and his work with the families of patients are important ways in which he can serve the purposes of the clinic. But largely as a result of the Second World War, there is much confusion as to whether the psychiatric social worker should also participate in the total treatment of the patient. Because of the shortage of psychiatrists during the War, psy-

[6]Hester B. Crutcher, *Foster Home Care for Mental Patients,* Commonwealth Fund, New York, 1944, pp. 127-131.

chiatric social workers were often called upon to encroach more and
more upon duties that were formerly regarded as exclusively those of
the psychiatrist.

The shortage of trained psychiatrists exists even today, and the increasing number of persons who are seeking the services of psychiatric
clinics further complicates the problem. (See Table 14.) What should

Table 14

COMMUNITY CLINICS IN THE UNITED STATES BY ORGANIZATIONAL AUSPICES
AND GROUPS SERVED, MAY, 1946

	Children Only	Adults Only	All-Purpose	School Children Only	Court Cases Only	Veterans Only	Restricted to Agency Clients	Total
Community clinics	67	22	174	16	5	12	14	310
Division of state or county government	193	12	141	9	18	0	0	373
Veterans Administration	0	0	0	0	0	5	0	5
Total	260	34	315	25	23	17	14	688

Source: National Committee for Mental Hygiene, *Bulletin on Psychiatric
Rehabilitation,* New York, 1946.

be the function of the psychiatric social worker? Should he be responsible just for the case histories and family situations of patients? Should
he be the psychiatrist's "assistant" in treatment? Or should he engage
in therapy directly, whether under the supervision of a psychiatrist or
not? At present the variations in practice are wide.

Mental Hospital Clinics. The distinctively mental hospital may also
have a psychiatric clinic, but its function may differ somewhat from
those of general hospitals. It may be used in large part, especially in or
near a large city, for the aftercare of mental patients who have been
discharged. It may be the headquarters for the "outpatient" division of
the institution's work. It may thus permit the continuing contacts of
the mental hospital with patients after they have been restored to their
families or placed in foster families. The clinic may also serve a direct
objective of providing more facile social service contact for serious

mental cases from the community to the hospital proper. In such a capacity the mental hospital clinic is usually able to make better use of hospital resources for psychiatric purposes than are clinics in general hospitals, simply because they are more directly and logically related to the total functioning of the hospital. Again, clinics in mental hospitals may be able to offer more intensive and extended treatment of patients who do not need to be hospitalized but who are in need of continuing and serious treatment.

Independent Clinics. There are some psychiatric clinics which are unattached to hospitals or which have working relations with hospitals, although they may not be under the direct supervision of a hospital. The Psychiatry Clinic in Boston is an example:

The Psychiatry Clinic was opened October 5, 1942, by the Boston Psychoanalytic Institute as a "psychotherapeutic clinic for ambulatory patients whose problems are related to the present war situation." The term "Psychiatry Clinic" was chosen to designate the interest of the organization not only in the direct treatment of patients, but also in research. The staff of the Clinic consisted of members or candidates of the Boston Psychoanalytic Institute. The social worker had training in family casework, child placing, and in a psychiatric clinic serving children and adults.

The Clinic did not use complete analytic methods, but an abbreviated form of psychotherapy based on analytic understanding. It was not the purpose of the Clinic to remodel the whole lives of patients but rather to deal with certain parts of the neurotic personality, with the aim of removing specific disabilities.

In the first six months of experience the Clinic accepted one third of its patients from the specifically war-related organizations (American Red Cross, rehabilitation agents, induction board psychiatrists), and another third from the usual medical sources in the community. The remainder came from social work agencies, colleges, churches, and other organizations and agencies in the city. The bulk of the patients had problems which were aggravated by wartime living. Diagnostically, the entire range of psychiatric problems was encountered by the Clinic among its patients.

The role of the social worker in the Clinic has been described by its worker in the following words: "The caseworker's responsibility varies with the individual situation, but it has two main aspects. First, it is the Clinic's opinion that if a short form of psychotherapy is to be developed, the most advantageous use must be made of the time of both physician and patient. Therefore, the psychiatrist should have, at the time he meets the patient, any factual information that is readily available and that can be secured without involving the patient or others in a way that might be contraindicated. Consequently, the worker has some contact with all the cases, not by referral from the doctor but at the point of application. In the second place there is a group of cases in which, because of the immaturity of the patient, the degree of illness, or the complexity of the family situation, it is necessary for a social worker to play an active supplementary part. This part may be taken by the Clinic social worker, by a worker in an outside agency, or by the two together."[7]

Other Places of Practice

In Public Health Nursing Agencies. Psychiatric social workers have been employed by public health nursing agencies to help nursing staffs appreciate the mental hygiene implications of their activities, to detect more readily those cases which need special psychiatric care, and to participate more intelligently in the community aspects of their work. The responsibilities of the psychiatric social worker in public health differ from those of a similar worker in another setting in that the public health organization usually provides a course or courses for its staff. These courses regularly contain a basic introduction to the field of psychiatry, methods of detecting serious psychiatric ailments, the use of community facilities, the basis on which referrals may and should be made by nurses to psychiatrists and psychiatric clinics, and other topics.

In addition to giving courses the worker oftentimes engages at appointed times in informal discussions with groups of nurses who have common problems and with individual nurses who present special problems. The psychiatric social worker may also accompany those nurses who engage in home visits in order to become more fully acquainted with the types of cases found in the field and to assist the nurse wherever possible in her approach to the patients. All of these duties, while assumed by psychiatric social workers in many public health organizations throughout the country, are not utilized universally because of varying factors: the availability and competence of psychiatric social workers, the experience and competence of the nursing staff, the personnel facilities of the organization, and the types of problems met with in the field. But they all are available as means by which the psychiatric social worker may strengthen the program of a public health organization. As was suggested in the preceding chapter, this type of work may also be performed by medical social workers.

In Educational Institutions. Educational institutions also are currently employing psychiatric social workers in a limited way. The activities of

[7]Helen E. Spaulding, "The Psychiatric Clinic," *The Family* (now *Journal of Social Casework*), volume 24, number 3, pp. 102–103.

the social worker in the general school setting have been previously described. Here it may be appropriate to mention three special types of situations in which the psychiatric social worker is being used increasingly. Private schools are more and more availing themselves of the services of psychiatric social workers. Undoubtedly, a further increase· in the numbers of fully trained workers available will see an increase in the number of workers employed by private schools. Nursery schools are also more and more interested in securing psychiatric social workers. It is seen that through the use of such workers the nursery school is better able to serve the needs of its children. This type of practice includes both the child within the nursery school as well as the child's home relationships. Colleges also are more interested in the possibilities of psychiatric social service than ever before. For many colleges an extended social service department as an intrinsic part of the educational program is seen as an important next-step in educational achievement.

In addition there are a small number of psychiatric social workers who are employed by mental hygiene societies. These workers chiefly do community organization work rather than casework and are used in preparing public relations materials, in coordinating the work of community agencies in the field, in planning conferences, and in assisting in community surveys.

It is possible too that in the future more psychiatric social workers will engage in private practice on a basis similar to that of the private physician.[8]

SELECTED READINGS ON PSYCHIATRIC SOCIAL WORK

Alexander, Franz, and French, Thomas, *Psychoanalytic Therapy: Principles and Applications,* Ronald, New York, 1946.

Allen, Frederick H., *Psychotherapy With Children,* Norton, New York, 1942.

American Psychiatric Association, *One Hundred Years of American Psychiatry,* New York, 1944.

Beck, Bertram M., in collaboration with Robbins, Lewis L., *Short-Term Therapy in an Authoritative Setting,* Family Service Association of America, New York, 1946.

Beers, Clifford W., *A Mind That Found Itself: An Autobiography,* Doubleday, Doran, New York, anniversary edition, 1935.

Brill, Abraham A., *Freud's Contribution to Psychiatry,* Norton, New York, 1944.

[8]See Lee R. Steiner, "Hanging Out a Shingle," *The News-Letter of the American Association of Psychiatric Social Workers* (now *Journal of Psychiatric Social Work*), volume 6, number 3, Winter, 1936, pp. 1–8.

Crutcher, Hester B., *A Guide for Developing Psychiatric Social Work in State Hospitals,* State Hospitals Press, Utica, 1933.

———, *Foster Home Care of Mental Patients,* Commonwealth Fund, New York, 1944.

Deutsch, Albert, *The Mentally Ill in America: A History of Their Care and Treatment From Colonial Times,* Columbia University Press, New York, new printing, 1946.

English, O. Spurgeon, and Pearson, Gerald H. J., *Emotional Problems of Living: Avoiding the Neurotic Pattern,* Norton, New York, 1945.

French, Lois M., *Psychiatric Social Work,* Commonwealth Fund, New York, 1940.

Gartland, Ruth, *Psychiatric Social Service in a Children's Hospital: Two Years of Service in Bobs Roberts Memorial Hospital for Children,* Social Service Monograph, University of Chicago Press, Chicago, 1936.

Horney, Karen, *The Neurotic Personality of Our Time,* Norton, New York, 1937.

Klein, David B., *Mental Hygiene: Psychology of Personal Adjustment,* Holt, New York, 1944.

Lee, Porter R., and Kenworthy, Marion E., with the collaboration of Sarah Ivins and others, *Mental Hygiene and Social Work,* Commonwealth Fund, New York, 1929.

Lowrey, Lawson G., *Psychiatry for Social Workers,* Columbia University Press, New York, 1946.

Plant, James S., *Personality and the Cultural Pattern,* Commonwealth Fund, New York, 1937.

Rennie, Thomas A., and Woodward, Luther E., *Mental Health in Modern Society,* Commonwealth Fund, New York, 1948.

Small, S. Mouchly, *Symptoms of Personality Disorder,* Family Welfare Association of America (now Family Service Association of America), New York, 1944.

Strecker, Edward A., *Fundamentals of Psychiatry,* Lippincott, Philadelphia, 3d edition, 1945.

Towle, Charlotte, *Social Records From Psychiatric Clinics,* with discussion notes, Social Service Series, University of Chicago Press, Chicago, 1941.

For other references, consult bibliographies at the end of other related chapters.

Public Welfare: Structure

Public social services have become increasingly important in recent decades. The passage of the Social Security Act in 1935 drew the federal government deeper into the business of social welfare and aroused the hopeful attention of many people. Questions regarding the legitimacy of federal participation were raised. Some of these inquiries pertained to the way in which responsibility for social welfare should be organized in the nation.

There is little doubt among public welfare personnel that many improvements can and should be made in the organization of services through local, state, and federal government. But any changes must be based wisely on that which already exists. The following summary statement of a county welfare department describes one aspect of public welfare organization:

SOME ASPECTS OF THE ORGANIZATION AND OPERATION OF SCOTT COUNTY WELFARE DEPARTMENT

Location and Office Facilities. The Scott County Department of Public Welfare is situated in the county seat which had a population in 1940 of 6,110 persons and is the largest community in the county.[1] The office in the Court House is fairly centrally located in the county and is easily accessible.

The office has a small waiting and reception room, with two semiprivate interviewing booths in an adjoining room. The visitors' desks are arranged in a larger room, one end of which is blocked off with file cabinets to arrange space for the stenographers. The case supervisor has a

[1]Scott County has a population of approximately 20,000. The name given for the county is fictitious.

424

small wall-board office on one side of the room to provide privacy for conferences. The child welfare worker's desk is blocked off from the rest of the room by a large bulletin board so that she can interview persons in privacy in the event the two interviewing booths are occupied. The county director has a large private office which opens into the visitors' room and also directly into the hall. A large table in the director's office is used for meetings of the staff and of the County Board. The entire space is small but well arranged and fairly adequate.

The County Board. The County Board of Public Welfare has had approximately the same membership since first appointed, most of the members having formerly been members of the County Child Welfare Board. It meets one afternoon each month, usually about the 15th. The minutes are brief, stating resolutions made, problems discussed, authorizations approved, wardships recommended, personnel action, and cases discussed. The county director and case supervisor always meet with the board and usually the child welfare worker attends. The members of the board have a sustained interest in public welfare matters and are all active participants. They were originally opposed to any fixed policies, preferring that all cases be handled on an individual basis. They now recognize the value of establishing some fixed policies, particularly in the area of budgeting, and have established a few definite policies by resolution.

The board members have done a great deal of interpretation of the program in the community and encourage the staff to speak whenever possible. They are less enthusiastic about written interpretation, fearing that it will be misunderstood.

Major responsibility and authority for administration of the agency's program has been delegated to the county director and his staff. In the beginning, the board studied individual cases before decision, but now case decisions are listed and approved after cursory review. The board always follows the county director's recommendation in individual cases and the director has been specifically authorized to: (1) close cases upon death, voluntary withdrawal, or refusal of grant; (2) approve or withdraw cases in which the State Department of Public Welfare has approved transfer; (3) increase awards for medical care; and (4) make commitments to hospitals. The board usually follows the county director's recommendations in the selection of staff and follows the progress of each worker with interest. The county director has been authorized to employ emergency clerk-stenographers without approval of the board. Working hours, holidays, and vacation policy were established by resolution of the board and the minutes state that they will base all salary changes on increased efficiency and length of service. The county director acts as secretary to the board. He discusses all problems of the agency with the board and never proceeds with changes until he secures their approval.

Agency Functions and Assignment of Work. The agency administers, in addition to the public assistance programs of old-age assistance, aid to the blind, and aid to dependent children, the programs for crippled children, child welfare, probation, and parole. One visitor handles all of the child welfare service cases and the county director handles probation and parole. The other programs are handled by the visitors according to geographic district.

The staff consists of the county director, one casework supervisor, and at present five welfare visitors. The full staff should consist of six welfare visitors but there is one vacancy. The vacant district has been handled by the case supervisor. A new worker has been employed to start work on December 1, 1943, thus bringing the staff up to the minimum State standard. Ordinarily, the problem of staff turnover has not been serious in this county as there has only been a total of 23 workers in seven years. No employee has ever been discharged but during the past two years they have considered workers whose qualifications were not up to the standards formerly used.

The responsibilities of the staff members have been clearly defined as set forth by an outline available in the office. The county director is responsible for interpretation of the programs, planning board meetings, supervision of bookkeeping and statistical processes, matters pertaining to financing the program, final approval of cases to be presented to the board, supervision of parolees and preparole investigations, probation services and problems relating to release of liens. In addition, he assists the case supervisor in planning staff meetings, works with the case supervisor in planning office practices and procedures, confers with the case supervisor on staff problems, develops county policies for the consideration of the board, and assists in decisions on case problems brought to his attention by the case supervisor. In addition to his office functions, the director is an officer in the State association of county directors.

The case supervisor is responsible for the review of all recommendations as to case decisions and the approval of cases for presentation to the board, supervision of the work of all visitors and stenographers, planning and direction of regular staff meetings, setting up proper controls for the supervision of the workers, distribution of case loads and assignment of special duties to the workers, assisting the county director in evaluating policies and procedures to gear the administration to changing conditions, presentation of summaries of cases to the board for action, and interviewing and taking applications in the absence of the regular worker.

The visitors are responsible for visiting and recording on all cases assigned to them, referring problems on which they require advice to the case supervisor, cooperating in special work planned to improve the county department, and attending staff conferences.[2]

Salaries and expense accounts are published in the local paper monthly for each employee along with other county expenses and salaries. The

[2]Duties taken from "Outline of Duties and Responsibilities of the Staff" in the Scott County Department of Public Welfare.

county director has attempted to have this procedure eliminated, but without success. The recipients sometimes compare these salaries with their assistance checks to show the inadequacy of the awards or congratulate visitors on increases, or complain that salaries are too high. The staff resents having the entire community know their salaries.

Case Loads. The case loads for public assistance workers varied from 144 to 167 cases as of September 30, 1943. The old-age assistance cases in these loads varied from 118 to 142 cases, aid to dependent children from 8 to 15, aid to the blind from 3 to 7, and to crippled children from 4 to 9. There were only eight cases pending on the last day of September, all old-age assistance. Wherever possible, visitors are assigned to districts other than those in which they reside.

Concept of Supervision. The case supervisor is responsible for the supervision of the visitors. She has been with the agency for six years and had some experience in emergency relief work in a larger city prior to her employment here. Staff meetings are planned by her and held regularly every other Saturday morning. New policies and common problems are discussed, representatives of other agencies and groups discuss programs and problems, books are reviewed, and conferences discussed.

Individual conferences with the workers are held by the supervisor biweekly, depending upon the need of the worker, at regular scheduled periods. Problem cases in the worker's load are discussed with a view to planning further work and to strengthening performance. The supervisor suggests reading material that she feels would be helpful to the worker and such material is discussed in conference. She makes notes on the visitor's work for discussion and maintains card controls and a notebook to follow up on problem cases as well as the routine work. A desire was expressed for more opportunity to discuss her work with other persons in similar positions or with persons with more supervisory experience in order to get new ideas and methods. She expressed a hope that a plan might be worked out whereby case supervisors from several counties might meet regularly for this purpose.

The county director and case supervisor attend as many meetings of social work groups as possible and give the staff encouragement and opportunity to do likewise. Both the supervisor and child welfare worker have had leaves of absence to attend school, and both are now taking one afternoon a week to attend courses. Other members of the staff are encouraged to take special work.

Staff evaluations are not prepared in this county. The county director, in replying to correspondence regarding individual workers, has made evaluations of the workers for that purpose only. The work of individual visitors is frequently discussed at board meetings to indicate their improvement but no formal record is made. Weaknesses and strengths of the workers are discussed in conferences.

The county director has conferences with individual workers on job analysis and maintains a chart for each worker covering such points as previsit planning, preparation for dictation, use of time, number of visits made, material covered in visits, office routine, and client attitudes.

Orientation of new workers is conducted mainly by the case supervisor. Workers are given State manuals, case records, and general literature on the work to read, and the material is then discussed with the supervisor and also, frequently, with the county director. The supervisor conducts a tour of the Court House to show how verifications can be secured from records and has the new worker accompany her to observe home visits and other investigations. As the worker assumes regular duties, frequent conferences are held to discuss planning for visits, content of interviews, recording, and follow-up, with a continual discussion of philosophy and attitudes. As workers become more proficient, conferences are scheduled for regular periods twice a week.

The county director has a great deal of confidence in the State Department's district representative and consultants and states they are perfectly free to discuss problems with individual workers concerned. The director likes to sit in on such conferences, where possible, to keep up with current activities and get ideas for better administration.

Relationship to Other Welfare Agencies and Activities. There are 11 townships in the county, the trustees of which are responsible for general relief. The budget standards of the township trustees are considerably lower than those of the county department. Fewer items are allowed and the amounts allowed for items are less. The township trustees are not particularly cooperative in supplying special needs in public assistance cases, according to the county director, but do supply medical care to other members of the family not covered by the county medical aid plan and occasionally furnish school books or other assistance. The county notifies the township trustees when assistance payments are made to active cases and checks with them orally for information on cases known to have been active.

The Welfare Society, a family welfare agency operating in the county seat only, is the oldest agency in the county and has been very cooperative in supplying special needs and assisting transients.

There is a Council of Welfare Agencies in the county but it has become inactive since the war-connected welfare activities have become so important. There were 35 to 45 agency members including the Tuberculosis Association, Boy and Girl Scouts, churches, schools, Parent-Teacher Associations, and clubs.

The local Red Cross chapter has only a volunteer staff. The county department has a written agreement with the agency setting forth working relationships and responsibilities. The Red Cross has been helpful in securing dependency allotments for families assisted by the county department.

Case Records. There is a case record for each old-age-assistance and aid-to-the-blind recipient and for each aid-to-dependent-children family group. Records of persons in the same household have not been combined but where such situations exist, carbon copies of the narrative are made so that the narratives are identical.

All data pertaining to a case are filed in the case record except medical reports in old-age-assistance and aid-to-dependent-children cases which are filed separately.

A clerk-stenographer is responsible for the safekeeping of the records, which are filed in steel cabinets and locked each night. A charge-out system is in effect.

Because of the lack of well-qualified staffs in other agencies in this community the county director rarely gives permission for use of records by other agencies. At times, records are discussed with representatives of other organizations or small portions read to them. Records may only be taken from the office to the visitors' homes to enable them to get "caught up," and then only with special permission from the director. A check list of records taken out is kept.

Lists of recipients have not been used for other than administrative purposes.

Application Procedures. Applicants for public assistance usually apply in person at the county office but the agency takes the application in the home when the applicants are unable to call at the office for any reason.

When applicants call at the office, they are received by a clerk-stenographer who takes the name, inquires as to the purpose of the call, checks the files to find any previous record, and notifies the visitor in whose district the applicant resides. The visitor interviews the applicant, informing him as to the program, policies, and eligibility proofs required, completing the application unless the applicant is obviously ineligible or decides he does not wish to apply at this time, and arranges for a later home visit. If the application is not completed, a record of the interview is made and filed with the informal rejections. If accepted, the intake interview is recorded very briefly at the time the investigation is recorded. In the absence of the regular visitor, the case supervisor conducts the intake interview.

Applications are usually taken at the time of the first request if the applicant is not obviously ineligible, or in any event if the applicant is insistent. Applications are counted statistically at the time of acceptance.

If the applicant appears to be eligible for more than one type of assistance, the agency attempts to consider the best interests of the applicant in advising him as to the program for which he should apply. Usually, persons who would qualify for old-age assistance or blind assistance are encouraged to apply for the latter because of the fact that local funds are not required.

The agency finds that applicants are cooperative in providing data for required proofs of eligibility. Cases are not rejected unless found ineligible or applications voluntarily withdrawn.

The entire investigation is conducted by the visitor who will continue to carry the case. All applications are checked with the master index and cross references are also checked. The agency has the central index of the County Council of Social Agencies but this has not been kept current since 1941. Information is secured from other agencies interested in the cases, usually by telephone, as few agencies maintain narrative records. Any information secured is summarized in the narrative record.

Investigations are usually completed within three weeks after the application, according to the case supervisor. The supervisor maintains a list of cases pending in addition to the application register maintained by a clerk-stenographer. These lists are checked with visitors during regular conference periods and before board meetings to determine what is delaying the investigation. Applications investigated during the month prior to the time of the board meeting are presented to the board for approval of payment to be made the first of the following month. Cases completed after the board meeting and prior to the first of the month may, in an emergency, be approved by the county director for payment on the first, and are then acted upon by the board at the next meeting.

Applicants needing immediate assistance are usually referred to the township trustee or, in one city to the Welfare Society (private). Every effort is made in these cases to speed up investigation. Payment in some instances is authorized before responsible relatives have been consulted.

Home visits were made in all applications reviewed, and State standards of investigation were met in all approved applications reviewed.[3]

Not all county departments of public welfare operate and are organized in the manner of that of Scott County. There are other structures, smaller and larger, to which the county department is related, at least in many localities. Usually, there is a state department of welfare which coordinates and plans the activities of the counties. In some places there are city divisions of the county system of public welfare which care for local needs. The federal government also influences county activities. All three types of governmental organization for social welfare—local, state, and federal—will be discussed in this chapter.

THE NATURE OF PUBLIC WELFARE WORK

The discussion which has been presented thus far in this book, especially that included in the chapters on family casework, child welfare work, medical social work, and psychiatric social work, refers mainly to the organization of social work services according to a

[3]These materials are based on excerpts from Federal Administrative Review Materials covering the period of July 1, 1942 to June 30, 1943, and published by the American Association of Schools of Social Work. For a discussion of the methods and purpose of the Administrative Review see Kathryn Goodwin, "Administrative Review in Public Assistance," *Social Security Bulletin,* volume 6, number 10, October, 1943.

widely held distinction between private and public agencies. This distinction was also carried out in the chapter on the history of social work, in so far as it seemed necessary to divide the history into private and public segments. Such a picture of social work, however, does not readily enable the observer to understand all of the complex ramifications of the field. Actually (as stated in Chapter 2), the distinctions between private and public social work are true chiefly for organizational purposes. The specialties of social work which have been considered up to this point are more properly to be deemed processes continuing within various agencies rather than airtight, compartmentalized types of practice. So in medical social work the fundamental process involved is the helping of persons who have social and emotional problems attached to physical illness. There naturally are agencies which give this process support. But the nature of agency organization in a community usually is not simple or determined by any special rule. The medical social worker may operate in a public hospital or a private hospital. He may work in a public hospital but be paid from the funds of a privately financed organization. Or the medical worker may be employed by a public health agency which is financed by the municipal, state, or federal government. On the other hand he may be engaged by a private child-caring agency concerned with special cases. There are many variations.

From this comment, then, it may be realized that social casework, like social work itself, is not limited simply either to its private or to its public expressions. There is considerable room at present for both private and public services.

Historical Development

Historically, private social work has been a feature of western development. This is in line with the general development of western individualism and the stress of bourgeois democracy upon the prerogatives of "private enterprise," even in the social welfare field. This stress can be seen in the social work setup of almost any American community, with its usual wide array of private casework agencies.

However, there has been another trend at work in western social welfare history, involving a larger operation than the private services, which has borne exceedingly important fruits in our time. That trend is the public welfare movement, which has sought to lodge responsibility for certain types of social well-being upon the community as a whole rather than upon special groups within the community. Organized private agencies are relatively recent compared to the public services, whose development dates back at least as far as the Statutes of Laborers in the fourteenth century. It includes the noted growth of the English Poor Laws which became leading influences in the developing patterns of social work in this country. The overseers of the poor, mentioned in Chapter 2, also contributed to the tradition. Indeed, alongside of the privately financed and managed social work agencies which carried heavy social welfare burdens for centuries, there has been the somewhat parallel growth of public welfare services.

Meaning of Public Welfare

While public welfare may be interpreted in a broad sense to include any benefit which is contemplated or achieved for the total community through private or public means, it should be borne in mind that the use of the term in this book and in this chapter does not carry such an inclusive connotation. In our consideration we wish it to mean, as it has already gathered meaning in practice, the scope of activities which are carried on by governmental, tax-supported, social work agencies. This definition of public welfare is still rather vague, but it may perhaps be clarified by listing the activities which are commonly considered as a part of public welfare.

R. Clyde White gives the following list of the persons treated and the activities included in public welfare in this special sense of the term:[4]

1. Insane and Epileptic:
  a. Hospital treatment
  b. Outpatient clinic treatment
  c. Custodial care
  d. Casework services
  e. Conditional discharge under supervision
2. Feeble-Minded:
  a. Special education in an institution
  b. Custodial care
  c. Sterilization
  d. Conditional discharge under supervision
  e. Placement and employment
3. Physically Handicapped (blind, crippled, deaf):
  a. Corrective treatment, outpatient or inpatient
  b. Special education

  c. Vocational rehabilitation
  d. Custodial care
  e. Casework services
  f. Assistance to the blind
  g. Placement in employment
4. Tuberculosis:
  a. Outpatient treatment
  b. Hospital treatment
  c. Casework services
  d. Vocational rehabilitation
  e. Placement in employment
  f. Health education
5. Criminals and Delinquents:
  a. Probation with casework services
  b. Fine
  c. Suspended sentence
  d. Confinement in institution, penal or correctional
  e. Vocational training

⁴R. Clyde White, *Administration of Public Welfare,* American Book Company, New York, 1940, pp. 5–6.

f. General education
g. Parole with casework services
h. Placement in employment
i. Preventive measures
6. *Dependent and Neglected Children:*
   a. Aid to dependent children
   b. Casework services
   c. Foster home care
   d. Adoption
   e. Institutional care
   f. General education
   g. Relief
   h. Recreation
   i. Placement in employment
7. *Invalid (permanently incapacitated):*
   a. Medical care
   b. Relief
   c. Custodial care
   d. Casework services

8. *Aged:*
   a. Old-age assistance
   b. Relief
   c. Institutional care
   d. Medical care
   e. Casework services
9. *Able-Bodied Unemployed:*
   a. Relief
   b. Work relief
   c. Medical care
   d. Casework services
   e. Placement in employment
10. Sick:
   a. Clinic treatment
   b. Hospital care
   c. Home treatment
   d. Relief
   e. Casework services
11. Maladjusted School Children:
   a. Casework services
   b. School relief

The above list provides a detailed conception of the persons and activities included in public welfare. Some of its categories, however, obviously are overlapping. There is no effort in the modern public welfare agency to press clients into any one category. Some workers also would question the social work nature of some of the items suggested. A fine, for example, is not in itself a part of social work, either public or private. Again, hospital treatment of the tubercular is more primarily a medical function than a part of social work. "Casework services" seem to be conceived also as a special contribution rather than a general method of relating individuals with needs to the appropriate resources.

Financial and Nonfinancial Needs

Within the list can be found various material and nonmaterial services. Public agencies are mainly concerned with the former, but it is obvious that many cases which involve financial needs also contain psychological and social needs. In fact, it is clear that the fundamental and ultimate purpose of the public agencies is not merely the distribution of material services. In the final analysis it is the strengthening of personal and social well-being in terms of the quality of total living.

Even in a public assistance agency, where financial aid is the keynote, many cases evidence both financial and nonfinancial aspects:

Mr. J, who grew up in a family where he was the mother's dependent son, has had a difficult time maintaining his place in the world by supporting his wife and children, apart from his parents. Now, in establishing his eligibility for assistance, he must draw the parents into the investigation. While he knows that with some sacrifice they not only could help him but would willingly do so, his very survival as an adequate adult male is at stake in his protest against turning to them or having them know of his predicament. Even his illness does not justify or ease the situation. His marriage is threatened, for again, as in its early days, his mother will hold the ascendant position, and the struggle to place his wife first which he had practically won could well be lost in the obligating return to dependence on his parents.

* * *

Miss C had long clung to her family in spite of early impulses to break away. Throughout her childhood and adolescence she had been outdone by a sister whom she felt her parents greatly preferred. Her resentment bade her break off and find a life of her own, but guilt over this same resentment, together with a persistent need to be needed, forbade the going. A seemingly curious reaction is this not uncommon one of staying because one wants to go. A normal separation would have been an enactment of her rejection, so she stayed, contributing to the support of the family group for many years. Finally the "life of her own" came about through the death of the mother, when the father went to live with the "preferred sister." Later, financial reverses in this family and the father's application for old-age assistance brought an inquiry as to her ability to support him. The worker found a woman who unquestionably was earning enough to contribute but offered many reasons for being unable to do so and who finally, under pressure, asserted strongly her right to her own earnings—in her words, a right to a life of her own. Perhaps she had an unconscious need to withhold love as she felt the father had withheld love from her, expressed in her words to the effect that B could be left to take care of him; he always liked her; he chose to go with her, and so on.

* * *

Mr. O, a successful engineer, was earning $400 a month in wartime. His wife also was earning, and yet, when approached regarding the support of his aged father, he gave depression debts, educational plans for his children, medical expenses, and the like as his reasons for being absolutely unable to give his father a home or to contribute to his support elsewhere. The real reason lay in this man's long-standing resentment toward his father who, in his opinion, "let him and his sister down" following their mother's death, when he married another woman. "Let her children support him" was his attitude, since it was their mother who enjoyed the most productive years of the father's life and spent his money. Rigid enforcement of the laws on responsibility of relatives brought compliance in this case, but with no feeling on the part of the son that social justice has been administered to him.[5]

Oftentimes, as these cases show, financial needs may heighten the intensity of nonfinancial needs within a family.

THE GROWTH OF PUBLIC RESPONSIBILITY

Public welfare has had a long and painful development. Its support historically has been manifold. Many streams have fed into this great reservoir of national strength. Two of them can be mentioned here to illustrate the factors which have contributed to modern public welfare.

Philosophies of Cooperation

It is apparent from common-sense observation that men are not born with equal advantages, from whatever angle advantages may be counted. Whatever equality persons may have, is imputed to them or granted by sources which are not wholly the expression of natural sentiment. The "dog-eat-dog" philosophy of life which admittedly has infested a great part of western civilization is a denial of men's equality and dignity. The "survival of the fittest" is a social doctrine, notwithstanding its prevalence in some quarters, which is questioned by many as inappropriate both to facts and to ideals.

Fortunately, there have been powerful positive philosophies of personal and social responsibility which have been alive in western culture for as long as it has existed. These have tended to support a cooperative society in which there would be mutual respect for the rights and dignities of all individuals. The plight of each is the responsibility of all. These fundamental beliefs have not always been dominant nor have they been expressed constantly in their ideal forms, but they persist nevertheless.

The philosophies of cooperation which support the well-being of individuals, no matter what their condition, have stemmed from both religious and secular sources. There were periods in which religion provided the main motivation toward cooperation, and it still does to a considerable degree even today. But there is also a variety of secular theories which are united with the Judeo-Christian tradition in assert-

[5]*Common Human Needs: An Interpretation for Staff in Public Assistance Agencies,* Federal Security Agency, Social Security Board, Bureau of Public Assistance, Public Assistance Report number 8, written by Charlotte Towle, United States Printing Office, Washington, D. C., 1945, pp. 81–83.

ing the importance of the individual person. Democracy certainly is the chief of these.

The Nature of Modern Society

One does not have to know much about life in these times to understand that modern society is exceedingly complex and more or less fortuitous in many of its aspects. Intertwined as it is in its various components, what happens in one part usually influences the whole. The influence, moreover, may strike individuals in ways which are usually described as "accidental."

Unemployment alone is a factor which makes clear the complex nature of modern society. It is naïve to assume that all individuals should be self-supporting in the face of an economic order which sometimes does not allow very much personal freedom. When a period of economic depression sets in, all of the striving of the individual may be in vain. He may be adversely affected by forces over which he has little control. His environment, through no virtue or fault of his own, may make his material prosperity impossible or greatly reduced.

It is too much to ask that the individual bear the responsibility for conditions which are not of his choosing or his creation. It would seem proper for the community to assume responsibility for his condition and to assure him that he will not be made to suffer for factors outside of his management. Groups of individuals who are negatively affected by social and economic conditions often do not remain passive in the face of their disaster, but form pressure groups which work for their own benefit. Such efforts cannot be construed to be inimical to the welfare of the whole, but actually in support of the whole. For, according to the philosophies of cooperation, if one suffers, then so does the whole.

The complexity of modern society also means that the challenge of mass trouble cannot be met by the private efforts of any one individual or group. The kinds of calamities which befall persons in our society are usually such that private efforts of cooperation are not sufficient to meet the demands. No one person or group of private citizens could have financed the depression needs of the 1930's. It was necessary, aside from being desirable, that the federal government assume responsibility for the well-being of the private citizen.

Responsibility for a Normal Existence

By a combination of a philosophy of cooperation which is loosely called "democracy" and the insistent facts of our modern, complex society, it is felt by almost everyone today that government must assume responsibility in the form of public welfare services. It has been made clear only recently, however, that government should assume responsibility for more than a minimum of personal and social well-being. There was a time when it was popular to believe that the least assistance given to an indigent person was the most desirable. It was thought that this practice would not deter the person from seeking employment on his own initiative. But this outlook is seriously questioned at the present. If a person is ill, it does him little good to receive the minimum of treatment. The good physician seeks to enable the patient to gain a full recovery. Likewise, providing only a minimum of financial assistance to an unemployed person, far from engendering very much initiative on his part, may actually deaden that which he has. The object, then, of public welfare is to assist threatened persons to live a normal existence in so far as is possible. This attitude has been expressed many times recently. It was also voiced as long ago as the sixteenth century, however, by a Spaniard, Juan Luis Vives, in an address to the Council and the Senate of Bruges, Belgium: "Just as in a wealthy house it were a disgrace for a father of the family to allow any to hunger or go naked or to be disgraced by rags, so it is not seemly that in a city by no means needy the magistrate should permit any citizens to be harassed by hunger or poverty. Everything in the city that falls into decay is renewed, whether walls or dykes or institutions; thus the citizens too should be relieved who have suffered damage from any cause." While Vives declared a relatively new and unorganized sentiment for his time, we today, after centuries of struggle, have within the accepted framework of government a more tangible expression of the attitudes he represented.

LIMITATIONS

Formal Controls

Public welfare activities, because they are supported through tax funds, are regulated to a considerable degree by the legislative bodies which represent the taxpayers. This fact reveals an interesting aspect of the subject. True, no agency, private or public, is without limitations. All have to meet some kind of requirements: in part, private; in part, public. The private agency, for example, must meet certain public and legal requirements, even though its financial backing may be wholly from private donors. In its very process of incorporation it confronts a form of public or legal regulation which is imposed by a legislative body as a means of safeguarding the general public from charlatans and of enabling an agency's nature and function to be formally recognized. There are other regulations which lawmaking bodies impose upon private agencies; in general, however, they do not disturb the fundamental principles of private agency organization which are private financing and administration.

Public and Private Restrictions

The public agency, of course, faces more restrictions of a legalistic character, both because of the administrative responsibility involved and the type of social service expressed. But in addition to the formal controls, it also encounters those of a more private nature. In this regard, public opinion has always played a large part in determining the policy of public welfare work. The public agency cannot do as it pleases in regard to what it deems its community responsibility. A private agency, as has been observed many times in the history of social work, has the possibility of favoring a particular category of need, if the agency believes some good end is thus being served. So it may provide care for a special group, such as spastics, far out of proportion to what they may from any general standard merit. The private agency may justify such procedure on the ground that someone, through a financial grant, specified that such a service be organized. Or the agency may feel that through its specialized interest in one group it may learn how better to begin the treatment of other groups. Or it may think that restricting treatment to one group will encourage other agencies to aid other groups requiring specialized treatment.

But the public agency usually cannot be so selective about its clientele. It cannot spend disproportionate amounts of money on special groups for whatever good reason it may be able to find. It is in this sense far more responsible, in terms of the broad and general needs of the community, for providing equal treatment facilities and possibilities. A public agency which initiated a program which was too far off-center from what the community felt was its direct and most general needs, would probably feel the pressure of disapproving private citizens. In fine, the public agency (like the private agency) must meet standards or limitations from both private and public sources. The private agency has its own particular standards. The public has its own, as well.

Of course, private and public agencies in some cases are not clearly separated. This is especially true in protective and correctional work and in child care services. In these instances the private and the public agency very often work in a cooperative relationship. Thus a public agency may not possess institutions for neglected children, but may "farm" them out to institutions which are privately owned and administered. The public agency may, however, grant money to the private institution on a per capita basis in order to meet its obligation toward the maintenance of children adjudged by a public agency (a court, for example) to be a ward of the government. Where such a cooperative relationship obtains, there obviously is a blending of responsibility and of administration.

Initiating Action. The fact that agencies have to meet certain limitations does not make them passive instruments in the hands of a legislature or of community opinion. Instead, they are active in pressing their own claims and viewpoints upon the community and the legislative body. Because of the experience a public agency secures through its activities, certain values are found and are cherished. Through experience in connection with a particular community need the public welfare agency often knows better than the general community or a legislative body what the next steps in social welfare should be. Because of the knowledge gained by the public agency new courses of action may be created from within the agency which, even though they may be without full community support (can it ever entirely be gained?), may be worthy and desirous of practical embodiment. So the public agency (and the same thing would hold true for the private agency as well) cannot sit back and wait until decisions have been made for it by the general community or by a legislative body, but must be courageous and pioneering to the extent that it uses every opportunity that is backed by sound opinion for the furtherance of new welfare goals for the community.

Legal Restrictions

But while this may be true, the public agency is faced with the necessity of operating under a specific set of legal restrictions. All that goes on in a public agency in relation to service for clients must be justified and sanctioned by reference to the welfare laws which pertain to the agency and to the special activities in question.

Usually, there is some overlap in the legal foundations of a public welfare agency. For one thing the various states have their own welfare laws. While there is fairly general agreement among the laws of the states, there are important differences. Variations even occur within a state because of different local ordinances. Finally, the federal government has its laws which relate to the states, the counties, and the local communities. The complications of this extensive overlap in legal and administrative function in the public welfare field are apparent to all who know it even in a casual way.

Political Interference

The fact that the public welfare agency is dependent upon legislative bodies implies all too often a degree of political domination which adds a restriction beyond those which purely legal regulations might provide. The rising importance of public welfare work and the increase through the years of public welfare budgets indicate that this is a ripe field for political management. Although, fortunately, the laws which regulate the activities of public welfare agencies almost everywhere take public assistance out of the hands of partisan groups and even of individual whim, the guarantee for the client of the public welfare agency is oftentimes at best minimal. This means that while certain standards must be kept by law, the law may not be so generous as it might in certain instances, because of political interference or conservatism. Thus actual needs of people may be unmet because the political requirements of meeting their needs are unfilled. No amount of sympathetic administrative foresight can take the place of the necessary legislative action.

On the other hand political management of public welfare may actually take the form of direct political interference. A state department of welfare, for example, may be seriously hampered in its program because of the necessary bipartisan composition of the department's governing board. If the board represents only one political party, the problem of political interference may be even more obvious.

The interference by politicians does not occur on one level of governmental administration, alone. It may be a factor in local, state, and federal programs. But our major interest is the actual organization of public welfare services on a local, state, and federal basis. We turn now to the task of describing the organization of public welfare services. This description will be followed in the next chapter with the types of services supplied to clients.

LOCAL WELFARE ORGANIZATION

In the discussion of the history of public welfare in Chapter 2, it was pointed out that the first type of welfare organization was the local. This fact is not surprising when one considers the general history and philosophy of the United States. Only in more recent years have citizens been contemplating coordinative action on state and federal bases, and even now there is considerable opposition to a further extension of the power of the states and of the federal government. This resistance operates regardless of the problem under consideration and derives, as has been suggested, from a faith in past ways of doing things. But whatever the distribution of welfare services among federal, state, and local governments, the fact remains that by some means or other the public services rendered clients must have an outlet in the local community. There is a difference, however, between state and federal assistance being administered by state and federal agencies in local communities directly, and the historically indigenous, locally organized public welfare departments which are in large part locally financed and managed. In this section of the chapter we are considering the latter type of public welfare organization; in the first section an example of this kind of organization was provided in the introductory case. (See also Figure 28.)

The actual area of responsibility the local agency may cover will vary according to the geographic definition of local responsibility and according to the enabling legislation provided by the larger sanctioning body, as will be seen.

Geographic Unit

Responsibility for public services exists in a number of patterns in this country. While there is but one federal government, there are forty-eight state governments and innumerable local units of government. Each division of government bears some relation to public welfare, whether positive or negative. In New England, in general, the local unit responsible for the public services is the city and town. But in the South and the West the county is the local unit of responsibility. The most confusing division of function, however, is found in the middle Atlantic states and the Midwest where a combination of county, city, town, and township can be holding responsibility. Also in several states that employ state administration of public assistance, or part of it, the local unit is the county (Illinois and Pennsylvania), while in others, districts embracing several counties or towns are established (Connecticut, Maine, New Hampshire, Vermont, etc.). There is obviously much overlapping, variation, and competition in the division of local public welfare services. New York State recently has surveyed its public welfare organization through a committee appointed by the Legislature, and has suggested certain revisions of the state-locality division of function which in operation seem to be superior to the older design.[6] The new system consists of 68 county and city public welfare districts, as against the 126 county and city agencies in existence prior to April 1, 1946.

[6] Harold C. Ostertag, "New York Revises and Simplifies Its Public Welfare System," *Social Service Review*, volume 20, number 1, March, 1946, pp. 11–17.

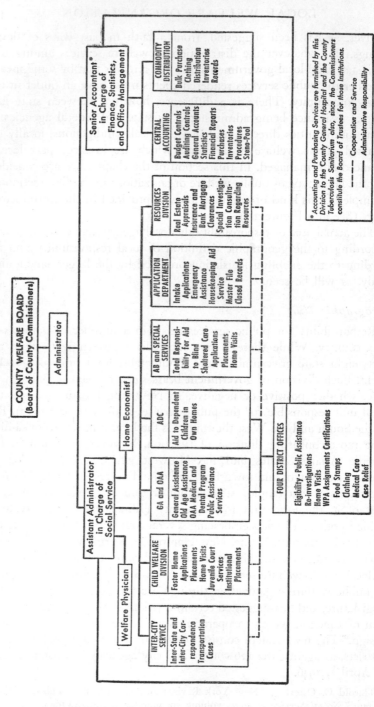

Fig. 28. Aspects of Organization and Operation of a Local Welfare Department†

ROCK COUNTY WELFARE DEPARTMENT

COUNTY WELFARE BOARD
(Board of County Commissioners)

Administrator

Senior Accountant*
in Charge of
Finance, Statistics,
and Office Management

Assistant Administrator
in Charge of
Social Service

Welfare Physician

Home Economist

INTER-CITY SERVICE
Inter-State and
Inter-City Cor-
respondence
Transportation
Cases

CHILD WELFARE DIVISION
Foster Home
Applications
Placements
Home Visits
Juvenile Court
Services
Institutional
Placements

GA and OAA
General Assistance
Old Age Assistance
OAA Medical and
Dental Program
Public Assistance
Services

ADC
Aid to Dependent
Children in
Own Homes

AB and SPECIAL SERVICES
Total Responsi-
bility for Aid
to Blind
Sheltered Care
Applications
Placements
Home Visits

APPLICATION DEPARTMENT
Intake
Applications
Emergency
Assistance
Housekeeping Aid
Service
Master File
Closed Records

RESOURCES DIVISION
Real Estate
Appraisals
Insurance and
Bank Mortgage
Clearances
Special Investiga-
tion Consulta-
tion Regarding
Resources

CENTRAL ACCOUNTING
Budget Controls
Auditing Controls
General Accounts
Statistics
Financial Reports
Purchases
Inventories
Procedures
Steno-Pool

COMMODITY DISTRIBUTION
Bulk Purchase
Clothing
Distribution
Inventories
Records

FOUR DISTRICT OFFICES
Eligibility - Public Assistance
Re-investigations
Home Visits
WPA Assignments Certifications
Food Stamps
Clothing
Medical Care
Case Relief

*Accounting and Purchasing Services are furnished by this
Division to the County General Hospital and the County
Tuberculosis Sanitarium also, since the Commissioners
constitute the Board of Trustees for those Institutions.

----- Cooperation and Service

——— Administrative Responsibility

442

Enabling Legislation

The local public welfare agency may maintain only those activities which the state has delegated to it. Thus a city which derives its power from the state will have the degree of its responsibility in local welfare activities defined for it. There may be a division of responsibility which the state and the locality share. This division may be financial, the state providing a certain share of local expenses and the city making up the difference. It may be administrative. The state may assume responsibility for the correctional care of all felonious criminals while the city maintains institutions for misdemeanants.[7] But whatever the division of responsibility, the number and scope of the activities which a local department of welfare may enjoy is in large part determined by its legal relation to the state as defined in a city charter.

State control of local public services may be permissive or mandatory. These alternatives are defined in the legislation pertaining to particular welfare activities. If it is permissive, the locality may or may not develop the services, according to the need or the ability of the local community. If it is mandatory, a definite obligation is placed on the locality to provide the service. The state, for example, under its mandatory powers, may declare that localities (towns, townships, counties, cities) must be responsible for needs of children, unemployment relief, medical service, and other welfare concerns. Under these conditions there would be no means, theoretically, by which the community could escape its responsibility to have organized services available in these categories for its members. But, practically, the situation may differ. Where the service is completely locally financed and there is no state agency to compel local action, the local community may ignore the state law. Several places, for example, have not utilized state and federal benefits for general assistance because of a failure on their part to cooperate financially (parts of Texas, South Carolina, and other localities).

The location of welfare responsibility may not always be clearly defined either by the locality or by the state. Like many developments,

---

†In Figure 28, the name of "Rock County" is fictitious. The county has a population of approximately 474,000, most of whom live in the city, which is the county seat. Fewer than 25,000 are rural-farm population. (Taken from: *Some Aspects of the Organization and Operation of Rock County Welfare Department*, American Association of Schools of Social Work, New York, undated; and Federal Security Agency.)

[7]Generally speaking, a *felony* is an offense which is punishable by a year or more of imprisonment. A *misdemeanor* is an offense punishable by less than a year of imprisonment.

public welfare has arisen in a topsy-turvy fashion. So it may not be possible to say in a particular state just who is responsible for a particular need; nevertheless, the organization to meet the need may be in existence simply because the need was met by the state or the locality or by both partially, without a too clear and formal definition of what each one's role should ideally be. There is, therefore, a "common law" tradition in public welfare work as well as elsewhere.

Personnel Practices

Use of Merit System. In most localities the lower ranking positions in public welfare are regulated through civil service. The possibility of political interference on this level is nonexistent. The lower staffs of local public welfare agencies also benefit in some places through the employment of persons who have some professional education. But since the size and scope of local agencies vary tremendously throughout the country, the specialization and skill of workers vary in accordance. A large city department of welfare may employ many grades of lower staff workers who may possess among themselves a wide array of specific talent. The staff of a small county organization may well consist of a few grades of workers, if not only one, and the degree of specialization involved may be relatively slight.

Under the 1939 Amendments to the Social Security Act, however, all persons in local departments of public welfare administering old-age assistance, aid to dependent children, and aid to the blind (federal programs) must by federal requirement be selected in accordance with a merit system. This requirement has caused more activity and change in this field than occurred in all previous history.

Election of Executives. A few of the higher administrative positions in local agencies, however, usually are not covered by civil service. The practice of securing executives varies from place to place, and no one pattern perhaps has evolved in the country on this point. Sometimes, usually in rural counties, the top public welfare official is elected along with those who fill other political positions. The dangers of this practice are almost too obvious to be commented upon. The person who is able to win an election may not be really qualified by any standard to be the executive of a public welfare agency. He may be more successful in running a political campaign than competent to perform his executive duties. Moreover, the elected welfare official may incur political debts through his having run for office, both to politicians and to special groups within the electorate, which may hamper the most objective consideration of the public welfare office. There also may be pressures which he uses upon employees to force them to work for his re-election. The practice has not been pure enough to prevent such officials from putting pressure even on clients.

Political Appointment of Executives. The executive of the local public welfare agency also may secure his office through direct political appointment on the part of a delegated official, such as a mayor. This practice is widely used. Instead of the welfare official having to run for his office, he is appointed by the party in power. This procedure obviates many of the more evil possibilities which are inherent in the direct election plan, but, nevertheless, does not entirely free the welfare official of political loyalty. In order, then, to get his position in the first place he may be dependent again not so much on his professional competence as upon his political influence and value. Similarly, the program of public welfare which is his responsibility may be turned into a quasi-political one which seeks the retention of the party in power.

Both the procedures of directly electing welfare officials and of having them appointed by political representatives also fail to take into sufficient account the fortunes of political life. The executive who is capable may be dismissed from office if he is not re-elected or if his party is not. This may mean for a local agency that its program will suffer because it will not have the guidance of a fairly permanent leader.

Selection of Executive by Public Welfare Board. A safer way of securing executive leadership for a local agency is by giving the responsibility for appointing executives to a public welfare board. The variations which exist in this method are considerable although its general lines are fairly well drawn. The public welfare board may be appointed by a political person, such as a mayor, or it may be elected. Preferably, terms of office should be overlapping so that the majority of the board membership may at no time necessarily represent the political party in power. A "staggered" system of appointments to the board can accomplish this. The appointee, under this method, owes only indirect loyalty, if any, to a political party. Thus he may be chosen more because of his ability for the job than for his value to the party in power. The turnover of leadership may also occur less frequently.

Of course, where the appointive board is simply and directly selected by the party in power, the same sorts of evils mentioned under direct appointment or election systems may hold.

Usually, appointed boards of public welfare have a larger function than that of selecting an executive (or several executives) for a local agency. The board assumes duties for policy-making, thereby regulating the activity of the executive and the whole department under his jurisdiction. Thus the board acts as a governing body, supplying for the agency the ultimate authority (except for the more final political authority).

Where public welfare agencies do not have governing boards which appoint executives, there may be need for a board which derives its authority from the executive. Such a board would have no absolute managerial function over the activities of the executive or his agency, but would act as a consultative and voluntary body to which the agency could turn for advice on agency problems and through which the agency is better interpreted to the community. The creation of this type of board would be one of the community-organizing responsibilities of an executive who saw its need.

Provisions of Security Act Apply. No matter what means are used to select a top executive for a local department of public welfare, the provisions of the 1939 Amendments to the Social Security Act must still be taken into account. These specify that executives who have direct responsibility for old-age assistance, aid to dependent children, and aid to the blind (federal programs) must be chosen by a merit system.

The political implications of public welfare, fortunately, are not universally significant. It has been possible in many localities to secure, oftentimes despite the political potentialities of the particular welfare system, those persons who have been both competent and publicly minded. Part of the explanation for this is expressed in the familiar adage, "No system is better than the people who make it up." This, however, is no excuse for those systems which by their very nature encourage political manipulation of public welfare.

Centralized Control Lacking. Local public welfare activities are not always coordinated, however, under the leadership of a single government agency, executive, or board. Some services are organized under the direct legislative function of a state government. Other services are more closely related to judicial responsibility. Still others pertain to the executive function of government. While there is no easy way of deciding practically which public services should come under the jurisdiction of the legislature, the executive, and the judiciary, this very fact has aided the present lack of centralized control over all public services, even on a local basis. Furthermore, the value of relatively disorganized public welfare agencies on a local basis may be too politically important to overcome, although it has been done in some sections of the country. It is a hope that as more and more rational and efficient interest develops in local communities, there will be a greater degree of coordination and centralized control than in the past. Divisiveness is, of course, more prone to hold sway in the larger local units because of the increased complexity of centralized control and administration. In small communities it is clearly not possible to have a large number of separate public services because of the low volume of business involved. Especially in rural counties the organization of the local agency must be all-inclusive in order that there be sufficient reason to have any one service in the first place and in order also to carry on effective work in particular areas of need.

Beyond the need for effective coordination of public welfare services within the community stands the need for greater coordination between localities. The fact that localities cannot of themselves completely solve (either financially or administratively) their local tasks makes a consideration of the state public welfare organization pertinent.

STATE WELFARE ORGANIZATION

Development of State Control

The state organization of welfare services came rather late in the development of American social work. Historically, it has been built, in many places at least, upon the already existing structure of the social services which local communities have provided. This type of growth oftentimes resulted in the states assuming primarily a coordinative function in relation to local agencies, especially in the earlier years. As coordinating agencies, state welfare organizations laid down the principles binding upon all local agencies and checked on local agencies for purposes of increasing efficiency. In the course of developing their local agency work, communities often found it necessary to call upon the states for financial assistance in order to carry on a particular program of activity. Thus a city might find itself in an especially depressed financial condition due to peculiar and special circumstances beyond its control. It might not be financially able to carry the kind of public assistance program it needed. Reliance upon state resources was indicated. In this way, states came to have responsibility not only for coordination but also for financing. In addition, state activity in public welfare has been even more direct on occasion.

Special Activities. From a relatively early time in American history, states have assumed responsibility for special groups of dependents. Criminals were among the first for whom the states provided. In time many other special groups were added: neglected children, the insane, the deaf, the dumb, the blind, the feeble-minded, the aged, the tubercular, the sick, dependent mothers and children, "impotent" poor, and able-bodied poor. As these services developed they were usually headed administratively through state channels to the legislature, the judiciary, or the executive branches of state government. Usually, each special activity was related directly to its appropriate administrative head, and the activities among the various departments of the state governments were not coordinated. Each one ran its own program and had access to the programs of others only along voluntary or high administrative lines. So the development of state welfare organization has been dependent upon the coordinative needs of local communities—needs which were larger than the resources of local communities—and upon the direct experience of the states with various types of welfare activities.

Historical Growth. The first serious attempt to organize public welfare on a state basis occurred in 1863 in Massachusetts when a State Board of Charity was constituted. The function of this Board was primarily regulative or coordinative. It did little to disturb the relationships which then existed among the local agencies and the direct service agencies managed by the state. But it was a valuable contribution for the time because it enabled the multitudinous services (of a public character) scattered throughout the state to cooperate in a mutual venture of discipline and growth.

Under the Massachusetts State Board of Charity, however, there actually was only a loose sort of coordination. It was not until 1917 in Illinois that the first really integrative state department of welfare was initiated. This department effectually brought together the various governmental activities and agencies under the administrative direction of a single public welfare department with state scope. The State Board of Charity of Massachusetts and the first department of public welfare in Illinois, however, were signposts in a general period of awareness of the need for more and more coordinative achievement in public welfare. The trend from the close of the Civil War to the present (and still operative today) is toward further state integration of welfare services. There still remains, however, considerable work to do.

State Welfare Functions

At the present time the states control various welfare functions. For the most part these functions stand somewhere between the local and the federal programs. For purposes of classification they may be grouped into three divisions: (1) supervision of locally administered welfare programs; (2) state-operated welfare services and institutions; and, (3) general activities of the state department. These will be briefly analyzed to show their meanings:

1. Supervision of Locally Administered Welfare Programs. State departments of welfare usually have control over a multiplicity of welfare programs. These may include many services which are not financed by the states, but over which the states have supervisory responsibility.

Basic to a state's supervision of local programs is research. State departments regularly survey various forms of aid to persons in need in order to determine their effectiveness. Where programs are not found to be effective, recommendations are made for their improvement. Visitations are also made to agencies and institutions to evaluate the quality of standards which prevail. This form of supervision is important for agencies and institutions which are seeking state licenses for practice, and also for those which have been practicing but which may need the stimulus which comes from an on-the-spot estimate of strengths and weaknesses.

In New York State, for example, the supervisory responsibilities include:[8]

441 hospitals
97 independent dispensaries
198 private homes for the aged
62 public homes
57 county welfare departments
11 city welfare departments
79 homes, temporary and special, for adults
45 convalescent homes
175 institutions
126 agencies, public and private
21 health agencies
26 shelters
27 vacation camps
24 other
135 special services

Obviously, the scope of such supervisory operations makes them a very important part of a state program. (See Figure 29.)

2. State-Operated Welfare Services and Institutions. State departments also maintain certain services which relate to persons in need. These services often include the following: child welfare services, institutions for delinquents and criminals, veteran services, aid to the blind, services to Indians, general relief, and assistance to the aged.

[8]*Public Social Services in 1946,* 80th Annual Report, New York State Department of Social Welfare, Legislative Document No. 76, Albany, 1947, p. 46.

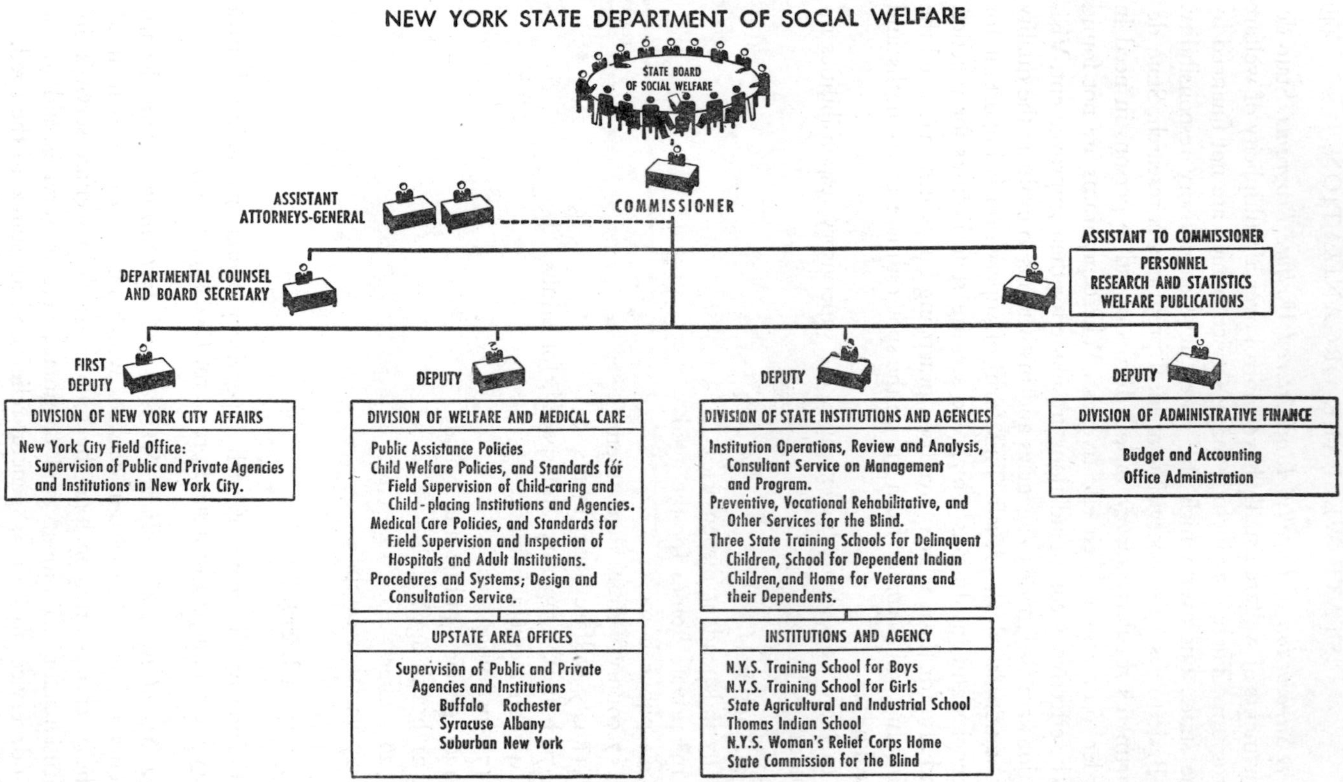

NEW YORK STATE DEPARTMENT OF SOCIAL WELFARE

FIG. 29. Social Welfare Services in New York State, 1947

A large part of these services are direct in their application to clients, but some are indirect. The direct services are maintained in some instances in connection with federal-local arrangements to which the state is a contributing factor both financially and in terms of supervision. Other services are more indirect. For example, a state department may organize a training program for the personnel of local departments or may publish manuals to aid local departments in the administration of their services as they are affected by the state requirements.

Prominent among the services which state departments offer for clients directly are institutions. These may affect many types of citizens: the sick, veterans, the aged, children, the mentally retarded, and others.

3. General Activities. State departments have responsibilities which pertain to public welfare activities. But they also have responsibilities for developing and setting standards and for supervision in the private welfare field as well. State departments are concerned with the matters which affect the well-being of citizens in all privately financed institutions and agencies. They formulate policies, rules, and regulations which are designed to fulfill these responsibilities.

The state departments of welfare act upon applications of charitable institutions, health insurance groups, and others seeking incorporation, dissolution of incorporation, and changes in their corporate powers and purposes. They license health dispensaries and issue permits for maternity care in public homes. They are responsible also for the visitation of private institutions and agencies as well as those under public auspices. In these and other ways, state departments of welfare maintain functions which cover all social welfare activities within the states, whether public or private.

The fact that state departments have responsibility for private agencies in certain respects tends to break down the common assumption of separation of public from private fields of welfare activity. As was noted previously, however, this popular conception is very largely false.

Coordination of Services

So far in the discussion of state welfare organization it has been assumed that the integration of public welfare services on a state basis is a desirable goal. At least two questions, however, may be asked regarding this assumption. First, is such integration desirable? Second, is such integration possible? Both questions are in many ways mutually dependent.

Disadvantages of Unity. The efficiency of any administrative unit which is as large-scaled as that of public welfare in a state needs to be qualified. While it may be easy to say that all public welfare services should be united, yet, through such unity, certain values of a more decentralized program may be lost. The larger the organization, the more difficult it usually is to effect executive action. The size of the administrative unit affects the number of executives it will need, and if the unit is too large there may be little opportunity for initiation anywhere within it because of the slowness with which any single action might stir a large number of interested persons. The placing of special administrative power (in military-like fashion) in the hands of chief executives hardly answers the problem, because there may be less need for initiating action from the top down than from the bottom up.

Furthermore, the organizing of public welfare services on a state basis without regard for the specialization of services implied in such a large enterprise may weaken the efficiency of the various specialties. There may be value administratively in having groups of interested specialists united only among themselves, rather than joined with others who may not be as well versed in their particular problems. Thus if all of the hospitals within a state are organized under one administration, it may be possible for the hospital heads to act more quickly and intelligently than if they had not only to meet among themselves but also with the representatives of old-age assistance or unemployment units of the state welfare department. There are values, however, in the other procedure too.

Integration and Coordination. The line of reasoning followed thus far has suggested that it probably is not desirable to integrate the welfare services of states too extensively. But this does not mean that public welfare activities should not be coordinated. There is a vital distinction between "integration" and "coordination" which bears examination. For one thing, state services can be integrated or consolidated to prevent unnecessary duplication of services. If several types of state-supported programs are doing essentially the same job, it usually is possible to decide through a centralized and administrative agency which department might well appropriate the service and which might cease performing it. Coordination, rather, signifies cooperation between two units of social welfare. These may be united under one administration or under two or more. The essential element is the cooperative. Through cooperation it may be possible for two agencies, each designed to give partial aid to veterans, for example, to understand what their partial roles are and to achieve the greatest degree of general service for veterans on a preconceived, deliberative basis. This cooperation may be possible without administrative integration, but if the services are voluminous and complex they probably will need a standing connection for the establishment of cooperative relationships.

Value of Planning. Coordination may also signify planning. In any state the changeability of the public welfare needs requires constant revision and planning of the ways to meet the needs. If there is a high degree of centralized coordination, such work may be done more easily than if it is left to haphazard opportunities and happenings. The possibilities of this type of coordination are seen in the case where a new service is to be added to already existing ones. Just how the new service should be related to the old, how it should be set up in the first place (from the viewpoint of internal organization), and what measures of cooperation it would require from the other state agencies are the proper responsibilities of a state department of welfare.

State Integration, Desirable or Possible? These three functions—planning, cooperation, and avoiding duplication—give an idea as to what the role of the state welfare department might be. Obviously, there are other possibilities, as the actual operations of state departments of public welfare ably testify. With these three in mind, however, the question "Is state integration desirable?" can be answered with a "Yes" and a "No." Yes, it is valuable if it means that a degree of coordination shall be achieved which shall overcome the disparate interests, partial views, and fragmentized services of local agencies. No, it is not desirable if it means a general absorption of all state welfare activities into a colossus of an administrative hegemony.

Of course, the second query "Is state integration possible?" is connected in many respects with the first. The question of "possibility" involves the traditional growth of the state welfare organizations. It has been said that there is a definite trend toward greater state participation in welfare services. In that sense one can be hopeful that the trend will not stop until further integrative and coordinative work is done to improve the organization of public welfare in many states. If the trend were to continue to the point where it would obliterate all decentralized possibilities, it would be dangerous because it would lead to inefficiency. On the other hand the real answer to the question lies in an appreciation of cultural dynamics (which reminds us that there seldom is a social problem which is attacked scientifically in a thoroughgoing fashion and solved in toto). Usually, as the term *trend* implies, the development of centralized services has been a slow growth, occasioned by much social pain. However, the fact that during the last two decades almost a third of the states have made definite progress along this line suggests that the rate of change is fairly rapid.

The reorganization which was effected in a number of states through the requirements of the Social Security Act is noteworthy in this connection. According to the 1939 Amendments to the Act every state must "either provide for the establishment or designation of a single state agency to administer the plan or provide for the establishment or designation of a single state agency to supervise the administration of the plan." This requirement especially affected those states in which there was a low degree of public welfare coordination and integration. As a result, there was much organization and reorganization of state agencies and services.

Forms of Organization. The organization of state welfare programs at present takes a number of forms. These are appropriate to the historical development of the states. They also reflect the activities of the various public welfare policies and administrations. The forms are briefly the following: (*1*) *Omnibus departments.* These are represented by Rhode Island, New Jersey, Georgia, and Wisconsin. In such departments there is a consolidation of practically all major welfare activities, broadly interpreted, within one administrative unit. (*2*) *Two departments.* These are represented by Pennsylvania and Tennessee. In these states the public welfare activities are centered in two administrative units, namely, institutions and public assistance. (*3*) *Three departments.* These are represented by New York, Massachusetts, Michigan, and California. (See Figures 30 and 31.) In these states the welfare activities are distributed among three administrative units, namely, public welfare, corrections, and mental health. (*4*) *Miscellaneous departments.* There are some states which combine features administratively, which have already been mentioned, but with their own individuality. Thus two states, Maine and Missouri, include public health and public welfare under one head.

There is no basis at present for deciding which of these types of state public welfare organization is most suitable. Historic reasons often make one preferable to another or to all others in certain states. It may be possible that through more extended experience and by greater administrative insight one or more of these plans may become nationally desirable, but this is not now the case.

Executive Administration

State departments of welfare have been organized traditionally in three ways. These ways differ in detail from state to state, according to the specific requirements of the states. They may be outlined here as "types," bearing in mind that as such they reveal the possibilities and,

ORGANIZATION OF THE CALIFORNIA STATE DEPARTMENT OF SOCIAL WELFARE

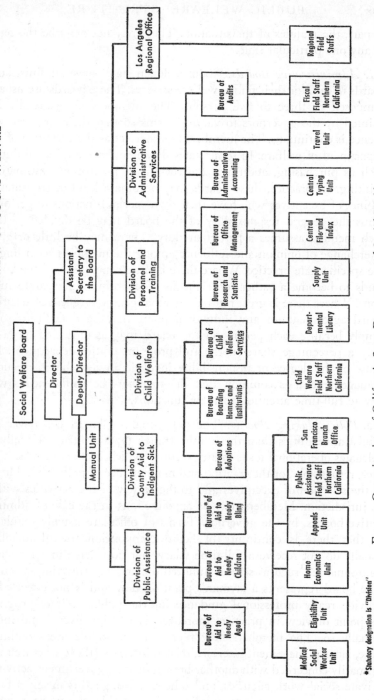

FIG. 30. Organization of California State Department of Social Welfare, 1946

*Statutory designation is "Division"

in part, the realities of the situation. They may not describe the setup of any one particular state.

1. Administrative Boards. About a dozen states have administrative boards to care for their public welfare services. These boards are usually composed of three to five persons. The members are generally appointed by the governors to varying terms so that their corporate existence is continuous. The members together act as the executive of the department of welfare. In some states they may have additional duties, such as purchasing, auditing, construction of institutions, estimating, printing. In practice, these boards may become a kind of consultative cabinet of executives who have their own special functions to perform. Thus the general responsibility of the board may be divided so that each member assumes a particular duty. There may be little or great interchange of opinion and influence among the members according to the specific state practice. Where there is little compensation, the board tends to become a rather loose means of coordinating separate functions. Where there is great mutual interchange, the problem of securing board agreement on any individual point may be difficult to solve simply because each person on the board may assume that he holds only a percentage share in the full program of the department. Because of the degree of responsibility involved in such board-executive management, it is common that the members be paid officials who devote full-time attention to their functions.

2. Policy-Making Boards. The policy-making board has fewer administrative duties than the administrative type of board. Usually, it delegates operational tasks to an executive which it chooses. It is, however, responsible for the creation and maintenance of policy, in addition to the selection of executives and to the review of the activities within its jurisdiction. Members may be appointed, as in the case of administrative boards, by the governor. Terms of office are usually regulated so that there is continuity of board composition. Board members usually do not receive a full-time salary, but do receive in some states a nominal fee, such as several hundred dollars, and traveling expenses. The board represents a layman's point of view and is not expected to provide really professional guidance for the public welfare program. Its point of view in practice, moreover, is usually diverse and intentionally so. The members may represent geographic areas within a state, labor-management interests, related interests (those who are more primarily concerned with another branch of state government activity), private social work agencies, and others. Through this means a fairly heterogeneous approach to public welfare problems can be secured.

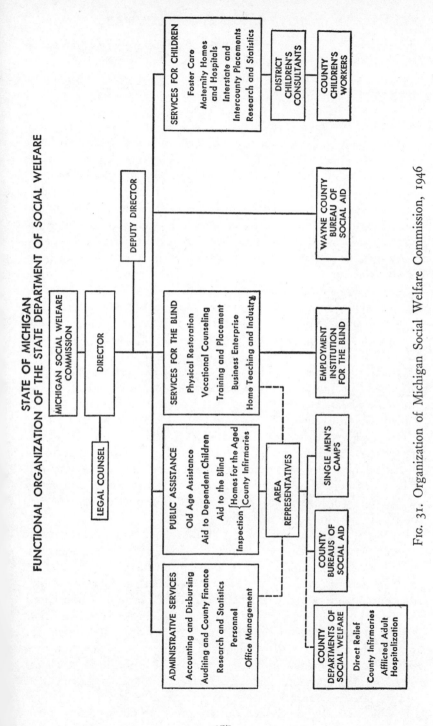

STATE OF MICHIGAN
FUNCTIONAL ORGANIZATION OF THE STATE DEPARTMENT OF SOCIAL WELFARE

MICHIGAN SOCIAL WELFARE COMMISSION

DIRECTOR

LEGAL COUNSEL

DEPUTY DIRECTOR

SERVICES FOR CHILDREN
Foster Care
Maternity Homes and Hospitals
Interstate and Intercounty Placements
Research and Statistics

DISTRICT CHILDREN'S CONSULTANTS

COUNTY CHILDREN'S WORKERS

WAYNE COUNTY BUREAU OF SOCIAL AID

SERVICES FOR THE BLIND
Physical Restoration
Vocational Counseling
Training and Placement
Business Enterprise
Home Teaching and Industry

EMPLOYMENT INSTITUTION FOR THE BLIND

PUBLIC ASSISTANCE
Old Age Assistance
Aid to Dependent Children
Aid to the Blind
Inspection { Homes for the Aged County Infirmaries

AREA REPRESENTATIVES

SINGLE MEN'S CAMPS

ADMINISTRATIVE SERVICES
Accounting and Disbursing
Auditing and County Finance
Research and Statistics
Personnel
Office Management

COUNTY BUREAUS OF SOCIAL AID

COUNTY DEPARTMENTS OF SOCIAL WELFARE
Direct Relief
County Infirmaries
Afflicted Adult Hospitalization

Fig. 31. Organization of Michigan Social Welfare Commission, 1946

457

There may be difficulties in this type of public welfare organization because the executive chosen to perform the administrative duties must relate himself essentially to a board with limited professional understanding.

3. *Individual Executives*. In some states the authority and responsibility for public welfare services are lodged in one person, an executive director of the department of welfare. He is usually appointed by the governor and is directly accountable to him. This means that he probably will have direct access to the governor on matters that concern his department. He may also be able to initiate action more promptly and directly within his department because authority is concentrated in him rather than in a board. On the other hand, if the executive is considered as being a political appointee, he may lose his position if the party loses an election and, as a result, the department may suffer from the change of leadership. Increasingly, however, the individual executive type of administration of state public welfare is being preferred by those who understand the problem of administration. While it has its own peculiar defects, it probably surpasses the other types in its clear delineation of responsibility and in its efficiency.

In some states, positions other than that of chief executive today reside in the hands of governors. The appointment of the department heads under the welfare official may also be the governor's responsibility. The lower positions in state public welfare, as in local public welfare, are at present under civil service. Also, as in local administration, those who are directly responsible for administering old-age assistance, aid to the blind, and aid to dependent children are regulated by the merit system. It is to be hoped that a further extension of civil service will enable state departments of welfare to be removed from the influence of even the best-minded of politicians.

Because of the wide scope of state welfare services it is necessary for all states that have centralized control to subdivide administrative responsibility. It is common to have divisions on the basis of specialized services operating within a department. Some of the more usual divisions are: public assistance, children's services, corrections, handicapped, hospitals, public relations, in-service training, inspection. Not all of these, however, may be found necessarily in any one state department.

Not only must state departments of public welfare maintain their own operational organization for services which are direct to clients, but also they must relate themselves effectively to local departments of welfare. This circumstance has in many states created a state organization which is highly diversified and responsive to differing sets of conditions and problems. Thus a state department may be more directly related to clients in certain categories of need or in certain areas of the state than it may in others. The degree of consistency of state programs is usually not very great, principally because of the random manner in which local responsibility has historically broadened into state responsibility and finally, in large measure, into federal responsibility.

FEDERAL WELFARE ORGANIZATION

Historical Policy

There are some who find it paradoxical that the federal government has a Department of National Defense and other departments but no Department of Social Welfare. This omission is, however, quite in keeping with the historical conception of the role of the federal government. Not until recently has the idea of a federal Department of Social Welfare come to have very much meaning, and its importance is not everywhere recognized even now.

The traditional view of the function of the federal government omitted any responsibility on its part for extensive social services to the national community. Local responsibility was everywhere accepted, and not without considerable reason. Throughout the long course of the English Poor Laws, the forerunners of so much in our American tradition, stress was placed upon local responsibility. Our social heritage made it exceedingly appropriate, even inevitable, that the emphasis in American public welfare should also be upon the local community.

Factors Effecting Participation

A number of factors arose over a period of time in this country to modify the thinking and practice of "individualism" and to affect, in turn, the locus of responsibility for public welfare. Some of these factors were primarily of a technological character. The inventions in communication and transportation helped shrink the size of the national community and made of what were formerly isolated, small communities, more or less appendages to larger social entities. Social space shrank to such an extent that what was originally a distance problem within a locality became suitably one between two communities, and what were problems between communities became state problems, and what were state problems became national problems. On these grounds alone it was desirable for the federal government to take a more active responsibility in social service affairs. But there were other factors also. Some were social. Of this category one of the most important is the fact that the national community grew in size from a few million inhabitants in its earliest years to almost a hundred and fifty millions. Originally, the sparsely settled regions of the country hardly called for federal action of many kinds, certainly not in the social services. A federal program would have been too expensive and too unwieldy to operate with efficiency. It was logical for local communities to assume responsibility for most matters.

Also among the factors which encouraged the rise of federal responsibility in public welfare were some which were philosophical or ideological. The older political theory which made little room for governmental participation in social welfare gave way under the impact of many forces to an outlook which saw fewer problems and disvalues in participation than it did in nonparticipation. Somewhat changed economic theories and practices contributed to this development too. The modification of the extreme individualism of Protestantism and the rise of the "social gospel movement" within the churches also gave strength to the newer viewpoint.

As was mentioned in the chapter on the history of social work, there were other reasons why the federal government has come to assume such a large share of responsibility for general welfare. Certainly, one of these is the fact that the federal government always has been responsible for the welfare of certain special groups within the population, such as the Indians and war veterans. This peculiar responsibility broadened over the years to include more people and varying categories.

Another of the reasons for the significant rise of the federal services was the depression of the 1930's. As was mentioned previously, the depression taxed the financial resources of the private agencies far beyond their limits. The voluntary agencies were simply unable to handle the situation because of their limited resources. There was no practical means of assuming the burden of economic support for the many persons and families in need during that period, as there has been none since, aside from the federal government. Because of the same factors most localities and states were unable to finance the needs of the time.

Vigorous National Approach Needed

Thus the current acceptance by the federal government of responsibility in the social services has been a result of many and varied forces. The fact which remains, whatever one's personal outlook on the question of federal participation may be, is that today, given the vastness and the complexity of many of our welfare problems, only a vigorous national approach is satisfactory for their solution. The federal government in social welfare is here to stay. No other adequate means of meeting the problems we face has received the same popular acceptance.

It should be pointed out, however, that federal participation has not lessened the local activity in public welfare, but rather has tended to build it up and make it more adequate to its needs. Each area of government—local, state, and federal—has its own peculiar place in the social work setup. Each one assumes complete responsibility for some programs, and cooperates on others.

It is entirely possible that in time a federal Department of Welfare will be created to integrate and coordinate the already existing federal social services. In fact, the impulse for such a Department has been a force, albeit a weak one, for a number of years. In 1921, under the Presidency of Warren G. Harding, a bill to initiate a Department of Public Welfare was introduced into the Senate, but it was defeated. Again, in 1937, under the aegis of President Franklin D. Roosevelt, this need was formulated by his Committee on Administrative Management. Although several bills were submitted to Congress, they were not passed.

Federal Social Welfare Agencies

In the meantime the social welfare operations of the federal government have been carried on through various channels. Some of the work is administered within the cabinet departments of the government. In addition, there are a few independent federal agencies established for just this purpose. Perhaps the chief of these is the Federal Security Agency.

Some of the social work agencies and activities of the federal government will be listed and described briefly. It is difficult to know, however, which functions of the federal government are within the boundaries of public welfare as described in this chapter. In a sense almost all of the activities of the federal government are concerned with the general social welfare of the national citizenry. But there are practical limitations to such a conception, and here a narrower list will be provided.

1. The Office of Indian Affairs. The Office of Indian Affairs, under the Department of the Interior, is primarily charged with the well-being of American Indians. The Indians are exceptional in regard to federal care. They are the only national minority group which has a special governmental agency interested specifically in their welfare. The underlying reason for this treatment is fairly obvious. Perhaps the Office of Indian Affairs is a means whereby the national community attempts to ease its conscience in regard to the past treatment of the Indians. At any rate the Office does maintain a number of special functions pertaining to Indians which might be termed social welfare activities. For example, it provides an educational program for the 417,000 Indians of the nation (about 30,000 are in Alaska). It operates some 400 day schools, boarding schools, and community centers. It also aids Indian children who are attending public schools. Through 70 hospitals and sanitariums, and more than 100 clinics, the health of the Indians is checked. Moreover, the Office offers social services for the needy, the sick, and the disabled, and aids tribal leaders in securing and maintaining peace. Because the Indians own about 56,000,000 acres of land, a special program of agricultural and industrial guidance is proffered which aids (by means of irrigation, erosion control, forestry management, planned land-use) the development of natural resources, and works for the securing of adequate land where nonreproductive land hinders Indian life. It, furthermore, administers tribal and individual money held in trust by the government and provides credit to individuals and groups who wish to develop their resources. The stated purpose of the Office of Indian Affairs is "to aid the Indians to become economically independent through the use of their own resources and skills, and to adapt indigenous Indian institutions and culture to modern conditions."

2. *The Bureau of Prisons.* The Bureau of Prisons is another of the special departments of federal social service. It was created by a Congressional act in 1930 and located within the Department of Justice. The Bureau is responsible for those persons who have violated federal laws. Its work includes prison management with all of its various details. It also entails the parole supervision of federal offenders. Its Director is appointed by the Attorney General of the United States. He, in turn, may appoint two deputies to help in the administration of the program. The lower ranking positions are under the control of civil service.

3. *The Veterans Administration.* The Veterans Administration provides another example of federal service to a special group within the population. It is a nondepartmental agency of the government although it necessarily cooperates with many branches of the government. It was created in 1930 by executive order under authorization of an act of Congress. This act enabled the President to consolidate and coordinate under a single control all federal agencies dealing with veterans. The agencies which previously had dealt with veterans were: Bureau of

Pensions, the United States Veterans Bureau, and the National Home for Disabled Volunteer Soldiers.

The purpose of the Veterans Administration is stated comprehensively in the *United States Government Manual* as follows:

> The Veterans Administration administers all laws relating to the relief of, and other benefits provided by law for, members of the military and naval forces. It is responsible for extending relief to veterans and to dependents of deceased veterans of all wars, and to veterans and to dependents of deceased veterans who served in the Government military and naval establishments during time of peace, as provided by the various acts of Congress. These laws include, in addition to compensation, pensions, vocational rehabilitation, and education, the guarantee of loans for purchase or construction of homes, farms, and business property, readjustment allowance for veterans who are unemployed, Government life insurance, death benefits, adjusted compensation, emergency and other officers' retirement pay, and physical examinations, hospital and outpatient treatment, or domiciliary care. The Veterans Administration also provides Government Life Insurance and administers the insurance section of the Soldiers' and Sailors' Civil Relief Act for persons in the active military service.

These purposes obviously entail a large organization for their achievement. The activities of the Administration have been divided into a number of Services, some of which may be mentioned: Veterans' Claims Service; Dependents' Claims Service; Vocational Rehabilitation and Education Service; Finance Service (responsible for the accounting of the money appropriated for the Administration's work); Insurance Service; Medical and Hospital Service; National Homes Service; Construction Service (responsible for the construction of governmental, rather than private, homes, and facilities for the care of veterans); Supply Service (responsible for all supplies and equipment used by the Administration); and others. In addition to this division into various Services, there are regional divisions throughout the country, numbering now about 150. These regional divisions are subdivided in order to provide easy geographical access to veterans. The subdivisions are called Branch Offices and Contact Units.

4. Special Wartime Agencies. The national government provided various temporary services during the Second World War.[9]

[9] The War Refugee Board aided refugees from enemy oppression. The War Manpower Commission sought the best possible utilization of manpower by means of training and proper placement. The War Relief Control Board controlled the giving of relief to various groups affected by the war. The United Nations Relief and Rehabilitation Administration (U.N.R.R.A.) aided the in-

5. National Housing Agency. The National Housing Agency, established in 1941, represents another public welfare agency in at least some of its aspects. Under it, the Federal Public Housing Authority seeks the improvement of public housing in the country.

6. Farmers Home Administration. An activity of the Department of Agriculture which might come under the heading of public welfare is the Farmers Home Administration (formerly called the Farm Security Administration), established in 1937. Under its program nearly 900,000 farm families have been aided by loans to secure various farm and home supplies needed to make a living and to increase production of farm commodities. In 1945 there were more than 2,500 veterans of the Second World War who were recipients of governmental aid of this sort. The loans are given along with technical guidance as to how the money might best be invested. The nature of this guidance is as broad and inclusive as agriculture itself.

In addition to such loans to individual farmers, the Administration provides loans to groups of low-income farmers for machinery and other facilities which they may jointly use. The Administration also helps those to whom it loans money by setting up group health services in cooperation with local medical practitioners.

Other divisions within the Department of Agriculture which might be classified as public welfare services are the Federal Crop Insurance Corporation and the Bureau of Human Nutrition and Home Economics.

7. The Women's Bureau. The Women's Bureau of the Department of Labor was established by Congress in 1920 and has as its purposes the formulating of standards and policies for promoting the welfare of wage-earning women, improving their working conditions, and advancing their opportunities for worthwhile employment. A Labor Advisory Committee composed of the representatives of ten of the larger labor unions of the country assists the Bureau in its activities.

8. The Federal Security Agency. The Federal Security Agency comprises what is possibly the most direct and largest of all of the federal programs in public welfare. Because of this, it merits a more detailed analysis than has been given to the other programs. The Federal Secu-

---

habitants of liberated countries, arranged for the return of displaced persons, and helped restore essential industries and services. This latter board was created as an international agency in 1943 through the signing of an agreement at the White House by the United Nations and other nations associated with them in the war.

rity Agency was established in 1939 as the result of a long series of reorganizations in the social and welfare sections of the federal administration. It first embraced the Civilian Conservation Corps, the National Youth Administration, the Office of Education, the Public Health Service, the Social Security Board, and the United States Employment Service (transferred to the War Manpower Commission in 1942). When the Agency was reorganized later, it was given the Film and Radio Services of the former National Emergency Council as a part of its Office of Education. These services, however, were closed in the summer of 1940. The participation of the government in the American Printing House for the Blind also was transferred at this time to the Agency. Another plan of reorganization of the Agency saw the inclusion within it of the Food and Drug Administration (formerly a part of the Department of Agriculture), St. Elizabeth's Hospital, Freedmen's Hospital, Howard University, and the Columbia Institution for the Deaf—all the latter from the Department of the Interior. In the spring of 1943 the functions of the Office of Defense Health and Welfare Services (including its Health and Medical Committee) were transferred to the Agency from the Office for Emergency Management. At this time also the Office of Community War Services and the Committee on Physical Fitness (the latter closed in the summer of 1945) were created. The Office of Vocational Rehabilitation was created and assigned to the Federal Security Agency in the summer of 1943.

In the summer of 1946, Congress passed Reorganization Plan II, which reorganized the Federal Security Agency in a number of ways. Three governmental services were transferred to the Agency: The United States Employees Compensation Commission, the Children's Bureau (previously a part of the Department of Labor), and the Division of Vital Statistics. Under this reorganization the Federal Security Agency has been constituted as four main operating branches with six staff offices. The four main operating branches are: (a) Office of Education; (b) United States Public Health Service; (c) Social Security Administration; and (d) Office of Special Services. The six staff agencies have the following titles which, in part, explain their function: Executive Assistant, General Counsel, Research, Information, Federal-State Relations, and Inter-Agency and International Relations. A description of the four main branches follows:

a. Office of Education. Although the Office of Education was in continual existence from 1867, it was not until 1939 that it became a formal part of the Federal Security Agency under the President's Reorganization Plan I. The Office maintains a number of activities. These may be listed briefly: (1) It collects statistics on almost all forms of educational activity, including schools, colleges, universities, libraries, programs of instruction, administrative procedures; (2) it makes studies of special problems in the field of education and issues reports which pertain to such problems; (3) it maintains a consultative and advisory service to educational institutions, to students, and to representatives of foreign countries; (4) it administers a program of grants-in-aid to education; (5) it conducts special programs not within the scope of those responsibilities noted above but of importance to the field of education.

The Office was active during the war period in adapting its facilities to the needs created by the war. It also has maintained an Inter-American Educational Relations program which has sought to develop understanding in that area.

In addition, the Office of Education has educational functions relating to the Columbia Institution for the Deaf, Howard University, and the American Printing House for the Blind.

The Columbia Institution for the Deaf, in existence since 1857, was transferred to the Federal Security Agency in 1940. The Institution cares for all deaf mutes of teachable age within the District of Columbia, without charge. The advanced department of the Institution, Gallaudet College, offers a course of studies which is unique of its kind.

Howard University was established in 1867 and was transferred to the Federal Security Agency in 1940. The University offers education to Negroes through nine colleges and schools, many of which are professional in character. The University is supported in part by Congressional funds and in part by private contributions.

The American Printing House for the Blind was established in 1858. It is privately owned. The federal government through the Office of Education, however, contributes to its support through annual appropriations.

b. United States Public Health Service. The United States Public Health Service, created in 1798, was transferred to the Federal Security Agency in 1939. What began as a special governmental service to merchant seamen has become one of the most extensive and comprehensive health services in the country. Its activities may be listed as follows:

1. Federal-State Cooperative Program. The Service cooperates with other federal agencies and with state and local agencies on matters relating to public health, health education, and sanitation. For this purpose an annual appropriation not to exceed $20,000,000 has been authorized, although the sums usually spent are not that large. A $10,000,000 program for the prevention, treatment, and control of tuberculosis is another part of this cooperative service. Sixteen million dollars was appropriated in 1946 for the combating of venereal disease. About $2,500,000 was granted in 1946 to care for special wartime problems in connection with the armed services. These large sums of money are an indication of the strength of the Service's activities in the area of federal-state cooperation.

2. *Research*. The Service, through the National Institute of Health, various field stations, and the National Cancer Institute, maintains a research program which investigates the causes and methods of prevention of disease. During the war especially, diseases of importance to the Departments of War and Navy were investigated. About $2,000,000 is currently being spent on research by the Service.

3. *Control of Biologic Products*. The Service controls, in interstate commerce, the manufacture and sale of biologic products used medicinally by means of inspecting factories, testing of products, and licensing in order to assure purity. Many persons benefited during the war by the standardization of high efficiency in the collection and use of blood plasma which was achieved by the Service.

4. *The Prevention of the Introduction and Spread of Disease*. The Service checks through its stations all persons who enter the United States, both immigrants and domestic travelers. It also is interested in preventing and controlling the spread of disease between the states.

5. *Hospitalization and Institutions*. The Service administers a wide array of medical facilities: 25 marine hospitals, 120 relief stations, 133 contact hospitals located in ports not served by the marine hospitals, a hospital for the care of lepers, two hospitals for drug addicts, Freedmen's Hospital in the District of Columbia (a general hospital connected with Howard University), and St. Elizabeth's Hospital (a mental hospital for members of the armed forces, certain residents of the District of Columbia, and other federal charges). It also maintains a medical program within federal penal institutions.

By the terms of the Hospital Survey and Construction Act of August 13, 1946, the Service is authorized to supervise the federal funds that are allotted to states as grants-in-aid under the Act for the conduct of state-wide surveys of the needs for hospitals and related facilities, and for the construction of such facilities.

6. *Dissemination of Public Health Information*. Through all of the popular educational means the Service provides information relating to public health.

7. *Administration of Regulatory Laws*. The Service is responsible for the administration of those laws which pertain to the development and maintenance of national public health.

The Division of Vital Statistics which, until the reorganization of the Federal Security Agency in 1946, was in the Department of Commerce, is now within the United States Public Health Service. This Division seeks to promote the adoption by the states of uniform and improved standards of registering births and deaths. It makes a monthly survey of mortality by a sampling method and publishes this and other reports pertaining to the vital statistics of the nation.

As was mentioned in the chapter on psychiatric social work, the United States Public Health Service has been given the responsibility for the administration of the National Mental Health Act, passed by Congress in June, 1946.

c. Social Security Administration. Perhaps the most significant of all of the activities of the Federal Security Agency to the student of public social work is the Social Security Administration. Its activities can be regarded with little question as constituent parts of public welfare.

The Social Security Administration was established (originally as the Social Security Board) under the provisions of the Social Security Act of 1935. It became part of the Federal Security Agency in 1939. The functions of the Administration are carefully defined by the Social Security Act of 1935 and its Amendments of 1939. They include responsibility for the general determination of policies and action in the following categories: (1) The administration of federal old-age and survivors' insurance. The amounts of money thus spent are certified by the Administration to the Treasury Department for disbursement. (2) The approval of state unemployment compensation laws and the certification of those states which are eligible, upon regular examination, for federal payments. The Administration also cooperates with the Treasury Department and employers to certify the amounts which may be counted toward tax payments. (3) The approval of state plans for old-age assistance, aid to dependent children, and aid to the blind, again reporting to the Treasury Department regarding those items which are of interest to the Department. (4) The making of studies and recommendations on ways in which the economic security of the nation's citizens may be strengthened through plans of social insurance and other methods. In addition to these functions, the Administration had specific wartime responsibilities.

The Administration operates through a commissioner and his staff. The commissioner is in charge of the general management of the program of the Administration. Supporting him are various divisions of activity-units such as: procurement and property, library and reference services, personnel and business management, publications and review, operations in regional offices, advisory services to the states, budget, general coordination, and procedures.

The major program of the Administration is organized under four Bureaus. These may be briefly noted and described.

1. Bureau of Old-Age and Survivors Insurance. This program involves a large amount of bookkeeping as to the amounts of money that employees and employers contribute to the general trust fund out of which insurance benefits and administrative costs are taken. Other functions are: determining the eligibility of workers for the insurance, certifying to the Treasury Department the amounts of money which should be paid to individual claimants, maintaining wage records on all persons so insured in order that their benefits may be accurately determined, and many additional activities which tend to help in making the insurance program effective.

The Bureau acts through five regional offices appropriately placed throughout the country. In addition there are 422 field offices, 38 branch offices, and 1,496 stations. Cases usually enter at the stations, but any person who is dissatisfied with the treatment may appeal to the next higher office.

In order to conduct its program effectively the Bureau maintains an interest in research regarding all of those happenings which might affect its program.

2. *Bureau of Employment Security.* This Bureau, which is responsible for the federal program of unemployment benefits, mainly coordinates the separate programs of the various states rather than dispenses benefits directly to recipients. It is the states themselves that are expressly concerned with the crediting of workers, the determining of benefit rights and eligibility, the collection of contributions, and the payment of benefits. The Bureau is, however, concerned with the state management of unemployment benefits. Because federal funds which reimburse the states for their maintenance of unemployment benefit arrangements have been restricted by standards of practice determined by the Social Security Act, as amended, it is the Bureau's responsibility to see that the states meet the requirements of the Act. When the Bureau is satisfied that these have been met, it certifies payment to the states.

The concrete provisions which restrict state activity do not require that all states pay the same unemployment benefits. Actually, there is wide variation among the states. But the provisions do require that state benefits be paid through public employment offices or such other agencies that the Bureau may approve. The Bureau also tries to protect the worker whose benefits are threatened because he refuses a position which fails to meet adequate labor conditions. It, furthermore, requires that the states deposit all money which they collect in the federal trust fund established for this purpose. Likewise, states can withdraw money from the fund only to pay benefits. The states are obligated to pay benefits promptly and to provide the means whereby dissatisfied workers may appeal their cases.

In addition to these concerns, which are specifically required of the Bureau, there are others of a more general nature. Thus the Bureau maintains a service to the states whereby state problems of an administrative or financial character may benefit from federal experience and knowledge. Also among the other activities of the Bureau is a program of research on the trends and needs most pertinent to the subject.

3. Bureau of Public Assistance. The Bureau of Public Assistance, like the Bureau of Employment Security, is not directly responsible for eligibility conditions and amounts of payments to those receiving public assistance. These are state responsibilities. The federal government has a more responsible role, however, in the Bureau of Public Assistance than in the Bureau of Employment Security, because it shares both in the administrative costs of the program and in the actual disbursements to individuals.

The Bureau regulates three types of public assistance, as definitely prescribed by the terms of the Social Security Act: old-age assistance, aid to dependent children, and aid to the blind.

The Bureau's responsibility toward the states is the same for all three areas of activity. Thus the states cannot require eligibility conditions which are more restrictive than certain maximums which are maintained by the Bureau. The states, moreover, must participate financially in the program in order to benefit from it. The states must have a central controlling and disbursing system. State benefits must be in effect in all political subdivisions, thus cutting off opportunities for political interference with this welfare program. Certain standards of administration must be maintained by the states. The states must hold information granted them by applicants and recipients of assistance in confidence. Hearings must be available for dissatisfied clients. A method of taking into account the financial resources of applicants must also be a part of the program of the states.

Before a state may receive federal funds it must submit a plan of operation to the Bureau for approval. When this has been granted, a state may receive from the federal government a portion of the total costs of assistance payments and administrative costs. The maximums to which a state may call upon the federal government for support are determined by law, although the states may be more generous in their program, paying out the additional funds necessary from their own treasuries. The Bureau requires that whatever sums are paid in specific cases be paid in cash rather than in goods or services.

The Bureau also maintains a research and counseling program for the states and for itself.

4. The United States Children's Bureau. The United States Children's Bureau, formerly a part of the Department of Labor until the summer of 1946, has engaged in social welfare activities since its creation by President Taft in 1912. Its original charter required that the Bureau "investigate and report to said Department upon all matters pertaining to the welfare of children and child life among all classes of our people, and shall especially investigate the questions of infant mortality, the birth rate, orphanage, juvenile courts, desertion, dangerous occupations, accidents and diseases of children, employment, legislation affecting children in the several States and Territories." This assigned task of research has been conducted on the whole with admirable skill. The reports of the Bureau comprise some of the best that are presently available within the field which it represents. They are the work, more specifically, of the several divisions of the Bureau: the Industrial Division; the Division of Research in Child Development; the Delinquency Division; the Social Service Division; the Division of Statistical Research; and the Editorial Division.

In addition to its duties of investigating and reporting on the welfare of children, the Bureau also maintains a social service program of its own. From 1922 to 1929 it administered the Maternity and Infancy Act of 1921, and prior to that period, the Federal Child-Labor Act of 1917. At present it administers the maternity and child welfare provisions of the Social Security Act of 1935 through the Division of Maternal and Child Health, the Crippled Children's Division, and the Child Welfare Division. Organizationally the work is divided into five regional offices for each service.

The responsibility for applying the Fair Labor Standards Act of 1938 in the field of child labor formerly was within the province of the Children's Bureau. By this Act, children under 16 years of age are excluded from employment in establishments which produce goods for interstate commerce, except that children of 14 and 15 may work in occupations other than manufacturing and mining (a special provision for farm labor) under certain conditions. Hazardous occupations may not use children under 18. The administration of the Act in regard to child welfare was left to the Department of Labor when the Children's Bureau became a part of the Federal Security Agency in 1946.

A further feature of the Bureau is its cooperation with other American countries in activities which relate to the promotion of child welfare.

During the period of the Second World War special problems were felt by the Bureau. To meet these, the National Commission on Children in Wartime was appointed. The Commission published effective literature on ways and means of meeting wartime children's needs. It also called conferences in various places to try to formulate techniques of acting on behalf of children. The Bureau, during the war, also managed a $44,000,-000 program of state aid for emergency maternity and infant care needs for the families of enlisted men of certain categories in the armed forces.

The problem of juvenile delinquency, especially significant in war years, also was approached by the Bureau. It sought the extension of services to children who might have become delinquent. It worked with other governmental agencies to originate plans of delinquency prevention and treatment. It conducted conferences on the problem. It also created several studies relating to wartime delinquency.

d. Office of Special Services. The Office of Special Services is new to the Federal Security Agency and was created by the reorganization of 1946. The following are within its jurisdiction:

The Bureau of Employees' Compensation and the Employees' Compensation Appeals Board are mainly concerned with the protection of federal employees and do not pertain to the public at large.

The Office of Community War Services, now liquidated, was developed in the war years to implement the Federal Security Administrator's responsibility for coordinating emergency services in health, education, welfare, recreation, social protection, and related fields.

The Office of War Property Distribution was set up in 1945 to work with the War Assets Administration in providing a channel whereby surplus property derived from the war could more easily be distributed to health, welfare, education, and other nonprofit organizations having by law special priorities. Its work ceased with the termination of the war.

The Office of Vocational Rehabilitation operates under the legislative sanction of Public Law 113 (the Vocational Rehabilitation Act and its amendments, 1943). It cooperates with the states to provide disabled persons with various rehabilitative services. Actually, any service which is required of a disabled person to fit him for normal participation in life is made available by the Office. Medical or surgical treatment is furnished to needy individuals if they are not able to pay for such services themselves. Hospitalization is given freely where needed. Artificial appliances may be provided. Counselors advise on vocational possibilities. Preparatory steps are taken to enable disabled persons to find special work. Any other handicaps which a disabled person may have in establishing a normal life will be met where needed and when feasible by the Office by provision of: licenses, maintenance, occupational tools, transportation, and training tools, among others.

The types of handicaps which are treated by the Office include defective vision, hearing defects, crippled limbs and back, tuberculosis, cardiac, diabetic, and neurotic disorders, and certain others. The Office not only offers its services freely to individuals throughout the country upon the application of eligible, disabled persons; it also operates a case-finding service through which individuals who are eligible and who do not apply are encouraged to make use of the federal services. It is estimated that about a million and a half persons could benefit from these services. In 1947 about 300,000 persons were registered with the Office.

The eligibility requirements of the Office are quite general and consist of three principal qualifications: (1) a person must be of employable age; (2) an occupational handicap must exist by reason of disability; (3) the individual may be rendered employable or more employable through rehabilitation services. (See Figure 32.)

The Office functions through eight regional branches, but its main work is done indirectly through various state programs. It was one of the provisions of the enabling legislation that cooperation between the Office and the states was required. The federal government finances state programs of direct service amounting to about $7,000,000 each year, and the amount is increasing as more persons take advantage of the program. The Office, in addition to supplying the states with money to support programs which in practice are essentially their own, provides an advisement service by which the states are able to secure the best possible information about national practices which will aid them in the solving of concrete local problems. The Office also runs a training program within states to increase the professionalization of rehabilitative staffs in state organizations. The Office also assists the states by placing disabled persons in suitable positions.

DISABLED PERSONS REHABILITATED INTO EMPLOYMENT

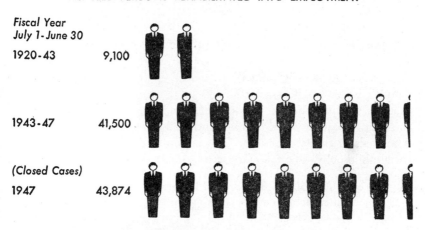

Fiscal Year *July 1 - June 30*		
1920 - 43	9,100	
1943 - 47	41,500	
(Closed Cases) 1947	43,874	

(Each Figure Represents 5,000 Disabled Persons)

FIG. 32. Disabled Persons Rehabilitated Into Employment, 1920 to 1947 (Office of Vocational Rehabilitation, Federal Security Agency.)

The Food and Drug Administration is another of the services of the Office of Special Services. It carries on the work of safeguarding the general public against harmful and misleading foods and drugs.

THE UNITED NATIONS

The primary scope of the present discussion of public welfare work concerns the United States. But it is not amiss in a world which is seeking unity to examine those activities of the United Nations which more or less fall into the public welfare field. They warrant attention, furthermore, because the United States is committed to the successful development of international government through the United Nations.

The United Nations, as is generally known, came into existence on June 26, 1945, at San Francisco to express the resolution of 1,700,000,000 people and fifty nations to "unite their strength." At present there are even more people and nations within the organization.

The United Nations has many purposes which are channeled through a variety of "organs." These include:

The General Assembly
The Security Council
The Economic and Social Council
The Trusteeship Council
The International Court of Justice
The Secretariat

Economic and Social Council

Naturally, not all of these "organs" conduct social work activities. Probably, the one which is closest to the heart of social work is the Economic and Social Council. (See Figure 33.) In some ways this Council is one of the chief supports of the total aims of the United Nations, for by it the fact that peaceful and friendly relations between the nations require world stability and well-being has been recognized. The goals of the Economic and Social Council give evidence of that social philosophy. The following are the purposes of the Council:

1. To promote higher standards of living, full employment, and conditions of economic and social progress and development.
2. To achieve cooperation in solving international economic, social, health, and related problems.
3. To promote international cultural and educational cooperation.
4. To encourage universal respect for, and observance of, human rights and fundamental freedoms for all, without distinction as to race, sex, language, or religion.

One of the Council's functions, the International Children's Emergency Fund, deserves special mention. It was created on December 11, 1946, by a special resolution of the General Assembly. Its immediate problem was to continue, at least in part, the work of U.N.R.R.A. in the meeting of children's needs. The financing of the Fund was to be derived from three chief sources: (1) any residual funds of U.N.R.R.A.; (2) contributions made available by governments; (3) money contributed by voluntary sources and individuals. The distribution of the assets of the Fund, of course, is on the basis of need, without discrimination as to race, creed, nationality status, or political belief. The Fund is to function in all countries in which children and adolescents were victims of aggression.

While the social work aspects of the United Nations are not too numerous or important at the present time, compared to the needs and possibilities, nevertheless there probably will be a further growth of such international social work. The more the world becomes united and the more the effects of the interdependency of world social and

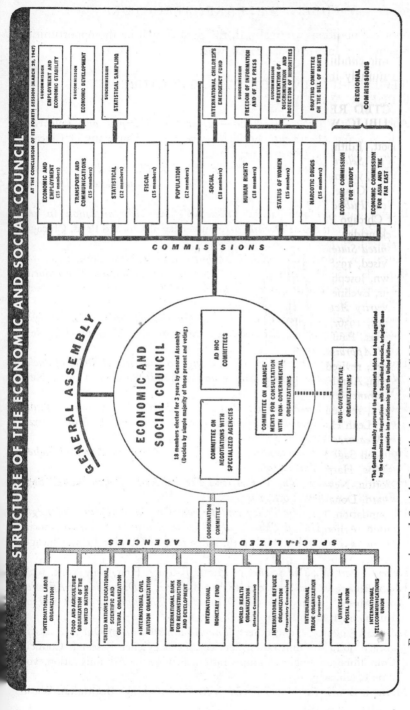

Fig. 33. Economic and Social Council of the United Nations   (Chart issued by U.N. Dept. of Public Information.)

economic conditions are realized, the greater will be the opportunities for genuinely international social work.

SELECTED READINGS ON THE STRUCTURE OF PUBLIC WELFARE

Abbott, Edith, *Public Assistance—American Principles and Policies—With Select Documents,* Social Service Series, University of Chicago Press, volume 1, Chicago, 1940.

Abbott, Grace, *From Relief to Social Security: The Development of the New Public Welfare Services and Their Administration,* University of Chicago Press, Chicago, 1941.

Breckinridge, Sophonisba P., *Public Welfare Administration in the United States: Select Documents,* University of Chicago Press, Chicago, revised, 1938.

Brown, Josephine, *Public Relief: 1929–1939,* Holt, New York, 1940.

Burns, Eveline M., *Toward Social Security: An Explanation of the Social Security Act and a Survey of the Larger Issues,* McGraw-Hill, New York, 1936.

Douglas, Paul H., *Social Security in the United States: An Analysis and Appraisal of the Federal Social Security Act,* McGraw-Hill, New York, revised, 1939.

Epstein, Abraham, *Insecurity: A Challenge to America; A Study of Social Insurance in the United States and Abroad,* Random House, New York, revised, 1938.

Feder, Leah H., *Unemployment Relief in Periods of Depression—A Study of Measures Adopted in Certain American Cities: 1857 Through 1922,* Russell Sage Foundation, New York, 1936.

Hopkins, Harry L., *Spending to Save: The Complete Story of Relief,* Norton, New York, 1936.

Howard, Donald S., *The W.P.A. and Federal Relief Policy,* Russell Sage Foundation, New York, 1943.

Johnson, Arlien, *Public Policy and Private Charities: A Study of Legislation in the United States and of Administration in Illinois,* Social Service Monographs, number 16, University of Chicago Press, Chicago, 1931.

Kelso, Robert W., *The Science of Public Welfare,* Holt, New York, 1928.

Klein, Alice C., *Civil Service in Public Welfare: A Discussion of Effective Selection of Public Social Work Personnel Through the Merit System,* Russell Sage Foundation, New York, 1940.

Lansdale, Robert T., and others, *The Administration of Old Age Assistance,* Public Administration Service, Social Science Research Council, Committee on Public Administration, Studies in Administration, volume 6, Chicago, 1939.

Meriam, Lewis, *Relief and Social Security,* Brookings Institution, Washington, D.C., 1946.

Millspaugh, Arthur C., *Public Welfare Organization,* Institute for Government Research, Studies in Administration, Brookings Institution, Washington, D.C., 1935.

Nelson, Lowry, *Rural Sociology,* American Book, New York, 1948.

Stevenson, Marietta, *Public Welfare Administration,* with the assistance of other members of the staff, American Public Welfare Association Publications, Macmillan, New York, 1938.

United States National Resources Planning Board, *Security, Work, and Relief Policies,* Government Printing Office, Washington, D.C., 1942.

White, R. Clyde, *Administration of Public Welfare,* American Book, New York, 1940.

For additional related readings, consult the bibliography at the end of the following chapter.

Public Welfare: Process

The following attempt on the part of a client of a public welfare agency to write her own case record provides a somewhat humorous but enlightening insight into the practices of social workers in the public welfare field. The introductory remarks are made by the social worker who was connected with the case:

> Mrs. Parks has received old-age assistance since the beginning of the federal assistance program. She is an agreeable person, has a fair education, and has always been pleasant to deal with.
>
> One day she came to the public assistance office to ask that a correction be made in her mailing address. The receptionist examined her case record for the present address. Mrs. Parks observed this and asked what was written in these pages about her. The receptionist explained that this was called a narrative, and told her something of how narratives are built. Mrs. Parks was fascinated. "I'm going to write one myself," she added. And she did.
>
> It was not to be expected that her narrative would conform to recording standards generally, for Mrs. Parks had little opportunity to learn what constitutes an acceptable case record. She does, however, present a client's point of view, and reveals her response to agency contacts and her impressions of them.

* * *

Home Visit, 2–1–44. A home visit was made to me this date. The visitor, Miss Manning, sat on the edge of her chair as usual. She looks like she is afraid to sit back against the upholstered back for fear it isn't sanitary. She talked about the weather a few minutes, said the room was nice and warm, and then asked about my health. For a minute I thought she was interested but when I said I had to call Dr. Spencer last week because of an attack of indigestion, she whipped open the notebook she carried and began to write. "What doctor did you say you had? Did you say acute indigestion? Oh, yes, what did you say he gave you? Are you still taking it? What is the dose? How often do you take it? How much does a bottle cost? How long does it last? How long will you have to take it? Oh, yes, hydrochloric acid with your meals—indefinitely. I was just asking so we could include its cost in your grant," she said, still writing.

I was tired and impatient by this time. I can't stand that notebook and pencil of hers. When she gets to asking me questions and writing down answers, it makes me feel I am in court on trial for my life and surely must be guilty. I decided the next time she came I would get a notebook and pencil and write down what she says.

Then she asked me about the utility bills. She agreed that fuel is awfully expensive this year and I was glad to talk to her about it, if only she hadn't kept writing down what I said. She seemed to understand about why I need more for utilities than I have been needing. Conditions have made them higher, she said.

She talked awhile, and then got out her budget sheet. She gave me one and I got a pencil and we made out the budget. I'd write what I need in the "estimated" column, and she filled in the "standard" column, and we figured up what I'd get. That is sort of fun, only it is so awfully important. It scares me about how much it is going to come out. For some things I need more than she could put in, but for some I didn't need as much. It figured out so I get a little raise. I don't know why I am always so scared when budget time comes. As I think back, my check never has been decreased and I have usually had a raise, but, in spite of myself, I'm always afraid for budget time to come, and I'm glad when it's over. I keep accounts and I like to show them what I really need. Miss Manning always lets me help make out the budget and explains what can go in. The visitor before her never did that, and never told me what I'd get. I like Miss Manning's way better.

She was ready to go and I was almost ready to like her, when she turned to me and said, "Now, on my next home visit we'll go into the cost of repairs on the house if you have decided what you want to do." "Home visit!" Why did she have to say that? It put me right back in my place. You visit people you like or whom you have business dealings with and want to see, but a social worker makes a home visit to a relief client because she has to hold her job.

Office Interview, 4-15-44. Something rather nice happened to me. My favorite grandson came to see me. He is on his way to visit his mother and wants me to go with him. He will go on from his mother's to a job that he believes will take him approximately three months and then will bring me back home. I was quite excited and hurried making my arrangements to go, but got Howard to bring me to the office so I could tell Miss Manning about my trip and ask to have my check sent to me while I am to be at my daughter's. I left Howard in the car and went in and asked for Miss Manning.

I thought she would never come in to talk to me, but finally she did come, looking pleasant, unhurried and easy. I started in rather breathlessly to tell her about my grandson and the trip. She seemed interested and hoped I'd have a nice visit. I gave her my address, and she wrote it down. Then she asked me what I'd need my money for while I was visiting—surely my daughter wouldn't ask me to share expenses while I visited her. I told her I couldn't help thinking I would be a much more welcome guest if I didn't have to begin asking for money as soon as I arrived. I suggested to her she must know the many little personal expenses one has when visiting. She didn't answer, so I said I didn't believe I'd go after all if my check would be stopped and I would be without money. She said not to worry about the check, that I would get it all right.

She asked about my health—if I thought I could stand the trip, and did I understand the Department would not pay my way back and would not be responsible in case of my illness or accident while out of state? I wanted to scream at her that all I asked her to be responsible for was changing my address. But I didn't. She told me to notify the office when I got back and I promised. She explained they would send me a letter reminding me to let the office know my plans after I had received my third check out of the state. I assured her she wouldn't need to write, that I would remember and let her know. I was only trying to save her trouble. I was on my feet trying to get away. She smiled indulgently, "Oh yes, we'll write you along with the others due home that month from visits. It's routine here and we couldn't keep in mind that you wouldn't need a letter. You must remember you are just one of several thousand we have to keep up with."

I went out too crushed to answer. Foolish tears blinded me so I could not see my way. I'm just one of several thousand—my first trip in twenty years. I thought I was sort of special.

Letter, 7–10–44. The letter Miss Manning said she'd write came today. She said she hoped I was enjoying my visit, and would I please let her know when I planned to return and should she change my address, and where do I want my next check sent. I'd write to her, "See your narrative—Office interview, 4–15–44. I told you then." But I couldn't do that, it might hurt her feelings. I am writing her I will be home as planned and my address will be the same as always.

Office Interview, 7–25–44. I went to the office today and reported to Miss Manning that I am home. She asked about my trip, and told me about a trip she had made to the Gulf Coast and some of the places she had been were the same I'd been. She didn't hurry me and acted like she enjoyed talking to me. She didn't cross-examine me. I liked her this time.

Home Visit, 9–12–44. Miss Manning came today to talk to me about the repairs on the house. The man from the lumber yard had called her to give her their estimate on the work. She got her notebook out, so I got one too. I started writing down what she said to show her how it is, but it seemed so discourteous I couldn't do it. I just can't be rude to people. She thought I should have the north door fixed to fit better, because it gets so cold in the kitchen, and suggested that I have new screens put on most of the doors and windows. I didn't want to ask for more than I had to have, but was awfully glad I could go ahead and have those things done. She looked around the house, helped me plan what to have done with a lot of good sense. She helped me quite a bit in planning the repairs and seemed interested in me being comfortable and having my house look nice besides.

She went to the lumber yard and asked for a price to include several things I had not had figured and then came back to talk it over with me. She said the entire bill would be $75 and that my check would be increased $15 for the next five months to pay it. She said the lumber yard had agreed to that. I'm always glad she tells me just what I'll get and when, so I can do business like anyone else.

Home Visit, 10–15–44. Miss Manning stopped in for just a minute to see the house since the work on it is done. I tried to thank her for the raise. I'd planned a nice speech to say, but she didn't seem to listen and sort of cut me off. "You don't need to thank me," she said. "I didn't give you anything. It isn't my money, you know. You are entitled to it. It is my business to help people get the amount to which they are entitled, so if I have any credit at all coming to me it is just that I am doing my job well." I felt for a minute like she had shoved me away. I was grateful and wanted to thank someone. Her tone was not ungracious though and I am glad she feels that way—that I am entitled to it, instead of thinking she's done a good deed. I'm grateful to her just the same. She was real pleased with the front steps instead of the tumbledown porch. She noticed my new curtains and said she thought I was awfully smart to have managed them. I was afraid she would think I was extravagant and spent my money wastefully, but when she seemed so pleased I showed her my new pillow covers I'm making out of two old linen dresses. She seemed to think they were very pretty and clever. She seemed more like it was just a little friendly call and not a "home visit." She didn't write anything in her notebook.

Home Visit, 2–4–45. Miss Manning came today. She said she wanted to ask me about the lumber yard bill and I told her it was all paid and showed her the receipts. She said my check would be decreased next month. I told her I expected that. Then I said she must have a good memory to remember when such bills are paid out. She said, "Oh, I don't trust my memory with anything. I set up a tickler card on each case which needs attention in each month." She had her notebook out and started to write. I froze up inside. She'd had a tickler card set up on my case! I'm just a case and the only way she ever thinks of me and what I need is to set up a tickler card. I should have remembered that I am just one of several thousand. I'll try and remember that from now on. No wonder she talks to me sometimes like I'm plain dumb.

When she got to talking about expenses, I knew it was budget time again, so I told her about the bills the best I could. I intended to tell her about the leak in the water pipe and that I am going to have a plumber bill to pay, but I was so upset I forgot it. I guess I ought to have some tickler cards, too. She asked me about the insurance on the house. I had forgotten about it. I saw she was looking in her notebook at some notes she had there, and for the first time I saw some good of her carrying it with her all the time. She got out her budget sheet and we moved up to the table and worked it out. Again, it was a little raise over what I was getting before the repair money was put on.

I was trying to get settled again after my usual fright that my budget would some way figure out a decrease in my check. I wish I could quit worrying about my check being cut down, but that's what I hear all the time from the other old people I know. They all worry about it, and every now and then it happens to some of them. Miss Manning spied my pillows and began about how well my linen covers had turned out. She examined them and talked about how clever and pretty they were, just like she would with any of her friends. She had remembered about my two old linen dresses and admired the way I had worked them up. Then she picked up the little Wedgewood vase that was once my mother's and before that my grandmother's. She handled it so carefully, like it was very precious, and looked at it as one looks on something of rare beauty. For a minute I was afraid she was going to ask me if I would sell it, but she didn't. She said, "I like to come here so I can look at this lovely vase." It made me feel rich somehow and like other people to have something she recognized was priceless. I felt better than I have since I first asked for assistance.

As Miss Manning left she told me she wouldn't be back for at least a year, as she is accepting another assignment for that length of time. She said a Miss Wesley would take over her work and would come to see me if I need to talk over any change in circumstances or adjustment in grant.

I wanted to hold on to Miss Manning and not let her go. It scares me to think of anyone else coming. I've been worrying only when a new budget is made, but now I'll worry all the time till this new visitor comes. I'm afraid she'll decide before she ever sees me that I don't amount to anything or I wouldn't receive assistance. I don't want to be classified and set apart. I want to be the same as I was before I got assistance—the same as other people.[1]

The record written by Mrs. Parks is not meant to describe public welfare in its entirety or at its best. Indeed, public welfare is a long story which cannot be completely told even in the two chapters devoted to it in this book.

[1]Mary Overholt Peters, "A Client Writes the Case Record," *The Family* (now *Journal of Social Casework*), November, 1945, pp. 258–261. Also, see the sequel to this article, "A Client Continues Her Case Record," by the same writer, *Journal of Social Casework,* volume 27, number 6, October, 1946, pp. 216–222.

THE ROLE OF PUBLIC WELFARE

In the preceding chapter the organization of public welfare has been briefly described on a local, state, and federal basis. From this discussion it is evident that there is considerable organizational overlapping of public welfare functions. This overlap, however, usually does not affect the individual client who comes to a public assistance agency for aid. If he applies in a local county office for assistance, for example, he will

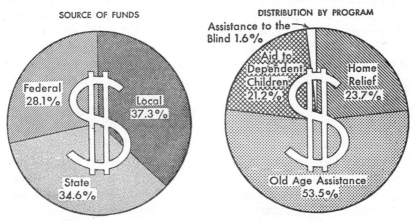

SOURCE OF FUNDS FOR PUBLIC ASSISTANCE IN NEW YORK STATE
AND DISTRIBUTION BY PROGRAM
1945
TOTAL - $88,268,000

SOURCE OF FUNDS

Federal 28.1%
Local 37.3%
State 34.6%

DISTRIBUTION BY PROGRAM

Assistance to the Blind 1.6%
Aid to Dependent Children 21.2%
Home Relief 23.7%
Old Age Assistance 53.5%

Fig. 34. Source of Funds for Public Assistance in New York State and Distribution by Program, 1945

(*Public Social Services in 1945*, New York State Department of Social Welfare.)

not be bothered with a reminder that so much of the money granted him has come from the federal treasury, so much from the state, and so much from the county. (See Figure 34.) He will be dealt with in terms of his need within the eligibility limitations and provisions set up for him and others by the various interested departments of government having jurisdiction in his case. Thus, to the client seeking assistance, the activities of the public welfare agencies seem more simplified than the previous chapter may have suggested to the reader. While this is so, and one can be grateful for the extent to which it is so, nevertheless there is room for improvement and for further coordination and integration of public welfare services.

Restrictions on Public Welfare Workers

Public welfare services have suffered somewhat, especially in times past, from various negative attitudes expressed toward them both by professional social workers and by lay people. No doubt there have been genuine provocations in actual practice for these attitudes, but, in general, they are much overemphasized. For some time the public welfare agencies, for example, because of their strict eligibility requirements, have been thought of as "snoopers" into the private lives of applicants. Furthermore, the public welfare worker is not allowed as much freedom for individual treatment as a worker in a private agency, simply because the public law does not always and everywhere allow for such a wide degree of individualization, that is, the treatment of clients strictly according to their concrete, peculiar needs without rigid reference to the applicability of general standards. It is true, though, that the degree of individualization possible in the public welfare field has progressively increased, so that today there is in many instances little difference between the freedom of the public and the private social worker. Nevertheless, it would seem that there always must be a greater degree of restrictiveness in governmental work than in the social work provided by privately financed agencies. This should not be taken to mean that private agencies are not mindful of their responsibility. They too must "answer" to the public, but not in so definite a legal manner. It also does not mean that such restrictiveness is necessarily disadvantageous; in fact, greater discretion on the part of the worker as to whether a person is eligible and how much is to be received may be a safeguard both to the client and the worker.

Public agencies have also been accused of being "hard" and impersonal. Clients have reported that public agencies have been conducted more as businesses while private agencies have been conducted more as professional organizations. Several comments may be made on this view. Certainly, the personnel standards in the past (and even at present) do not generally permit public agencies to provide the high degree of specialized, professional care which characterizes the private agencies. However, there are undeniable signs of improvement; recently, most public agencies have sought to raise the quality of their personnel. The shortage of professional workers has contributed to this deficiency to some degree, although the low salaries prevalent in public social work probably have contributed more. But the impersonality of the public agencies perhaps has another basis than that of personnel. This condition is rooted in the history of the public services, especially since the period of the 1930's.

Expansion During Depression

The greatest extension of public welfare work has come about in the last decade or two. Prior to that, while public welfare work did exist, there was little public activity, quantitatively speaking. The modern era of public social work actually began with the economic depression of the early 1930's of this century. It was at that time that public assistance became so immense an activity that in the resultant confusion many negative features were included. Because of the exigency of the great numbers of people unemployed at that time, it was necessary to establish, on entirely inadequate financial bases, public means of assistance. Lack of money gave rise to the hiring of nonprofessional staffs by the public welfare agencies. (Even if there had been adequate financing, however, it is doubtful, as suggested previously, that enough professional workers could have been secured.) Furthermore, the rush measures that the depression forced upon public welfare were not conducive to the development of the best personal relations between workers and clients. But to a considerable extent these difficulties are now being overcome. It is regrettable that today such a large part of the population still characterizes public welfare work in terms of their experience with it during the relatively inefficient days of the 1930's.

Inadequate Financial Assistance

The public welfare agencies in the past, and to a considerable extent at present, moreover, have the reputation of providing inadequately for clients. Here again there is much reason for agreement with the complaint, especially for the past. The fact that the amounts of financial assistance provided for needy clients were often woefully inadequate has not been obscured by social workers. On the contrary, social workers have been in the vanguard of those who have advocated a liberalization of the financial assistance programs of government and the creation of more sensible arrangements, such as social insurance, for the meeting of problems. After all, the financial limitations placed upon public agencies are not placed by the agencies themselves, but by legislatures which are publicly responsive. One needs only to be reminded of the fact that there has been and still is the widely accepted opinion that recipients of public assistance are receiving not too little, but too much. A cursory reading of the newspapers during the past two decades, on the subject of liberalizing the financial activities of public agencies, will convince one that the actual legislation has often been realistic and generous. If it is to be even more realistic and generous, an enlightened and active electorate must make it so.

Social workers in public agencies have tried to contend with the inadequate financial basis on which their agencies operate by aiding clients to make the best possible use of the limited funds which they may receive. The following is an example of family budgeting and counsel offered by a public worker:

Visited D family after receiving message that Mr. and Mrs. D had come in to report that after attempting for a month to get along on the relief allowance, they had gone into debt with the grocer in order to pay their rent and utilities. They asked to have their relief allowance increased.

Investigator found Mr. and Mrs. D were home awaiting her visit. Mrs. D looked tense and worried; Mr. D, discouraged and resentful. He said that when he and Mrs. D decided to apply for relief, they had understood they would get enough money to provide for the children until he secured another job. He did not expect to be out of work long, but in the meantime his family must live. In order to pay his rent he had gone into debt with the grocer. Mrs. D said she never had had any difficulty and they had never gone into debt before. She has always prided herself on being a good manager. Mr. D gave her his full wages, out of which she gave him an allowance, and from the balance she met all other expenses.

Worker suggested that it must be difficult to live on the reduced income and that it must require all the experience and ingenuity that Mrs. D possessed to get along as well as she had. Worker wondered how the $14 every two weeks for food compared with the amount Mrs. D formerly spent. Mrs. D said that it was impossible to feed her family on that amount and that was the difficulty. Worker wondered whether Mrs. D was aware of the equally nutritious value of certain low-cost foods that she may not have considered when she had more money to spend on food. Worker added that although Mrs. D could not buy as great a variety of foods on this allowance, with her experience it should be possible for her to provide the family with a nutritious, well-balanced diet. Worker explained that she could give Mrs. D a list of low-cost foods and Mrs. D might go over them to see if she is making the best use of them.

Worker explained that the agency had on its staff specialists in this field who have made a study of how and what to buy on this limited amount of money, and that Mrs. D might find some of their information helpful. Mrs. D doubted whether she could get much help, but she would be glad to try. The agency, she felt, was asking the impossible; even the allowance for gas and light was inadequate. Her bill for gas and light was always at least $6. Worker asked Mrs. D if she cooked more than one food at a time in the oven. Mrs. D showed surprise. Was that possible? Worker stated that a number of devices like this had been developed out of the experience of many people, and that probably Mrs. D knew of some of them, but she would be glad to make them available to her. Mr. D interrupted to suggest to his wife that "she let the lady help her if she could. Maybe we'll get something out of this relief."

Worker suggested that Mrs. D keep a list of her expenditures for the week and come into the office to discuss them with the worker and the home economist.[2]

Dignified Treatment of Client

A philosophy widely accepted in public welfare today is that the client should be viewed as a self-respecting member of the community. Having a problem does not necessarily impair one's value to the community, and any client is entitled to assistance in solving his problem so that he may maintain his normal place in the community. This respect for the client means that he is treated with appropriate dignity by the workers of the agency. It means that whatever financial assistance is granted shall not be given in the spirit of "charity," but in the belief that the client is entitled by law, if eligible, to whatever the provisions of the law may provide. The worker in the public agency, therefore, does not "help" another individual but, rather, mediates what has already been specifically declared through law to be the public welfare rights of citizens to a client who seeks to benefit by them. Obviously, this conception of public welfare work rules out the giving of assistance on the basis of the "worthiness" of the client.

Many clients who come to public agencies for the first time may labor under a false sense of failure. They will not need the public agency to point out their "unworthiness" as clients. They may misinterpret the meaning of their plight and castigate themselves unduly. Such clients need to be helped to see themselves as having rights. They also need to be encouraged to regain their composure and confidence. The following case points this out:

Mr. B, unemployed, applied for assistance. His opening statement of need was accompanied by comments to the effect that he had no idea of the existence of such an agency as this until now. He felt it was disgraceful that he had permitted himself to seek "charity" and had hardly been able to get inside the door when he arrived. Only the thought of his child spurred him on. He feels he must submit to any humiliation in order to save her suffering. He interrupted the worker's initial attempt at interpretation of the purpose of the agency and of his right to assistance as though he had not heard, to recount how his financial difficulty began; how formerly he could turn to his family for help in time of need just as formerly they could turn to him. The worker replied to this with a remark that in the general economic situation many individuals and families could no longer help one another.

[2]Adele R. Glogan, "Practical Counseling in Family Budgeting in a Public Department," *The Family* (now *Journal of Social Casework*), volume 23, number 1, March, 1942, pp. 26–27.

Mr. B refuted the worker's attempt to ease his discomfort, insisting staunchly that it was not the state of society but his own fault that he could not earn. The worker then directed his inquiry toward why he felt it was his fault. There followed, with much feeling, a self-blaming account of his several recent job failures after a long record of success. In the course of his recital he brought out that his wife had a right to expect him to support her and the child. Before their marriage she had been a business success and she had no comprehension of failure. Since their marriage she had depended completely on him and did not understand what was happening in the world. But neither did he believe that this trouble of his was due to economic conditions in general. (Subsequent investigation showed that his wife was fully aware of the economic situation, that she was understanding of his situation, and that she too had repeatedly tried to reassure him by attributing his business failure to general economic conditions.)

We have here another example of how a person's emotions can influence his thinking. Because Mr. B feels to blame for his failure and cannot understand and accept it himself, he thinks others feel the same way about his problem. We see here that Mr. B's feelings about being unemployed and having to ask for help determine what he does in applying. They make him deny that he is asking help for himself. They make him present his child as the person for whom help is requested. Obviously, he finds the experience too painful to enter into fully, so unconsciously he justifies his request and pretends to himself and to the world that he is only here because of someone else. Since he has not yet fully entered into the experience, he is not yet ready to relate himself to the agency, and he is not yet ready to understand what he hears about the agency, nor is he ready to use the service as a right.

We do not fully understand his discomfort or why this experience causes him to blame himself, but it is glaringly clear that he has an inner need to place his failure in himself rather than in the social structure. Why? Assuming that he is tending to do what makes him more comfortable, we conclude that this self-blame or his assumption of responsibility eases his discomfort. If his reaction is purely self-blaming, it would seem that the present catastrophe makes him feel guilty and we could suspect that the present problem activates old disturbed and self-accusatory feelings about himself and may be more than a response to the present situation. In this instance, the self-blame would be self-punishment and would ease guilt, perhaps thus relieving him of the fear of worse punishment through further economic reverses. The final economic reverse which could come to him now would be rejection of his application for financial assistance. Therefore, fear of the outcome here may be eased by "admission of wrongdoing." If, on the other hand, his reaction is part of a characteristic tendency to assume full responsibility for his own affairs, then perhaps claiming the failure as his own eases anxiety, for he is accustomed to being able to cope with the world. It may be a more threatening idea to him to think that the social order is against him than to think there is something wrong with himself, for he could deal with his own ineptitudes more readily than with a changed world.

Subsequent developments show us the meaning of his response. After placing the problem on himself and expressing considerable feeling about it, Mr. B spontaneously brought the conversation back to his application for assistance. There followed a careful review of his financial situation during which he presented a plan for moving into the rent-free house of a relative. The worker gave him encouragement in this plan. As the agency's need for certain information was conveyed to Mr. B, he anxiously raised questions about the agency's investigations and records. He eagerly set about procuring evidence of eligibility and showed lessened discomfort on hearing of the agency's way of working, the confidential nature of records, and so on. At one point he asked the worker whether she thought a man could take money and retain his self-respect. Interpretation of his right to assistance and of financial help as a temporary boost which anyone might need at some point, obviously relieved tension and brought comment to the effect that now he was going to be able to face "this thing. I couldn't see my way out."

There was initial resistance to having his home visited since he had not had the courage to tell his wife he was coming here and had hoped to keep the agency contact from her. On his return visit to the office, he expressed willingness to have the home visited and great relief because his wife had been so pleased at his coming here. Instead of being angry and humiliated, she had been gratified at "his courage in applying for help." Shortly after assistance was given, Mr. B moved quickly to look for kinds of employment which formerly he had considered beneath him and managed to get a part-time job. His account at the time of application showed that for some months he had been drifting along, using his savings and hoping against hope that "something good would turn up." Now he became more realistic and, in contrast to his original denial that the economic situation had changed, he was able to say that "in these times" it would be better to take anything.

It would seem from his response that Mr. B's disturbed feelings about his problem were those of the man who, accustomed to manage his own affairs, finds himself suddenly helpless. He still could not give up completely and so he eased his anxiety over his helplessness by insisting that he alone was responsible. He was able to make constructive use of his right to assistance, not only because of the way his application was handled but also because his anxieties stemmed from his strengths and from the reality of his economic dilemma. Had his attitudes been more purely self-condemning, because his present failure was bringing to the surface basic feelings of inadequacy, his response to the help given might have been quite different. Financial assistance might have eased some of his anxiety. He might, however, have continued to feel humiliated and inferior and, if so, would not have moved so quickly into resuming the management of his own affairs. He might instead have been more inclined to succumb to dependency and to pay his way through self-blame.[3]

Increased Scope of Public Services

One of the present major trends in the whole field of social work is toward the increased participation of public agencies in providing welfare services. Whereas the social work field just a few decades ago was largely dominated by the privately financed agencies, it is today composed of a weakened, private social work emphasis and a greatly strengthened, public social work stress. It would seem that the future will see the further development of the public services and possibly a further decline in the influence of the private agencies. A familiar and oft repeated theme at various social work conferences and meetings is that of future relations between private and public agencies, and it is not at all clear that all private agencies feel that they will have a significant place in the future in relation to the publicly financed agencies. Usually, the private agencies say that they are and will continue to be the experimenters in the social work field, providing, after trial, for the public agencies those practices and policies which can be applied on a large scale. On this point the private agencies may overlook the fact that while there is relatively little experimentalism among the public agencies in this country, due in part to their legal organization, such a limitation is not inevitable or permanent and public agencies could be as experimental as the private agencies, if they were permitted to be. It is also true that there are relatively few private social agencies that are engaged in anything that could be called experimentation or research. That is their role, but few are filling it.

Likewise, the argument, sometimes presented by those who favor private agency services, that through such agencies certain needy groups within the community may advantageously receive a disproportionate amount of care (more care than would be permissible if these groups were to be treated out of public funds), does not fully solve the future of private social work agencies, even though it may rationalize for some the distinctiveness of such agencies. For, if certain groups within the community are genuinely in need of a disproportionate amount of care, and if their cases are so recognized by the general community, there is little logically or necessarily to prevent the community from providing such care. The veterans are an example of this special consideration. And actually, it would be difficult to argue that

[3]*Common Human Needs: An Interpretation for Staff in Public Assistance Agencies,* Federal Security Agency, Social Security Board, Bureau of Public Assistance, Public Assistance Report number 8, written by Charlotte Towle, United States Printing Office, Washington, D. C., 1945, pp. 15–17.

at any time there is absolutely equal treatment of the various groups already within the province of public welfare.

All things considered, then, it is hard to understand how the scope of the public services can be strictly confined. The trend, as has been mentioned, has been toward increased participation in social welfare on the part of the government. There appear to be no factors of significance which are reversing this trend.

This discussion of the role of public agencies in the general social work field today gives us an incentive to analyze the actual, present-day public welfare process in order to see how extensive the public services are. Because public welfare is popularly conceived to be the equivalent of financial assistance, it may be well to begin by examining the various aids of this nature offered by government.

Following this discussion it will be appropriate to look at the other channels through which government seeks to secure and improve the public welfare.

MEANS OF ASSISTANCE

Direct Financial Aid

One of the most popular means of government aid to needy persons is through direct financial assistance. In former times, and to some extent even today, this form of assistance was of three sorts: money, goods, and services. Assistance in the form of money has come to be accepted by social workers, as well as by their clients, as preferable to the other two types. Money enables the client to meet his needs through the use of his own individuality and his own efforts. If he needs food and is given money, he will be able to go to the store himself and buy the food. If he needs clothes, he will have his personal integrity respected to the fullest if he can go to a clothing store and there purchase what he needs, even as a nonassisted individual would. The granting of money, then, lessens any possible stigma attached to the client's use of assistance for his welfare. It also makes it easier for the agency to control the value of the assistance because the money will represent more standardized value than either goods or services.

Giving of Goods

The giving of goods, however, has been a popular practice in the past and is still utilized to some extent today. Thus instead of giving clients money with which they can buy their food, clothing, and other essentials, some agencies provide the actual items. This giving of goods may be direct or indirect. The agency may keep a storehouse where the client who needs a new coat may call for one. Or, in the indirect method, the client may be given vouchers or coupons which he can redeem in local stores or in other special places. During the 1930's the government utilized surplus crops, under a complicated economic arrangement, to meet indirectly (through the use of a coupon system) the needs of families who were lacking in income.

This giving of goods, whether direct or indirect, has the advantage that the person who needs a particular commodity will actually receive it. There can be (or so it is supposed) very little dissipation of public funds for nonessential purposes. The pet argument is that the man who needs food for his family will get the food, whereas the man who receives cash may spend it on drink. This argument sounds more reasonable than it actually is. The man who receives goods assistance in place of cash may be deterred from spending the value of the assistance on "riotous living," but again he may not. If he is anxious to use the assistance for himself rather than for meeting family needs, he will probably be ingenious enough to convert the goods allotment into cash.

The receipt of goods instead of money may, moreover, detract from the client's sense of personal dignity. If he must present coupons at a local store in order to receive food or clothing, thus publicizing the fact that he is on "relief," his self-respect may be threatened. Or, if the goods are presented to the client at the agency or its warehouse, the feeling of charity may be intensified, and this is contrary to the best thinking on the subject today. Finally, if goods are given the client, he will probably have to forego those regular and normal procedures of living—budget planning and keeping, making personal decisions as to colors and quality—and all the other factors which make for responsible, mature money-management within the home. On the other hand cash allotments also have their dangers, such as the client's unwise use of the money.

Providing Services

Aside from cash or goods allotments, clients have also been helped by various services. One such service is that of medical care, either direct or indirect. If direct, the agency may, for example, maintain a medical clinic where clients can receive medical treatment. If indirect, the agency may have worked out relations with local physicians, dentists, and hospitals, whereby clients can be treated for no fee or at reduced rates. A form from the agency may be the client's means of receiving these services from extra-agency sources. What is true of medical care may be true also of other types of services which clients need. While this means of aiding clients has its own advantages, it also suffers from the disadvantages which the granting of goods entails. In practice today there is broad acceptance of the money assistance method of public agency operation. It seems to serve best the aims which modern public agencies have for themselves and for their clients.

Institutional Care

Another means of assisting clients materially is that of institutional care. This differs from the means just mentioned in that it assumes the placement of the client in an institution in order for him to receive aid. This insistence that the client live within an institution gave rise to the term of *indoor relief* for this method of assistance. The aged, especially, are often cared for in this way.

Formerly, institutional care was one of the chief methods of helping needy persons. The *workhouse test* for unemployed individuals in the history of social work implied that a client show his genuine need and good faith by accepting placement within an institution. Such means of assisting the materially needy, however, have lost their prestige in recent years, and today these are much less used than previously. Today, *outdoor relief*, or assisting persons in their own homes, has become the dominantly accepted avenue of public assistance. This change, in part, has been due no doubt more to social workers' and society's belief in the value of family life than to overcoming the suspicion regarding the client who asks for material assistance. Also, indoor relief in many institutions created more problems than it solved for the individual who was institutionalized.

CATEGORIES OF ASSISTANCE

The public welfare programs of government are many and varied. First, the following will be discussed: (1) general public assistance, (2) assistance to the blind, (3) aid to dependent children, (4) old-age assistance, and (5) other governmental services. Then the governmental social insurance programs will be described. (See Figure 35.)

General Public Assistance

The history of general public assistance dates back to the English Poor Laws which guided the development of British social work and which, in turn, became the foundation for American practice. Under the English Poor Laws, responsibility for the general care of indigent persons remained with the locality.

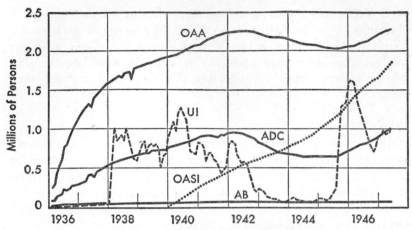

FIG. 35. Social Insurance Beneficiaries and Public Assistance Recipients Under the Social Security Act, February, 1936 to June, 1947. (AB: aid to the blind. ADC: aid to dependent children. OAA: old-age assistance. OASI: old-age and survivors insurance. UI: unemployment insurance.)

(Federal Security Agency, Social Security Administration.)

General public assistance, as the title implies, is the most general of all forms of public aid. It is historically that type of assistance or relief out of which the various other and more specialized types of public aid have arisen. In the beginning all persons in need, whether unemployed, insane, sick, aged, or whatever, were cared for by this generalized means. Only through the recognition of special categories of need in the more recent years has a more specialized program of assistance been formulated.

As indicated in Chapter 11, the actual administration of general public assistance shows wide variations throughout the country. In about fifteen states the old practice continues of permitting each county or municipality to be responsible ultimately for its own program of general public assistance. On the other hand about half of the states have taken steps to insure a more efficient program of general public assistance. Here the control of local activities by the state departments of welfare has been a prominent feature. This cooperation on the part of local units has usually meant increased services to clients, a less costly administrative program, and a more rational and understandable instrument of general assistance administration.

Requirement of Legal Settlement. A point which illustrates the inadequacy of county and municipal administration of general public assistance is that of legal settlement or residence. In fact, state administration of the general assistance program may also be deemed inadequate because of this same point, although the difficulties of legal settlement are much more apparent and harmful on a local than on a state basis. Under the provisions of legal settlement the client is required to live within a particular jurisdiction for a specified amount of time before being eligible for assistance from that jurisdiction. (See Table 15.) Many states—Massachusetts, for example—require five

Table 15

STATE RESIDENCE REQUIREMENTS FOR PUBLIC ASSISTANCE, 1936 AND 1945

State residence requirements*	Number of States With Specified Requirements					
	Old-age assistance		Aid to the blind†		Aid to dependent children	
	1936	1945	1936	1945	1936	1945
5 years	41	35	24	27	0	0
3 years	0	2	0	2	0	0
2 years	1	1	0	2	0	0
1 year	0	12	2	14	26	46
None	0	1	0	1	0	4
No approved plan	9	0	25	5	25	1

*For simplification, the residence requirements of the states were grouped in classifications which included variants, e. g., "5 years out of 9 years," "5 years out of 10 years," and so on.
†In 1936, 11 states waived residence requirements if the applicant became blind while resident in the state. In 1945, 19 states made such provision.

Source: A. J. Altmeyer, "People on the Move: Effect of Residence Requirements for Public Assistance," reprinted from the Social Security Bulletin, Federal Security Agency, Social Security Board, Washington, D.C., January, 1946, p. 3.

years residence without receipt of relief to gain settlement; Connecticut requires four. This means (on a state basis of interpretation) that John Doe of Indiana could not expect to call upon Illinois, if he moved there, for general public assistance until he had lived within the state of Illinois the required amount of time. The same procedure would hold for a person who moves from Illinois to Indiana. This example also has its counterpart in local practice. Oftentimes, especially in those states which are most closely the inheritors of the practice of the English Poor Laws, a person cannot secure assistance if he moves from one county to another within the same state until he has lived in the new locality the required amount of time. Such a requirement has the force of law and cannot be circumvented by public social work agencies. Settlement and residence barriers are highest in states that have one hundred percent local financial responsibility for general relief; they have been abolished between counties in states with state financing.

The fact of legal settlement does not necessarily mean that a client who does not meet the time requirements of the locality in which he is living would go without assistance. He could always turn to private agencies, if the private agencies were prepared to meet his needs. He might also receive assistance from the jurisdiction in which he was living and have it "charged" to the locality in which he had established legal residence, although this practice operates only in a few states that provide for it specifically by state law. The "charge-back" system may seem relatively simple, but it is not so in actual operation. For one thing, it signifies that the client must be able to establish legal residence somewhere and have that residence recognized by the jurisdiction in which he is living. Sometimes this requires legal action for him or for the agency and may be costly. Moreover it involves both localities in a complex and wasteful bookkeeping activity which works two ways. While a jurisdiction may be interested in maintaining accurate records regarding those which owe it money, it also must be the recipient of bills from others which bear examination and testing. The cost of this activity in itself makes the practice a questionable one.

The factor of legal settlement, therefore, is an example of the complications which can result from a too strict adherence to concepts of public welfare more suited to a prior time. Despite the advance in the direction of more and more state control of local welfare activities, there still is need of much more.

Exhaustion of Familial Resources. Another important requirement of general public assistance pertains to the ability of relatives to contribute to the solution of the applicant's financial problems. Briefly, the thought of the legislation which regulates general public assistance on this point (as well as other and more specialized types of assistance) requires that a person seeking public financial aid should have exhausted or nearly exhausted his familial resources. In most states family support is required where feasible, although there is no general agreement among the states as to which relatives should be called upon for such support. In some states the requirement of family aid is more or less nominal, while in others its force is expressed through court orders requiring support. Behind the stipulation of family assistance is the belief that by calling upon relatives for support the public treasury is protected and family life is strengthened.

In line with participation on the part of relatives, public agencies also demand that the clients themselves have exhausted or nearly exhausted their own resources. Persons who possess property, who hold life insurance, and who have various other assets are generally required to liquidate these before being eligible for public assistance. Some minimum may be allowed, but it is usually only large enough to care for essential needs, such as burial. Property and insurance exemption is more frequent and more generous in old-age assistance, aid to dependent children, and assistance to the blind, than in general assistance.

The requirements that the applicant for assistance depend upon his relatives where possible and that he have exhausted his own personal resources do not always work to the permanent advantage of the client and the community. They tend to label the client as a community liability who should assume the major burden of his circumstance himself, rather than as someone who needs helps in a particular circumstance which may not affect the whole of his life organization. This, in many cases, is out of line with the best knowledge of how persons come to need financial assistance. It may reduce the applicant from a person who needs momentary assistance or partial assistance to a "pauper." It may, moreover, disrupt what otherwise would be for him a "normal" existence. Requiring relatives to support needy applicants also places considerable strain upon the relatives in many instances. This strain, far from strengthening family ties, may in some cases cause family friction and actual hardship. Probably, relatives should be called upon only after careful budgetary analysis shows that such a course would be advisable.

Types of Needs. Implied so far in the discussion of eligibility requirements for public assistance is the problem of need. While it is relatively easy to declare that on this point the public agencies recognize chiefly material wants, it is difficult upon further thought to define the nature of such wants. Thus a client who is unemployed may require financial assistance in order to support his family, but if he were also able to secure further education or "retraining," he might be able to get off the relief rolls. The first type of need, granted that all other eligibility requirements are met, would be recognized as a legitimate need treatable by a public agency. The second need, that of education, in most places would not. In fact, the types of needs which are recognizable by public agencies are definitely restricted, and a client who seeks assistance must be able to show that his need specifically fits into the conception of need which is held by the public agency.

Requiring a client to have exhausted his own resources before receiving assistance from a public agency may also raise problems of a moral nature, in addition to any which may exist of a material sort. The following case of "Frank Schultz" illustrates this point:

> After he was on relief for a month or so, it was discovered that he had a bank account of considerable amount. The worker accused him of this and he vociferously denied it. He denied it even in the face of actual facts to the contrary. Finally, the supervisor, who had known him for some time, attempted to gain his confidence. Failing in this she was forced to threaten to have him prosecuted if he did not make restitution. The next day he came into the supervisor's office with the money to repay all he had received. The supervisor looked at him searchingly; she was honestly trying to understand why this apparently upright man had been dishonest. She asked him, with no unkindness in her voice, "Won't you tell me why you did this?" The man answered her sincerity with frankness and said, "We were always brought up to keep some money in the bank for a rainy day; it is easy to get relief now; I thought maybe later it would be hard so I had better save the money for that time. I couldn't bear to see my children hungry."[4]

The two types of need which have been mentioned are material. They pertain to the ways in which a client may or may not receive assistance from public funds. The public agency, however, has other than financial bases of operation. Sometimes the chief need of a client is not financial, but psychological. Thus a man may be unemployed and in need of financial assistance not because of economic conditions but through personal inadequacies. The case of Mr. "G" points out this kind of problem and the way in which a public worker can meet it:

> Mr. G, aged 43 when he reapplied for financial assistance in 1940, had had a long record on public assistance rolls. Married at 29, he had come to this country from Scotland in 1926 and had brought his family over shortly thereafter. From 1926 until 1934 he had been self-maintaining, although the family had had a precarious struggle. Trained as a draftsman at a polytechnic institute in Scotland, he was unable to obtain that work in this country, so he had taken employment as a harnessmaker, repairing saddles for riding horses. In the depression years this work became increasingly irregular, so he bought a taxicab to help provide for his family. He was not able to earn enough for his family as an independent "cabbie" and found it necessary in 1934 to apply for public relief. He

[4]Ella Lee Cowgill, *A Guidebook for Beginners in Public Assistance Work,* Family Welfare Association of America (now Family Service Association of America), New York, 1940, p. 20.

continued to earn part of the total expenses of the family with his taxi during the time he received public assistance and after he was transferred to a work-relief project. From 1934 to 1940 the family had been continuously on general relief or work relief for partial support. During this time, Mr. G showed unusual stability and both he and his wife were noted as having ability to manage resourcefully on a very meagre income.

In 1940, Mr. G reapplied for financial assistance on being laid off W.P.A. At this time there were five children, the family was living in a rent-free apartment in return for janitor service, there were no debts, they had managed to maintain some insurance, and the children were well cared for and were attending school regularly. Mr. G had been exerting every effort to get work as a draftsman, for which he had received further training and experience under W.P.A. He recounted the numerous employment contacts which he had made and was deeply discouraged at his failure to get a job in a defense plant where there was now a growing demand for workers in this skill. He attributed his failure to employers' prejudice against W.P.A. workers. Careful inquiry revealed that he had become so convinced that employers would not hire workers from W.P.A. that in his recent applications he had withheld information on this connection, creating in his employment record a gap of a period of years which also operated against him. He said that he valued this experience highly and was convinced that he could do this work, but he felt so keenly that others looked down on W.P.A. that he could not sell himself or persuade others that it had been a worth-while experience.

At the close of the interview the worker offered to see the employment manager at the aeronautical plant where he had applied, to help him get a job. Mr. G eagerly accepted this help. The worker learned that the employer had reservations about Mr. G because his record showed no recent work and a long-standing record of irregular work. Interpretation of the man's feelings about his W.P.A. experience, interpretation of W.P.A. projects, and a statement regarding Mr. G's good record on W.P.A. won the employer's interest, not only in this man but also in W.P.A. employees in general. He said that he had no idea that the city took this kind of interest in people receiving relief and that he would be interested in giving such men a trial. Mr. G immediately took the job proffered, arranged to get supplementary training in the use of certain instruments, and quickly and happily terminated his contact with the agency.

In this case we encounter a man whose failure to get work was attributed to circumstances over which he had no control. The worker, out of his experience with other W.P.A. employees, knew that there was some reality for his belief that some employers were prejudiced. By December, 1940, it is probable that labor shortages were fast eliminating these prejudices and that Mr. G's inability to "sell himself" stemmed from disturbed feelings over past defeats. At this time, it is possible that there was considerable tendency on Mr. G's part to ascribe his own feelings of inferiority to others and to believe that they thought his qualifications inferior because, through job rejections, he had come to feel that way to some extent himself. The decisive points here, however, are that these feelings had some basis in reality, that Mr. G did not feel wholly inferior in his qualifications, and that, in general, he was a responsible person who still was actively striving to manage his own affairs and was not given in general to placing blame and responsibility on others.[5]

Other Eligibility Requirements. In addition to the previously mentioned eligibility requirements, there are several others which bear note. In some cases the applicant's age determines the type (and therefore the amount) of assistance he may be qualified to receive. For example, a person's status in relation to the public agency changes considerably if he is over 65 years of age. Children also are regarded as being eligible to specialized treatment. Aside from age, the moral character of the applicant is a consideration. While the older and more moralistic notions of the "worthiness" of the client have greatly disappeared from the private and public practice of social work, there are tinges of it in the eligibility requirements of many localities where the applicant must show that he is "fit" to receive public aid. The citizenship status of the applicant may also determine his eligibility. Thus in some places the applicant is ineligible for certain types of assistance unless he is a citizen. In a similar vein, persons who have lost their civil status through imprisonment, or whose civil status is questionable by reason of having a prison record, are not eligible for public assistance. In some states a person's physical condition would determine the type of public assistance he would receive. The applicant's occupation or lack of occupation is also a factor. Finally, the honesty of the client in giving a record of himself and his need and his general willingness to cooperate with the mechanics of agency procedure are often taken as requirements by public agencies.

Agency Interrelations. Because of the limitations of the present eligibility of the public agencies, not all clients who have genuine needs can be helped. It is the obligation and the opportunity of the public worker when he meets such cases to help clients in contacting agencies that can assist. The following is an illustration of this procedure:

Mr. T, aged 55, tall, thin, neatly dressed, of Swedish-American stock, nervously explained as he took his seat that he was coming here as a last resort, without his family's knowing, and that he never had applied for public or private "charity." After working 30 years selling foodstuffs, averaging about $40 per week, he was laid off a year prior to this application. Since that time, he had exhausted unemployment compensation benefits, insurance cash value, credit with friends, grocer, and landlord. In

[5]*Common Human Needs, op. cit.,* pp. 26–28.

his home, besides his wife, he had kept his daughter, Mary, his son-in-law, Tom, and their baby, Marie, without asking any contribution from them over a period of three years.

His son-in-law's income was $20 a week, which was used for clothes and personal medical expenses (Mary now being pregnant again), and for their savings in order that they might start housekeeping. Further discussion indicated that the two groups were actually a closely knit family unit. They were ineligible for assistance on the basis of the income in the household.

Mr. T became very dejected when he was told that the agency could not help him. He argued that, as head of the house, he could never go to his son-in-law for money nor ask him to take over the total household expenses, including medical expenses for his mother-in-law. Mr. T felt that he would thus become a "burden and liability" and he would rather put himself "out of the picture."

As the interviewer saw it, the major difficulty for Mr. T was not simply economic and would not have been solved by a relief check. Economically, his position had been undermined, but just as important was his emotional heartbreak. He was losing status in his family as the provider and patriarch he wished to be. Socially, his friends avoided him, since he was always asking for money. As a wage-earner, he was finding himself shelved as a has-been. With this tentative diagnosis, the interviewer suggested a course of action which might help him focus more clearly on the way in which life was actually evolving for him, and which might relieve some of the pressures that were breaking his spirit.

The current intra-agency report of firms now hiring was discussed with him. His method of seeking employment was reviewed, with some suggestions for a more effective job search through changing his registration at the State Employment Office to include more kinds of unskilled jobs and through contacting other sources of information. Regarding the medical needs of Mrs. T, the services of the medical clinics were discussed, since he could not afford to continue the expensive treatments she now received.

As for tensions which were mounting in the home and the validity of requesting his daughter and son-in-law to accept more responsibility, the interviewer recognized that it was beyond the treatment scope of the present contact, for his total behavior symptoms were deeply rooted. Since the help he needed was in making the transition from middle age to being an "older man," it was suggested that he might feel better and more hopeful if he were to discuss his problems with an interested person in a private agency. The type of service they could offer him in his present dilemma was also explained. Mr. T thought this might be of value since "even this talk had helped." He requested that the interviewer make an appointment with the family agency for him.[6]

[6]Sylvia Sacks, "Public Agency Intake and the Case Work Goal," *The Family* (now *Journal of Social Casework*), volume 23, number 2, April, 1942, pp. 66-67.

In meeting the conditions under which public agencies must operate, social workers can do much of a casework character in interpreting the function of the agency. While some private agency workers derogate the effectiveness of public agencies, still most try to interpret the restrictions of the public agencies in a constructive way. The following case illustrates how a social worker in a private agency can accomplish this task:

Mr. and Mrs. B came to the private agency without an appointment and said they wanted information about how to get relief. They were young, shabbily dressed, and appeared uneasy and uncertain. Mrs. B sat in the waiting room. Mr. B wandered around, looking out of the window, handling papers and books on the desk, always followed by his wife's searching eyes. Frequently, he stopped in front of her chair and talked to her in inaudible tones.

When the worker was ready to see them, he started immediately on his story. Until a few weeks ago, he had been working for the iron works in a town nearby, averaging $21 a week. He had had no work since and his money was all gone. The rent of $12 was in arrears and his wife was expecting to be confined at any time. He did not know what his wife was going to do. He had wanted her to go to a private physician and have her baby at home. She went to the Hospital Prenatal Clinic during the early part of her pregnancy, but hadn't returned recently, for her husband was sure she could have a doctor at home.

His father had been giving him enough food to get along on and supplying Mrs. B with milk but could not keep this up—he had his own family to support.

The worker explained the procedure for procuring relief, emphasizing the fact that Mr. B would need to obtain an appointment to make application for it, and at that time give the relief agency all the necessary information to establish his eligibility. She gave him the address of the relief agency and talked with him about getting his appointment at once. He had not thought there was anything for him to do except to say he was out of work and needed help. The worker explained that both he and the relief agency had a part in this: his part was to apply and show them why he needed help; their part was the result of what he did.

They talked further about Mrs. B's plans. She decided to go to the Hospital and explain to them why she had not returned to the Prenatal Clinic; she was sure they would understand; they were very kind to her. She was a patient there for a number of weeks, just after she was married, and that was how she had been referred to the Prenatal Clinic.

Mr. B was in the office five days later, his wife outside in the car. He was on his way to town. Yes, he had an appointment at the relief office and his wife was going to stop at the Hospital, but he couldn't wait like this. Goodness knows what he'd do—starve he guessed—almost another week had gone by and he was no nearer relief than the last time he was in the office. "Are you sure?" the worker asked. He—well—he supposed he was sure. The worker suggested they take account of stock together. He had made an appointment and would make application for relief when? Oh yes, 2:00 p.m. (It was then 11:30 a.m.) And what had he done toward getting that relief? Oh yes (he dug down in his pocket), he had done just what the worker suggested, listed everything they asked for on the slip they sent him and was taking that with him. But that didn't help him that day—he hadn't any money, he had to get gas for the trip from his oldest brother, he hadn't any food, and he didn't see any chance of getting any soon. The worker persisted, "Do you really believe you have all the facts they want and that everything you are going to tell them can be verified?" Yes, he was sure. Then, if this were so, the worker would suggest he ask the interviewer at the relief office about how soon he could expect help.

As he left, he said, "Will you be here when I come back—for I have to have help and if they don't give it to me . . ." The worker replied, "If you come back this way, stop in and tell us all about it."

Mr. B did not return that day but was in the office bright and early the following day. He hadn't come back this way and so hadn't gotten in. He wondered if the private agency could give him some help—he hadn't gotten anything at the relief office.

The worker asked him just how he had managed since his work stopped and at first he answered, "Oh, every kind of way—but it's no way to live," but when the worker suggested he mention these ways, he reiterated what he had said at his first interview, that his father had been giving him food and milk but couldn't keep that up forever. The worker said of course his father couldn't, but if Mr. B had given all the necessary information to the relief agency and if it was all just as he had stated, his father wouldn't have to keep it up forever. Did he think his father could keep on helping for a week—or at the most, say, ten days more? Well, if his father knew that would be all he would have to do, he guessed his father wouldn't mind that long. The worker explained that if he had done his part she was sure it would not be longer than that. Mr. B sighed as though relieved, commented, "Well I guess he'll come across for a while," and left the office.[7]

Assistance to the Blind

One of the first groups to achieve specialized public treatment was the blind. While for some time and in many places they were classified in the general category of public assistance, their needs were quickly recognized by the public as meriting more specialized care.

[7] Claire Thomas, "What Is the Private Agency's Responsibility Toward a Client of the Public Agency?" *Cooperative Case Work,* Family Welfare Association of America (now Family Service Association of America), New York, 1935–1939, p. 11.

New Understanding of Problems of Blindness. The blind have unfortunately been viewed by society as not being very useful members. It has been assumed that they would need help even while some other needy groups did not receive it, for blindness commonly has been viewed as entailing total disability. It has been only in more recent years that the blind have not been looked on as totally incapacitated individuals, but were recognized to have some talents even surpassing those of seeing persons. Today, the blind person is considered to be merely a handicapped person, and his problems are viewed as nothing strangely set apart. But the rise of this newer understanding of the problem of blindness had little to do with the origination of aid to the blind. Rather was it due in some measure to the social recognition of the blind person as having a decidedly serious handicap which merited serious attention.

Assistance to the blind today is organized through a complicated system which extends from the Federal Security Agency of the federal government to the local governmental agencies which actually disperse the assistance. Under the conditions of the Social Security Act the

SOURCES OF 143,649 NEW CASES REFERRED TO STATE REHABILITATION AGENCIES AND COMMISSIONS FOR THE BLIND, FISCAL YEAR ENDING JUNE 30, 1947

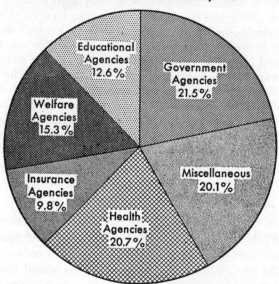

FIG. 36. Sources of 143,649 New Cases Referred to State Rehabilitation Agencies and Commissions for the Blind, Fiscal Year Ending June 30, 1947

(Office of Vocational Rehabilitation, Federal Security Agency.)

blind may be assisted through federal, state, and local funds, operating through states which have approved programs. The fact that the Act was passed in 1935 and the states developed approved plans later, some only in very recent years, indicates a lag in the full realization of the federal program, which is not wholly the responsibility of the federal government. (See Figure 36.)

Meaning of Blindness. Aid to the blind naturally is allocated to those persons who are adjudged to be blind and who have unsatisfied needs. The meaning of blindness and its detection differ in the various states. In a majority, an examination must be made by a physician in order to establish eligibility for such assistance. Some states, however, have no such provisions. Moreover, the actual seeing ability of the person applying for blind assistance is variously interpreted among the states, some being more generous than others. The condition of blindness, once established, is reviewable in many of the states, that is, periodic examinations by physicians are required (usually instigated by the agency) in order to determine whether or not the client should continue to receive public assistance. In some states, however, no periodic examination is required and the person who establishes eligibility at one time secures it for the rest of his life. This interesting practice holds true in some of the most populous states: Illinois, New York, and Pennsylvania, for example.

Qualifications for Assistance. While blindness itself is one of the conditions whereby an individual may qualify for public assistance, another is that of actual need. The blind person generally cannot automatically, because of his blindness, receive public aid. He also must require public assistance in order to meet his needs. Today's program of aid to the blind is primarily intended to meet the needs of those blind persons who are living at home. Where states are so prepared and where the needs of the blind are appropriate, institutional care may, however, be provided. This is especially true of vocational schools for the blind, where they may learn some means of self-support. Vocational training may be provided in addition to the cash payments which are intended for the general support of the blind. In some states special funds are provided for those blind students who are in college so that they can hire readers and in other ways help meet their expenses. But whether the needs of such people are met through institutional care or direct financial support, there usually must be clear evidence that needs exist before eligibility is established.

In a number of jurisdictions, additional requirements are made of the blind. About half of the states rule that public begging will disqualify blind persons from state support. More than a dozen others require a blind person to undergo an ophthalmic operation before becoming eligible, if medical judgment indicates that sight can be saved or improved materially. In addition, the more general requirements discussed under eligibility for public assistance largely apply to the blind as well.

Amounts Provided. The amount of money provided for the blind varies throughout the states. The maximum amounts allowed vary from $180 to $600 a year. California and Nevada appropriate the maximum of $600 for blind persons. This, of course, does not mean that all persons within these states receive the maximum payment, although in several states the minimum and the maximum have been made identical. Where this is the case, blind persons receive a single determined amount, notwithstanding their needs or assets. Aid to the blind tends in these states to become something of a pension device. It may be fair also to say that these states fail to use public funds constructively in so far as there is no noticeable means under this arrangement of treating blind persons individually. Each one is entitled, when his eligibility has been established, to so much aid and no more, notwithstanding his specific requirements.

Arranging for the financial assistance of the blind has other than purely material aspects. In the following case the worker enables two blind people to achieve a solution to a very pressing human problem which pertained only in part to their financial need:

When we work with the adult whose handicap has been lifelong, it may be too late to bring about basic personality change. Understanding his response may, however, enable us to be more helpful in many ways. For example, in the case of Mr. and Mrs. N, the worker encountered a young couple who were both blind. They were living in basement rooms in a dilapidated building, quarters provided by the township authorities for families receiving assistance. Mr. and Mrs. N had met in the State institution for the blind and had been married shortly after leaving there while both were employed at broom-making in a blind and disabled-worker's shop. Mrs. N, aged 20, applied for and received aid to the blind when she became pregnant and could no longer work. Because of his age, 19 years, the husband was not eligible for aid to the blind. When she was unable to accompany him back and forth from the shop and in their rounds in broom selling, he gave up his work, maintaining that he could not get along without her. During the subsequent months he became increasingly dependent on her. He became increasingly irritable and difficult after the birth of a child with normal sight, since the mother became quite absorbed in this fulfillment of her fondest hopes.

It was at this point that Mrs. N unburdened to the worker her great discouragement over Mr. N's inability to assume the responsibilities of a husband and father. She described him as always having been childish, which she attributed to the fact that he lost his parents during infancy and was left to the care of a grandmother who gave him excessive care because of his disability. Upon marriage he immediately looked to her to plan for both of them. She contrasted her own situation with his in that she had come from a family in which there was hereditary blindness, five of eight members having been sightless or having had markedly impaired vision. She said that her disability had been taken for granted. Her family was sociable and of great solidarity. The children took responsibility and participated almost normally in the life of the community. Mrs. N impressed the worker as being an outgoing sociable woman with unusual self-dependence in managing her affairs and in caring for her child.

As Mrs. N talked of her concern over her husband the worker directed her to consider what the child meant to him, and she was able to identify his difficulty as one of rivalry, though at the time this did not help her to feel any more tolerant of his limitations. The worker's suggestion that she put more responsibility on him did not bring results. Later the worker tried to get acquainted with Mr. N, who had until this time remained almost unknown because all financial planning had been done with Mrs. N. She found him very unhappy because he was not working and earning, and also because his wife had money and he did not. He disliked broom-making. He claimed to be mechanically inclined and said that he enjoyed working on old radios. He recalled his life in the institution with some pleasure, particularly as he talked of having studied the violin, of having played in the orchestra, and of having participated in musical activities at the church. In this community he had missed his religious and musical activities and had wanted work of a different sort but had felt that he would not be considered for anything. He was discouraged and depressed about their physical surroundings, and the worker got the impression that their living arrangements had operated against community contacts. The worker agreed that there might be difficulty in getting a job but, in view of the labor shortage and the fact that some industries were now employing blind workers, held out hope that he might get work. She made suggestions as to where he might apply. She showed interest in his musical ability also, and interest in the possibility that they might find community activities and church connections similar to those which they had enjoyed in the past. Later Mr. N obtained work, and shortly thereafter the worker helped him apply for residence in a housing project.

Some months later the worker learned from Mrs. N that he had continued to be fairly regularly employed; that they were planning to have the child admitted to a nursery-school group; that Mr. and Mrs. N had become affiliated with a group of young married couples who lived in the housing project and gave parties. Both Mr. and Mrs N were playing in the orchestra for their dances. In their last conversation Mrs. N stated that her husband had become tolerant of the baby; that he had bought him an electric train for Christmas and since the baby was too young to enjoy this toy, Mr. N was playing with it a great deal. She complained that he had spent a considerable sum of money on a watch, which was foolish in that he could not use it. The worker directed her to consider the importance of this possession to him in terms of "being like other men." Mrs. N reported general improvement in their relationship, their only present difficulty being over the spending of money. She recounted that their worst quarrel had occurred over some curtains—Mrs. N wanted pink ones, while Mr. N wanted blue![8]

Aid to Dependent Children

Just as the blind as a special group have touched the emotions of the American people and have had public assistance programs designed particularly for them, so also have dependent children. They comprise another of the important categories of specialized assistance which the local, state, and federal governments have sought to administer.

The exact meaning of "dependent children" is not generally clear in the public mind. To some persons it suggests "mothers' pensions"; to others it connotes "survivors' assistance." While these terms have some meaning, it is perhaps better to use the term "aid to dependent children" as being more inclusive. Originally, the assistance was formulated to care for widows who had dependent children, and to a large measure this connotation still holds. But today the term has been greatly broadened, especially in certain states, to include much more. In a majority of the states this type of assistance is available to mothers whose husbands have deserted. In twenty-one states, assistance is extended to children of divorced parents. In an equal number of states the assistance is liberal enough to include any dependent child. This last type of aid to dependent children was clearly defined in the Social Security Act, which for the past years has been the bulwark of the state programs of aid: "The term 'dependent child' means a child under the age of sixteen who has been deprived of parental support or care by reason of the death, continued absence from home, or physical or mental incapacity of a parent and who is living with his father, mother, grandfather, grandmother, brother, sister, stepfather, stepmother, stepbrother, stepsister, uncle, or aunt, in a place of residence maintained by one or more of such relatives as his or their own home." Most of the states have approved programs of assistance for dependent children under these terms.

The eligibility standards for this type of public assistance are by and

[8]*Common Human Needs, op. cit.,* pp. 75–77.

large generous. Only a few states insist upon citizenship. Residence requirements generally stipulate either that the parent be a resident of the state for a year or that the child should have been born in the state. A few states also require that the property holdings of the recipients be limited. Definitions of the amount of income permissible in establishing eligibility for dependency are mentioned by a number of states. In general, however, the states have limited programs which do not utilize all of the funds which are available through federal support.

Of interest in regard to the governmentally financed program of aid to dependent children is the fact that the provisions are in general less ample than those for the blind and for the aged. The anomalous condition is explained by some as being due to the vote-securing possibilities of assistance programs for the blind and the aged. This may well be so. But it is of extreme importance that children who have no votes (except potentially) but who are the nation's most significant assets, from almost any angle of evaluation, be protected to the utmost. It is hoped, therefore, that the years ahead will see a further financial liberalization of this type of program.

As in the case of the other types of assistance mentioned in the chapter, the social worker in a public agency oftentimes deals with clients who have nonfinancial needs which are attached to their need for material support. The following is an illustrative case in the child welfare field:

Mrs. L, a widow who had been receiving aid for her three dependent children ranging in age from 7 years to 6 months, sought the worker's help in finding a place for the children in order that she might go to work. As this request was considered with her, she showed marked anxiety about leaving the children lest they not get good care and also lest her husband's people condemn her as an irresponsible and unloving mother. As the possibility of remaining at home with a plan for continuing the financial assistance was explored with her, she revealed that she was deeply discouraged over managing the two boys. Their father had spent so much time with them and he had been such a help in disciplining them. They missed him and had not been the same since his death.

She had had difficulty managing the money—her husband did the major part of the family purchasing and planning and she had been lost and confused in trying to make ends meet. She felt lost even in meal-planning as she always planned around his likes and dislikes. She had been depressed and lonely and her moods affected the children. Her husband was a sociable man who liked a good time. He would pile them all into the car and off they'd go for picnics or to visit friends he'd made at the plant. Now they had no car and she had lost touch with his friends. On this occasion the worker proffered the agency's help in budget-planning, in advising her on child care, and also offered to help her find certain community resources which she might find useful in rearing her family on a smaller income than formerly they had. Mrs. L was appreciative of the worker's interest and in the subsequent months made eager and productive use of the supportive help given.[9]

Old-Age Assistance

Old-age assistance was formerly a part of general public assistance, as were aid to the blind and aid to dependent children. But today it too is a special category of assistance. The rise in awareness of the problems of the aged has been almost phenomenal in recent years. Perhaps its most radical expression was the Townsend plan which sought to secure for the aged a more liberal livelihood than even the most generous of the governmentally sponsored programs ever envisaged. The rise has been influenced no doubt to a considerable degree by the fact that the population of the United States is aging; increasingly, there are larger proportions of aged persons within the total population. They have become a special pressure group of significant force upon government, and there is every indication that their influence will be enlarged in the coming years.

Programs of assistance for the aged existed before the Social Security Act of 1935, but they were, with the possible exception of that in New York, decidedly inadequate. From the financial standpoint, most of the states provided sums which were ridiculously small. Eligibility regulations also were stringent. The methods of administration were almost notoriously bad. Fortunately, the Social Security Act had the effect of greatly strengthening and improving the old-age assistance programs. The provisions of the Act have been mentioned in the previous chapter and need not be recalled here.

Comparison With Other Programs. The old-age assistance program should be sharply differentiated from the old-age pension program of government. Pension plans usually require no establishment of need and are granted because the person has served as a governmental employee for a stipulated number of years. He receives the pension whether or not he has actual need of it, although in most cases there is a real need. In the old-age assistance programs, on the other hand, the recipient is not necessarily a governmental employee. Moreover, he must have needs which meet the definitions of the old-age assistance

[9] *Ibid*, pp. 30–31.

legislation. He must be eligible for aid, as eligibility in public welfare has been discussed.

The old-age assistance program should also be differentiated from various systems of retirement which are not of a pension character. Such a program of retirement assistance is that provided by many teachers' organizations. Usually, under such plans the individual and the employing agency contribute over a period of years to a general fund from which payments are made upon retirement, again without a need-basis having to be established. The Federal Old-Age and Survivors Insurance plan is another example in point. Old-age assistance is granted, conversely, because the applicant can show that he does not have the means of supporting himself. Only on the satisfaction of this requirement can the assistance be given.

Administration by States. Several state peculiarities in the administration of the national program of old-age assistance may be noted here. Some states have disqualifying conditions such as that of begging, having committed a felonious offense within the previous ten years, failing to support children under a specified age. Some states do not require citizenship; some do. The property holdings of an aged person determine his eligibility in many states, although the trend is to establish eligibility on the basis of income rather than that of property. Many states require that the assistance granted during the lifetime of the aged person shall be retrieved from his resources, if any, upon death.

The amounts of money which are provided by the various states are inadequate today, and a great deal needs to be done to improve the program. But with the development of social insurance plans operated by government, this deficiency may be lessened, although even in regard to the insurance plans considerable improvement is called for if they are to serve the aged well.

Nonmaterial Aspects. While the financial problems attached to the assistance of the aged are many and diverse, there also are nonmaterial problems with which the social worker in a public agency deals. Some aged people have a difficult time accepting change. They may resist the efforts of the workers to benefit them. The psychological type of need is just as important in some cases as the material. The case of Miss "S" is an example:

Miss S, a recipient of old-age assistance, was growing so infirm as to be unable to care for herself adequately. The public assistance worker tried to help her face her need for institutional care, only to have the suggestion staunchly repudiated. Finally, eviction by three successive landlords because of neighbors' complaints about the state of her rooms and inability to obtain a fourth lodging led to her placement in a home for the aged where she subsequently led a more comfortable and satisfying life. On the day of removal, she angrily reproached the worker for not having "made her" do this earlier, and at this time she recounted the discomforts and loneliness of the past months.[10]

Other Governmental Services

The services which have thus far been discussed in this chapter have their locus within the Social Security Administration and are dispersed through state and local facilities. Actually, these do not comprise all of the social services offered by government, nor indeed by the Federal Security Agency. From a broad point of view, there are a number of others which may be classified as being more or less within the field of social work in its public welfare aspects.

Mental Disability. The local, state, and federal governments are regularly providing various kinds of services to the mentally disordered (psychotics). These services are usually of two types: institutional, and clinical. In many localities there are local, state, or federally financed and managed institutions which house and treat mental patients. State governments alone operate about 200 such institutions. In some states these mental hospitals are grouped under the state department of welfare; other states have created independent departments of mental hygiene. Clinics likewise abound, usually being attached to hospitals.

Closely related to the care of psychotics by the government is the care of the feeble-minded. The largest number of institutions for the feeble-minded are today under state auspices. As in the case of mental hospitals the institutions for the feeble-minded are in some states under the control of state departments of welfare, while in others they are responsible to other departments.

Criminality. Criminals and delinquents are also the charges of the government. Local, state, and federal facilities exist for the treatment of both adult and juvenile offenders. The facilities generally consist of correctional institutions, probation and parole services, and services in connection with trial. These have been discussed in Chapter 8.

Medical Care. Medical care comprises another of the governmental means of serving the population. The largest single medical service provided by government is that of hospitalization. While a significant portion of the cost of maintaining hospitals is borne by private means, nevertheless an even larger share is carried by public funds. In many instances medical care is supplied to public clients through private

[10]*Ibid*, pp. 69–70.

medical resources on referral from public departments. This service may be paid in part or in full by the government.

Responsibility for venereal diseases, as well as for certain other damaging and highly communicable diseases, has always been assumed to be a significant medical responsibility of government. Even departments of health, from the broad point of view of public welfare, contribute to social work goals.

Public Works. In the past the government offered a public works program for the unemployed which might be termed a part of public welfare. The period of the 1930's evidenced the greatest display of this type of governmental assistance.

Employment Counseling. Another example of federal assistance of a social work character is the United States Employment Service. This was initiated as a unit under the Department of Labor in 1933 and transferred to the Federal Security Agency in 1939. The Wagner-Peyser Act which gave it birth provided for a national system of public employment offices. During the war the service was operated on a federal basis under the War Manpower Commission. In 1946 it was returned to the states for administration, with the federal government still financing the program.

In addition to these services there are others, many others, which the local, state, and federal governments extend to the people.

SOCIAL INSURANCE

Another of the methods used to maintain the public welfare is that of social insurance. The rights of individuals under assistance programs are determined by eligibility standards. Under insurance programs a contractual right is possessed by the participant whereby he shares benefits automatically upon his fulfillment of the statutory qualifications.

Several of the insurance programs, especially as supported by the federal government, will be examined. They will be reviewed rather fully in order to point out, among other things, the degree of detail which characterizes the public welfare field in its concrete operation.

Old-Age and Survivors Insurance

A program for the relief of the needs of the aged and of survivors, which possesses considerable promise for the future of public welfare administration, is that of insurance. While it is not accurate to say that the insurance method of meeting personal needs will some day become the only means (because probably no insurance program can cover all emergency conditions), it is fair to say that it will greatly take the place of the older and more direct types of public assistance. The granting of old-age assistance is necessary only because a more foresighted arrangement has not previously been worked out to care adequately for the aged.

Payments Into Fund. Insurance programs do not need the qualifying eligibility rules which direct assistance requires. Under the insurance conception of public welfare, the person who reaches old age does not ask for government funds to which he has contributed nothing. Rather, for a large part of his employed lifetime he has been making payments along with other employees into a governmental trust and, after proper conditions are met, he is entitled to a share of the money. Thus, as under certain pension and retirement arrangements, an applicant would not have to establish his need before receiving governmental funds but would receive them whether he had need of them or not.

The Federal Old-Age and Survivors Insurance plan instituted under the Social Security Act (and its amendments) involves, among other things, a trust fund derived from various financial sources: the employer, the employee, and the government. The fund is governed by a Board of Trustees who have the following duties to perform: (1) they hold the trust fund; (2) they report to Congress on the first day of each regular session on the operation and the status of the trust fund during the preceding fiscal year and on its intended operations for the following five years; (3) they report to Congress whenever in their judgment the trust fund is too small to meet its obligations for the coming five-year period.

Benefits at Age of Sixty-Five. The benefits of the plan cover a wide range of people. Every person who is a full-fledged member of the insurance plan, has attained the age of sixty-five, and has filed an application for benefits, receives benefits for each month beginning with the month in which the individual becomes eligible until the month preceding the month in which he dies. The wife of an insured member is also eligible for benefits under certain conditions. She must have attained to age sixty-five, have filed application for benefits, and have lived with her insured husband at the time that the application was made. She would not receive benefits from the husband's insurance, however, if she herself is similarly insured, unless her own insurance is less than half of her husband's. In this case she could forfeit her own insurance in favor of her husband's. The wife may receive benefits until she dies, her husband dies, they are divorced, or she receives benefits which violate the conditions previously mentioned. The amount of

Table 16

EXAMPLES OF OLD-AGE INSURANCE RETIREMENT BENEFITS

(For a single insured worker, and for a worker and his wife, or for a worker and one dependent child)

Average monthly wage*	Number of years in which worker was paid wages of $200 or more in covered employment	Monthly benefit payments to—	
		Worker	Worker and wife
$50	5	$21.00	$31.50
$100		26.25	39.38
$150		31.50	47.25
$250		42.00	63.00
$50	7	$21.40	$32.10
$100		26.75	40.13
$150		32.10	48.15
$250		42.80	64.20
$50	10 (maximum possible through 1946)	$22.00	$33.00
$100		27.50	41.25
$150		33.00	49.50
$250		44.00	66.00
$50	20	$24.00	$36.00
$100		30.00	45.00
$150		36.00	54.00
$250		48.00	72.00
$50	30	$26.00	$39.00
$100		32.50	48.75
$150		39.00	58.50
$250		52.00	78.00
$50	40	$28.00	$40.00
$100		35.00	52.50
$150		42.00	63.00
$250		56.00	84.00

*For "average monthly wages" under $50 the benefits are smaller, but they cannot be less than $10 a month for the worker and $15 a month for the worker and wife.

Benefits are payable only on account of "fully insured" workers. Amounts of benefits illustrated above depend on "average monthly wage."

Source: *Insurance for Workers and Their Families: Federal Old-Age and Survivors Insurance,* Federal Security Agency, Social Security Administration, Washington, D.C., January, 1947, p. 14.

benefit which a wife may receive is approximately one half of the husband's primary benefit. (See Table 16.)

Entitlement of Children. The plan also covers children. Every child of an individual living or dead entitled to primary benefits who has made application, is unmarried and not eighteen years of age or older at the time of application, and was dependent on the insured individual, is entitled to insurance benefits. These amount to one half of the insurance benefits of the parent of whom the child is a dependent. Benefits to the child stop whenever any of the following occurs: the child marries, dies, is adopted, or attains the age of eighteen. A child is not eligible if he is neither the legitimate nor adopted child of the insured person, if he has been adopted by some other individual, or if, at the time of the insured person's death, he is living with and supported by a stepfather.

Eligibility of Widows. Widows also are eligible for insurance benefits under this plan. The following conditions are made of them in order that they qualify for benefits: they must be the widows of husbands insured under the plan; they must not have remarried; they must have attained the age of sixty-five; they must file an application for such benefits; they must have been living with their insured husbands at the time of the husband's death; they must not be entitled to receive primary benefits of their own. Widows may receive benefits equal to three fourths of the insured person's benefits until they remarry, die, or in other ways become ineligible. Under another arrangement the widows of insured members who are not eligible under the previous plan, but who have children who are eligible under the qualifications for children, may also receive insurance benefits equal to three fourths of the benefit which the insured person would receive. (See Figure 37.)

Dependency of Parents. Parents of insured individuals may also benefit from the plan if the insured person has left no widow or surviving, eligible children. The parents must also be sixty-five years of age, have been dependent upon the insured individual before his death, and have filed proof of such dependency two years before the time of the insured individual's death, have not married since the individual's death, and have no status entitling them to any benefits which exceed one half of the benefit provided by the insurance of the deceased individual. The benefit for parents equals one half of the benefit of the insured individual and holds until the parents or parent dies, remarries, or otherwise becomes ineligible.

Conditions of Payment. Lump-sum death payments are also possible under the insurance plan. The lump sum provided upon the death of

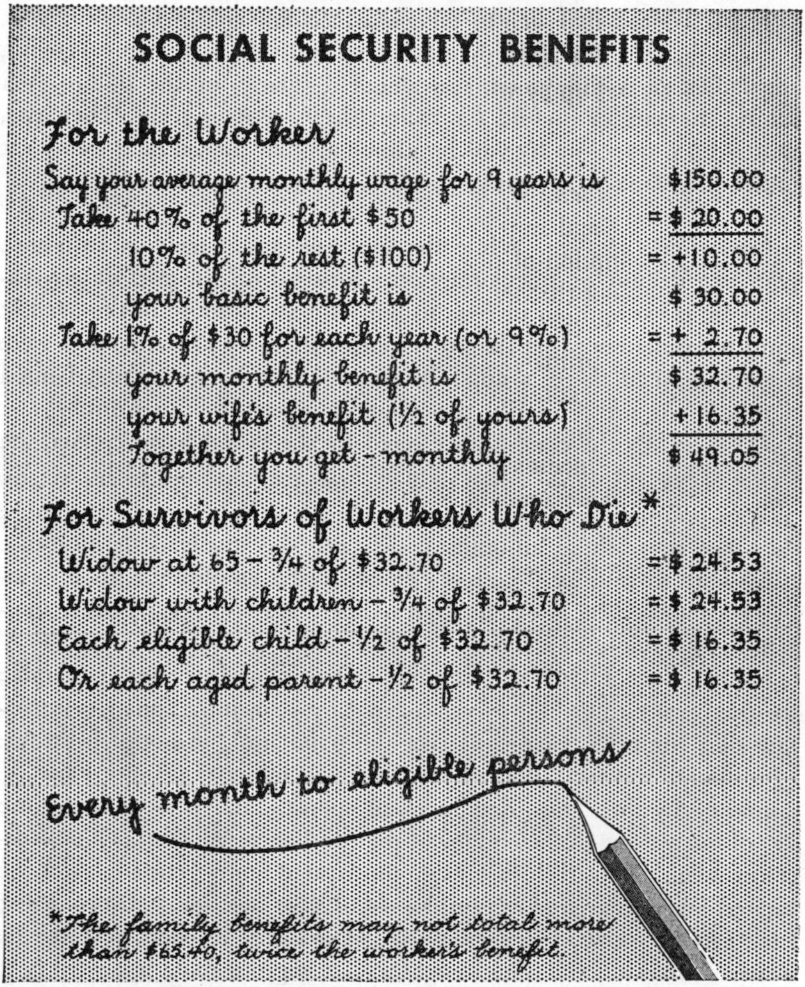

SOCIAL SECURITY BENEFITS

For the Worker

Say your average monthly wage for 9 years is	$150.00
Take 40% of the first $50	= $ 20.00
10% of the rest ($100)	= +10.00
your basic benefit is	$ 30.00
Take 1% of $30 for each year (or 9%)	= + 2.70
your monthly benefit is	$ 32.70
your wife's benefit (½ of yours)	+16.35
Together you get - monthly	$ 49.05

For Survivors of Workers Who Die *

Widow at 65 - ¾ of $32.70	= $ 24.53
Widow with children - ¾ of $32.70	= $ 24.53
Each eligible child - ½ of $32.70	= $ 16.35
Or each aged parent - ½ of $32.70	= $ 16.35

Every month to eligible persons

*The family benefits may not total more than $65.40, twice the worker's benefit.

FIG. 37. Social Security Benefits for the Worker and for His Survivors
(Federal Security Agency, Social Security Administration.)

an insured individual is six times the primary payment. The following persons may share in the distribution of the lump sum: the widow or widower of the deceased, any child or children of the deceased, any other persons who are entitled to share in the benefit, in such proportions as the laws may determine. Application for such payment must be made within two years' time of the death of the insured individual.

In addition to these provisions there are others which regulate the minimums and maximums which can be received as benefits. There are rules also which pertain to the conditions under which the benefit may be reduced in order to take into account contingent situations, such as the part-time employment of an individual receiving benefits, the failure of a child to attend school regularly, or the failure of a mother to care for a child for whom she is receiving aid. There are, moreover, ways set up by which individuals may appeal their treatment under the plan.

Limitations of Plan. While the Old-Age and Survivors Insurance plan is a definite and important step forward on the part of government in its assumption of responsibility for the welfare of the aged, it must be pointed out that the provisions of the Social Security Act were severely limited in their application to the population of the United States. There are primarily two qualifying sets of limitations.

a. Wages. By the conditions created by the Social Security Act, the terms of the insurance cover only income paid by employers to employees up to and including $3,000 a year. Furthermore, the insurance does not cover those amounts which may be involved in insurance plans entered into by the employee or by the employer with his employees for the benefit of employees. There are also several other limitations of a minor character.

b. Employment. Only certain groups of employed persons are eligible for the plan. Groups not as yet covered by such provisions are important and comprise a large part of the population. Among them are: agricultural workers; domestics in private homes; persons who are employed by their sons, daughters, or spouses, and persons under the age of twenty-one in the employ of their fathers or mothers; ship workers on non-American ships outside the United States; employees of the United States government; employees of state and local governments; fund raisers, social workers, foundation workers, teachers, researchers, writers, librarians, and others engaged in nonprofit making enterprises; those working for foreign governments; most fishermen; and children under eighteen.

Obviously, these limitations exclude many people who should rightly benefit from the provisions of the Old-Age and Survivors Insurance plan. While there has been constant agitation to change the legislation to include more and more groups, nothing actually has been accomplished up to the present. Probably, however, the need for a more extensive insurance program for old age and for survivors will make an appeal in the near future sufficient to bring about new legislation.

But granting the serious limitations of the Act which gives the insurance its existence, one should not overlook the Act's real virtues. Contrasted to old-age assistance, which is administered without the financial participation of the recipient, this type of insurance contains many hopeful gains and promises.

Unemployment Compensation

One of the most serious fears which modern society has produced among countless of its members is the fear of unemployment. And rightly so, for the results of unemployment in terms of family misery, personal disorganization, and lack of social well-being, are by now so generally known that little comment is necessary. True, the facing of old age has been a difficult problem for many, but the prospect of being thrown out of work before retirement has perplexed even more persons and for more years of their lifetime. As part of its welfare program, therefore, the government has seen fit to set up those arrangements which will cushion the shock of unemployment and make life more tolerable for many. While the person who is unemployed has been, and to some extent still is, aided by the general public assistance provided by local, state, and federal governments, he has not been insured against general unemployment until rather recently. Previous to the Social Security Act there was no general system of unemployment insurance. It was this Act that made real to a considerable extent the protection of workers and their families in times of unemployment.

Fig. 38. Unemployment Insurance Helps in Reducing the Cost of Relief
(Federal Security Agency, Social Security Administration.)

Many workers have been protected, however, even prior to the Social Security Act, from unemployment suffered because of disabilities incurred on the job. This protection has been provided both by private insurance companies and by the states. As yet there is no general federal program of disability insurance which would supplement or integrate the various nonfederal methods of meeting the problem. It is also important to note that there is as yet no federal provision for support in case of permanent disability, aside from the previously discussed categories. Thus a man who suffers permanent disability at the age of fifty-five would have to wait until he became sixty-five (with accompanying losses in his benefits) before he would be eligible for permanent federal support. There would be, however, other means of aiding such a person, although they would not be federal.

Regulations States Must Comply With. The Social Security Act does provide a general system of unemployment insurance or compensation which is a clear example of public welfare work. The plan under the Act, while centralized in the federal government, gives notable responsibility to state and local communities. The purpose of appropriations under the Act is that "of assisting the States in the administration of their unemployment compensation laws." Payments to the states are regulated by a Board which uses the following criteria: (1) the population of the state; (2) an estimate of the number of persons covered by the state law and the cost of the administration of the state law; (3) such other factors as the Board finds relevant.

The Board can make no payment to a state which does not meet certain requirements. The states must maintain standards of personnel for aiding in the efficient and full distribution of the compensation due insured individuals. There is suggested here a civil service system of personnel selection and tenure. The payments of compensation to individuals must be made through public officers or such other agencies as are given approval by the Board. Opportunities for fair hearings must be supplied to all aggrieved individuals. States must immediately transfer to the Federal Unemployment Trust Fund all money received into the unemployment funds of the states. All money within the states' unemployment funds must be used for the purpose of compensation (with the exception of administration costs). States must also provide reports to the Board of their activities, whenever they are requested. A further responsibility is to make available to any federal agency concerned with the administration of public works the personal data regarding insured individuals and their right to unemployment compensation. In addition to these requirements, states must maintain adequate money resources for this purpose and must have a definite system of benefit allotments for individuals.

Amount of Payments. The fund originally set aside by the federal government in 1936 for the unemployment program was $4,000,000. This was increased for each fiscal year, according to plan, until it reached $80,000,000 in 1940. The states also contribute large sums of money for compensation. From all financial resources including the states' treasuries, the states paid $71,200,000 in benefits in the fiscal year 1944–1945, a rise of about $10,000,000 over the previous year.

The actual money received by the unemployed individual, however, is rather small. In April–June of 1945 the weekly benefit for total unemployment averaged $17.30 for the country as a whole. Wide variations among the states went into this average. In North Carolina the payment meant $8.95 for that period, while in Michigan it was $19.46. Both figures are obviously inadequate for workers with dependents; the goal for unemployment payments, according to the Social Security Administration itself, has been set at $25.00 a week.

Persons Excluded From Coverage. The provisions of the Act in regard to unemployment leave much to be desired. As with Old-Age and Survivors Insurance the omission of members and groups of persons from the plan does not make for a wide coverage of the American population—only about half are now included. There are still technicalities which prevent certain individuals and groups from sharing fully in the program. These would be eliminated if a more intelligent insurance plan for unemployment was achieved. The fact, too, that only those workers employed in a covered industry having eight or more employees under one employer are eligible to enter the plan means that its benefits are denied to those persons who do not work in large economic units. It would seem on this point that the national plan should cover all industries, regardless of the number of workers hired. More than half of the states, however, do have unemployment compensation programs which include firms with less than eight workers.

Variations in Benefits. There also is wide variation regarding the duration of the benefits receivable. At the start most states limited the maximum duration to 16 weeks, after a period of waiting of at least two weeks. More recently, many of the states cut the waiting period to one week; Maryland has eliminated the waiting period entirely. In 1945 there were only five states which had extended the period of maximum benefits to twenty-six weeks. In some states, the past earnings of the individual also influence the amount he will receive under the plan and the length of time for which he will receive benefits. For example, the duration period in some states may be only three or four weeks for workers with low past earnings. In other states, however, the amount of past earnings does not influence the duration of the benefits. And notwithstanding the calculations of states regarding past earnings and duration periods, they often have maximum regulations of payment which seriously restrict the amounts of benefits which the jobless many receive. Thus in some states today the maximum is set at $15.00 a week (which was the maximum for all of the states in 1937). Recently, the maximums of twenty-seven states were increased to $20.00 or more. Even this figure, as has been mentioned previously, is noticeably low.

A National Social Insurance Plan

One of the needs apparent from the discussion of governmental operations in social insurance, is that of integration. The integration of social insurance on a national scale should mean the extension of the insurance plan to cover more adequately those persons who are now participants and also to include within the plan those needs which are presently left out. The fundamental design of a national plan should provide minimum protection against all major risks for all people who have to face them. While the program should be national in scope, it could very well profit by previous experience and be run on a decentralized administrative basis. Through a decentralized system of management an individual could secure any or all types of covered assistance from one local office.

An integrated national plan should include all those services which already exist and others. There should be an adequate medical insurance section in the program. There should be a national disability program. There should be more generous assistance in all of the present categories in line with social adequacy rather than political expediency. The formula for the determination of benefits should be standardized so that individuals are equal in regard to the benefits which they may receive from various sections of the plan. The benefits should be more rigidly standardized throughout the country. The plan, finally, should be operated on the insurance basis rather than on the assistance basis. This would obviously mean increased financial demands for its upkeep, not only on the individuals participating, but also on the local, state, and federal governments.

CASEWORK IN PUBLIC WELFARE

For some time there has been a doubt as to the validity of thinking of public welfare services as utilizing casework techniques. Especially was this so in the earlier days of the modern period of public welfare (from the early 1930's to the present). The personnel practices of public welfare agencies often seemed to confirm this judgment, for the agencies very largely did not employ professional social workers but relied on nonprofessional persons to administer their programs. This is still true to an extent which is lamentable. But large governmental programs like public welfare are slow to change, even on so important a point as quality of service. Thus from the standpoint of actual fact there may be some reason to suppose that the public agencies have not been and are not yet ready to administer their services in a fully professional manner. There has been, however, over a period of years, a decided improvement from the professional point of view in the quality of the services rendered by these agencies.

Another doubt regarding the use of casework techniques in public welfare rests upon the fact that the regulations of the public agencies seem to a considerable degree to cut off those possibilities of meeting individual client's needs, which in many instances have so excellently characterized the private agencies. The worker who is not required to individualize the client further than most public legislation permits has a doubtful casework status. So it has been claimed. This limitation, however, is not intrinsic or unchangeable.

Result of Regulatory Limitations

The erroneous assumptions underlying this limitation to the functions of a public welfare agency have been pointed out on several occasions. In an article which tackles this subject, Meta L. Landuyt provides a case which shows how the very regulatory limitations of a public agency may form a basis for the casework process:

Mr. B applied for old-age assistance at the instigation of his son. Mr. B had been acting as caretaker of two small apartment houses and earning his rent and a small cash allowance of about $18 a week which supported him and his wife, who was not quite old enough to apply for Old-Age Assistance. Mr. B had been ill with pneumonia and, although he was recovering, his son felt that his plan to return to work would be too much for him. The son telephoned the office and requested that a worker call at the home and take the application.

The worker called at the home and talked with both Mr. and Mrs. B. Mr. B was aware that his son had asked us to call. Worker explained the eligibility requirements for Old-Age Assistance and the service our agency could offer. Mr. B stated that he understood but that he had always been able to take care of himself until his recent illness and did not wish to accept relief. The landlord had been very good to them and would continue to give them their rent in return for Mrs. B's answering the telephone and making rental collections. Mr. B stated that he still had a few dollars cash (about $50) and thought he could make that last until he was able to get back to work. In the meantime, Mrs. B was attempting to fire the furnace, and they had paid a high-school boy to carry out ashes and shovel snow from the walks. Mr. B was worried about cleaning floors and halls, which they had not been able to do.

Mr. B apologized for the necessity for the worker's making a call but stated that he preferred to get along on his own. Worker assured him that he had not caused any inconvenience and that she would be glad to help him if she could. However, she understood his desire to be self-supporting and suggested that he get in touch with us at any time if things did not work out as he planned. At this point Mr. B asked how long it would take to get help if he needed it. He had heard that there was a long waiting list. Worker explained that it had formerly been true that the list was quite long but since funds had been made available this list had been taken care of, and now applications made during one month could receive payment the following month. Checks were written in the state office and mailed. Worker then asked if he would like to fill out an application that day so that it could be acted upon if he wished. Mr. B thought he would like to do this although he was pretty sure he wouldn't need it if he could just get his strength back. Worker took the application but told Mr. B that she would not take any action on it until she heard from him telling her what he wanted done.

Worker then called on Mr. B's son who had telephoned the referral. She explained that Mr. B appeared to be eligible for Old-Age Assistance but seemed strongly opposed to receiving aid. The son said he knew that his father was very proud but he was worried about Mr. B's health. Worker pointed out that, in view of Mr. B's strong feelings on the subject, forcing Mr. B to accept help might also retard his recovery. Worker then discussed with the son how Mr. B could get along until he was either able to work or could bring himself to accept Old-Age Assistance. The son stated that he would be glad to help but was financially unable to do so as he had four children to support and was earning only $40 a week. Worker spoke of Mr. B's concern about his job remaining open for him. The son thought he might be able to help out there. He could go over on his day off and do some of the cleaning and could stop in an evening or two each week and carry out ashes so that his father would not have to pay for that.

Worker explained that we had taken the application but had promised to wait until we heard from Mr. B before we acted upon it.

Almost a month later we received another telephone call from the son stating that Mr. B was feeling much better and the doctor had said it was all right for him to resume his work. Mr. B had requested the son to call and ask us to cancel the application. The son would continue to give him a hand with the heavier tasks for a while. Since the manager had not had to hire someone to take Mr. B's place, his salary had continued. The son thanked us for the interest we had taken in his father.

Worker wrote a note to Mr. B telling him that she was glad to hear that he was feeling better and that according to his request the application was being canceled. She again told him that if we could ever be of service to him to feel free to call upon us.[11]

The fact that the public agencies have largely offered material service while the private agencies have been more concerned in the recent years with what may be described as "counseling" or the treatment of personality problems indicates to some the failure of the public agencies to practice casework or to need casework procedures. This distinction may hold generally, but it does not in all particulars, for there are private agencies whose main function is the dispersal of material aid while there are public agencies which undertake intensive psychological treatment.

Intensive Application

The following case of the "D" family illustrates how a medical social worker employed by the St. Louis Social Security Commission (which administers general relief, aid to dependent children, and old-age assistance) demonstrated the value of intensive casework with ill clients:

In the D family were the father, aged 29, the mother, 23, and five children, the oldest aged 7. The family applied for assistance for the first time in February, 1942, because of the man's illness. Diagnosis was rheumatic fever, and it was recommended that Mr. D have complete rest for several months. However, Mr. D could not accept his dependency on the agency, and several weeks after applying for assistance took a job doing carpentry, his regular trade. He became severely ill after two days' work, and was forced to stop work and apply again for assistance. The family was soon referred by their visitor to the medical social worker. It was found that Mr. D had a great deal of anxiety about the situation, that he could not accept his dependent role, and that in order to avoid facing the fact that he would have to be dependent for a long time, he was insisting that he was not very ill and that he was able to do some kind of work.

The medical social worker visited the home about twice a week, gave Mr. and Mrs. D an opportunity to talk out their feelings about being on relief, gave assurance in various ways of their social acceptability, assured them that their needs would be met, interpreted to them the nature of Mr. D's illness and the necessity for carrying out medical recommendations. In addition to this, various services were secured, such as volunteer motor service to the clinic, occupational therapy in the home, and referral to an agency where glasses could be secured. As time went on, Mr. D became noticeably less agitated in manner, and appeared to be accepting the situation with less protest. He attended the clinic regularly and

[11]Meta L. Landuyt, "Case Work in a Public Assistance Agency," *The Family* (now *Journal of Social Casework*) volume 25, number 2, April, 1944, pp. 44–45.

avoided strenuous activities. Several times he telephoned the worker to ask whether he should undertake certain activities.

Nevertheless, Mr. D's underlying need to be independent persisted and eventually expressed itself in action. One morning about three months after the worker's first contact, Mrs. D telephoned the worker that Mr. D had gone to work at a carpentry job that day. She was worried about it and was afraid of the consequences. She was asked whether she thought Mr. D would be willing to go to the clinic the next day to discuss his employment with the doctor. She was sure that he would do so, and the worker arranged for a clinic appointment the next day, enlisted the help of the clinic social worker in obtaining recommendations from the doctor. Mr. D did attend the clinic and upon the physician's recommendation quit the job. Six weeks later, Mr. D was told by the doctor that he could return to his regular employment, and he was back at his old job the next day.[12]

Referral to Other Agencies

If a public agency cannot, because of eligibility limitations, for example, enter into a sustained relationship with a client, it can still utilize the casework process in making reference to other agencies. The following is an example:

Mrs. W, a middle-aged woman, applied for public assistance for the first time. She brought with her a stack of envelopes and papers tied in a tight little bundle, and in a business-like manner, explained briefly that she had left her husband four weeks ago and she and her 14-year-old daughter were living in a furnished room. Her husband was employed as a pressman and earned about $25 a week. She had thought it over very carefully and felt she could not live happily with her husband, and, therefore, had left him. There was one complication, however, and that was the fact that she was unable to work and support herself. She had $15 when she left her husband, out of which she paid her first room rent and food bill. Now she owed two weeks' rent and a store bill of $8. She was afraid her landlord would ask her to move and the grocer refuse to grant her additional credit; she, therefore, needed immediate assistance.

She gave this information almost in an itemized, rehearsed fashion, without any outward expression of emotion. As each point of eligibility was raised in filling out the application form, she produced evidence from her little stack of papers: her rent books for several years back, her rent receipt at her present rooming house, her husband's pay envelope, her clinic cards and her grocery bill.

It was explained that in a case of separation, if the husband was employed, the woman was required to place a Court Order on him for her

[12]Evelyn Gross Cohen, "A Medical Social Worker in a Public Assistance Agency," *The Family* (now *Journal of Social Casework*), volume 25, number 1, March, 1944, p. 17.

support. Mrs. W promptly pulled from her bundle of papers her Court Card showing that she had already done this and also unearthed a card with the name of the Probation Officer, who, she said, advised her to apply for assistance. He could verify all this information if we called him. The interviewer commented that it would hardly be necessary to get further verification other than that for she seemed to have brought almost everything that could be requested. Mrs. W said she heard these things were necessary and she wanted to be prepared. Furthermore, she did need our help as soon as possible and she thought this would help.

The interviewer asked whether she had made any attempt to get funds from her husband since she had left him. Mrs. W said he refused to give her any and that was why she was taking the matter to Court. He used to give her only $16 a week out of his salary and expected her to pay all the bills, including rent and clothing, and yet expected her to keep up a nice home and "elaborate table." It couldn't be done. Now she would make him give her money through the Court. Besides, the Probation Officer had told her she could not take any money from him until her case came up in Court within several weeks. The interviewer asked whether she also thought it would hurt her case of nonsupport against her husband if she accepted money at this point, and very matter-of-factly, Mrs. W said she thought it would.

In discussing the situation over the telephone with the Probation Officer, the worker learned that Mr. W was willing and anxious to contribute to his wife's support even before the matter came up for a hearing, but he had not heard from her since she left him, and that he did not know where to send any money. As the Court is not permitted to divulge addresses, they could not tell him where she was. The husband seemed very anxious for reconciliation and the Probation Officer thought the Judge would work toward this in their hearing.

It was necessary for the interviewer to explain to Mrs. W that her husband's salary was considered a resource, and although it was easy to understand why she did not want to use it, that part was really her own problem. The agency was using public funds to help those who had no other way of providing for themselves. If, as she had mentioned previously, her husband had really refused to give her any money during this time, it might be possible to grant assistance pending Court action. However, under the circumstances, it would be necessary to verify her husband's refusal to support, and this would make it necessary to refer her application to the visitor for further investigation before any assistance could be granted. The interviewer added that she wished she could give assurance that the agency could grant her the help she needed at this time, as it must be pretty hard for her to have made up her mind to leave her husband and take him to Court, and then find difficulty in obtaining enough money on which to live until her case came up for hearing.

The interviewer asked whether in all of her well-thought-out plans she had not anticipated any difficulty in getting outside financial help. Now that this had arisen, did she have any plans of her own to tide her over? For the first time, Mrs. W showed some signs of relaxing the firm, tense hold she appeared to have of her situation. Almost in a tone of self-pity, she said that she had thought of trying to find some work, even as sick as she was.

The interviewer asked whether it was really as important to her as all that to take her husband to Court. Was she reasonably sure that was what she wanted? Mrs. W said she had thought it seemed the only thing for her to do, but maybe it wasn't all as simple as it appeared at first. The interviewer then asked whether she would like to think through this decision a little further with someone in another agency who might be able to help her with it. Mrs. W admitted that she did have some problems in her mind she wasn't sure about. There were two things especially on which she would like to get someone else's opinion. The interviewer explained that the worker in the family agency would be glad to talk with her about something she really wanted help with, but financial assistance might not enter into the situation at all. Mrs. W said she would welcome an opportunity to talk with someone about these two problems she had in mind. If the interviewer could tell her where to go, she would do so right away. She had felt so free since her separation from her husband, in spite of all the struggle it had meant for her, but she did want to be so "awfully sure" about herself before the hearing.

The interviewer suggested that she think it over a little further as to whether she really wanted to have help on her problem from this kind of an agency, especially since it might not be able to give her financial help. After telephone consultation with the family agency, a card of introduction was given to Mrs. W which she could use when and if she wanted to go further with this referral. She took the card and thanked the interviewer for her interest.

A call from the family agency later in the day told us that Mrs. W was in that office.[13]

Responsibility of Public Agency

The responsibility of the public agency, then, is essentially the same as that of the private agency: to provide those resources within its jurisdiction, limitations, and possibilities which will, upon reflection, help meet the examined needs of clients. This responsibility implies that highly trained leadership is required for the administration of the process in public welfare work, as in private social work. All of the professional casework elements which are present in private social casework are also present in public welfare work, except that they are on occasion somewhat differently utilized.

[13]Helen R. Spitz, "The Interviewer's Responsibility in Determining Eligibility," *Intake Policies and Practices,* Family Welfare Association of America (now Family Service Association of America), New York, 1940–1941, pp. 12–13.

SELECTED READINGS ON THE PROCESS OF PUBLIC WELFARE

Browning, Grace, *Rural Public Welfare: Selected Records With Introductory Notes and Comments,* Social Service Series, University of Chicago Press, Chicago, 1941.

Colcord, Joanna, *Cash Relief,* Russell Sage Foundation, New York, 1936.

Cowgill, Ella L., *A Guidebook for Beginners in Public Assistance Work,* Family Welfare Association of America (now Family Service Association of America), New York, 1940.

Cox, Cordelia, and Reed, Ella W., *Interviews and Case Studies in Public Welfare: For Use of Discussion Groups,* American Public Welfare Association, Chicago, 1945.

Daly, Dorothy B., *Case Work Practice in Public Assistance Administration: A Manual To Be Used by the Practitioner in Public Assistance to Develop the Effectiveness of His Methods and the Quality of His Service to Clients and Community, and by Supervisors as a Framework for Staff Development Through an In-Service Training Program,* American Public Welfare Association, Chicago, 1942.

de Schweinitz, Karl, *People and Process in Social Security,* American Council on Education, Washington, D.C., 1948.

Glassberg, Benjamin, *Across the Desk of a Relief Administrator,* American Public Welfare Association, Chicago, 1938.

Houwink, Eda, *The Place of Case Work in the Public Assistance Program,* American Public Welfare Association, Chicago, 1941.

Kurtz, Russell, *The Public Assistance Worker: His Responsibility to the Applicant, the Community, and Himself,* Russell Sage Foundation, New York, 1938.

LaBarre, Maurine, editor, *Practice of Case Work in Public Agencies,* Family Welfare Association of America (now Family Service Association of America), New York, 1940.

Lawton, George, editor, *New Goals for Old Age,* Columbia University Press, New York, 1943.

Russell, Elizabeth, *Professional Growth on the Job: A Guide for the Public Assistance Worker,* Family Service Association of America, New York, 1947.

Smalley, Ruth, and others, *Meaning and Use of Relief in Case Work Treatment,* Family Welfare Association of America (now Family Service Association of America), New York, 1941.

Street, Elwood, *The Public Welfare Administrator,* McGraw-Hill, New York, 1940.

Towle, Charlotte, *Common Human Needs: An Interpretation for Staff in Public Assistance Agencies,* Federal Security Agency, Social Security Administration, Bureau of Public Assistance, Public Assistance Reports, number 8, Washington, D.C., 1945.

Tyre, Nedra, *Red Wine First,* Simon and Schuster, New York, 1947.
Wessel, Rosa, editor, *Method and Skill in Public Assistance,* Journal of Social Work Process, Pennsylvania School of Social Work, volume 2, number 1, Philadelphia, December, 1938.

For additional related readings, consult the bibliography at the end of Chapter 11.

13

Social Group Work

Social group work is concerned with the social development of individuals. Many agencies assume group work responsibility. They differ significantly among themselves, making it hard to represent the whole field by any one example. The following story, "Just What Is A BoyscluB?" describes one organization which falls within the group work classification:

Throughout the year, more than one hundred eighty boys daily are finding fun, companionship, and constructive activities at "their club," the BoyscluB of Muncie. Woodworking, handicrafts, boxing, glee club, art classes, and scores of other interesting programs are conducted by understanding and capable leaders during out-of-school hours for members seven to seventeen years of age.

These members have worked as well as played in their new clubrooms. During the past three years the boys themselves have carpentered, painted, and remodeled to completely transform seventeen rooms into cheerful, well-equipped quarters where youthful interests, busy hands, and eager minds can participate in wholesome play and informal classes. The former hospital building, now the Community Service Center, vibrates with the sound of happy voices from the lower floor rooms and the adjoining playground to which the boys throng. Over nine hundred boys are members, and during the past year they participated 65,221 times in the variety of activities.

"Just what is a BoyscluB?" you ask. The BoyscluB is a place where a boy can go when he wants to do something with his spare time. It is always open to him after school, evenings, Saturdays, and vacation-time. Each boy pays a membership fee of fifty cents, and boys who cannot afford the dues are given the opportunity to earn their membership through work. Members are enrolled by personal interview and the filling out of pertinent information on an application card.

Let's take a few minutes to look into the BoyscluB. School's out, and there's a gang of boys hurrying toward the entrance now.

"Hi, Jimmy," the desk clerk greets the ten-year-old who stops at the registration counter and check room. Jimmy replies as he wriggles out of his coat and hands it to the junior leader in charge. Pocketing his check number, Jimmy makes a beeline to the game-room to see what's doing there.

Scores of boys are busily engaged in playing ping-pong, billiards, checkers, puzzles, construction sets, and other popular table games. Over at one side, a duck-pin bowling game is in progress, and beside the improvised alley, a closely contested game of shuffleboard attracts our attention. Jimmy sees his pal, Charlie, over at the box hockey game and moves over to challenge him. With broom stick handles they try vigorously to outdo each other in pushing the wooden puck through the small openings in the partitioned, boxed-in area, to the other fellow's goal.

After playing awhile, the two boys feel the urge to "let off more steam," so they enter the adjoining exercise gymnasium. Slipping off their shoes, they seem to almost disappear in the mass of arms, legs, and bodies of boys who are rough-and-tumbling on the large wrestling mat. All around, boys are socking the punching bag, jumping the rope, swatting the heavy training bag, and exercising on the stall bars which line the wall. A boxing bout is in progress in the enclosed ring, and other boys are watching while they await their turns to don the gloves. Over in the opposite corner, several boys are stunting on the horizontal bar.

"Time for tumbling period," the instructor calls, and the boys voluntarily clear the mat and wait around the edges for a period of somersaults, body rolls, and pyramid building.

Cooking Class. But Jimmy remembers that today is Tuesday, and it's five o'clock. "Almost late for cooking class!" Off to the kitchen-classroom he goes to help cook soup, spaghetti, meatballs, and cocoa. Cookies are baking in the oven for dessert, and several boys are chopping vegetables for the salad. Jimmy introduces us to the home economics teacher, saying, "This is Miss Nelson. She teaches us all about health and good manners, too. We graduate next week and earn our diplomas as good cooks!" We are told that the boys find it lots of fun learning to cook, set the tables, and, of course, eat their own cooking. Each boy helps to clean up and wash the dishes when it's his turn. Jimmy is one of the twenty boys in the two cooking classes that meet once a week for a ten weeks' course.

A buzzer sounds in the hall, and we go out to see boys preparing to leave. Program Director Woody Greenlee informs us that experience had proved that closing for supper was a necessity. Otherwise, boys would rather remain to play than go home to eat.

Muncie's BoyscluB is rather typical of others in Indiana. Indianapolis, Terre Haute, Columbus, Rushville, Franklin, Bedford, Warsaw, and Edinburg have similar programs and are affiliated with the Boys' Clubs of America, the national organization which serves in an advisory capacity to some 300 BoyscluBs throughout the country.

The Muncie BoyscluB is a Community Fund supported agency governed by an advisory board of eighty men and women who elect a board of directors to guide its operation. The staff is made up of the executive director, and the program director, who are full-time employees. They are assisted by part-time workers, college students, adult volunteers, and members of the Junior Leaders' Corps. A clerical worker and a janitor complete the staff.

The purpose of the BoyscluB is to promote the physical, mental, and moral well-being of boys; and to develop dependable and approved social conduct. We all know that boys seek fun and the companionship of their fellows. The kind of fun and companions—and more especially, the kind of leaders they follow—determines to a large extent their behavior and their attitudes.

A boy may be left to his own devices most of the time, or he may be at loose ends because of some upset. Where could he find better fun, fellowship, and guidance than in the activities of the BoyscluB? What better leaders can he follow than men who devote their lives to the leadership and counsel of boys?

The method by which the BoyscluB achieves its objectives is by furnishing facilities for the operation of all types of constructive programs that attract boys into voluntary membership under supervision of a trained staff. Leaders build upon the basis of the boy's interests and create wants that challenge him to measure up to his own progressive best. This draws boys of all ages and all types at all times.

Returning for the evening program, we find the BoyscluB already a beehive of activity. The normal noise of boys engaged in activity is about us, for real boys do not play quietly.

The handicraft room is open, and we look in to see boys busily sawing and filing plastic rings; cutting and linking leather belts; making knifeholders and pocketbooks from leather; and also knotting and braiding lanyards, key chains, and other projects. For only a few pennies a boy may weave a mat or hot-pad holder. He may prefer to work with metal, glass, or plaster. Making articles from scrap or low-cost materials teaches resourcefulness and useful hand skills. Many boys find that they can easily sell the products of their handicrafts and take orders for their work.

Other boys like Jimmy attend the woodwork shop where they can make toys, furniture, and other wooden articles. The large well-equipped shop has plenty of saws, hammers, and even power tools. There is plenty of lumber from packing boxes and crates. "The instructor, Jerry, is a cabinetmaker, and he's a swell guy, too! He'll help you fix anything, even repair your broken wagon or chair. Then, you give it a coat of paint and it's just like new!"

Older boys have a separate department off to one side of the building. Here the teen-agers have a lounge, game-room, and club meeting room to themselves. Comfortable furniture, a radio, phonograph, and plenty of magazines and reading material make the lounge a popular place. Billiards, ping-pong, dart games, and chess are being played in the game-room. In the club room, a group of Junior Optimists are conducting their regular weekly meeting with the assistance of an adult advisor. This group-club, like several others, elects its own officers, sets its own dues, and chooses its programs and entertainments.

A class in art and drawing under the leadership of a Ball State College student always attracts a roomful of would-be artists who try sketching, water colors, and finger painting. On other evenings, interest groups in model plane building, woodburning, and woodcarving occupy the same classroom.

The Library. The library is the only quiet room in the midst of all the activity. Here boys are gathered around tables, browsing through magazines, and others are seated in comfortable chairs reading of adventure and excitement. Hundreds of books are available for home use, and the librarian will even help boys with their homework if she's not busy. Story telling and papercrafts for the "Midgets" are also conducted in the library.

Educational movies are shown twice weekly in the "Little Theatre," where boys have built their own stage and seats for a hundred and sixty boys. On other evenings, dramatics, stunt nights, and glee club meetings use the auditorium.

Almost too numerous to mention are the many special events such as the Halloween Carnival which was attended by 550 members, the Pet Show, Christmas Festival, Valentine's Day Party, and the Prettiest Sister Contest. Intramural athletic competition in boxing, wrestling, broad jumping, pull-ups, and basketball free throw receive the participation of large numbers of boys. Game-room tourneys in ping-pong, checkers, and other games highlight each week.

Community service projects such as the Christmas toy repairing for the Salvation Army afford the opportunity for boys to be of service to others. Leadership training among older boys is emphasized in the regular on-going program. Junior leaders meet regularly and assist in classes and activities.

Summer Vacation. Summer vacation means Camp Adventure and a real outdoor camping experience to hundreds of boys who might otherwise miss out on a camping opportunity which is so dear to the heart of a boy. Last summer 290 BoyscluB members took part in the camping program. Two-day trips with boys sleeping overnight at camp were especially planned for boys as young as seven years of age and others who had never been away from home. From early morning the campers engage in swimming, boating, fishing, hiking, exploring, nature study, crafts, sports, woodcraft, and "eating." Evenings are capped off with campfire programs that encourage boys to sing, tell stories, and do stunts. Older boys attend regular camping periods. Camping provides experiences that a boy cannot possibly get at home or at school; and each camper takes home with him more than the memory of a pleasant trip.

Camp fees are low—one dollar covering all charges for the two-day trips. Community Fund and Golden Gloves Tourney contributions make up the balance of actual costs. But even lacking the camp fee does not exclude any member; for if his parents cannot pay, and he cannot earn the money, arrangements are made for work at the BoyscluB beforehand to earn a camping trip.

Personal adjustment is an important part of BoyscluB training. This is facilitated by the warm and friendly atmosphere, the group associations, and the understanding guidance of those whom the boys know can be trusted. Leaders attempt to do more than keep boys busy! Getting along with each other, the devolopment of skills and healthy attitudes, and good sportsmanship are emphasized.

Guidance and counseling are a vital part of the BoyscluB's services as it strives to sustain and strengthen parental effort. Work with individual boys is continued through conferences and home visitations. Fathers and mothers are frequent visitors, and last year 586 parents visited the clubrooms. Close cooperation with other social agencies, the schools, juvenile aid department, and the probation officer is maintained. Boys referred for membership by other agencies are contacted and encouraged to participate.

Referral to proper agencies for further assistance is made where family contact is made and the conditions warrant it. Knowledge of the home situation makes it easier to understand the boy and his problems.

The BoyscluB appeals to boys because it has no fixed or settled program. They may come in when they wish, stay as long as they like, and go when they are ready. There are always other boys around to play with and an instructor who can demonstrate the fine points of almost any game. Nothing fancy about it; sensible rules, and lots to do so that any fellow can have fun after school and in the evening.

One wonders where these boys would go and what they would do with their time if we had no BoyscluB or camp for them.[1]

Many of the aspects of group work are expressed in the BoyscluB of Muncie, Indiana. These and others will be elaborated upon in the remainder of this chapter.

INTERRELATIONS

In the first chapter it was stated that social work consists of component parts: casework, group work, and community organization. These three illustrate social work's concern with the individual, with

[1]Raymond E. Bogden, "Just What Is A BoyscluB?", *Public Welfare in Indiana,* volume 57, number 4, series 349, April, 1947, pp. 10-11, 18, 19.

small groups, and with communities. They have each developed specialized techniques to enable them to meet the needs of those they serve. Corporately, they work together for the enrichment of human life.

In preceding chapters considerable emphasis has been given to the specialties of casework. In the next chapter community organization will be treated. In this chapter the subject of group work is the special topic of interest.

Group work appropriately stands between casework and community organization because it deals primarily with small groups of individuals. It is concerned with the individual, but not the individual in his solitariness. It is interested in the community, but not as the focus of initial activity. It is involved with specific groups. These groups lead to the strengthening of individual abilities; they also lead to the strengthening of community movements for the general welfare.

From one point of view, group work is the most general of the social work processes, because it stresses the small group basis of all social work activity. As has been said previously in regard to casework, there is no such thing as an individual problem or a problem of an individual. What so often seems to be a problem of an individual is in actuality a group problem which has cropped up most dramatically in the life of one individual. No one can have a problem in his aloneness, and all problems which individuals present to caseworkers are in reality group problems. This fact explains, in part, the interest which caseworkers constantly maintain in the group configurations of individual problems. The boy who is being treated in a child guidance clinic usually cannot be treated alone; he must be aided along with his parents. The wife who has a quarrel with her husband cannot be helped very much unless the husband is also seen. The mental patient in a hospital cannot be cured in and by himself without regard to the family and community conditions which to some extent induced his problem. So, wherever casework operates at its best, it includes a type of group responsibility.

Likewise, it may be argued, again from a special point of view, that community organization is deeply rooted in group work. While the task of the community organizer is the relating of community resources to community needs, the actual process often does not involve the whole community but the special groups which are more vocal and aggressive than the community as a whole. Thus, although a committee in a neighborhood may represent to a considerable degree the true interests of the neighborhood, they may in reality only represent a very small numerical minority of the total population. But the community organizer does not stop his work because he is unable to make direct contact with whole communities at a time. He operates on a group work basis in so far as he is constantly in touch with relatively small groups who claim to represent the true interests of the community. In his skill in working with people, such an organizer most closely resembles a group worker; he holds committee meetings; he maintains the leadership position and philosophy of group leaders; he possesses in the main those professional traits which characterize the group worker.

And yet, despite this similarity between group work, casework, and community organization, there are specific and important differences between the three. The actual focus of attention differs among them. Casework, for all it may seek to work with the group implications of individual problems, works principally with and through the individual. Community organization, for all that it must operate through smaller groups than whole communities, still is chiefly concerned with effecting community benefits. Group work, for all that it seems to be closely related to both casework and community organization, has its own special activities and focus of interest. These will be made clearer as the chapter proceeds.

THE AIMS OF GROUP WORK

Group work grew up under an educational philosophy quite different from that maintained today. The features which inspired the early settlement house founders and the creators of other group work forms no longer hold the attention of most group workers.

In the beginning and during the development of group work a number of points were aimed at. Some of those purposes will be stated briefly.

Americanization

Without doubt a large part of the early initiative in group work arose from the desire to facilitate the assimilation of large numbers of immigrants and their children into the American scene. Group work, mainly a phenomenon of urban life, sought to aid newcomers to the country so that they could take their "place" along with old-line Americans. The programs of the early settlement houses, programs which provided instruction in all things American—language, political participation, civics, vocational education—indicate that this aim was a significant one. The activities oftentimes were not in line with the interests of the particular nationality and so-called racial practices of the persons who used the settlement houses.

Prevention of Juvenile Delinquency

The prevention of juvenile delinquency was another strong aim supported by group work in its earlier period. In so far as there was an attempt to produce good citizens, this purpose was related to the prior one of Americanization. The thought of many of the earlier leaders in group work was that "taking children off the streets" and supplying them with relatively harmless activities (which might also be pleasurable) was a noble and worthy task. By means of a polite recreational program, children who otherwise would "run the streets" would be saved from wrongdoing. At times this concern for the well-being of children was inspired not so much by a genuine interest in children as by a sense of self-protection. This was also true of the Americanization programs. When children from depressed areas of the cities made forages into sections which were economically better off, they were immediately judged to be in need of "saving." Because such children often expressed in their actions (more than in words) a social philosophy which did not always agree with that of the more propertied groups in the community, they were assumed to need an educational program which would curb their "antisocial" expressions. For some, the Americanization of such children meant their removal as a potential threat to the "better element" in the community. For others, there was a desire to protect children in slum areas from the inevitable consequences of their slum living. It is significant that the leadership of the early settlement house movement was derived from the "better element" in the community, usually from those sons and daughters of wealth who could afford voluntarily to give their time and energy to the betterment of the conditions of the poor.

Religious Philanthropy

A number of organizations were founded in the early days of the group work movement for essentially religious purposes. Many which no longer adhere to religious approaches in group work did in their beginnings stress group work as a means of saving souls, of preserving morality, and of increasing righteousness. The number of religious mission stations in large cities attests even today to the fact that religiously inspired group work has not completely disappeared.

Recreational Interest

While there are a number of aims which the leadership of the early group work movement possessed, it is important to differentiate between the motives of the leadership and those of the people who responded to group work activities. It is clear that many persons responded because they were attracted to the purposes of the leaders. It is equally clear that many were attracted to group work centers simply because of the activities offered. This interest, spontaneously expressed, is not difficult to explain. Play is a fundamental expression of human sociality, and every community needs some ways of satisfying the recreational interests of its members. If these means are not provided, they will be created by persons indigenous to the community. Many of the early group work activities were provided in forms quite different from those which might have been initiated by the people themselves. In fact, even today some group workers are disturbed because not all of the recreational pursuits of young people within slum areas are directed to the accepted activities provided by settlement houses and other group work organizations. For the most part, however, group workers, especially the professionals, know the importance of indigenous groups, understand the reasons for their formation and for their desire not to be identified with agencies, and wish to establish relationships with them. But the many immigrant families who entered our large cities were not always able, especially on a mass basis, to organize their own methods of recreation (or at least not to the satisfaction of interested outsiders), and they easily turned to the forms which were provided for them.

Recent Aims

While some of the old aims still prevail, group work, as it progressed, assumed new aims in line with changes in other fields. The more recent knowledge of group organization and function also affected the purposes of group work. A changed philosophy regarding the rights of the individual in education and in group work bore its fruits. The increased secularization of modern society relieved many of their religious motives for group work. The Americanization program so popular at one time gave way to a different outlook which encouraged pride in national and special cultures. The flow of immigrants lessened. The group work approach to juvenile delinquency was no longer regarded as the only "perfect" preventive instrument.

These changes in the aims of group work brought concomitant changes in practice. Programs of settlement houses changed. Activities were viewed not merely as bait to keep children out of trouble. They had to have meaning, real meaning in themselves. In the place of programs which minimized the importance of national backgrounds, settlement houses sought to explain various cultures to their members. Religious values practically disappeared.

This period saw the introduction of a wide array of activities into group work methodology. Group work became a full-fledged system of organized recreation. How it differed from other forms of recreation and from some forms of education, few workers cared to say. But its acceptance as a legitimate recreational device in itself was not doubted.

Stress on Personality. More recently, the stress which formerly was placed on activities has been somewhat overshadowed by the interest of group workers in personality. Out of the groping of the past five or six decades a more integrated and positive philosophy of group work practice is evolving. It suggests that there is nothing more important to the whole operation of group work than the individuals who comprise its program. No longer are the activities of the group virtually viewed as more important than its members. Accordingly, *what* a group does today is often not considered so important as *how* it does it and what effects this will have on the personalities of the group members.

Psychologists and sociologists in particular have contributed to this most recent conception of group work. The formative influence of the small, informal, face-to-face primary group devoted to play purposes has been an accepted part of sociological and psychological thought for some years. But group workers have put the idea into practice in deliberative and planned ways only within recent years. This concept and its concrete applications suggest the tremendous potentialities that group work has for the formation of character. The concept of the primary group has influenced the activities as well as the philosophy of group workers. In place of the mass activities which characterized former practice (and which are present to some extent even today), there is a trend toward smaller group formations in which a greater degree of individualization is possible.

New Types of Leadership. To a considerable extent the newer outlook on group work also has increased the respect which the group leader has for the individual member and for the group as a whole. Formerly, especially under some of the aims previously outlined, the leader was eager to impose his help upon groups. He believed that he had some "good" which he was charged to deliver (perhaps as painlessly as possible) to groups. Leadership implied that the leader determined the activities, settled disputes, safely guarded each and every child, and sought always to indoctrinate his own values into the others. Group work as a means of individual discipline of children fitted closely into the supposedly effective program for the prevention of delinquency. It was thought that by a child's accepting authority in the group work situation he would better appreciate the need to accept lawful authority elsewhere. There was obviously something of the "military academy philosophy" of personal discipline in earlier group work.

However, increased respect for personality and the rights of individuals has largely changed the picture. The authoritarian form of leadership almost everywhere accepted in this work previously is no longer in favor. Today, the leader respects the personalities of the group members by not seeking to enforce upon them any aims, either tacitly or overtly, except those which are deemed essential for reasons of health, personal safety, or the actual avoidance of serious negative consequences. This means that the professional group leader does not impose his will upon the members. He hopes that whatever leadership aid he can provide will enable them to express their own values and purposes. He believes that his leadership consists of furnishing the knowledge and techniques whereby the group process may be facilitated.

GROUP THERAPY

The recent interest of group workers in the personality of the members has encouraged the rise of group therapy. While such therapy is not usually classified as an intrinsic part of group work, it undoubtedly is closely related to it. Historically, much that has happened in group therapy has been derived from casework. Today, the therapy, with various theoretical approaches, is concerned with assisting through specialized group placement and specialized group activities individuals who reveal abnormal social relations. While group work is closely affiliated with casework, group therapy is perhaps even more so.

Group therapy has mainly been developed as an adjunct service of child guidance clinics or of child welfare agencies which deal with emotionally disturbed children. The experience of the Jewish Board of Guardians in New York City provides an example. In the spring of 1934 a group activities program was developed in connection with the casework services of the Board. Some of the children being treated were found to be unresponsive to individual approaches. Also, there was then current an impression that group activities might benefit certain emotionally disturbed children. After the more usual types of group activities were set up for the children, such as hikes and picnics, trips to interesting places, and arts and crafts, it was realized that the group approach to individual treatment might be utilized more planfully. From the outset the Board recognized that not all individuals requiring treatment would benefit from group therapy, but that some would benefit immensely. It also was seen that group therapy in itself is rarely sufficient, and that the best results in such therapy could be obtained where there was close cooperation with casework.

While there are various forms of group therapy used throughout the country at the present time, the type which Samuel R. Slavson, the director of the group therapy program at the Jewish Board of Guardians, has developed, is called *activity group therapy*. By this, Slavson signifies that the therapeutic benefits sought in group experience are derived from the activity provided for groups and not from the impositions of a group leader. Thus he claims that "members of therapy groups have a catalytic effect upon each other, which facilitates catharsis in language and action. Disturbed and neurotic persons have repressed their spontaneity because of a fear of consequences. They are unable to establish satisfactory relations for the same reason. The uninhibited expression in acts and words by some of the other members in groups reduces the neurotic's fear and he acts out or talks about his problems."[2] In the group experience each individual can express himself without rebuke for any destructive action or thought and with the assurance that he will be praised for his constructive accomplishments. Slavson defines his conception of group therapy in the following manner:

> *Group Therapy,* as we employ the term, is treatment in which no discussion is initiated by the therapist; interpretation is given only in rare instances and under specific conditions. Emotional re-orientation comes from the very fact that the child experiences actual situations, lives and works with other children, comes into direct and meaningful interaction with others, and as a result modifies his feeling tones and habitual responses. We conceive a group as an aggregation of three or more persons in an informal face-to-face relation where there is direct and dynamic interaction among the individuals comprising it, and as a result the personality of each member is fundamentally modified. Applied to Group Therapy, this definition implies small numbers and age and sex homogeneity.[3]

Four Types of Groups

On the basis of the work done by Slavson at the Jewish Board of Guardians, four types of groups have been set up to meet the group therapy needs of clients.

[2]Samuel R. Slavson in *Better Times,* a publication of the Welfare Council of New York City, volume 28, number 36, May 30, 1947, pp. 1–2.

[3]Samuel R. Slavson, *An Introduction to Group Therapy,* Commonwealth Fund, New York, 1943, p. 2.

1. Therapeutic Play Groups. These are organized for preschool children and provide an atmosphere where they can freely play out their tensions or fantasies. Special materials, such as water, water-color and finger paints, plasticine, animal toys, and dolls are given to the children. Interpretations are made of the children's responses to these materials.

2. Activity-Interview Groups. These are organized for children between the ages of six and ten and are intended for fairly severe neurotics. The activities of the children are interpreted in accordance with psychological and psychiatric understandings. In addition to the materials provided for therapeutic play groups, the following are also used: toy guns, copper and wood, ten-pins, and ping-pong. While these groups seem to be similar to therapeutic play groups they employ a higher degree of psychotherapy.

3. Transitional Groups. These are organized for children of school age and are directed toward those children who have progressed in other forms of therapy groups and who are ready for placement in more normal groups in their neighborhoods.

4. Interview Groups. These are organized for adolescent girls and mothers of clients and seek to aid adjustment through conversational methods. No materials or food are provided for these groups. The members are encouraged to talk about their emotional problems and to gain assistance from the group.[4]

The effect of group therapy of the Slavson variety is shown in the following case summary of "Paula":

Paula was a shy, withdrawn girl of twelve. Her mother died when Paula was young; her father was going blind. There were four other girls in the family, two of whom were married. None displayed any interest in our client. After her mother died, Paula was sent to live with Mrs. Wentz. She did all the housework before school and helped in Mr. Wentz's cigar store after school hours. When referred to the agency Paula was living at home again, but continued to be neglected and used as a drudge by her sisters. She did most of the heavy cleaning in her own home and continued to do the housework for Mrs. Wentz. She received no spending money from her sisters and only a very small sum from her employer. Paula had no friends and no contact with girls or boys of her own age.

At the first meetings Paula was on the defensive. When playing word games, for example, she would show off. When the other girls could not give the correct answer, she at once volunteered "I know," with an air

[4]A summary article by Samuel R. Slavson can be found in *Better Times*, a publication of the Welfare Council of New York City, volume 28, number 36, May 30, 1947, pp. 1–2.

of superiority and implied ridicule of the others in the group. She never looked the other girls in the face and appeared very sly. When the girls washed the dishes at the close of the meetings, Paula did not help.

Paula seemed very resentful of the other girls' possessions. One of the members wore a wrist watch. Paula wanted to know what she was doing in the "club." She thought it was only for poor girls! Because of her work at Mrs. Wentz's, Paula could not come regularly to the meetings. She usually came late and told the worker that she "got the devil for not coming home right after school."

After seven weeks the report on Paula reads, in part, as follows:

Paula seems to have lost her resentfulness and has made two friends. She insists on helping them and is always the first to offer to put away the materials. The girls are very helpful toward her, too. They seem to realize that she has a hard time of it, but do not show it in any way except by being friendly toward her. She enjoys working on materials, and says she hates "to lose one minute." At first she would not try anything unless she was sure she could do it as well as the others. Last meeting she started to paint, telling the worker that she was "very poor at it."

Her whole attitude seems to have changed. She is now always pleasant to everyone at the meetings and, though she herself is dressed very shabbily, admires the clothes the other girls wear and takes suggestions from them.

We may add that Paula is now, at nineteen, earning her own living, is a member of a settlement house club, has a boy friend, and is a happy, though a very limited, person.[5]

American Group Therapy Association

In 1943, group therapists organized the American Group Therapy Association with headquarters in New York City. Those who hold membership include psychiatrists, psychologists, psychiatric social workers, and group therapists. At present there are about 150 members. The Association fulfills the following functions: it coordinates efforts in the field, publishes researches in group therapy, provides consultation service, and formulates standards and policies of practice, in addition to other activities.

THE NATURE OF GROUP WORK

The previous description of the development of group work as philosophy and as practice does not entirely explain the nature of present-day group work. A more comprehensive statement is needed.

Not all workers in the field and the classroom would agree on any

[5]Samuel R. Slavson, *An Introduction To Group Therapy*, Commonwealth Fund, New York, 1943, pp. 23-24.

one definition of the nature of group work. Some speak of it as a "field," some as a "process," some as a "specialty" of social work, and others use different terms. In part the problem is one of verbalization. But there has grown up in recent years, aside from the words employed, a general agreement as to what group work shall mean. It is possible to state here the components of group work on which there would be wide agreement and to develop these components descriptively in the succeeding parts of this chapter. Group work, then, may be defined as comprising the following: (1) an educational process; (2) carried on in leisure time with voluntary groups; (3) with the aid of a group leader; (4) under the auspices of an agency; (5) for the satisfaction of the social needs of individuals; and (6) for the development of legitimate group goals. Each of these aspects will be discussed in detail.

An Educational Process

The group work process differs from the casework process in that the first is educational while the second is therapeutic. This distinction does not hold absolutely, however, especially where casework clients are counseled rather than treated (this distinction is sometimes made), or where the group work process borders upon group therapy. But, in general, it may be affirmed that the caseworker is constantly dealing with personal problems in a way in which the group worker is not. The group worker assumes a degree of normality on the part of group members and proceeds from there to benefit the members. The caseworker assumes, on the other hand, that the client is to some extent not capable of making his own way in the community without some type of additional "outside" support. In this sense, then, the casework process is therapeutic while the group work process is primarily educational.

The fact that casework is essentially therapeutic and group work educational oftentimes makes cooperative relations between casework agencies and group work agencies highly desirable. An illustration of such cooperation is given in the case of "Jane":

> Jane tried to come to the "Y" alone one Saturday morning in October, 1935, but she was so scared that she was afraid to get off the street car and rode to the other end of the line without asking the motorman where to get off. The caseworker knew that this had happened, and offered to bring the girl the first time or to make arrangements for her friend to come also, so that she would have the companionship of a person she knew. In talking with Jane, the caseworker reassured her and gave her confidence to come to the "Y" alone. If she had not done this, the girl would never have had enough courage to meet this new

situation. The first few weeks Jane talked about nothing in the club and expressed no definite opinions on any subject.

It was not until the first week in December when the girls were sitting around informally making Christmas cards that she expressed herself definitely. The girls were talking about teachers and she said, "Some teachers can be terribly mean, can't they?" The next week Jane and another girl worked together to make a tray on which they could serve the Christmas cookies for the club party. Gradually, in this way, she began to take an interest in the club, its activities, and to have a definite feeling about the girls in the group. In January, when the leader asked the girls if they would like to have officers, Jane was one of the first to speak up and say that she did want officers. When there was a new girl who came in to be shown around the building, the leader asked Jane and her friend if they would not like to show this girl around. This gave them a feeling of importance and they were confident that they knew the "Y" and had a contribution to make.

In February, when the officers were elected, Jane was elected secretary and in this way she felt important and a vital part of the group. During the spring she began to show more initiative, enjoyed the company of the other girls, was very regular in her attendance, kept her minutes fairly well and entered into all the club activities enthusiastically. She benefited by the free atmosphere created by the club and felt at ease. She might never have liked the "Y" at all if the caseworker had not reassured her and the group worker had not made her feel wanted and important, giving her responsibilties which she could assume. The caseworker in this instance showed interest in all of her activities at the "Y" and cooperation took place on a very natural basis.

The next year Jane was elected president of her club and this meant that she was even more important to the group than she had been before and with this backing from the group she became more interesting as a person, more attractive and less self-conscious. She began to talk about boys in the group and the caseworker felt that the group contributed in her heterosexual adjustment. When she first came to the "Y," the caseworker described her as an unattractive, dull child from a simple, country, foster home background. Two years later she had made new friendships, had gained self-confidence, and was a girl who had a positive personality. During the two years that she was at the "Y" the caseworker and group worker evaluated her adjustment four or five times, and it was felt by both that the group had been a definite factor in her becoming a well-adjusted individual.[6]

Group workers and caseworkers are increasingly developing mutually helpful relationships so that the benefits of the two types of agency

[6] Adelaide Dorn, "An Experiment in Case Work-Group Work Correlation," *Cooperative Case Work,* Family Welfare Association of America (now Family Service Association of America), New York, 1935-1939, p. 64.

work can be brought to persons in need. The fact that group therapy is practiced in conjunction with the casework activities of child guid-- ance clinics and other casework agencies indicates a rising respect for the benefits of group work on the part of caseworkers. Similarly, group work agencies are today more aware than ever of the need for close contact with caseworkers. A sign of this cooperative feeling on the part of group workers is expressed in the arrangement in Cleveland whereby a caseworker from the Associated Charities undertakes casework responsibilities in a group work agency—Goodrich House:

> Goodrich House asked that a member of the Associated Charities staff come in the afternoon and evening—in the afternoon to observe the children especially—so the young people would have the benefit of contact with her and it would be a more or less natural referral. They had had difficulties with referrals from other agencies—children referred failed to get there or came wandering in alone, perhaps coming once and never returning. A caseworker who knew the program thoroughly could take the time for a conference with the child and help him get into a group suited to his need.
>
> The caseworker visited almost all the classes and clubs. She stayed on in the evening to meet with the agency people. Six girls from 14 to 20 years had interviews with her. In one case the family was taken for service by the Associated Charities. The caseworker had conferences with staff and volunteer group leaders who were having difficulties understanding members of their groups.[7]

Some of the larger group work agencies are now employing caseworkers on their staffs, on either a full-time or part-time basis. The functions of the caseworkers include: facilitating and intensifying referrals to casework agencies and from casework agencies, following up such referrals, working with group work leaders in understanding the individuals in their groups, improving the intake procedure in the agency, and doing casework on a short-time basis with certain individuals and families as circumstances require.

Media Utilized. Group work as an educational process utilizes many educational media for its expression. There is a wide array of activities which the worker can offer as meeting the requirements of the group work process. The working out of a play, for example, may be a suitable activity. The children in a settlement or other agency may gather on afternoons to write the script, to construct and paint the needed scenery, and to act out the parts. Or some teen-age girls may get to-

[7] Gertrude Wilson, *Group Work and Case Work: Their Relationship and Practice,* Family Welfare Association of America (now Family Service Association of America), New York, 1941, pp. 90–91.

gether once a week as a club to enjoy their own association, to plan projects (like a hike, a dance in a community center, a shuffleboard tournament), and to carry them out. Or a mixed teen-age group could meet in a public or private school after the formal classes are finished to work on hobbies. There might be one hobby for the whole group or many among the various members. A group may also consist of a cabin crew of boys in a summer camp where there is the possibility of cooking meals out-of-doors, of cooperatively keeping the cabin clean, of

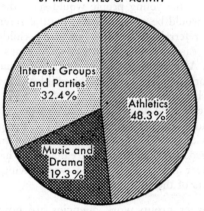

COMMUNITY RECREATION
EXPENDITURES IN 1940
BY MAJOR TYPES OF ACTIVITY

FIG. 39. Percent of Expenditures for Community Recreation in 1940, by Major Types of Activity

(Bradley Buell, "Let's Look at the Record," *Survey Midmonthly,* Vol. 82, No. 2, February, 1946.)

undertaking kitchen tasks together, and of engaging in other summer camp activities. Or there may be a cottage group in an institution where the boys have been assembled for special leisure-time activity; they may be engaged, for example, in a handicraft session or preparing gifts for the coming Christmas season. All such situations could fall within the boundaries of group work.

These examples of the group work process have been mentioned (there are many others) because they illustrate the educational character of group work. They all imply in one way or another the presence of an educational interest. Without being as highly organized and formalized as it may be in some compulsory schools, the educational element in group work is nevertheless rooted very firmly in the fundamental motives of the group members.

Concern for Activity and Personality. In group work, in its aspect of being an educational process, there is a concern on the part of the worker both for the activities offered and for the personality products which result. There was a time when it was possible to debate whether group work was more concerned with the activities in themselves or in the psychological benefits derived from engaging in any activity of an educational nature. This, as has been widely seen, is an artificial problem. The group worker is interested in the specific activities a group may undertake because the activities will structure the kind and amount of psychological benefit the members will receive from the experience. But he also realizes that no group program, regardless of how important it may seem in itself, is a substitute for the more personal values being sought through the use of group activities. The program, both for its intrinsic values and its products in terms of individual achievement, is important to the group worker.

Educational Differences. The question may arise as to how group work in its educational aspects differs from formal education. Formal education stresses the educational values which may be derived from group activity, but it sometimes imposes this stress to the detriment of the pleasure to be gained concomitantly from the activity itself. Also, the possibility of the freest sort of group activity is restricted in formal education. Here the group, so it would seem, is composed more of individuals who relate to a leader than of members who are vital parts of a group process. There are other differences which will be discussed later under other aspects of group work.

Progressive education, on the other hand, seems to approximate group work rather closely. In it there is notable emphasis upon the need for spontaneous and vital group participation. The leader bears a somewhat different relation to the group than does the leader in formal education. The basis of group activity in projects also reminds one of group work. In fact, in recent years, group workers and progressive education leaders have recognized that their interests are exceedingly close. It is common for them to attend each other's meetings and to hold joint conferences about their work.

Values Derived. So it can be said that group work is an educational process. As an educational process it implies the use of activities which will make personal achievement possible. In order to fulfill the educational goals implicit in group work there must be derived from the activities important values for the individual and for the group. This means concretely that almost any group activity can be a group work activity and the list of the activities which would qualify is too long to be mentioned here. But it also means that no activity is undertaken in group work simply because of the sheer attraction of the activity (although there may be significant attraction). The activity must educationally serve personal and group ends.

The following illustration suggests the ways in which group work qualifies as an educational process. It makes clear some of the points regarding group work which have been mentioned and shows certain other aspects of it. It is significant because it shows how a group work program can be initiated (really a phase of community organization):

When the high-school students in Owosso began to agitate for the establishment of a youth center, it was not a new or unique movement. Students of the same age with the same desire for an outlet had been doing the same thing all over the country. They had been asking questions and making an organized effort within various communities to determine the procedure they should follow. They were asking: "If adults want to cut delinquency down, why don't they help by working with us in an effort to provide some place where we can go to have fun?" "If no one will help us to find good clean entertainment, can they wonder that we go where we can to have whatever fun is available?" They were asking something which many towns had not previously given young people—complete cooperation and a recognition of the fact that they had a responsibility to the youth of the community.

By April of 1945 there was a great deal of precedent for this type of action. In the state of Michigan alone a great deal of progress had been made with youth activities. Governor Kelly had set up a youth administration, and, under the guidance of the Department of Public Welfare, dozens of youth canteens had been set up and were running smoothly in towns and cities throughout the state.

In Owosso the recreation commission accepted the responsibility of guiding the young people of the city in the organization of a recreation center. When the committee of high-school students presented their plan to the commission, they were well enough impressed to appoint one member of their body to act as direct supervisor of the enterprise—to direct the young people, and to go with them to the mayor with their program.

The mayor was impressed with the importance of the demand the students were making as well as by the seriousness displayed by them. He made it possible for the students to use Curwood's Castle, the most logical place in town for the location of a center. It is an ideal building for it has a large room and several small ones.

Curwood's Castle is one of the historical landmarks of Owosso—the studio of James Oliver Curwood. It had been given to the city some years before by Mrs. Curwood, and had, until last summer, been a complete liability to the city, since it served no more purpose than to satisfy an occasional visitor who wanted to see the place where Curwood had worked. Despite this, some of the townspeople objected to making the Castle available to the young people, but this disapproval greatly diminished when they saw the program in action.

The high-school students with their own chairman drew up a constitution and set of bylaws under the direction of the recreation commission and the high-school principal. Several committees were chosen to work on the finance, decoration, and membership.

The group's plans were beginning to take shape when the school year ended. This set back the plans for the center a great deal and though most of the students recognized that there was a great need for a recreation center during the summer when many of them were on jobs, they had lost interest in the project. The chairman of the high-school group was unconcerned. She and the adult adviser put the blame for the lethargy on the other students.

It was after two weeks of trying to work with these two nominal heads of the project, when I received a telephone call from one of the students. His name was familiar although he was a newcomer to Owosso. It was he who had written an attack in the public forum column of the local newspaper against the townspeople for neglecting the recreational needs of the young people in the community.

During our telephone conversation he told me that a group of students, some of whom had formerly been on the committees for the Castle, were determined to get things going again. He asked me if I would come to the meeting of the group and act as temporary chairman.

· We met at the high school and, to my great surprise, there were twenty enthusiastic young people present. They were, for the most part, not the "prominent" students. I had never seen many of them at the regular Castle committee meetings. They were a group of "ordinary" high-school students who knew very definitely what they wanted and were determined to get it.

This first meeting proved to be pretty much of a grievance rally. They wanted me to know the real reasons why nothing had been accomplished in the last two months, and why some of them had neglected even to help with the plan up until now.

"Why should we help with all the dirty work when we knew that it was going to be run only for the '400'?"

"Yeah, it'd be nothing more than a country club for the same bunch of kids who were appointed to start it. They could decide who'd get in and who wouldn't. Why should we help them and then not even get to belong?"

I could see that essentially what this group was revolting against was the undemocratic way in which the whole program had been conducted. They disliked the fact that the daughter of the chairman of the school board had been appointed to lead the movement. They objected to the fact that this girl and her friends would be the charter members of the organization and would thereby have the privilege of passing on all new members. Certainly, their grievances were valid, and they had all of the spirit and ideals necessary to make a success of the Castle. The one thing they needed and wanted was someone to help them get things going. They asked me to be their chairman, and I accepted.

This was the first of a series of meetings during the next five weeks. During this time both the former high-school chairman and the adult adviser resigned their positions and the recreation commission handed over full responsibility to our group which had now grown considerably.

The constitution was revised in such a way that anyone could become a member of the Center merely by paying his dues. We also made provision for students who could not afford the dollar a year dues to earn their membership by working a few nights at the Castle. We arranged for the election of officers by all the members in the fall after the initial membership drive was completed.

We elected new committees to take care of finances, cleaning and decorating, music, and the opening rally. We felt that if we could first collect enough money to cover the expenses of redecoration, we would be in a much more secure position. This was accomplished by soliciting donations of money and merchandise from nearly all of the manufacturing concerns and prominent individuals in town. One of the girls wrote an article for the open-forum column in the local paper telling what we were going to do, when the work would start, and what kinds of help we wanted. Eighteen more students joined us the very first day. They contributed in every way from washing windows to hauling ping-pong and card tables from all parts of town. We spent days washing windows, scrubbing and painting walls, mowing the lawn, washing rugs, sand papering and varnishing floors. We were all very happy to see the building gradually evolve into the ideal bright spot for the kind of recreation everyone wanted. We brought our box lunches down each day and took turns going to the corner grocery store for milk. We worked hard, but we sang and talked and had more fun than most of us had thought possible. It was a true group spirit. We enjoyed the work because we were doing it together. No one had to nag or complain. We understood perfectly why we were there and what we had to do, and we liked it.

Two days before the opening, three of us had stayed late in the afternoon to finish up some work. We were out on the front lawn of the Castle painting chairs when a boy rode up on a bicycle and stood for several minutes, rather aloof, watching us paint. Finally he walked up the lawn and started talking with us. At first he was extremely antagonistic. He was curious to know just what was being done with the Center: who was going to run it, who could belong, and how we were organizing it, in general. When we told him what our plans were, he seemed quite amazed.

"You mean it's not going to be just a gay spot for the same old clique?"

"No, it's open to everyone and we hope that everyone will come and really take part in the activities. There's everything here for a good time. We just hope that people will cooperate by coming, having a good time, and making the Castle a success."

By this time his attitude had changed from the original antagonism to genuine interest. He asked if he could go in and look the place over. When he came out he told us that he wouldn't be able to join because he was going away in the fall to boarding school (which he told me later was a detention school), but would like very much to help us if he could. The next two days he proved to be one of our most valuable helpers— painting signs, contributing some clever advertising schemes, getting a coke machine, and generally making himself handy. This was the kind of boy who could gain so much from a healthy group activity. It was boys like this one whom we wanted to teach—just the kind who would have been excluded from the Center under the original membership plan. We reached Gary. He was given his membership for the help he gave, and comes to the Castle when home for "vacations." This one instance was enough to prove to us that what we were doing was worth any amount of effort we would expend.

But there were so many other things which made us feel the worth-while effect of our effort. After we had completed our advertising campaign, which consisted of signs, newspaper articles, announcements at the theaters, and hand-bills, only one thing remained for us to do. It was the thing for which we had been working for six weeks—*the opening*.

The day of the opening we all met and made our plans for the evening. We assigned jobs, such as tending the coke bar, taking tickets, playing records during the orchestra's intermission, and showing people through the building. The high-school students who were donating their services to play the music came to set up their instruments, and the agent came with our five cases of soft drinks.

When we ordered the five cases of drinks, we felt awfully optimistic. But ever practical, we knew that we could always use the left-over cases another night. We all nearly collapsed that evening when, about nine-thirty, the boy who was tending the coke-bar came down to the door to tell us that someone would have to go out for some more drinks. We were even more surprised when we counted the money that night (admission was charged until the membership drive could start with the opening of school in the fall) and found that we had over sixty dollars —close to 400 fifteen-cent admissions. Owosso did come through for us. The Castle received a tremendous send-off.

The second night, and the last night of my vacation, we had in the treasury a clear profit of $118.60 which we turned over to the city recreation commission to put it in a special account for maintenance of the building and the development of a broader program of activities at the Center.

Meanwhile, what had happened to our town's skeptics? From all of the letters we received and the others that appeared in the newspaper, it seemed evident that at least a great many of them had turned about face and were willing to admit the success of a project they had not believed could succeed. We now had the support of many who had been dubious. What does this project mean to a town like Owosso? It certainly means that a problem has been met, that young people have a place to go to find the right kind of fun. But more than this, it is an indication of progress. The whole movement is proof of the fact that a city can solve its problems through working together. The fact that the Castle has received much more support since its opening proves that people can be shown the value of a project of this type.

And the work of the small group of rebellious high-school students shows the cooperative group spirit under directive, but democratic, group leadership can overcome innumerable obstacles. The achievements of this group prove that real democracy can make people want to work, want to add their efforts toward the realization of a common goal. If youngsters can manifest such willingness to accept responsibility and to cooperate, surely adults can do likewise. In the dynamic interrelations of such a group an example can be found that might well be adapted to other efforts in the community. If this adaption does take place, our work will have had ramifications extending far beyond the field of recreation. It will have been a real experiment in democratic action.[8]

Carried on in Leisure Time With Voluntary Groups

The discussion of the relationships of group work with formal education and progressive education takes on a new light when it is stated that group work is carried on in leisure time with voluntary groups. On this score formal education hardly fits into the same mold as group work, for it is based on compulsory attendance. Progressive education fares somewhat better. It is evident that the latter does not in spirit rest as much upon compulsory techniques as does formal education. But even for those public and private schools which operate on a "progressive" basis, there is almost everywhere the accepted requirement that the children be in regular attendance. On the other hand one might ponder whether the requirement that group work be carried on in leisure time with voluntary groups might restrict it from exercising a wider influence in such places as formalized school programs. Perhaps it should be said that the group work process *in the main* is carried on in leisure time by voluntary groups. This does not mean, however, that, conversely, everything which is conducted in leisure time with voluntary groups partakes of the nature of group work.

Differences Between Group Work and Recreation. In this connection how does group work differ from *recreation,* as usually defined? For

[8]Elizabeth Malcolm, "Youth Builds a 'Castle,'" *The Group,* volume 8, number 3, March, 1946, pp. 12–15.

COMMUNITY RECREATION, PER CAPITA EXPENDITURES IN 1925 AND 1944

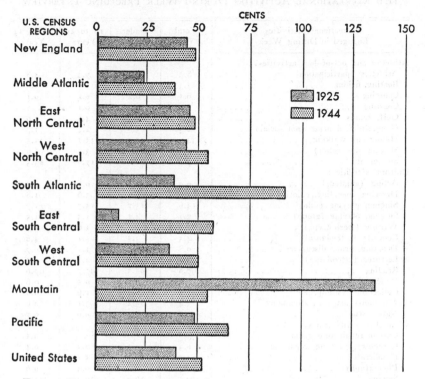

FIG. 40. Per Capita Expenditures for Community Recreation, by Region, in 1925 and 1944

(Bradley Buell, "Let's Look at the Record," *Survey Midmonthly,* Vol. 82, No. 2, February, 1946.)

one thing recreation does not necessarily signify group participation. A child working on a stamp collection may be said to be engaging in recreational activity. But even where groups are involved, there is a difference between recreation and group work. The former centers in large part simply in the enjoyment of activity (see Tables 17 and 18*), whereas the latter, as indicated previously, makes more of the educational benefits to be derived. Another way of distinguishing between group work and recreation is to consider recreation primarily as a field of activity (like child welfare) and group work as a process that may be used within it to bring about various individual and group goals.

*Tables 17 and 18 are taken from: Nettie P. McGill and Ellen N. Matthews, *The Youth of New York City,* copyright, 1940, by The Macmillan Company, New York, and used with their permission, pp. 228 and 229.

Table 17

PERCENTAGE OF FEMALES OF SPECIFIED AGE GROUP WHO ENGAGED IN SPECIFIED RECREATIONAL ACTIVITIES DURING WEEK PRECEDING INTERVIEW

Recreational Activities Engaged in During Week	Total (*)	Under 18 Years	18 to 20 Years	21 to 24 Years
Athletics and out-of-door activities:				
Athletics (participation)	8.3	17.5	7.4	3.8
Boating, fishing	1.3	1.0	1.9	1.0
Camping	0.1	0.2	0.1	0.1
Coasting	0.2	0.5	0.1	...
Golf, tennis	4.3	4.5	4.8	3.9
Gymnasium, dancing (not social)	2.4	3.6	2.4	1.7
Hiking and walking	34.0	35.4	33.7	33.5
Skating (ice, roller)	4.5	10.5	3.5	2.0
Swimming	17.0	22.0	17.9	13.5
Cultural activities:				
Acting (amateur)	0.9	2.1	0.6	0.4
Drawing, modeling, painting	3.6	6.9	3.6	1.8
Singing, playing (solo)	14.0	15.7	15.7	11.7
Singing, playing (group)	2.1	4.1	1.5	1.5
Writing (stories, etc.)	1.7	2.2	1.6	1.4
Concerts (attendance)	4.5	3.5	5.1	4.6
Debating, group discussion	0.8	0.8	1.1	0.7
Lectures (attendance)	2.2	2.2	2.1	2.3
Reading	97.8	98.3	97.7	97.6
Civic, political, philanthropic	0.4	0.1	0.5	0.6
Collections (stamp, etc.)	1.4	2.4	1.6	0.8
Museums (art, etc., attendance)	3.4	5.2	3.1	2.6
Nature study	0.8	1.4	0.6	0.7
Manual arts and crafts:				
Care or repair auto, radio	(†)	...	...	0.1
Carpentry, painting, repairing	0.3	0.3	0.3	0.4
Handicraft	14.7	13.0	15.1	15.2
Photography	0.4	0.5	0.3	0.6
Sewing	39.5	36.9	39.3	41.2
Social recreations and pastimes:				
Automobile riding	13.6	11.7	13.4	14.9
Card games	17.9	13.5	17.1	21.0
Church social activities	3.4	4.5	3.0	3.1
Clubs (not political or civic)	6.4	8.7	7.4	4.4
Dancing (social)	19.3	21.5	22.3	15.6
Movies (including theater)	78.1	79.0	80.2	76.1
Parties, socials	15.2	17.1	15.5	14.0
Picnics, outings	1.2	1.8	1.0	1.0
Pool	0.3	0.2	0.3	0.3
Puzzles, table games	7.5	7.5	8.3	6.8
Radio (listening)	83.5	84.5	84.8	81.8
Shopping	37.2	29.2	36.2	42.6
Trips	4.0	3.1	3.8	4.7
Visiting, entertaining	79.1	78.4	79.2	79.4
Miscellaneous:				
Letter writing	19.1	16.6	19.9	19.7
Pets (care of)	9.7	11.8	9.8	8.5
"Walking or hanging around"	6.4	8.3	6.8	5.0
"Nothing special"	38.4	40.1	39.5	36.5
Other	4.9	4.7	4.6	5.4

*Based on reports for 4,639 females.   †Less than one-tenth of 1 percent.

Table 18

Recreational Activities Engaged in During Week	Total (*)	Under 18 Years	18 to 20 Years	21 to 24 Years
Athletics and out-of-door activities:				
Athletics (participation)	46.8	66.6	48.3	32.9
Boating, fishing	4.5	5.2	4.5	4.0
Camping	0.2	0.1	0.3	0.1
Coasting	0.3	0.6	0.3	0.2
Golf, tennis	3.4	3.1	2.9	4.0
Gymnasium, dancing (not social)	3.5	5.2	3.5	2.2
Hiking and walking	32.3	31.1	34.6	31.1
Skating (ice, roller)	4.6	9.5	4.2	1.8
Swimming	24.8	27.8	26.3	21.5
Cultural activities:				
Acting (amateur)	1.0	1.5	0.8	0.9
Drawing, modeling, painting	5.4	7.6	5.1	4.2
Singing, playing (solo)	9.8	10.2	10.4	8.9
Singing, playing (group)	2.5	3.7	2.4	1.9
Writing (stories, etc.)	1.7	1.7	2.0	1.5
Concerts (attendance)	3.7	3.7	4.5	3.0
Debating, group discussion	1.4	1.4	1.3	1.5
Lectures (attendance)	3.0	3.7	3.3	2.3
Reading	98.1	98.2	97.7	98.3
Civic, political, philanthrophic	1.8	0.8	1.3	2.7
Collections (stamp, etc.)	3.2	5.4	3.2	1.7
Museums (art, etc., attendance)	3.7	4.1	4.1	3.2
Nature study	0.7	0.9	0.6	0.6
Manual arts and crafts:				
Care or repair auto, radio	9.6	6.5	9.7	11.6
Carpentry, painting, repairing	12.7	12.7	13.3	12.1
Handicraft	0.1	0.2	0.2	0.1
Photography	1.6	2.4	1.5	1.2
Sewing	0.4	0.3	0.3	0.5
Social recreations and pastimes:				
Automobile riding	15.9	10.1	17.5	18.2
Card games	25.2	19.9	25.9	27.7
Church social activities	3.3	4.3	3.5	2.5
Clubs (not political or civic)	10.4	10.0	12.2	9.2
Dancing (social)	14.8	9.9	16.4	16.5
Movies (including theater)	80.2	81.0	80.5	79.3
Parties, socials	14.7	11.1	17.4	14.7
Picnics, outings	1.1	1.3	1.2	0.8
Pool	6.2	5.0	7.2	6.2
Puzzles, table games	8.0	9.6	8.3	6.7
Radio (listening)	85.7	85.8	85.3	85.8
Shopping	7.6	5.5	7.6	9.1
Trips	4.5	3.7	4.4	5.1
Visiting, entertaining	67.9	63.1	66.8	71.7
Miscellaneous:				
Letter writing	10.1	8.0	9.9	11.6
Pets (care of)	9.5	12.9	9.5	7.2
"Walking or hanging around"	21.1	24.0	24.1	16.8
"Nothing special"	44.7	44.7	43.8	45.3
Other	7.1	8.0	7.1	6.5

*Based on reports for 4,246 males.

Group work agencies, however, cannot be clearly differentiated in practice from recreational organizations. A neighborhood house may offer a program which consists both of recreation and group work. Obviously, the members of the agency's program are not called upon to make a theoretical decision as to whether they would like to participate in a recreational or in a group work program. Commonly, the members will want both, perhaps one at one time and the other at another, although probably very few will be consciously differentiating between the two.

The fact that group work is identified to an important degree with leisure time indicates its possibilities for the group-minded age in which we live and probably for the period just ahead. It is generally assumed that the leisure time of people will increase, as it has increased in the past, through technological and social advances. This extension of leisure time presents a problem to group workers, for the responsibility in part rests upon them for the development of our leisure-time resources. The growth of group work practice in recent years is testimony to the fact that group workers have not reneged entirely on this responsibility. But much remains to be done.

Group work in the past has been very largely identified with the child welfare movement. This association arose from its practice in settlement houses, Young Men's and Young Women's Christian Associations, the Boy Scouts and Girl Scouts, Camp Fire Girls, the 4-H movement, and many other youth-serving organizations.

Adult Education. Group work in the future, however, should also take a more active obligation toward those of other ages in the general population. The adult education movement, aside from any particular organization in that field, has just begun. As for adult group work, at present it is more of a promise than a reality. There is room for almost unlimited expansion here.

Adult education has been growing much closer in recent days than ever before toward social work in general. The beneficial value of educational activities for those who can no longer engage in full-time education are increasingly recognized. Social work agencies, particularly group work agencies, have realized that they have a distinctive and important role to play in aiding adult education. They also understand the relation between adult education and the prevention of some of the problems with which they are faced in one form or another. Moreover, the adult population has been "discovered" in the recent years by social workers, even as it has by other professionals and organizations. The schools of social work are curricularly responsive to the educational needs of adults. The New Orleans Council of Social Agencies, an example of a coordinating agency in a city, has recently added a Section of Adult Education. The trend for group work agencies is indicated by the Group Work Council of the Cleveland Welfare Federation in its creation of an Adult Education Section to develop the possibilities of adult education within the group work agencies of Cleveland.

Activities for the Aged. Among adults who could benefit from group work, the aged are of special significance. Like children, many of the aged are free of economic responsibility and thus have time on their hands which can be spent in group work activities. The prospect of developing activities for them has been realized recently in a number of communities.

In New York City, under the auspices of the Department of Welfare, the Hodson Community Center provides an example of group work with the aged. The originator of the Center describes its philosophy and activities in the following manner:

> The Hodson Community Center was started in the summer of 1943. It was started as a step in planning towards an adjustment of the older person in his natural environment. We wanted to lessen the period of dependency, to make possible the continued usefulness, dignity, and self-respect of the unwanted, complaining, ill-at-ease, and continuously larger group of older persons in the community. The Center was introduced as a social club where the older person could come and talk, play cards, read newspapers, or listen to the radio, have tea, coffee, and cake every day. It has become what we did not presume to expect in so short a time.
>
> The forms of expression at the Hodson Center are as varied as the pattern of living, but most important is the freeing of personality so that it can express itself in its own way. What we have been achieving is a healthy striving towards fulfillment.
>
> Our members write and mimeograph a magazine regularly, conduct weekly poetry reading sessions, participate in an English and citizenship course, refurbish toys for hospitals and nurseries, build household furniture, participate in discussions of current problems and on the psychological and physical difficulties of older persons, paint and draw, knit, sew, make artificial flowers, and do leather work.
>
> We work with people who have a lessening of physical energy, a separation, physical or emotional, from family and friends, and a loss of occupation. We have used our skills to develop areas of competency which do not cease to exist after sixty-five. We have substituted activity for fears and obsessions about aches and pains. Members who used to make a frustrating project out of a clinic visit now tell us that they have no time to worry about themselves. Members who complained that their arthritic condition was so bad they could not write their names, are now

participating in arts and crafts. The newer thinking in psychosomatic medicine supports our program. It is being increasingly recognized that physical ailments cannot be separated from their psychological components. We have substituted interest and friendship for crotchety complaints, quarrels with landlords, and recurring dissatisfaction with hospitals and public assistance services. Our trained group leader is ready to give individual counseling. As the person becomes more assured and more involved in activities, however, his problems tend to decrease and his capacity to cope with them improves.

For the younger person, recreation is the healthy expenditure of excess energy, a factor which has no place in planning for the older person. For him it is rather based on conservation of energy. The significance is psychological rather than physical.[9]

The growing proportions of the aged in our population probably will lead to an increase in the amount of attention given to them in the future.

Basis of Organization. The fact that group work is organized on a voluntary basis affords a dynamic which is often lacking elsewhere. The basic assumption behind all group work is that the members have expressed a desire to be a group. This does not mean that all members of such groups belong because they have identity of motive. The reasons why individuals will wish to associate are as manifold and variegated as human nature itself. But, because of (or despite) the special factors involved, the actual creation of a group depends upon the willingness of the members to conjoin their interests at some point of focus. Once a group has been formed on a voluntary basis, however, it possesses a dynamic of its own. This dynamic is an indispensable asset to the leader, who uses it as a basis for directing the group activities. In those cases where the basis of organization seems too narrow or trivial to the worker, he may build upon and enrich it by introducing new materials and fresh ideas.

With the Aid of a Group Leader

There are many reasons which could disqualify a group from being considered as falling in the category of group work. For example, the nature of the leadership is important. In group work the leader comes from the "outside."

Assumption of Authority. Most groups, of course, have indigenous leaders. A group on the street may appear to the casual observer to

[9] Harry Levine, "Recreation Revitalizes Older People," *The Welfare Reporter,* published by the New Jersey Department of Institutions and Agencies, volume 1, number 9, January, 1947, p. 12.

be without a leader. Boys may choose "sides" for a baseball game by tossing bottle caps on the pavement to see which lands nearest a line. The two nearest the line will be temporary captains of the two teams needed, the one landing nearest actually having first choice in selecting teammates. Or a bat may be flung from one member to another and through a process of grip elimination the choosing of teams may be started. Such processes do not always imply that any individual in the group is the primary leader. But, usually, no matter how the choosing of teammates may be accomplished (and it may be by direct assertion of leadership as well as by the means mentioned), there appears an allocation of authority in the course of the social operations necessary to playing baseball. Perhaps this takes place on the grounds of age, the oldest boy holding power and the younger boys agreeing with him in all decisions. It may be on the basis of self-assertion. One boy may "take over the group" without relationship to his age or the wishes of others, and the others may follow him. Authority may also be divided and distributed according to the "toughness" of the members, the most "worldly" becoming the chief. There are many ways in which the authority of a group may be dispersed. The fact of its division without outside interference is as natural as the phenomenon of group formation itself.

Sometimes in group work practice the dominance of the "chief" will determine the decisions of the group, aside from whatever specific organization the group may have. A group leader in describing such a situation tells how a girl, "Paula," overrides the particular group, the "Gay Girls," of which she is a member. She has been its president, but no longer is. Her influence, however, is such that she is still the president in effect. The group leader's account summarizes very briefly his impressions of the meeting:

The girls talked so much and were so full of "pep" and enthusiasm that it is rather difficult to attempt to give a picture of them: Paula, to whom all the girls turn for leadership; Bertha, slangy, with a way of expressing herself all her own; Maria, very loud and good-natured; with the others, with the exception of Olga and Rose, saying plenty. Olga and Rose were enthusiastic even though they said very little, for once readily agreeing with the others in their plans.

Occurrences at this meeting demonstrated more than ever that Paula is the natural leader of the group. They turn to her for everything but she does not always do everything for them as they want her to. When she does not initiate activities, however, they usually do nothing. The group is unusually cooperative.[10]

[10]Grace Longwell Coyle, editor, Studies in Group Behavior, Harper and Brothers, New York, 1937, p. 23.

Problems of Leadership. The breakdown of power within a group and the tendency of groups to have leaders, whether elected or not, are of significance to group work operations. At least two questions emerge. One relates to the nature of group work. Is it possible that a group which forms without an "outside" leader is properly a group work group? The second concerns the acceptance of the outside leader by the group members and his subsequent relations with them.

The first problem has usually been answered by saying, as indicated previously, that there must be some direction by an outside leader. In this connection the distinction must be made between the usual group process and that of group work organization. The group work process occurs only when there is a leader (enabler, guide, counselor, adviser) present who is consciously effecting the process. Usually, a professionally trained worker, a graduate of an accredited school of social work with a major in group work is implied. One reason for this is the fact that such a group often needs to be related to a source of knowledge and skill in conducting the group process which it otherwise would not have. Leadership in group work means, in part, that the group will be directed by a professional individual who has studied the group process and has had experience in group living. The leader's principal responsibility is to create advantages in procedure. At few points is it considered necessary or proper for him to decide or contribute to issues other than procedure.

The second problem involves the relation of the group leader to the members. Of primary importance is his initial assignment to the group. Much of his success, especially with adolescent and adult groups, is determined at the earliest stage of his contact with the members. Forcing of the "outsider" on the group by the agency administration can be disastrous for the group, the leader, and the agency.

Democratic Procedures. After this first hurdle has been passed, the achieving and maintaining of satisfactory relations with the members is no easy matter. Not all leaders would approach the problem in the same way, and the method could differ from group to group according to the specific organization of power within the group. However, the leader, for one thing, would be interested in furthering democratic procedures and would use every means to encourage the adoption of democratic values. Power which is achieved and maintained through democratic means should be encouraged by the leader, while power which is arbitrary and dictatorial should be frowned upon. As was mentioned earlier, however, the leader cannot require ideal conditions in every regard but must accept to some measure the conditions as found, if there is to be any group work. But, "accepting as a starting point" and "accepting as a permanent inevitability" are obviously different. The worker may have to permit an arbitrary distribution of power within a group in order to establish a relationship with the group in the first place, but he should seek to develop more democratic bases for authority in time.

It is not always easy for the group leader to further democratic aims. Democracy is much easier to verbalize than to make effective. Sometimes a leader may fail to establish a cooperative spirit between the group and himself. The following is an account written by a group leader who, recognizing his failure to develop the kind of leadership he desires, is making plans to overcome the difficulties:

> Two days later the club attended the Gloom Chasers' party.
> During this period the Leader had some doubts as to his own relation to the group. Steve had commented that he was old-fashioned which made him consider his methods of approach to the conflict of standards. The Leader comments on this:
> "The effect of the Leader's words in the discussion of the outing when mentioned several weeks ago had seemed only to estrange the group from him because the club now refrains from talking in his presence about its parties outside of the Community House. The fellows seem to think that the Leader is an old timer and doesn't know any better. The problem is not very serious but it is plain enough that the Leader should not pursue his original plan of making suggestions for the planning of these outside affairs. Possibly a solution for next year would be for the Leader to become a member of the club. He can then suggest entirely different activities from their old type of outing but make them when no other plans are being considered. Probably what was wrong this year was that the Leader interfered with the club's plans. At the time the Leader did not recognize it as interference but the group seemed to take it that way.
> "What the club needs is to be directed into constructive channels. The Leader is hoping, more or less blindly that he may, by pointing out their deficiencies, change the members somewhat. This is not a good method, the Leader realizes, because it is hollow but when ordinary types of indirect group or personality control apparently fail, the point-blank type may bring results."[11]

The group leader also seeks to strengthen the leadership potentials of the members. The worker never wishes to rob the group and its members of the opportunity to lead; rather, his purpose is to insure the possibility that leadership tendencies on the part of the members will

[11]*Ibid.*, pp. 102–103.

be encouraged. These leadership potentials cannot be enhanced if the group leader dominates the situation, or if one member undemocratically dominates the group.

The grounding of the group work process in democratic procedures reveals one of the social values of such work. It represents, along with other expressions of democracy in the community, a "grass-roots" foundation of democratic living. In many cities there is surprisingly little opportunity for children to be influenced and educated along democratic lines. Homes may provide a weak example because of the dominance of one parent (or both parents) over their children. Schools may be so utilitarian-minded with vocational programs that the achievement of genuinely democratic social experience may be sidetracked. Churches may be more concerned with the indoctrination of revealed truths than in developing strong democratic (and to some extent Christian) ways of interpersonal living. In fact, in many communities there are few opportunities for young people to have primary contact with democracy and to explore its practical possibilities through creative group experience aside from the opportunities offered by group work agencies.

Under the Auspices of an Agency

Group work usually operates with the sanction and support of an agency. The agency has a bearing upon the work of the leader and upon the activities of the members.

Imposing of Limitations. A chief influence of the agency is that of setting limitations for the group leader and for the group. A social work agency sponsoring a group maintains relationships of responsibility to the community, for one, which call for special examination. The group leader is responsible to the community for his activities, but usually indirectly through the agency. As a representative of the agency which pays him or which secures him on a volunteer basis to do a particular job, his actions will usually be interpreted by the community not simply as his personal actions, but as the policy of the agency. His achievements will not be merely his achievements, but a part of the work of the organization which has given him the opportunity to achieve. Because this is so, and for other reasons, agencies assume responsibility for the determination of policy regarding group work. So an agency may determine that certain ways of representing it to the community are highly desirable and should be furthered at every instance. It may also decide that other ways draw unfavorable attention to the agency and so are undesirable. Thus agencies in attempting to fulfill their community obligations must impose some limitations upon the activities of groups under its sponsorship.

This control by an agency is not meant necessarily to entail hardships for workers and groups. Any activity, whether casework, group work, or community organization (or any nonsocial work activity for that matter), which derives its support from an agency, must operate within certain predetermined boundaries. To proceed in any other way would connote an anarchistic and meaningless condition harmful to the positive intentions of the organization. In regard to group work, a group cannot maintain a policy toward the community which is "yes" one day and "no" the next. The consistency of its policy will to a considerable measure determine its effectiveness in community relations. This does not mean that policy cannot be changed, but that its changing should be orderly. It also implies that there must first of all be a policy from which deviation can be rightfully made.

Actually, agency-imposed limitations may afford many positive advantages. The policy of a group work agency that there will be no segregation of people according to racial or religious backgrounds in the program is certainly socially desirable. An agency's decision to allow the Young People's Political Party to meet in the gym of an evening, because it believes that such groups in the neighborhood should be helped, may be of positive advantage to the Party. The judgment of an agency that a schedule regulating the use of a swimming pool makes for order and fairness may mean that more people are able to use the pool than otherwise. Often whether a policy is restraining or positive will depend upon the attitude of the group itself toward the policy.

It is necessary to interpret the conditions which agencies impose on their groups. The rules of an agency are viewed as discussable. They can be modified. They can also become a valuable teaching tool in the hands of a skilled group leader. The following illustration shows how a discussion was held by a leader with his group on the very matters of agency policy:

At this meeting the discussion on the purpose of the agency was continued. The Leader had given some material about the agency to several of the club members. Several members of the Red Jackets, a younger boys' club, were present.

The first point in the minutes from last meeting was the report on the agency. Steve asked the Leader for that but the Leader referred it to Jake and he read the report. This report emphasized the fact that the Community House hopes in time to turn over its work to organizations already in the neighborhood. The fellows took this point up and asked how this was being done. Reference was made to work done by the agency at the Polish Church and at the schools. The Leader pointed out the role of the Advisory Committee from the neighborhood in respect to the policy formulation of certain work of the House.

The House Council was referred to as an example of neighborhood control. Frank said, "If the House Council has some control, why does it pay two hundred dollars to the House for light and fuel? Why doesn't it use that money from dues for improvement of equipment?" "Yes," added Steve, "two hundred dollars wouldn't mean much to the House if the Community Fund pays for it." The Leader replied that every little bit counts and that if the House Council would use the money for equipment the budget on light and fuel would be increased. The House had to count on the house dues to help pay expenses, the Leader explained, and added that in most organizations the members pay for the privileges and that some of the money generally goes for upkeep of the buildings. Steve and Frank maintained that the House Council should not make that donation, intimating that the suggestion in the first place had come from a staff member. The Leader professed ignorance of this but suggested that the group might investigate the matter in a House Council meeting.

The discussion then turned to the purpose of having clubs. Steve pointed out that most clubs do not know what they are organized for. "What are you organized for?" asked Steve, referring to the Red Jackets. Andy, the president, said something about, "for fun, trips, and recreation." He was not definite and Steve told him, "How do you fellows expect to accomplish anything if you don't know any better than that what you want?" The Hudsons laughed at this. The Leader asked what they wanted from their leader if they did not seem to get what they want now. Tom interrupted and said that the leaders did not help the clubs enough. "They should give games, new ones and not the old ones, and the House should provide better equipment," he said. The Leader asked, "You wouldn't want the leaders to provide entertainment for you, would you?" They intimated that they did and Frank said, "The House aims to satisfy the recreational needs of the people but they do not have enough equipment. The Community House just provides a meeting room."

"What do you mean by recreation?" asked the Leader and Frank mentioned basketball or pool. To this the Leader replied that a lot depended on the definition of recreation and stated that in many ways club activities are recreational. The basketball need is met outside the House in the High School and the Church gymnasiums which are cooperating with the agency. The Leader said, "One of the aims of a good club should be to become self-sufficient and to be able to furnish its own recreation and program without very much help from the leader." "But the leader ought to give lots of suggestions at first," said Frank. "Quite right," replied the Leader, "but most clubs expect the leader to be an entertainer all the time and many clubs which don't seem to do anything, definitely resist advice and suggestion." Steve remarked that such clubs should be thrown out.

At this point, some of the Red Jackets told about their leader and complained that he was always talking—either "beefin' " (bossing) or else talking about politics or the like. They said that if they talked about politics they could stay at the House longer but they indicated that they did not like such talking. After this speech Jim particularly looked at the Leader and grinned and let out a hollow laugh as if to say, "That's what we think of you." Steve asked the Red Jackets if they did any "crabbing" and they admitted that they did sometimes. Steve pointed out they were probably at fault. The Leader asked them if they ever went to their leader about their dissatisfaction with the club and offered to work the problems out together. They said "No", so the Leader advised them to do this.

Later he talked to them further on the subject, with emphasis on the idea of cooperation with their leader. The Leader told the group that he was glad to get all of these points of view because unfortunately the group did not express itself on these things very often. He said, "I hope I'm not carrying this too far (Jim and Frank squirmed in their chairs as they had been doing) because I don't want to bore you, but I'm learning a few things." The Leader indicated that the points which were suggested in the evening's discussion should be written up and presented to Mr. K and perhaps later to the House Council. The Leader said, however, that they should not be disappointed if some of their suggestions bore no fruit because in the matters of finance no one could very well dictate what should be done with the persons financially responsible.

The Leader comments on this:

"The discussion, the Leader feels, was valuable in that the fellows did think about the policies of the House. Some of their criticisms of clubs' not doing anything worth-while were true even though their interpretation of worth-while activities does not correspond with the Leader's. On the other hand, such statements as 'The House doesn't do anything for clubs which aren't active and for members who fail to take part,' indicated that the fellows in their hypercritical state are mentally lazy. Of course, it can be understood that they would not be aware of the fact that through a group work process some of the inactive people would eventually be 'brought out'. The Hudsons certainly show that they attribute their club growth almost entirely to their own work. The Leader is willing that this should be because it gives them the feeling that they are independent.

"In the discussion the Leader decided that discussions as such must never be forced nor carried too long. Often a leader goes home feeling that he had a wonderful discussion meeting when, as a matter of fact, the group goes home feeling that they never heard such a 'windy' leader before. This meeting certainly made the Leader more awake to the fact that all work with groups must consider the immediate effect on the group, as well as the ultimate effect.

"The best part about the whole discussion was the fact that the fellows made up a list of suggestions which will be handed to Mr. K and from that there will probably be some results in the form of a report on the House that can be passed out to groups. The club pointed out one very important thing—that too many clubs are meeting for no good reason at all that the clubs themselves can state."[12]

Increase in Group Work Organizations. Group work in recent years has been utilized by increasing numbers and types of agencies. At first there were only a few organizations which found group work suitable and advantageous for their purposes. Some of these have been mentioned in Chapter 2: settlement houses, Boy Scouts and Girl Scouts, the various Y groups. Among others which traditionally have had programs in group work are: Boy Rangers, Boys' Clubs of America, Camp Fire Girls, Catholic Boys' Brigade, 4-H Clubs, community centers (notably those under Jewish sponsorship), Junior Red Cross, and Pioneer Youth. The activities of all of these organizations would make interesting study for the growing effects of group work upon American communities. (See Figure 41.)

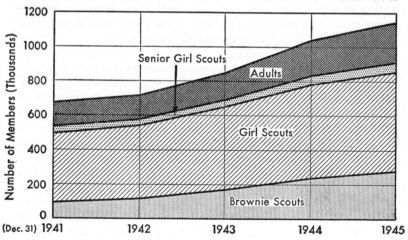

FIG. 41. Growth in Girl Scout Membership During Second World War
(Chart through courtesy of Girl Scouts of U.S.A.)

Boys' Clubs of America. The Boys' Clubs of America bear attention because as of the summer of 1948 there were about 300 local units with approximately 250,000 youthful members. Each local unit is affiliated with the national Boys' Clubs of America. The Clubs exist to provide children in underaverage localities with the opportunity to use their

[12]*Ibid.,* pp. 129–132.

leisure time constructively. They are concerned with the enhancement of health, the development of recreational and vocational talents, and other activities which will encourage leadership and good citizenship. Boys' Clubs place no restriction upon membership because of race, religion, or social status. While the majority of the members of Boys' Clubs are between twelve and sixteen years of age, the Clubs are open to those between eight and twenty-one. The members are usually classified according to age: eight to ten year olds are called "midgets"; eleven to thirteen years, "juniors"; fourteen to sixteen, "intermediates"; seventeen to twenty-one, "seniors." There are about 600 full-time, 1,000 part-time, and 1,000 volunteer workers throughout the nation in Boys' Clubs.

4-H Clubs. The 4-H clubs predominate in rural areas. They are part of the extension work of several agricultural organizations and groups: the United States Department of Agriculture, various agricultural colleges within the states, and the county organizations interested in farming. The aims of the 4-H clubs are the following, among others: acquiring farm and home skills, understanding nature, developing ideals of collective living and action, homemaking, and social and recreational opportunities. These objectives are pursued by approximately 1,700,000 young people between the ages of ten to twenty in about 75,000 local clubs, under the leadership of about 180,000 voluntary leaders.

Camp Fire Girls. The Camp Fire Girls is another leisure-time, group work type of organization which exerts a wide influence over girls throughout the country. There are three age groupings within this organization: the Blue Birds, seven to nine years; the Camp Fire Girls, ten through junior high-school age; and the Horizon Clubbers, who are of senior high-school through junior college ages. The local organizations are oriented toward the education of girls in the management of home responsibilities, the development of avocational skills, and the requirements of social participation. Girls are awarded honors for their skill in various crafts. Volunteers provide the leadership for the groups. Like the other character-building institutions, they usually have a sponsoring board composed of interested local citizens. About 360,000 girls are presently members.

Junior Red Cross. The largest youth organization in the country (about 20,000,000) is the American Junior Red Cross. (See Figure 42.) This consists of the school members of the American Red Cross. It is primarily interested in service along the line established by the parent organization. In many schools the projects of the American Junior Red

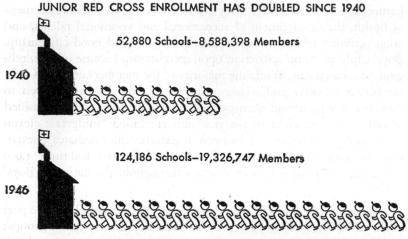

JUNIOR RED CROSS ENROLLMENT HAS DOUBLED SINCE 1940

52,880 Schools—8,588,398 Members

1940

124,186 Schools—19,326,747 Members

1946

Fig. 42. Increase in Junior Red Cross Enrollment Between 1940 and 1946
(*Red Cross Service Record: Accomplishments of Seven Years,* American National
Red Cross, 1946.)

Cross have become an accepted part of the curriculum. While the primary stress of the Junior Red Cross is upon health education, it does not neglect the need for good citizenship. The organization is definitely tied up with services extended throughout the world—as near and far as the International Red Cross operates. At the present time considerable effort is being shown in local schools to help meet the health and educational needs of children in other countries. There are both voluntary and paid workers who direct the program.

Settlement Houses. While the work of the settlement houses has been mentioned previously, especially in the second chapter, it may be well to say a few more words about it here in terms of its current influence. There are today over 200 settlement houses in the country coordinated in the National Federation of Settlements, and approximately 150 other settlements, church houses, and other local community organizations not affiliated with the National Federation. Whether the title of "settlement" is a good one or not is debatable. It is still used in the majority of cases, but "neighborhood house" runs a close second. In addition there are other terms which are used, such as: community center, association, hall, inn, commons. But whether or not the agencies in this category are correctly named, there still persists the force and feeling of the settlement house idea. All settlements, however, operate on the basis of the sociological unit of the neighborhood.

Settlement houses thrive on club organizations. Club organization is utilized by other group work agencies, but with the settlement houses there is a long tradition whereby small, spontaneous groupings of children use the facilities of the settlement for their own group ends. The work of the settlements, however, is becoming more specialized as other than club interests are developed and workers with special skills are employed. Today, in many large settlements, there is a wide array of group formation and activities.

The houses are increasingly concerned about the quality of their staffs. In the earlier days group leaders were secured from those within the community who were highly imbued with ideals of social change and betterment. Currently, settlement houses, while not devoid of that previous spirit, have become professionalized. The rise in most communities of relatively independent services, such as playgrounds, health agencies, kindergartens, public baths, and other group work agencies, has supplanted a large part of the activities and responsibilities which formerly were assumed by settlement houses. (It should be pointed out, however, that the settlement house leaders pioneered in developing these services and in urging public officials to have them continued on a permanent basis by public agencies.) On this basis alone there is probably justification for settlement houses developing more of a specialized program. Settlements, however, are still interested in community improvement and do not think that their efforts of other years along this line are complete or satisfactory. They recognize their own present-day obligation to take part in the healthy growth of the neighborhood.

Neighborhood houses are often thought to deal almost exclusively with children. This, of course, is not true, either in fact or theory. Practically, settlements have groups of all ages. One of the special possibilities for them today lies in the establishment of groups for the aged, as has been explained. Theoretically, the houses are concerned for family welfare and believe that they exist to be used by neighborhood families. Thus it is not enough to say that the settlement house is a place where children can be kept from becoming delinquents. It is just as much concerned with the home and neighborhood and the improvement of both.

Camping. Among the group work services offered to many people of all ages is camping. A distinctly American creation, camping not only has been spreading to other countries but is expanding in several directions in this country. First, it is growing in the number of people who take advantage of this form of recreation. Today, there are more persons who enjoy the benefits of vacation camping than ever before.

Also, camping has been increasing in its efficiency. Originally it was relatively unorganized. The values of leisure-time camping were thought to be so "natural" that no serious control of camping experience was necessary. The essential stress was upon activity, often merely for the sake of activity. The possibilities of camping for educational objectives, however, were quickly seen. The summer camp, while still relatively unorganized, provided a fortunate learning period for many. The stress here seemed to be upon the learning of avocational skills and the attainment of "character." At the present time the emphasis in camping, while not excluding the other two, is upon the social orientation of the camper, his opportunity to absorb democratic procedures at an elementary level of experience. The view is held by many agency-sponsored camps that camping should be an integral part of the total educational experience of the child. As summer camps approach these newer aims, they fall more and more within the province of professional group work.

The camp situation is fairly well described in a statement of Camp Raritan in New Jersey:

A visitor to Camp Raritan sees first a group of buildings forming the central village. Here, campers call for their daily supply of food at the camp store, deposit their pennies in the bank, take books from the library, receive tools and supplies from the repair shop, make their bed-rolls, check equipment for short camping trips, and visit the clinic for any treatment demanding the attention of the camp doctor. This central village houses neither campers nor counselors. They will be found in the woods nearby. One small group lives in three long houses resembling wind tunnels. The boys, themselves, have built these out of saplings.

A canvas shelter provides dining room and kitchen. The boys are busily engaged in repairing an oven and fireplace constructed from rocks, clay, an old five-gallon metal ice-cream freezer, and a few iron bars. Their task must be completed today because tomorrow's menu calls for a meat loaf and two berry pies. Another camper is building a small wash water dam. He becomes more interested in catching salamanders and crayfish. He has never seen them before. The visitor suspects that the wash water dam will soon turn into an aquarium.

Some boys are following a team of horses. The team is dragging a ten-foot log. The horses belong to the covered wagon group which travels about the country camping in pastures of friendly farmers. Now the boys are back at camp and a neighboring group has borrowed the animals to pull a log to its special camp. The log will be sawed up and used for seats at the dining table.

Here is another group of boys, aged thirteen and fourteen years. They have been at camp two weeks and are establishing a new site. Under the direction of their counselors, they have cleared a place in the woods, erected three tepees, a dining room shelter, and a temporary kitchen. A fireplace and oven have been completed and a play area cleared. A hole has been dug in the side of a bank near the small stream. This is the first step toward a refrigerator!

After supper, which the boys themselves have prepared, the campers hold a pow-wow around their fire. Stories are told. They sing. But more important to this group is a discussion of what they are going to do next day. A hike is suggested, a game, a visit to another camp, a swim in the river, a raking and cleaning up of their camp site. Finally, the group decides to do jobs about camp in the morning, hike in the afternoon (visiting the other camps on the way), and to end the day with a swim in the river.

Sitting around the camp fire with the counselor, the visitor hears some amusing stories of what happens when city children like these are given their first outing in the country.

Joe, a new eleven-year-old camper, came to camp with a distinct distrust of other people. He was particularly afraid that the other campers would steal his belongings. Consequently, on hot days he insisted on wearing his sweater and carrying his tooth brush, paste, comb, stamps, stationery, and flashlight all day long. With the help of his counselor and older campers, Joe, after ten days, began to see that he could trust his camp mates to treat his belongings with respect. At the end of his camp period, he even loaned some of them.

*   *   *

The camp doctor, a westerner, unused to the language of New York City children, questioned a boy who came to the clinic concerning his trouble. "I boined my finger," the boy said. The doctor asked, "Can't you say burned instead of boined?" The boy replied, "Chee, Doc, I don't wanna talk like no sissy."

*   *   *

Bob, on his first day in camp, was running across a field to the shower when a camp director saw him stop and stare at the ground in front of him. He had discovered his first grasshopper. The camp director asked him what he had found. With amazement written all over his face, he exclaimed, "Look, Chief, a flying cockroach!"

Breakfast is at seven. A lazy mist of smoke hanging over the trees tells that breakfast is being prepared in many small camps.

A walk down to the village shows a small group of campers making sandwiches for lunch and packing them in knapsacks. They are going on a three-day camping trip to the farm of a friendly neighbor some seven miles away, from which another group has just returned. Excitedly they tell how the farmer exhibited his stock, explained the rotation of crops and the necessity for keeping the soil in good condition. They had a chance to milk a cow, too, but few were able to draw any milk.

An all-camp affair has been planned by an elected committee of campers and counselors for Saturday afternoon and evening. The program has been inspired by "barnraising" as practiced by the early pioneers. The object of this program is to gather, chop, and saw enough logs to supply firewood for the entire winter camping season. The program starts with a swim for the entire camp. Then the campers reassemble for the wood-gathering program. Soon, saws, axes, sledges, and wedges have provided enough wood for all winter.

By this time the boys are ready for dinner. Corn in the husk is buried in a long trench fire and covered with canvas and dirt. A large oblong fire is built on the ground. When the red bed of coal is ready, large steaks are thrown on it. Long forked poles turn the steaks as they cook. The boys call this a Buffalo Steak Fry and the fact that buffalo is not used does not matter to them one bit. After a meal of steak and sandwiches, corn on the cob, tomatoes, and lemonade, the evening program is started. This consists of skits and stunts adapted from various phases of camp life. One is presented by each of the twelve groups of campers. As darkness overtakes the group, songs around the campfire end a day filled with new experiences—experiences about which these children could not have dreamed before. To them the U.S.A. had meant city streets!

They will not forget camping in the forest. They cannot forget the fun they had. They won't forget the real America.[13]

Group Work in New Settings. At the present time, group work activities are pioneering in new settings. There is some indication that governmentally sponsored group work activities will be developed in the future. The use of group work for the aged by public departments of welfare has already been mentioned. It is possible, too, that public departments of education will more and more see the possibilities of integrating summer camp programs with the more formal winter programs which they offer. Public schools also are developing afterschool activities to an extent unparalleled in our national history. Even in some of the institutions of higher education there have been a few pioneering efforts to use group work procedures to provide a full education. In this connection the programs of Brooklyn College and the University of Minnesota bear special attention. They have been described as follows:

In 1941, Brooklyn College and the University of Minnesota each established a Bureau of Student Activities within the Office of the Dean of

[13] *Adventures in Camping,* by the Johanna M. Lindlof Camp Committee for Public School Children, William Jansen, Chairman, The Publications Committee, New York, 1943, pp. 13–15.

PERCENT OF TOTAL SUPPORT

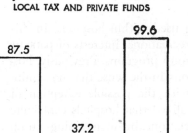

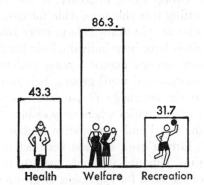

FIG. 43. Sources and Percent of Total Support Provided for Health, Welfare, and Recreation

(Bradley Buell, "Let's Look at the Record," *Survey Midmonthly*, Vol. 82, No. 2, February, 1946.)

Students. Its location within the office of the Dean of Students more definitely integrates group work on the campus into the total personnel program of the institution. As an agency, the Bureau of Student Activities deals with all students. It is as much concerned with so-called normal students as with those who have more serious emotional problems. Group work and casework, campus version, are thus recognized as equally important aspects of the major personnel program.

In such co-educational situations as Brooklyn College and the University of Minnesota both men and women are employed on the group work staff and both men's and women's organizations as well as mixed groups are served, in a fashion similar to practices in community centers. As in a group work agency, staff members serve both as group work supervisors and program advisers. They work with students in a cooperative relationship while plans are in process of formation. They are tentative in expressing their opinions. The question method is frequently used as a technic for guiding discussion or clarifying a situation. Dominative methods are avoided. Social situations, committee meetings, panel discussions, symposia, round tables and the like are regarded highly as means for helping students in the modification of attitudes and opinions. The atmosphere of conferences and meetings is friendly and stimulating; there is rapport developed between faculty and student members while they are working together on solutions to problems of interest to both students and faculty.

As in group work agencies in the larger community, not all group work is concerned with work in groups. Individual conferences are frequent, especially preparatory conferences which precede group meetings. There is a great deal of individual work and guidance.[14]

Group work, moreover, is also being used within hospitals. In this setting it is able to provide for certain recreational interests of patients who are physically able to enter into group programs. Previously, hospitals have been individualistic institutions in the sense that no significant groups existed among patients, with the possible exception of unorganized ward groups. It is now realized that hospitals contribute to the normality of patients' social relations by maintaining group work activities wherever possible. Where they have been wisely tried, the social and recuperative benefits of such programs are evident.

Group work also has been active in the institutional field for some time, although it is only recently that there has been open recognition of the need for expansion of group work programs within institutions. Institutions for children especially can benefit from the use of group work knowledge and skill. This knowledge and skill may be utilized within cottages in terms of cottage management. It also may be used in the direct organization of the leisure time of cottage children. The spread of group work to institutions other than those for children has not taken place very widely, although this is possibly one of the trends which group work may take.

National Associations. Some of the agencies and organizations for group work mentioned in this chapter are related to national, voluntary associations. Among these are the following:

The Associated Youth Serving Organizations (A.Y.S.O.) was organized in 1943. It was comprised of seven national agencies (including Camp Fire Girls, National Jewish Welfare Board, National Federation of Settlements, National Board of the Young Women's Christian Association) and conducted a program which coordinated their work. It, however, is no longer in existence, being now a part of the Youth Division of the National Social Welfare Assembly along with other organizations.

The Youth Department of the National Catholic Welfare Conference coordinates many Roman Catholic group work services. It is not a super-authority placed over other Roman Catholic youth groups and organizations, nor does it seek to turn the attention of its membership to national needs. But it does provide for the interpretation of the problems of youth for Roman Catholic as well as non-Roman Catholic

[14]Louise Price, "Group Work: Campus Version, 1945," *The Group,* volume 7, number 3, March, 1945, pp. 6–7.

organizations. It further supports the National Catholic Youth Council, a federation of all existing and approved Roman Catholic youth groups in the country. There are two sections to the Council: (1) the Diocesan Section, and (2) the College and University Section. The Diocesan Section cooperates with various youth groups which are organized primarily on a diocesan basis; the College and University Section cooperates with the National Federation of Catholic College Students and the Newman Club Federation.

The National Jewish Welfare Board, mentioned in Chapter 2 under Jewish social work, represents a significant nation-wide coordinative effort on the part of Jewish group work organizations.

The United Christian Youth Movement is the organization which has developed a cooperative program for the various Protestant youth-serving groups and agencies in North America. About 90 per cent of Protestant young people (approximately ten million in number) are coordinated on an interdenominational scale. The United Christian Youth Movement represents the combined efforts of about 185 state, provincial, and community youth councils and councils of religious education. The Movement was established in 1934 and is supported by forty-two of the Protestant denominations. The Movement does not believe in superimposing a new organization on the existing ones. It does try to cooperate wherever possible in strengthening the work of each individual organization by providing a united perspective on youth, religion, and society. The Youth Division of the International Council of Religious Education publishes program materials, furnishes field services to local groups, plans for the annual observance of Youth Week, sponsors six regional conferences each year and the Christian Youth Conference of North America every fourth year.

The National Federation of Settlements provides assistance to local settlements on personnel, programs, and administration through materials, field service, and conferences. The Federation also represents local neighborhood houses in their relations with other national organizations.

For the Satisfaction of the Social Needs of Individuals

There has been some discussion as to whether group work exists primarily for the individual or for its own collective purposes. This discussion has never been very widespread, fortunately, because it is too obvious to most people that a group can serve, and serve adequately, both personal and group ends. There is no necessary conflict between the two. It is true that individuals within a group often have to modify their personal wishes in order to maintain sufficient group solidarity.

Likewise, it is known that groups often modify their activities to take specifically into account the special interests and talents of individuals. The individual and the group, therefore, are in a process of interaction and neither need dominate the other. At least the group exists in part for the satisfaction of the social needs of individuals.

That individuals have social needs is not difficult to establish in the abstract. There are today numerous special terms which psychologists and sociologists use in seeking to describe the social needs of individuals, but despite differences over terminology, there is general agreement that social needs do exist.

Concretely, however, the group worker is always interested in the relationship of designated social needs of individuals to the activities which groups perform. At the outset, then, there is need for the worker to understand how he can appropriately appraise the social needs of individuals. A number of ways are open to him. Some of them are:

Personal Interview. Some group work agencies realize the importance of having personal interviews with all individuals before permitting them to join in group activities. From an interview it may be determined, for example, that one child would like to act in a play rather than engage in any of the other activities which the agency offers. If this is so, there is already an indication of the needs of the individual. Another child may prefer to play basketball to the exclusion of all other activities. These needs are rather plain and may easily be detected. The interview, however, may also be used to uncover the basic needs that can and should be met in the group or groups (such needs as security, response, recognition, etc.). In many of the present-day interviews only the surface facts (interests) are discovered, but as intake procedures are improved a better understanding of the basic needs of the person should be possible. The interview may also be of value after placement in further uncovering the requirements of the individual.

Tests. The use of tests for determining the social needs of individuals has not been too fully developed by group workers. But, clearly, if group workers wish to know enough about their clients to place them properly in organized groups and to provide the best possible group experience for them, the use of tests must become more widespread. Commonly known and standardized tests can point out to the worker the kinds of skills that individuals have. This knowledge is important in group placement. The worker, moreover, can determine what rates of learning to expect of individuals. This may save him from the unfortunate experience of expecting more or less from individuals than he rightfully should. When individuals fail to function according to the development of their groups, tests may give the answer why. The group worker can also use the findings from tests to evaluate the work of the agency, so that the agency will be better able to spend its energy in the meeting of actual, instead of assumed, needs.

The administration of tests by an untrained person, however, is scarcely desirable. In this regard the special services of a psychologist can be used to advantage. A caseworker from a neighborhood agency may also be able to make a contribution. The group worker, moreover, may be able to use the test findings of other agencies within the community (schools, casework agencies, hospitals) which already have appropriate information. Aside from individual tests, there are group tests, but in general these are not so reliable.

Observation. Not all individuals can be interviewed or tested upon their entrance into a group work agency. The group leader, for example, who takes a "cellar club" into a settlement house can hardly impose interviews and tests for all members to determine whether or not they should all be in the same group. Probably, the condition on which they will enter will be their right to determine their own membership and to plan their own activities. Later, when they have been within the agency for some time and have discovered that it is seeking to serve them in ways which will further their own development, they may decide that they can "listen" to the group worker more and more. Only then may they be amenable to interviewing or testing. There are other situations, too, in which the group worker could not expect to use the interview and testing methods.

The worker can, however, observe the operation of groups to discover what their effects are upon the individuals who compose them. For example, the child who at the start insists upon being only in a dramatic group may be observed in action to show interest in handicraft work. Perhaps he admires the backdrop which another group has made in conjunction with the dramatic presentation. Perhaps he has taken part in the creation of stage scenery because that has been an accepted part of the activities of the dramatic group. If the worker observes such a latent interest, he may encourage the child to enter more actively into a handicraft group which does more than create stage scenery. Thus through observation the leader may discover the strengths and inclinations of various individuals and help to channel these appropriately.

So far, the discussion has indicated how the group leader can determine the needs of the group members by means of interviewing, testing, and observation. Just what are the social needs which can be met by group work?

Group Benefits for Individual. The group should provide for the individual a place in which he finds a degree of security, where he is able to express himself freely, both vocally and in activity. The group should, through the granting of security, enable the individual to gain confidence in himself and in his own abilities. It should be the experimental testing ground on which abilities are freely located and developed. The group should help a person to express himself without fear that his mistakes will be dealt with too harshly. It should, moreover, place its own resources at his disposal at certain times to strengthen him in his "ego" feelings and also in regard to the social situation in which he can express himself.

The individual should also find in the group a healthy devotion to nonindividual ends. The person may expect the group in some ways to serve him. He must also expect in some ways to serve the group. He does not stand alone, with the group at his side assisting him in his every wish. He needs to know the extent to which the group will cooperate with him and the extent to which the group must expect cooperation from him. Through this devotion to group goals the individual loses a degree of his individuality, gains greater security, and takes part in a goal-conscious operation which calls upon him for his more creative and responsible talents. He becomes a part, and an integral part, in a plan or program of activities. He sees his role in relation to those of others. He secures self-responsibility regarding his place within the group.

The individual, furthermore, learns from the group work process those elements of behavior which are intrinsic to the process of other groups. He finds himself in relationship to a leader who has some degree of authority over him. He must interact with others within the group in order to discover and maintain his own position. He comes in contact with the very obvious processes of group interaction: cooperation, conflict, accommodation. These strengthen his social abilities to get along in all groups. He becomes socialized. He is taught, not so much by a single leader or teacher but by the group itself, what the requirements of group living really are. This participation in the group process enhances the skill of the individual in making friends. It contributes to his feelings of belongingness. The feelings of belongingness, in turn, contribute to his feelings of status and importance.

These social needs of individuals are important. They comprise for the group worker the social-individual goals he uses to judge the success or failure of group work in a specific case in relation to a specific individual.

The following excerpts from a record show among other things how the leader is able to relate himself to the needs of individuals within the "Playtime Club":[15]

11–4–36. The supervisor asked if Carrie could join the Playtime Club. Group worker referred her to Mary, the president.

Annie wanted the group worker to come to her side and tie the knot. (Group worker had already shown her how.) Worker refused.

11–11–36. Carrie looked as if she might have lost her temper had group worker not been looking at her.

11–18–36. Group worker started games while candy cooked. (This ended the dispute over who should stir.) Group worker got members to sit down and decide where they wanted to go on a trip—(introducing new ideas).

12–9–36. Group worker insisted that they all sit around the table and discuss what a president should do—(authority). Group worker told group that next time they got into such a noisy argument they would have to go out on the playground where they wouldn't disturb people— (limiting whole group).

12–16–36. Mary decided that each should draw for parts in the play. (Group worker did not interfere although she records that the play could not materialize because of the conflict this caused.)

1–20–37. Girls objected to parts in the play. Group worker said this could be changed if she assigned the parts, but Mary said no, it could not be done that way.

2–3–37. Josephine said group should assign parts, the others agreed, and the group worker took the responsibility.

2–16–37. Group worker said if there were any changes in parts she would make them—(limiting the whole group).

* * *

1–6–37. Trouble broke out again on both sides of Stella and she moved to sit beside the group worker.

1–13–37. Frances tried to put Stella in the corner and group worker refused to permit this.

2–10–37. Stella interrupted, Mary told her to keep still. Group worker suggested that she join in the discussion, too, and say what she thought.

Group worker brought Carrie into the activity by suggesting that she mix blue and yellow and make green.

[15]Gertrude Wilson, *Group Work and Case Work: Their Relationship and Practice,* Family Welfare Association of America (now Family Service Association of America), New York, 1941, pp. 49–50.

2–16–37. Group worker intervened to explain what Stella meant, but there were harsh words back and forth. Stella was greatly agitated and group worker sent her for pencils.

2–24–37. Frances insisted that she could not come at night. All attacked her. Group worker interrupted the argument by saying that she had some moccasins and other Indian tools she would like to bring in and asked who wanted to go with her to get them . . . Playing with the objects gave the girls a chance to calm down and then group worker turned to Mary and said, "You were not through with the business meeting." Mary proceeded.

For the Development of Legitimate Group Goals

It has been mentioned previously that there is no genuine conflict between the individual and the group in group work. Both represent values which the worker seeks to further. The person's individuality cannot be neglected in the group process if personal interests are to be realized. The group also cannot be viewed as a mere collection of individuals, each standing simply in relation to himself. The person in a group is an individual plus the interaction which the group provides and which in part defines him as an individual. At times the private interests of the individual may be supreme for him, but at other times he will be called upon to serve larger interests. The serving of broader values is not a denial of his individuality, but a supplementing and a fulfillment of it.

The group goals in group work are of various sorts. On one hand the satisfaction of the social needs of the members is a legitimate goal. But the group also has goals which may be viewed from a different perspective than that of the individual and his needs. The group goals are those to which the individuals as a group give assent regardless of the personal motives or desires of any one member. The methods of achieving a goal might show individual differences. Also there may be differing degrees of emotional attachment on the part of the various members toward a goal. To some it may be more important than any of the views of any of the members. To others, however, the rights of the individuals in the group may be respected to such an extent that the group goal may be hampered or even threatened in its expression.

The group goals in group work are not imposed by the agency although it may have a stake in the group's arriving at a particular decision. They are not granted to the group by the group leader, even though he may think he has in mind the ideal aim. They are discovered at best within the group itself. The agency may provide its facilities for the achievement of the goal, where it agrees with its purpose. The leader may develop the expression of the goal through conscious direction of the attention and interest of the members. But, basically, the collective goal belongs to the group; it is begun in the group and it comes to its fruition there (although its effects may be felt by others).

Focusing Attention on Others. Groups may focus their attention not only upon themselves, but upon others, especially the community. The interest of groups in community affairs is not difficult to stimulate. In fact, group sessions usually reflect in one way or another the topics of the day. For example, during the serious depression days of March, 1933, a group of girls who could have discussed their private interests turned their attention on a national interest:

> By this time the national catastrophe to the banks had broken and was affecting many members of the group. In spite of the interest in a recent dance which they had all attended, the following discussion arose in the club meeting:
> The question of the banks came up and Stella said the Warner factory had closed down for a week. "They had a big meeting and asked us if we were willing. They have plenty of orders and to spare, but they figure they'd lose money if they couldn't pay us the week's wages, so we just closed." She thought it would be funny not going to work but a vacation would be nice too. At this point Rose and Olga came in and became much interested in the subject since they too had discussed it at their factory. Olga said her place had had a meeting, too, but had decided to run the next week without pay. She said only one girl had said she would not work and she had changed her mind when she saw she was the only one. "Gee, I wouldn't have the nerve to say 'no' and I don't think anyone else would either," she explained.
> Stella began asking questions about the President's proclamation and the reason for it. The Leader explained that it was the only way in which the banks could be made safe, the only way in which confidence could be restored. Rose said her factory had been closed for two weeks and she had no idea when it would open. If the banks became safe, she wondered if that would make any difference. Angela asked how long the bank holiday of the President would last and the Leader said she did not know but she doubted if it would be over on Thursday, the appointed time. The group began telling stories of people having no money and how funny it was to buy things on credit. They mentioned the fact that movies were operating on a check basis.
> The Leader then told of the similar situation of 1907 when the banks had all closed and scrip had been issued. "That was before we were born, wasn't it?" Angela asked. "Oh, let's forget it," Olga suggested. "There's enough of that all day long."[16]

[16]Grace Longwell Coyle, editor, *Studies in Group Behavior,* Harper and Brothers, New York, 1937, pp. 76–77.

The social interests of groups may be more inclusive than community problems. It may extend, even as it does in many groups at the present time, to the whole world. The following illustration is an example of how a Jewish community center channeled interest along very broad lines:

> One Center recently conducted a project for the "intermediate" clubs in which the young people presented their conception of the United Nations peace conference in terms of five major issues: (1) Who Shall Pay for the War? (2) What Shall Be Done With Axis Nations After the War? (3) What Type of International Order Shall Be Established? (4) How Shall We Solve the Jewish Problem? (5) What Are Your Country's Demands?
>
> Each club represented one of the United Nations at the hypothetical peace table. The conference was divided into five panels and groups sent two representatives to each. At the final plenary session, resolutions adopted by the panels were discussed and voted upon. The project was rounded out by an interesting exhibit of United Nations materials that gave expression to the ideas and opinions of the groups represented. The interest of the young people in the project was a reflection of the vital concern they had in their future.
>
> Inter-Center conferences on major social issues and current problems reveal considerable experience and knowledge. At one such conference, the representatives called for greater utilization of Center facilities, expansion of program, and increased democracy-in-practice. They urged that Jewish problems be discussed in every Center, and that local leadership strive to keep youth informed on legislative matters, community developments, and social action.
>
> The young people were divided into "functioning panels" or round tables, each under the leadership of a chairman and a consultant. They had ample opportunity to think together in the more informal atmosphere of a discussion group. Records were kept of the discussion in each round table, and the recorders reported to a general session.[17]

Aside from mere interest and discussion, such groups may be an instrument of social action. To the extent to which community conditions operate at a disadvantage to the members of a group, their stake in social action is obvious. Not all such groups, however, mature to the point where action becomes a vital basis for the establishment of group goals. Many proceed to the point of choosing goals for themselves without seemingly being able to think in terms of the factors operative in the community outside of the agency which gives them

[17]Meyer Bass, "Meeting Jewish Youth Needs," *The Group*, volume 8, number 4, June, 1946, p. 7.

shelter. On the other hand some groups are able to transcend their own rather narrow interests to formulate aims which definitely pertain to the improvement of community conditions, and this is as it should be. All group experience should result in some kind of action, and more of it in group work should result in social action. Here again the leader can make an important contribution by stimulating the members of his group to action on matters of concern to them.

PROFESSIONALIZATION IN GROUP WORK

The group worker very often must relate himself to nonprofessional people who hold positions of responsibility in group work agencies. It is much easier for the relatively untrained person (in the professional sense) to secure a position in group work than in casework. The group work field has progressed markedly in recent years in improving the quality of its leadership, but much remains to be done. In many instances, persons who have completed a liberal arts course in a recognized college, especially with majors in the social sciences, are able to find group work positions. The need, however, is for professionally trained workers.

Knowledge Is Needed

The group leader's qualifications should include both knowledge and skill. In regard to knowledge the group leader should have understanding of the general society in which he lives. He should know something about the cultural, ethnic, economic, social, religious, and governmental aspects of the community which he serves. This should be bolstered by a background which includes the history of the country and the history of the group work movement. The group work leader also should have a vital understanding of the co-processes of group work, namely, social casework and community organization.

The group leader should know human nature, the development of personality, the implications of group experience for individual behavior growth, and the influence of environment upon the person. He should be acquainted with the nature of group life, the various forms of group experience which exist, the role of the leader within the group, and the effects of the community upon group behavior. He should also know how to provide content for group work programs. This means that he should have a variety of possibilities to offer his groups in the way of activities. All of the general understanding of the individual and of society cannot suffice for concrete knowledge regarding the group work activities themselves. It would be well for such a leader to be aware of the problems of record-keeping, of supervision, community planning, social research, and social action. All of these together indicate that the group leader needs to have a very wide background of serviceable knowledge about his profession. It is usually necessary for him to spend two years in a graduate school offering group work education to secure this kind of preparation.

Skill Is Required

In addition to the knowledge the group worker should possess for the effective conduct of group activities, he should be skilled. Skill implies a quality of leadership which cannot be developed simply through formal educational training. This does not mean that knowledge and skill are antithetical. One complements the other. But there are aspects of the two which can be distinguished. The group leader needs to be such a personality as will act as a positive catalytic agent for the group process. He needs the "knack" of group leadership. The amount of skill which group leaders possess varies from person to person, but from this it cannot rightfully be concluded that one is born with leadership possibilities or without them. Skill in group work can be cultivated through experience. The leader's training, then, should include not only "book learning," but also practical activity. The present programs of graduate schools which give instruction for group leadership recognize this need and provide for field work experience in which skill can be developed.

Group work as a growing profession has recourse to an increasing mass of data for its guidance, much of which is scientific. The continued growth of these data will encourage the fuller professionalization of the field. Probably, the future will find group work requiring graduate, professional training to the same degree as casework. Perhaps time alone will be the determining factor.

Problem of Supervision

The sharp division between professional and nonprofessional training in group work presents to the group worker a set of problems which generally do not exist for the caseworker. The professionally trained group worker usually finds supervision an important and general part of his work. While there is some opportunity for supervision in casework, as when a worker within an agency directs a student from a graduate school of social work or is assigned the responsibility of offering guidance to the agency staff, the group worker may find that supervision entails a large part of his schedule.

The number of nonprofessional workers in many group work agencies makes the problem of their supervision of no small concern to the professional staff.

The type of supervision in a group work agency also differs from that of casework agencies. In casework agencies the person doing the supervising generally assumes either professionalization on the part of the individual guided (as with professional workers on the staff) or at least interest in securing professional training (as with a graduate student). Of course, the group worker also has occasion to direct already professionalized personnel and students of graduate schools. But the fact that the bulk of the professional group worker's responsibility oftentimes relates to nonprofessional personnel makes for definite differences in the aims and scope of group work supervision which the group work adviser must take into account.

Aims of Supervisor. The group work supervisor, for one thing, seeks to orient the group worker to the agency and to the community. This can be done through private conferences, as in most agencies, or through a lecture series, as in some large agencies. The worker is provided through this orientation with a keener perspective of what the community is like and what the agency is attempting to do in the community. Through this process he also receives understanding about the ways in which he can develop his work with the groups of the agency.

The adviser also seeks to orient the worker to the specific nature of his task in regard to assigned groups. To do this the professional worker should know something of the background of the person who is under his leadership. He will further need to know something of the group members so that he will be able to make the group work process, as previously described, a reality instead of a textbook formula.

The group work supervisor, moreover, must provide opportunity for regular conferences with the workers. These conferences will enable the supervisor to supplement the worker's orientation to the community, the agency, and the groups within the agency. The supervisor will be able to check on progress made by the workers. The conference gives him opportunity to offer assistance with especially difficult group problems which baffle the workers. Greater integration of the work of the agency may be achieved. The conference may also influence leadership attitudes on the part of workers so that they will grow professionally.

An example of a conference between a group worker and his supervisor is provided in the following record:

SUPERVISOR'S RECORD OF CONFERENCE
WITH GROUP LEADER

Agency: N.C. Group: B Date: 2/12/38
Leader: C.D. Supervisor: S.J.L.
Duration of interview: 1 hr.
Following observation: 2/5/38

Write a narrative account of conference with group leader, giving name of group, matters, and individuals discussed; with suggested procedure, development, and outcome.

Supervisor indicated that he was interested in talking a little bit with leader about the meeting that he had observed the previous week. First of all, he asked the leader what she considered her function would be within her group while the Center craft teacher was teaching them to make rings? Leader felt that she might learn a great deal about the members and their interests through informal conversations that would take place while the project was being carried on. In talking about her relationship with the craft teacher, after much thought, the leader felt that it probably would be a good idea to talk to the craft teacher about how the two of them might cooperate; and the leader might be given the opportunity to follow up on interests of the members without interference. During the time that the leader took to arrive at this point in her thinking, she brought up a problem arising in another group of hers. (This is a dramatic group which is made up almost entirely of her club members.)

This problem centered about one of her members who was not able to get along with another girl that did not belong to the B Club. Leader felt that this enmity between the two girls was disrupting the dramatic group. She couldn't quite arrive at any method for handling the situation. She thought that she ought to see these girls in individual conferences, but wondered how she might ask them to see her personally without giving them the impression that anything was wrong. Probably she could do this on the basis of something the girls were doing; but she couldn't figure out just what approach to take, and was left with the idea that she must think this through a little further.

Supervisor then indicated that, in the meeting he had observed, the president of the club seemed to be the motivating force for everything that happened within the group. Leader could not see this until supervisor mentioned the various things that he had observed going on. Leader agreed that the observations were correct; so supervisor asked what ideas the members had about the duties of a president. All the leader's remarks showed that the group's idea probably was that a president was the boss. Supervisor wondered if under such conditions a leader could expect democratic procedure to be carried out?

He also asked what the leader felt her function within the group was? Was the leader supposed to be just the passive observer? Leader was not quite sure. She thought that a group ought to be allowed to do pretty much what it pleased. This made supervisor ask whether there was any necessity for a leader in a group's meetings? Could her group have done exactly the same things that they did in the meeting that was observed, if she hadn't been present? Leader had to admit that they probably could have. What then was the leader's function? Leader mentioned that she seemed to be getting a new idea at the conference; and that the idea was that there were points for her to step into group discussions to see that procedures were facilitated, and that group suggestions were worked through to the group's satisfaction.

Supervisor wondered also why the leader had seen the meeting of her group in an almost entirely different light than the supervisor. Leader mentioned that probably she looked for different things. As conference closed, supervisor wondered whether there was a likelihood that leader was reading into the group's actions those things she wanted to see there? Also, in writing reports, wasn't leader using group work terms too readily and easily? As leader rose to leave the conference, she said rather quietly, "I guess I am a little glib with group work vocabulary."

Use of Records in Interview or Suggestions Regarding Records. Both the leader's and supervisor's reports of meetings were used throughout.

Attitude of Leader During Conference. Leader seemed at ease when she came in, but seemed a little embarrassed as conference progressed.

Supervisor's Evaluation. Leader has a tendency to try to insert new thoughts at points in conference where she doesn't feel herself ready to continue along the lines of conversation where she has to admit poor leadership technique. It does seem that the conference helped the leader toward an entirely new idea of her function within the group. But she is not sure of herself in this direction, and probably will take some time to arrive at a way of handling situations within her group with greater ease. I feel that the leader now realizes that we are aware of her easy use of terms, and of her method of reading her own feelings into situations. This may change her entire outlook on her job.[18]

Record-Taking

Involved to some extent in supervision is the practice of record-taking. Record-taking in group work is less universally practiced and less perfected than in casework; nevertheless it is important, and increasingly so. The group worker, whether professional or nonprofessional, has need of accurate information regarding what he is attempting to do. This need is primarily personal, inasmuch as it relates to the understanding he has of his relations with his groups and

---

[18]Sidney J. Lindenberg, *Supervision in Social Group Work,* Association Press, New York, 1939, pp. 82–84.

the inner dynamics of the group processes he seeks to lead. It is possible for some leaders to maintain objectivity regarding the process in which they are involved without recourse to writing, but the number is small. Most workers find that record-taking increases the objectivity with which they view their work.

The following illustrates the kind of record a group leader would keep of a meeting. The values of the record are largely apparent from the reading of it.

LEADER'S RECORD OF GROUP MEETING

Agency: N.C.　　　　　　Group: B　　　　　　Date: 3/19/38
Leader: C.D.　　　　Time and length of meeting: From 7:15 to 8:45
Activities (list, be specific): Rings, Dancing, and Social
No. enrolled—8; No. present—8; No. absent—1; No. visitors—1

Description of Meeting Place and General Setting. Met in auditorium. Lighting for ring-making poor, but only place we could meet where eating was allowed and where we should be able to dance. Victrola available, piano, enough space; stuffy at first; later, window opened.

Narrative Account. (Include participation of individuals outstanding or difficult—give names of members and adult leaders participating.)

Girls brought potato chips to eat as had been agreed—(to bring anything they wanted instead of their dues). Miss F, a Center staff member, explained situation about cooking and gym facilities. Leader explained further to lessen the group's feeling of discrimination about use of such facilities. Agreed before Miss F left that they would use the gym next week, and the dining room the following week. No other direct planning, although a few remarks were made during the meeting about doing acrobatics and wearing gym suits the following week. Also, one of the girls asked later about what they would make in the dining room, and another answered that they would keep the same arrangement as had been made in their original plans for cooking.

Miss A, the Center crafts teacher, had the girls begin work on rings immediately; continued until 8. Everyone worked at the same time—interested. Some difficulty about tools, but settled, and they exchanged them back and forth easily. New girl visitor had been introduced—brought in by Fay. Knows Fay and Matilda from school; some of the others also. Desultory conversation going on about clothes; leader asking about new visitor, talking with her, looking at other girls' rings, helping Rose. References to boys kept cropping out. Also much discussion about feats of new girl in the way of acrobatics.

Frances, the president, called meeting, while working, to save time. Leader asked why have meeting? General chorus of, "In case somebody wants to say something." Rush through, since everything had already been settled. Frances had been exercising authority to grant permission to other members to go out for drinks. Leader took it away a few times by giving girls permission—(not too humiliatingly for Frances). Several times during this period Matilda had questioned president's authority—"Who are you?"—when Frances had said or done something too authoritatively.

At 8 p.m. Frances called a halt on the rings. Leader had requested this. Frances heard and took initiative. Rings collected and group went on smoothly to dancing. Leader operated victrola. Several of the girls were excellent dancers—Frieda, Fay, Frances especially. Shirley unexpectedly good. Matilda good, posture poor. Rose E. not so popular, too stiff. Girls did not want to dance with her. Leader did. Suggested to her that she loosen up and then she danced a few times, still hurt a bit, however, because other girls did not want to dance with her. Soon tired of the same records, tried others, tried piano, back again to dancing, then watched new girl while she tap danced. Led to asking her to do it for group. Then everybody did something.

Great trouble getting started. No one would go first. Frances seized control and called on people. Perhaps leader should have asked someone else to do it. Frances obviously likes power and wants to be able to be authoritative as much as possible. Shirley and Frances did a dance together. Helen did her tap dancing. Called on leader, who tried to introduce group singing—something new. Then Helen did another dance, and then six girls danced together. Rose in this—a folk dance they had all learned in a dancing class at the Center. Leader tried a Virginia Reel, but the girls did not want to do it. No one seemed to have any other ideas, so the girls dispersed, some to show Helen, the new girl, around the Center.

Evaluation. Meeting enjoyed by girls because of appeals of food and ballroom dancing—obviously interested both. Shirley able to participate successfully. Satisfaction because all able to participate successfully. Connected by one girl to party—"Girls should learn to dance for anniversary." Rose enjoys participating. Doing folk dance and being in the limelight helped her—helped that feeling of insufficiency she had felt about ballroom dancing.

Helen is the first non-Jewish girl to be brought into the group. No feeling of estrangement. Obviously brought in and accepted for her accomplishments. Girls look up to her. (Healthy attitude to admire her?) Value in breaking down cliquishness, and lines of demarcation. Informal programming; breakdown of attitude about facilities and need for planning ahead brought home.

Program Ideas and Suggestions Growing Out of the Above. The ballroom dancing seems a vital point. Work in again. Really teach, use better music. Use social graces.

Leader should learn music to be able to play it right away. Also, work in group singing whenever possible.

Leader had heard how orderly they were the week before when she was absent. Asked why. Girls said because they were responsible for themselves, better attitude and development. Obviously they like the feeling. Could be utilized to good advantage in developing their ability to get along and manage a group.

Try another sort of folk dance with them some time—one which would appeal. The more who danced and thought they were doing well, the more there would be who enjoyed it and would be willing to go on.[19]

Records are also important to the agency which sponsors the worker. The agency, through the supervisor, has a means of knowing what is going on if there is a record. By aiding the worker through guidance, it can improve its own program. In some agencies the records are regularly used in staff conferences to provide a basis for staff discussion and learning. The value of records to group work clients is indirect but nonetheless real.

American Association of Group Workers

The technical problems of increasing the quality and effectiveness of social group work do not rest upon the individual group worker or agency alone. They are also the responsibility of the American Association of Group Workers. This organization is designed "to promote association among education, recreation, and group workers, to raise the standards of competence among practitioners, to encourage continued study of the basic body of knowledge and skills essential to professional practice, to improve personnel practices (including professional education), to encourage research, and to provide individual and corporate action on matters affecting the field of practice." There are at present over 2,000 members of the Association and about 20 local chapters. The Association publishes *The Group: In Education, Recreation, Social Work,* bimonthly October through May; and *Proceedings,* annually.

SELECTED READINGS ON GROUP WORK

American Association of Group Workers, *Proceedings,* New York, annually.

Baxter, Bernice, and Cassidy, Rosalind F., *Group Experience: The Democratic Way,* Harper, New York, 1943.

Blumenthal, Louis H., *Group Work in Camping,* Association Press, New York, 1937.

Bowman, LeRoy, *How to Lead Discussion: A Guide for the Use of Group Leaders,* Woman's Press, New York, 1934.

Busch, Henry M., *Leadership in Group Work,* Association Press, New York, 1934.

[19]*Ibid.,* pp. 85–88.

Carr, Lowell J.; Valentine, Mildred H.; and Levy, Marshall H., *Integrating the Camp, the Community, and Social Work*, Association Press, New York, 1939.

Collins, Alice H., *Methods in Group Work: Learning from Case Work Experience*, Woman's Press, New York, 1938.

Coyle, Grace L., *Group Experience and Democratic Values*, Woman's Press, New York, 1948.

——, *Social Process in Organized Groups*, Richard R. Smith, New York, 1930.

——, editor, *Studies in Group Behavior*, Harper, New York, 1937.

Crow, Lester D., and Crow, Alice V., *Our Teen-Age Boys and Girls*, McGraw-Hill, New York, 1945.

Du Vall, Everett W., *Personality and Social Group Work: The Individual Approach*, Association Press, New York, 1943.

Hall, Frances A., *Statistical Measurement in Group Work*, United States Children's Bureau, publication number 248, Washington, D.C., 1939.

Hawkins, Gaynell, *Educational Experiments in Social Settlements: Studies in the Social Significance of Adult Education in the United States*, American Association for Adult Education, New York, 1937.

Hendry, Charles E., *Decade of Group Work*, Association Press, New York, 1947.

Hjelte, George, *The Administration of Public Recreation*, Macmillan, New York, 1940.

Jennings, Helen H., *Leadership and Isolation: A Study of Personality in Interpersonal Relations*, Longmans, New York, 1943.

Jones, Anna M., *Leisure Time Education: A Handbook of Creative Activities for Teachers and Group Leaders*, Harper, New York, 1946.

Kellerman, Henry J., *Personal Standards in Social Group Work and Recreation Agencies*, Welfare Council of New York City, New York, 1944.

Kennedy, Albert J., and others, *Social Settlements in New York City: Their Activities, Policies, and Administration*, New York City, Welfare Council Research Bureau Studies, number 2, Columbia University Press, New York, 1935.

Klapman, Jacob W., *Group Psychotherapy: Theory and Practice*, Grune, New York, 1946.

Leigh, Robert D., *Group Leadership: With Modern Rules of Procedure*, Norton, New York, 1936.

Lieberman, Joshua, editor, *New Trends in Group Work*, National Association for the Study of Group Work (now American Association of Group Workers), Association Press, New York, 1938.

Lindenberg, Sidney, *Supervision in Social Group Work*, Association Press, New York, 1939.

Lippitt, Ronald, *An Experimental Study of Authoritarian and Democratic Group Atmospheres*, Studies in Child Welfare, University of Iowa Press, Iowa City, 1940.

MacIver, Robert M., editor, *Group Relations and Group Antagonisms: A Series of Addresses and Discussions,* Harper, New York, 1944.

McBurney, J. H., and Hance, K. G., *The Principles and Methods of Discussion,* Harper, New York, 1939.

Moreno, Jacob, *Who Shall Survive?: A New Approach to the Problem of Human Interrelations,* Nervous and Mental Disease Publishing Company, Washington, D.C., 1934.

Pendry, Elizabeth R., and Hartshorne, Hugh, *Organizations for Youth: Leisure Time and Character Building Procedures,* McGraw-Hill, New York, 1935.

Price, Louise, *Creative Group Work on the Campus: A Developmental Study of Certain Aspects of Student Life,* Bureau of Publications, Teachers College, Contributions to Education, number 830, Columbia University Press, New York, 1941.

Simkhovich, Mary K., *Neighborhood: My Story of Greenwich House,* Norton, New York, 1938.

Slavson, Samuel R., *An Introduction to Group Therapy,* Commonwealth Fund, New York, 1943.

———, *Character Education in a Democracy,* Association Press, New York, 1939.

———, *Creative Group Education,* Association Press, New York, 1937.

———, *Recreation and the Total Personality,* Association Press, New York, 1946.

Sullivan, Dorothea F., editor, *The Practice of Group Work,* American Association for the Study of Group Work (now American Association of Group Workers), Association Press, New York, 1941.

Tead, Ordway, *The Art of Leadership,* Whittlesey House, New York, 1935.

Trecker, Harleigh B., *Group Process in Administration,* Woman's Press, New York, 1946.

———, *Social Group Work: Principles and Practice,* Woman's Press, New York, 1948.

Wald, Lillian D., *House on Henry Street,* Holt, New York, 1915.

———, *Windows on Henry Street,* Little, Brown, Boston, 1934.

Wilson, Gertrude, *Group Work and Case Work: Their Relationship and Practice,* Family Welfare Association of America (now Family Service Association of America), New York, 1941.

Woods, Robert A., and Kennedy, Albert J., *The Settlement Horizon: A National Estimate,* Russell Sage Foundation, New York, 1922.

14

Community Organization

Not all of the purposes of social work can be carried out simply by working with individuals and groups. At some points social workers must work with the interrelationships of groups. When they do seek to effect relationships between two or more groups, they are engaging essentially in community organization.

Community organization, as will be explained, is a complicated structure and process. In order to get some understanding of it, however, the following story of Los Angeles' answer to the 1943 zoot suit riots is told. It does not relate the whole nature of community organization, but it does graphically portray a number of its elements:

On the morning of June 9, 1943, the front pages of newspapers all over the country carried stories of a crisis in Los Angeles. Tales of clashes and riots between servicemen, Latin-American and Negro youths, lurid accounts of "zoot suit" gangs made dramatic reading. The people of Los Angeles were themselves deeply shocked and concerned.

Fortunately, however, the leaders of the community retained their perspective. They knew that the areas in which the riots occurred were in the section of the city least served by youth agencies. They realized that here were to be found the poorest housing, the lowest income levels, the heaviest concentration of minority racial groups. They appreciated that here was no situation to be dealt with by mere emergency action, but one which called for a constructive antidote to the disintegrating factors producing the crisis. So the Los Angeles Youth Project came into being.

Today, Los Angeles can point to two results. In the area itself, roughly covering a quarter of the city, 25,000 children and youths are enrolled in 1,113 organized and supervised groups. Three years ago, only 8,000 were so enrolled. Moreover, the project's capacity to enlist the participation of long neglected cultural groups is evidenced by the fact that their proportion among these 25,000 members now almost exactly corresponds to their proportion in the total population of the area. The contrary was the case three years ago. Group programs have been enriched in variety and content. There has been a significant increase in the enrollment of older teenage youth, a group always difficult to reach and retain. For the first time, people in this area of great need are receiving intelligent and concentrated attention, and are responding to it.

But the Youth Project has also been a practical experiment in the co-ordination of youth services. Here, too, results have been achieved which have fundamental, long-range implications. Eleven agencies are cooperating in the program—the All Nations Foundation, Boy Scouts of America, Camp Fire Girls, Catholic Youth Project, Church Welfare Bureau, Girl Scouts, International Institute, Jewish Centers Association, Woodcraft Rangers, Y.M.C.A., and Y.W.C.A.

A total of over three quarters of a million dollars has been spent under their auspices: $234,000, allocated by the community chest in 1943; $249,-000, in 1944; and $290,000, in 1945. Most of this money has been spent for trained personnel—none of it for capital expense. Sixty professional men and women are working in the area, who would not be there otherwise. The recent community recreation survey conducted by Roy Sorenson and a staff of experts recommended that coordinating procedures similar to those worked out by the project be extended to all areas of the city. (See *Survey Midmonthly*, February, 1946.)

Dynamic Purposefulness. For many years, communities, councils of social agencies, and group work leaders have talked about the need for coordinating youth service. In Los Angeles this talk is being translated into action. The foundations have been laid in philosophy, structure, and practice. We think we have found at least some of the answers to that perennial and perplexing community organization question: "How do we effect coordination?" It is to that phase of the Los Angeles experiment that this article primarily is directed.

Perhaps the crisis of 1943 made it easier to launch the project with a clear-cut purpose than might otherwise have been the case. But the fact that from the very outset everyone has understood that it is a *deliberate attempt to extend youth service into an area of greatest need* is the touchstone which has opened up the opportunities for cooperative practice. There were no confusing generalities about this purpose. The area was there where one could see it, the needs were there for people to examine; "expansion" has real, practical meaning to group work agencies. Nor was there any confusion about the triple breakdown of this over-all purpose, which was articulated early by the project:

1. To meet the normal needs of normal youth for group work and recreational activity;

2. To encourage those who are least apt to join a group with a traditional program to participate in some type of supervised activity;

3. To work directly and constructively with groups of delinquent youth.

Just as important as this clear statement of purpose, was its wholehearted acceptance by all eleven participating agencies. For two decades, Los Angeles had been slow to increase funds for group work services. The wartime experience of U.S.O., beginning in 1941, had demonstrated the practicability of a united approach. These agencies wanted to make and carry out the plan *together*. From the start, they have regarded it as an experiment in joint planning, joint program making, joint operation. They have been searching *for the best way* to extend their common group work services.

The seriousness of the situation, the evidence of common purpose among the agencies, and the vision of chest leadership—all helped to bring about the allocation of chest funds which made the project possible. Without this investment of money, obviously little could have been accomplished.

Structure. Although the project is under the general sponsorship of the youth services division of the Welfare Council of Metropolitan Los Angeles, it has a board of directors of its own, vested with operational responsibility. This board is composed of both lay and professional representation from the participating public and private agencies. Under it are three important working committees: a committee on programs; a committee on program analysis; and a delinquency committee.

The program committee is made up of executives, supervisors, and other workers from the cooperating agencies. They study the needs of the area and recommend the programs to be undertaken. The seminar quality of committee meetings has been an important by-product. Members have learned from each other, developed personal working relationships, and successfully created an atmosphere conducive to constructive change. Thus the group process itself has contributed directly to the development of the project's leadership.

The committee on program analysis and evaluation works closely with the program committee in conducting a continuous evaluation of operations.

The work of the delinquency committee would make a fascinating story in itself. Under its guidance is a special service unit charged with the task of working with difficult neighborhood gangs which the agencies are unable to reach through their regular approaches.

The coordinating staff consists of a director, who also serves as the director of the youth services division of the Welfare Council, two assistant directors, and four full-time and one half-time area coordinators. The professional group leaders, working in the area, serve as members of the staffs of the participating agencies.

The Coordinators' Key Role. The experience of three years has demonstrated that the community organization skill of the coordinators is the key to successful coordination. It has become increasingly apparent that the *process* by which the coordinator helps agencies work together is more important than the structure within which they work.

The need for a staff skilled in community organization processes was not recognized at first. The early planning group thought that the project director could do the necessary organizing. But the size of the project alone, including, as it does, ten substantial areas, soon made it apparent that practically he could not. And as experience developed, it became clear that cooperation within the area does not just happen, it comes only as the will of the agencies is combined with the professional skill of the coordinator.

There is perhaps no better evidence of the project's experimental emphasis on the development of these skills and processes than the negative fact that no one has yet produced the usual manual "How to Organize a Community in Six Easy Meetings." Nor has the project prescribed "A Typical Type of Organization for the Area." But more and more, experience is enabling us to identify at least some of the crucial points at which the coordinator must exercise his skill.

He must in the first instance help bring *understanding* of the area to the people who are planning for and working in the different communities. Within its ten geographic divisions can be found vivid contrasts and varying needs. These communities differ just as individuals and groups differ. Even within these subdivisions, which are relatively large, neighborhoods present distinctive patterns. The approach to each must be *individualized*.

The cooperative relationship between the project and the research department of the Welfare Council makes it possible for the coordinator to secure basic social data about the communities to which they have been assigned. These include population characteristics; shifts and changes; national and racial make-up; age groupings; facts about housing; education; employment.

Essential knowledge about other factors in the areas and neighborhoods can come only as a result of day-to-day working experience. But its systematic collection and analysis is no less important. Who are the leaders in whom people have confidence? How much experience have organizations had in working together? Does the community have a clear conception of its needs and potentialities?

Not only must the coordinator help the people planning for and working in the area to gain an understanding of its characteristics, he must also help them gain acceptance from the community. Naturally, this means that he himself must be accepted. He must understand his own feelings about the community and the people in it. He must meet them on their own ground, in terms of their own attitudes and interests. He must participate in their affairs. His contacts must be natural, easy, grounded in personal understanding, and without prejudice. As he establishes his own identity with the community, he can help the professional leaders gain a similar identity.

The coordinators have discovered another principle of successful community organization. They must take the community where it is and begin by helping its leaders produce what *they* want. One coordinator who had worked in several different areas remarked that the biggest thing she had learned was that these communities were at different stages in their development. Instead of bringing to them an already prescribed program, the thing to do was to help a local community committee locate its own needs, arrive at the goals and objectives which it recognized as desirable, and make practical plans to reach them. Thus the process and habit of working together becomes established and as time goes on, larger goals and broader objectives can be naturally evolved.

Finally, underlying all the skills and processes which the coordinators have developed is the fact that they must work with people. A study of their records shows that their essential task has been to change the attitude of the people of the community toward themselves, to influence their behavior toward cooperative and constructive action. Their work with leaders and key individuals, their handling of the dynamics of personal and group relationship, is the key which unlocks the solution of problems and the practicalities of program making.

Underpinning Philosophy. We have come to the conclusion, however, that the clear statement of purpose, the money investment by the community chest, and the expert skills of the coordinators could not have guaranteed success for the project, of and by themselves. Equally essential has been the philosophy of approach, buttressing these organizational and administrative attributes. We can articulate, at least tentatively, four of its component parts.

The first stems from the fact that the agencies accepted the desirability of pooling their resources. That meant that in this particular area they determined to compete no longer for the establishment of youth groups under their own auspices. They gave up competition for money, resources, and leadership. Instead, they decided to meet with local community representation, collect facts, study needs, and *together* decide which agency was best suited to do what and where. As a basis for judging the over-all success of the project, they accepted a new criterion—"How well are needs being met?"—in place of the old one—"How much work is my agency doing?"

Second, every effort has been made to emphasize and encourage the grass roots characteristics of the area organization and program. Over-all planning and guidance inevitably must come from "Downtown," but the people in the area have been given every opportunity to assume direct responsibility for specific planning and execution. As a result, the organization structure and the program in each district have been kept flexible and indigenous to it. Progress has been measured in terms of community growth rather than in patterns artificially conceived apart from community reality.

Third, and following logically, the whole approach has been positive rather than negative. That is, we have not started out by asking, "What's *wrong* with this community?" Instead we have asked: "What's *right* with it? What does it need? On what can we build to make it possible to meet these needs?"

Fourth, we have realistically faced the fact that planning and budget making must be an integrated, continuous, and orderly process. The people responsible for inaugurating and planning the program also have accepted the responsibility for allocating funds to the several agencies and the various districts. The community chest has shown its confidence in the project by delegating this responsibility within the over-all allocation which it makes. The agencies working together have demonstrated their competence to discharge it. Plans are not made without regard to money, and money is not spent without relation to planning.

The Project at Work. Perhaps an account of what happened in connection with a new area recently added to the project will serve to illustrate the working methods which have resulted from this combination of community organization skill and underlying philosophy. This area is in the southwestern part of the central section of Los Angeles. It has long been underserved, and its rapidly increasing population includes a concentration of minority groups.

The initiative came from the area itself, when a representative group of citizens asked the project board to extend its work to their community.

The board assigned a coordinator to study the request and to be generally responsible for guiding the planning and negotiations which might ensue. Her first step was to assemble information for use by the project board in deciding whether or not to extend its service to the area. The research department of the Welfare Council put together facts and findings from the general community recreation survey and from other sources, which gave a composite picture of the characteristics of the area and the needs which the project would be called upon to meet. The coordinators then met with representative people in the area, to get a first-hand view of their concept of its needs, possible solutions, and their capacity to assume responsibility.

On the basis of this assembled evidence, the board voted affirmatively to add the area to its jurisdiction.

The next step was a joint meeting of community representatives and representatives from the agencies, called by the board, and planned and organized with the assistance of the coordinator. As a result, this group organized itself into a planning committee for the whole area.

In a successful series of meetings, this committee, assisted by the coordinator, established the boundaries for the program, explored needs, and agreed on a specific program to meet them.

The practical implementation of the program then became a matter for the agencies immediately involved. Staff representatives from those already carrying on some work in the area, were appointed to a committee charged with working out details.

The project assigned several new workers to these agencies. The committee decided that these should work under the supervision of one agency and that the new programs should be conducted as joint programs under this single supervisor.

After this administrative setup had been perfected and the new workers were on the job, two committees made up of young people from the schools, churches, and youth organizations of the area were appointed to help carry out the plan.

Thus the Los Angeles Youth Project has been and continues to be a daring departure from the traditional. But as a result, our youth services are becoming coordinated.[1]

The story of the Los Angeles Youth Project indicates how various groups in the community can work together for the welfare of the community. While this process can include many more groups than those interested in social welfare, it can be clearly seen among social welfare groups.

INTERRELATIONSHIPS

Casework is concerned with the activities of individuals. Group work pertains to group activities. Community organization is concerned with the activities of communities. But casework is not related to all individuals, and neither is group work interested in all groups. Community organization, likewise, from the point of view of the social worker, is not responsible for all of the functions of a community. To make community organization, in its social work sense, coexistent with the total operations of communities would make community organization not simply a branch of social work activities, but a complete rationale of community life.

There is a sense in which the term *community organization* may legitimately be used to designate the total activities of a community. After all, communities do have particular organizational structures. But this connotation is seldom used by social workers because it includes phases of community life which lie outside the scope of social work, no matter how interesting these may be to the workers as individuals. Similarly, social workers cannot be held professionally responsible for the total activities of communities, for such is the rightful function of government and other agencies or organizations. Community organization, then, is not a substitute for government; it is not a "secondary government" hiding in the shadows of primary and genuine government. Its place is less pretentious than that.

[1] Harleigh B. Trecker, "Pioneering in Coordination," *Survey Midmonthly,* volume 83, number 1, January, 1947, pp. 15–17.

To say specifically what is the nature of community organization is a task which no one to the present has been able to accomplish to the satisfaction of all others. To define community organization as "a process whereby community resources are organized to meet community needs" probably says too little about the salient features of the definition: resources, needs, process. But a better way of creating insight regarding the character of community organization is that of listing some of the responsibilities which community organizers commonly accept as rightfully being theirs. Such a list would include the following:

1. To enable communities to increase their well-being through democratic procedures.
2. To understand the factual basis of community life on which social welfare programs can be based and improved.
3. To help organize those programs in the community by which social welfare goals may be more readily achieved.
4. To coordinate existing social work services in ways that will make them even more effective.
5. To plan for the best possible use and development of community facilities in social welfare.
6. To educate the community, through the various accepted publicity channels, as to the conditions and possibilities of successful community living.
7. To assist in the raising of money for the support and extension of existing social services.

These responsibilities of the community organizer may not be contained in the activities of any one organizer or organization, but they are a summary of the aims of a complex of persons and agencies. Possibly, a few other responsibilities could be added to the list, but those provided are representative enough.

While the three approaches to human need outlined in this book (casework, group work, and community organization) are sometimes viewed as being three separate instruments of community improvement, at their best they are not so separate and distinct as some would wish to make them. Actually, they are quite coordinate. Each needs the others. None can say, in St. Paul's phrase, "I have no need of thee." The casework, the group work, and the community organization agency each depends to a considerable degree upon the others. To the extent to which the interrelations of these three types of organizations within a community are complete and mature, a considerable part of the function of community organization is complete and mature. Where the various specialties, in the forms of agencies, are separate and relatively independent, the task of the community organizer has just begun. Thus to say that community organization is primarily tied to casework and group work, for the purposes of its social work definition, is to indicate a condition which it of necessity must both possess and preserve.

COMMUNITY ORGANIZATION AND
SOCIAL WORK ADMINISTRATION

From this discussion the impression may be formed immediately that community organization, in large part, is allied to if not identical with social work administration. Of course, there is from the common-sense point of view notable overlapping between community organization and social work administration. To a considerable extent the activities of the community organizer seem to be administrative functions, and from a broad point of view they are. But there are distinctions which can be drawn between the two. These are relative and typologic, and should not be taken as explaining any concrete activity either of a community organizer or of an administrator.

Difference in Interests

The differences between the two rest largely upon the fact that the interests of the administrator belong basically to the internal operations of a particular social work agency, while the community organizer is fundamentally interested in the interrelationships between social work structures. Thus, by way of example, an executive who wishes to increase the efficiency of a social work agency by rearranging its consultation practices is primarily an administrator. The executive who arranges for regular conferences between the medical social work staff of a hospital and the hospital's staff of physicians is primarily an administrator. The executive who decides in conjunction with his social work staff that his agency should not accept clients who have problems connected with tuberculosis, because there are community facilities elsewhere which are adequate for the care of such persons, is primarily an administrator.

On the other hand the head of a child guidance clinic, for example, who arranges with the school board to have school playgrounds available in the summer. time is primarily a community organizer. An individual who is hired for the purpose of aiding an agency in its public relations program (sending news items to the local papers, raising money through mailings) is primarily a community organizer. A person who is on call to handle the problems of social work agencies (as, for example, a field worker of the Family Service Association of America) is primarily a community organizer.

Relationships

To understand the relationships which may exist between administration and community organization one must take into account the concept of "roles" as used in sociology. This concept indicates that one individual at different times may be both an administrator and a community organizer. Sometimes his actions may be more of an administrative character; at other times they may be directed more toward community organization. There are, however, some individuals in social work who regularly work more in one role than in the other.

The basic distinction between community organization and administration in social work is, then, that devotion to activities which relate to the community, however narrow or broad in scope, fundamentally characterizes the community organizer. The social work administrator in his administrative role is usually concerned with a social work situation, the organizational structure of which pertains to a particular agency.

New Stress on Administration

The administration of social work agencies is an undeveloped field, but one which is exceedingly important. Social workers in casework and group work have been so concerned with direct service to individuals and groups that oftentimes they have neglected the weightier issues of the organization and operation of their agencies. In recent years, however, there have been some signs that administration is receiving increased attention. In 1946, for example, for the first time in the seventy-two-year history of the National Conference of Social Work there was a section on administration. A number of the graduate schools of social work are encouraging the study of administration by offering courses on the subject and providing concrete experience in various aspects of such work. A great deal needs to be done, however, before social work administration becomes mature.

In one listing of the ingredients of administration for social work agencies the following tasks are assigned:[2]

1. The determination and clarification of objectives, functions, and policies.

[2]Arthur Dunham, "Administration of Social Agencies," *Social Work Year-book, 1947: A Description of Organized Activities in Social Work and in Related Fields,* ninth issue, Russell H. Kurtz, editor, Russell Sage Foundation, New York, 1947, pp. 15–16.

2. The mobilization and maintenance of resources—personal, financial, material, even psychological—to the end that the agency may carry out its purposes and fulfill its functions effectively.
3. The development of program.
4. Organization and coordination.
5. Leadership, direction, and supervision.
6. Planning, standardization, and evaluation.
7. Recording, accounting, and related activities.
8. Processing, or routine procedures.
9. Public relations.

It may be noted that the views previously presented might modify at least the ninth task for social work administration as outlined here.

THE MEANING OF THE COMMUNITY

It is difficult to say what is meant by the *community* as the term is used by the community organizer. The entity to which he refers is not always clear in his mind or in the minds of others. The sociologist, on the other hand, usually possesses a more definite conception. He commonly refers to the community as being a geographic area in which people carry on the major human functions: in which families reside, children are sent to school, business is transacted, religious life is centered, local problems are expressed through local government, and a spirit of neighborliness is maintained. (This conception must be further elaborated and conditioned when applied to the more complex centers of modern living, such as large cities, in which communities in a sociological sense are not simple and are not "naturally" formed.)

Based on Religious Faith

The community to which the community organizer refers in his work is at times the community of the sociologist. But he has also a number of other meanings for the community. For example, he may think of the community as being composed of persons who share a particular religious faith. So it is assumed by some community organizers that they are working with a community when the only significant binding tie (and that may be weak at times for many within the so-called community) is that of religion. In this vein, community organizers often speak of "the Jewish community" even though the body of Jews is scattered throughout the whole country, has no general agreement on any particular point, not even religion, and even though the membership may not always recognize themselves as belonging to such a community. This practice is commonplace among the various religious groups.

The community organizer may work with a special group, believing it represents a community, without invalidating the community organization process. Such practice only limits the scope of the process. Since sectarian services comprise a notable portion of the total social work services in the country, and since those working with such sectarian groups consider themselves community organizers, at least in certain of their activities, the use of the term *community organization* on such a basis becomes simply a description of fact.

Considered as Special Groups

Community organizers also refer to other special interest groups as being communities. A council of child-caring agencies may seek to develop understanding of a particular program relating mainly to children. Its "community" consists of those persons who are definitely interested in such programs. These persons may live near the headquarters of the council; they may live near the units involved, or they may not. They may never have visited a child-caring agency. They may have no more than a philanthropic or prestige interest in identifying themselves with the program. On all other points of significant life contact they may be either positive, neutral, or ill-disposed. And yet, whatever the circumstances, if the group declares and maintains an interest in the program of the council it is often referred to as a community by community organizers. Usually, in reference to the particular agency, such a group of persons is "our community" or "our supporting community."

This way of speaking of communities possesses more "freewheeling" in that it terms a community as being any interested public, whether there are definite geographic limits or not. Put another way, the community for some community organizers is any group which can answer the question, "Who will be interested in this particular social welfare problem?" Thus there may be as many communities as there are problems of a community nature. Accordingly, in one instance the community may be a neighborhood, in another it may be the nation. At times the community becomes a political entity (especially where political action is sought). In another moment it may be a religious entity, as when a denomination seeks financial support for its child-caring institutions. The possibilities are many.

It may be, as one worker has suggested, that the exact meaning of community is unimportant except for working purposes since "it can be defined and redefined as new projects are undertaken." This might be viewed as too hopeless an attitude, however, when compared to the accomplishments in definition of other fields and especially in view of the basic importance of the meaning of community to community organization.

TERMINOLOGY

Use of Term Community

Not only is the word *community* somewhat confused in its usage by community organizers, but other terms also fall short of the desired exactness. Perhaps this condition is to be expected in a field of activity which is relatively so new in its scientific aspects. For, although community organization is older than social work itself, it has been only recently that community organizers have sought to clarify exactly what they are seeking to do.

The use of the term *community organization* is a further example of the difficulties which the logician finds with the terms in the field. Inasmuch as the word *community* varies in connotation, its serviceableness in the title for the activities of social workers as they relate to the community may be questioned. To some the term might well be dropped and another used. Just which term might be substituted is not yet clear. Many feel that the word *social* might improve the title since it is broader and more in keeping with the usage which community organizers generally give to *community*. The word *social*, on the other hand, is vague and seems to suggest an interest on the part of the community organizer in broader areas of community life than those of a social welfare nature. The term *social*, however, would bring community organization in line with casework and group work since they very often are called social casework and social group work.

Meaning of Organization

Organization as a word linked with *community* also raises certain questions. It seems at first to suggest that some specific community is actively being organized. *Organization* further suggests that the community organizer is a person who works on instead of with the community. But the community organizer does not use the community as an instrument for the fulfillment of his own objectives; he seeks to serve the community in the achievement of its aims. From another angle, the word *organization* seems to refer to a stated condition of things existing within the community—an expression of the status quo arrangements. This interpretation would also be deemed inadequate by many community organizers because they think of community organization as a process more than as a definite and prescribed social structure. In this regard, *planning* has been suggested a number of times to replace *organization,* but it has failed of general acceptance probably because it describes only a part of the community organizer's function.

Other Terms

The following terms have been used in place of community organization, some with more success than others: social welfare planning, community organization work, social welfare organization, social organization work, social engineering, social community work, community work, community organization for social work, intergroup work, social planning, welfare organization work. Since the securing of a better term for community organization is not a matter which can be decreed by any individual scholar or any group of authorities meeting in plenary session, the older and more familiar term of *community organization* still is popularly used today and probably will be for some time.

We do not need here to settle the problem of terminology, however, as ultimately it concerns chiefly those who are vitally and deeply involved with the practice of community organization. In the field itself, there are weightier problems and contributions than that of terminology.

Professional Development

Many of the problems connected with the theory and practice of community organization will probably be solved by the Association for the Study of Community Organization, formed in 1946. The Association, open to membership both from individuals and organizations, states its purposes as follows: "To increase understanding and improve professional practice of community organization for social welfare." It acts as a clearinghouse for relevant projects, studies, and activities. The development of a professional literature is a special interest. It is hoped that a number of local discussion groups will spring up to assist the Association with some of the problems on the subject.

THE STRUCTURE OF COMMUNITY ORGANIZATION

The more recent opinion in the social work field considers community organization both as a social structure and as a social process. In other words there are organizational forms which community organization itself takes within communities and there are processual elements which operate in some cases without regard to organizational forms. Previously, in speaking of the differences between social work administration and community organization, we have said that the executive of an agency may be both an administrator and a community organizer. Such an example suggests community organization as a social process because it shows that such activities can be carried on without precise reference to a particular agency. But there are in existence agencies which have community organization as their sole business, and this fact suggests that community organization is a social structure. A council of social agencies would be an example.

The distinction between structure and process, however, does not solve all problems in regard to the nature of community organization. For example, a group of social workers reporting to the National Conference of Social Work in 1939 pointed out that there is difficulty in defining the function of certain workers within agencies which have community organization as their chief purpose. Are statisticians, secretaries, copy writers, janitors, and others who work in community organization agencies, actually community organizers by reason of such employment? While some may be able to deny that some of these workers are community organizers, it may be difficult for them to establish a practical and realistic criterion for judgment. The same question obviously could be asked of workers within casework and group work agencies in relation to the primary functions of these two specialties.

The structure of community organization cannot, therefore, be determined with ease. There are many ramifications and complexities which baffle clear analysis. But in the main it is possible to describe some of the organizations which partake in the community organization process. These are of six types: individual agencies, neighborhood councils, supraneighborhood councils, state and regional councils, national organizations, and international cooperation in social welfare.

Individual Agencies

Each individual casework and group work agency to some extent participates in community organization. While the primary function of a particular agency may be that of casework, it is usually difficult for a casework agency to fulfill its aims without some degree of community interaction. The degree to which a casework agency comes in contact with the community signifies its practice of community organization. The community organization practiced may be poor or well done, but it is essentially community organization. Likewise, for a group work agency. In fact, quantitatively, the bulk of community organization for social work in America is done by caseworkers and group workers, yet not under the heading of community organization.

Fund-Raising. Local agencies, for example, are regularly perplexed by the problems of fund-raising. This is especially true for those privately financed. In a small private agency the task of obtaining sufficient money for its operation may fall to the executive. When it does, the executive actually becomes a community organizer by the definition employed in this chapter. But in a large agency the work of securing funds is too much for any one individual. The agency may use some of its workers for campaigning, but it may also hire a professional money-raiser to organize and direct the campaign. On this account many of the larger agencies in the country require the services of a staff of professional workers whose chief business is that of meeting the budget. Whether the local agency uses its own executive or another specifically trained to the job, community organization is being practiced.

Education. Usually, fund-raising is conducted along with an educational campaign. Today, agencies believe that it is not enough simply to ask people for their money. It is necessary also to tell them why their money is needed and what it will do. It may be possible in connection with fund-raising to accomplish other goals than these, but these probably are the principal ones. A publicity program can also be utilized by a local agency even when it is not seeking money. Thus a public relations person on an agency staff may be responsible for a variety of community organization tasks of a publicity nature. He may organize a group of interested citizens in the community for regular meetings to inform them of the work of the agency, and, in turn, to inform the agency of community needs. Such a group might include: school people, ministers, allied social workers, public officials, physicians, nurses, representatives of business, and others who would be of importance for this type of program.

Community Relations. An example of the way in which a composite local group can help an agency and a community is provided in the experience of the St. Louis Family and Children's Service:

> After a district committee in the Southwest District office of the St. Louis Family and Children's Service had been active for six years, a rather thorough review was made of its organization and function. This study revealed that although its purpose did not change from year to year, there were different emphases, depending on the particular interest of members of the group and specific district needs. Early in its history, the committee had stated its purpose as follows:
>
> *1. To participate in the definition of problems and the exploration and mobilization of resources to meet the needs on a local basis.*
>
> *2. To interest itself in the fuller use of resources already existing and to help in developing an understanding within the community of these resources.*

3. To channel interest in community planning in such a way that there will be a minimum of overlapping of effort.

4. To share knowledge of the community and its problems and resources so as to bring about a more general understanding of some of these same factors.

The committee membership included staff members and individuals living or working in the district. New members were chosen by the District Committee because of their interest in the community and because they would contribute to the thinking of the group. The total membership ranged from twelve to eighteen people and included, among others, school principals, ministers, businessmen, a dentist, and a university professor. In all, twelve staff members and sixteen nonstaff people served on the committee. The thirty-one regular meetings held during the six-year period showed remarkably consistent attendance. In addition to regular meetings, some members of the group also worked on special committees.

A wide range of topics was discussed. Some of these led to committee projects that drew others in the community into participation. Discussion of topics such as the effect upon family life of poor housing, serious health problems, the absence of the father from the home, working mothers, and some of the juvenile delinquency and child behavior problems growing out of these stimulated a keen desire to "do something" about these conditions.

Problems and questions for discussion came from the committee members and their own knowledge of these matters was first pooled. This was supplemented by material from available written reports, plus data from other people in the community. Material was summarized and evaluated by the committee to define the problem more clearly and to outline a plan of approach to modify it. The proposed plan was then presented to whatever group in the community was most likely to be able to implement it.

Three of these periods of focused activity revolved around: (1) the Tower Grove Area project; (2) an effort at interpretation of the agency to the community served by the district; (3) a study of child care needs in the district.

In our early discussion of the district as a whole, the Tower Grove Area stood out because of the clear-cut problems of its people and the lack of resources to meet these problems. As compared with the rest of the district, this area showed a disproportionate range of family problems. Overcrowding, heavy relief lists, unemployment, relatively higher incidence of ill-health and delinquency were evident. The committee was concerned about the apparent helplessness of a group of rural people transplanted to an urban community. Consultation with ministers, school principals, nurses, and others in the area indicated that we had a problem beyond the time and ability of our group to explore further. A study of the area made by a social work student led the committee to propose to the executive committee of the agency and to the Social Planning Council a project for intensive work in that neighborhood. The purpose of the project was twofold: to help those people to live more comfortably, and to help social workers to learn more about the dynamics of working with such a group. The project was carried out by an agency worker designated as director and working with an advisory committee of representatives of social agencies in the area and the chairman of the district committee. After the project was well established, the district committee received frequent progress reports but took no more action.

Discussion of this project developed an awareness in the committee of a need for close working relationships between the agency workers and people in the area, resulting in our second period of activity—experiments in interpretation to our community. A cross section of about a hundred people living or working in the district was invited by the district committee to a dinner meeting in a neighborhood church. In direct and non-technical language we told who we were and what we did. We told them, too, of the understanding they could give us of the needs and resources of that community and the people in it.

The following year the committee invited two key groups, ministers and school principals, to meet with us separately and together. When children and grownups were unhappy, the principal and the minister tended to know it. Discussion around case material helped us to learn more of the kinds of problems coming to these men and the services they offered or felt they needed as well as telling them more clearly what we had to offer.

Sharing our concern about people with these two professional groups led us to our third period of clearly focused activity—a study of the needs of children whose mothers were employed in war industry. Interviews with sixty-seven key people in the district confirmed our feeling of need for more adequate planning for children. A written report of our local experience was submitted through the agency executive to the committee of the Social Planning Council which was studying day care needs of the entire community.

Any review of the experience of the District Committee must try to define why it has been worth-while. The seven men who maintained interest and participation over this period summarized the values to themselves thus:

1. The District Committee gave interested citizens and people in leadership roles in the community an opportunity to participate in community thinking and planning.

2. Members found it useful to them in their work to get an idea of general conditions in the area in which they were active, as it reinforced and confirmed, or corrected, their own impressions.

3. Members acquired an increased understanding of the resources and function of social agencies through District Committee activity and found this useful in their individual work.

District Committee activity had an effect on agency structure and program and on the casework service to the individual client. As a small segment of the community, the nonstaff members served for the executive as a sounding board for reactions of the community to certain policies and practices. The designation of one worker as director of the Tower Grove Area project and the close participation through an advisory committee with representatives of the social agencies in the area were definite modifications in the district program. The casework process with the client felt the effects of District Committee activity. As members of the committee developed an awareness of the possibilities and limitations of the agency program, they made more and better referrals at an earlier and more treatable stage. Through members of the District Committee the district staff gained access to responsible people and groups in the community. The working relationship within the committee helped staff members to gain greater ease in approaching and using other key people. Examining one small area in detail—as in the Tower Grove Area project—helped the staff to see more clearly some of the methods and results of working within the accepted standards of the client. The approval and sanction of the agency program by members of the District Committee gave to staff members an acceptance in many situations and with many groups which could have been achieved in no other way.[3]

Other Goals. Aside from this example there are other ways in which local agencies take part in community organization. To the extent to which a local agency is part of a council of social work agencies, it is participating in community organization. This participation may be, as in most instances, of a voluntary or mutual nature which tends to emphasize the close tie between community organization and the local agency. The latter's cooperation with a council of social work agencies might indicate a community interest on the part of the local agency in such aims as regulating the standards of individual agencies, using collective means of finance, or utilizing the advantageous social service exchange.

The fact that local agencies, for the fulfillment of their functions, must have some skill in community organization suggests the importance of the subject for all social caseworkers and social group workers. All of the major social work goals require the acceptance of the general public. To secure this acceptance, caseworkers and group workers must use community organization techniques. They should have a definite understanding of the means by which individual agencies extend themselves into the community and express the needs of the community. Graduate schools of social work provide such instruction.

On the other hand it is also true that the community organizer must have a concrete knowledge and appreciation of the functions of case-

[3] Ruth M. Baldwin, "How a District Committee Operates," *Highlights,* volume 7, number 7, November, 1946, pp. 104-107.

workers and group workers. He cannot afford to be lacking in an understanding of the methods and problems of these allied workers, for if he is employed by a local agency he may be responsible for the fulfillment of a program basically not his own.

Neighborhood Councils

A more complex type of community organization is found in the neighborhood council. The neighborhood council movement is a relatively recent one in social work compared to the community organization operations of local agencies. The movement is especially strong in the larger cities where the neighborhood and its needs may be somewhat forgotten by the larger city population, as it may indeed be neglected also by the neighborhood population. Previously, neighborhood councils have often been outgrowths of the settlement house movement. Usually, the needs for which they are created are more specialized than those which might pertain to a whole city or to a larger geographic unit of a city. This does not mean that neighborhood councils are always able to solve their problems and to meet their needs without taking recourse in one way or another to the larger community. In fact, at times the neighborhood council is a pressure group in social welfare upon the larger population unit for benefits which are felt by the neighborhood to be essential for its own well-being. On the other hand there are many problems and needs which the councils can meet without going outside their jurisdiction.

Formed for a Specific Purpose. Neighborhood councils are commonly organized at the beginning around one specific neighborhood need. This need may be of a social work nature or not. The residents of a neighborhood may, for instance, be anxious about the recreational facilities of the neighborhood, believing that they should be increased or that better leadership should be provided for the existent facilities. Or the people may be concerned with the adequacy of the garbage-disposal practices of the city. Poor housing or lack of housing may be the prime objective. High consumers' prices have been known to be the impetus for the formation of such councils. But whatever the basis for formation, the neighborhood council may simply represent a highly specialized and even transient interest of the residents of a neighborhood.

When this is so, the problem of the permanency and scope of such councils is intensified. In the past, in many localities, neighborhood councils have been difficult to keep alive. They arise to meet a specific need and when it is met they sometimes tend to become disorganized, at least until another need is potent enough to arouse enthusiasm. The scope of activities of a neighborhood council likewise may be extremely limited. Being organized in many instances around a particular need, the council may not be interested in the broadest possible program of neighborhood action. The trained community organizer can be of help to such councils. He should be able to provide that type of leadership which will enable and encourage councils to continue their community responsibilities and to develop new interests. This does not mean that he can force a particular program of activities upon them or that he can keep them from disbanding if they so desire, but that he can through leadership seek to introduce attitudes and concerns which will encourage permanency and breadth on the part of the groups.

The council which is formed because of a particular need, however, has many assets, chief among which is intensity of interest. If a council has a special concern, it at least has that much; some councils have nothing so moving that their memberships can be permanently sustained at a high degree of effectiveness. Moreover, if a council newly formed about a particular need achieves success, it may through a sense of pride and accomplishment look about for "new worlds to conquer." These assets are among those upon which the community organizer would wish to build.

While there are some neighborhood councils which present a more or less volatile community organization program, there are many, probably the majority, which maintain serious, continuous, broad programs. These councils find a constant need for neighborhood consultation, planning, coordination, and financing of their social services. They may have a permanent staff of professional leaders to whom the direction of their activities is committed.

Three Types of Councils. Organizationally, neighborhood councils consist of three types. First, there is the council which originates out of recognized local needs and which may include other groups within the neighborhood than those interested in social welfare. Second, there are neighborhood councils which are established by the existing social welfare agencies because they see the need for coordination to gain strength. The first is likely to be run more by lay people—a citizens' council; the second tends to be dominated by professional social workers. The third type stands midway between the first two, including features of both. Each type of organization has its own particular advantages.

The degree of democratic participation in neighborhood councils has been praised on more than one occasion. In a sense the councils comprise for these modern times a foundation stone of democracy, for they provide the private citizen with a channel for the expression of his social interest which is often lacking in political organizations. The councils serve as training centers in democratic awareness and achievement.

Supraneighborhood Councils

While neighborhood councils are the organizations most directly related to the welfare needs of local areas, aside from individual agencies, they generally are in need of supraneighborhood councils in order that their wants may receive the widest possible coordination and attention. Large cities, with their many neighborhoods, tend to have numerous neighborhood councils. For example, New York City, previous to some recent modifications of the neighborhood council structure, had at least thirteen. Where this is so, there is a legitimate place for another agency which seeks to integrate the work of the local groups. Also, because of the specialized organization of some of the neighborhood councils there actually may be several councils in one neighborhood, whatever the names applied to them.

The integration of neighborhood councils may take the form of a city-wide council of social agencies, composed in membership of the

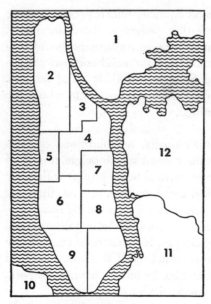

FIG. 44. Affiliated Regional Councils in New York City

("Planning Center," Welfare Council of New York City, May, 1947.)

(1) Bronx Council for Social Welfare
(2) Riverside Civic Council
(3) Central Harlem Council for Community Planning
(4) East Harlem Council for Community Planning
(5) Park West Neighborhood Association
(6) Chelsea-Clinton Council for Community Planning
(7) Yorkville Civic Council
(8) East Midtown Council for Social Welfare, Inc.
(9) Lower West Side Council on Social Planning
(10) Staten Island Council of Social Agencies
(11) Brooklyn Council for Social Planning, Inc.
(12) Queensboro Council for Social Welfare

various neighborhood councils and individual agencies. This method of neighborhood coordination is popular in both large and small cities. The large cities may even have intermediary coordinating councils for boroughs, for several neighborhoods, or for special interests of neighborhood groups. The foregoing map (Figure 44) shows the various subcouncils of the Welfare Council of New York City.

In more rural areas the coordinating council may represent the whole county. Most rural areas, however, do not have the equivalent of the urban neighborhood council at all.

Growth of Movement. The council of social agencies movement began as long ago as 1909 in Milwaukee and Pittsburgh when the need was seen for greater coordination of welfare services. Since that time the council movement has grown noticeably. Today, there are over 350 cities in the United States which have such organizations. Almost every city with a population of over 100,000 has some kind of community-wide council. In addition there are several hundred localities where a community chest program includes many activities elsewhere assumed by a community council. Where there is no over-all agency which coordinates, there sometimes are specialized agencies coordinating in recreation or health, in social work, or in some other aspect of general awareness.

Functions of Councils. The functions of a supraneighborhood council (usually called council of social agencies, social planning council, or community council) vary from place to place according to the conditions of its establishment. In some areas some or all of the activities overlap the functions of neighborhood councils and other agencies. But the following are commonly found:[4]

a. Coordinating service. Councils enable their members to get together to share experiences, to develop mutual understanding, and to create cooperative bases of action. Many councils, in addition, take responsibility in defining the scope of member agencies so that duplication of services is diligently avoided. Councils also have programs of enlightenment and research which are maintained by members from various agencies, thus making for cross-fertilization of ideas and attitudes. They act as clearinghouses on information for lay people and professionals in the community. In these and other ways coordination of social welfare activities is achieved.

[4] Merrill F. Krughoff, "Councils in Social Work," *Social Work Yearbook, 1947: A Description of Organized Activities in Social Work and in Related Fields,* ninth issue, Russell H. Kurtz, editor, Russell Sage Foundation, New York, 1947, pp. 132–133. The categories of responsibility have been taken from this article.

b. Fact-finding. If a council is to act in the interests of the community, it is important that there be a fundamental knowledge of community conditions and possibilities so that intelligent planning can be accomplished. A council of social agencies also needs to know about the cost and distribution of the social services so that proper planning can be done in this regard. It may not always be possible for a council to make its own studies. Occasionally, "outside" consultants and groups are used to gather important information regarding the community and its social services. Also, a few experts are beginning to realize that lay leaders must take part in gathering the facts if they are to accept the findings. "Interpretation by participation" is being recognized increasingly as the most effective way.

c. Joint action. After the facts have been gathered and interpreted, preferably simultaneously, community action may be needed to bring about some improvement. Herein lies another responsibility of a council of social agencies. Perhaps the need is the elimination of an old service, the strengthening of an already existing one, or the creation of an entirely new service. Whatever the need, the council can speak with concerted authority and interest.

d. Improving the quality of service. Councils usually have means of rating social work agencies. They discriminate against those which are lacking in such professional standards as are unquestionably required to protect clients. But they also seek to improve the standards of the accredited agencies by providing special conferences, training institutes, consultations, and other means of betterment.

e. Common services. Councils seldom operate services which benefit clients directly. Direct aid is not considered one of their responsibilities. But they do operate services for one another which indirectly benefit clients. The prime example of this is the social service exchange. More will be said of the social service exchange later in this chapter. In addition to the exchange a council may have a central volunteer bureau, an information service, a joint publicity program, and other common services.

f. Developing public understanding. The council of social agencies acting on a supraneighborhood basis is able to engage in community-wide education for the strengthening of social services. For social work it is especially true that very little of a permanent or worth-while character can be done when it is not ultimately based upon popular response. It is one of the obligations of a common council to keep popular understanding alive and developing. Not always, however, does popular knowledge need simply to be improved. Many times it exists only superficially and even prejudicially. In some communities the general council has the responsibility to impart relatively simple, basic information about the existence and quality of its member agencies.

These, then, are the types of services which a supraneighborhood council can provide.

Accomplishments of Councils. The accomplishments of a council of social agencies in carrying out its functions can be very great for community welfare. Over a period of years, especially, the gains add up until they command attention and respect. In the case of the Welfare Council of New York City, for example, there have been some significant accomplishments. For the period from 1925 to 1946 the following items have been selected by the Council to show its benefits:

Mobilized the Council membership to meet problems of unemployment during the depression.

Developed, in cooperation with city government, service for persons out of work and in need of relief.

Set standards for Home Relief Bureau.

Created a Central Registration Bureau for the homeless.

Organized a Harlem Advisory Committee to get relief for Negroes.

Gathered weekly statistics from nonprofit bureaus on jobs available and applications.

Studied, in behalf of State Employment Service, placement services for refugees from dictator-ridden countries.

Supported federal aid to transients; state social security proposals; an adequate governmental employment service.

Trained 500 persons on W.P.A. to assist in recreational and educational activities.

Obtained modification of licensing of newsstands which gave opportunity for employment of the handicapped.

Pressed for more adequate service in Domestic Relations Court, which resulted in increase of its budget and employment of 26 additional staff workers.

Established need for construction of the hospital on Welfare Island for the chronically ill.

Developed improved standards in child care institutions.

Revised at request of Commissioner of Health the sanitary code for day nurseries, kindergartens, and nursery schools.

Cooperated with physicians, city, and state governments in organizing medical and nursing care for dependent families.

Promoted enforcement of housing laws and urged public housing program.

Compiled standards of sanitation and convenience for rented rooms for young women.

Developed standards for comfort, efficiency, and medical care in homes for the aged.

Recruited 500 social workers to staff emergency wartime welfare centers.

Gave training courses for volunteers in cooperation with C.D.V.O., Department of Health, and New York Junior League.

Arranged with War Manpower Commission to call meeting of 70 federal, state, and local public and voluntary agencies to consider necessity of integrated service for veterans which resulted in establishment of the Veterans' Service Center.

Cleared over 86,000 names through the social service exchange for the Selective Service as part of the program of screening out men likely to become psychiatric casualties.[5]

Along with the organization of supraneighborhood councils of social agencies there are in many localities overlapping councils set up for more special purposes than those served in a general council. Thus, for example, sectarian groups regularly have area-coordinating councils for integrating the operations of their member agencies. Other special interests may also have their coordinative units. A city may have a child welfare council to represent the interests of the child welfare agencies within its geographic jurisdiction. (See Figure 45.)

Disadvantages of Councils. The present method of organizing councils of social agencies has several disadvantages. Currently, councils operate on a delegate basis, each member agency being entitled to one vote. This practice tends to weight the influence of private agencies unduly, since there are usually more privately financed agencies than public. To arrange the distribution of power within the supraneighborhood council on the basis either of budget size, of agency size, of a principle regulative of the participation of private and public agencies, or by some other means than that regularly used would, however, also raise significant problems.

The granting of membership on an agency basis also tends to make the council a large and unwieldy body for efficient purposes. Although the functions of the councils for the most part are given over to committees, even such committees must be large if they are to be representative, and usually committee reports must appear before the total delegate body. In other words the size of the supraneighborhood council is apt to be self-defeating.

A third disadvantage to the delegate system of organizing councils is the lack of executive responsibility. Usually, little is done without the

[5] "Planning Center," Welfare Council of New York City, New York, May, 1947, pp. 13–14.

SUGGESTED ORGANIZATION CHART FOR A COMMUNITY COUNCIL OR WELFARE ORGANIZATION

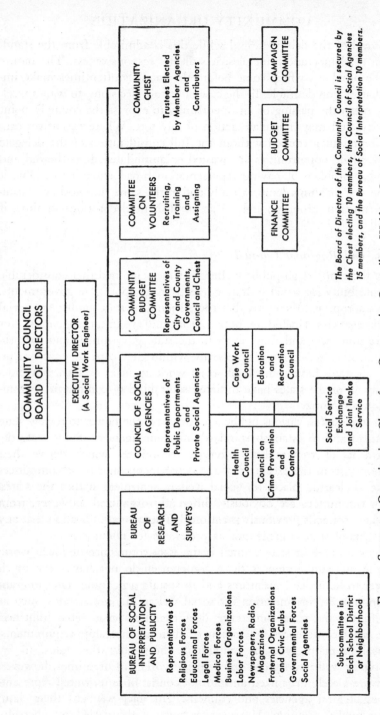

FIG. 45. Suggested Organization Chart for a Community Council or Welfare Organization

(June P. Guild and Arthur A. Guild, *Social Work Engineering*, Harper, New York, 1940.)

approval of the delegates, and while this is admirable from the stand-point of democratic principles, it stultifies responsiveness. The nature of the problems which come before the councils oftentimes make im-mediate action desirable. In the case of certain decisions, to wait a week may mean the passing of an opportunity to express the council's point of view and may invalidate action of any sort. Where executives can-not represent a council without the full consideration of the delegate body, many opportunities are wasted or annihilated. It is the old and familiar problem of having representation broad enough to enable it to possess meaning democratically and at the same time to have execu-tive function strong enough to accomplish needed actions in time, if at all.

State and Regional Councils

In the chapters on public welfare it was mentioned that considerable responsibility for social welfare currently rests upon state governments. It is appropriate, therefore, that there should be state councils of social work agencies (including both official and voluntary agencies) for expressing local and state needs to the state government and for pro-viding other services not necessarily within the scope of government. Not all states have councils of social work agencies as such, but prac-tically all of the states have initiated some kind of community organi-zation program.

In some states, various public agencies have the power to review state practices and to establish standards for state agencies. Some state de-partments of welfare have advisory committees which derive their authority from the executive of the departments, and these committees serve as clearing places for social welfare sentiment within the states. Such committees are obviously differently organized, however, from the state councils previously mentioned. There is no indication that any one type of state organization is preferable for all states.

Another type of state council is the state conference of social work. While in many instances these conferences do not have very much power to influence legislatures and to sustain a genuine state program of community organization for social welfare, in some states, such as California, the state conference does exercise considerable influence. The state conferences, by reason of their membership requirements, appeal to many types of individuals throughout the states, to lay people as well as to professional social workers. Oftentimes, however, they are loosely organized and do not consist of empowered represent-atives of local agencies and councils. This fact weakens their claim upon public attention. Moreover, because of the varied membership, state conference activities often are of such a general and nonpolitical character as to deny the effective treatment of certain important considerations.

In relation to the various forms of state councils for social welfare it may be pointed out that there can be serious difficulty in securing harmonious relationships between urban and rural areas. In some cases the effectiveness of state councils has been lessened (sometimes eliminated) because the required action could not meet with the approval of both urban and rural delegates.

Regional Councils. There are, in addition to state councils, several organizations which work on a regional basis, although their roots are usually in national bodies or in voluntary associations of state bodies. Probably, to the degree that regionalism, or at least the awareness of regionalism, is developed in this country will there come into being agencies for coordinating the welfare activities of whole sections of the country.

A good example of a regional agency is the Southern Regional Council, whose existence dates from 1944. The membership of the Council is composed of 1,500 individuals (white and Negro), and cooperating agencies on a regional, state, and local basis. The Council works for the improvement of economic, civic, and racial conditions in the South. It seeks to foster equality of opportunity for all peoples in the region. To attain these ends the Council does research, makes surveys, publishes educational materials, coordinates existing agencies in the field, consults with agencies concerning their problems, and holds conferences.

National Organizations

It is natural, given the complexities of social welfare development on local, state, and national bases, as we have it in this country, that there should arise organizations which should seek the coordination of social welfare activities on the national level. These organizations possess all of the advantages of a highly rational, sectionless type of approach to social welfare problems and suffer from all of the disadvantages of remoteness from concrete local conditions. The national organizations are of various kinds. They exist for casework and for group work interests as well as for others. It would be too tedious to present a complete list, but a few may be profitably mentioned.

The American Association of Social Workers is composed of professional social workers who have been admitted to membership after meeting certain carefully defined standards. Its status in social work is similar to the professional organizations in medicine and law. At present it has a membership of under 12,000 persons who represent 98 local chapters. Although the Association is mainly concerned with the problems of professional social workers, problems of a wider nature are also part of its interest. Its responsibility in regard to various national issues in social welfare is expressed through committees and through the national body. Its official publication is the *Social Work Journal*.

The National Conference of Social Work, in existence since 1873, is another national organization in the social welfare field. The Conference is composed of about 7,500 individuals and 450 organizations. Once a year it holds a general meeting of a week's duration. The main contribution of the Conference to the better functioning of social workers and social work agencies is the discussion of various significant topics of interest: casework, group work, community organization, social action, economic conditions, public welfare administration, and other themes. The main weakness of the Conference is its inability to take a stand on any issue. This weakness is written into its Constitution. Thus on most matters there may be discussion but no action.

Sectarian. Of a type similar to the National Conference of Social Work are the conferences of professional workers which coordinate sectarian interests on a national scale. Jewish social work is organized in the National Conference of Jewish Social Welfare. Catholic social work is organized nationally in the National Conference of Catholic Charities. Protestant social work is organized nationally in the Church Conference on Social Work.

Special Interests. Along with these sectarian bodies there are several which represent other special interests. The American Association of Medical Social Workers, for example, represents medical social workers and their constituencies. The American Public Welfare Association, as the title implies, operates in the public welfare field. The Family Service Association of America is the national expression of local family casework agencies. The Community Chests and Councils, Inc., is composed of local community chests and councils which have grouped themselves together for their mutual benefit. There are others of this type.

Governmental Services. Aside from the commendable work of the American Public Welfare Association, the governmental services have yet to achieve a really effective over-all agency of official status which will coordinate their many activities. For a time it seemed as though the National Resources Planning Board would assume this role, but it was disbanded. More recently the growing influence of the Federal Security Agency has seemed to point to a development which may provide national coordination, although there is yet much to be desired.

The reorganization plan of the President which was acted upon in the summer of 1946 further centralized the authority of the Federal Security Agency in social welfare.

In addition to the national organizations listed, there are many more which present many variations in size, resources, types of program, authority over members, and in other details. Those mentioned provide some idea of the organizations already in the field.

Benefits of Coordination. Coordination on a national scale can be very beneficial. The types of problems, however, and the resistances which often stand in the way of genuinely cooperative action are complex and deep-seated. Most of the national agencies are definitely weaker than is desirable and the techniques of releasing them from the grip of size are ineffective, if not unknown.

At present the whole structure of community organization, as represented by the various national agencies active in the field, seems to point to a lack of integration of the coordinating agencies. The large number which exist, by their very number, call for a more consolidated program for social welfare on a national basis. The National Social Welfare Assembly (formerly the National Social Work Council) seems to be a step in the right direction in that it seeks to have within its membership all avowedly national organizations in the social work field (it has in its membership about 44 national agencies including 11 federal agencies). It was organized in December, 1945. As yet, however, the Assembly has not been able to present a very vigorous program. It is indeed one of the limitations of the Assembly, as with the National Conference of Social Work, that it is able to assist only in the communication of ideas among its constituency without providing for a social action program to relate the ideas so derived to practical achievement.

International Cooperation in Social Welfare

The complex relationships which exist in our world, in many of its aspects, exist to a considerable extent in social welfare. As was mentioned in other chapters some phases of present-day social work are international in outlook and scope. The welfare activities of the wartime U.N.R.R.A. and the peacetime United Nations fall within this category. The problems of the refugee also have directed attention toward international horizons. The American Red Cross from the start of the Second World War carried on relief programs in over 46 countries abroad, although this figure has shrunk to some 17 countries at the present time. The total cost of this work has amounted to more than

$175,000,000. These patterns of international cooperation represent merely a sampling from a much broader number of instances.

Among the cooperative efforts of a community organization character, there are several which merit mention. The American Council of Voluntary Agencies for Foreign Service, while not a strictly international agency from the point of view of structure, does coordinate the activities of agencies whose primary concern is international social work. The Council, founded in 1943, contains 62 national agencies which have individual programs of relief and rehabilitation for the populations of countries abroad. Its existence is based on the feeling that the work of so many agencies has to be coordinated and consolidated for purposes of efficiency. Information has been shared by the members through the Council, and the collective resources have been organized in such ways as to make them most practical. It is noteworthy that the Council, in undertaking this significant task of coordination, unites sectarian and nonsectarian organizations, agencies interested in particular nationalities, the relief services of labor organizations, and other types of agencies. In 1945 the Council also achieved the creation of the Co-operative for American Remittances to Europe (C.A.R.E.) which sends packages from persons in the United States to relatives and friends abroad, at no profit, at low cost, and in considerable quantity. In addition the Council has worked with the problems of displaced persons.

The International Labor Organization (I.L.O.) can in part be termed a social work organization which operates on an international basis. It was created by the peace treaties at the close of the First World War. The assumption underlying the I.L.O. is that satisfactory labor conditions are basic to the maintenance of peace and that the labor situation in any one country affects that in others. The form of cooperation in the Organization is unique of its kind. It includes elected representatives of employers, workers, and governments who meet at stated times to enact measures for the common international well-being. Since 51 nations belong to the Organization, its decisions directly affect a large number of people. There are three divisions within the Organization: (1) the International Labor Conference (its parliamentary assembly); (2) the Governing Body (its executive council); and (3) the International Labor Office (its secretariat). Recently, the Organization became affiliated with the United Nations.

World Conferences. Social workers also have held international conferences for themselves. The first of these occurred in 1928 in Paris, with about 2,500 delegates present from 42 countries. Two hundred seventy-nine persons from the United States were in attendance. The second Conference was held in 1932 in Frankfort on the Main. The third and last before the Second World War was held in London in 1936. At a meeting in Brussels in 1946 the officers of the International Conference on Social Work decided to hold the next meeting in 1948 in the United States. The meeting was held in conjunction with the seventy-fifth anniversary meeting of the National Conference of Social Work.

These activities of an international character remind us that social work is developing on this front, if slowly. It seems that at the present time there is a surging of social work interest from the local community to the broader population—to supraneighborhood associations and even state organizations. It may be that the interest already well-grounded on a national basis will grow, supplanting the smaller loyalties. Finally, though it seems very distant, there may be the creation of extended interrelationships between the social welfare programs of the various nations. The United Nations gives at least a semblance of such a hope.

THE PROCESS OF COMMUNITY ORGANIZATION

Community organization operates both as a structure and as a process. As a structure it is represented by various organizations within the community which are purportedly designed to relate community resources to community needs. As a process it is represented by those activities by which agencies actually do relate community resources to community needs. As a process, moreover, it usually is carried on within the organizational structure intended for that purpose in the community, but, on the other hand, as has been said, it is also expressed by individuals whose main function is not community organization. Theoretically, the process precedes the organization, the structure merely giving more effective possibility to the process.

While it is difficult to list a series of activities which in combination compose the whole of the community organization process (and there is no general agreement in the field of social work on what activities should be included), some of the more obvious will be commented on here to show their nature in some detail.

Coordination

Perhaps the most obvious of the elements of the community organization process is that of community coordination.[6] The arranging of

⁶The overemphasis on coordination as the chief example of community organ-

community relationships for cooperative ends is an intrinsic part of community organization. It takes place so often and in so many ways that it is difficult to comprehend the whole scope of this type of community organization process.

There is the kind of coordination which might be termed mutual self-help. Many agencies find that they cannot maintain their best functioning without setting up cooperative relationships both of a social-work and nonsocial work character with other agencies. Such relationships comprise a form of community organization.

In addition to the mutual self-help patterns which individual agencies may create, there are many other ways in which cooperation may be expressed. A council of social agencies, for example, provides a different example of community organization in its coordinative aspects because there usually are no direct services to clients implied in the program of such a council. The chief function of a common council may be said to be coordinative. This is also true for the neighborhood council, the state and regional councils, and the national and international efforts in community organization.

The cooperation which is possible between an individual agency and a council of agencies is illustrated by the following "case study":

The city of D, like many other cities, is faced with a housing shortage. This has been growing more and more acute, not only for families in the lower-income brackets but for all families. The families in the lower-income brackets, however, are those that most often come to the attention of the agency.

There is diversity of opinion in D among groups concerned with housing as to the ways in which the shortages can best be met. This diversity of opinion is sharp enough to evoke open criticism by the interested groups of various suggested ways for handling the problem.

The agency has gathered facts about what is happening to families known to it. It is, however, in no position to offer expert or technical advice on the best method of creating new housing or making present housing more effective. The facts that the agency has collected have been given to its board and other groups, among them the council of social agencies. The agency sees the problem as being community-wide and too large for a single agency. The council, through its intake committee, has found that the problem is common to all agencies and has gathered from

ization was probably due to the fact that the community chests organized as the American Association for Community Organization in the early part of the 1920's. After other experts objected to their pre-empting this name, they dropped it, assuming the title of Community Chests and Councils, Inc. Historically, coordination came late. For years, community organization resulted in the formation of individual agencies, until coordination became imperative.

all agencies evidence of social breakdown being caused by this housing shortage. Speaking for the agencies as a group, the council has published one effective news story, citing growing social breakdown because of housing lack. There is continued emphasis on the problem in the intake committee, and the way is open for the agencies to continue to speak on this subject through the council.

Again we have an agency recognizing that its clientele or its program is affected by a community condition. The first principle followed was that of recognizing in what area of this problem the agency could offer testimony and facts. Second, material was gathered and distributed to appropriate other agencies including the council. Third, the agency participated with other agencies through the intake committee of the council and helped gather the evidence of social breakdown. The council acted in gathering this evidence from all agencies and spoke for the group.

In its relationship with the council the agency is participating in a cooperative enterprise. This does not preclude the agency in D, or other agencies in D, from gathering further material. It does not preclude further agency action but it does oblige the agency to clear with the council on such proposed action. The council is also obligated to seek the opinion of the agency.[7]

Social Service Exchange. The social service exchange, known in some localities as the "confidential exchange" and in others as the "social service index," is a clear illustration of the means cooperating agencies have devised for the improvement of their individual functioning. Usually, the exchange is operated by a council of social work agencies as one of its many services. The exchange itself does not possess casework records of clients. It does have such essential information, however, as the names and addresses of persons who have been clients of social work agencies in the community, with a listing of the agencies involved. The cards, filed either alphabetically or phonetically (or both ways) and usually according to several systems of reference, comprise a source of preliminary information for social workers in casework and group work agencies (and in some communities for certain other individuals and organizations). Agency workers generally "clear" with the exchange regarding their clients. This clearing provides basic data regarding the previous agency history, if any, of the new client. If more information concerning the client is desired, the agencies listed by the exchange may be contacted. Usually, an agency contacts the exchange through a card application, although in certain cases telephone clearings can also be made.

[7]Robert F. Nelson, "The Executive and the Community," *Some Dynamics of Social Agency Administration,* Family Service Association of America, New York, 1946, pp. 34-35.

At present there are three ways of financing the exchanges. In some places the costs are met by tax appropriation, in others by the community chest, and in still others they are divided among the agencies using the service. Some exchanges are operated by private agencies, but in an increasing number of communities the exchange is maintained under public auspices. This latter means seems appropriate for many localities where there is considerable public agency activity. The rapid growth of the public services and the volume of their activities place stress upon the need for publicly operated exchanges. There does not seem to be any essential argument against this practice proffered by the private agencies, since the service can be maintained without political meaning either for the public or for the private agencies. The actual experience of publicly financed exchanges in about 65 cities presents a generally favorable argument for public support.

It is not easy to decide which agencies within the community, outside of the obvious social work agencies, should have registration privileges. The question has been raised whether the tenants of public housing projects should be registered with the exchange. Further, should the public schools have access to the information of the exchange? Should certain public departments, such as police, probation, parole, and courts, be allowed the use of the confidential files of the exchange? Should the service be available to industries, whether management or labor? These and other questions regarding the use of the social service exchange have been raised. It would seem that none of these questions can be solved without taking into account the concepts of practice of the various agencies that wish to use the exchange. The basis on which the information is received, the responsibility of the exchange, and the ends to which the information may be put seem to be some of the determining factors in any decision regarding the extent to which exchanges should be inclusive or exclusive of agencies other than those which have social work specifically as their purpose.

More and more it is being realized by social workers who have an intimate knowledge of the exchange movement that larger geographic areas have to be covered. The common coverage is the county, the city, or a unit even smaller. It is felt by some workers that there is need for state, regional, and national coverage, especially for certain cases. The mobility of clients makes this need apparent. On the other hand a national exchange, particularly, would involve obvious difficulties, such as financing.

The social service exchange is one example of practical community coordination. There are in addition to it many other illustrations of the coordinative interests of community organization.

Financing

The joint financing of social work services comprises another of the elements of the community organization process. At first glance, joint financing may seem to be simply one of the components of agency coordination. But the actual practice of joint financing and its importance to the social work field suggest its significance as a basic element itself.

There are still many agencies which do not rely on joint financing, but they are few in number compared to those which appreciate the advantages of cooperation on this score. Historically, the typical method of agency financing was noncooperative. In fact, the past history of the financial activities of individual agencies shows a high degree of vicious competition. It has been only in relatively recent years that agencies have overcome their competitive practices and banded together as far as financing their programs was concerned. Actually, however, the first joint financing agency was established as early as 1887, in Denver. Another notable step was the formation of the Federation of Charities and Philanthropy in Cleveland in 1913. It was not for some years after that time that the movement spread to other cities.

The joint financing of social work agencies is most frequently maintained by community chests. The practices of the chests in securing money may differ, but most localities have an annual drive. This annual drive for funds requires a high degree of community organization. There must be preparation, usually for a long time preceding the actual campaign, on the part of the staff of the chest. Like a military movement, the strategy must be carefully planned. The work of the drive is commonly divided among various groups and areas within the community. The community's leading citizens, for example, may be asked to serve on a committee to solicit the larger gifts. These individuals would also be sought after by the chest to have their names attached to the campaign—on letterheads, in public statements, at dinners. There also may be an industrial committee to solicit funds from workers and from management. There may be a women's division to make a special appeal to the women of the community. There may be a residential committee to engage in door-to-door canvassing for contributions. The Community Chests and Councils, Inc. arranges for all local campaigns to be conducted at the same time, during one chosen week of the year.

Community Chests and Councils, Inc. Community Chests and Councils, Inc. stands as a most important national coordinating body responsible for the raising of money through community chests. It also has other important functions. It was founded in 1918 and today coordinates about 475 community chests and councils of social agencies.

Its purposes and activities include the following: "To assist in the development of community organization for health and welfare; and to give service and leadership to local community chests and councils of social agencies in joint financing, joint planning, and interpretation of social work through committee activities, research, correspondence, field visits, local studies of chests and councils, regional and national conferences, staff training institutes, and publications." The organization sponsors two annual institutes for social work executives, in Wisconsin and North Carolina. Its monthly news bulletin is called *Community*.

The money collected through the community chest campaign is apportioned to community agencies through a budgeting procedure. Some communities wait until they know how much money they have to divide, while others decide on a plan before the campaign is run. The budgeting procedure is initiated by the agencies themselves by filing an application for funds for the succeeding year. The application generally requires that the agency describe its minimal needs (without which it could not maintain its current program) and its maximal (including new developments in program). The applications are reviewed by committees of the chest in order to determine the validity of the requests and their priority. If an agency does not agree with the decisions of the chest committee, it may appeal at a special budget hearing. If there is agreement, the chest pays the apportioned share to the agencies in monthly payments for the year, unless special circumstances arise which require a change in the amounts given.

The accompanying chart shows how money collected by the community chest of New York City is distributed. (See Figure 46).

Coordination and Cooperation Needed. The fact that both councils of social work agencies and community chests have been separately created in many American communities raises an important problem regarding joint financing. To the councils of social agencies have largely fallen the responsibilities of coordination, with the exception of financing. But this division of labor has meant that all too often a council of social agencies can plan a program of community coordination without having the active and intimate support of the community's money-raising agency. Likewise, the community chest in many places raises money without a too detailed understanding of the plans of the council of social work agencies. To many social workers and others, it would seem that integration of the money-raising activities with the social planning requirements of a community would result in increased efficiency.

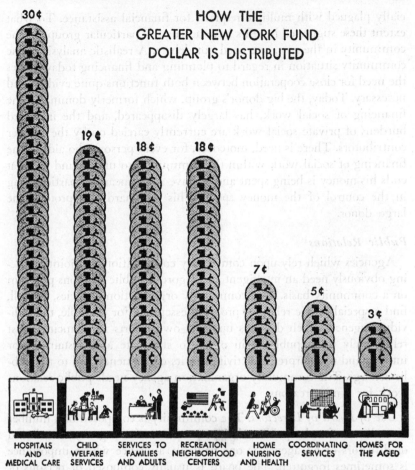

HOW THE GREATER NEW YORK FUND DOLLAR IS DISTRIBUTED

30¢ — HOSPITALS AND MEDICAL CARE

19¢ — CHILD WELFARE SERVICES

18¢ — SERVICES TO FAMILIES AND ADULTS

18¢ — RECREATION NEIGHBORHOOD CENTERS

7¢ — HOME NURSING AND HEALTH

5¢ — COORDINATING SERVICES

3¢ — HOMES FOR THE AGED

Fig. 46. How the Greater New York Fund Dollar Is Distributed

("Facts, Facts, Facts," a publication of the 10th Annual Campaign of the Greater New York Fund, New York City.)

The fact that these two allied types of community agencies are not consolidated in many localities makes it necessary for close cooperation between the two. In some communities they have been organized under a single board of trustees. This arrangement in part tends to solve some of the weightier problems which individual agencies and separate programs otherwise might entail.

The view has been expressed that councils of social agencies tend to serve professional groups (social workers mainly) more than they appeal to certain donor's groups. Community chests, on the other hand, are thought to serve the larger donors who otherwise would be especially plagued with multiple requests for financial assistance. To what extent these suggested benefits have accrued to particular groups in the community in the past, one need not debate. A realistic analysis of the community situation in regard to planning and financing today makes the need for close cooperation between both functions quite evident and necessary. Today, the big donor's group, which formerly dominated the financing of social work, has largely disappeared, and the increased burdens of private social work are currently carried on by the smaller contributors. There is need, moreover, for every person who aids in the financing of social work within the community to understand to what ends his money is being spent and to have some means of participating in the control of the money spent. This safeguard also protects the large donor.

Public Relations

Agencies which rely upon community coordination and joint financing obviously need an intelligent and vigorous public relations program on a community basis.[8] Noncommunity organization agencies, as well, find a special public relations program essential. For example, the individual agency which depends upon its own efforts in financing must rely closely upon publicity in order to stimulate and sustain donor interest and to interpret its activities to its constituency and to the public at large. The community organization agency needs public relations work for similar reasons.

Use of Board of Directors. The community is composed of a number of audiences for the public relations purposes of an agency. The board of directors of an agency is one valuable audience whose importance is sometimes forgotten. The board is usually composed of persons of wide influence in the community, persons who represent various lines of special activity: business, women, religion, education, wealth. Because of their position in the community and their varied interests, the board members may be a really potent source of community contact. If, for example, the director of an agency wishes to correct popular impressions about the use of welfare funds for the unemployed, he may find that presenting the facts to the board will be an indirect but effective way of diffusing them throughout the community.

The fact that boards of directors are suitable audiences for the promulgation of social work ideas in a community has meant in some

---

[8]*Interpretation* is the older and still widely used term among social workers for *public relations. Public relations* refers to a set of activities directed toward the maintenance and improvement of the quality of relationships between an agency and a community.

localities that boards need to be educated to their unique opportunities. Plans to increase the efficacy of boards have developed in recent years in many communities. Usually, the plans both represent a form of community organization and aid in the furtherance of community organization objectives. The Brooklyn Council for Social Planning, as an example, created an Institute for Board Members. The Institute is described as follows in the yearly report of that agency:

A course for Board members was formulated by a committee of the Council in the belief that social work does not stand still but changes with the times and that it is the responsibility of board members to understand the over-all picture of Brooklyn and its needs as well as the role of the individual agency in fulfilling those needs. Called "Brooklyn Faces the Future," the course consisted of six sessions held at the Brooklyn Bureau of Social Service in January and February. There were 101 who enrolled and the attendance indicated that the course met with popular approval. Subjects covered by prominent speakers included: (1) background and concepts of social work; (2) family problems today; (3) children's agencies; (4) health and rehabilitation; (5) the relation of public to private agencies; and (6) the responsibilities of board members.

Summaries of each session were prepared and a few are still available. Questionnaires were sent to all who registered, requesting their opinion of the course and suggestions for future courses. Answers to date indicate that another course is desired, preferably after January 1, 1947. An article, "How Brooklyn Faced the Future," written by the Chairman, appeared in *Better Times* on April 5th, giving a fuller analysis of the course.[9]

Use of Agency Workers. The workers on an agency's staff are another public relations audience. Since these workers through their daily contacts with individual clients, groups, and community movements represent the agency in the community, it is important that they themselves have an awareness of the role that they should play. In casework agencies, for example, the caseworker, without specifically saying anything about community relations when interviewing clients, will be a personal embodiment of the meaning of social casework and will influence individual opinion in these situations regarding the work done by such agencies. This, of course, does not preclude more active means of accomplishing specific ends. The worker in his contacts beyond the office with community groups also has opportunities of a public relations nature. If he speaks before a Parent-Teacher Association, for example, about the contribution his agency can make to the well-being of school children, he is in a significant way interpreting his

---

[9] *Something Is Being Done!*—Annual Report 1945–1946, Brooklyn Council for Social Planning, Brooklyn, N.Y., p. 10.

agency. The worker who serves on a community committee for the prevention of juvenile delinquency similarly has opportunities for the presentation of the viewpoints of social work agencies. Thus an agency can capitalize upon its community contacts for the extension of common knowledge regarding general needs and social agency functions.

General Publicity. There always remains, however, the need for general publicity regarding the work of an agency. This work may be managed by a special staff employed for this specific task. More often it is one of the responsibilities of the executive. In the past the main type of publicity work done by agencies was aimed at increasing financial support. Today, there is increasing use of other goals. Currently, social work agencies realize that they have a responsibility to educate community members not merely to give money for worthy causes but also to understand and respond to conditions with which they may be unfamiliar in the community and to the role of the social work agencies in meeting these conditions. This type of educational outlook will probably not harm the money-raising ambitions of agency executives in the long run, but it certainly should not be viewed merely as a means of increasing financial support. It should stand on the facts, needs, and possibilities of community action.

An effective form of publicity-education for a social agency is that which seeks to inform lay people on a case-discussion basis of the work of the agency. This type of public relations has been used valuably in many communities. An example of its use in Milwaukee will clarify its procedure and meaning:

> Agency and community both benefit when lay people participate in the work of an agency. Participation has traditionally taken the form of direct volunteer service and advisory activity, usually in a neighborhood office. The development of professional skills by caseworkers, and the gradual disappearance of neighborhood offices, has reduced opportunities for such volunteer activity. To preserve lay interest in the agency, new avenues of participation must be found.
>
> In many large cities, including Milwaukee, district offices have been consolidated in recent years and case committees can no longer be grouped around neighborhood problems. In their place, board and staff have sometimes organized case-discussion groups around community-wide conditions of special concern to the agency and to people interested in the work of the agency. Five such groups of the Family Service of Milwaukee met once a month last year for lunch and discussion. Six groups will start meetings this autumn: Day Nursery Care, Services to Veterans and Their Families, Motherless Families, Marriage Counseling, Central Case (sampling of different agency services), and Parent-Child Problems.

Case material without identifying data is presented by a professional worker and followed by general discussion. Emphasis is upon community needs and the work of the agency. Although members do not advise about techniques of treatment, suggestions from specialized resources such as personnel managers, teachers, doctors, and veteran's agency workers are of real help.

The board of directors takes major responsibility for these meetings. Each group has a chairman and an alternate, both of them board members. They are assisted by a staff consultant. Board members recruit most of the group members with an understanding that membership and attendance are flexible and that they may choose the group that most interests them. However, they may shift from one group to another.

Chairmen try to sample the thinking of members, and often reasons given for shifting to another group or for dropping out altogether are extremely helpful to the agency. The total membership of each group is thirty; attendance at each meeting averages twenty. An attempt is made to include a variety of members, to represent the whole community, but at present a majority are from professions and are people who traditionally have given time and money to voluntary social agencies. One group next year plans to meet evenings, hoping that this will make it possible for a broader group to participate.

Board and corporation members find that discussion groups enrich their knowledge of social work in general and of their agency in particular. The groups are considered an important testing ground for prospective board members. The agency also looks upon these meetings as (1) a channel for interpreting its program to the community and (2) an opportunity to test its ideas and activities against the thinking of civic-minded persons.

At the close of this year's meetings, the agency polled the members with a questionnaire composed by group chairmen and staff consultants. They hoped to learn if the agency and the group members agreed about the purpose of their participation and if there were suggestions for future meetings. Sixty per cent of the membership replied.

The great majority considered that the average attendance was good for free discussion. A few preferred groups smaller than twenty; none wished for larger ones. Concerning which agency services were most and least familiar, a marked difference was revealed between opinions of group members and staff.

Comments heard about the agency were noted: for instance, "Your organization spends too much time on complicated casework and ignores relief needs," and "Your agency is seen as a place where only poor people get help." One of the most revealing factors was the great number who replied, "I hear nothing about the agency outside these meetings." Members suggested many individuals who had had no previous contact with the agency but who were interested in participating.

About half the membership desired to switch to another group, to widen their knowledge of problems and services. A large majority preferred luncheons to evening meetings, indicating that present members come from a restricted group who are free to attend noon meetings. This re-emphasized the need for a broader base of participation.

The questionnaire suggested five purposes for lay participation in discussion groups and asked each member to indicate by number the relative importance of each. Here is the total result:

1. To become acquainted with the work of the agency so I can tell others.

2. To learn more about local social conditions.

3. To reflect public opinion, so that the agency knows better what the community is thinking about certain problems.

4. To gain information that might be helpful to troubled people I know.

5. To register approval of the agency work through attendance.

Replies to the questionnaire indicate that members have good understanding about the purposes of the groups. They show, too, that community people are willing to be channels for interpretation and do not always expect to advise or to do direct practice. Most heartening, many recognized the responsibility to keep the agency in touch with community thinking so that the program can be geared to changing needs.[10]

Vigorous Program Needed. The tasks facing social work in its public relations aspect are momentous. For one thing it is clear that social work, if it is to keep pace with other developments in society, must "market" its contributions even as other organizations do theirs. In a former time when social work was thought very largely to pertain to the poor in terms of informing them about the availability of social services and to the rich in terms of soliciting their money, it may have been proper for social work to conduct special and minimal public relations programs. But, today, when social work is dependent for its support upon everybody and seeks to help everybody, it is imperative that thoroughgoing, vigorous, and widespread publicity be achieved.

Social work will have to develop training facilities for public relations workers to a greater degree than is available at present to care for the rising need. The number of positions available now is probably not much more than 1,000, but these require a high degree of professional skill. Some of the graduate schools of social work offer courses in the subject. Much more of a coordinated and detailed nature must be done, however, if social work is to develop as it should.

Agencies Engaged in Public Relations. The work of the National Publicity Council for Health and Welfare Services is providing a gen-

[10] Roy Dulak, "Milwaukee's Experience With Case Discussion Groups," *Highlights,* volume 7, number 6, October, 1946, pp. 86–88.

uine service to social work agencies throughout the country. Organized in 1921, the Council is composed of approximately 2,000 governmental and voluntary social and health agencies. It has the responsibility to stimulate interest on the part of its member agencies, and generally, in publicity. It acts as a clearinghouse for materials and ideas. Its publication called *Channels* is a valuable tool for any agency concerned with its public relations.

The Department of Social Work Interpretation of the Russell Sage Foundation also operates in the public relations field. Its main contribution is that of preparing materials dealing with the development of programs and resources of interpretation (or publicity) and with the adoption of general publicity procedures to social work.

Techniques Used. The public relations programs of agencies may be carried on by three means. These naturally must be related to the requirements of the audiences to which an appeal is being made. It is clear, too, that not all of the content an agency may wish to publicize will be appropriate to all three.

First, there is the *spoken word*. This method has been described previously. It implies the executive speaking to his board, the worker to his client, the worker to community groups, and, in turn, these groups reaching other individuals and groups. The possibilities of interpreting social work over the radio and by community lecture series have also been somewhat explored in recent years.

Second, there is the medium of the *written word*. The agency which is concerned about community relations can profitably use leaflets, flyers, booklets, annual reports, and other devices to disseminate knowledge about its work. These may be directed to the general community or toward some special section of the community (such as laborers, the church, the unemployed). The best work of this type (and probably of all types) has been accomplished by private agencies, but in recent years many of the public agencies have realized that they also have an important stake in publishing programs. The annual reports of public agencies which formerly were extremely forbidding because of their exaggerated statistical nature, their lack of human-interest items, and their failure to include pictures and other interest-securing content have changed for the better and are in some instances outstandingly attractive avenues of community appeal.

The third technique in public relations is related in part to the second: *the use of pictures and other visual methods*. The use of photographs, either posed or not, in the publishing program of an agency increases the effectiveness of the materials in this "sight-seeing" age.

The use of motion pictures in social work has been noticeably slow and lacking, although this medium has been utilized to a considerable extent in the public health field, and elsewhere. There hardly seems to be any conclusive reason why the social work field should not be able to enlist public sentiment through motion pictures more than it has in the past.

Research

The community organization movement rests firmly on the need for research. Nothing less than action based on accurate social research will satisfy the persons and groups with which the community organizer works. Because of the nature and youth of community organization, however, there are many aspects of it which have not yet known the patient quest of the fact-finders. But, increasingly, there is a scientific effort to approach the needs of the community, the resources for meeting them, and the techniques to relate them effectively. This means, concretely, that the community organizer is necessarily involved in research. The whole program of community organizers, whether in community coordination, financing, public relations, or any other activity, should ultimately rest upon facts.

There are several ways of approaching the needs of communities and their resources. Some are more preferred than others. They may be classified as either indirect or direct, although it is readily admitted that there may be combinations of the methods. In the indirect approach the conclusions of the community organizer are not derived from primary association with the data investigated, but are accepted by him on the basis of intuition or on the authority of another researcher. In the direct approach the community organizer has first-hand contact with the basic data being investigated.

Indirect Approach. a. Use of Intuition. Community organizers may arrive at a basis for their activities through intuition. At first glance, especially in this so-called scientific age, one may laugh derisively at such an approach. On many occasions this derision will be merited. But there are several aspects regarding the reliability and function of intuition which we should consider. There is little in intuition on the part of a sensitive and expert mind which of itself is necessarily unworthy. If one wishes to know what the basis is for a particular physical ailment and consults a physician, one soon may come in contact with intuition operating in the field of medicine. The physician may have amassed many facts. He may know many theories. But, after all is known that humanly can be known, and despite and because of the extent of experience, the physician will have to make up his mind regarding the diagnosis and the treatment which he will employ. In many cases, fortunately, there have been built up through medical researches of a laboratory character the kind of knowledge and judgment which mitigate the need for a high degree of intuition. But in other cases the main tool of the physician may be his insight, not entirely related to facts on a strictly empirical foundation. Here, intuition may be termed "an expert's guess," and it may be the best that is available at the time or under the circumstances.

Similarly, there is a place for intuition in community organization, as perhaps in all types of research to a greater or lesser degree. The community organizer, because he deals with constantly changing materials of human, collective experience, may be unable on a strictly scientific basis to determine a proper course of community action. He may be able, by comparing the juvenile delinquency records of the local police districts in his city with the recreational facilities of the districts, to arrive at a conclusion regarding the need for increased recreational facilities in some of the districts. He may be right. It would not be well for anyone facing the problem to disregard any factual material assembled. But he might be wrong, too. The differences in juvenile delinquency records in various police districts may be more a matter of different police standards than of differing recreational opportunities. If the researcher takes this discrepancy in standards into account, which may be difficult, he may be involved in a further difficulty. The more related factors that are involved, the more difficult it is for the social researcher to draw significant conclusions for community organization practice.

It would seem that somewhere along the line there is a rightful and unavoidable place for intuition in its refined connotation. George Bernard Shaw remarked once that he always knew in a moment what it took Sidney Webb a long time to validate through his social investigations. Granting that this is a witty exaggeration, there is, nevertheless, a place for the Shaw as well as the Webb method. But both work best when not used as exclusive methodologies but when combined properly within the experience of a single individual. Intuition of itself is too insecure, partial, and doubtful to be used exclusively. Strictly scientific investigation is too fragmentary, relative, and uncertain to be made into a totalitarian methodology. The community organizer must use both.

b. Use of Research of Others. Another indirect method which the community organizer can profitably use is that which uncovers community conditions through the use of the research of others. It is not always possible for the community organizer to make first-hand or direct studies of community life. He may not have the funds available to begin such an undertaking (and social research properly managed is expensive). He may wish to devote his time and that of his staff more to those interests which derive from research—as social action. Again, research on his part may be unnecessary because the aspect of the community on which he seeks information may have been studied by others. If the community organizer wishes to show that certain conditions increase absenteeism, for example, he may receive information on the problem from the employers of local industries, from labor unions, or both. If he wishes to know whether juvenile delinquency has increased or decreased, he may simply have to consult the Police Department. If he wishes to know how much money the social work agencies have expended in specialized fields, he may be able to secure appropriate statistics from the community chest. If he wishes to know the number of persons on relief and their family size or their rentals, he may be given this knowledge by the public welfare agency in his community. In other words the community organizer does not always have to undertake direct investigation of the social phenomena which concern him, for he can utilize the researches of others in so far as they exist and are reliable. This assemblage of the data of others can be termed research of a sort. But, at best, it is indirect.

Direct Approach. a. Partial. The community organizer may appraise community conditions directly in either of two ways. For one, he may make a study of one particular section of the community or of one particular problem. To illustrate: he may himself discover or it may be brought to his attention by a group of interested citizens that there is need for public housing. It would not be well for him to trust his own insight, no matter what his sensitivity may be, nor to accept the opinion of others, even for their own benefit. He may first look at the literature of various organizations to discover what has been done in the way of uncovering and defining the public housing needs of the community. But if no material exists or if the work of the other organizations does not quite answer his questions, the community organizer may then instigate his own research upon the subject. Such research would be of a partial type, inasmuch as it would include only the one problem, that of public housing.

Partial researches comprise one of the direct methods of social research the community organizer may employ. They are important whenever data are not available and there is keen interest in a specific need which cannot wait for a complete analysis of the whole community. Most of the research of community organizers, quantitatively speaking, is of this variety.

b. Total Analysis. In recent years, however, a different type of direct research on the part of community organizers has been developed. This is the social investigation of entire communities.

Analysis of the complete community has a number of advantages for the community organizer. It permits him to see conditions from the perspective of the whole community. This will enable him to put into its proper place the felt need of any active group within the community. It may uncover need which no group has been organized to meet. It will involve the community organizer appropriately in the problem of community planning.

On the other hand the use of their energies for a complete study of the community may take the organizers away from more specifically required activities. The cost of such community surveys also is tremendous, and, usually, limited budgets make them more utopian than practical. Also, the community organizer may fail to realize that his primary function is not that of research exclusively, but that research is simply the foundation for other things.

One of the finest examples of complete community studies in social welfare was that accomplished by Philip Klein with a staff of collaborators, *A Social Study of Pittsburgh*. The subtitle of this volume further indicates the nature of the study: "Community Problems and Social Services in Allegheny County." The study was begun in 1934 and the report published in 1938. It included two interests of major importance to the researchers and to the community: (1) the social and economic life of the community; (2) the social and health work organizations attempting to serve the community. Both interests were examined in detail and with care.

Not all communities, as has been mentioned, can afford to engineer a complete community analysis such as that done in Pittsburgh (the cost of the Pittsburgh survey to the Buhl Foundation was $85,000). For those communities which seek a less expensive and less involved study there is a helpful guide in the book, *Your Community*, compiled by Joanna C. Colcord. While the book brings up questions of importance to any community organizer who wishes to know his community, it merely provides the questioning framework of what would have to be an actual social investigation. It can also be used advantageously by others.

From the foregoing description of the role of research in community organization, it must not be hastily assumed that research is simply an adjunct of community organization alone. True, it is important to community organizers, and their programs should be based upon it. But casework and group work also are research-minded and need the contributions of research in their programs. Naturally, the scope and functions of research in casework and group work differ somewhat from research in community organization. It is primarily from the viewpoint of community organization that research has herein been discussed.

Community Planning

The health and welfare services of many communities have grown up in a topsy-turvy fashion. The result of isolated innovations and discrete needs has been that social services in many places have no basically coherent or efficient organization. Community planning is an effort on the part of the community to introduce modifications into its social welfare facilities so that a more coherent and efficient program will result. In most localities the task of community planning is given to the council of social work agencies. Councils are commonly interested in only the health and welfare needs. Some city governments, however, now have departments of social planning concerned with community planning in respect to every phase of city life.

Getting Up-to-Date. Social welfare is a constantly changing phenomenon. The changes of our modern society are relatively fast and devastating to time-bound organizations and institutions. What was a need properly and without qualification ten years ago may not be a need now. Many organizations have been immobile in the face of changing economic and social conditions. They have sought in their own entrenched way to preserve their special place and function in the community without regard to the new conditions which have developed. The doctrine of "social lag" may be proved in social work no less than elsewhere.

The community organizer seeks to bring agencies and community social welfare practices up-to-date with existing social conditions and knowledge. On the basis of a knowledge of conditions derived through community research, he will attempt to improve the social welfare of the community by modifying agency procedure. To illustrate: it may be seen on the basis of investigation that there are far too many agencies of one type in a community and entirely too few of another. In such an event a council of social work agencies will discourage new agencies of the first type (where needs are met to a considerable extent) from forming, and will urge the creation of agencies of the second type (where needs are going unmet). The council may also encourage competing agencies to relocate themselves or to modify their programs of service in order to increase the social service coverage of the community. If, as in some communities, agencies feel that they cannot financially (or in other ways) support a new program adequately, the council of social work agencies may assist in setting up a cooperative arrangement whereby several agencies may together create the desired service. In many ways the community organizer may help plan for the better utilization of the welfare facilities of a community.

The community organizer may also try to improve the community generally so far as its organization and life affect social work responsibility. For example, he will not only attempt to see that there are enough agencies to care for juvenile delinquents, but he will also try to curb delinquency by the establishment of more playgrounds or other such methods.

Anticipating Needed Services. In recent years there has been some stress placed on the community organizer's role in the anticipation of social welfare needs. While the community organizer desires to work on the basis of expressed community support, there is a place in his thinking and activity for the planning of future services, although there is no general need at the present. A striking example of this occurred at the end of the Second World War. The community organization agencies of many American cities realized, before the war was over and before there was any pronounced need, that there should be special agencies for the assistance of veterans released from military service. While the Veterans Administration and the War and Navy Departments had their own programs to meet certain of the problems of veterans, these were at best temporary in some categories and incomplete in others. Some communities, however, before the close of the war actually created agencies to meet special needs of veterans. This kind of anticipation of social welfare developments will probably become an increasing responsibility of community organizers.

Initiation of Community Service

The planning of community welfare reminds us that, at some point or other, changes in the actual organization of the welfare services of the community must be effected in order that the elements of the community organization process previously mentioned may function adequately. Thus there can be no effective community planning which does not somewhere lead to action. The initiation of community service properly becomes a significant element in the community organization process.

The initiation of community service, however, is a varied and multiformed phenomenon. There is no single pattern of community action which alone expresses this element. In recent years considerable stress has been given to social action. It has been seen, not alone by community organizers but by many lay people of varying occupations, that the final means of resolving many community conflicts, of extending governmental social services, of preventing certain social harms, of integrating important groups of community needs, and of realizing other desired values is through political action. True, informal and voluntary organizations of people can accomplish much and their importance should not be minimized. But government is also a primary expression of the will of the people. Because it is, community organizers have come to realize that the influencing of legislation is one of their responsibilities.

Types of Influence. There are two principal types of influence which a community organization agency can bring to bear upon political leaders. First, the agency can speak for itself (and, indirectly, for its following). It can send its own delegates to places where legislation is being considered in order to express the agency's outlook. Of course, the position and activity of the agency should be interpreted to the community so that the community will be aware of the value which the agency finds in its particular decision.

The second type of action which can be taken is that of arousing public opinion on a legislative issue before trying to influence directly, if at all. A community organization agency may feel that its function has been fulfilled if it stirs the people of the community into realizing the meaning of the political action to be taken, believing that the community itself should take its own steps through existing channels.

Obviously, there are combinations of both of these methods of social action on the part of an agency. Neither is suitable at all times nor in every legislative situation.

The following illustration shows, among other things, how an agency in the city of "L" influenced legislators and public issues when state-wide legislation threatened changes which the agency saw as detrimental to the public welfare program:

A legislative commission composed of senators and representatives was named to investigate the public welfare department of the state. The investigation took place in the year preceding a meeting of the state legislature. The commission hired no professional aid, but conducted its own investigation, consisting largely of interviews with disgruntled clients and subpoena of public welfare employees. The latter interviews were prejudiced and consisted largely of "grilling." From time to time prejudiced newspaper articles were released, containing little factual material but full of innuendoes to discredit the public welfare department.

The welfare department began to lose the confidence of the public. Employees sought other positions and it appeared that sweeping political changes would be made. The executive and staff of the L agency followed the investigation closely. From time to time board members as individuals were brought up-to-date. Five months before the legislative session the president of the agency, in setting up the year's program, listed this investigation as one of the three most important items on the agency docket. In the September meeting of the board he introduced this subject.

Later in October the legislative commission released its report and recommendations. The agency staff analyzed the report and rushed copies to the board with a covering letter pointing out the few good recommendations and the many poor ones. The report was discussed by the board in its November and December meetings. The board decided in December to adopt a resolution, stating the reason for the agency interest, commending the good recommendations, and questioning the poor ones. They also recommended further study by experts. This was released to the newspapers and timed to coincide with statements by the state League of Women Voters, various labor unions, the State Committee on Child Welfare, and others. Additional agencies and organizations followed.

In the meantime the agency, through the executive and board members, aligned itself with the State Committee on Child Welfare, the League of Women Voters, the Council of Social Agencies, the Community Fund, and others to form a group to follow legislation. As legislation came out, the staff helped analyze it and forward it to the board. In the January board meeting a board member reviewed all pending legislation for the board of directors. As the month went on, changes in proposed legislation were followed closely. The agency accepted the leadership of state-wide organizations and worked along with them on an over-all state approach.

Board members attended public hearings. Board and staff members spoke, representing the agency at public hearings. Board and staff sent letters and telegrams to members of the legislature and the governor's office on various pieces of legislation. Persons from the membership of the agency were asked to help as individuals. Staff, board, and membership took the initiative in discussing the question with key people and other interested persons. This was all done in cooperation with other interested agencies, many of which were in a position of state-wide leadership. The outcome was that much of the proposed poor legislation was modified, other legislation defeated, and additional good legislation passed. In the March board meeting a board member reviewed the results for staff and board. The agency was pleased with the results.

The agency in the city of L illustrates again the importance of having an understanding of the agency program, and highlights the principle of participation in community planning where this is needed to protect agency program, through either preserving or strengthening the program of a related agency or agencies. Good public welfare is essential to private agency programs. The agency recognized this and took responsibility accordingly. Second, it cooperated with and used other interested agencies. While the family agency in L played an important part in the action, it recognized its limitations and accepted leadership from organizations of greater size and with a state-wide program. At the same time, because of its own conviction and readiness to participate, it had a voice in directing the program.

Third, the agency acted as a unit. The staff was concerned about the commission and its handling of the investigation. It used the board early in the investigation, as individual counselors, in order to be sure its own ideas were sound. Later the board members began to use the staff to get the intimate professional knowledge board members needed. Finally, staff and board came to a conclusion regarding the dangers of the commission report and the proposed legislation. With their recognition of the agency stake in the matter, action as an agency became possible.

Among the various devices used were some that deserve comment. Letters and telegrams were sent by board and staff. One of the uses of these communications was to demonstrate the interest and concern of as many persons as possible in the matter. Another was use of a carefully worded letter from one or perhaps a few individuals to one or two key persons, based on sound reasoning and expressed persuasively. This calls for careful selection of the author, and well-considered thoughtful content embodying technical knowledge from several sources assembled for the use of the author.

Careful publicity was also given to a board resolution. Resolutions need to be carefully written and to be based on complete agreement from the group. In the case of an agency this always needs board or authorized committee approval. One of the strengths of resolutions for public release is that they not only afford a way to express a point of view but they also offer opportunity to interpret the agency and exactly why the agency is interested in the matter.

Individuals, including staff, board, persons from the membership and community, were used. Highly personal contact can often go a long way in interpretation. Care must be exercised, however, to see that persons are not asked to represent a point of view for which factual backing does not exist, or which calls for more technical knowledge than is available to the selected individual.

Much has been written about newspaper and other publicity. It is, however, important to re-emphasize here that, in community planning, a public statement must represent the view of the agency as a whole. It should be carefully planned and written and should be made as effective as possible.[11]

[11]Robert F. Nelson, "The Executive and the Community," *Some Dynamics of Social Agency Administration,* Family Service Association of America, New York, 1946, pp. 31-33.

Creating New Services. Aside from engaging in social action, the community organizer also has the important job of creating new services for the community. While one might think this is a relatively simple matter, experience shows that it is not. Margaret Byington in her *Organizing a Public Welfare Committee in Spring County* indicates just how complicated the procedure may be. The community organizer in this case sought to create a committee, composed of private citizens, which would be attached as it were to the public welfare department of "Spring County," New York, for the purposes of bringing community opinion to the department and of interpreting the department's function to the community. The creation of this committee took several months. It had to be planned carefully before its inception and through its development. It rested ultimately upon the relationships the community organizer made and maintained with many individuals and organizations in the county.

Creating new services may also mean the setting up of an entirely new agency. The complications of this type of initiation of community service are portrayed by Francis McLean and Ralph Ormsby in the study, *Organizing a Family Agency.*

The setting up of a family agency has also been described from the viewpoint of a volunteer group's activities in this regard. The community organization process is clearly evidenced in this example:

Desiring to put the Christian principles they believed in into action in their community, a group of women of the Woman's Auxiliary, Christ Church, Cranbrook, Bloomfield Hills, Michigan, set out some years ago to work with the social agencies in their county. Soon a program of family visiting developed. These volunteer workers accepted referrals from the agencies in their area, but despite the time and interest these agencies showed, the volunteers found themselves facing many situations they could not handle, and missing opportunities to expand into allied projects in the community because they did not know how to develop them. To solve these problems, they secured the services of a professional social worker as their consultant for six hours each week.

Under the direction of the caseworker, the whole volunteer program broadened. New areas of activity were started in an effort to have jobs suited to every type of skill the volunteers had to offer rather than trying to turn all the workers into one way of expression. One group, however, continued to do "family visiting." Under the supervision of its consultant, over a six-year period this group demonstrated its ability: (1) to provide long-time supportive visiting to families that needed follow-up help but no longer required the specialized services of the referring agency; (2) to secure the extra services and material aids which the established agencies could not provide and which held special significance in helping certain families to regain their independence; (3) to grasp the significance of individual family problems and define them for the entire committee. Thus the observations of these visitors became a springboard for discussions and analyses of both casework procedures and community problems.

By the fall of 1944 these volunteers had found themselves facing many situations which they themselves were not equipped to relieve and for which they could find no agency qualified to assume responsibility. The impact of having to turn their backs on unhappy people and on children growing into delinquency brought them to a point where action was imperative. "How can we turn these thwarting and upsetting experiences into something constructive?" was the question they asked.

They decided to sponsor a professional setup that could help fill the gap. But where and how? Many possible approaches were discussed and a former Board member of the Family Welfare Association of America happened to be present at one of these meetings. She urged them to feel free to ask for help from the F.W.A.A. and this resulted in their writing for advice. Back came an offer to have a member of the war-service program survey the area in February, 1945.

The die was cast; this was a tremendous opportunity in the eyes of the group and the way must be prepared for the New York specialist. The enthusiasm of the group was fanned by the clear definition of the twofold purpose of a family agency stated in *Organizing a Family Agency*. The volunteers set to work. Starting with the social agency heads who were friends of the church group and had worked with it, they branched out to the unknown and interviewed all agency executives and key people in the community. Naturally, the leadership and interviewing fell to a few members adept at it and available at the time, and even then it was interesting to see how their clarity and confidence developed as they proceeded. When the F.W.A.A. representative arrived, this sponsoring group was able to present her with a schedule of appointments knowing that everyone on this list had had an explanation of who was coming to see him and why, and that there would be a follow-up program.

The report of the F.W.A.A. representative was that a family agency was badly needed in the area. She had uncovered a few spots where there might be active opposition to the organization of such an agency, and she noted that the community might be distinguished by its general apathy. Then, with a few challenging and inspiring remarks, and a list of practical suggestions, the hand and voice of the expert left.

During the next two months the volunteers at the church spent many hours thinking together, but they were also busy. A brief was made of the F.W.A.A. report and mimeographed copies of this, along with a letter of explanation and requests for specific backing, were sent to everyone who had been seen to date. Many individuals were seen, bringing the total number interviewed to about one hundred. There were a few leaders who needed to be brought along with the program and they were seen three or four times. Other groups in the parish were visited and assistance was solicited from three interested, influential businessmen who were members of the church. They agreed to make preliminary contacts with several community chest board members, but they urged more direct action. The women who had been selling the idea of an agency decided the time for a general meeting had come.

The Christ Church Committee had, as its dinner guests on May 2, one hundred agency board members and executives. The County Probate Court judge acted as chairman of the after-dinner meeting; Dr. Fritz Redl, outstanding psychiatrist and teacher, spoke lucidly and fascinatingly for thirty minutes on the universal need for casework and its values as a preventive of social ills; and an open discussion period followed. There was free and general participation in the discussion and four professional social workers answered questions. The discussion moved from whom this agency would serve, to types of social problems, their treatment, ways and means of organization, and on to how an agency would tie in volunteer work. The guests were given pamphlets, "The A.B.C.'s of a Family Agency," prepared and printed by the Christ Church group to help interpret the who, what, where, when, how, and why of a family agency in their county. The meeting closed with the appointment of an executive sponsoring committee that would work on questions of finances and the selection of a board. The husband of one of the church committee members remarked that he couldn't see what they had been working on so hard, since everyone seemed in hearty accord. This comment depicts the good feeling that existed that evening and tells the story of what had been accomplished.

Seven weeks later the first meeting of the sixteen board members of the new family agency took place. There are three members of the Christ Church Social Service Committee serving on the board; each was chosen for the particular contributions he would be able to make. The volunteer group that pioneered for this agency has again become just a supporting community group and their project has been launched with its own representative board. This experience seems to illustrate how convictions built on sincere concern and realistic experiences contain the vitality and maturity necessary to withstand the stresses and discouragements encountered in a job of community organization, and to carry through to accomplishment.[12]

COMMUNITY ORGANIZATION AT WORK

In this chapter, community organization has been described as to structure and process. In actual practice, however, these two aspects are

[12]Mrs. Albertina Mabley, "A Volunteer Group Organizes a Family Agency," *Highlights,* volume 6, number 8, December, 1945, pp. 121–123.

rarely distinguishable. The following example shows some of the elements of structure and process in combination:

Let us consider a situation which a few years ago involved a family agency, the community chest, a newly organized council of social agencies, and a suburban area of a city. The family agency in B, a city of over 300,000 persons, was a well-run, competently staffed family agency. Public relief was fairly adequate but many families asking assistance did not conform to the rigid regulations and financial restrictions of the public agency. In meeting the relief needs of such cases, the family agency in B had a considerable relief function in the community. Adjacent to and really part of the city of B for all practical purposes, was a suburb of 40,000 persons, not incorporated in the city and not in the same county. Public relief in this county and suburb was entirely inadequate, in fact nonexistent. Many persons living in the suburb were employed in the city of B. They contributed to B's community chest. There were industries in the suburb, however, which, because they were not in the city, were not included in B's community fund campaign.

A group from the suburb approached the family society asking it to serve the suburban community. They felt they had a right to this since many of them contributed to the community chest. The executive secretary and board members helped this group analyze what they wanted. In short, they wanted a relief program. The group were taken to the community chest and the council of social agencies, where the matter was discussed. At first the chest saw the practical money-raising question, but not beyond. It asked the family agency to go ahead but limited the funds for the job to an inadequate sum and did not see the implication of the suburban public relief picture.

The board and staff of the family agency made a hasty estimate of the minimum number of applications that could be expected and gathered some factual material. As a result of their findings the board decided that it would not be constructive in the long run to accept this responsibility, but at the same time pointed out ways that the suburb could be helped to get public relief. Subsequently, the chest, the family agency, and the council of social agencies together helped the suburb organize a citizens' committee, which was instrumental in getting the suburb help from its county for a public relief program. Limited casework service not including relief was begun later by the family society.

This situation demonstrates the application of a number of principles important in community organization. First, the agency saw itself as part of the community. The request from the suburb in a different county might have been denied routinely with no further consideration. This was not done because the agency recognized a responsibility for the community welfare regardless of narrow jurisdictional boundaries.

Second, the agency had a well defined purpose and good understanding of its own function. The agency's responsibility for financial assistance was well thought out and met the community need. Harmony existed between the community, the agency, and the community chest on this score. Progress was being made in the direction of strengthening the public agency so that it could take more responsibility. Third, the agency recognized a new problem affecting the entire community. New needs were arising. These were related to the already sound understanding the agency had of public relief problems in the city of B.

Fourth, the program of another agency was also touched, that of the community chest. The agency recognized that the chest had a money-raising problem. It also recognized that the newly formed council of social agencies had a stake in program planning. Fifth, there was a constant stream of interpretation of agency program in a series of individual and group contacts. Sixth, the suburban group was given a positive reception and effort was made to help them see their problem in its true light.

When the chest was shortsighted in terms of program and could see only one side of the picture, the family agency board and staff explored thoroughly what acceptance of such a responsibility would mean. They then stood firmly on their conviction about the agency job, but at the same time took responsibility for pointing out ways to meet the real problem. The community chest recognized the agency's knowledge in this area as well as its competence to give a casework program. With this recognition the way was open for help and planning and action. When action was taken to set up a basic relief program, casework services were extended on a sound basis to help meet the suburban community needs.[13]

SELECTED READINGS ON COMMUNITY ORGANIZATION

Alinksy, Saul D., *Reveille for Radicals,* University of Chicago Press, Chicago, 1946.

Atwater, Pierce, *Problems of Administration in Social Work,* University of Minnesota Press, Minneapolis, new edition, 1940.

Baker, Helen C., and Routzahn, Mary B., *How to Interpret Social Work,* Russell Sage Foundation, New York, 1947.

Bond, Elsie M., *Methods of Securing Social Welfare Legislation,* State Charities Aid Association, New York, 1941.

Brown, Esther L., *The Use of Research by Professional Associations in Determining Program and Policy,* Russell Sage Foundation, New York, 1946.

Bruno, Frank J., *Trends in Social Work: As Reflected in the Proceedings of the National Conference of Social Work, 1874–1946,* Columbia University Press, New York, 1948.

[13]Robert F. Nelson, "The Executive and the Community," *Some Dynamics of Social Agency Administration,* Family Service Association of America, New York, 1946, pp. 29–30.

Byington, Margaret F., editor, *Organizing a Public Welfare Committee in Spring County,* New York School of Social Work Publications, Columbia University Press, New York, 1941.

Cohen, Martin, and Wallace, Elizabeth, *Some Problems of Administration in Social Work,* University of Toronto Press, Toronto, 1944.

Colcord, Joanna, *Your Community: Its Provision for Health, Education, Safety, and Welfare,* Russell Sage Foundation, New York, 3d revision by Donald S. Howard, 1947.

Community Chests and Councils, Inc., *Community Organization for Health and Welfare on a State-Wide Basis,* New York, 1946.

——, *Health and Welfare Planning in the Smaller Community,* New York, 1945.

——, *The Neighborhood Approach to Community Planning,* Bulletin number 94, New York, 1937.

——, *What Councils of Social Agencies Do,* Bulletin number 100, New York, 1939.

Dimock, Marshall E., *The Executive in Action,* Harper, New York, 1945.

Dunham, Arthur, *The Future of the State Conference of Social Work,* published for the Association of State Conference Secretaries by the National Conference of Social Work, Columbus, 1941.

Follett, Mary, *Creative Experience,* Longmans, New York, 1924.

Guild, J. P., and Guild, A. A., *Social Work Engineering: An Outline of Topics for Survey, Planning, and Appraisal,* Harper, New York, 1940.

Hanchette, Helen W., and others, *Some Dynamics of Social Agency Administration,* Family Service Association of America, New York, 1946.

Hawkins, Gaynell, *Education for Social Understanding: Programs of Case Work and Group Work Agencies: Studies in the Social Significance of Adult Education in the United States,* American Association for Adult Education, New York, 1940.

Holbrook, David H., *Relationship Between Community Organization and National Agencies,* National Social Work Council (now National Social Welfare Assembly), New York, 1938.

Johns, Ray E., *The Cooperative Process Among National Social Agencies,* Association Press, New York, 1946.

King, Clarence, *Social Agency Boards and How to Make Them Effective,* Harper, New York, 1938.

King, Edith S., *The Social Service Exchange: A Device for Facilitating the Exchange of Confidential Information Among Welfare and Health Agencies,* Federal Security Agency, Social Security Administration, Bureau of Public Assistance, Bureau Circular number 16, Washington, D.C., 1943.

Kinneman, John A., *The Community in American Society,* Crofts, New York, 1947.

Klein, Philip, and others, *A Social Study of Pittsburgh: Community*

Problems and Social Services of Allegheny County, Columbia University Press, New York, 1938.

Levy, Harold P., *A Study in Public Relations: Case History of the Relations Maintained Between a Department of Public Assistance and the People of a State,* Russell Sage Foundation, New York, 1943.

——, *Building a Popular Movement: A Case Study of the Public Relations of the Boy Scouts of America,* Russell Sage Foundation, New York, 1944.

Lindeman, Eduard C., *The Community: An Introduction to the Study of Community Leadership and Organization,* Association Press, New York, 1921.

Lundberg, George A., *Social Research: A Study in Methods of Gathering Data,* Longmans, New York, 2d edition, 1942.

Matthews, William H., *Adventures in Giving,* Dodd, Mead, New York, 1939.

McClenahan, Bessie A., *Organizing the Community: A Review of Practical Principles,* Century, New York, 1922.

McLean, Francis H., and Ormsby, Ralph, *Organizing a Family Agency,* Family Welfare Association of America (now Family Service Association of America), New York, 1944.

McMillen, Wayne, *Community Organization for Social Welfare,* University of Chicago Press, Chicago, 1945.

Metcalf, Henry C., and Urwick, L., editors, *Dynamic Administration: The Collected Papers of Mary Parker Follett,* Harper, New York, 1942.

Metropolitan Conference for Social Planning, *How to Organize a Community Council: A Guide,* Boston Council of Social Agencies, Boston, 1941.

Morgan, Arthur E., *The Small Community: Foundation for Democratic Life; What It Is and How to Achieve It,* Harper, New York, 1942.

North, Cecil C., *The Community and Social Welfare: A Study in Community Organization,* McGraw-Hill, New York, 1931.

Norton, William J., *The Cooperative Movement in Social Work,* Social Welfare Library, Macmillan, New York, 1927.

Ogden, Jean, and Ogden, Jess, *Small Communities in Action: Stories of Citizen Programs at Work,* Harper, New York, 1946.

Paradise, Viola, *Toward Public Understanding of Casework,* Russell Sage Foundation, New York, 1948.

Pettit, Walter, *Case Studies in Community Organization,* Appleton-Century, New York, 1928.

Philips, Wilbur C., *Adventuring for Democracy,* Social Unit Press, New York, 1944.

Rhoton, Anne, *Regional Conferences of State Conferences of Social Work,* Missouri Association for Social Welfare, Jefferson City, Missouri, 1944.

Routzahn, Mary B., and Routzahn, Evart G., *Publicity for Social Work,* Russell Sage Foundation, New York, 1928.

Sanderson, Dwight E., and Polson, Robert A., *Rural Community Organization*, Wiley, New York, 1939.

Seymour, Harold J., *Designs for Giving: The Story of the National War Fund, Inc., 1943–1947*, Harper, New York, 1947.

Steiner, Jessie F., *Community Organization: A Study of Its Theory and Current Practice*, Appleton-Century, New York, revised, 1930.

Street, Elwood, *A Handbook for Social Agency Administration*, Harper, New York, 1948.

Tead, Ordway, *Democratic Administration*, Association Press, New York, 1945.

Trecker, Harleigh B., *Group Process in Administration*, Woman's Press, New York, 1946.

Urwick, Lyndall, *The Elements of Administration*, Harper, New York, 1943.

Withers, Gertrude V., *Effective Rural Social Work Through Community Organization*, American Public Welfare Association, Chicago, 1942.

Zimmerman, Carle C., *The Changing Community*, Harper, New York, 1938.

APPENDIX A

Periodicals and Serials
in the Field of Social Welfare

(*This unclassified, selected list represents material that is being published currently in the United States*)

(The following abbreviations are used: (m)—monthly; (bi-m)—bimonthly; (q)—quarterly; (s-a)—semiannually; (irreg)—irregularly.)

American Child. (m, Oct.-Je.) National Child Labor Committee, 419 Fourth Ave, New York, N.Y.

American Journal of Economics and Sociology. (q) N. Queen St. & McGovern Ave., Lancaster, Pa.

American Journal of Mental Deficiency. (q) American Association of Mental Deficiency, 372 Broadway, Albany, N.Y.

American Journal of Orthopsychiatry: A Journal of Human Behavior. (American Orthopsychiatric Association.) (q) George Banta Publishing Co., 450 Ahnaip St., Menasha, Wisc.

American Journal of Psychiatry. (bi-m) American Psychiatric Association, 9 Rockefeller Plaza, New York, N.Y.

American Journal of Sociology. (bi-m) University of Chicago Press, 5750 Ellis Ave., Chicago, Ill.

American Sociological Review. (American Sociological Society.) (bi-m) Conrad Taeuber, U.S. Dept. of Agriculture, Washington, D.C.

Annals. (American Academy of Political and Social Science.) (bi-m) 3457 Walnut St., Philadelphia, Pa.

Best Years: A Magazine By and For Old Persons. (q) Smithtown Branch, New York.

Bulletin. (American Association of Medical Social Workers.) (6 times a year) The Association, 1129 Vermont Ave., N.W., Washington 5, D.C.

Bulletin. (Child Welfare League of America.) (m, Sept.-Je.) The League, 130 East 22d St., New York 10, N.Y.

Bulletin. (National Association of School Social Workers.) (irreg) The Association, 1367 Clover Road, Rochester, N.Y.

Catholic Action. (m) National Catholic Welfare Conference, 1312 Massachusetts Ave., N.W., Washington, D.C.

Catholic Charities Review. (National Conference of Catholic Charities.) (m, Sept.-Je.) The Conference, 1317 F St., N.W., Washington, D.C.

Channels. (8 times a year) National Publicity Council for Health and Welfare Services, Inc., 130 E. 22d St., New York 10, N.Y.

The Child. (U.S. Children's Bureau.) (m) Supt. of Documents, Washingington, D.C.

Child Development Abstracts and Bibliography. (Society for Research in Child Development.) (bi-m) National Research Council, 2101 Constitution Ave., Washington, D.C.

Child Study: Journal of Parent Education. (q) Child Study Association, 221 W. 57th St., New York, N.Y.

Community: Bulletin. (m) Community Chests and Councils, Inc., 155 E. 44th St., New York 17, N.Y.

Employment Service Review. (U.S. Employment Service.) (m) Supt. of Documents, Washington, D.C.

Federal Probation. (U.S. Probation Service.) (q) Supt. of Documents, Washington, D.C.

The Group. (q) American Association of Group Workers, 670 Lexington Ave., New York 22, N.Y.

Highlights. (m, Oct.-Jl.) Family Service Association of America, 122 E. 22d St., New York 10, N.Y.

Jewish Social Service Quarterly: A Record of Communal Trends and Developments. (q) National Conference of Jewish Social Welfare, 67 W. 47th St., New York, N.Y.

Journal of Abnormal and Social Psychology. (q) American Psychological Association, Inc., Northwestern University, Evanston, Ill.

Journal of Criminal Law and Criminology, including the *American Journal of Police Science.* (American Institute of Criminal Law and Criminology.) (bi-m) Northwestern University Press, 357 E. Chicago Ave., Chicago, Ill.

Journal of Criminal Psychopathology. (q) Medical Journal Press, Woodbourne, N.Y.

Journal of Educational Sociology: A Magazine of Theory and Practice. (m, Sept.-May) Payne Educational Sociology Foundation, Inc., 32 Washington Place, New York 3, N.Y.

Journal of Exceptional Children. (International Council for Exceptional Children.) (m, Oct.-May) Harley Z. Wooden, Flint, Mich.

Journal of Gerontology. (q) Gerontological Society, Inc., 507 S. Euclid St., St. Louis 10, Mo.

Journal of Psychiatric Social Work. (q) American Association of Psychiatric Social Workers, 1790 Broadway, New York 19, N.Y.

Journal of Rehabilitation. (bi-m) National Rehabilitation Association, 1114 56th St., Des Moines 11, Iowa.

Journal of Social Casework. (m, Oct.-Jl.) Family Service Association of America, 122 E. 22d St., New York 10, N.Y.

Journal of Social Hygiene. (m, Oct.-Je.) American Social Hygiene Association, Inc., 1790 Broadway, New York 19, N.Y.

Marriage and Family Living. (q) National Conference on Family Relations, 1126 E. 59th St., Chicago, Ill.

Mental Hygiene. (q) National Committee for Mental Hygiene, Inc., 1790 Broadway, New York 19, N.Y.

Monthly Labor Review. (U.S. Bureau of Labor Statistics.) (m) Supt. of Documents, Washington, D.C.

Nervous Child: Quarterly Journal of Psychopathology, Psychotherapy, Mental Hygiene and Guidance of the Child. (q) Grune and Stratton, 443 Fourth Ave., New York 16, N.Y.

Occupational Therapy and Rehabilitation. (American Occupational Therapy Association.) (bi-m) Williams and Wilkins Co., Mt. Royal and Guilford Aves., Baltimore, Md.

Personnel Administration. (m, Sept.-Je.) Society for Personnel Administration, Box 266, Washington, D.C.

Personnel Journal: The Magazine of Labor Relations and Personnel Practices. (m, Sept.-Je.) Personnel Research Federation, 60 E. 42d St., New York 17, N.Y.

Prison World. (American Prison Association.) (bi-m) Bruce Publishing Co., 2642 University Ave., St. Paul, Minn.

Probation. (bi-m) National Probation and Parole Association, Inc., 1790 Broadway, New York 19, N.Y.

Psychiatric Quarterly. (New York State Department of Mental Hygiene.) (q) State Hospitals Press, Utica, N.Y.

Psychiatric Quarterly Supplement. (New York State Department of Mental Hygiene.) (s-a) State Hospitals Press, Utica, N.Y.

Psychiatry: Journal of the Biology and the Pathology of Interpersonal Relations. (q) William Alanson White Psychiatric Foundation, Inc., 1500 Greenmount Ave., Baltimore, Md.

Psychoanalytic Quarterly. (q) Psychoanalytic Quarterly, Inc., 372 Broadway, Albany, N.Y.

Psychoanalytic Review: An Educational American Journal of Psychoanalysis Devoted to an Understanding of Human Conduct. (q) Nervous and Mental Diseases Monographs, 64 W. 56th St., New York 19, N.Y.

Psychological Abstracts. (13 times a year) American Psychological Association, Inc., Northwestern University, Evanston, Ill.

Psychosomatic Medicine: Experimental and Clinical Studies. (Supplements.) (bi-m) Division of Anthropology and Psychology, National Research Council, 2101 Constitution Ave., Washington, D.C.

Public Administration Review. (q) American Society for Public Administration, 1009 Sloan St., Crawfordsville, Va.

Public Welfare. (m) American Public Welfare Association, 1313 E. 60th St., Chicago 37, Ill.

Recreation. (m) National Recreation Association, 315 Fourth Ave., New York 10, N.Y.

Rural Sociology: Devoted to Scientific Study of Rural Life. (Rural Sociological Society.) (q) North Carolina State College of Agriculture and Engineering, Raleigh, N.C.

Smith College Studies in Social Work. (q) Menasha, Wisc.

Social Forces: A Scientific Medium of Social Study and Interpretation. (4 times a year) Williams and Wilkins Co., Mt. Royal and Guilford Aves., Baltimore, Md.

Social Security Bulletin. (U.S. Social Security Administration.) (m) Supt. of Documents, Washington, D.C.

Social Service Digest. (m) 373 Spreckels Bldg., San Diego 1, Calif.

Social Service Review: A Quarterly Devoted to the Scientific and Professional Interests of Social Work. (q) University of Chicago Press, 5750 Ellis Ave., Chicago, Ill.

Social Work Journal. (6 times a year) American Association of Social Workers, 130 E. 22d St., New York 10, N.Y.

Sociology and Social Research: An International Journal. (bi-m) University of Southern California, 3551 University Ave., Los Angeles, Calif.

Sociometry: A Journal of Interpersonal Relations. (q) 259 Wolcott Ave., Beacon, N.Y.

Survey Graphic: Magazine of Social Interpretation. (m) Survey Associates, Inc., 112 E. 19th St., New York 3, N.Y.

Survey Midmonthly. (m) Survey Associates, Inc., 112 E. 19th St., New York 3, N.Y.

Understanding the Child: A Magazine for Teachers. (q) National Committee for Mental Hygiene, 1790 Broadway, New York 19, N.Y.

APPENDIX B

Suggestions for a Book Collection on Social Work

GENERAL

Bruno, F. J. *The Theory of Social Work.* 646 p. Boston, Heath, 1936.

Clarke, H. I. *Principles and Practice of Social Work.* 450 p. New York, Appleton-Century, 1947.

Fink, A. E. *The Field of Social Work.* 518 p. New York, Holt, 1942. (Includes bibliography.)

Harrison, S. M., and Andrews, F. E. *American Foundation for Social Welfare.* 249 p. New York, Russell Sage Foundation, 1946. (Includes bibliography.)

Kurtz, R. H., editor. *Social Work Year Book, 1947: A Description of Organized Activities in Social Work and in Related Fields.* Ninth issue. 714 p. New York, Russell Sage Foundation, 1947.

Lee, P. R. *Social Work as Cause and Function,* and other papers. 270 p. New York, Columbia University Press, 1937. (New York School of Social Work, Publications.)

Queen, S. A. *Social Work in the Light of History.* 327 p. Philadelphia, Lippincott, 1922.

Warner, A. G., and others. *American Charities and Social Work.* 4th edition. 616 p. New York, Crowell, 1930.

Watson, F. D. *The Charity Organization Movement in the United States: A Study in American Philanthropy.* 560 p. New York, Macmillan, 1922. (Includes bibliography.)

Witmer, H. L. *Social Work: An Analysis of a Social Institution.* 539 p. New York, Farrar, 1942. (Includes bibliographies.)

CASEWORK

(see also Medical Social Work and Psychiatric Social Work)

American Association of Social Workers. *Social Case Work, Generic and Specific, an Outline: Report of the Milford Conference.* 92 p. New York, The Association, 1929. (Studies in the Practice of Social Work, No. 2.)

Aptekar, H. H. *Basic Concepts in Social Case Work.* 201 p. Chapel Hill, University of North Carolina Press, 1941.

Brown, J. C. *The Rural Community and Social Case Work.* 165 p. New York, Family Welfare Association of America (now Family Service Association of America), 1933. (Includes bibliography.)

de Schweinitz Karl. *The Art of Helping People Out of Trouble.* 231 p. Boston, Houghton, 1924.

Dollard, John. *Criteria for the Life History, With Analyses of Six Notable Documents.* 288 p. New Haven, Yale University Press, 1935.

Garrett, Annette. *Interviewing, Its Principles and Methods.* 123 p. New York, Family Welfare Association of America (now Family Service Association of America), 1942.

Hamilton, Gordon. *Principles of Social Case Recording.* 142 p. New York, Columbia University Press, 1946. (New York School of Social Work, Publications.) (Includes bibliography.)

——— *Theory and Practice of Social Case Work.* 388 p. New York, Columbia University Press, 1940. (New York School of Social Work, Publications.)

Hollis, Florence. *Social Case Work in Practice: Six Case Studies.* 313 p. New York, Family Welfare Association of America (now Family Service Association of America), 1939. (Includes bibliography.)

Lowry, Fern, editor. *Readings in Social Case Work, 1920–1938: Selected Reprints for the Case Work Practitioner.* 810 p. New York, Columbia University Press, 1939. (New York School of Social Work, Publications.)

Reynolds, B. C. *An Experiment in Short Contact Interviewing.* 101 p. Northampton, Mass., Smith College School for Social Work, 1932. (Smith College Studies in Social Work. Volume 3, No. 1, September, 1932.)

Richmond, M. E. *Social Diagnosis.* 511 p. New York, Russell Sage Foundation, 1917.

——— *What Is Social Case Work?* 268 p. New York, Russell Sage Foundation, 1922.

Robinson, V. P. *Changing Psychology in Social Case Work.* 205 p. Chapel Hill, University of North Carolina Press, 1930. (Includes bibliography.)

——— *Supervision in Social Case Work: A Problem in Professional Education.* 199 p. Chapel Hill, University of North Carolina Press, 1936.

——— editor. *Training for Skill in Social Case Work.* 126 p. Philadelphia, University of Pennsylvania Press, 1942. (Pennsylvania School of Social Work, Social Work Process Series.)

Strode, Josephine, and Strode, P. R. *Social Skills in Case Work.* 195 p. New York, Harper, 1942. (Includes bibliography.)

Taft, Jessie, editor. *A Functional Approach to Family Case Work.* 208 p. Philadelphia, University of Pennsylvania Press, 1944. (Pennsylvania School of Social Work, Social Work Process Series.)

Wilson, R. S. *The Short Contact in Social Case Work: A Study of Treatment in Time-Limited Relationships in Social Work.* 2 volumes. New York, National Association for Travelers Aid and Transient Service, 1937.

Young, P. V. *Interviewing in Social Case Work: A Sociological Analysis,* with an introduction by J. C. Colcord. 416 p. New York, McGraw, 1935.

SOCIAL WORK ADMINISTRATION

Atwater, Pierce. *Problems of Administration in Social Work.* 319 p. Minneapolis, University of Minnesota Press, 1940.

Guild, J. P., and Guild, A. A. *Social Work Engineering: An Outline of Topics for Survey, Planning, and Appraisal.* 136 p. New York, Harper, 1940.

King, Clarence. *Social Agency Boards and How to Make Them Effective.* 108 p. New York, Harper, 1938. (Includes bibliography.)

Street, Elwood. *A Handbook for Social Agency Administration.* 467 p. New York, Harper, 1948.

Tead, Ordway. *Democratic Administration.* 78 p. New York, Association Press, 1945. (Includes bibliography.)

EDUCATION FOR SOCIAL WORK

Abbott, Edith. *Social Welfare and Professional Education.* 2d edition, · revised and enlarged. Chicago, University of Chicago Press, 1942.

American Association of Schools of Social Work, Study Committee. *Education for the Public Social Services: A Report of the Commiteee.* 324 p. Chapel Hill, University of North Carolina Press, 1942.

Brown, E. L. *Social Work as a Profession.* 4th edition, revised. New York, Russell Sage Foundation, 1942.

Reynolds, B. C. *Learning and Teaching in the Practice of Social Work.* 390 p. New York, Farrar, 1942.

Steele, Evelyn, and Blatt, H. K. *Careers in Social Service.* In collaboration with Vocational Guidance Research. 256 p. New York, Dutton, 1946.

COMMUNITY ORGANIZATION

Alinsky, S. D. *Reveille for Radicals.* 228 p. Chicago, University of Chicago Press, 1946.

Colcord, J. C. *Your Community: Its Provision for Health, Education, Safety and Welfare.* 2d edition. 261 p. New York, Russell Sage Foundation, 1941.

Klein, Philip, and others. *A Social Study of Pittsburgh: Community Problems and Social Services of Allegheny County.* 958 p. New York, Columbia University Press, 1938.

Lindeman, E. C. *The Community: An Introduction to the Study of Community Leadership and Organization.* 222 p. New York, Association Press, 1921.

MacIver, R. M. *The Community: A Sociological Study; Being an Attempt to Set Out the Nature and Fundamental Laws of Social Life.* 3d edition. 446 p. London, Macmillan, 1924.

—— *Society: A Textbook of Sociology.* 596 p. New York, Farrar, 1937.

McMillen, Wayne. *Community Organization for Social Welfare.* 658 p. Chicago, University of Chicago Press, 1945. ("Readings" at end of each chapter.)

Morgan, A. E. *The Small Community: Foundation for Democratic Life: What It Is and How to Achieve It.* 312 p. New York, Harper, 1942. (Includes bibliography.)

Norton, W. J. *The Cooperative Movement in Social Work.* 373 p. New York, Macmillan, 1927.

Pettit, W. W. *Case Studies in Community Organization.* 345 p. New York, Century, 1928. (Includes bibliographies.)

Phillips, W. C. *Adventuring for Democracy.* 380 p. New York, Social Unit Press, 1940.

Steiner, J. F. *Community Organization: A Study of Its Theory and Current Practice.* Revised edition. 453 p. New York, Century, 1930. (Includes bibliography.)

CHILD WELFARE

Abbott, Grace. *The Child and the State: Select Documents With Introductory Notes.* 2 volumes. Chicago, University of Chicago Press, 1938. (Social Service Series.)

Baylor, E. M. H., and Monachesi, E. D. *The Rehabilitation of Children: The Theory and Practice of Child Placement.* 560 p. New York, Harper, 1939.

Gesell, A. L., and others. *Infant and Child in the Culture of Today: The Guidance of Development in Home and Nursery School.* 399 p. New York, Harper, 1943.

Healy, William, and others. *Reconstructing Behavior in Youth: A Study of Problem Children in Foster Families.* New York, Knopf, 1929. (Judge Baker Foundation, Publications, No. 5.)

Hopkirk, H. W. *Institutions Serving Children.* 244 p. New York, Russell Sage Foundation, 1944.

Hutchinson, Dorothy. *In Quest of Foster Parents: A Point of View on Home-Finding.* 145 p. New York, Columbia University Press, 1943. (Includes bibliography.)

Isaacs, Susan. *Intellectual Growth in Young Children.* 370 p. New York, Harcourt, 1930.

—— *Social Development in Young Children: A Study of Beginnings.* 480 p. New York, Harcourt, 1933. (Includes bibliography.)

Lundberg, Emma O. *Unto the Least of These: Social Services for Children.* 424 p. New York, Appleton-Century, 1947.

Polier, J. W. *Everyone's Children, Nobody's Child: A Judge Looks at Underprivileged Children in the United States.* 331 p. New York, Scribner, 1941. (Includes bibliography.)

Ribble, M. A. *The Rights of Infants: Early Psychological Needs and Their Satisfaction.* 118 p. New York, Columbia University Press, 1943.

Sayles, M. B. *Substitute Parents: A Study of Foster Families.* 309 p. New York, Commonwealth Fund, 1936.

Taft, Jessie, editor. *Social Case Work With Children: Studies in Structure and Process.* 237 p. Philadelphia, Pennsylvania School of Social Work, 1939. (Journal of Social Work Process. Volume 3, No. 1.)

Thurston, H. W. *The Dependent Child: A Story of Changing Aims and Methods in the Care of Dependent Children.* 337 p. New York, Columbia University Press, 1930. (New York School of Social Work, Publications.) (Includes bibliography.)

White House Conference on Child Health and Protection, 1930. Reports. Published by Century and Appleton-Century. (Two volumes entitled *The Dependent Child* and *The Delinquent Child* are particularly important.)

White House Conference on Children in a Democracy, 1939–40. Proceedings and Final Report. Washington, D.C., Government Printing Office, 1940–41.

MEDICAL SOCIAL WORK

Bartlett, H. M. *Some Aspects of Social Case Work in a Medical Setting: A Study in the Field of Medical Social Work.* 270 p. Chicago, American Association of Medical Social Workers, 1940.

Cannon, I. M. *Social Work in Hospitals: A Contribution to Progressive Medicine.* Revised edition. 247 p. New York, Russell Sage Foundation, 1923.

Cannon, W. B. *The Wisdom of the Body.* 312 p. New York, Norton, 1932.

Champion, W. M., editor. *Medical Information for Social Workers.* 529 p. Baltimore, Wood, 1938. (Includes bibliography.)

Hinsie, L. E. *The Person in the Body: An Introduction to Psychosomatic Medicine.* 263 p. New York, Norton, 1945.

Richardson, H. B. *Patients Have Families.* 407 p. New York, Commonwealth Fund, 1945.

Robinson, G. C. *The Patient As a Person: A Study of the Social Aspects of Illness.* 423 p. New York, Commonwealth Fund, 1939. (Includes bibliography.)

Sigerist, H. E. *Civilization and Disease.* 255 p. Ithaca, Cornell University Press, 1943.

Thornton, Janet, and Knauth, M. S. *The Social Component in Medical Care: A Study of One Hundred Cases From the Presbyterian Hospital of the City of New York.* 411 p. New York, Columbia University Press, 1937.

Weiss, Edward, and English, O. S. *Psychosomatic Medicine: The Clinical Application of Psychopathology to General Medical Problems.* 687 p. Philadelphia, Saunders, 1943. (Includes bibliography.)

PSYCHIATRIC SOCIAL WORK

Aichhorn, August. *Wayward Youth,* with a foreword by Sigmund Freud and a note about the author by the editors; revised and adapted from the second German edition. 236 p. New York, Viking Press, 1935.

Alexander, Franz, and French, T. M. *Psychoanalytic Therapy: Principles and Application.* 353 p. New York, Ronald Press, 1946. (Includes bibliography.)

Allen, F. H. *Psychotherapy With Children.* 311 p. New York, Norton, 1942.

Davies, S. P. *Social Control of the Mentally Deficient.* 389 p. New York, Crowell, 1930. (Includes bibliographies.)

Deutsch, Albert. *The Mentally Ill in America: A History of Their Care and Treatment From Colonial Times.* 530 p. New York, Columbia University Press, 1946. (Includes bibliography.)

Deutsch, Helene. *Psychoanalysis of the Neuroses.* 236 p. London, Hogarth Press, 1932.

English, O. S., and Pearson, G. H. J. *Emotional Problems of Living: Avoiding the Neurotic Pattern.* 428 p. New York, Norton, 1945. (Includes bibliographies.)

Fenichel, Otto. *Psychoanalytic Theory of Neurosis.* 703 p. New York, Norton, 1945. (Includes bibliography.)

French, L. A. *Psychiatric Social Work.* 344 p. New York, Commonwealth Fund, 1940.

Freud, Anna. *The Ego and the Mechanisms of Defence.* 196 p. London, Hogarth Press, 1937.

Freud, Sigmund. *A General Introduction to Psychoanalysis.* 412 p. New York, Liveright, 1935.

Horney, Karen. *Our Inner Conflicts: A Constructive Theory of Neurosis.* 250 p. New York, Norton, 1945.

Lee, P. R., and Kenworthy, M. E. *Mental Hygiene and Social Work.* Prepared with the collaboration of Sarah Ivins and others. 309 p. New York, Commonwealth Fund, 1929.

Lewis, N. D. C., and others, editors. *Modern Trends in Child Psychiatry.* 341 p. New York, International University Press, 1945.

Lorand, Sandor, editor. *Psychoanalysis Today.* 404 p. New York, International University Press, 1944. (Includes bibliographies.)

Lowrey, L. G. *Psychiatry for Social Workers.* 337 p. New York, Columbia University Press, 1946.

Stephen, Karin. *Psychoanalysis and Medicine: A Study of the Wish to Fall Ill.* 238 p. New York, Macmillan, 1933.

Towle, Charlotte. *Social Case Records From Psychiatric Clinics;* with discussion notes. 455 p. Chicago, University of Chicago Press, 1941. (Social Service Series.) (Includes bibliographies.)

Zachry, C. B. *Emotion and Conduct in Adolescence.* Prepared for the Commission on Secondary School Curriculum, Progressive Education Association. 563 p. New York, Appleton-Century, 1940. (Includes bibliography.)

GROUP WORK

Baxter, Bernice, and Cassidy, R. F. *Group Experience: The Democratic Way.* 218 p. New York, Harper, 1943. (Includes bibliography.)

Busch, H. M. *Leadership in Group Work.* 306 p. New York, Association Press, 1934.

Coyle, G. L. *Social Process in Organized Groups.* 245 p. New York, Smith, 1930.

————— *Studies in Group Behavior.* 258 p. New York, Harper, 1937.

Du Vall, E. W. *Personality and Social Group Work: The Individual Approach.* 234 p. New York, Association Press, 1943. (Includes bibliography.)

Jennings, H. H. *Leadership and Isolation: A Study of Personality in Interpersonal Relations.* 240 p. New York, Longmans, 1943. (Includes bibliography.)

Lieberman, Joshua, editor. *New Trends in Group Work.* 229 p. New York, Association Press, 1938.

Lindenberg, J. J. *Supervision in Social Group Work.* 141 p. New York, Association Press, 1939.

MacIver, R. M., editor. *Group Relations and Group Antagonisms: A Series of Addresses and Discussions.* 237 p. New York, Harper, 1944.

Slavson, S. R. *Creative Group Education.* 247 p. New York, Association Press, 1937.

————— *Introduction to Group Therapy.* 352 p. New York, Commonwealth Fund, 1943.

Tead, Ordway. *The Art of Leadership.* 308 p. New York, Whittlesey House, 1935.

Wilson, Gertrude. *Group Work and Case Work: Their Relationship and Practice.* 107 p. New York, Family Welfare Association of America (now Family Service Association of America), 1941. (Includes bibliography.)

PUBLIC WELFARE AND SOCIAL INSURANCE

Abbott, Edith. *Public Assistance.* 1 volume. Chicago, University of Chicago Press, 1940. (Social Service Series.)

Abbott, Grace. *From Relief to Social Security: The Development of the New Public Welfare Services and Their Administration.* 388 p. Chicago, University of Chicago Press, 1941.

Breckinridge, S. P. *Public Welfare Administration in the United States:*

Select Documents. 2d edition. 1229 p. Chicago, University of Chicago Press, 1938. (Includes bibliography.)

Brown, J. C. *Public Relief, 1929–1939.* 524 p. New York, Holt, 1940. (Includes bibliography.)

Browning, G. A. *Rural Public Welfare: Selected Records With Introductory Notes and Comments.* 578 p. Chicago, University of Chicago Press, 1941. (Social Service Series.) (Includes bibliography.)

Burns, E. M. R. *Toward Social Security: An Explanation of the Social Security Act and a Survey of the Larger Issues.* 269 p. New York, Whittlesey House, 1936.

de Schweinitz, Karl. *England's Road to Social Security: From the Statute of Laborers in 1349 to the Beveridge Report of 1942.* 281 p. Philadelphia, University of Pennsylvania Press, 1943. (Includes bibliography.)

Douglas, P. H. *Social Security in the United States: An Analysis and Appraisal of the Federal Social Security Act.* 2d edition. 493 p. New York, Whittlesey House, 1939.

Epstein, Abraham. *Insecurity, a Challenge to America: A Study of Social Insurance in the United States and Abroad.* 2d edition, revised. 939 p. New York, Random House, 1938.

Howard, D. S. *The W.P.A. and Federal Relief Policy.* 879 p. New York, Russell Sage Foundation, 1943.

Klein, A. M. C. *Civil Service in Public Welfare: A Discussion of Effective Selection of Public Social Work Personnel Through the Merit System.* 444 p. New York, Russell Sage Foundation, 1940.

Kurtz, R. H. *The Public Assistance Worker: His Responsibility to the Applicant, the Community, and Himself.* 224 p. New York, Russell Sage Foundation, 1938. (Includes bibliography.)

Meriam, Lewis. *Relief and Social Security.* 912 p. Washington, D.C., Brookings Institution, 1946.

Rubinow, I. M. *The Quest for Security.* 638 p. New York, Holt, 1934.

Stevenson, Marietta. *Public Welfare Administration.* Prepared with the assistance of other members of the Staff of the American Public Welfare Association. 352 p. New York, Macmillan, 1938. (Includes bibliographies.)

Street, Elwood. *Public Welfare Administrator.* 422 p. New York, McGraw, 1940.

United States National Resources Planning Board. *Security, Work and Relief Policies: Report of the Committee on Long-Range Work and Relief Policies.* 640 p. Washington, D.C., Government Printing Office, 1942.

White, R. C. *Administration of Public Welfare.* 527 p. New York, American Book, 1940. (Includes bibliography.)

MEDICAL SERVICE

Binger, C. A. L. *The Doctor's Job.* 243 p. New York, Norton, 1945. (Includes bibliography.)

Cabot, Hugh. *The Patient's Dilemma: The Quest for Medical Security in America.* 284 p. New York, Reynal, 1940.

Committee on the Costs of Medical Care. *Medical Care for the American People: The Final Report of the Committee.* 213 p. Chicago, University of Chicago Press, 1932.

Davis, M. M., Jr. *America Organizes Medicine.* 335 p. New York, Harper, 1941. (Includes bibliographies.)

Falk, I. S. *Security Against Sickness: A Study of Health Insurance.* 423 p. Garden City, New York, Doubleday, 1936.

Goldman, Franz. *Public Medical Care: Principles and Problems.* 226 p. New York, Columbia University Press, 1945. (Includes bibliography.)

Gunn, S. M., and Platt, P. S. *Voluntary Health Agencies: An Interpretative Study,* with a foreword by L. I. Dublin. 364 p. New York, Ronald Press, 1945.

Sigerist, H. E. *Medicine and Human Welfare.* 148 p. New Haven, Yale University Press, 1941. (Terry Lectures.)

Stern, B. J. *Medical Services by Government; Local, State, and Federal.* 208 p. New York, Commonwealth Fund, 1946. (New York Academy of Medicine, Committee on Medicine and the Changing Order, Studies.)

Index of Authors and Others

(*For Index of Subjects, see pp. 676–695*)

Index of Subjects

(*For Index of Authors and Others, see pp. 671—675*)